Fundamentals of Public B
and Finance

Aman Khan

Fundamentals of Public Budgeting and Finance

Aman Khan
Department of Political Science
Texas Tech University
Lubbock, TX, USA

ISBN 978-3-030-19228-0   ISBN 978-3-030-19226-6   (eBook)
https://doi.org/10.1007/978-3-030-19226-6

Cover image: © HGEsch Photography

This Palgrave Macmillan imprint is published by the registered company Springer Nature Switzerland AG
The registered company address is: Gewerbestrasse 11, 6330 Cham, Switzerland

To
My two little grandchildren—
Sofia Clare and James Cole

Preface

Without question, budgeting is the single most important function in government; it is the lifeblood without which a government will come to a standstill. Without budgeting, there will be no public goods and services and a host of other benefits that we take for granted. In other words, there will be no roads, no bridges and highways, no public safety, no health care and education for those who cannot afford it, no guaranteed income and sustenance for the poor and the needy, no national security and environmental protection, no protection against unfair trade, no protection against unfair price and monopoly in the marketplace, no incentive for economic growth and technological innovation, and the list goes on. Put simply, without budgeting there will be no government of any kind—the two go hand in hand.

Budgeting is an involved process. It is the only function in government where all three branches of government, in particular, the executive and the legislative branch are actively involved in decision making—the executive branch in all stages of the process, especially during budget preparation and execution, and the legislative branch during the appropriation phase of the budget. Although the role of the judicial branch is minimal, it can be significant in terms of the impact its decisions have on the budget process, especially when the budget decisions of the other two branches are challenged and found unconstitutional, as it happened many times in the US budget history. Interestingly, although not as conspicuous, the public also has a role in budget decision making; in particular, at the subnational level where the governments are required by law to call for a public referendum before introducing any major tax or expenditure legislation. Public is also involved during the preparation phase, especially at the local level, where the process requires a public hearing on the proposed budget before it is formally presented to the local council or commission for appropriation.

Why Study Public Budgeting?

Given the level of budgetary activities that take place throughout the year, in particular the amount of economic resources these activities consume and the complexity of the political process a budget has to go through, it should not be difficult to understand why one should study budgeting or, in the least, have an interest in the subject. John Wanat (1978), asking the same question, provides several explanations as to why we should study public budgeting. These include, among others, the budget size, priorities of the government, public accountability, the complexity of the decision process, intergovernmental relations, and the needs of the practitioners.

Both, in absolute dollar terms as well as a percentage of gross national, state or local product, budgeting plays a critical role in the overall functioning of a government. In its bare essence, budgeting is the means by which a government allocates its resources to meet the competing needs of society. But resources are finite and needs are many. Therefore, government must prioritize its policies so that the available resources can be used efficiently to produce the best possible results, consistent with those priorities. Since budgeting deals with public money, the government is accountable to the public as to how that money is spent. To highlight, the bulk of the revenue a government collects to finance its activities comes from taxes; as such, government has an obligation to make sure that the budget is used efficiently and effectively for the greater good of the public. The budget process ensures that the agencies and departments that are responsible for spending money vis-à-vis providing public goods and services can be held accountable for failing to do so.

Budgeting also improves coordination between different agencies and departments within a government, as well as between different levels of government through intergovernmental transfer of funds. Although individual agencies and departments within a government carry out their budgetary activities based on own mission, goals, and objectives, budgeting requires that these activities are coordinated with the larger mission, goals, and objectives of the government. From that point of view, the agency mission, goals, and objectives constitute a subset of the mission, goals and objectives of the government. Coordination helps minimize internal conflicts and improve better working relationship between agencies and their subunits, thereby improving the overall performance of the government.

Finally, what makes budgeting interesting is the amount of time a government spends each year on the budget process, from preparation, to appropriation, to implementation, to evaluation. It takes somewhere from six months to two years to prepare a budget, depending on the size of the budget and the level of government. During the appropriation phase, much of the time is spent discussing and debating how best to allocate the resources of the government; more precisely, who should get what, how much, and why? Once the funds are appropriated, the entire fiscal year is devoted to spending the allocated funds consistent with the appropriation decisions. Even after the fiscal year is over, additional time is spent on evaluating how efficiently and effectively the government has been able to carry out its activities; in other words, achieved its mission, goals, and objectives with the allocated resources.

Eclectic Nature of Public Budgeting

Unlike most fields of study, public budgeting is eclectic; it is multidimensional. According to Albert Hyde (1991), a public budget has four important dimensions: It is partly economic, partly political, partly accounting, and partly administrative.

First of all, a budget is an economic instrument that can help a jurisdiction's economic growth and development. This is certainly true at the national level where the federal budget serves as the principal mechanism by which the government directs income redistribution, promotes full employment, stimulates economic growth, and insures price stability.

Secondly, it is a political instrument that allocates resources among multiple, conflicting, and competing interests within a jurisdiction. Understanding the political process is important because, while the needs of the jurisdiction are mostly economic, the process that determines the budget allocation is largely political. Interestingly, this role of budgeting as a political exercise is not unique to the federal budget; it takes place at all levels of government. However, the process is much more complex at the federal level because of the sheer size of the budget.

Thirdly, it is an accounting and legal instrument. As an accounting and legal instrument, it provides a ceiling on government spending making it legally binding for the government to stay within its means. Ceiling establishes control over the traditional line-item budget. Line itemization makes it easier for an average layperson to understand the basic behavior of budget allocation and how control is exercised on budgetary activities. Budgetary control is particularly relevant for funds that operate on an annual basis and how various revenue and expenditure transactions take place throughout the fiscal year (Lynch 1995).

Finally, it is a managerial and administrative instrument that specifies the ways and means by which the public goods and services are provided and establishes criteria by which they are monitored, measured, and evaluated for efficiency and effectiveness. A budget manager must try to articulate the needs and demands of the organization, as well as those of the public, by explicitly taking into consideration economic, political, and financial conditions of the government and the needs of the public.

Budgeting is also analytical. An important aspect of public budgeting that often gets ignored in most discussions on the subject is that it is analytical in content. To be a successful budget practitioner, it is important that one has a basic knowledge of quantitative methods and techniques such as statistics, econometrics, decision science, and tools of program evaluation that are increasingly becoming commonplace in budgeting today. For instance, the knowledge of statistics and econometrics is vitally important, especially during the preparation phase, for analyzing past budgetary data and use that information for budget forecasting—forecasting of revenues and expenditures. Budgeting ultimately is about the future—future revenues and future expenditures. Although most practitioners will not do the forecasts themselves, the knowledge of basic forecasting methods will help them better understand how the forecasts were made, the direction of the forecasts, and the causes that underlie the direction.

Budgeting takes place under resource, environmental and other constraints. This makes it necessary for a government to carefully evaluate its allocation decisions. Since budget deals with the allocation decisions of a government, the knowledge of decision science is important, as it provides the decision makers with a set of tools and techniques that are useful in evaluating budget decisions, in particular how best to allocate the limited resources of a government to achieve its goals and objectives. Finally, the knowledge of program evaluation, especially pre- and post-analysis of government programs, is important during the evaluation phase. For most large programs, including those that come up for normal appropriations every year, it is expected and, in some cases required, that an evaluation report is included with the budget requests. This is necessary for the decision makers to see how well the government has been able to utilize past budget allocations to justify future allocation.

The Budget Document

Budgeting is applied. This is clearly evident in the two major documents that a government puts together each year—one, before the fiscal year begins, which is the budget document, and, the other, immediately after the fiscal year is over, which is the annual financial report. Both documents contain a wealth of information about the government that a reader will find useful. Given the breadth of information the documents contain, in particular the budget document, the budget serves as a government's most important reference document. As Hyde puts it, "in their increasingly voluminous and complex formats, budgets simultaneously record policy decision outcomes; cite policy priorities and program goals and objectives; delineate a government's total service effort; and measure its performance, impact and overall effectiveness" (Hyde 1991).

Familiarity with the budget document, therefore, is an important first step in learning about a government and the jurisdiction it serves. More importantly, familiarity with the document will allow a reader to learn about a jurisdiction's economy, in particular, about its revenue base, its expenditure history and future direction, its fund structure and basis of accounting, its budget process, budget systems that guide its budget development, financial policies that guide its budgetary and financial activities, capital improvement activities that are vital for its long-term growth and development, its past budget accomplishments and future challenges; above all, the extent to which it has been able to utilize the allocated funds to achieve its goals and objectives in the past, and how it plans to achieve its objectives in the future.

Structure of the Book

To a considerable extent, the emergence and success of public budgeting as a field of study is due to its eclectic nature, in particular its ability to draw from the richness of other disciplines and due to its ability to contribute to the other disciplines at the same time. The book is an attempt to reflect this multidimensional nature of public budgeting.

It begins with an introduction to market system and the role of government; in particular, market failure and the need for government intervention. This is important because government intervention in the marketplace has a direct bearing on the budget. In general, the more the intervention, the greater is the need for budgetary activities vis-à-vis the bigger the size of the budget to support the range of measures that will be needed to address the failure. This is followed by, in Part I, budget background that serves both as a prelude to and foundation for many of the budgetary activities in government. It begins with a general discussion of taxation, which is the primary means by which a government collects its revenues, and the criteria for evaluating a tax system. This is followed by an overview of government expenditures, their growth trends and underlying causes of growth, and a detailed discussion of its revenues, in particular the various sources from which it collects its revenues and their underlying structure.

All governments, except for the federal government, prepare two budgets—an operating budget and a capital budget. The operating budget deals with routine (recurring), everyday operation (activities) of a government, while the capital budget deals with activities that are non-recurring and long-term in nature. The next two parts of the book, Part II and Part III, discuss these two activities in considerable details. Part II, which looks at the operating budget, focuses on three areas—budget process, budget systems, and elements of budget forecasting. Interestingly, the budget process and the budget systems most governments currently use have gone through extensive developments over the years. The chapters try to capture this development in as much details as possible, especially the budget systems, followed by a broad discussion of budget forecasting. Forecasting is integral to public budgeting, but it is a vast area. Given the range of forecasting methods that are available to a budget practitioner vis-à-vis a forecaster, it is difficult to cover every single forecasting method in a single chapter; as such, the chapter focuses on those that are simple and relatively easy to use.

Part III of the book, which looks at the capital budget, also focuses on three areas—capital budget process, methods commonly used in evaluating capital projects such as payback period and cost-benefit analysis, and capital rationing. It is difficult to discuss capital rationing without shedding some lights on decision tools that have become commonplace in dealing with capital rationing problems; in particular, optimization models such as those used in mathematical programming. To keep the discussion to a minimum, the chapter focuses on two basic programming models, linear and integer, both of which have been extensively used in capital rationing. The book concludes with an overview of some of the contemporary issues in public budgeting. While no book can capture the essence of every single aspect of a field or discipline, it has made an attempt to cover as much of the fundamentals as possible.

Finally, as noted earlier, budgeting as a field of study has an analytical undertone, although that may not be obvious by looking at a budget document which largely consists of numbers and narratives. It does not show what went behind those numbers—the enormous amount of calculations and the analytical details to put together the document. There is a reason for this: The document is prepared for policy debate in the legislature and for public consumption. Nevertheless, at its core, it is analytical that requires a basic knowledge of quantitative methods and techniques, especially when preparing, implementing, and evaluating the budget. The book has made every effort to keep the analytical details of these tools to a minimum and as simple as possible, while recognizing the importance of these skills for a budding budget practitioner. Also, the book is structured in such a way that the readers can easily skip the chapters that are more analytically oriented as well as for expediency of time; in particular, the chapters on budget forecasting (Chapter 7) and capital rationing (Chapter 10) without losing the focus of the book.

Lubbock, USA   Aman Khan

References

Hyde, A. C. (1991). The Development of Budgeting and Budget Theory: The Threads of Budget Reform. In A. C. Hyde (Ed.), *Government Budgeting: Theory, Process, and Politics* (pp. 1–6). Pacific Grove, CA: Brooks/Cole Publishing.
Lynch, T. D. (1995). *Public Budgeting in America*. New York: Prentice-Hall.
Wanat, J. (1978). *Introduction to Budgeting*. Monterey, CA: Brooks/Cole Publishing.

Acknowledgements

Several of my former professors and colleagues took their time to read various chapters of the original manuscript at different points of its development. My sincere thanks and gratitude to each one of them; in particular, to Professors James Kenkel, Jack Ochs, and Louis Vargas of the University of Pittsburgh; Professors Peter Summers of University of Illinois, Vic Valcarcel of the University of Texas at Dallas, Susan Opp of Colorado State University, and John Gerlach of Western Carolina University; and Professors Drew Winters, Robert Ricketts, Dakshina De Silva, Robert McComb, Masha Rahnama, and Klaus Becker of Texas Tech University. Thanks also to two anonymous reviewers for their comments and suggestions. Again, my sincerest thanks to each one of these individuals who took the time from their busy schedule to read parts of the manuscript, but I alone bear the responsibility for any error the book may contain.

In the same vein, I want to extend my special thanks to several individuals at Palgrave-USA without whose help, patience and unfailing support this publication would not have been possible; in particular, to Ms. Michelle Chen, the editor of Palgrave, who had the patience to bear with me and never failing to extend her support when I needed it, and Mr. John Stegner, Associate Editor, for his patience and unfailing support during the entire process. Thanks are also due to the entire production team, in particular, Mr. Sham Anand, Project Manager, and Ms. Prathipa Raju, Production Editor, as well as the team that designed the cover, for making sure that everything was in order during the production process. I owe each one of them my heartfelt thanks and gratitude.

Finally, a very special thanks to my family—Terri, Junaid, Jasmine, Tyler, and my two little grandchildren, Sofia and James, without whose love and affection this book would have never seen the light of day; I am proud to have them all in my life.

Contents

List of Figures

List of Tables

Introduction: Market System and the Role of Government

The level of budgetary activities in a government is directly related to the economic system of which it is a part. In a command economy, where there is no private sector, budgeting is central to all economic and noneconomic decisions of the government. In a free market economy, such as the United States, while the presence of a strong private sector limits the role of government, it is still substantial considering the size of the federal budget that runs into several trillion dollars each year. Although not as high as the federal budget in percentage terms, state and local budgets also constitute a significant percentage of their respective gross products. Therefore, to understand the nature of budgetary activities in a government it is important to understand how the market system operates—its strengths and limitations and, more importantly, the role government plays in a market system. As the conventional wisdom goes, the more efficient the market system, the less the role of government.[1] In budgetary parlance, it means less government expenditures, less taxes, and less regulations. Ideally, if the market system could address all our needs and fully regulate its own behavior, there will not be any need for government intervention, but, in reality, that is seldom the case. A market system, by itself, cannot perform all the functions necessary to meet the needs of society nor can it fully regulate itself, hence the need for government intervention. This chapter briefly discusses how the market system operates, the problems an unchecked market system creates for society, and why government intervention is necessary, including an overview of some of the measures commonly used to address the problems.

1.1 A Simple Illustration of How the Market System Operates

Let us begin with a brief discussion of how the free market system operates to understand why collective action vis-à-vis government intervention is necessary. A market system, in particular a free market system, is a system of interactions

© The Author(s) 2019
A. Khan, *Fundamentals of Public Budgeting and Finance*,
https://doi.org/10.1007/978-3-030-19226-6_1

between the buyers (consumers) and sellers (producers) in a market without any, or as little as possible, intervention by the government. It is based on the notion of a "perfectly competitive market," characterized by a number of conditions such as a large number of buyers and sellers, full information for both buyers and sellers, no barriers to entry into or exit from the market, perfect mobility of resources (factors of production), and absence of public goods and externalities. If these ideal conditions were to exist, the free market system should be able to meet all the needs of society, guaranteeing maximum welfare for the public and maximum profit for firms and businesses. However, in reality, such a system does not exist; nevertheless, it provides a conceptual framework for understanding market behavior in all its forms and variations.

To illustrate how the system operates, let us begin with a simple market economy consisting of households (HHs) and firms and businesses (FBs), with no government intervention.[2] In this simple and uncomplicated economy, households demand goods and firms and businesses supply the goods that the households demand. The interaction between supply and demand takes place in the economic marketplace, following the rules of free market competition. The interaction determines a price at which the goods brought to the market will be cleared off, setting an equilibrium condition in the market. The price is called the equilibrium price, P^0, and the quantity sold—the equilibrium quantity, Q^0. However, in order for firms and businesses to be able to produce goods, they need factors of production (land, labor, capital, etc.) which the households must supply. As before, the interaction between supply and demand will determine the price, P^0, at which all the factors of production brought to the market will be cleared off, establishing equilibrium in the respective factor market—labor in the labor market, capital in the capital market, and land in the land market (Fig. 1.1).

In the event that the market conditions change, say, supply increases from S to S', as shown in Fig. 1.2a, the price will come down from P^0 to P' and at the reduced price the surplus goods will be cleared off the market, creating a new equilibrium condition. The converse will be true if demand increases from D to D', but supply remains constant. It will increase price, from P^0 to P', and with increased price more suppliers will join the market, which will increase supply but will also lower the price to P''. The process will continue until all the goods brought to the market are cleared off, creating a new equilibrium, Q'' (Fig. 1.2b). An identical situation will also take place in the factor markets where the interaction between demand and supply of land, labor, and capital will determine the price (rent for land, wage for labor, and interest for capital) at which all the factors brought to the market will be cleared off, creating a new equilibrium in each factor market. When all the markets are in equilibrium, the result will be a "general equilibrium" in the market.

A general equilibrium in the market does not mean that the markets are independent of each other; in reality, they are interdependent in that what happens in one market can easily affect the equilibrium in another market. Thus, if the demand for a commodity, say coffee, increases, it will not only increase the price of coffee, but will also increase the demand for tea (a close substitute), assuming

Households demand goods and services

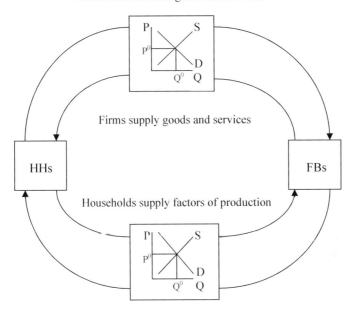

Firms supply goods and services

Households supply factors of production

Firms demand factors of production

Fig. 1.1 A two-sector free market economy

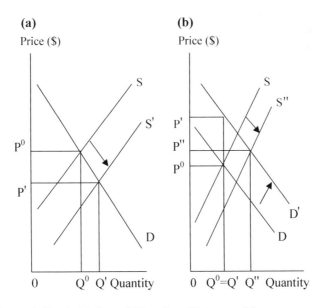

Fig. 1.2 Changes in Supply (**a**), demand (**b**), and equilibrium conditions

more consumers will move to tea. Similarly, if the demand for input factors, say capital, in one market increases, there will be less capital available for investment in another market, and so forth. In other words, a change in demand and supply will change the equilibrium condition in a given market, as well as in all other markets with which it has a direct or indirect relationship until a new equilibrium is established.

1.2   Market Failure and the Need for Government Intervention

As simple and uncomplicated as the system appears, it also has a tendency to create certain conditions in the marketplace that economists call "anomalies," which, if left unchecked, will lead to "market failure" (Bator 1958). The failure occurs because of market's inability (1) to operate efficiently, (2) to deal with aggregate (macro) economic problems, (3) to provide goods that are necessary for collective consumption called public goods, and (4) to regulate itself. Richard Musgrave, in his classic text "The Theory of Public Finance," recognized three essential functions a government performs in response to these failures—allocation, distribution, and stabilization (Musgrave 1959). The allocation function, according to Musgrave, deals with the process by which the resources of society are divided between private and public goods. The distribution function adjusts the inequities in income and wealth to ensure that they conform to what society considers "fair" or "equitable," while the stabilization function deals with measures necessary to maintain high employment, a reasonable degree of price stability, economic growth, and balance of payment equilibrium. The fourth function—regulation—is a process that regulates the behavior of firms and businesses to ensure competition in the marketplace.[3]

1.2.1   Failure to Operate Efficiently

Although in principle the market system is supposed to operate efficiently, it often fails to do so. The failure occurs when the market deviates from the rules of free market operation, creating inefficiency in the marketplace. This does not mean that the market disappears literally—only that it creates certain conditions that are detrimental to free market operation and, consequently, to society at large. Important among these conditions are monopoly, externality, imperfect information, incomplete markets, and income inequality.

1.2.1.1 Monopoly
At the opposite end of free market competition is monopoly, where a single firm dominates the market. Monopolies occur because of economies of scale (lower average cost of production), where it may be advantageous for a firm to have control over a vast amount of resources, including capital to achieve economies for

large-scale production, such as steel, heavy industries, and public utilities.[4] What this means is that it may be cheaper for a large firm to produce the entire output rather than allowing a number of small firms to produce parts of it because it will be less costly. High start-up or fixed costs for products, such as public utilities, may also discourage small firms to compete. These types of monopolies are called natural monopolies. Monopolies may also occur when a government gives exclusive rights to a firm to conduct business such as the British East India Company during the mercantile period, or more recently the rights given to firms such as AT&T to have full control of local and long-distance calls until 1984 by protecting it from competition. These types of monopolies are called legal monopolies. A somewhat different form of legal monopoly that is not so direct would be patent rights given to a firm for invention for a certain number of years. Although patent rights can serve as an incentive for innovation, it can also stifle competition depending on the condition and the time length of protection.[5]

Theoretically, there is nothing wrong with monopoly as a market condition; in particular, a natural monopoly since it allows some competition in the market, but the problem with monopoly, in particular a pure monopoly is that it can control price by controlling output. Additionally, monopolies can exercise undue influence through political and non-political means to control raw materials and prevent others from entering the market. Since none of these conditions are in the best interest of the consumers, some interventions are necessary to prevent monopoly formation and encourage competition. Government intervention through regulations, such as antitrust laws, is an effective way to deal with this, especially where there is no natural monopoly. The earliest antitrust law passed in the country was the Sherman Antitrust Act in 1890. A number of other acts have been passed since then such as the Clayton Act in 1914, the Public Utility Holding Company Act in 1935, the Cellar-Kefauver Act of 1950, and so forth. The primary objective of these and other similar acts is to ensure competition by allowing unrestricted entry into the market by other firms and prevent unfair competition by firms of all sizes.

In reality, the market is neither perfectly competitive nor dominated by a single firm, but rather lies somewhere in between. A good example is oligopoly, where a few large firms dominate the market. Interestingly, to have control over the market oligopolies often collude with each other and behave like a monopoly firm, as in a cartel such as the Organization of the Petroleum Exporting Countries (OPEC) and, occasionally, they would compete with each other to maximize individual profit. As the number of oligopolies increases, an oligopolistic market would resemble a competitive market and the oligopolies may assume some of the same characteristics of a competitive firm. In fact, the competition will produce equilibrium in the marketplace, called Nash equilibrium—a non-cooperative equilibrium, where each firm tries to maximize its profit by taking into consideration other firms' output, as given. Since the market is in equilibrium, no single firm has an incentive to unilaterally adjust output, thereby producing a profit margin that will be less than the profit for a monopoly firm but more than a competitive firm. From the point of view of consumers, however, the effect will be essentially the same as a monopoly.

A Note on Natural Monopoly

It is worth expanding a little on a term we introduced earlier called natural monopoly. Unlike pure monopolies, natural monopolies are not necessarily undesirable from society's point of view, as long as the benefits to society of lower price from economies of scale outweigh the higher price generally associated with pure monopolies. Under these circumstances, society may be better off allowing some monopolies to exist or it can assume the responsibility by producing the goods itself or use regulation to control the price a monopoly firm may charge for the provision of the goods. Goods such as electricity, water, sewer, gas pipelines, and other capital intensive goods are classic examples of activities that have built-in economies of scale that can be produced at a lower cost without the complications of higher prices. Also, as noted earlier, the initial setup costs of these activities are quite high making them prohibitive for small firms to enter the market to provide the goods. This may explain why a government often allows large private firms to undertake these activities and, in some cases, assumes the ownership of these activities itself such as electricity or gas, thereby serving the role of a natural monopolist.

1.2.1.2 Externality

Externality simply means spillover or third-party effect; it is the unpriced cost or benefit the action of an individual or a firm produces for a third party. Unlike normal market operations, where the market determines the price the individuals must pay for the choices they make (e.g., goods and services they consume), most of these costs and benefits take place outside the market system such that when an externality occurs there is no market mechanism to allocate the costs and benefits for the affected party. In other words, they are not reflected in the market price. Therefore, if left up to the market to allocate the costs and benefits, especially costs, the market does not have the incentive or the means to correct the problem. The end result is inefficient allocation of resources.

Externalities can occur at any stage during the consumption of a good, called consumption externality, such as eating contaminated food that can cause serious health problems, or during production of a good, called production externality such as the action of a firm X affecting the action of a firm Y. Regardless of whether they occur during consumption or production, externalities can be positive or negative, depending on the consequences they produce for the affected party. Positive externalities occur when the action of an individual or a firm produces a benefit for others that is not reflected in the price. A good example of positive externality will be when a neighbor keeps his property in good condition which increases not only the value of his property, but also the value of the property of his neighbors for which they did not have to contribute but, nevertheless, receive the benefit. The opposite is true when the neighbor fails to do so, which will lower not only the value of his property, but also the value of the property of his neighbors, creating a negative externality. Another frequently cited example of negative externality is when a firm pollutes water that reduces water quality, imposing an external cost on individuals living and working around, but not necessarily on the firm. Interestingly, the firm does not include the external cost of pollution in the market price of the good; if it has to, it will invariably increase the price, thereby giving it the appearance of being less costly than it really is (had the cost been included in the price).

Since the market fails to take into account the costs externality produces for the affected party, it has no way of knowing the "true" demand and, as such, has a tendency to overproduce goods that produce negative externality. Similarly, the market has a tendency to underproduce goods that produce positive externality when it fails to take into account the benefits externality produces for the affected party vis-a-vis society at large since it does not have the knowledge of the "true" demand. Therefore, for both positive and negative externalities, the result will be inefficient allocation of resources for failing to produce what society would consider desirable. Take, for instance, education. As shown in Fig. 1.3a, given a choice, the public would be willing to consume a higher quantity of education at point at Q', but may actually receive Q^0 because of higher costs, among others. Take, on the other hand, the example of a meat processing plant that pollutes water (Fig. 1.3b). The plant will produce Q^0 at price P^0, because it costs less due to economies of scale, while the public may be willing to consume less at Q'.

A classic example of negative externality with a long history is the "tragedy of the commons," where individuals, as well as firms and businesses, acting in self-interest can destroy public resources, thereby affecting their consumption by

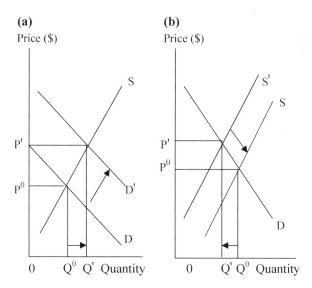

Fig. 1.3 Under production of goods for positive externality (**a**); Overproduction of goods for negative externality (**b**)

the collectivity (Shafriritz et al. 2009). Popularized by Garrett Hardin (1968), the concept was first introduced in 1892 when the naturalist John Muir founded an environmental activist group called the Sierra Club, to protect the Sierra Nevada, also known as the Yosemite National Park, from the abuse by mountaineers and vacationers in undeveloped northern California at the time. Muir, along with several interested groups, lobbied Congress to turn the State Park to the federal government, which incorporated it into a national park. The movement created mass consciousness among the public that eventually led to other kinds of legislations, protecting environment, natural resources, and endangered species.

Causes of Externality

Given that externalities are a common occurrence and can easily lead to inefficient allocation of resources, the question then is what causes externalities to occur. In general, externalities occur when there are no property rights or they are not well defined. Property rights are laws that allow individuals to own and voluntarily exchange property in the marketplace for a price, as determined by the interplay of supply and demand. What this means is that for a market system to operate freely and efficiently it must have well-defined property rights. Without clearly defined property rights, individuals will behave in self-interest without due consideration for others, especially in situations where resources are scarce, resulting in externality problems that can cost society both in monetary terms and loss in aggregate welfare (Bator 1958). In the extreme case, it can lead to social anarchy. Therefore, property rights serve as a necessary condition for maintaining social order by removing problems externalities produce for individuals, as well as for society at large. In reality, the rights do not necessarily remove externalities since it is difficult to remove them entirely, but they can create conditions for exchange between the parties involved to negotiate a resolution to externality problems.

Measures to Correct Externality

Externalities are real and can produce serious economic and social costs, if not addressed properly. The simplest way to deal with an externality problem is to allow the parties to resolve it through direct negotiation or bargaining without any external intervention. This would be possible if the number of individuals involved in an interaction is small and the parties have the same ability to influence the outcome, but, unfortunately, that is seldom the case. Parties do not necessarily have the same ability to influence the outcome of any negotiation, meaning that some interventions by government are necessary.

In general, the government can intervene through its allocative policy by regulating the amount of externality a firm can produce such as the amount of pollutants it can discharge. Alternatively, it can respond by introducing pecuniary measures such as taxes in proportion to the amount of externality that will require firms to produce an equitable level of output. While there are circumstances where it may be possible to accurately measure externality, such as industrial pollution, it may not be the case in every situation which may make it difficult to use proportionate taxes as an effective alternative. Ideally, if enforcement costs are not an issue, taxing would be economically preferable to regulation because it would encourage the producers who are in a better position to know the costs of externality to choose the least cost way of reducing the problem. Furthermore, regulations of individual processes may not control the overall level of externality, such as pollution from all sources, without additional regulations that specify who may or may not operate. However, a pollution tax requires no such administrative discretion since the total level of pollution from all producers can be controlled by simply adjusting the tax rate at which all producers must pay.

Interestingly, there are circumstances where taxing as a method can be difficult to use because of the difficulty to determine who should be taxed and how much, especially in situations where multiple organizations are involved with poorly defined property rights. The result may require the government to maintain a balance between regulation and tax that will be most cost-effective, depending on the nature and the extent of the problem. On the other hand, it can use the same policy in reverse by creating incentives for positive externality, such as giving a price or tax break for firms that underproduce goods that are socially desirable since, from society's point of view, they need to produce more.

1.2.1.3 Imperfect Information

Information is vital for making rational choices by consumers. An important requirement of free market operation is that consumers must have full knowledge of the goods and services they consume and, consequently, the price they must pay for their consumption. Given a choice, most firms will not voluntarily provide full information about their products, which creates an information gap between what consumers need to know to make a rational choice about their consumption and the level of information available in the market. Even with recent advancements in information technology, it is likely that information will not be readily accessible to all consumers or they may not have the necessary means or knowledge to acquire the information they need, creating what one would call a "rational ignorance"—a condition that deprives individuals not only from learning the truth about the goods and services they consume, but also the additional price they may have to pay for lack of information. Therefore, some interventions are necessary in the marketplace to ensure that the consumers have the information they need to make rational economic decisions about their consumption.

A good example of government intervention to correct the problem imperfect information creates for consumers is the Truth-in-Lending bill that Congress passed some years ago, which requires all lenders to inform the borrowers the exact rate of interest they will pay on their loans before signing contracts. Another good example is the Truth-in-Advertising bill Congress passed under the Lanham Act in 1946 to protect consumers from false advertising. Together with the Clayton Act, the Lanham Act allows the consumers who have been harmed by false advertising to press charges and receive compensation for the damage. Similar examples can be found in a variety of other areas. In fact, many of the labels on consumer products that have become commonplace today are the results of the initiatives by the government as part of its contents disclosure policy to keep consumers informed that otherwise would not have been provided by the market.

1.2.1.4 Incomplete Markets

In our two-sector economy, we assumed that market is quite capable of meeting all the needs of the consumers, as long as they have the effective demand in that they have the purchasing power to back up their demand. In reality, the consumers may not have the same means or the ability to purchase what they need, leaving them with very little or no options. A good example is higher education. Although the private sector has the ability and can provide higher education in sufficient quantities, it will not provide for those who cannot afford the price since it will not be profitable to do so. The result will be a level of output or consumption that is less than what is socially desirable. Put differently, if education can be treated as an investment, which it is, in particular higher education, then failure to invest in education will have a negative effect on society, resulting from loss of income, loss of productivity, increase in crime and violence, and so forth. Therefore, some interventions are necessary to ensure that it is available to those who want higher education. A good example is the 1965 Higher Education Act the government passed, providing guarantee on student loans to ensure that students can receive loans at low or reasonable interest rates to finance their education, among others.

Another, but a slightly different example will be insurance on bank deposits. Because of the possibility of financial risks, banks will not automatically provide insurance to their depositors, which may make sense from an economic point of view, but may not be desirable from society's point of view. Consider a bank run (which occurs when a large number of customers decide to withdraw their deposits thinking the bank might be insolvent) which is often contagious because it can lead to a chain effect, resulting in massive withdrawals and eventual collapse of the banking system. Therefore, like education, some interventions are necessary to reduce the possibility of a bank run and also to ensure that the depositors are guaranteed a minimum safety on their deposits. Consequently, in 1933, following the collapse of the banking industry, the government established the Federal Deposit Insurance Corporation (FDIC), as part of the Glass-Steagall Act, to provide insurance for depositors against potential loss of savings in the event of bank failures, among others. Interestingly, the act was repealed in 1999 under the Gramm-Leach-Bliley Act that some believe may have partially contributed to the financial market collapse of 2007–2008.

While it is understandable why firms will not provide goods for those who cannot afford the price in a market system or, in some cases, not produce at all, there are other explanations as to why that may be the case. A good case in point is information asymmetry (the differences in the level of information individuals have during a transaction), where an individual with less information is in a weaker position to bargain or negotiate a contract and, as such, may end up paying a higher price than he should. Take, for instance, health insurance. The insurance company may have a general sense of the risk the buyer may possess, but it has to be careful how the premium is charged. If the firm underestimates the risk, it will charge less than what it ideally should, in which case it will incur a loss. On the other hand, if the firm overestimates, it may charge more than what it ideally should and may lose the buyer, as a result. The outcome may be a no-win situation for the firm and the firm may decide not to provide the service at all, which may not be in the best interest of either the consumer or society, at large. Since health care is a socially desirable good, some interventions are necessary to ensure that a minimum level of the good is available to those who need it. It should be emphasized, however, that information asymmetry is not necessarily the reason for individuals who do not have health insurance; they may choose not to have an insurance because the cost is higher than what they can afford or are willing to pay. There are plenty of other similar examples where government interventions are necessary because of the market's inability to meet the needs of the consumers.

1.2.1.5 Income Inequality

The economic decisions of firms and households are often guided by a simple economic rule called the marginal condition which provides a basis for firms and businesses to determine what goods to produce, how much to produce, and at what point the production will be inefficient. In its bare essence, for a profit-maximizing firm to operate efficiently it must produce up to the point at which the marginal cost, MC (the cost of producing an additional unit of a good), is equal to its marginal revenue, MR (the revenue earned from the sale of an additional unit of the good); that is, $MC = MR$. To produce more will result in a loss because marginal cost will be higher than marginal revenue ($MC > MR$), just as to produce less will not be profitable because marginal cost will be less than marginal revenue ($MC < MR$), indicating that opportunities exist to produce more without incurring a loss. In other words, the firm can continue to produce additional units with positive marginal revenue until the point where it will no longer be profitable, which will be at the point where $MC = MR$, and price reflects this relationship.

The marginal conditions described above can also be used to explain how the free market system rewards the factors of production. Take for instance, labor. How much an individual will receive in wage (price of labor) is determined by how much his labor is worth in the marketplace at the margin, that is, the revenue the employer will earn for an additional unit of labor. Thus, if it costs $12.50 an hour to produce an additional unit of a good and the revenue generated from that unit is also $12.50, such that $MC = MR$, then, by definition, price must be equal to both MC and MR. In other words, that is how much the individual should receive for an hour's worth of labor because to pay more will not be profitable for the firm, just as to pay less would mean that more labor could be absorbed at that price (assuming additional labor will be available at a lower price). Similarly, if it costs $75 an hour to produce an additional unit of a good or service that is how much the individual should receive, and so forth.

There is nothing inherently wrong with this fundamental economic rule since the price is determined by the interaction of supply and demand for labor. However, the problem with this is that it can leave a vast pool of unemployed or underemployed labor whose marginal worth is zero or barely above the subsistence level. This may produce an income gap that is not in the best interest of society, especially if the gap is wide enough that it can lead to social and political unrest. From an economic point of view, the income gap can be construed as a measure of welfare loss not only for individuals who are unemployed or underemployed, but also for society at large. Assume for a moment that income inequality produces a welfare loss, especially for those who are at the lower rung of income ladder, indicating that some interventions are necessary to minimize the income gap. This can be done by guaranteeing a minimum wage, as long as it does not significantly diminish the profit margin of the firms, or through direct financial benefit for the working poor such as Earned Income Tax Credit (ERTC), or through various other transfer programs, as long as these measures do not affect the welfare of those whose incomes will be affected by the decision. In reality, whether there will be a welfare gain or loss from intervention depends on the relative marginal utility of income and the amount of transfer.

1.2.1.6 Emerging Issues

As market conditions change due to changes in technology, businesses practices, and other factors, they tend to create new problems, requiring new sets of policies to deal with. A good example is networking, which is the practice where firms form an alliance for buying and selling commodities online that requires a new set of compliance rules, price relations, and market conditions that are different from the rules of exchange in the conventional marketplace. There are plenty of other examples that will continue to define emerging trends in the marketplace. The point is that in a dynamic, free market, economy the market conditions will constantly change, creating new problems that will require new and innovative ways to deal with the problems as they emerge, while ensuring free market operation.

1.2.2   Failure to Deal with Macroeconomic Problems

A second important consequence of market failure is the inability of the free market system to deal with macroeconomic issues such as unemployment, inflation, slow economic growth, and balance of payment disequilibrium. Unemployment occurs when an economy fails to create sufficient jobs to absorb the available labor force, while inflation occurs when there is a consistent increase in the general price level. Slow or poor economic growth is a condition where the real output of society remains constant or grows at a rate slower than the rate of growth in population, as measured by gross national product, GNP (the market value of all final goods and services produced in an economy in a single year or quarter, including net import) or gross domestic product, GDP (the market value of all final goods and services produced by factors of production within a country in a single year or quarter, excluding net import). Finally, the balance of payment disequilibrium occurs when an economy imports more than it exports, resulting in a greater outflow of capital than inflow. All of these have a cumulative effect on the aggregate economy that is difficult to address without some interventions by the government.

1.2.2.1 Unemployment

Unemployment is a common occurrence in a market economy. There are several reasons why unemployment occurs. First, when there is a structural change in the economy such as when an economy moves from a labor-intensive agrarian economy to a capital intensive industrial economy (capital-labor substitution), or from an industrial to a service-oriented economy, creating a mismatch between demand and supply in the skills of labor. The transition forces some individuals out of work, especially those whose labor is no longer required by the market called structural unemployment. Second, when firms regularly layoff employees to cut costs or increase productivity called frictional unemployment. Theoretically, it is not always possible to separate frictional unemployment from structural unemployment if layoffs are related to structural causes, in which case structural unemployment essentially becomes an extension of frictional unemployment—only that it lasts longer. Third, when demand declines for labor during certain times of the year because of slow economic activities, such as during summer months or immediately following the holiday season called seasonal unemployment. Fourth, when there are changes in the level of business activities, resulting from changes in the internal forces of an economy such as production, income, the demand for credit, interest rate, and inventories, called cyclical unemployment.

Of the above, cyclical unemployment is more complex to explain because economists do not precisely know when the cycle will start and how long it will last. Figure 1.4 shows a typical business cycle. In general, a minor cycle is less intense and is associated with a slowdown of the economy, called recession, and a major cycle can last for several years and is associated with a prolonged recession, with a partial breakdown of the economy, called depression. There is a fifth category of unemployment, called disguised unemployment, which occurs when individuals give up looking for jobs and become a part of what is known as hidden unemployment. This is different from underemployment, which occurs when individuals

Fig. 1.4 A typical business cycle

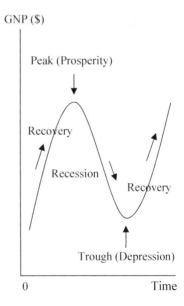

GNP ($)

Peak (Prosperity)

Recovery

Recession

Recovery

Trough (Depression)

0   Time

work in jobs that require less skill than they were trained for or for less number of hours than a full-employment job.

Regardless of what contributes to it, unemployment has serious economic consequences for individuals, who lose their jobs, and also for firms and businesses, as a result of lost production and income. People who cannot work do not produce, which makes the aggregate output smaller. According to Arthur Okun, known as the Okun's law, unemployment rate goes down when the real GNP (adjusted for inflation) is above 2.5%. More specifically, for each percentage point increase in real GNP, unemployment rate tends to decrease by 0.4%, and vice versa (Dornbusch and Fisher 1990). Recently, Romer and Bernstein (2008) suggested a "rule of thumb" approach, according to which a one percent increase in GDP would result in one million new jobs. Although these are not perfect measures of the relationship between unemployment and GNP or GDP, they do provide a useful guide for policy makers as to what measures to take that would bring down unemployment rate and promote economic growth. Interestingly, the market can be in equilibrium even when an economy is in recession, that is, when it is working at less than full-employment level.

The conventional notion of full employment is a situation where an economy is able to absorb all those who are looking for jobs, but an ideal definition would be a situation where all the factors of production are fully employed, that is, working at their fullest capacity. Unfortunately, it is almost impossible to have a full-employment or zero-unemployment economy. Economists, in general, believe that there is a "natural rate of unemployment" that is likely to be present in any economy since it is difficult for an economy to avoid elements of structural, seasonal, or frictional unemployment at any given time, even under the best of circumstances. Cyclical unemployment is usually excluded from this calculation because it follows a different pattern. Considered as the baseline rate of unemployment, the natural rate reflects the long-term market condition, consistent with the aggregate output in the economy in the absence of temporary changes in price and wage (Gordon 2018). However, the natural rate is not a fixed rate because it changes over time, depending on how well an economy is performing at the aggregate level, but the rule of thumb is that it should be above 0% (the full-employment rate in the absence of business cycle).[6]

1.2.2.2 Inflation

Inflation ordinarily means too much money chasing too few goods. Formally, it can be defined as an increase in the general price level. This does not mean that the price of every single commodity in the market is increasing at the same rate, although the overall trend is upward. Several factors contribute to inflation. First, when the demand for goods and services exceeds the available supply in the marketplace in the short run, especially when the economy is working at the full-employment level called demand-pull inflation. Second, when the price of factors of production (costs of labor, materials, and capital) increases resulting in higher prices of goods and services, called cost-push inflation. Third, when wages and prices show a downward rigidity, but are flexible upward, called structural inflation. This may be due to administered prices set by government, such as minimum wage or due to negotiated prices set by agreements between a labor union and the management, as in labor contracts, leading eventually to an increase in the general price level. Fourth, when government expenditure on social goods, such as social security payments, unemployment benefits, healthcare benefits, various welfare programs, including rent subsidies, and a host of other social services increases, called social inflation.

These programs increase the purchasing power of the consumers vis-à-vis the public, without a corresponding increase in productivity which results in inflation. Interestingly, many of these programs are indexed to inflation to adjust for costs of living increases, called cost of living adjustment (COLA), especially during times of economic prosperity when the inflation rates are usually high. A special case of social inflation is budget inflation when government expenditure as a whole increases in a full-employment economy without a corresponding increase in taxes; thereby, creating inflationary pressures.

There is a fifth category of inflation that has received considerable attention in recent years, which occurs in the midst of high unemployment called stagflation (a stagnant economy with high inflation). It drew serious attention in the late 1970s and early 1980s, especially following the OPEC oil embargo in 1973, creating a major price shock in the global oil market with severe consequences on the US economy. Although not a common occurrence, stagflation became a major economic challenge for the policy makers when the combined unemployment and inflation rate reached about 20%.

For a long time, economists believed that we cannot have both high unemployment and high inflation at the same time. In other words, there is a trade-off between unemployment and inflation in that when unemployment is high the inflation will be low, and vice versa. Theoretically, this makes perfect sense because during times of high unemployment people will have less purchasing power (effective demand) to clear off all the goods that are brought to the market. The opposite will be true, when unemployment is low. This relationship between unemployment and inflation was based on the empirical work of Arthur Phillips, a British economist, who studied the relationship between unemployment and wage increases in Britain between the years 1861 and 1913 and found that there is an inverse relationship between unemployment and inflation, which subsequently came to be known as the Phillips curve (Fig. 1.5).

The inverse relationship between unemployment and inflation convinced the economists that since we cannot have both high unemployment and high inflation at the same time, the policy makers have to be concerned only with one at any given time. Unfortunately, the stagflation of the late 1970s changed the dynamics of this long-held relationship, forcing the economists and policy makers to think of policies not in terms of one or the other (inflation or unemployment), but both. From a theoretical point of view, the relationship was challenged by the natural rate hypothesis on the ground that unemployment rate would eventually return to a rate determined by real variables in the economy such as real wage, independent of inflation. For instance, if unemployment is above the natural rate, more

Fig. 1.5 The Phillips curve

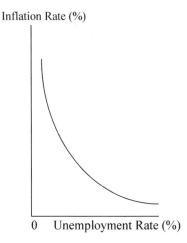

people would be willing to work at a lower wage which will bring the wage down, although fewer people may be willing to work at that rate. This will bring unemployment down to its natural rate. The converse will be true when unemployment is below the natural rate. Since fewer people are available, the real wage would increase, attracting more people into the labor force and raising the unemployment rate to its natural rate. Therefore, according to Friedman and Phelps (Gordon 2018), the curve would be vertical in the long run, not inverse.[7]

From a practical point of view, the primary concern with inflation is that it directly affects the purchasing power of the consumers and, consequently, their real income. In other words, it lowers the value of money over time. For instance, if a gallon of milk cost $3.75 last year and it costs $4.25 today, while income remains the same, the purchasing power vis-à-vis the real value of money has essentially declined as a result of the increase in price; in the aggregate, it lowers the real income of the consumers. Incidentally, the measure most commonly used to reflect the changes in price is the consumer price index (CPI).[8]

1.2.2.3 Policies to Deal with Unemployment and Inflation

For a long time, economists have been more concerned with unemployment than with inflation because of the experience of the Great Depression in the 1930s when the unemployment rate rose to about 25% (24.9% in 1933). Prior to that, the dominant economic principle was the classical economic principle led by the economists of the time, in particular by J. B. Say, a French economist, who believed that if left up to the market, the market should be able to correct any disequilibrium condition through the interaction of supply and demand.[9] The disequilibrium was considered temporary until the market adjusted itself, but the longevity of depression proved that it is possible to have equilibrium in the market with surplus labor and unsold goods. It was to the credit of the British economist John Maynard Keynes, who first suggested that prolonged recession is not a temporary condition, but rather the inability of the market to adjust itself due to lack of effective demand by the consumers, as well as by firms and businesses.

According to Keynes, the higher spending by consumers leads to greater effective demand for consumer goods and by firms and businesses for capital goods, which, in turn, leads to higher production, employment, and income (Keynes 1936). Conversely, a lower spending on consumer and capital goods reduces effective demand, leading to lower production, employment, and income.[10] The result is a vicious cycle of unemployment, recession, and eventually depression. Therefore, when the market conditions contribute to a lack of effective demand, the government needs to intervene to produce this demand and the policy the government uses to create this demand is known as the fiscal policy.

Fiscal Policy

The fiscal policy of a government operates through two principal instruments: tax, called tax policy, and expenditure, called expenditure policy. The government can use either policy to deal with the problem of unemployment and recession, but to have the desired effect it often needs both.[11] Let us look at how a government tax policy can help address the problem of high unemployment during an economic downturn, as shown below:

which simply says that lower taxes, which will increase savings, which, in turn, will increase investment and, finally, employment, but, in reality, it is much more complex because of the time it will take for the economy to move from one stage to the next to produce the desired result.

Also, there is no guarantee that tax cuts to induce job growth will work if there is excess capacity in the market, meaning that the firms are operating at less than their optimal (fullest) capacity, which is usually the case if the aggregate demand is less than what the firms could potentially supply. Theoretically, any increase in total spending that can be induced by a tax cut, leading to an increase in private investment, can also be induced by increasing government expenditure. However, the choice between increased government expenditure and reduced taxes must depend not only on economic rationale, but also on political considerations. When resources are underemployed (and interest rates are low, as a result) the social profitability of public investments in expenditure is usually high, and private firms with excess capacity will have little incentive to invest.

While, in principle, and assuming no excess capacity in the market, the tax policy should increase employment, but economists are uncertain as to how much time the process will require to generate the needed employment. There are three possible explanations for this apparent time lag: time to recognize the problem (recognition lag), time to implement the policy (implementation lag), and time for the policy to respond (response lag). From a policy perspective, it takes time to recognize the problem, determine the underlying causes, and take the appropriate course of action. From an implementation perspective, it takes time to plan, obtain new equipment, construct new plants, or refurbish the existing ones, before employment could be generated. Finally, from the point of view of actual results, it takes time for a policy to respond after it has been put in place, depending on how effectively the first two have been addressed (Dornbusch and Fisher 1990). Furthermore, if there is seepage in the economy, such as capital flight or if some savings are held back in that they are not funneled back into the economy, the process might take a much longer time than is necessary to recover. Therefore, in addition to lowering taxes, direct government intervention through public expenditure is often necessary to produce employment in the short run. The question is what kind of public expenditure will be most appropriate: economic or social?

Economic expenditures primarily include investments in infrastructure, such as roads, bridges, highways, and other construction projects, that will immediately absorb the surplus labor. Investments in social expenditure, such as education and job training, on the other hand, will create employment in the intermediate and long term, especially if unemployment is due to structural changes. In other words, both economic and social expenditures are necessary, along with private investments to produce the necessary growth in employment, as can be seen from the following relationship:

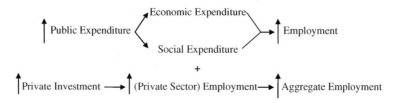

However, there are disagreements among the economists as to how much employment these measures will produce. Part of the reason for this is that, while the results of economic expenditures are relatively easy to determine, it is much harder for social expenditures which rely heavily on how fast the private sector will respond to a government's tax policy and create opportunities for the existing, as well as the retrained labor. Much also depends on the multiplier effects, in particular employment multiplier, these policies will produce for the economy.[12]

Besides employment multiplier, economists also use a variety of other multipliers, such as output multiplier, income multiplier, value-added multiplier, and so forth, to measure the effects of a change in an exogenous variable on the economy at large. The conventional wisdom here is that economic expenditures have a much higher multiplier effect than social expenditures, especially in the short-term, because of the time it takes to realize the full benefits of social expenditure. This is the essence of the Keynesian argument, known as the Keynesian multiplier, that since the macroeconomic problems of high unemployment and recession are the results of the lack of aggregate demand in the marketplace, an increase in exogenous spending vis-a-vis government expenditure (economic, as well as social), will increase the demand by some multiples.

Interestingly, multipliers do not remain constant over time—they change as the aggregate economic conditions change. Some economists believe that they can even be negative after a certain number of years, usually 5 or 6 years, which means that the fiscal instruments may not produce the exact same result once their purpose has been effectively served (Choudhury 1976). In other words, macroeconomic policies that have worked perfectly five years ago, $t-5$, may not work in exactly same manner next year, $t+1$.

Analysis of Tax and Expenditure Policy

Looking purely at the taxation side, the effectiveness of a government's tax policy depends on three things: who receives the tax breaks, how much, and how those benefits eventually translate into investments and employment.[13] Common sense tells us that tax breaks should be given to individuals with high incomes because they have a much higher marginal propensity to save, MPS (amount saved for each additional dollar of income) than any other income brackets, but, as noted earlier, if there is seepage in the economy or if some of the savings are held back it may not produce the desired result, even with a higher margin of savings. On the other hand, if tax breaks are given to the middle-income bracket it may go to both savings and consumption, but no one knows precisely in what proportion. However, one could argue that aggregate savings are likely to be higher for the middle-income bracket if the number of individuals belonging to the bracket is considerably larger than any other income brackets.

Now, looking at the expenditure side of the policy, when a government spends money (G), it usually comes from three sources: taxes (T), borrowing (B), and printing money (P), where each one can have a different effect on the economy depending on how they are used. We can express this relationship between government spending and the three measures as

$$G = T + B + P \qquad (1.1)$$

From a policy perspective, if spending comes entirely from taxes (G=T | B, P=0) there will be less money available, after paying taxes, for individual consumption, savings, and investment. If an economy is heavily dependent on consumption, then the decision has to be carefully weighed in making sure that it does not have a serious negative effect on aggregate consumption. On the other hand, if spending comes entirely from borrowing (G=B | T, P=0), or a combination of borrowing and taxes (G=B, T | P=0), | it will increase debt and raise the interest cost. Some economists, in particular Milton Friedman, have argued that the measure will "crowd out" the capital market, leaving less capital available for borrowing by the private sector, with no serious effect on output vis-à-vis the economy. The alternative will be external borrowing by the government to avoid the problem of crowding out, but creating one in the long term (political dependency, capital shortage in the global market, among others), if it has to rely on external borrowing for an extended period of time. However, the idea may not hold altogether if there is a surplus in the capital market from lack of investment opportunities, as it may be the case during times of prolonged recession or depression. In other words, government borrowing will not necessarily crowd out the capital market if there is a surplus in the capital market resulting from the decision by the private sector to hold back investments due to lack of investment opportunities or uncertainties in the market.

The notion that government borrowing crowds out the capital market with any visible effect on output vis-à-vis the economy dates back to David Ricardo, a nineteenth-century British economist, who believed that government borrowing can function like increasing current taxes and reducing current household and business expenditures. Known as the Ricardian Equivalence, the theory argues that it does not matter whether government raises taxes or borrows (which will eventually be financed out of taxes), the effect will be the same on the economy—private spending will go down by an equal amount withdrawn through borrowing or taxes, or both.

The theory was based on the notion that consumers are rational in that when government borrows to finance spending, say, during recession, while cutting taxes to induce savings and investment, consumers tend to save more than usual to pay for higher taxes in the future, but it is not clear to what extent the consumers make the choices about postponing current consumption in order to pay for increases in future taxes. However, it is also not clear to what extent the theory takes into account the multiplier effects of spending, which can easily undermine the support for it. Interestingly, the theory was extensively studied by Barro (1974), Feldstein (1976), and others, providing arguments on both sides of the issue.

Finally, if government spending comes entirely from printing money $(G = P \mid B, T = 0)$, it will create severe inflationary pressure on the economy and, as such, should be used as a last resort, but only as a temporary measure with proper monitoring, along with other measures.

Effects on Inflation While the fiscal policy of a government is most effective when it comes to unemployment and recession, economists believe that it can also be used in reverse to deal with inflation, as can be seen from the following relationship:

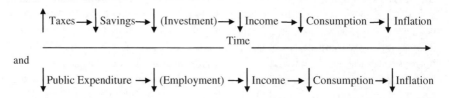

The assumption here is that inflation is caused by high aggregate demand (demand-pull inflation), which usually occurs when an economy is working at the full-employment level. Consequently, slowing the economy down through lower investment and income will reduce the purchasing power of the consumers, which, in turn, will lower inflation, but the process could be time-consuming. Also, an overuse of the policy may produce an opposite effect in that it can result in higher unemployment, creating a variety of social and economic problems that may not be in the best interest of society. The idea is to have a policy that will maintain a balance between unemployment and inflation.

Effects on Government Budget   Government policy using tax and public expenditures to deal with the problem of unemployment and recession has a direct bearing on the budget in that it can produce a deficit, a surplus, or a balanced budget. When a government increases expenditures and cuts taxes during an economic downturn, it will produce a budget deficit since it is taking less in revenue and spending more. This is known as expansionary policy. However, the deficits incurred during an economic downturn will be recovered from the surpluses when the economy bounces back since there will be less government spending and more tax revenue from a healthy economy. In other words, the budget surpluses produced when the economy bounces back will offset the deficits produced during the economic downturn.

Similarly, when a government lowers expenditures and raises taxes or keeps it at the same level as it was before, it will produce a budget surplus. This is known as contractionary policy. As noted above, the policy is often used as an anti-inflationary measure during times of economic prosperity, especially when an economy is working at the full-employment level which, unfortunately, has a tendency to create strong inflationary forces in the economy. Since the government spends less than it collects in taxes, this will cause the total spending to decline, producing a deflationary effect on the economy. Put differently, when a government collects more in tax revenue than it spends, especially during times of economic prosperity, it creates a fiscal drag (a restraint on the expansion of the economy as a consequence of tax policy) to help ward off inflation. On the other hand, when it spends more than it takes in revenue, as in a recession, it makes it necessary for government to raise taxes, or borrow, or both, creating a fiscal stimulus (opposite of fiscal drag) for the economy.

Finally, when a government spends the same amount as it collects in taxes, it will produce a balanced budget. In general, a balanced budget tends to have a neutral effect on the economy in that it will neither stimulate nor diminish demand as a result of taxes and government spending. Put simply, the neutral effect indicates that government through its spending will feed back into the economy what it withdraws in the form taxes; therefore, the net effect on the economy vis-à-vis on consumption, savings, and investment will be zero, but that may not always be the case. A balanced budget may have a non-neutral effect on the economy, depending on the sources of taxes and the direction of government spending.

Policy Implementation
The implementation of the fiscal policy as a means to stabilize the economy falls primarily on the chief executive—the President. Under the 1946 Employment Act, the President is given the authority to develop policies that would promote

full employment, increase production, and improve purchasing power. It was amended in 1953 to promote a stable dollar value. The act created the Council of Economic Advisors, headed by a chair and two additional members, to help the President put together the President's Annual Economic Report to be submitted to Congress each year on the state of the economy. The Congress has a counterpart of the Council, called the Joint Economic Committee, which receives the President's Economic Report after the President's State of the Union address. In recent years, the power and influence of the committee has significantly declined, especially with the establishment of the Congressional Budget Office (CBO) in 1974.

A Note on Supply-Side Economics

Macroeconomic policies based on Keynesian economics, which is often referred to as demand-side economics because it focuses on aggregate demand, also came under serious attack under the generic term "supply-side economics," especially in the 1970s for largely ignoring aggregate supply (Laffer 2004; Wanniski 1978). Supply-side economists believe that the best way to achieve economic growth and prosperity is by reducing barriers for firms and businesses through lower income and capital gains taxes, as well as by lowering government regulations. With lower taxes and regulations, both firms and individuals will have a greater incentive to work, save, and invest, which, in turn, will increase the supply of goods and services, reducing price and increasing consumption, and so forth. While there is a certain appeal to this argument, there is no guarantee that labor, savings, and investment will respond positively to after-tax real wages. For instance, with a reduction in real wage from tax cuts, it is possible that labor will substitute work for leisure, which in all likelihood will reduce but not increase the supply of labor. Similar arguments can be made of savings and investment. Interestingly, the comparison with Keynesian economics appears to be somewhat moot because the Keynesian policy focuses on stabilization, not on economic growth, which is an important focus of supply-side economics.

Reagan administration is credited with popularizing the supply-side economics by lifting price control introduced under the Carter administration, cutting down government regulations, and making several major tax cuts to boost the economy (Canto et al. 1983). The measures appeared to have produced tangible results in lowering inflation and unemployment, both of which were in the double digits when the administration came to power. However, it is difficult to assess the full effect of supply-side economics because, as the administration was cutting down taxes, it was also increasing spending on military and highways, creating serious deficit problem that required Congress to pass the Balanced Budget and Emergency Deficit Control Act in 1985.

According to Krugman (2019), the results of supply-side economics are mixed. For instance, the Clinton Administration raised taxes in the early 1990s and the economy experienced a bigger boom. The Bush Administration cut taxes in the early 2000s and there was hardly any effect. The Obama Administration also raised taxes in 2013, but also no effect on the economy. The Trump Administration's tax cuts in December 2017, while an endorsement of supply-side economics, remains to be seen what effect the policy will produce in the long run because it was introduced at a time when the economy was bouncing back with unemployment rate already low at 4.1%.

Monetary Policy

The experiences of the Great Depression left a deep sense of realization among the economists and policy makers that unemployment problem is a far more serious problem than any other macroeconomic issue, including inflation. The passage of the Employment Act in 1946 was a reflection of the concern the government had about the potential effects of a deepened recession on the national economy. Intuitively, in particular from a psychological point of view, this makes sense, because for an average person it is far more important to have a job and pay a little more in prices for everyday goods than not to have a job at all, but the cumulative effect of inflation on the economy can be just as severe as unemployment and recession. The double-digit inflation the country experienced during the late 1970s further proved how fast the real income can drop with rising inflation.

The policy that primarily deals with the problem of inflation is known as the monetary policy. However, unlike the fiscal policy, the monetary policy is not the purview of the federal government, but is the discretion of the Federal Reserve Board (the Fed, in short)—a semi-autonomous entity, created by Congress in 1913.[14] The Fed is comprised of a chairman, a board of governors, twelve reserve districts, three advisory councils, member banks, depository institutions, and a number of committees, among others. The chairman is appointed for a four-year term by the President and approved by the Senate, but can be reappointed. The board of governors consists of seven members, appointed by the President and confirmed by the Senate for a 14-year term. Each of the twelve districts has a Federal Reserve Bank, named after the city in which it is located and is headed by a 9-member board of directors—3 representing commercial banks, 3 representing non-banking interest, and 3 appointed by the board of governors. The council consists of twelve members, one from each district, selected annually by the board of directors representing each reserve bank.[15]

The single most important instrument that guides the monetary policy is money supply, which consists of 3 Ms—M1, M2, and M3. M1 primarily includes currency (coins and paper in circulation), travelers' checks, demand, and other checkable deposits. M2 includes M1, plus savings deposits, small-denomination time deposits such as CDs (certificates of deposits), and retail money market mutual funds such as T-bills and other short-term securities. And M3 includes M2, plus large time deposits, short-term repurchase agreements, institution only money market funds, and other large liquid assets. The Fed, through its Reserve Bank which serves as the central bank of the United States, controls (increases or decreases) the money supply as it sees fit to deal with inflation, and also unemployment and recession. However, to control the money supply, the Fed uses three principal instruments: reserve requirement, discount rate, and open market operations.

Reserve Requirement

All member banks, which account for over a third of all commercial banks in the country, are required to maintain a fraction of their transaction deposits (checking accounts and other deposits that can be used to pay third parties) with the Federal Reserve. Large banks usually maintain a greater percentage in reserve than small banks do, which can range from 3 to 10%. By raising the reserve requirement, the Fed can reduce the money supply. The way the process works is that when the reserve requirement is raised, it reduces the members' ability to extend credit and with less money in circulation it will reduce inflation. Conversely, when the reserve requirement is lowered, it increases the money supply by increasing the banks' ability to lend credit, but the measure can have an opposite effect if too much money is pumped into the economy.

Discount Rate

Discount rate is the interest rate at which the member banks can borrow funds from the Federal Reserve Banks. There are two ways in which a bank can borrow from the Fed. The first is by rediscounting its customers' notes and other eligible commercial papers and selling the eligible papers to the Fed. The second method, which is more convenient than the first, is by borrowing on the bank's own promissory notes secured by its customers' notes, government securities, and other acceptable collateral. Borrowing by the first method is called discount and by the second method is called advances, although both are popularly known as discounts.[16] Raising the discount rate will discourage banks to extend credit, which will lower money supply and with less money in circulation it will reduce inflation. The opposite will be true, when the discount rate is lowered.

In general, the Fed does not encourage direct borrowing from the Federal Reserve Banks, but instead, it allows the member banks to borrow from other banks with excess reserve on deposits with the Federal Reserve of other member banks, known as the Federal Funds Market. The rate at which a member bank can borrow from the Federal Funds Market is called the federal funds rate. The rate may be higher or lower than the prevailing rate at the discount window, depending on the situation on excess reserves.

Open Market Operations

Of the three instruments the Fed uses to affect the money supply, the most important is the open market operations. Controlled and run by the Federal Open Market Committee (FOMC), it deals with buying and selling of government securities such as Treasury notes, Treasury certificates, Treasury bills, and Treasury bonds. To increase the money supply, the Fed buys securities from the member banks, which increases their excess reserves and allows them to extend credit. Likewise, to lower money supply, it sells securities to the banks, which decreases their excess reserves and reduces their ability to extend credit, but the process is not arbitrary. The way it works is that the FOMC sets a target growth rate at stable prices and defines that goal in terms of GDP and inflation, and then works backward, identifying the rate at which the money supply must grow to achieve the desired growth in GDP. While the process may appear simple, there is no guarantee that the member banks will respond the way the Fed wants. It may be necessary for the Fed to induce the members to buy or sell such as offering them a premium price (above the market rate) when buying or giving a discount (below the market rate) when selling.

Effects on Unemployment and Inflation

Although developed as an operational tool to deal with inflation, monetary economists believe that it can be just as effective, if not more, as the fiscal policy to deal with the problem of unemployment and recession. By increasing the money supply, it can produce the same effect on unemployment as it can on inflation by lowering the money supply, although it may take longer for unemployment than inflation, as shown in the following relationship:

The process is similar to that we discussed earlier: increase money supply, which will lower the interest rate producing a spur in borrowing, which, in turn, will increase investment vis-a-vis employment. However, what if, the interest rate is already low to a point that the conventional means will not spur borrowing, called the liquidity trap, in which case the government can use unconventional means to pump money into the economy? For instance, the Fed can buy financial instruments issued by the government such as treasury bonds or it can buy financial assets held by private firms such as pension funds, mortgage-backed securities, and so forth to inject a predetermined quantity of money into the economy. This is known as quantitative easing of money, or simply QE. The Fed can do this (create new money electronically) without printing more banknotes[17] by simply increasing the balance on a reserve account, meaning that when it purchases an asset from a financial institution it simply credits the institution's reserve account with additional funds. This will expand the supply of Fed's money.

There are potential risks though with quantitative easing if the Fed overestimates the amount of money it needs to inject, which may result in higher inflation than desired. On the other hand, the inflationary pressure will be minimized if the economy grows faster than the pace of growth in the money supply. Interestingly, the growth in money supply can depreciate a nation's exchange rate against other currencies, which can be a blessing in disguise since it can boost exports and also lower the value of existing debt. However, the long-term effect may be negative as it may lower the inflow of capital by discouraging future investors from investing in government securities and other financial assets. Historically, the quantitative easing has not included high-risk securities, such as derivatives, but if they are to be included in the Fed's portfolio it could qualitatively change the dynamics of the entire process.

With regard to inflation, the policy can be used in reverse; that is, lower the money supply, which will raise interest rate and lower borrowing. Since it is difficult to borrow at a higher interest rate, it discourages lending and slows down the monetary growth and reduces inflation. Higher interest rate also makes earnings on accounts such as demand deposits more attractive because of higher return. This, in turn, encourages individuals to postpone current consumption for future consumption and, with reduced spending, inflation will also come down.

As for the effects on government budget, the results are not cut-and-dried. Since neither tax nor government expenditures are directly used to deal with unemployment, the effect of monetary policy on the budget is more indirect— one of the reasons why economists who advocate less government intervention in the marketplace, in particular the monetarists, prefer it to the conventional fiscal policy.

Monetary and Fiscal Policies Together

Most modern economists are neither Keynesians nor monetarists. They believe that to have any serious effect on the economy, whether it is high unemployment or high inflation, or both, the government must use both fiscal and monetary policies together, in combination—not one or the other. This was clearly evident in the late 1970s when the conventional macroeconomic policies were not sufficient to address the economic problem resulting from stagflation the country was facing. To illustrate the point further, while tax breaks are necessary during recession to produce savings and investments, without an expansionary monetary policy lowering the interest rate investments may not take place to the degree they are needed. To what extent the policies should be used in combination depends obviously on the severity of the problem and the relationship between the Federal Reserve Board, which is responsible for the monetary policy, and the government, which is responsible for fiscal policy. Operationally, however, it is much more difficult to predict how the policy mix will work and the result it will produce for the aggregate economy, although the overall quality of macroeconomic forecasts has improved considerably over the years (McNees 1988).

1.2.2.4 Other Macroeconomic Problems

Two other macroeconomic problems that are of some concern to the policy makers are economic growth and the balance of payment disequilibrium. Economic growth is generally defined as a secular (long-term) increase in per capita income. If growth takes place immediately following the recovery from recession, it is considered cyclical rather than secular. To ensure that growth is real, per capita income must also grow at a rate higher than the rate of growth in population. The use of population growth as a barometer for measuring economic growth goes back to the days of the classical economists. The balance of payments disequilibrium, on the other hand, takes place as a result of imbalance between exports and imports; in particular, when imports exceeds exports, creating a net negative import for an economy.

The Issue of Economic Growth

The classical economists, such as Adam Smith, David Ricardo, Thomas Malthus, and others, were seriously concerned about economic growth because they believed that economic growth will eventually disappear as a result of population pressure, based in part on the Malthusian theory that population grows geometrically (1, 2, 4, 8, 16,........), while food production grows arithmetically (1, 2, 3, 4, 5,.........). They focused predominantly on land as an important factor of production and emphasized the law of diminishing returns, arguing that as population pressure would increase and capital accumulate diminishing returns would set in.[18] The result would be a decline in real wage and profit. Some may argue that classical economists were not cognizant of technological progress; indeed, they were. Classical economists believed that technology would slow down the process to the eventual stationary state, but not eliminate it. Later economists were more optimistic, arguing that technology has the potential to overcome the law of diminishing returns.

The Great Depression turned the attention of the economists to the problems that were more immediate in nature. Once the depression was over, economists began to address the issue of economic growth. Economists Harrod (1948) and Domar (1957) were among the first to seriously look into the issue, providing a theoretical foundation that came to be regarded as the neoclassical growth theory.[19] Their works, especially of Harrod's, were later criticized as being too simplistic (Solow 1956; Baumol 1970).

Balance of Payment Disequilibrium

Balance of payments summarizes all economic transactions between households, firms, and government agencies in a country against the rest of the world during a given period of time. The transactions include exports, imports, and various capital flows. For accounting purposes, the transactions are recorded into two accounts: current account—to account for the movement of goods and services, and capital account—to account for the movement of financial assets. As in a double-entry accounting system, if there is a surplus in the current account, there must be a deficit in the capital account to balance the ledger, and vice versa. The deficits and surpluses tell us whether a country is a borrower or a lender to the rest of the world. For instance, a deficit in the current account indicates that a country is running a surplus in the capital account, while a deficit in the capital account indicates the opposite. A deficit in the current account is also an indication that a country running the deficit must borrow an amount equal to the deficit in the account to generate the necessary funds to balance the ledger. In most cases, the funds are generated by selling bonds and other debts of the country running the deficit to the rest of the world.

In recent years, the United States has been consistently running a deficit in the current account, indicating that it consumes more than it produces (more inflow of goods than outflows) and had to sell financial assets, as well as borrow substantial sums of money from the rest of the world to finance its current account deficits; thereby, creating a surplus in the capital accounts (more inflow of funds than outflows). Borrowing in such huge amounts to balance the ledger makes it a net debtor nation, meaning that we owe more to the rest of the world than it is owed to us. Economists, policy makers and others with a general interest in the future of the economy are concerned that if this trend continues it will create a serious balance of payment disequilibrium problem that will cripple the ability of the country to sustain economic growth and prosperity, and may even make it politically vulnerable, although it is not clear to what degree that will be the case.

Effects on Government Budget. Both poor economic growth and the balance of payment disequilibrium have consequences not only for the economy as a whole, but also for the federal budget. Federal budget constitutes a significant portion of GDP, running on average above 20% during normal years and much higher during times of economic crisis. Thus, any increase in economic growth vis-à-vis GDP or GNP will lead to an increase in the size of the government budget consistent with economic growth and a decrease will produce an opposite effect. The same goes for changes in the balance of payments. A favorable balance of payments (net negative import) will result in a higher GNP growth, which, in turn, will increase the size of the government, in particular the budget, as more revenues will become available from increased economic activities. The opposite will be true when an economy experiences an unfavorable balance.

1.2.3   Failure to Provide Public Goods

The third important consequence of market failure is the inability of the free market system to provide public goods. As consumers, we consume a variety of goods most of which are "private goods" because the utility we derive from the consumption of these goods is strictly to fulfill our own personal needs and satisfaction as individual consumers. However, we also live in collectivity and as members of collectivity we need to consume certain goods, called "public goods," that not only benefit us as individual consumers, but also society at large. What distinguishes most public goods from private goods is that they are indivisible in that they must be produced in lump sum, as a whole, and not in discrete quantities.

Paul Samuelson (1954), who pioneered the concept of public good, defined it as the good the consumption of which by one individual does not diminish the quantity available for consumption by others. In other words, the same quantity is available for consumption by all after the consumption by the first individual. For a private good, the quantity available diminishes as more individuals consume the good in that the less of it would be available for consumption by others. Suppose that there are n television sets in the market for consumption at any given time, where n is an unspecified large number. Therefore, the purchase of a set by an individual will leave one set less, $n-1$, in the market for purchase by others and the purchase of all the sets, n, will clear the market off the good. If it were a public good, the same quantity will be available for consumption by all.

1.2.3.1 Characteristics of Public Goods

Samuelson's definition of public good, which provides the foundation for much of the discussion on the subject, has two distinct characteristics: nonrivalness and nonexclusion. Nonrivalness, also known as the jointness characteristic, means that each individual's consumption of the good leads to no subtraction from any other individual's consumption of the good such that there is no reduction in the quantity available for consumption. In other words, once produced, the same quantity is available for consumption by all. Nonexclusion, on the other hand, means that once produced it is difficult to exclude anyone from the consumption of the good. Part of the reason for this is that since these goods must be produced in lump sum (as a whole) and not in discrete units, it is possible for more than one individual to consume the goods at no additional cost to the producer. In other words, the cost to the producer of the goods for consumption by an additional individual (marginal cost) will be zero; that is, $MC = 0$. To give an example, suppose that the cost of producing a good that can serve n individuals at a cost of \$1000, which is the total cost of production, and assume that it is a public good, the consumption by $n + 1$ individuals will not add any additional cost to the producer.

The fact that individuals cannot be excluded from consumption once a good is produced also means that it is possible for an individual to consume the good without having to pay for it, thereby creating a free-rider problem. To give an example, suppose that a community needs several street lights that will benefit everyone in the community equally. It will cost the community $\times$ amount of dollars to have the lights that must be borne equally by the members since they will receive the same benefits. However, if one member decides that he does not need the lights and, as such, refuses to pay, the individual can still enjoy the benefits of the lights and get a free ride should the rest of the members decide to cover the full cost of the lights. In other words, they will have to absorb the cost of provision if they want the streetlights or they could forgo the decision to have the lights.

In general, the free-rider problem is more likely to occur when the group size is large because it is difficult to avoid paying for a good when the group size is small without significantly affecting the quantity available for consumption. Free riding can also occur across political jurisdictions. For instance, individuals residing in one community can easily travel to another community and enjoy its facilities, such as public parks, public library, public safety, and other services, without having to pay for their consumption. In other words, it is difficult to exclude them from their consumption. However, free riding produces an immediate problem for the producer. Since it is difficult to exclude individuals from their consumption, it makes it difficult to determine the exact quantity of the goods the producer must produce and the price he must charge for their consumption. Without knowing the price he must charge and the quantity he must produce, both of which are necessary to determine the profit margin, the producer vis-à-vis the private sector will not have the incentive to provide the goods. The unwillingness of the private sector to provide the goods, therefore, makes it necessary for the government to provide them.

The paradox of the free-rider problem is that everyone loses when everyone pursues his own self-interest, as in the street light problem, because there is no guarantee that restraint by one will lead to restraint by others (Hirshleifer 1980).

Not only that, it can easily lead to allocative inefficiency when the costs of provision fail to reflect the "true" demand and society ends up paying a higher price than is necessary. Unfortunately, the free-rider problems are difficult to avoid, but they can be minimized through an appropriate mixture of price and tax policies, together with clearly defined property rights and laws to enforce them.

Pure vs. Impure Public Goods

Samuelson's definition of public good that it must be available in equal quantity for consumption by all (nonrivalness) and that once produced it is difficult to exclude others from its consumption (nonexclusion) is in essence the definition of a pure public good. However, most public goods we consume are impure public goods, in that they violate one or both conditions of pure public goods. The classic example of a pure public good that satisfies both nonrivalness and nonexclusion characteristics is national defense. Other examples of pure public goods would be lighthouse signal, street lights (mentioned earlier), public firework displays, and clean air (assuming government has a role in it), among others, where the provisions are both nonrival and nonexcludable.

An impure public good, on the other hand, can be defined as a good the consumption of which by one individual will diminish the quantity available for consumption by others. Although there is a similarity here with private goods, the rationale for diminishing quantity is not the same for impure public goods. In most instances, the reduction is due to congestion when a large number of individuals consume a good at the same time. These types of goods are often called "common resource goods" because they are nonexcludable, but rival. To give an example, when we use a road, a recreation facility, or a public swimming pool, they can easily get congested (overcrowded) as more individuals use them at the same time, leaving less of the goods available for consumption by others. In economic terms, it imposes a cost on the users because of overcrowding, called congestion cost that increases with additional consumption (Bruce 2001). As such, the term frequently used to define these goods is "congestible public goods." Besides creating congestion, overcrowding can also affect the quality of provision. For instance, the quality of health care a patient receives from a healthcare facility may decline as the number of patients using the facility at any given time increases. Likewise, the quality of education that depends on class size may decline as the class size increases. In fact, most public goods we consume on a daily basis are impure public goods with varying degrees of rivalness.

Variations of Impure Public Goods

While any public good that violates one or both conditions of a pure public good, by definition, is an impure public good, there is a wide range of these goods a government provides that varies in size and complexity. This section discusses various types of impure public goods, characterized by size, geographic location, the manner of provision, and how society values the provision. In addition, it also sheds some lights on two other types of impure goods that are somewhat different in characteristics from conventional public goods—proprietary goods and e-goods.

Hierarchy of Public Goods

All public goods have a spatial dimension in that they are provided for individuals who live within a defined political jurisdiction, or geographic area, and benefit directly from the provision. Based on where individuals live, consume the good, and the manner in which it is provided, a public good can be defined as global, regional, national, and local. A global public good, by its very nature, produces benefits that cover multiple countries and population groups. For a good to be considered global, it must have three essential characteristics: it must be nonrival, it must be nonexcludable, and it must cover multiple nations; preferably, the globe. Preserving global biodiversity, maintaining global financial stability, and controlling communicable diseases globally are good examples of global public goods. Clean air, if it is the result of global effort, will be another good example.

A national public good has the same characteristics as the global public good, except that its benefits are restricted to the confines of a national boundary such as national defense, national parks, national museums, public health infrastructure, and government published statistics. In contrast, a regional public good generally has a range that is larger than a nation, but equivalent to some well-defined set of nations such as the poverty alleviation program for Sub-Saharan Africa, which covers most of the countries south of the Sahara desert. A regional public good can also have a range that is smaller than a nation but larger than a state. A good example of this type of public goods will be the Anti-Poverty and Job Growth Program operated by the Appalachian Regional Commission (ARC) serving 13 US states. State-funded higher education, health care, and human services that often require a range that is larger than a single community, but smaller than a state, are also good examples of regional public goods.

Finally, local public goods are provided primarily for individuals living within well defined, but relatively smaller political jurisdictions such as a city, a township, a county, a school district, or a special district. Most public goods we consume on a regular basis such as public safety, public works, public library, public swimming pool, public parks, public schools, recreation facilities, and so forth are typical examples of local public goods. Local public goods in most instances are congestible public goods in that excessive demand on them can easily reduce their availability for consumption in equal quantity. As noted earlier, congestion can also lead to poor quality. In both cases, they fall within the general category of impure public goods. However, some local public goods are mixed in that they are partly local and partly extra local. An interstate highway that runs through a local jurisdiction is a good example.

Proprietary Goods

There is a category of impure public goods that have a lot in common with private goods in that they are provided in a business-like manner such that individuals consuming the goods must pay a price in accordance with the quantity they consume. Since these goods have some of the same characteristics of a private good in that they are proprietary in nature, we can define them as "proprietary goods." Proprietary goods are provided by all three levels of government. The US Postal

Service is a classic example of proprietary good. Other examples of proprietary goods that are local in character will be water, sewer, electricity, public transit, parking meters, and so forth. Since many of these goods are provided by government enterprises, the US Postal Department being one, they can also be defined as "enterprise goods."

Proprietary goods have a distinct characteristic that separates them from the conventional impure public goods in that they are nonrival, but price-excludable meaning that individuals can be excluded from their consumption for nonpayment. In other words, additional consumption will not necessarily diminish the quantity available for consumption by others but individuals can be excluded from consumption if they fail to pay for their consumption. There is a parallel here with club goods—a concept developed by Buchanan (1965), where the goods are nonrival but price-excludable in that it is possible to exclude individuals from consumption for nonpayment of membership fees. Club goods have an additional feature which also applies to proprietary goods in that there are economies of scale when additional members join the club which keeps the average cost of production low, but additional membership will not necessarily lead to overcrowding or congestion; as such, their consumption will not be rivalrous.

e-Goods

There is a new generation of public goods that has emerged in recent years as a result of technological advancements, called e-goods that are bought and sold on Internet, as distinct from goods that are bought and sold in the traditional marketplace. This includes information on a wide range of subjects that is readily available for consumption by the public. Also included in this category are materials such as public-domain software, provided both by the government and the private sector that are available to anyone with access to a computer. While the provision of these goods serves an important public purpose, such as information dissemination, they have also created a new set of challenges for the government that requires constant monitoring of what goes on Internet to minimize the potential for misinformation that may not be in the best interest of society.

A Note on Merit Goods

A special category of public goods that deserves some attention because of their unique characteristics is merit goods. The term "merit good" is often used to define those goods that society considers meritorious, based on the common perception of what is good for society. Although the market can provide these goods since they are excludable, but, if left up to the market, it will either not provide them or provide for only those who can afford the price, which can easily lead to underprovision. Two good examples of merit goods are education and health care. A somewhat different type of merit good will be corrective actions, such as seat belt or public decisions that do not interfere with individual choices, but permit the choices to be made more efficiently such as subsidies for low-cost housing for the poor or homeless shelters. There is often a sense of egalitarianism that underlies the provision of these goods, meaning that society has an obligation to provide them because of the benefits they produce for society at large and do not rely entirely on the ability to pay. The egalitarian values are generally strong when it comes to the poor and the needy.

Who Provides Public Goods?

The conventional wisdom that public goods are provided only by government is not necessarily true; they can also be provided by the private sector, in which case they are called privately provided public goods. Similarly, many of the public goods that a government provides are inherently private, meaning that they violate one or both characteristics of pure public goods, in which case they are called publicly provided private goods. The following sections provide a brief description of both and an emerging trend, called public–private partnership.

Publicly Provided Private Goods

Although the government provides these goods, ideally, they should be provided by the private sector since they are inherently private. To a large extent, the provision of these goods by the government depends on the private sector's willingness to provide the goods. Theoretically, the private sector can and should be able to provide these goods for anyone who wants to consume the goods, but will not do so if they cannot afford the price; the result will be underprovision. A good example of a publicly provided private good is education. The private sector can and will provide education for anyone as long as the individuals consuming the good are willing to pay for it, but it will not provide for those who cannot afford to pay. The unwillingness of the private sector to provide education for those who cannot afford the price makes it necessary for the government to intervene and provide it for those who will otherwise be left out by the market.

The question then is: Why should a government provide a good such as education that by all measures is a private good, even if the private sector fails to provide it for all. Two sets of arguments can be made in support of the government providing education: First, the provision can be justified on the meritorious nature of the good in that society will be better off in the aggregate when everyone has an education. There will be less crime and violence. Besides, an educated society will be more productive and contribute more to national income. Second, which directly relates to the traditional distribution question, with a moral undertone, that individuals who cannot afford to pay should not be deprived of the opportunity to receive education. More importantly, children should not be penalized for their parents' lack of means (Stiglitz 2000). Another good example is health care. The market will not simply provide health care for individuals who cannot afford the price yet there is a need to provide health care, even for those who cannot afford to pay because we all benefit collectively from a healthy society. A healthy society will lower health-care costs, work harder, be more productive, and create more income and wealth.

The flip side of the argument for the government providing a good that is inherently private is the question of cost. As with private goods, the cost of publicly provided private goods will also increase with increased consumption, as more individuals consume the goods. There is also the potential for overconsumption by the public if the goods are provided free of charge, or at a substantially lower price than the price in the private market. Take, for instance, public utilities such as electricity, which can be provided both by the government and the private sector. If it is provided entirely by the government, say, free of charge or at a substantially lower price than what it would cost to produce, individuals are more likely to be careless in their consumption, leading to wasteful consumption. This will also add to the aggregate cost of provision, and in the long run, society will be worse off, unless the consumption is carefully monitored and cost-cutting measures are taken to prevent cost increase from overuse. The same argument can also be made of health care and a variety of other goods and services a government provides.

Privately Provided Public Goods
There is a common perception among the general public that the government is not as efficient as the private sector and that, given a choice, the private sector would do a much better job of providing public goods, especially those that are provided in a business-like manner. This has led to the growth of privatization and outsourcing, or leveraging many of the traditional public goods to the private sector, such as garbage collection, court services, recycling, and even traditional public goods such as infrastructure, but often with mixed results (Halachmi and Boydston 2003; Rosell 2003). In fact, a close examination of outsourcing would reveal that governments across the board (federal, state and local) have made significant strides in recent years in providing many of these goods as efficiently as the private sector, contrary to common perception (Davis and Christensen 1980; Peltzman 1971).

The argument that private firms are inherently more efficient than government is based on the conventional wisdom that they have the necessary expertise, technology, and the organizational structure suitable for efficient production and delivery of goods and services. While there are some justifications for this argument, it is not necessarily the case in every situation if one would look carefully at the number of firms that go out of business each year because of their inability to successfully compete in the marketplace. Even the corporate mergers that are often highlighted as a measure of efficiency can be construed as the inability of the firms to survive on their own in a fierce, competitive market. In the same vein, one could also argue that protection from competition and a guaranteed profit may induce many of these firms to gravitate toward government to provide goods that have been traditionally provided by the public sector.

Let us look at the efficiency point again. Assume, for the sake of argument, that a private firm can produce many of the goods a government provides at a lower cost; however, there is no guarantee that the cost savings from efficiency will translate into lower price for the public. The lower cost invariably will result in a higher profit for the firm, but if there is no reduction in price the net gain to the public will be zero. To give an example, suppose that it costs a government $15 to collect a ton of garbage that a private firm could collect for $12.50. The difference will produce a net profit of $2.50 per ton for the firm. Assume that it charges the public the same price as the government before outsourcing, even though the cost of collection is lower and there is no visible increase in quality. From the perspective of the public, it would make no difference as to who provides the service since there has been no reduction in the price and, therefore, no change in their welfare. Assume now that the firm decides to charge the public more per ton of collection with no visible increase in quality, which is possible since garbage collection, like many other public goods, is a monopoly good where the producer can sell the good at a higher price than a competitive firm, in which case the public will be worse off.

Besides efficiency, there are other factors that can also prompt a government to outsource services such as the need to raise money to deal with cash-flow problem, especially for governments that are financially hard pressed. While outsourcing services, such as electric utility or trash collection to a private firm may offer a temporary financial relief, it is unlikely to produce a long-term solution for the government that may require a more careful analysis of the problem. It is quite possible that the problem is much more fundamental than it appears on the surface. Ideally, if technology and operating costs are not prohibitive, a government should be able to do as good a job as the private sector with greater control, manpower training, and oversight. As noted earlier, public organizations have made significant strides in recent years to improve the efficiency of service provision using various improvement measures, such as utilizing new tools of business management, developing innovations, adopting creative cost-cutting measures and, in some cases, working collaboratively with the private sector, to reduce costs and increase efficiency (Manion 2003).

A slightly different issue that has a direct bearing on efficient provision of public goods is the lack of coordination between government and the private sector providing the same public goods, which raises an interesting question: Does the dual provision in any way contribute to market failure? Since both sectors provide public goods, although in varying proportion, it is important that there is coordination between the two to determine the level of provision that would be "optimal." Unfortunately, any measure that attempts to coordinate service provisions between sectors and even within the same sector is often difficult in a free market economy that discourages intervention, although public–private partnership (a recent development in public goods provision) tries to address it, but in a limited fashion. The absence of coordination can easily lead to overproduction of goods, resulting in inefficient allocation of resources. On the other hand, provision by both sectors of the same goods increases competition, improves efficiency, and keeps prices low.

A Note on Public Goods Problem

The provision of public goods by both government and the private sector raises an interesting question—if such dual provision in any way contributes to market failure. Since both sectors can provide public goods, whether they are publicly provided or privately provided, it is important that there is coordination between the two to determine how much goods should be provided at any given time. Unfortunately, any measure that attempts to coordinate service provisions between sectors and, even within the same sector, is difficult in a free market economy that discourages intervention, even though the two sectors may not necessarily compete for the same consumers or have the same share of the market. On the other hand, the absence of coordination can easily lead to over- or underproduction of goods, creating additional problems for government, as well as the consuming public.

Theoretically, one would expect the market to be able to adjust itself through the interaction of supply and demand, especially for the public goods the private sector provides. However, the same logic may not apply to the goods a government provides in response to the void created by an incomplete market, discussed earlier. The over- or underprovision may also produce a cobweb-like situation, where one tries to catch up with the other but never quite addressing the issue. This is partly known as the public goods problem.

Public–Private Partnership

Recent years have witnessed a significant increase in the cost of provision of public goods at all three levels of government, resulting, in part, from rising costs of production and delivery and, in part, from rising demand for public goods, without a corresponding increase in the revenue streams of the governments. This has seen a resurgence of interest in alternative methods of public goods provision, from privatization and outsourcing (both of which have been in use for sometimes), to collective agreement (joint production of public goods that is becoming increasingly common in agri-environmental areas), to public–private partnership, among others. Of these, public–private partnership, also known as PPP or P3, in short, has been receiving the most attention, especially for large-scale projects such as infrastructure that are in dire need of government attention and would cost the government enormous sums of money to rebuild.

PPP is essentially a contractual arrangement between a government agency and a private entity to provide a public good or service that serves the interest of both parties. Government Accountability Office (GAO) summarizes this arrangement as one in which the agency may retain the ownership of the asset, but the private party generally invests its own capital to design and develop it (GAO 1999). According to Van Slyke (2013), the arrangement allows the skills and assets of each party to be shared in delivering the goods and services for general use of the public. In addition to sharing of resources, each party also shares the risks and rewards from the delivery.

Considered as the mid-way between complete provision by government and complete privatization, where the private sector assumes full control and the delivery of the goods, some welcomed it as the greatest development in the history of public goods since the introduction of welfare state (Harris 2004). There are obviously advantages to using PPP, the most important of which is efficiency since the private sector is considered more efficient than government, although, as it should become obvious by now, it may not be the case in every situation. Quality is also considered a hallmark of PPP since it draws in from diverse organizational cultures and professional backgrounds that offer opportunities for creativity and mutual learning. Another important consideration for PPP, one that lies at the heart of it, is the financial certainty it can provide for government that is desperately in need of financial relief yet needs to provide the badly needed public goods.

However, PPP is not a panacea. There have been concerns where PPP was applied, such as lack of transparency and public accountability (which also applies to outsourcing, if not properly monitored), and lack of safety and security that comes from reduced government control. Concerns have also been raised about the need for effective dispute resolution systems because of the intricate nature of contracts, as both sides try to quantify and minimize risk acceptance in the event of a potential failure. Another area of concern is the extended length of contract agreements that can bind both sides, eventually producing a diminishing return. Nevertheless, strengths can easily outweigh the weaknesses, as long as both parties realize that it is the public interest that must be central to the partnership. In other words, its success depends on how well both parties work together in the best interest of the public.

Interestingly, although PPP has been at work in the US for sometimes, actual commitments to the partnerships in dollar terms have been much lower compared to other industrialized countries such as the United Kingdom and France. Part of the explanation for this apparent slow growth comes from the fact that operationally PPP is a complex undertaking requiring sound political, administrative, legal, and institutional structures on both sides, which takes time to build. However, the potential for growth is considerable and the market remains positioned to become one of the largest in the world (Moody's 2016).

A Note on Tiebout Hypothesis

Public goods provision often reflects the location preferences of individuals, especially at the local level. What this means is that individuals have preferences as to where they want to locate, as long as it meets certain expectations they consider important. According to Charles Tiebout (1956) who initially brought the idea to the attention of public economists, if people are not happy with the mix of public goods in a community, given the tax package, they can easily move to a community that will meet their needs or expectations. This ability of individuals to constantly move between political jurisdictions creates a market-like solution to the public goods problem. In other words, people "vote with their feet" and locate in communities that offer them the bundle of goods and services for a tax package they prefer the most. This is known as the Tiebout hypothesis.

Based primarily on the principles of free market competition, the Tiebout hypothesis assumes a competitive spatial market with a large number of communities from which consumers can choose, free consumer mobility between communities, complete knowledge about the differences in public goods and tax packages in each community, and no spillover of service benefits (externalities) among the communities. Additionally, each community does its best to attract the right-size population to take advantage of economies of scale in public goods provision in order to keep the average cost of provision to a minimum. Under these conditions, the theory suggests that consumers will locate in the community that best satisfies their preferences and in the process an optimal size community will emerge. The result will be a quasi-market equilibrium, where individuals will reside in communities which would best satisfy their preferences, subject to the constraint that all communities are providing public goods at a constant cost (convergence of different tax rates of different communities to an average). Assuming all communities can supply public goods at a constant cost such that there are no economies or diseconomies of scale, the equilibrium will be identical to market equilibrium.

While the theory makes good sense if the fiscal considerations (different tax and spending packages) are the only factors individuals would take in their location decisions, but when other factors such as income, employment opportunities, community life, and so forth are brought into focus, it begins to lose some of its appeals. The point is, in reality, people do not always vote with their feet.

1.2.4   Failure to Regulate Itself

In a perfect world in which the market would operate freely and efficiently without creating any of the problems discussed above, there would be no need for government intervention. In other words, there will be no need to deal with economic and noneconomic issues, no need to provide public goods and, more importantly, no need for government to regulate the behavior of firms and businesses. Ideally, if economic agents, such as firms and businesses, could regulate their own behavior, none of these actions would be necessary, but, unfortunately, that is not always the case. Economic agents often create conditions, knowingly or unknowingly, that have social costs and without some form of intervention, in particular regulation by the government they will not have the incentive to correct the problems their actions produce for others. Therefore, the real issue facing the government is not whether regulation is necessary, but how much regulation is appropriate that would allow the firms and businesses to operate efficiently with as little social costs as possible.

Given that regulation is necessary, while the amount of regulation needed varies depending on how much inefficiency the market system produces for society and how much regulation society wants in return, the government has an obligation to supply it. The demand and supply of regulation make it possible to treat regulation as a public good since government is the sole provider of the good. George Stigler (1971), who studied regulation extensively, was among the first to suggest that, as an economic good, regulation has equilibrium price and quantity determined by the interaction of supply and demand (similar to Fig. 1.2a, b). Society demands regulation because it expects certain tangible results from it and government supplies regulation in response to that demand and other market conditions.

Interestingly, Stigler took the discussion on regulation a step further by suggesting that government agencies responsible for regulation are often captured (dominated) by large firms and industries whose behavior they are supposed to regulate. This produces a major gap between supply and demand that resembles a form of market failure. A good example is the series of questionable accounting practices by a large number of firms in the early 2000 such as Enron, Tyco International, WorldCom, Adelphia, and others that forced Congress to pass the Sarbanes-Oxley Act in July 2002 to oversee the practices of public accounting firms. A few years later, Congress passed new regulations, following the bankruptcy of financial conglomerate Lehman Brothers in September 2008, along with the risk taking practices of major mortgage lending institutions, such as Fannie Mae and Freddie Mac, after the repeal of the 1933 Glass-Steagall Act[20] in 1999, which, as noted previously, may have partly contributed to the housing market collapse in 2007–2008 and ushered a prolonged recession that came to be known as the Great Recession.

There is a parallel here with early institutional economics[21] which suggests that regulatory capture is possible because the dominant firms use their resources to influence the policy decisions that favor their own interest, rather than the interest of the public. This may partly explain why the large firms are able to influence so easily because they have more resources and a much better knowledge of how the regulatory process works than the average public. The off-shoot of this argument is that it is in the best interest of the public to protect the regulatory agencies from outside interest, so that the government is able to provide the good (regulation) efficiently without any external influence.

1.3   Non-market Failure

Just as the government needs to intervene when the market system deviates from the rules of free market operation, too much intervention in the marketplace can also lead to what one would call "non-market failure." There are several ways in which interventions can lead to non-market failure. First, interventions may lead a government to artificially inflate the demand curve for public goods since there is no clear-cut price mechanism to determine the demand and supply of these goods, as one would expect in a competitive market (Downs 1967). Second, interventions through social and political pressures may also distort the demand and supply of public goods. Political actors, who are responsible for decision making, such as during the budget process, often take a short-term view of their decisions, rather than long-term consequences of budget actions. The end result may produce a budget that may not reflect the true costs of goods and services a government provides. Third, too much intervention can also work as a disincentive rather than incentive for individuals to work hard, consume, save, and invest, causing more inefficiency in resource allocation than without intervention. The end result in each case produces non-market failure that is not in the best interest of the public or the firms and businesses.

1.4   Summary and Conclusion

By all measures, a free market system based on perfect competition is the most efficient economic system, as it fosters innovation, keeps prices low, and rewards efficiency. In reality, such a system does not exist because an unchecked free market system, absent any intervention by government, will create conditions that will lead to "market failure." This chapter has presented an overview of some of the conditions that contribute to market failure and why government intervention is necessary, as well as some of the measures to address the problems. On the other hand, too much intervention in the marketplace can have an opposite effect, creating what one would call a "non-market failure" that would hinder competition, discourage productivity and, in the long run, stifle the economy. There are obviously arguments on both sides of the issue—just as too little intervention would allow an unchecked market system to operate inefficiently, so would too much intervention. The objective then is to maintain a balance between the two. One way to achieve this is to recognize that there are areas where the private sector through free market operation does a better job than government and there are areas where a government does a better job. The point to keep in mind is that both sectors have important roles to play in a market system, where each can complement the workings of the other— government improving and extending the functioning of the market system and the market system improving the functioning of the government (Wolf 1988). The end result would be a genuine reduction in incidents of market and non-market failures that would benefit both the government vis-à-vis the public and the private sector.

Review Questions

Q1. What is market failure? What contributes to market failure and why is it necessary for government to intervene? What effect does market failure have on a government budget?

Q2. What is the difference between a pure monopoly, a legal monopoly, and an oligopoly? Why is monopoly not in the best interest of the public? What can a government do to control monopoly? Give examples of measures the government has taken to control monopoly.

Q3. What is a natural monopoly? What are the strengths and weaknesses of natural monopoly? Why government is often called a natural monopolist?

Q4. Define externality. What is the difference between positive and negative externality? What causes negative externality? How does externality contribute to inefficient allocation of resources? What measures are commonly used to correct negative externalities?

Q5. What is an incomplete market? What effect does an incomplete market have on society? What can a government do to correct the problems of an incomplete market?

Q6. What are the two major macroeconomic problems with which the policy makers are mostly concerned? Why? What contributes to the problems? What effect do the problems have on a government budget?

Q7. What policy does a government commonly use to deal with the problem of unemployment and recession? How is the policy used to address the problem? Can the policy be used to control inflation?

Q8. What is an employment multiplier? Why do economic expenditures have a higher multiplier effect on unemployment than social expenditures?

Q9. What is supply-side economics? How does it differ from demand-side economics? Which administration is credited with the supply-side economics the most? Why?

Q10. What is monetary policy? What are the principal instruments of monetary policy and how are the instruments used to affect money supply? What role does Federal Reserve Board play in this?

Q11. What is quantitative easing? Under what circumstances should a government use quantitative easing?

Q12. What is a public good and how does it differ from a private good? Why does the private sector fail to provide public goods? What is the difference between a pure public and an impure public good? Give an example of each.

Q13. Would you consider the following goods as pure public, impure public, or private: (a) higher education, (b) health care, (c) national defense, (d) toll road, (e) street lights, (f) amusement park, (g) fire service, (h) street repair, (i) parking meter, and [j] garbage collection? Why?

Q14. What is the difference between a publicly provided private good and a privately provided public good? Discuss the role public–private partnership plays in providing public goods.

Q15. Why should a government be concerned with economic growth and balance of payment disequilibrium? What effect do the problems have on government budget?

Q16. Why is it difficult for the private sector to regulate itself? Can government regulation be treated as a form of public good? What produces the gap between demand and supply of regulation? Can the gap be treated as a form of market failure?

Q17. What is non-market failure and why too much intervention in the marketplace is counterproductive to efficient operation of the free market system?

Notes

1. The idea of an efficient free market, also known as "the efficient market hypothesis," has its roots in the works of Milton Friedman, an ardent advocate of free market system. The hypothesis, which has been refuted by most economists, simply says that market works better than individuals who intervene in a discretionary manner. Nevertheless, it does provide the basis for a system that, according to Friedman, if left alone, could address many of the economic problems, at least, in principle.
2. No government intervention does not mean that there is no government; there is, but only that its role is minimal. According to Adam Smith and his classic work, the Wealth of Nations, this should include defense against foreign aggression, maintenance of internal peace and order, and public development work, among others. All functions besides these were considered beyond the scope of the state.
3. Musgrave, in fact, mentions regulation but subsumes it under allocation function because, according to Musgrave, it does not constitute an appropriate budget policy.
4. Economies of scale occurs when there is an increasing returns to scale; that is, output increasing more than proportionately for a given quantity of inputs. For example, if we double the amount of factor inputs (land, labor, and capital) and the output increases by more than double, it will lower the average cost of production as output increases.
5. In recent years, however, patent-right violations have become a global phenomenon, creating a new set of problems for the policy makers.
6. If inflation is brought into the picture, it should be the rate that is necessary to control inflation. Thus, if a 3% rate of unemployment is necessary to control inflation, than it should be the natural rate. Economists use a term to define this rate called non-accelerating inflation rate of unemployment (NAIRU). In fact, NAIRU is often treated as the full-employment rate.
7. Other curves developed in recent years depict a rightward shifting of the curve, indicating a higher price level-unemployment relationship in which both the price level and unemployment rates are higher, as one is traded-off against the other.
8. The CPI is based on the price of a fixed basket of goods and services (about four hundred basic commodities and services out of fourteen hundred needed for an average family of four) that includes food, clothing, shelter, transportation, medical expenses, and entertainment compiled by the Bureau of Labor Statistics (BLS). Two other indexes are also used for measuring inflation: the producer price index (PPI) and the implicit price deflator (IPD)—the latter often in the context of gross national or gross domestic product. The PPI measures the prices of goods and services at various stages of production process. The index is measured at the production stage, as well as at the commodity level. However, for analytical purposes the stages of production indexes are often considered more useful than the commodities index since the latter has a tendency to overestimate price increase. To give an example, suppose that the price of lumber goes up, which will increase the price of wood, which, in turn, will increase the prices of homes. The higher prices would be reflected in the final goods three times, as lumber (assuming it is a final good), as woods used in the construction, and as homes.

    The IPD, on the other hand, measures the changes in the prices of all final goods and services produced in a national economy during a given period. Produced by the Department of Commerce, it is obtained by taking the ratio of the current dollar value of all goods and services at a given time (called the nominal value) to its corresponding chained-dollar value (called the real value), multiplied by 100, that is, $IPD = [(\text{Nominal GNP/Real GNP}) \times 100]$. To give an example, suppose that the GNP of a government in 2011 in current dollar terms was $1560 billion, while its real GNP when adjusted, say, for 1982 prices was $1250 billion. Therefore, the implicit price deflator for GNP for the government in 2011 would be 124.8 [($1560 billion/$1250 billion) × 100]. Translated what this means is that the prices of all goods and services for the government in 2011 on average were 1.248 times their base-year price. In general, an IPD greater than one means inflation and less than one means deflation. Since IPD takes into consideration the prices of all final goods and services in an economy, it is considered a better measure of the general price level than CPI.

9. Classical economists, who mostly included economists of the pre-Keynesian era, believed that production, which creates supply, also creates an equivalent amount of monetary purchasing power (demand) and further assumed that all incomes will eventually be spent. Therefore, supply and demand will always be equal. This is known as the Say's Law, which became the foundation for supply-side economics of the 1970s.

10. According to Keynes, the effective demand is measured by the spending of current income. If spending for consumer and capital goods is high, it will lead to high effective demand, meaning that a continued (high) spending will assure a strong effective demand, which, in turn, will assure a (high) continued rate of production, employment, and income. This is what produces the circular flow of economic activity, described in Fig. 1.1.

11. We can also explain it in terms of aggregate output, Y, assuming a closed economy, $Y = C + I + G$, where C is consumption, I is investment, and G is government expenditure. Thus, for Y to increase, all three must increase, which will require a concerted government fiscal policy.

12. Multipliers measure the results of a change in an activity as a result of some changes in another activity. For instance, if a firm invests X amount of dollars that produces 500 new jobs and the employment multiplier is 2.5, it will result in 750 additional jobs [$(500 \times 2.5) - 500 = 1250 - 500 = 750$], as a result of creating the initial 500 jobs. This is the multiplier effect of investment.

    To understand how multiplier works, it is important to understand the meaning of three types of effects a multiplier produces: direct, indirect, and induced. A direct effect is associated with businesses and industries that are directly affected by the economic activity; an indirect effect is associated with backward-linked industries that supply the direct businesses and industries, and an induced effect is associated with the changes in household behavior, such as additional household spending from these activities. Multipliers can also be expressed as Type I or II multipliers. A Type I multiplier is calculated by dividing the sum of direct and indirect effects by the direct effects, while Type II is calculated by dividing the sum of direct, indirect, and induced effects by the direct effects. There is a third category, Type III Multiplier, which is similar to Type II Multiplier, except that indirect effects are calculated differently. There are a number of organizations, such as Moody's Investor's Service, that regularly calculate the multiplier effects of public and private investment decisions.

13. Theoretically, an increase in demand can lead to an increase in employment without any increase in investment. Indeed, in a severe recession there is so much excess capacity that one would not expect to see any increase in investment spending until there had been a substantial increase in demand that as met by increased employment of previously unemployed labor and production capacity.

14. Interestingly, while federal law secures the independence of the Federal Reserve on monetary policy and protects it from Congressional oversight, to a large extent, its independence comes from the fact that it does not have to rely on Congressional appropriation for its revenue, unlike the federal agencies. On the contrary, it relies on interest earnings from its holdings of US Government securities that it acquires through open market operations, as well as on loans it extends to the member banks at discount rates.

15. The twelve districts and their banks are Boston, New York, Philadelphia, Cleveland, Richmond, Atlanta, Chicago, St. Louis, Minneapolis, Kansas City, Dallas, and San Francisco.

16. Put simply, the discount rate is the rate at which the Fed loans to member banks or when commercial banks loan to each other. Interestingly, commercial loan rate is greatly influenced by a rate, called the prime rate. The prime rate, which is an index, is the rate at which a borrower with ideal credit rating and creditworthiness can borrow. Banks typically set their own rates and then add them to the prime rate when calculating consumer interest rates such as mortgages, personal loans, etc. It is simply the discount rate plus an added rate. Thus, if the discount rate is 5% and the added rate is 3%, the prime rate will be $5\% + 3\% = 8\%$. In general, when the discount rate is lowered, the commercial loan rate will go own, which will encourage individuals, as well as firms and businesses, to borrow. The effect will be opposite, when the discount rate is increased.

17. Incidentally, the Fed does not print money; it is the responsibility of the Department of Treasury through the Bureau of Engraving and Printing. The Fed orders from the Bureau

appropriate amount of denominations at a cost of a few cents a note, which varies depending on the size of the denomination. Each Federal Reserve Bank (FRB) is required by law to pledge collateral, which, at a minimum, must equal the amount of currency it has issued in circulation. Most of the pledges are based on the form of federal securities and gold certificates the banks hold.

18. Also known as the law of diminishing marginal returns, it says that when additional units of a factor of production are combined with fixed quantities of other factors output will increase initially at faster pace, then slow down, and eventually decline.

19. The neoclassical growth theory is based on several assumptions: (1) investment is equal to full-employment level saving, (2) saving is a constant fraction of output, (3) population would grow at a constant rate independent of real wage and other economic variables, and (4) factor substitution (e.g., capital for labor and labor for capital) was allowed, which was missing in the Harrod model. Most of these arguments were later challenged, especially the assumption of full employment.

20. Following the stock market crash of 1929 and a nationwide commercial banking failure, Congress passed the Glass-Steagall Act in 1933 to prevent commercial banks getting involved in the stock market, which many think contributed greatly to the stock market crash.

21. Institutional economics deals with how government institutions, such as Congress, the Presidency, the court system, and the bureaucracy, shape economic behavior. Traditionally, institutional economists viewed government as predominantly serving the private interest, especially the interest of large firms and businesses such as monopolies and oligopolies. Their argument was based on the notion that in an age of large business, it is unrealistic to expect the market to behave in a traditional manner, following the rules of a competitive market. Large firms set their own terms in the marketplace and use their combined resources to create support for their products through advertising, market manipulation, and public relations. In short, they are the real owners of power and require stability in the market through favorable monetary and fiscal policies to ensure profit without the necessity of taking risks (Galbraith 1967).

References

Barro, R. (1974, November–December). Are Government Bonds Net Wealth? *Journal of Political Economy, 82*(6), 1095–1117.

Bator, F. M. (1958, August). The Anatomy of Market Failure. *Quarterly Journal of Economics, 72*(3), 351–379.

Baumol, W. J. (1970). *Economic Dynamics: An Introduction* (3rd ed.). New York, NY: Macmillan.

Bruce, N. (2001). *Public Finance and the American Economy*. New York, NY: Addison-Wesley.

Buchanan, J. M. (1965). An Economic Theory of Clubs. *Economica, 32*(125), 1–14.

Canto, V. A., Joines, D. H., & Laffer, A. B. (1983). *Foundations of Supply-Side Economics: Theory and Evidence*. New York, NY: Academic Press.

Choudhury, N. N. (1976, July). Integration of Fiscal and Monetary Sectors in Econometric Models: A Survey of Theoretical Issues and Empirical Findings. *International Monetary Fund, Staff Papers, 23*, 395–440.

Davis, D. W., & Christensen, L. R. (1980). The Relative Efficiency of Public and Private Firms in a Competitive Environment: The Case of Canadian Railroads. *Journal of Political Economy, 88*, 958–976.

Domar, E. (1957). *Essays in the Theories of Economic Growth*. New York, NY: Oxford University Press.

Dornbusch, R., & Fisher, S. (1990). *Macroeconomics* (pp. 18–20, 149–157). New York, NY: McGraw-Hill.

Downs, A. (1967). *Inside Bureaucracy*. Boston, MA: Little, Brown.

Feldstein, M. S. (1976, July–August). On the Theory of Tax Reform. *Journal of Public Economics, 6*, 77–104.

Galbraith, J. K. (1967). *The New Industrial State*. Boston, MA: Houghton Mifflin.

General Accountability Office (GAO). (1996). *Executive Guide: Effectively Implementing the Government Performance and Results Act*. Washington, DC: Office of the Comptroller General of the United States.

Gordon, R. J. (2018). Friedman and Phelps on the Phillips Curve Viewed from a Half Century's Perspective. *Review of Keynesian Economics, 6*(4), 425–436.

Halachmi, A., & Boydston, R. (2003). The Political Economy of Outsourcing. In A. Khan & W. B. Hildreth (Eds.), *Case Studies in Public Budgeting and Financial Management* (2nd ed., pp. 65–76). New York, NY: Marcel Dekker.

Hardin, G. (1968, December 13). The Tragedy of the Commons. *Science, 162*, 1243–1248.

Harris, S. (2004, July 8). "Promoting Public-Private Partnerships" in the Section on Business Supplement. *The Times*, p. 3. Allied Newspaper Limited, Valletta.

Harrod, R. F. (1948). *Toward a Dynamic Economics*. London: Macmillan.

Hirshleifer, J. (1980). *Price Theory and Applications* (2nd ed.). Englewood Cliffs, NJ: Prentice-Hall.

Keynes, J. M. (1936). *The General Theory of Employment, Interest and Money*. Cambridge, UK: Cambridge University Press.

Krugman, P. (2019, January 17). Learn About Supply-Side Economics: History, Policy, Effects. *Politics and Society*. https://www.masterclass.com/articles/learn-about-supply-side-economics-history-policy-effects#what-is-supplyside-economics.

Laffer, A. (2004, June 1). The Laffer Curve: Past, Present, and Future. *The Heritage Foundation*. https://www.heritage.org/taxes/report/the-laffer-curve-past-present-and-future.

McNees, S. (1988, July–August). How Accurate Are Macroeconomic Forecasts? *New England Economic Review*. Federal Reserve Bank of Boston Issue, 15–36.

Manion, P. (2003). Financial a Recycling Facility Through a Public-Private Partnership. In A. Khan & W. B. Hildreth (Eds.), *Case Studies in Public Budgeting and Financial Management* (2nd ed., pp. 763–772). New York, NY: Marcel Dekker.

Moody's Investors Service. (2016, March 10). *US Public-Private Partnership Market Steadily Growing*.

Musgrave, R. A. (1959). *The Theory of Public Finance*. New York, NY: McGraw-Hill (Chapters 1–2).

Peltzman, S. (1971). Pricing in Public and Private Enterprises: Electric Utilities in the United States. *Journal of Law and Economics, 14*(1), 109–147.

Romer, C., & Bernstein, J. (2008/2009, January 13). *The Job Impact of the American Recovery and Reinvestment Plan* (p. 4). Office of the President-Elect. http://otrans.3cdn.net/45593e8ecbd07413m6bt1te.pdf.

Rosell, E. (2003). The Chickens Come Home to Roost: The Publicization of Private Infrastructure. In A. Khan & W. B. Hildreth (Eds.), *Case Studies in Public Budgeting and Financial Management* (2nd ed., pp. 773–784). Yew York, NY: Marcel Dekker.

Samuelson, P. A. (1954, November). The Pure Theory of Public Expenditure. *The Review of Economics and Statistics, 36*(4), 387–389.

Shafriritz, J. M., Russell, E. W., & Borick, C. P. (2009). *Introducing Public Administration*. New York, NY: Pearson Education.

Solow, R. (1956, February). A Contribution to the Theory of Economic Growth. *Quarterly Journal of Economics, 70*, 65–94.

Stigler, G. I. (1971). The Theory of Economic Regulation. *Bell Journal of economics and Management Science, 2*(Spring), 3–21.

Stiglitz, J. E. (2000). *Economics of the Public Sector* (pp. 456–468). New York: W. W. Norton.

Tiebout, C. (1956). A Pure Theory of Local Public Expenditure. *Journal of Political Economy, 64,* 416–424.

Van Slyke, D. M. (2013, March 9). *Building Public-Private Partnerships.* Presented to National League of Cities' Conference. https://www.nlc.org/sites/default/files/2017-06/Building%20 Public-Private%20Partnerships.pdf.

Wanniski, J. (1978). *The Way the World Works: How Economics Fail and Succeed.* New York, NY: Basic Books.

Wolf, C., Jr. (1988). *Markets or Governments: Choosing Between Imperfect Alternatives.* Boston: MIT Press.

Part I
Budget Background

Evaluating a Tax System and Related Measures

2

To a large extent, the effectiveness of a government depends on how well it can provide public goods that will meet the demands of its citizens. However, for a government to be able to provide the goods consistent with public demands, it must be able to collect the necessary revenue, in particular tax revenue, without overburdening the taxpayers. The decisions to raise taxes that can realistically support the range of goods a government provides must be based on a sound understanding of the principles that underlie those decisions. The budget process expects the decision makers to have a basic understanding of these principles before making any decision on how much goods they must provide, the amount of revenue they must collect, the sources from which the revenues must come, and the economic and financial impact their decisions will have on the taxpayers vis-à-vis society at large. This chapter discusses several widely regarded principles that serve as the basis for making tax decisions in a government, known as "the desirable characteristics" of a tax system. It also briefly looks at some of the methods commonly used in tax collection. A central issue in any discussion on taxation is not how much revenue a tax system generates, but who ultimately bears the tax burden, known as tax incidence. The chapter concludes with a brief overview of incidence of taxation, including some of the methods commonly used for measuring the incidence.

2.1 Objectives of Taxation

There is an old saying that two things are certain in life—death and taxes. As individual consumers, we pay taxes on our income, goods we purchase, properties we own, assets that have increased in value, and inheritances we receive. By the same token, firms and businesses pay taxes on incomes they earn, goods they buy (intermediate goods), and the salaries and wages they pay their workers. The conventional wisdom that if a government can find a way to tax, it will, is not a cliché if

© The Author(s) 2019
A. Khan, *Fundamentals of Public Budgeting and Finance*,
https://doi.org/10.1007/978-3-030-19226-6_2

one would look at the myriad of taxes from which a government collects its revenues and the public perception of tax, in general. A tax is not a choice, but rather an involuntary payment to government by a taxpayer for which there may not be a *quid pro quo* return or benefit; in other words, the taxpayer may not receive a good or service that is in equal value of the tax contribution.

Tax decisions are not random or arbitrary. They are based on sound social and economic objectives that a government strives to achieve. At a minimum, they must produce enough revenue for a government for it to be able to provide goods and services without producing serious financial hardship on the taxpayers. Tax decisions are also important for redistributing income and wealth so they are not concentrated in a few hands and are used for common good. Not only that, taxes are essential instruments for stabilizing the economy, in particular, for reducing unemployment, maintaining price stability, promoting economic growth, maintaining balance of payment equilibrium, and protecting industries from unfair competition. Furthermore, well-thought-out tax decisions can increase efficiency of market operations resulting from market failure or imperfections, such as those discussed earlier.

As important and desirable the objectives are, given a choice, no one would like to pay taxes, but without taxes of one form or another no government will be able to fully function. Put simply, without taxes there will be no government, no provision of public goods, no distribution of income, and no policies to regulate the behavior of firms and business. If taxes were voluntary, as in charitable contributions, it is unlikely that most individuals will volunteer and, even if they do, it may not be sufficient to cover the full cost of goods and services a government provides. Consequently, the government needs to use its legal and, at times, coercive authority, to raise the needed revenue through taxes and other means.

2.2 Criteria for Evaluating a Tax System

All tax decisions, large or small, have a direct bearing on the economic well-being of the taxpayers, as well as society at large. This means that the decision makers must carefully analyze and evaluate their choices before deciding what to tax, how much to tax, and who should ultimately bear the tax burden. There have been extensive studies over the years on what should constitute a good tax system, going back to Adam Smith and his 1776 classic work, The Wealth of Nations (McCreadie 2009). Smith recognized four cannons of taxation that to this day serve as the foundation for modern taxation: equality (proportionality), certainty (guaranteed revenue), convenience (ease of taxpayer payments), and economy (efficiency in collection). Recently, the Association of International Certified Public Accountants (AICPA 1992) recommended twelve principles as indicators of a good tax policy, including the four suggested by Smith over two hundred years ago.[1]

This chapter looks at several principles, or criteria, as they are often called, to evaluate the tax policies of a government that economists call "the desirable characteristics" of a tax system (Stiglitz 2000; Mikesell 2014). Although the actual number of these criteria can vary, the chapter looks at five that lie at heart of most tax decisions of a government; they are efficiency, equity, flexibility, simplicity, and feasibility.

2.2.1   Efficiency

Efficiency is primarily concerned with the production of the greatest amount of social value from a given activity at a minimum cost. Efficiency is realized when the net social value such as net welfare gain or social benefit is maximized without affecting the workings of the free market system. In tax parlance, it means that a tax system is efficient when it does not distort, or affects as little as possible, the workings of the free market system yet produces maximum revenue for a government without producing an excess burden for the taxpayers. In other words, a system will be efficient if it produces maximum revenue for a government without imposing an excess burden, called deadweight loss, on the taxpayers, such that it does not affect their ability to consume, save, and invest. If it does, it will produce a welfare loss not only to the individual taxpayers, but also to society, as a whole. Welfare loss occurs when the tax policy of a government causes a consumer vis-a-vis a taxpayer to change his behavior by consuming less, or a producer by producing less to avoid the tax burden than what is socially desirable.

To give an example of how a tax decision creates excess burden, suppose that a government imposes a new tax on a commodity, say, gasoline, by *t* amount, shown in Fig. 2.1. Let us say that the amount is 30 cents and the current price, before the

Fig. 2.1 Incidence of a tax decision

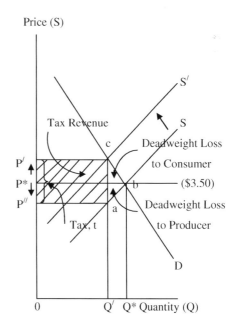

tax increase, is $3.50 per gallon. Given a choice, most firms would prefer to shift the entire tax burden on the consumers (forward shifting), but unless it is a monopoly it will be difficult to do so. Let us assume that they cannot also shift the entire burden on the suppliers (backward shifting). Since the firms cannot shift the entire tax burden to the consumers or the suppliers, forward or backward, they will lower the supply to S′, from S. In other words, they will lower the quantity to Q′, from the equilibrium quantity Q*. This will obviously increase the market price, let us say, by 20 cents, to $3.70 [$3.50 + $0.20 = $3.70] from the initial equilibrium price of $3.50, which was the price before the tax increase. This is given by the increase to P′, from the equilibrium price, P*. Since the firms can shift only 20 cents to the consumers, they are still left with 10 cents of the 30 cents in new tax; the net price to the firms will be $3.40, at P″, given by P′ − t = [$3.70 − $0.30]. The reduction in quantity with a concomitant change in price as a result of the tax decision by the government will thus measure the excess burden of the tax, given by the triangle Δabc. This is the burden both the firms and the consumers will have to absorb, respectively, from the after-tax loss to the firms for not being able to shift the entire tax increase and to the consumers from the after-tax increase in price.

David Hyman (2014) provides a simple expression for measuring efficiency loss or excess burden of a tax for each dollar of tax revenue; he calls it the efficiency-loss ratio of a tax. It is obtained by dividing the excess burden per dollar of tax revenue by total tax revenue and is given by the expression

$$ELR = (\text{Excess Burden}/\text{Tax Revenue}) \qquad (2.1)$$

where ELR is the efficiency-loss ratio.[2] For instance, an efficiency-loss ratio of 0.25 would mean that for each dollar of tax revenue raised a year, the excess burden will be 25 cents. Since the goal of any tax decision is to ensure that it does not create an excess burden on the taxpayers, or produces as little as possible, without lowering the tax revenue, estimating the efficiency-loss ratio from various tax measures can produce useful information for government to help achieve that goal.

Interestingly, the effects a tax decision produces for individuals as well as firms and businesses are often complex and numerous, but their presence in a tax system can affect its efficiency. This section briefly looks at some of the effects a tax decision produces for individuals as well as firms and businesses vis-a-vis society at large. They are behavioral effects, financial effects, organizational effects, distortionary versus nondistortionary effects, and partial versus general equilibrium effects (Stiglitz 2000).

2.2.1.1 Behavioral Effects

When a government imposes a tax, it directly affects an individual's ability to consume, save, and invest. Obviously, the more an individual has to pay in taxes, the less will be the portion of his after-tax income that will be available for consumption, savings, and investment. If, for instance, 90% of an individual's after-tax income goes into direct consumption, only 10% will be available for savings. Since the rate of savings ultimately determines the level of investment in an economy, it is necessary for the government to carefully weigh the effects a tax decision will have on savings vis-à-vis investments. However, the effects of a tax decision are not necessarily restricted to individual decisions on direct consumption; they also apply how individuals make personal decisions such as marriage, the size of the family, sending children to college, buying health insurance, and so forth (Stiglitz 2000).

2.2.1.2 Financial Effects

As noted earlier, the tax decisions of a government and the manner in which the taxes are collected have a direct bearing on the well-being of individuals, as well as firms and businesses. For instance, it makes very little difference whether an employer contributes to an employee's retirement plan or pays an equivalent amount directly to the employee so far as the employer is concerned, but it makes a real difference on the employee's overall income situation. If the contribution is made directly to the retirement plan, it will directly add to the employee's overall benefit package and indirectly to his real income for which the employee will not have to pay any taxes (under the current law). On the other hand, if the payment is made directly to the employee, it will add to the employee's aggregate income, thereby increasing his overall tax liability (Mikesell 2014). Similarly, business decisions will also be affected by government taxes. Since business profit, interest, dividends, and capital gains (increase in net worth of an asset) are not treated the same way under the current tax system, it will have a real effect on how firms and businesses make their financial decisions. For instance, if dividends on stocks are taxed at a much higher rate than returns on government securities, there will be more incentives for firms to invest in government securities than in stocks, which will affect long-term private capital investments.[3]

2.2.1.3 Organizational Effects

Similar to the effects a tax decision has on individual behavior, government taxes also have a direct effect on organizational behavior—in particular, how business organizations make financial decisions that involve risks. Business organizations can take different forms such as proprietorship (a single owner), partnership (two or more owners), and corporations (a legal entity created by the state with multiple owners or stockholders).[4] How each of these organizations makes their financial decisions and the risks associated with those decisions depends on the nature of the tax structure. For instance, prior to 1986, corporations were paying at 5 different rates ranging from 11 to 50%, which were substantially changed under the Tax Reform Act of 1986. The act simplified the tax structure, lowered the top marginal tax rates (from 50 to 28% for personal income and from 46 to 34% for corporations), shifted more of the direct tax burden to corporations, and reduced a number of tax breaks that were embedded in the tax code. A higher tax burden would obviously discourage firms and business from taking risks. In general, how firms and businesses take risks is determined by how the tax system treats tax liabilities. Corporations, for instance, have a much higher liability than either proprietorship or partnership, which may impede their ability to raise capital or may force them to take less risky ventures.

2.2.1.4 Distortionary vs. Nondistortionary Effects

Like most firms and businesses, individuals react differently to tax decisions of a
government. If an individual can do nothing to alter his tax liability (amount of tax
the individual must pay), it is a nondistortionary tax. Nondistortionary taxes are
also called lump-sum taxes. A good example of lump-sum tax is a head tax, also
known as poll tax that one has to pay regardless of income or wealth. Thus, if an
individual has to pay $150 in taxes independent of his earnings or circumstances,
it is a lump-sum tax. On the other hand, if an individual can alter his tax liability
in some ways, it is a distortionary tax. Income tax is a good example of distortionary tax since individuals can change their tax liabilities by deciding to work less in
order to pay less in taxes. Taxes on commodities are also good examples of distortionary tax because individuals can decide to lower their tax liability by consuming less. In fact, many of the taxes we pay have distortionary characteristics.

2.2.1.5 Partial vs. General Equilibrium Effects

The effects of a tax decision are often measured by a term called elasticity. Elasticity
measures the change in a variable in response to a change in one or more variables.[5]
For instance, if the demand for a commodity changes because of a corresponding
change in price, it is called the price elasticity of demand. Similarly, if the demand
for a good changes in response to a change in tax decision, it is defined as the tax
elasticity of demand. To give an example, suppose that a government imposes a new
tax on returns on capital invested in the housing market, say, new constructions. This
will affect the supply of capital that goes into the housing market depending on the
rate at which the return is taxed; if the tax is high, it will invariably lower the amount
of capital that will go into the housing market, which, in turn, will affect housing
construction. Assume, for the sake of argument, that the decision will affect only the
housing construction and nothing else; that is, it will not have any effect on any other
market other than the housing market. Since the decision affects only the housing
market and nothing else, it is called a partial equilibrium effect.

Partial equilibrium effects of a tax decision, while easier to understand and analyze because they tend to deal with a single market that is directly impacted by the
decision, do not provide a complete picture of how an economy responds to a tax
decision, especially if the effect of the decision filters over other markets. Since
the markets are interdependent, any major decision on a tax is likely to have an
effect not only on the intended market, but also on all other markets in the economy that are directly or indirectly related to it producing a general equilibrium
effect.[6] Thus, the decision to impose a new tax on returns on capital invested in the
housing market in our example will also affect all other sectors or industries, such
as labor, materials, supplies, and so forth, that are directly or indirectly related to
housing construction producing a general-equilibrium effect in the market.

2.2.2   Equity

Equity, or fairness, as the term commonly used, is concerned with the relative distribution of resources among individuals and groups, according to some

established notions of fairness and justice. Most general discussions of a tax system begin with the assumption that it is "unfair," but it is not quite as simple to say what is "fair" or "not fair"—much depends on how the tax burden is distributed among the various income brackets under different tax alternatives. There are two basic concepts of equity that economists and policy makers use to deal with the fairness issue: horizontal and vertical. Horizontal equity is concerned with the treatment of individuals with equal incomes, while vertical equity is concerned with the treatment of individuals with unequal incomes. Since much of the problem in taxation revolves around how to deal with individuals with unequal incomes, economists and policy makers are mostly concerned with vertical, rather than with horizontal equity.

2.2.2.1 Horizontal Equity

In general, a tax system is considered horizontally equitable if it treats individuals with equal incomes equally, which means that if two individuals have identical income they must pay exactly the same amount in taxes. Put differently, if two individuals with identical income had the same welfare before tax for it to be horizontally equitable they must have the same welfare after the tax, everything else remaining the same (Feldstein 1976). Horizontal equity is not a serious issue for economists because it does not deal with real distributional concerns of society as much as with the principle of justice or fairness that involves some value judgment.

Stiglitz (2000) uses an interesting example that is worth mentioning here. Two individuals with identical income and background go to an ice-cream parlor—one orders a vanilla ice cream and the other a chocolate ice cream. Assume that both ice creams cost exactly the same to make regardless of the flavor, but are taxed differently (vanilla ice cream a little higher than the chocolate ice cream because it is more popular) and the seller passes the extra tax to the consumer. If the individual ordering the vanilla ice cream pays a little more to absorb the burden of tax increase, does it mean that the tax system is inequitable? According to Stiglitz (2000), the answer is no. The tax system did not discriminate because the individual paying more had an option to order the chocolate ice cream, but preferred not to. In other words, they had the same opportunity set to choose from, but one decided to forgo the opportunity.

Another example that is frequently used in this context is the marriage tax. For instance, two individuals with identical income who live together pay at a lower rate than a married couple, each with identical income as the single individuals because their combined income puts them into a higher tax bracket. Interestingly, the current tax structure under the joint rate schedule (married, filing jointly) allows for some benefits only if the income of one spouse is considerably higher than the other. This is known as the income-splitting effect because it splits the incomes of both spouses equally for tax purposes. For instance, if one spouse earns $60,000 and the other has no taxable income, then $60,000 would be divided equally between the spouses as if each had earned $30,000 income for the year, which will lower their marginal tax rate (defined as the rate on the differences between two income brackets). This obviously benefits a single-earner family.

On the other hand, if both spouses work and have identical income, their combined income will put them into a much higher bracket and, consequently, will be paying at a much higher rate.

This raises an obvious question: Is it fair (horizontally equitable) for two individuals with identical income to pay at a higher rate simply because they are married? This is known as the marriage penalty or marriage tax. Unfortunately, the economists do not have a precise answer to this. Part of the reason for this is that even though it gives the appearance of an economic problem, it is considerably different from conventional economic problems because of its value orientation. From an economic point of view, however, one could argue that, like the ice-cream case, the individuals had an opportunity set to choose from. In reality, given a choice, most economists would prefer not to deal with issues that are highly sensitive, with a moral undertone, rather leave them to the policy makers to decide what is in the best interest of society.

2.2.2.2　Vertical Equity

Vertical equity, as noted earlier, deals with how individuals are treated with unequal incomes. In general, a tax system is considered vertically equitable if it treats individuals with unequal incomes differently. However, dealing with vertical equity is far more complex than dealing with horizontal equity because it requires the use of some scales by which to measure the well-being of individuals with different incomes. Several different constructs can be used for measuring vertical equity, but the two most frequently used in economic analysis of taxation are the ability to pay and the benefit principles.

The Ability to Pay Principle

According to this principle, taxes should be levied in accordance with the taxpayer's ability to pay and often serve as the basic criterion of fairness in taxation. The assumption here is that those who have greater ability should pay more than those who do not.[7] In other words, if an individual has high income and in a position to pay more, then he should pay more, but how much more is a complicated question. Economists and policy makers do not have a precise answer as to where the cut-off line should be; that is, how much more in taxes an individual should pay. Instead, they rely on value judgment about the distributional effects a tax decision will produce on the aggregate welfare of society (Haveman 1976).

Consider a society consisting of two individuals—a rich man and a poor man. The rich man decides or is asked to sacrifice a small fraction of his income, say, through tax transfer for the welfare of the poor man. As shown in Fig. 2.2, a little sacrifice by the rich man will have a far greater effect on the poor man than on the rich man. It will substantially increase the welfare of the poor man, from $W_{P,B}$ to $W_{P,A}$ (where P stands for the poor man and the subscripts B and A stand for welfare level before and after the income transfer, respectively) compared to the welfare loss of the rich man, R, from $W_{R,B}$ to $W_{R,A}$. Part of the reason for this is that the marginal utility of a dollar to a rich man is much lower than the marginal utility to a poor man. In other words, a poor man will derive more satisfaction

Fig. 2.2 Welfare effects of income transfer

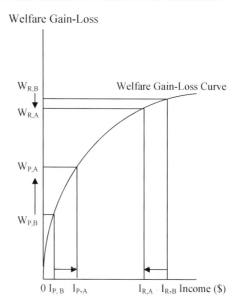

Welfare Gain-Loss

from an additional dollar than a rich man. Since the welfare gain of the poor man from a marginal dollar is considerably more than the welfare loss of the rich man, that is, $W_{P,B} - W_{P,A} > W_{R,B} - W_{R,A}$, in the aggregate, both will be better off by the income transfer. Simply put, it will increase the aggregate welfare of society.

While the example above may appear simple, in reality it is much more complicated, especially where income transfers are concerned. The question at stake here is at what point the transfer will no longer be feasible since it is simply not possible to ask the rich man to continue to pay more in taxes. Although there is no cut-and-dried answer to the question, one way to deal with the problem is to apply the well-known Pareto optimality to determine if there is an optimal transfer of income. The Pareto optimality is based on two conditions: Pareto improvement, also called Pareto superiority, and Pareto optimality. Theoretically, as long as the transfer will continue to improve the welfare of the poor man without lowering the welfare of the rich man, it will be a Pareto improvement, and at the point where no additional improvement is possible, it will be Pareto optimal. In other words, so long as the transfer improves the welfare of the poor man without lowering the welfare of the rich man society in the aggregate will be better off.

Unfortunately, there is no guarantee that the transfer will produce an efficient outcome because there is no way of knowing if it will not lower the welfare of the rich man, even if it is only by a small fraction. Put simply, the individuals who think that they are being disadvantaged from income transfer under Pareto efficiency may not necessarily agree to use this as a mechanism for resource allocation, regardless of their level of income and wealth. They may very well be content with Pareto inefficient allocations, as long as the level of utility they derive from the existing level of allocation is higher (Stiglitz 2000). The frequent conflict in Congress over

trade-off between tax increase and income transfer for various redistribution programs is a good case in point. Another problem with the criteria is that there is no
one Pareto efficient resource allocation, but a whole range of Pareto efficient allocations. What this means is that while an individual may be better off in one situation,
he may not be better off in another. In other words, the same individual may not be
better off in every situation. The problem can become even more complicated if one
would bring in *n* individuals with multiple income levels into the picture, involving
multiple different transfers and welfare calculations.

In as much as the ability to pay principle has an intuitive appeal, one could
also argue if it is fair to ask someone to pay more simply because one earns more
income, or has greater ability to pay more. The answer to the question may lie
in the value judgment that underlies the tax decisions of a government—in particular, income tax and the degree to which an individual must pay more in taxes.
Others may argue that paying more by those who have the ability to pay more
makes good sense because if a given tax policy benefits some individuals more
than others, then those who benefit more from that policy have an obligation to
pay more vis-a-vis compensate those who lose in the process. This is known as
the compensation principle.[8] The assumption here is that if the gain from the decision is large enough to compensate those who lose, it should, and the result will
be Pareto superior since society will be better off in the aggregate. However, the
question still remains as to how much more and what will be an optimal level of
tax that will be satisfactory to all.

Finally, it should be pointed out that the ability to pay is based on how one
defines "ability." The presupposition that individuals with higher incomes must
pay more is somewhat of a misnomer because, in reality, they may not be in a
position to pay more. For instance, two individuals with identical income but different financial conditions may not have the same ability to pay. If one has more
liability than the other, then even with the same income the individual with greater
liability may not be in a position to pay more. Interestingly, the tax provisions
under the current structure were built essentially with this purpose in mind—to
allow the individual taxpayers some flexibility in dealing with their financial liabilities. Consequently, taxes are paid not on gross, but on net income after adjusting for allowable provisions.

The Benefit Principle

According to this principle, individuals should pay in proportion to the benefit
they receive from the consumption of a good. Since the government expenditures
financed by taxes provide benefits to individuals, the magnitude of these benefits
could be used to determine the size of the tax burden individuals should bear, but
the question is how to tie the two together since individuals do not receive the
same level of benefit for their taxes. The essence of the argument is that it is unfair
to use income as the sole basis for taxation when individuals do not receive the
same amount of benefit as they contribute in taxes. In other words, the taxes the
individuals pay for the consumption of public goods should be based in accordance with the benefits they receive, not on their ability to pay.[9]

To give an example, suppose that a government plans to undertake a program at a cost of, say, $100 (in reality, it will be much more) that will benefit three individuals—A, B, and C, each with a different level of income. Assume that A has the highest income of the three, B has the second highest, and C has the lowest. If the ability to pay principle were to apply here, A will bear the most of the cost because he has the highest income, B will bear the second most, and C will bear the least. Now, suppose that the benefits the individuals will receive from the program are the exact opposite of their income in that C will receive the most benefit, B the second most (in fact, B's position remains unchanged), and A will receive the least, in which case it will be unfair under the benefit principle to ask A to pay more in taxes when he will receive the least amount of benefit from the program, even though A has the highest income. Let us say that we are able to convert the benefits in monetary terms such that A will receive $20 worth of benefit, B will receive $35 worth, and C will receive $45 worth. Therefore, according to the benefit principle, A should pay $20 in taxes (20% of the total benefit), B should pay $35 (35% of the total benefit), and C should pay $45 (45% of the total benefit), which will make up the total cost of the program (Table 2.1).

There are several fundamental problems with the benefit principle, as it should become obvious from the above example. One, it is not always possible to assign a precise dollar value to the benefits individuals receive from a public good, especially if the goods are intangible such as education, health care, recreation, and so forth, such that one is able to establish a one-to-one correspondence between the cost of provision and the amount of benefits received. Two, for those public goods where there is a free-rider problem, it is difficult to determine the exact quantity individuals will consume because of the revealed preference problem and, therefore, the price they must pay for their consumption. However, the benefit principle makes perfect sense for goods that are provided in a business-like manner, such as water, sewer, electricity, toll roads, and so forth, where non-exclusion condition does not generally apply. Since these goods are divisible, it is possible to assign a dollar value to the quantity consumed and, therefore, the price the individuals must pay in proportion to the amount of benefit they receive.

Three, it is unfair, if not difficult, especially from a moral ground, to ask individuals at the lower rung of income strata to pay the full value of the benefits they receive from the consumption of a good when they can least afford. Four, from a purely economic point of view, when individuals do not have the ability to pay, it may discourage society from providing the good at all, or it may force them

Table 2.1 Distribution of cost burden: the ability to pay vs. the benefit principle

Individuals	Benefits received ($)	Cost share in equal amounts ($)	Cost share by ability-to-pay ($)	Cost share by benefits received ($)	Income status
A	$20	$33.33 (33.3%)	$45 (45%)	$20 (20%)	High income
B	35	$33.33 (33.3%)	35 (35%)	35 (35%)	Middle income
C	45	$33.33 (33.3%)	25 (25%)	45 (45%)	Low income
	$100	$99.99 (99.9%)	$100 (100%)	$100 (100%)	

to consume less, such as less education, less health care, less public safety, and so forth, than what is socially desirable which will be an inefficient allocation of resources. Collectively, it will lower the aggregate welfare of society. Finally, by itself, the benefit principle may not be sufficient to generate the needed revenue for a government. A good example is state sales tax. While it produces the bulk of the tax revenue for most state governments, it is often supplemented by revenue from income tax and other non-tax revenues. This may partly explain why both principles are necessary, so as to provide a government with a much larger tax base from which to collect its revenues.

2.2.2.3 Efficiency-Equity Trade-Off

Although in theory it is possible to design a tax system that would be equitable, in reality it may be quite difficult to implement it. There are several reasons for that. First, it would require the decision makers to obtain full information on individual preferences for goods and the quantity they want to consume, which may not be easily obtainable. Second, even if it is possible to obtain such information, it is quite likely that individuals will not voluntarily reveal that information in order to reduce their tax burden. The government will then have to find other alternatives such as income, wealth, the quality of public goods, or some other measures to obtain that information which may not produce a perfect index of their preference. Third, when a government imposes a tax, in particular a progressive tax, on individuals to improve vertical equity, it will invariably impinge on their ability to consume, save, and invest, causing a deadweight (welfare) loss not only to the individuals, but also to society at large.

Put simply, a progressive tax on income, while may provide a strong ground for vertical equity, could lead to inefficiency due to the distortionary effect it may have on aggregate income, savings, and investment. If so, the government will have to make a trade-off between progressive taxation that would ensure vertical equity and the deadweight loss to society that would result from the excess burden of taxation. As noted earlier, the deadweight loss or excess burden occurs as a result of welfare loss from the tax decision of a government. Theoretically, every tax decision a government makes creates an excess burden, as it limits the choices by steering resources away from their best and most productive use based purely on economic ground. Therefore, the objective of any tax decision should be to keep the excess burden to a minimum, or as low as possible.

There are several ways in which one can minimize the excess burden of taxation, but the one that has drawn considerable attention in the literature on tax efficiency is the Ramsey rule. According to this rule, taxes should be placed in inverse proportion to the elasticity of demand for goods. The argument is based on the conventional wisdom that the more inelastic the demand for a good, the higher should be the tax on the good. Therefore, higher taxes should be placed on goods with inelastic demand since the consumption is less likely to be affected by higher taxes, although it is likely to produce an excess burden resulting from the higher tax (Holcombe 2006).

This may partly explain why taxes are high on goods such as alcohol and tobacco. Since these goods are considered less desirable from society's point of view, while the demand for the goods tends to remain more or less unaffected by taxes (inelastic demand), they are likely to produce less excess burden for society. As such, they are often considered efficient, but not necessarily equitable. The efficiency argument comes from the fact that since the demand for these goods is price inelastic, any increase in taxes on these goods will not have any real effect on their demand. However, a higher tax would impose a heavier burden on individuals with low income who may end up spending a disproportionately higher percentage of their income on these goods and, consequently, paying disproportionately more in taxes for their consumption than individuals with higher income.

The point that is important to recognize here is that, regardless of what type of tax a government imposes, it is likely to produce a disproportionately higher burden on some individuals than others. Consequently, it will be difficult to avoid a deadweight loss when the burden is shared disproportionately. This may partly explain why governments use multiple sources of revenue, rather than any one in particular, so that the burden does not fall heavily on any particular income group. In other words, distribute the liability among multiple income groups and sources as much as possible to minimize the excess burden, although it may increase the cost of tax administration (Yang and Stitt 1995).

2.2.3   Flexibility

All economies, in particular a market economy, go through periodic ups and downs creating frequent revenue challenges for a government. This means that the tax base from which a government collects its revenues must be flexible in order to meet the changing needs of society. In general, the more flexible a tax base vis-à-vis a tax system, the greater the ability of a government to generate the needed revenue from that base, or system. In principle, all taxes are flexible in the long run, but the degree of flexibility depends on the nature of the tax, the condition of the economy, and the public's willingness to support any changes in the tax system, in particular tax increase. Nevertheless, there are ways in which a government can increase its revenue from an existing tax base, or system. There are three principal means, for instance, a government can use to increase its tax and non-tax revenue: expand the tax base, raise taxes, and find new sources of revenue. The following provides a brief overview of each.

2.2.3.1   Expand the Tax Base

A tax base is a legally defined source from which a government collects its tax revenue. Considering the fact that much of the revenue a government collects comes from taxes, its economic well-being must depend on its tax base. In general, the growth of a tax base depends on the method a government employs to generate the needed revenue from that base without necessarily raising taxes. For instance, if a government relies largely on property tax, then expanding the full value of taxable property, such as allowing the appraised value to fully reflect the market value without raising tax rates, will increase its tax base. Similarly, if a government relies predominantly on income tax, then lowering some of the provisions in the tax code without necessarily raising taxes will increase its tax base. However, to increase the size of a tax base, it must have the growth potential or the capacity to generate the additional revenue. Given a choice, most governments would prefer to collect their revenues from a tax base that is stable and has the potential to grow, rather than the one that is stagnating or unpredictable, but that is not always the case. Unfortunately, the revenue base items with the highest growth potential are frequently the least stable, such as the income tax base that grows with income and rises or falls with the general condition of the economy.

2.2.3.2 Raise Taxes

A government can also raise revenue by raising taxes either by increasing the tax rate on an existing source or by introducing tax on a source that was not previously used. However, raising revenue by increasing tax rates is not an attractive alternative by any measure; there are frequent legal and political obstacles that can prevent a government from raising taxes. Public reluctance to support tax increase, even in the best of times, can frequently work against any decision to raise taxes. Also, from a theoretical point of view, there is a limit to how much revenue a government can raise by raising taxes from a given base. According to the famous Laffer curve (2004), which provided much of the conceptual foundation for supply-side economics in the late 1970s and early 1980s, higher taxes tend to produce a diminishing rather than an increasing return in tax revenue, meaning that an increase in tax rate will increase revenue up to a point beyond which it will not produce any additional revenue. Put simply, if a government does not have sufficient revenue capacity that can be tapped from a given tax base, then raising tax rates will simply not produce any additional revenue for the government from that base. On the contrary, the revenue may actually decline because at higher rates people will have less incentive to work hard, and firms and businesses less incentive to take risks, if a significant portion of their additional income is going to be taxed away. Figure 2.3 shows this relationship between tax rate and tax revenue. As the figure shows, the revenue will be maximum at point R^0, which is the highest point on the curve, corresponding to the tax rate at r^0, and will continue to decline as the rate crosses this point toward 100%.

Theoretically, the Laffer curve can be applied to any tax—not just income. The essence of the argument will be the same that, for any tax base, there exists a rate that can produce the maximum revenue from that base. Therefore, any effort to raise more revenue beyond that maximum by raising the rate will not simply produce more revenue.

Fig. 2.3 Laffer curve

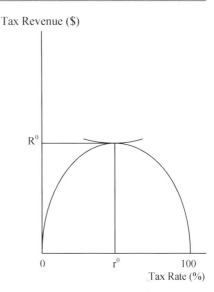

2.2.3.3 Find New Sources of Revenue

Finally, a government can always try to generate new revenues from sources that have not been previously tapped or explored, especially non-tax revenue. These are revenues that do not rely on taxes and, as such, can provide an effective tool for raising revenue for government without burdening the taxpayers. Non-tax revenues generally include user fees and charges, fines and forfeitures, licenses and permits, and intergovernmental transfers. Additionally, a government can use creative financing to raise revenues that do not include raising taxes or using fees and charges. This may, for instance, include selling surplus government assets that do not serve any useful purpose, renting out unused properties such as vacant land, buildings, and equipment, investing idle cash to generate interest earnings, and encouraging public–private partnership, among others.

Unfortunately, the number of sources or avenues from which a government can collect new revenue has declined considerably in recent years, as governments compete with each other for new sources. Also, the amount that can be raised through creative financing may not be sufficient to make up for the revenue gap, although there may be exceptions. The point to keep in mind is that regardless of how revenues are raised, the taxpayers, for the most part, do not like to see their government grow too big or collect more revenue than is necessary, especially from taxes. Given a choice between tax and non-tax revenue, most taxpayers would prefer the latter, as long as it does not involve paying more taxes.

2.2.4   Simplicity

A tax system must be based on laws and procedures that are easy to understand by the taxpayers and also easy to enforce by the administration at the lowest cost.

The US tax system is extremely complex, consisting of a myriad of laws and regulations, built over time that is not easy to grasp by an average taxpayer. Even some legal scholars, going as far back as 1947, expressed concerns at the complexity of the US tax laws (Hand 1947). Keeping track of records and filling out forms to comply with the tax laws under the current system can consume an enormous amount of time. The Internal Revenue Service (IRS), a bureau of the Department of Treasury, estimates that completing and filing the basic tax return form (Form 1040) requires more than 13 hours on average (Higgins 2007). If one could just imagine every single taxpayer filing multitudes of forms and schedules to detail their financial activities for the year, the time and money it would take them to comply with all the tax laws and prepare the returns would be astronomical.[10]

2.2.4.1 The Tax Codes

The problem with the current tax system, especially at the federal level, lies in part with the federal tax codes, also known as the Internal Revenue Codes (IRCs), which are administered by the IRS.[11] While the tax laws are primarily used for and directly related to revenue generation for the federal government, the tax codes are mostly used for policy purposes—in particular, to achieve social, economic, and political goals. For instance, to encourage home ownership the current tax law allows for deduction of mortgage interest expense on debt if the property is used as the primary residence. Similar provisions are built into the system for sales and other taxes. On the other hand, a tax code such as IRC Section 162 indicates when an individual can claim a business deduction. However, the use of the codes as an instrument of government policy raises serious questions about the principles that underlie the codes since the tax policies of the government do not remain constant—they change as the administrations change. As a result, the codes are frequently amended by Congress to reflect the changes in government policies which can easily add to the number, as well as to the complexity of the system.

2.2.4.2 Costs of Administration and Noncompliance

Complexity often has an economic cost that can increase exponentially over time. The complexity of the current tax structure has produced two sets of costs that have been a concern for the government, in particular for the IRS for a long time: administrative cost and compliance cost. Administrative costs primarily include the costs of administering and enforcing the tax laws, and are reflected in the budget of the IRS. The IRS budget has gone up considerably in recent years, although it constitutes a small fraction of the total federal budget running at around one-half of 1% of the total receipts (GAO 2008). If one would add to this the noncompliance costs that result from tax evasion and tax avoidance, the combined cost to the administration and the public, as well as to firms and businesses, would run into billions of dollars a year. Tax evasion takes place when the taxpayers do not comply with the tax laws by failing to pay taxes that are owed to the government, while tax avoidance occurs as a result of the effort by the taxpayers to reduce tax liability.

Tax evasion is clearly a violation of the tax law, and without effective enforcement of the law, the government will collect far less in tax revenue than if it has to rely entirely on voluntary compliance. Tax enforcement is costly, so is tax evasion. One of the more difficult forms of tax evasion is the underground economy, such as the drug trade and other forms of clandestine transactions that take place without any consideration for taxes. This has created a major tax gap for the government costing it billions of dollars each year. Interestingly, unlike tax evasion, tax avoidance is not against the law, although there are obvious cases that can be considered tax evasion by the taxpayers and avoidance by the government. A common practice of tax avoidance is income shifting, where an individual shifts his income to a family member, usually with less income, to avoid higher tax liabilities. Another form of tax avoidance is to take advantage of different tax rates on different types of incomes. Capital gains tax is a good example because the rate is much lower on capital gains than on "regular" income such as wages and salaries. Besides, they are not subject to payroll taxes. It is possible to have more complicated forms of tax avoidance, but that may require sophisticated knowledge of the tax laws and how they are interpreted, and often outside the realm of an average taxpayer.

Historically, noncompliance has been more of a problem with income tax than with sales or property tax. Property tax, in particular, is difficult to avoid because properties are tangible and fixed, and as noted earlier, their proximity to the government makes it difficult to avoid the tax. Consequently, the collection rate has been much higher for property tax than for most other taxes, running over 90% in most cases. Overall, the high running costs of taxation are direct results of the complex structure of the current system. Simply put, if a tax system is too complex for a government to administer and for the public to understand and comply with, it is not likely to be perceived as a good system. In other words, for a tax system to be desirable, it should be simple and relatively inexpensive to administer.

2.2.5   Feasibility

In a democratic system, all decisions, including those of government taxes, have to go through a political process where they must have the support of the public. Public support is necessary for a government to pass legislations on major tax decisions. For instance, if a government wants to introduce a new tax, be it a state income tax or a local option sales tax, it has to have the approval of the voting public. The process often requires that the initiatives go through a public referendum before the legislature can act on them. This has two immediate implications for a tax policy: One, it gives the public an opportunity to carefully evaluate the proposed policy before voting on it and, two, it allows the decision makers to recognize the choices made by the public and to ensure that the policy reflects those choices.

   Although politics can occasionally sidetrack the real benefit a tax policy produces for society, it is the risk a government has to take when introducing a new tax initiative; it is part of the democratic process under which the government operates. To give an example with which the author is familiar: It involved a local government that introduced a local option sales tax (LOST) several years ago. According to the local charter, the government was required to go through a public referendum within the first six months of its introduction. The revenue from the tax was to be used for economic development that was badly needed, in particular from the loss of revenue from a military base closure earlier that served as a major source of revenue for the government for a long time. The local Tax Watchers' group, which strongly opposed the policy from the beginning, was able to generate enough support to convince the public to vote against it. The initiative was repealed, which cost the government millions of dollars in potential tax revenue that it badly needed for economic development. Interestingly, the policy was subsequently reintroduced and the voters approved the decision.

   In spite of the initial failure, the concept of engaging the voting public on issues such as a major tax initiative makes perfect sense for two simple reasons: One, for most local governments, public referendum is a constitutional requirement that must be observed regardless of the nature of the tax proposed. Two and, more importantly, the public, in particular the taxpayers, must have a say in the process since it is the taxpayers who are ultimately responsible for bearing the tax burden. The upshot of the story is that there is no point of having a tax policy, or any policy for that matter, if it does not have the support of the public, especially in a democratic society. However, to have public support, a government must earn the trust of the public. Although there is no precise agreement among public officials and academics as to what constitutes public trust, most would agree that there has been a significant erosion of this trust in government in recent years. This means that in order to have an effective economic policy, whether it deals with taxation or public expenditure, the government must make serious efforts to regain the public trust (Christensen and Laegreid 2003; Putnam 1995).

   While earning public trust in general is not easy in a democratic society, it is much harder when it comes to taxes. A study by Martin Daunton (2001) suggests three principal means a government can use to create or rebuild public trust, especially with regard to taxes. First, by assuring the taxpayers that their tax dollars will not be misused or wasted. In order to ensure this, the government must have a sustained program of expenditure control. Second, by bringing about administrative reforms designed to control political pressure for higher spending. Third, by creating a philosophy of balance and fairness in the tax system which can be achieved through a gradual change in the political culture, especially among those who are directly involved in everyday tax decisions. None of these tasks are easy for any government and may take a long time to earn public trust, but, in the end, it is in the best interest of the government to have an informed and engaging public when making decisions that will affect their collective welfare.

2.2.6   Other Related Criteria

In addition to those mentioned above, there are other criteria that must also be considered when making a tax decision, four of which are worth noting—stability, transparency, convenience, and security. Used often in conjunction with flexibility, a tax system must be stable in that the sources a government uses for tax purposes must produce a stable income for it to be able to carry out its normal operations. A tax system must also be transparent. Individuals paying taxes must have a good understanding of the taxes they pay, the amount of their liability, how the liability is calculated, who collects the taxes, and the government that uses the tax dollars. Similarly, a tax system must be convenient in that the timing of payment and the manner of tax collection should be convenient for the taxpayers. Finally, a tax system must be secure in that the government must protect taxpayer information from improper and unlawful disclosures.

2.3   Optimal Tax Structure

Tax decisions are often more complex than any other decision a government makes, in part, because of the process it has to go through, especially the political process and, in part, because of the effect it has on the taxpayers, as well as society at large. Yet, without taxes there will be no government, no provision of public goods, and no improvement in collective welfare. Therefore, one needs to ask if there is an optimal vis-à-vis the best tax system—one that will generate maximum revenue for a government and will also produce the least burden on the taxpayers. Unfortunately, it is difficult to have a tax system that will fully satisfy all the stakeholders equally or at the same time. Theoretically, if one could have a tax system that would meet all the criteria and also produce maximum revenue for a government, it would be possible to achieve some measure of optimality, but, in reality, it is much more complex than that—economic and political realities often make it difficult to have a tax system that will fully meet these criteria.

However, one can argue that when a tax system is less than optimal, it is still possible to achieve some degrees of optimality. A good example is the theory of the second best, which allows for the achievement of second-best optimality when some of the conditions of first-best optimality are violated (Lipsey and Lancaster 1956–1957). The first-best optimality generally refers to Pareto optimality. Pareto optimality, in this case, refers to a tax structure such that there exists no other tax structure that can make some individuals better off without making others worse off (Stiglitz and Rosengard 2015). As noted earlier, there is not one, but multiple different optimal tax structures which would satisfy the Pareto conditions meaning that, in each case, no one can be made better off without making someone else worse off. Put simply, if an individual is better off under tax structure A, he may not be better off under tax structure B or C, and so forth.[12]

This raises an interesting question whether it is possible to apply the optimality condition strictly when we know that tax decisions can produce distortions. Stiglitz (2000) makes an important point that it may be better to have two small distortions than one large one. For instance, if a tax decision produces welfare loss, say, to 5% of the population, or two small distortions that make 10% of the population worse off, it is a better decision than the decision that will make 75% of the population worse off, which would lower the aggregate welfare by a substantially greater margin.

One could also argue that if some distortions or inefficiency in a tax system are unavoidable, it may be prudent to have a single tax, such as a lump-sum tax, instead of multiple different taxes to keep the structure simple and distortions less. Theoretically, it would make sense only if we all had identical incomes or preferences and our collective needs were kept low, so that the government can institute a uniform lump-sum tax on all taxpayers to keep the deadweight loss to society to a minimum. In reality, it will be difficult to have such a system because of our varying needs, incomes, and preferences, which may partly explain why it is necessary to have a tax system that better reflects the economic and political structure of a society, consistent with its value preferences.

2.4   Methods of Tax Collection

The primary means by which a government collects its revenues are taxes. However, as noted earlier, raising revenue from taxes imposes a burden not only on the taxpayers, but also on the government. While a government must raise sufficient revenue to meet the expenditure needs of its citizens, it must also make sure that its tax decision does not impose an excess burden on the taxpayers. This balancing act between the need to raise sufficient revenue, on the one hand, and the desire not to overburden the taxpayers, on the other, makes it necessary for the government to carefully weigh the pros and cons of the methods it must use to raise tax revenues. This section provides a brief summary of three such methods that are frequently used for raising tax revenues: (1) according to tax base, (2) according to tax responsibility, and (3) according to rate structure. The methods are interdependent in that any tax decision involving one is likely to have an effect on the others. For instance, a decision to expand a tax base will have an effect on how individuals pay their taxes, the rate at which they pay, and the burden they ultimately have to bear.

2.4.1   According to Tax Base

As noted earlier, a tax base is a legally defined source from which a government collects its revenues. There are three principal sources from which a government collects its tax revenues: income, consumption, and wealth. Income, especially taxable income, is the portion of earnings of individuals, as well as firms and businesses that are subject to taxation. Consumption is the after-tax income that is not saved. In other words, it is the portion of an individual's after-tax income that is spent on consumption goods. Wealth is the net value (after taxes) of the individual's stock of accumulated savings or investments. Collectively, it is the net value of all financial assets (e.g., stocks and bonds), capital assets (e.g., machines, tools, and equipment), and land (e.g., real and personal property) that make up the accumulated savings and investments for an economy.

2.4.2   According to Responsibility

One of the earliest methods used in tax classification is how individuals pay their taxes, known as tax responsibility. According to this method, a tax can be direct or indirect. A tax is considered direct if it is imposed directly on individuals such as individual income. On the other hand, a tax is considered indirect if it is imposed not on individuals, but on the goods and services they consume. Sales tax is a good example of indirect tax. The difference between a direct and an indirect tax is the anonymity of the latter.

2.4.3   According to Rate Structure

Individuals do not pay taxes at the same rate as their income changes—some pay more and some pay less. This is known as the rate structure of tax. In common parlance, the rate structure of tax means the application of a tax rate to a tax base to produce a given amount of revenue from that base. The rate can be fixed, or it can vary according to a predetermined formula. Thus, based on a rate structure, a tax can be progressive, regressive, or proportional (Fig. 2.4). A tax is considered progressive if an individual or firm pays at a progressively higher rate as income increases; it is considered regressive if the rate decreases as income increases; and it is considered proportional if the rate remains the same, regardless of changes in income.

The distinction between the different components of a rate structure is important to understand the relationship between the tax rate and the tax base—in particular, how the rate varies with changes in the base. Two general terms are frequently used to explain this relationship: average tax rate (ATR) and effective tax rate (ETR). An ATR shows the relationship between tax liability (how much an individual or firm has to pay in taxes) and taxable income that is subject to tax. It is obtained by dividing tax liability by the amount of taxable income. For instance, if an individual has a tax liability of $1875 on an (adjusted) taxable income of $28,750, the individual's ATR will be 6.52% [$1875/$28,750 = 0.0652 × 100 = 6.52%]. On the other hand, the ETR, which is often referred to as the actual rate, because it is based on gross rather than adjusted income, is obtained by dividing the tax liability by the gross income. Thus, if the individual in our example has a gross income of $41,000, while his tax liability remains the same, the ETR will be lower than ATR at 4.57% [$1875/$41,000 = 0.0457 × 100 = 4.57%].

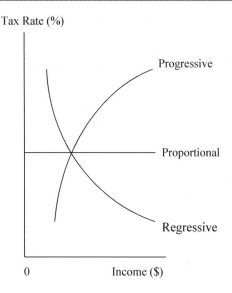

Fig. 2.4 Rate structure of a tax

Table 2.2 Rate structure of income tax

Progressive			Proportional		Regressive	
Taxable income ($)	Tax rate (%)	Tax liability ($)	Tax rate (%)	Tax liability ($)	Tax rate (%)	Tax liability ($)
5000	10.0	500.00	10.0	500.00	10.0	500.00
10,000	15.0	1500.00	10.0	1000.00	9.0	900.00
15,000	20.0	3000.00	10.0	1500.00	7.5	1125.00

Table 2.2 gives an example of each type of rate structure. As shown in the table, under a progressive tax structure, the tax liability constitutes a higher percentage of taxable income at higher levels of income. Under the proportional tax structure, the tax is levied at a flat rate, say, at 10% on taxable income. In other words, the ATR is 10% at all levels of income, while under the regressive structure the tax liability constitutes a lower percentage of taxable income at higher levels of income. In general, if ATR remains the same at all levels of the tax base, regardless of increases or decreases in income, the tax is proportional. If, on the other hand, it increases with an increase in the tax base, it is progressive. Finally, if it decreases, as the tax base increases, it is regressive.

The rate structure of a tax can also be determined by comparing ATR with the tax rate applicable to additional income as income moves from one bracket to the next, called the marginal tax rate (MTR). For instance, when the structure is progressive, the MTR is above the ATR (MTR>ATR). When the structure is regressive, it is below the average rate (MTR<ATR), and when it is proportional, the two are the same (MTR=ATR). The comparison makes it possible

for the decision makers to see what kind of effect a tax decision will have on the taxpayers.

Consider again the example in Table 2.2. When the taxable income of the individual goes up by $5000, from $10,000 to $15,000, and the tax liability goes up by $1500, from $1500 to $3000 for a progressive tax, the MTR is 30% over this range [(3000–$1500)/($15,000–$10,000) = $1500/$5000 = 0.3 × 100 = 30%], which is greater than the ATR of 20% [$3000/$15,000 = 0.2 × 100 = 20%]. Similarly, when the taxable income goes up by $5000, from $10,000 to $15,000, and the tax liability goes up by $225, from $900 to $1,125 for a regressive tax, the MTR is 4.5% over this range [($1125–$900)/($15,000–$10,000) = $225/$5000 = 0.045 × 100 = 4.5%], which is below the ATR of 7.5% [$1125/$15,000 = 0.075 × 100 = 7.5%]. Finally, when the taxable income goes up from $10,000 to $15,000 and the tax liability goes up by $500, from $1000 to $1500 for a proportional tax, the MTR is 10% over this range [($1500–$1000)/($15,000–$10,000) = $500/$5000 = 0.1 × 100], which is the same as the ATR of 10% [$1500/$15,000 = 0.1 × 100 = 10%].

Interestingly, the current tax system has elements of all three taxes. Although it is mostly progressive, it has elements of both regressivity and proportionality. For instance, income tax is generally considered progressive since the rate at which individuals pay taxes goes up with higher incomes, but only up to a point beyond which the rate remains the same, which may be considered as regressive. A good example of proportional tax, on the other hand, would be sales tax where individuals pay at the same rate, regardless of their income. Another example of proportional tax would be if individuals pay at the same rate, say, at 15% in taxes of their income. However, it would be considered regressive if individuals with higher income pay at the same rate relative to their income as those with low income.

2.5   Incidence of Taxation

The central issue in any discussion on taxation is who ultimately pays the tax or bears the tax burden, known as incidence of taxation. Whether a tax is paid directly or indirectly the incidence of taxation deals with the final payment of the tax. The individual who ultimately pays when a tax is collected bears the tax burden. Although the location of the tax burden determines its incidence, its effect on the economic well-being of the individual paying the tax may not be the same, depending on the income status of the individual and the tax rate at which he has to pay. Thus, if the incidence falls on an individual who is rich, the income effect on the individual is likely to be much less than if it falls on an individual who is poor. Tax incidence analysis provides an important building block for understanding the fairness of a tax system—in particular, the effect tax decisions can have on the taxpayers.

Interestingly, the incidence depends on the elasticity of demand and supply. Going back to the example of gasoline tax increase we discussed earlier, if demand was perfectly inelastic, the sellers could easily shift the entire burden of tax increase on the consumers. Likewise, if the supply was perfectly elastic, the consumers could shift the entire burden on the sellers. Since, in reality, demand and supply are neither perfectly elastic nor perfectly inelastic, both sellers and consumers have to absorb the burden in varying proportions, as we saw in our example, but how much each side will pay depends on the degree of elasticity.

From a practical point of view, however, measuring the actual incidence can be complicated, especially if the tax is indirect. The difficulty stems from the fact that the burden can be easily shifted forward to others such as when a firm shifts the burden of a tax increase to consumers by increasing the price of a good, or backward by shifting the burden to the suppliers by asking them to lower their price. Both forward shifting and backward shifting are possible when there are no easy substitutes either for the consumers or for the suppliers. The problem is further complicated if the burden is shifted multiple times, from one firm or individual to another, and to another, and so forth, thereby making it difficult to trace the steps down to the last firm or individual who is ultimately responsible for paying the tax.

2.5.1 Measurement of Tax Incidence

While it is important to understand who bears the tax burden, it is also important to understand the distributional consequences of tax incidence, so that appropriate measures can be taken to correct the problem. At a broader level, measuring the distributional consequences allows us to understand the underlying structure of a tax system—whether it is progressive, regressive, or proportional. Several methods have been developed over the years to measure the distributional consequences of tax incidence, but the two most frequently used are Lorenz curve and Gini index. The following provides a brief discussion of the two methods.

2.5.2 The Lorenz Curve

Developed by Max Lorenz in 1905, the curve has been extensively used to show the distribution of income within an economy between different households or income brackets, as well as between different communities, regions, and countries. Figure 2.5 shows a typical Lorenz curve, where the percentage of households is given on the horizontal axis and the percentage of real income (adjusted for inflation) on the vertical axis. The line OX is called the line of equal distribution since it is drawn at the perfect 45° angle, which indicates that if all the coordinates on real income and percentage of households would fall on this line (such as 25% of the households with 25% in real income, 50% of households with 50% in real income, and so forth), there will be no inequalities in income distribution. In reality, no income distribution of any society will form a perfect 45° line; rather, it will resemble the curve OABY. As shown in the figure, at point A the bottom 25% of

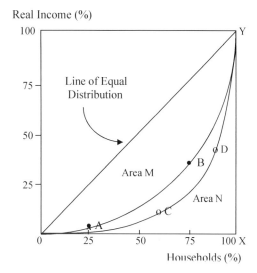

Fig. 2.5 A typical Lorenz curve

the households have about 5% of the real income, while at point B the top 25% have about 60% of the real income (reading from top-down on the curve).

Consider now the effect of a tax policy on the distribution of income. Imagine that we have two Lorenz curves—one representing the old tax policy, given by OABY, and the other representing a new tax policy, given by OCDY, after making adjustments on all possible effects of the tax (Fig. 2.5). To find the difference between the two policies in terms of their effects on income distribution, we can take the differences in observations between the two curves at different points. The differences will allow us to compare the income distribution under the new tax policy against the policy before the policy change.

2.5.3   The Gini Index

Information contained in a Lorenz curve is often summarized with the help of a measure called the Gini index. The purpose of this index is to measure the degree of inequality in an income distribution and is given by the ratio of the area under the Lorenz curve (Area M) and the entire area below the line of equal distribution, covering the entire lower triangle (Area M+Area N),[13] as shown below:

$$G = \text{Area M}/(\text{Area M} + \text{Area N}) \qquad (2.2)$$

where G stands for Gini coefficient. The coefficient ranges between 0 and 1 $(0<G<1)$ and is sometimes multiplied by 100 to range between 0 and 100.

In general, a low Gini coefficient indicates more equal distribution, with 0 being perfect equality, and a high coefficient indicates more unequal distribution, with 1 being perfect inequality. To be valid, the computation requires that there should not be any negative value in the data set. In other words, if the coefficient is to be used to describe household income inequality, then no household should have a negative income. A good example of Gini coefficient applied to tax incidence was by Joseph Pechman (1985) who studied the incidence of overall 1980 tax structure, involving all federal, state, and local taxes. The study found that, based on the observed coefficient, the overall distribution of tax burden was roughly proportional to income, with the exception of very high and very low-income brackets. Although a Gini coefficient provides useful information on income distribution resulting from tax and other decisions, it is usually considered a rough assessment of how income is distributed. As such, its value as an effective tool on which to base policy decisions should be considered with some caution.

2.5.4   Other Indexes

Besides Gini index, there are other methods that can also be used to measure income inequality. A good example is the McLoone index, which is obtained by dividing the total amount of income below the median by the median times the number of observations below the median:

$$MI = \sum M_b/(m \times n), \tag{2.3}$$

where MI is the McLoone index, ΣM_b is sum of the values below the median, m is the median value, and n is the number of observation below the median. For instance, suppose that we have a society consisting of 11 individuals with the following income distribution: 2—$1 million, 2—$500,000, 1—$250,000, 1—$100,000 (which is the median income), 2—$75,000, 2—$50,000, and 1—$35,000. Therefore, the McLoone index for the income distribution of eleven individuals will be 0.57 [($75,000 × 2 + $50,000 × 2 + $35,000)/(($100,000)(5)) = ($150,000 + $100,000 + $35,000)/($500,000) = $285,000/$500,000 = 0.57]. Like the Gini coefficient, the McLoone coefficient ranges between 0 and 1 (0 < MI < 1) but, unlike the Gini index, a low index indicates unequal distribution, while a high index indicates the opposite. Although much simpler to construct, the index has a major weakness in that it ignores values above the median.

Another measure that has considerable merits in measuring income distribution is the Theil index. Initially developed for measuring entropy (maximum disorder) in economics, it has been extensively used for measuring income inequality (Theil 1967). Like the Gini index, the Theil index also ranges between 0 and 1, 0 being no inequality and 1 being total inequality. However, unlike the Gini index, it has one additional advantage in that it is additive across sub-groups meaning that the sum of the coefficients of the sub-groups equals the coefficient for society.

2.6   **Summary and Conclusion**

The primary means by which a government collects its revenue are taxes, although there are other sources from which it also collects revenue such as user fees and charges, fines and forfeitures, intergovernmental revenue, and so forth. Taxes, nonetheless, remain the mainstay of a government's revenue. Therefore, any decision to raise revenue from taxes will have a direct bearing not only on the government, but also on the taxpayers vis-a-vis society at large. However, tax decisions are not arbitrary and can be a long-drawn process; as such, it is important to understand the principles that underlie those decisions. The principles, also called criteria, are necessary to evaluate the effectiveness of a tax system. This chapter has provided a brief overview of some of these criteria. Conventional wisdom suggests that when a tax system is able to fully utilize these criteria, it should be considered a desirable system, but the political and economic realities often make it difficult to do so. The result is less than an optimal tax system. Economists and policy makers believe that it is possible to achieve some measures of optimality, even when a tax system fails to fully satisfy these criteria. It will not be the most efficient or desirable system, but it will be close—the second best.

Review Questions

Q1. What are the objectives of taxation? Why is it important to evaluate a tax system and what criteria are commonly used to evaluate the system? Why the criteria are often called "the desirable characteristics" of a tax system?

Q2. What is the notion of efficiency important in tax decisions of a government? Why should policy makers be concerned with excess burden of taxation? How would one measure efficiency loss? Give an example.

Q3. What effects does the tax decision of a government have on tax efficiency? Discuss with example, at least, three of these effects.

Q4. What is equity in taxation? Why is it important in tax decisions of a government? What is the difference between horizontal and vertical equity? Why are policy makers less concerned with horizontal than with vertical equity?

Q5. What two criteria are commonly used to measure vertical equity? What does the ability to pay mean? Why should an individual pay more in taxes, even if he has the ability to pay more?

Q6. What is Pareto efficiency? What role does Pareto efficiency play in tax decisions of a government?

Q7. What is benefit principle? Why should a government use the benefit principle as a basis for taxation? Give an example of how the principle can be used. What are some of the limitations of the benefit principle?

Q8. Why is it necessary to have an efficiency-equity trade-off? What can a government do to minimize the excess burden of taxation? What is

Ramsey rule and how is the rule used to minimize the excess burden? Why is the rule not always considered as equitable?

Q9. What is flexibility in taxation? What measures can a government use to increase this flexibility?

Q10. Why is it difficult to raise taxes? Is there a limit to raising taxes? How does the Laffer curve explain this limit?

Q11. Why is it important that a tax system be simple? What makes the current tax system complicated? What can a government do to make the tax system simple?

Q12. What is an optimal tax structure? Is it possible to achieve some measures of optimality when some of the conditions of optimality are violated? How? Give an example.

Q13. What is a rate structure of tax? Suppose that we have the following information on taxable incomes and the corresponding tax rates (Table 2.3).

Table 2.3 Review question (Q10)

Progressive			Proportional		Regressive	
Taxable income ($)	Tax rate (%)	Tax liability ($)	Tax rate (%)	Tax liability ($)	Tax rate (%)	Tax liability ($)
15,000	10.0	–	10.0	–	10.0	–
20,000	12.5	–	10.0	–	8.5	–
25,000	15.0	–	10.0	–	7.5	–

Given the information above, calculate the tax liability in each case and indicate if it will progressive, regressive, or proportional.

Q14. For Q10, calculate ATR and MTR, and determine if the rate in each case will be progressive, regressive, or proportional based on the relationship between ATR and MTR.

Q15. What are the three primary methods of tax collection? What is the difference between an average and an effective tax rate? What is marginal tax rate? How can the two, average tax rate and marginal tax rate, be used to determine the tax structure of a government? Explain with an example.

Q16. What is incidence of taxation? What is Lorenz curve and how is it used to measure tax incidence? What is Gini index? How is the index used to measure tax incidence? Explain with an example.

Q17. Define McLoone index. Suppose that we have a society consisting of 15 individuals with the following income distribution: 3—$10 million, 2—$2 million, 2—$1 million, 1—$800,000 (which is the median income), 1—$500,000, 3—$300,000, 2—$150,000 and 2—$100,000. Calculate the McLoone index (MI) and interpret the result.

Notes

1. The 12 tax principles of AICPA are (1) equity and fairness, (2) certainty, (3) convenience of payment, (4) effective tax administration, (5) information security, (6) simplicity, (7) neutrality, (8) economic growth and efficiency, (9) transparency and visibility, (10) minimum tax gap, (11) accountability to taxpayers, and (12) appropriate government revenues.
2. Hyman uses the following expression to measure the excess burden or deadweight loss of a tax: $W = (1/2)T\Delta Q$, where W is the area of the triangle or excess burden, T is the tax per unit, ΔQ is the change (usually decrease) in the quantity of a good consumed as a result of the tax-induced increase in price. Thus, if ΔQ is 1,000,000 per year, and T is 30 cents, then the excess burden of tax, W, will be $150,000 per year, that is, (0.5) (0.3) $(1,000,000) = \$150,000$.
3. Interestingly, the current tax law gives firms and their stockholders incentives to have the firms retain earnings in order to fund expansion that will increase the value of shareholder's stock, rather than pay out earnings that become immediately taxable. The corporate tax law also encourages firms to increase their debt-equity ratios, since interest on debt is treated as a business expense, thereby reducing corporate taxes. This can lead firms to borrow money in order to buy out another firm, or simply to increase their debt-equity ratio and reduce their tax bill.
4. Most corporations are chartered by the individual states, but there are some that are federally chartered, such as national banks by the Controller of Currency, the Federal National Mortgage Association (Fannie Mae) chartered by Congress, and so forth.
5. The elasticity, ε, is usually defined in terms of unit elasticity, elasticity, and inelasticity. A unit elasticity has a coefficient of 1 $(\varepsilon = 1)$, elasticity a coefficient of greater than 1 $(\varepsilon > 1)$, and inelasticity a coefficient of less than 1 $(\varepsilon < 1)$. In general, a high elasticity means greater responsiveness to a given change and a low elasticity means the opposite (for more discussion on the subject, see Chapter 10).
6. Arnold Harberger (1974) was among the leading authors to develop a model to study the general equilibrium effects of taxation, in particular tax incidence. His model was applied to a variety of taxes such as commodity tax, income tax, general tax on labor, etc.
7. The most commonly used measure for the ability-to-pay principle is the comprehensive income based on the works of two notable economists (R. M. Haig in the early 1920s and H. C. Simons in the early 1930s), which include all incomes of an individual, regardless of their source or use.
8. Another term for compensationprinciple is the Kaldor–Hicks criterion, named after the two economists who developed the concept (Kaldor 1939). It is based on a simple precept that if individuals, as well as firms and businesses, benefit from an imperfectly functioning tax policy, they have an obligation to compensate those who lose from the same policy.
9. The principle has its roots in the works of Swedish economist Erik Lindahl of early twentieth century and the market principle applied to taxation for public goods, called Lindahl tax, which says that individuals should pay tax based on the benefit they receive from the consumption of the good at the margin.
10. In recent years, computer filing of tax returns has simplified the process considerably, especially if there are no complicated supporting documents needed to be included.
11. The Internal Revenue Codes (IRC) is the main body of domestic statutory tax law of the United States, organized topically. It includes laws, covering the income tax, payroll taxes, gift taxes, estate taxes, and the statutory excise taxes. It is published as the Title 26 of the United States Code (USC) and is also known as the internal revenue title.
12. This is an inherent weakness of Pareto optimality in that there is no *optimum optimorum*—the best of the best, or global optimum. However, there have been attempts in recent years to use multi-objective optimization to determine a Pareto global optimum (Deb and Gupta 2005).

13. Since the Gini index is defined as the ratio of $M/(M + N)$, with $M + N = 0.5$ (since it constitutes 50% or lower half of the area under the perfect equality line), then $G = M/0.5 = 2M = 1 - 2N$. A simple, yet practical way to compute the coefficient was suggested by Angus Deaton (1997). It is given by the expression: $G = \frac{N+1}{N-1} - \frac{2}{N(N-1)\mu}\left(\sum_{i=1}^{n} P_i X_i\right)$, where μ is the mean income of the population (P) of ith individual with income X, such that the richest person has a rank of 1 and the poorest a rank of N. The ranking provides a relatively higher weight to the poor people in the income distribution than the rich, providing some justification for income transfer.

References

AICPA. (1992). *Guiding Principles of Good Tax Policy: A Framework for Evaluating Tax Proposals.* https://www.aicpa.org/advocacy/tax/downloadabledocuments/tax-policy-concept-statement-no-1-global.pdf.

Christensen, T., & Laegreid, P. (2003, March 15–18). *Trust in Government—The Significance of Attitudes Towards Democracy, the Public Sector and Public Sector Reforms.* Paper Presented at the 64th National Conference of the American Society for Public Administration (ASPA) on "The Power of Public Service," Washington, DC.

Daunton, M. (2001). *Trusting Leviathan: The Politics of Taxation in Britain, 1799–1914.* Cambridge, UK: Cambridge University Press.

Deaton, A. (1997). *Analysis of Household Surveys: A Microeconomic Approach to Development Policy.* Baltimore, MD: Johns Hopkins University Press.

Deb, K., & Gupta, H. (2005). Searching for Robust Pareto-Optimal Solutions in Multi-objective Optimization. *Proceedings of the Third Evolutionary Multi-criteria Optimization (EMO-05) Conference (Lecture Notes on Computer Science), 3410,* 150–164.

Feldstein. M. S. (1976, July–August). On the Theory of Tax Reform. *Journal of Public Economics, 6,* 77–104.

Government Accountability Office (GAO). (2008, March 13). *Internal Revenue Service: Fiscal Year 2009 Budget Request and Interim Performance Results of IRS's 2008 Tax Filing Season.* Washington, DC: GAO-08-567.

Hand, L. (1947, December). Thomas Walter Swan. *Yale Law Journal, 57*(2), 167–169.

Harberger, A. C. (1974). The Incidence of the Corporate Income Tax. In A. C. Harberger (Ed.), *Taxation and Welfare* (pp. 132–162). Boston, MA: Little, Brown.

Haveman, R. H. (1976). *The Economics of the Public Sector.* New York, NY: Wiley.

Higgins, M. (2007). *Concepts in Federal Taxation.* Jersey City, NJ: Thomson-Southwestern.

Holcombe, R. G. (2006). *Public Sector Economics: The Role of Government in the American Economy.* New York, NY: Prentice-Hall.

Hyman, D. N. (2014). *Public Finance: A Contemporary Application of Theory to Policy.* New York, NY: Cengage Learning.

Kaldor, N. (1939, September). Welfare Propositions of Economics and Interpersonal Comparisons of Utility. *Economic Journal, 49,* 549–552.

Laffer, A. (2004, June 1). The Laffer Curve: Past, Present, and Future. *The Heritage Foundation.* https://www.heritage.org/taxes/report/the-laffer-curve-past-present-and-future.

Lipsey, R. G., & Lancaster, K. (1956–1957). The General Theory of the Second Best. *Review of Economic Studies, 24,* 11–32.

McCreadie, K. (2009). *Adam Smith's the Wealth of Nations: A Modern-Day Interpretation of an Economic Classic.* Oxford, UK: Infinite Ideas.

Mikesell, J. L. (2014). *Fiscal Administration: Analysis and Applications for the Public Sector.* New York, NY: Wadsworth.

Pechman, J. A. (1985). *Who Paid the Taxes: 1966–1985?* Washington, DC: The Brookings Institution.

Putnam, R. D. (1995, January). Bowling Alone: America's Declining Social Capital. *Journal of Democracy, 6*(1), 65–78.

Stiglitz, J. E. (2000). *Economics of the Public Sector* (pp. 456–468). New York: W. W. Norton.

Stiglitz, J. E., & Rosengard, J. K. (2015). *Economics of the Public Sector* (pp. 606–635). New York: W. W. Norton.

Theil, H. (1967). *Economics and Information Theory.* Amsterdam: North Holland.

Yang, C. W., & Stitt, K. R. (1995, January). The Ramsey Rule Revisited. *Southern Economic Journal, 61*(3), 767–774.

An Overview of Government Expenditures

3

Structurally, all budgets have two sides—a revenue side that deals with the amount of revenue a government collects each year from various sources and an expenditure side that deals with how that revenue is spent on various public goods and services. The amount of money a government spends each year on public goods and related activities ranges from a few million dollars, to hundreds of millions, to billions and even trillions of dollars, depending on the size and level of government. Historically, government expenditures have been growing consistently over the years, especially at the federal level, raising some serious concerns in recent years. While the growth trend remains a concern, government expenditures serve a number of vitally important purposes. In addition to dealing with market inefficiencies, such as those discussed earlier, government expenditures are necessary to stabilize the economy, to maintain a strong national defense, to provide public goods, and to deal with specific needs of society such as redistribute income that a free market system will not or cannot address on its own. This chapter provides a broad overview of government expenditures, in particular, the differences between different types of expenditure, the nature of growth in government expenditure, and some of the causes of this growth. However, government expenditures cannot grow without limits since no economy can sustain an uncontrolled growth and, if not carefully monitored, will have serious economic, social and political consequences. The chapter concludes with a brief discussion of limits to growth in government expenditure.

3.1 Types of Government Expenditure

The simplest way to understand the behavior of government expenditure is to classify the expenditures based on the specific purpose they serve. For instance, government expenditures can be classified by functions such as agriculture and transportation, by programs such as Social Security and Medicare, and by cost

© The Author(s) 2019
A. Khan, *Fundamentals of Public Budgeting and Finance*,
https://doi.org/10.1007/978-3-030-19226-6_3

objects such as salaries and wages, materials and supplies, contractual and capital outlays. The expenditures can also be classified by the level of discretion a government has on the expenditures such as mandatory versus nonmandatory, as well as by the level of aggregation that divides expenditures into broad categories such as domestic versus defense.

Functional classification, also known as budget classification, generally follows the structure of an organization based on specific functions, programs, and activities the organization performs. This makes allocation decisions relatively simple than if the decisions have to be made based on criteria that rely on value judgment. For instance, the federal budget classifies the budgetary activities of the government into a number of distinct functional categories and associated subcategories based on the specific purpose each function serves. The categories provide a broad statement of budget goals, objectives, and priorities and help facilitate analysis of individual programs within each category. They also serve as a basis for Congressional budget allocation, spending limits, and revenue projections. Currently, there are 20 functional categories included in the federal budget such as national defense, international affairs, science and technology, agriculture, health, education, Social Security, Medicare, veteran's benefits, general administration, and so forth. Similarly, state and local governments also classify the budgetary activities into distinct functional categories such as health, education, transportation, welfare, public safety, recreation, and general administration, among others. The categories are not iron-clad in that they can be changed with legislative approvals, especially for the federal government, with the approval of the appropriations committees.

Classification according to the level of discretion divides expenditures into those that are mandatory, known also as nondiscretionary spending, and those that are nonmandatory, known otherwise as discretionary spending. Mandatory expenditures are direct expenditures on programs, such as Social Security, Medicare, Medicaid, unemployment compensation, student loans, and retirement programs for federal employees that do not have to go through the normal appropriation process. Instead, these expenditures are governed by statutory criteria that entitle the recipients the benefits of the programs, hence, the term entitlements. Some mandatory expenditures such as Social Security are indefinite, while others, such as minor agricultural programs such as subsidy for specialty crops such as fruits and vegetables expire at the end of a certain period. However, Congress can change the size of the spending by changing the authorization rules with 60 votes in the Senate. In contrast, nonmandatory expenditures have to go through the normal annual appropriation process and are subject to various budget enforcement rules. Most defense, education, transportation, and a number of other federal programs would fall into this category. Approximately, 62% of all federal expenditures are currently mandatory (Amadeo 2018).

Mandatory expenditures have an important implication in that they restrict a government's ability to deal with potential budgetary challenges, especially in the short run; as such, these expenditures are often called uncontrollable expenditures. Thus, with over 60% of the federal budget being mandatory, it leaves the government with less than 40% over which it has control. Four areas make up the bulk of the mandatory spending: Social Security, Medicare, Medicaid and interest cost on debt. Of these, Social Security alone constitutes about 25% of the budget, Medicare and Medicaid combined make up roughly 25%, and interest cost about 8% (Amadeo 2019). Other areas of mandatory spending, although minor, include food assistance programs such as Supplemental Nutrition Assistance Program (SNAP), temporary assistance to needy families (TANF), and earned income tax credit (EITC). This leaves very little room for discretionary spending and, consequently, the flexibility the government has in dealing with new economic challenges.

Put simply, much of the government expenditure is uncontrollable, which diminishes its ability to undertake any major economic initiatives without borrowing, or substantially cutting down discretionary spending, or lowering current expenditure on nondiscretionary programs. This may partly explain the historical growth in government expenditure. Unfortunately, any decision to slow down or substantially reverse the current trend through legislative actions seems unlikely in the current political climate.

According to the level of aggregation, government expenditures can be classified into two broad categories—defense and domestic. Currently, defense expenditure constitutes about 20% of the federal budget, but can vary over time, while nondefense or domestic expenditure constitutes the remaining 80%. Important among the domestic expenditures are health and human services, followed by education, Veterans affairs, homeland security, energy, housing, and urban development. Interestingly, most of these expenditures fall under discretionary spending.

Government expenditures can also be classified by consumption and investment. With some exceptions such as water and electricity, governments do not produce goods; governments procure goods for current consumption that directly benefit the public. As such, these expenditures are often called government final consumption expenditure (GFCE), as opposed to expenditures that are made for future consumption of the public, called investment expenditure. Unlike the state and local governments, the federal government uses a more expanded definition of investment expenditure, which includes, among others, investments in intangibles such as research and development (R&D), intellectual property that has a life span of two years or more, as well as investments in human capital to improve worker productivity, investments in physical assets such as land, structures, equipment, and infrastructure that are considered necessary for capital formation (GAO 1997). Together, the expenditures on final consumption and capital formation make up a significant portion of aggregate output, or gross domestic product (GDP).

A Note on Off-Budget Expenditure

Another way to classify government expenditures, especially at the federal level, is to exclude certain items from appearing on the budget that do not go through the normal appropriation process, called off-budget items, as opposed to those that go through the process, called on-budget items.

Two good examples of off-budget items are Social Security Trust Funds and the US Postal Service (USPS). The Social Security Trust Funds consist of two funds: Old-Age and Survivors Insurance and the Disability Insurance, both of which have been accumulating surpluses well into the early 1980s. However, Congress requires that surpluses be invested in government instruments such as federal Treasury Bonds because of their guaranteed security. Although, in principle, Congress is not supposed to use these surpluses to finance tax cuts or expenditure increases, unfortunately, that has not always been the case. However, for reporting purposes, both off-budget and on-budget revenues and expenditures are included when reporting the federal budget deficit, but only on-budget items when reporting debt.

In addition to Social Security Trust Funds and the USPS, there are other entities such as the Federal Reserve System (FRS) which are also excluded from this process, largely to allow it the flexibility to use the monetary policy without political pressure. Also included in this category are Fannie Mae and Freddie Mac, the two major federal mortgage finance enterprises that came under serious scrutiny in recent years, especially during the financial crisis of 2007–2008.

3.2   Growth in Government Expenditure

Government expenditures do not remain constant or grow at a constant rate. Historically, the expenditures have been growing at a fairly rapid pace at all three levels of government, but the growth has been more conspicuous at the federal level because of sheer size of the government vis-à-vis the budget, which currently runs at several trillion dollars a year. Although much of this growth took place during the second half of the last century, the trend seems to be continuing. Beginning with the Great Depression in the 1930s and continuing through the rest of the century, federal expenditure grew from about 5% of GDP at the beginning of the early 1900s, to over 40% at the height of the war years in the 1940s, to about 20% at the close of the century (OMB 2011). Although there were a couple of small spikes since then, the overall trend seems to be around 20%, for now (OMB 2018).

To highlight, the federal outlays[1] grew from a meager $525 million in current dollars at the turn of the last century in 1901 to about $93 billion in 1945 at the close of World War II, dropping to its lowest level to about $30 billion in 1948, then growing to a remarkable sum of $504 billion in 1979. The trend continued through the remainder of the century. For instance, between 1980 and 2000, the growth tripled, from $591 billion in 1980 to about $1.8 trillion in 2000, and more than doubled to about $4.17 trillion in 2018. At the current rate of growth, it is estimated to grow to over $6 trillion by 2028 (OMB 2019). Although not as conspicuous at the subnational level, the state and local governments also experienced considerable growth during this period. For instance, between 1948 and 2010, the combined state and local expenditures grew from about $21 billion in 1948 to a little over $3 trillion in 2010. The combined spending by all three governments totaled approximately $7.1 trillion dollars in 2018 (US Government Spending 2018).[2] Given the growth trend, it is quite likely that it will continue well into the future, although the process may slow down from time to time either due to public pressure or due to a general slowdown in the economy, or both.

From a slightly different perspective, the growth in federal spending can be attributed to the growth in both domestic and defense spending. Although much smaller than domestic spending as a percentage of GDP defense spending has fluctuated considerably over the years. For instance, it was quite low at the turn of the last century constituting about 1% of GDP, but rose to 22% by the end of World War I, then increasing further to 41% at the height of World War II. It began to decline gradually following the war, with occasional spikes for subsequent wars and disasters, but not to the same level as it was during the two world wars (US Government Defense Spending 2018). Currently, it stands at about 4% of GDP and is expected to remain around that number for a while, barring any major war, or natural or man-made disasters. In budgetary terms, the government currently spends around 50% of the discretionary budget on defense spending, or roughly 20% overall, which is a significant amount, given the size of the federal budget (US Government Defense Spending 2018).

While the growth in defense spending showed major ups and downs, increasing considerably during times of war and decreasing when the war is over, as one would expect, the growth in domestic spending also showed similar ups and downs. For instance, following a period of high growth in the 1960s resulting from of major expenditure initiatives under Johnson Administration's the Great Society Programs and the introduction of two major healthcare programs, Medicare and Medicaid, it began to slowdown in the 1970s. The decline was due in part to a major energy crisis that hit the country in 1973, following an OPEC oil embargo, and continued through the early 1980s. It picked up somewhat in the 1990s, but not to the same level as it was in the 1960s. This was possible because of cuts in defense spending, following the break-up of the Soviet Union, some reductions in domestic spending, especially in government redistribution programs, and the overall positive growth in the economy. The pace of growth began to slow down again in the early 2000s resulting, in part, from a general slowdown in the economy and, in part, because of the internal political climate that did not look favorably to rising government expenditure. Slow economic growth, combined with a budget deficit that has been growing steadily, further contributed to the nostalgic attitude toward increased domestic spending.

3.2.1 Shifts in Government Expenditure over Time

An interesting pattern emerges when one makes a comparative assessment of growth in government expenditure over time in that the federal government alone is responsible for about three-fifths of the total spending, while the state and local governments account for the rest. The pattern was considerably different at the turn of the last century when local spending was much higher than what it is today. For instance, local governments accounted for over 60% of all public expenditures in 1910, whereas the federal government accounted for about 30% and the state governments for the rest (Statistical Abstracts of the United States, multiple years). It has been declining ever since for local governments bringing it to the current level. Several factors have contributed to this trend: one, the rising demand for public goods, along with the growth in population; two, increase in the overall quality of living and rising public expectations for better and more expenditures; and three, the inability of the local governments to keep up with this demand due to a declining revenue base, especially property tax. Given the current state of the economy and the general growth pattern, it is unlikely that this scenario will reverse any time soon.

Economists try to explain this shift in government expenditure from local to state, in particular to the federal government as a shift in centralization ratio (the proportion of direct expenditure, excluding intergovernmental transfers, to total expenditure). In general, the higher the ratio the greater the shift, but centralization may mean more than just increasing the share of public expenditure by the federal or state government; it may also mean greater authority and control by the upper-level government of the lower-level governments. For instance, when the federal government provides grants and other financial assistance to state and local governments, they often come with a host of terms and conditions the recipient governments must observe in order to qualify for these grants. From the federal government's point of view, the conditions are necessary to increase accountability, minimize revenue gap, and, more importantly, to ensure equity in service provision (Holcombe 2006). The same also applies to state contributions to local governments. However, from the point of view of the recipient governments, the conditions impinge on their flexibility to utilize the funds as the governments see best fit their needs and, given a choice, most would prefer transfers with as few conditions as possible.

A Note on New Fiscal Federalism

One of the important contributing factors affecting the growth in government expenditure, especially in the 1980s, was the "new fiscal federalism" initiated under the Reagan administration, which saw a systematic decline in federal contribution to state and local governments. Of particular significance was the phasing out of many unconditional grants such as General Revenue Sharing. The policy was based on two fundamental concepts: one, making the federal government more efficient by trimming the size and influence of the federal government; two, to achieve this objective, by shifting the responsibility of social and economic assistance to state governments and, from there, to local governments. There was also an implicit objective to the policy, which was to reduce the inflation rate that was in the double digits during the first couple of years of the administration. Cutting down federal expenditure was one way to achieve this, at least, in part. Interestingly, the inflation rate declined significantly in the subsequent years, although not entirely due to this policy. However, the policy had two immediate effects: One, it saw a gradual increase in state contribution to local expenditure to make up for federal revenue loss; two, from a political perspective, it saw a reemergence of state influence on local governments.

3.2.2   The Distributional Aspects of Government Expenditure Programs

Government expenditures include measures that are specifically designed to address the distributional issues that an unchecked free market system creates for society. Historically, the government has used two sets of measures to deal with various distributional issues resulting from free market operation: (1) social insurance programs, such as Social Security, worker's compensation, and unemployment insurance, to provide insurance against old age, disability, and economic uncertainty and (2) public assistance programs, such as EITC, TANF, public housing, and SNAP, known previously as food stamps,[3] to provide direct financial relief for low-income working families, as well as for the poor and the needy.

While both social insurance and public assistance programs are generally known as entitlement programs, social insurance programs fall into a different category because of the contributory nature of the programs, where individuals are required to contribute in order to be eligible for benefits. Public assistance programs, on the other hand, are mostly non-contributory, tax-financed assistance, designed to help the poor and the needy. Regardless, the programs provide a "social safety net" for those who need the most help by guaranteeing a minimum level of economic well-being.

In addition to providing a social safety net, there is also an underlying economic rationale that justifies many of the government redistribution programs in that the programs increase the purchasing power of the recipients. Without this additional purchasing power, many of the goods brought to the market will remain unsold leading to loss of income for firms and businesses that produce the goods, and hurting the economy in the aggregate. Put simply, the programs help the poor and the needy, as well as those who produce the goods, and the economy at large.[4] As such, the term frequently used to describe the role of these programs play in stabilizing the economy is automatic stabilizers, discussed earlier, although it is not clear to what extent the programs stabilize the economy.

A breakdown of government redistribution programs would indicate that the bulk of federal expenditure goes to social insurance programs, in particular Social Security and Medicare, followed by public assistance programs such as Medicaid, SNAPs, TANF, and public housing. As noted earlier, a further breakdown of government expenditures would indicate that roughly 60% of the expenditures go to three areas: Social Security, health care, and welfare. More specifically, about 25% go to Social Security, while between 25 and 30% go to health and welfare—the bulk into health care (US Government Spending 2018).

The rapid growth in government expenditure for many of these programs has also raised questions about their long-term viability, especially during economic hard times when the economy fails to grow at a pace that can sustain this growth. Added further to this concern is the relative cost burden of the social insurance programs, in particular, Social Security and Medicare resulting largely from a growing retirement population relative to the population entering the job market. By most counts, this would put a heavy burden on an already strained economy, especially on the younger generations. The growth in interest cost on debt, which currently runs at about 8% of the budget, has also become a major concern as it continues to increase mirroring the growth in government expenditure and a general shift in debt burden on the future generations. According to a recent OMB estimate, the percentage is likely to increase to almost 13% by 2024 (Amadeo 2019).

The scenario presented above does not appear to be much different at the subnational level. For instance, at the state level, the largest percentage of state expenditure presently goes to health and welfare, followed by education, retirement, transportation, and the rest to grants and subsidies, interest cost on debt, and corrections. For example, around 38% of the state budget currently goes to health care, about 20% to education, around 15% to retirement, and 7% each to welfare and transportation, and the rest to a variety of other programs (US Government Spending 2018). Similarly, at the local level, the largest percentage goes to education, followed by public safety (police and fire), transportation (including public works), health care, and the rest to interest cost on debt, welfare, and recreation. In terms of percentage breakdown, over 37% of all local expenditures go to education, about 10% each to public safety and health care, about 8% to transportation, and the rest to miscellaneous other programs (US Government Spending 2018).

Interestingly, like the federal government, the state and local governments also do not have much flexibility once the expenditure commitments have been made. Additionally, unlike the federal government, the choices for the state and local governments are considerably limited since these governments do not have the ability to print money or borrow to the same degree the federal government can. However, as with the federal government, it is unlikely that there will be any major changes in the current scenario for the state and local governments anytime soon.

In short, four areas make up the most of government expenditures: health and welfare, defense, education, and pension. While much of the discussion on pension obligations has focused on Social Security in recent years, it has not received the same level of attention at the state and local level. In fact, pension funding at the state and local levels is increasingly becoming a major concern for many of these governments, as the deficits in their own pension funds continue to mount. According to one estimate, the shortfall currently stands at over $3 trillion dollars and, in all likelihood, will grow even larger creating severe financial predicaments for many of these governments for years to come (Elliott 2010). If these trends are any indication, it is likely that government expenditure will continue to grow in all four areas consuming the lion share of these governments' operating budget, although it is possible to reverse the trend with strong political will, combined with appropriate policy changes, but, again, in the current political climate it does not appear to be a likely scenario.

3.3 Causes of Growth in Government Expenditure

It should be worth noting that the unabated expenditure growth the country has been experiencing over the years is not unique to the United States. Most industrialized countries have experienced similar growth—some more than others, thereby, raising the question: What contributes to growth in government? There are several causes or explanations as to why governments grow, ranging from simple, common sense explanations to theories that are based on human psychology, to theories of economic growth and development. This section highlights four of these theories or causes of growth in government expenditure.

The first and foremost cause is the growth in population. Government expenditure grows as the population grows, in order to meet the increasing needs of the growing population. The higher the growth rate, the greater the demand for goods and services; consequently, the higher will be the expenditure, although the rate of growth will vary depending on the general condition of the economy. Secondly, public expenditure grows in response to growth in the general price level (inflation), which means that even if the population does not increase, or its growth rate remains constant, the public expenditures will still increase to keep pace with the rising costs of inflation. Thirdly, during times of economic slowdown such as prolonged recession, or crises such as war and natural disaster, government expenditure tends to grow at a much faster pace than during normal economic times. However, when the crisis is over, the expenditure or the tax structure that helped support this growth seldom returns to the original level. Some call it path dependence, which allows a government to have an inertia meaning that once a social or economic program has been established and the agency that runs the program is in place it is difficult to remove it (Garrett et al. 2010). Finally, when an economy grows, political pressure also grows, especially in a democratic society, for social expenditures such as education, health care, income support, retirement benefits, and so forth. In other words, as the level of development increases, so does the relative size of the government.

Of the four primary causes of growth in government expenditure, the relationship between economic development and the growth in social expenditure is particularly noteworthy because of the amount of attention it has received in the literature. The relationship was first observed by German economist Adolf Wagner during the times of Bismark when he was trying to explain the relationship between the rate of growth of an economy and the growth in social expenditure (Musgrave 1969). Known widely as "Wagner's law" or "the law of increasing state activity," it simply says that the propensity for long-term increase in government expenditure is higher during times of economic growth and prosperity than at any other times. In other words, the more developed an economy the higher will be the level of government expenditure, especially on social goods.

Although as a concept the relationship makes good sense, empirical support for the law has been mixed, in spite of volumes of studies that have been done on the subject over the years. Perhaps the most notable study lending support to Wagner's law was that by Peacock and Wiseman (1961). Examining the growth in public expenditure in the UK from 1890 to 1955, the authors observed three inter-esting effects of government expenditure: One, when an economy is expanding, government expenditure tends to increase at a higher pace, usually at the national than at the subnational level, called the concentration effect. Two, major events such as natural disaster, war, and other man-made crises can force a government to increase expenditure by increasing taxes to raise the needed revenue to address the crises, displacing old expenditure and old taxes with higher expenditure and higher taxes, called the displacement effect. Three, once the crisis is over, the new tax rate and the tax structure may not return to the original level, as the taxpayers get used to the increases raising their tolerance level for higher taxes, called the inspection effect.

Subsequent studies on the law produced mixed results. For instance, a multi-national study consisting of eighty-six countries in 1995 found only a third of the countries supporting the law, while the rest did not (Koop and Poirier 1995). On the other hand, a number of studies, including a recent study involving a single country produced strong support for the law (Mohammadi et al. 2008), but, sur-prisingly, it failed to lend support when the law was applied to a different country in a different part of the world (Ighodaro and Oriakhi 2010).

The conventional wisdom that economic growth affects growth in govern-ment, in that it leads to growth in government expenditure has also raised ques-tions if there is a converse relationship between economic growth and expenditure growth; in other words, if the growth in government expenditure also leads to eco-nomic growth, in particular long-term economic growth. There are two ways to look into this question: one, from the point of view of investment expenditures and, the other, from the point of view of consumption expenditures, mentioned earlier. There is a general understanding among the economists that government consumption expenditures such as those spent on redistribution programs have a negative effect, while the investment expenditures such as those spent on infra-structure development have a positive effect on long-term economic growth (Barro 1991; Aschauer 1989; Landau 1983). The explanation as to why the consumption expenditures have a negative effect is because these expenditures produce a leak-age in the production process; in other words, they do not contribute to private production function, as the investment expenditures. Put simply, the consumption expenditures are not as productive as the investment expenditures.

3.3.1   A Cursory Examination of the Causes Applied to US Expenditure

A cursory examination of the growth of government expenditure in the US, going back to the beginning of the last century, especially at the federal level, would reveal that all four causes have been at work in varying proportions at different times. For instance, the New Deal policy that came out of the Great Depression in the 1930s called for greater government involvement that set the pace for much of the expenditure growth in the 1930s and 1940s, and continued through the rest of the century, including some that are still in place today. Similarly, the two major world wars, especially the World War II, saw a significant growth in government expenditure reaching as high as 45% of GDP at the height of the war and then climbing down once the war was over. The tax rate also increased significantly during this period reaching its peak at 94% (on taxable income over $200,000). Interestingly, the rate never dropped below 70% for over thirty years, thus, providing further support for the third tenet of Wagner's law—the inspection effect. However, the Economic Recovery and Tax Reform Act of 1981 reduced it to 50% and then again to 28% under the Tax Reform Act of 1986.

During the early part of the second half of the last century, in particular in the 1960s, the government introduced a number of expenditure programs (under President Johnson's Great Society Programs) in response to demands for changes in social and economic conditions that many considered were long overdue, which further added to the growth in government expenditure. Fortunately, the country was experiencing a rapid economic growth during this time which made it possible to undertake these programs.

Population growth also was a key factor in the growth of government expenditure, as the country's population grew tremendously from a little over five million at the beginning of the nineteenth century to about 300 million at the close of the twentieth century (U.S. Bureau of Census 2005). During the same period, the country transformed from a predominantly semi-industrial, agrarian economy to a major industrial power in the world, along with the cost of running the government which also increased considerably during this period, even after adjustments for inflation. In all likelihood, this growth trend in government expenditure will continue into the future, but the rate will fluctuate depending on the general condition of the economy, population growth, and the political climate of the country.

3.3.2   Other Causes of Expenditure Growth

In addition to those discussed above, there are a number of other explanations of what contributes to growth in government. Important among these are interest group politics, unbalanced productivity expenditure growth, fiscal illusion, and the economic theory of bureaucracy. Of the four, the interest group politics received the most attention among the academics, in particular political scientists, policy theorists, and budget practitioners because of its intuitive appeal. Based on the concept of political pressure, interest group politics argues that groups with common interest can organize themselves to exert political pressure on government (Olson 1965). For instance, groups frequently use lobbying as an instrument to influence decisions in support of policies that benefit them, but the costs of which are dispersed among the taxpayers and, in some cases, across jurisdictions. The result is expanded government expenditures that do not necessarily serve the collective interest.

One of the earlier theories that received considerable attention in the literature on the growth of government is the unbalanced productivity expenditure growth theory of William Baumol (1967). The theory is based on the wage differentials between the public and the private sector. Wages are generally high in the private sector because of higher productivity, resulting from innovation, capital formation, technology, and economies of scale. Whereas the public sector which is service-oriented, the labor is often the end product and technology does not have the same impact on productivity growth, as in the private sector. Despite such differences, Baumol argues that there cannot be too large a wage gap between the two sectors, as it may increase the potential for large flow of labor from public to the private sector. Since the public sector requires more labor relative to the private sector, given the nature of its work which is labor-oriented, but does not necessarily have a serious negative effect on economic growth, this will raise the cost of labor in the public sector and, consequently, increase government expenditure.

The fiscal illusion theory, as it relates to government expenditure and growth, assumes that government, elected officials, and the bureaucrats can create fiscal illusion by not revealing the true size of the government (Buchanan 1967). The government is able to do so because it can take advantage of lack of knowledge of the taxpayers. Taxpayers generally assess the size of their government by the amount of taxes they pay, which allows the government to use measures such as tax collection that are less visible to the taxpayers. Income tax withholding from payroll (payroll tax) is a good example in that although the tax is direct, withholding creates a fiscal illusion of an indirect tax. Some economists would argue that, while the theory has its merits, by itself, it may not be sufficient to explain the growth in government (Mueller 2003).

Finally, much of the credit for the economic theory of bureaucracy goes to William Niskanen (1971). The theory is based on the premise that bureaucrats and elected officials often behave as collusive oligopolists, where the bureaucrats try to maximize their budget, subject to cost constraints, and the elected officials try to maximize their political interests such as power, authority and, more importantly, getting reelected. The result is an oversupply of public goods, where the supply exceeds the point where the marginal benefit (MB) of the goods to the public must equal the marginal cost (MC) to the bureau of providing the goods, considered as the point of efficient provision. According to Niskanen, since the bureaucrats hold a monopoly position, they are better able to exert their influence because of their knowledge of the government and easy access to information. Some view the bureaucratic monopoly argument as oversimplified, but, nevertheless, recognize that the bureaucrats serve an important role for the elected officials, as well as the public (Casas-Pardo and Puchades-Navarro 2001; Breton and Wintrobe 1975).

A Note on Keynesian Policy and Expenditure Growth

As we noted earlier, Keynesian economic policy provides an alternative approach to classical economic thinking for dealing with the problem of unemployment and recession that is largely based on government expenditure. The essence of Keynesian approach is that increased government expenditure, both social and economic, especially in the short run, will increase employment. It will create effective demand vis-a-vis give the individuals the necessary purchasing power to clear the goods off the market and the process will help rejuvenate the economy through a cycle of expenditure, employment, income, and growth. In other words, government expenditures will have a multiplier effect that will eventually increase national income and promote long-term economic growth. However, the growth is not without constraints in that increased government expenditure can easily contribute to inflation and other problems such as crowding out, if the policy makers are not careful. In other words, they must exercise caution when applying the policy.

3.4   Limits to Growth in Government Expenditure

Two things become apparent from any discussion of growth in government expenditure: One, the expenditures have increased significantly over the years; two, there is a general consensus among the economists, policy makers, and taxpayers that at the current rate of growth it is unlikely for the government to be able to maintain the trend indefinitely. There have been several attempts in recent years to deal with the problem. A number of states have adopted expenditure growth limits since the mid-1970s, following the nation-wide movement on all kinds of propositions to control growth in government expenditures, in particular taxes. These growth restrictions are mostly limited to the percentage of growth in state population, personal income, and other restrictive measures. A good example is California's Proposition 4, which limits the state spending, as well as spending by most local governments. Introduced in 1979 at the height of the taxpayer revolt, under Article XIIIB of the state constitution, the proposition established the appropriation limit, called the Gann Limit, named after one of the authors of the measure, to keep the spending level under the 1978–1979 levels, after adjustments for inflation. The measure provides for redistribution of any excess revenue between the taxpayer rebate and additional spending by the state resulting from the appropriation limit for two successive years, allowed under a different proposition (Proposition 78). Interestingly, the Gann Limit has lost some of its appeal in recent years and, according to one observation, will not receive the stature of Proposition 13 (New 2004).

The enforcement of California's spending limit involves a series of complex calculations or the spending to conform to the limit, while other states have established more direct measures. For instance, Idaho currently restricts the spending to 5.33% of state personal income, which allows it to grow at the same rate as the personal income (Rueben and Randall 2017). Some states have introduced even stricter limits, such as Colorado's Bill of Rights and Oregon's "Kicker" rebate (which allows the rebate calculation for both individual and corporate taxpayers), while others require the surpluses to be sequestered to rainy day funds. The number of states with spending limits has increased considerably in recent years. As of

2015, twenty-eight states have spending limits of one form or another, with varying results. According to Rueben and Randall (2017), Colorado's Bill of Rights unfortunately did not boost the economic growth. Interestingly, the states with spending limits are more likely to maintain stabilization funds to hedge against economic instability than the states without the limits.

While restrictions on expenditure growth have produced some dividends for the state and local governments, limiting tax or expenditure growth for the federal government, on the other hand, has been much more difficult at least for a couple of reasons: One, it does not have the balanced budget requirement of the state and local governments and, two, it has to deal with macroeconomic issues that require a different set of tax and expenditure commitments which the state and local governments do not have. Theoretically, it is possible to have a balanced budget requirement for the federal government but it will need a constitutional amendment to do so. However, unlike the state constitutions or local charters, amending the federal constitution is far more difficult because it requires a two-thirds majority in both chambers of Congress, or a constitutional convention calling for two-thirds majority of the state legislatures, which may partly explain why the federal constitution has been amended only twenty-seven times, as opposed to some state constitutions, such as Texas, which has been amended over 450 times since 1876 (Maxwell et al. 2012).

Let us assume, for the sake of argument, that the federal government is able to balance its budget constitutionally, there is still no guarantee that it will be able to resolve the problem of expenditure growth easily because balancing the budget would affect only the operating budget, not the capital budget. Unfortunately, the federal government does not have a separate capital budget, as most state and local governments do. Separating the two will create additional problems that the government has not been able to resolve; in particular, how to define and measure the useful lives of a capital asset, how to depreciate the value of the assets over time, how to deal with uncertainty in the budget process, and finding ways to finance projects that will be acceptable to the public and the various interest groups, among others. This may partly explain why to this day the government does not have a separate capital budget, even though it was recommended by the Hoover Commission going back to 1949 (Lederle 1949).

3.4.1   Approaches to Limiting the Growth in Government Expenditure

From a purely theoretical point of view, especially following the work of Wagner, a number of studies have been conducted over the years to determine the cut-off level for government expenditure; in particular, what will be an acceptable level of expenditure, given the tolerance limit of the public for increased taxes. Colin Clark, a British economist, looked extensively into this question using data from a number of Western countries for the inter-war period and came up with an interesting suggestion that it should be 25% of GDP. Known as the Critical Limit hypothesis, Clark's proposition was based on the argument that when government expenditure reaches 25% of total activity in a country, it will exhaust the public's ability to pay more in taxes; in other words, it will exhaust their tolerance level (Pechman and Mayer 1952). His theory was based on two fundamental assumptions: One, crossing the critical limit vis-a-vis when tax collection crosses the 25% of gross national product, it will reduce incentive for work and, as a result, affect productivity and, two, increasing government expenditure beyond this limit would produce inflation. Although his theory did not receive widespread attention among the economists and policy makers at the time, the concept itself has provided foundation for some of the recent theories of tax and expenditure such as the well-known Laffer Curve, discussed earlier, and the Armey Curve, discussed next.

Richard Armey, a former representative of US Congress (1995), developed an interesting approach, similar to that suggested by Colin Clark, called the Armey curve, to explain the relationship between GDP growth and the growth in government expenditure as a percentage of GDP. His theory is based on a quadratic relationship between government spending and the GDP (Fig. 3.1). According to Armey, the GDP growth will be higher for governments with a good mixture of public and private decisions on resource allocation and will be considerably lower for governments where all decisions are made by the central government, as in a centralized economy, or in an economy where there is no formal government or the rule of law. Put differently, as the size and expenditure of a nation's economy grows, so will its GDP, everything else remaining the same, but only up to a point at which the output will be maximum. Anything beyond that maximizing level of expenditure, the output will start to decline, as the government begins to crowd out the market by taking away more resources and functions from the private sector.

Fig. 3.1   The Armey curve

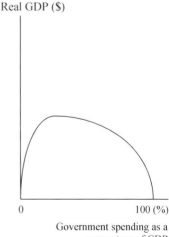

Several empirical tests have been conducted on the Armey curve since it was suggested; one study, in particular, found that the curve peaks at about 17.45% of GDP, which are several points below the average rate at which the federal government has been growing for some times (Joint Economic Committee 1995). In other words, if the relationship between the GDP growth and government spending were to hold for the Armey curve, the federal expenditure should be about 17% of GDP, not higher. However, a major weakness of the curve is that it does not take into consideration the economic and other crises that may add to the growth in government expenditure. Theoretically, the Armey curve can be easily extended to state and local governments to determine an appropriate "cut-off" level for these governments as a percentage of gross state or local products, in which case some of the same constraints will also apply.

A Note on Median-Voter Theorem

While from a purely academic point of view, it is difficult to pin-point a single factor that would limit the growth of government, one could argue that in a democratic society the political pressure that contributes to rising expenditure can also limit its growth. The voting public would resist the growth of their government *ad infinitum*, forcing the process to slow down to a level acceptable to the majority. There is a parallel here with the median voter theorem of the public choice theorists, which says that the push and pull between those who demand more expenditures, especially social expenditure, and those who demand less will eventually bring the provision to a level somewhere in the middle that will be politically acceptable to the majority of the voters.[5]

To give an example, suppose that we have three groups of voters in a political system—conservative, mainstream, and liberal. As shown in Fig. 3.2, each group of voters has a unique level of preference for government expenditure based on the utility they derive from those expenditures, as given by their preference curves. Given a choice, the conservatives would prefer less government expenditure once the utility level crosses the peak (maximum), just as the liberals would prefer more, but up to the point where the utility level reaches the peak (maximum), and the mainstream the same. However, in a complicated world with limited resources, the push from the liberals for more and the pull from the conservatives for less will bring the expenditure level to the center (median). This is the essence of the median voter theorem. In general, one would expect the relationship to hold during times of normal economic growth but in times of economic crisis, such as deep recession, the position may shift to the right on the horizontal axis to reflect the condition of the economy. The converse would be true during times of high economic growth and prosperity, when the demand for economic and social expenditures is expected to be less.

An important weakness of the median voter theorem is that voter preferences may not be single-peaked, as shown in the above figure; they can be bi-modal or multi-modal, in which case it may be difficult to determine

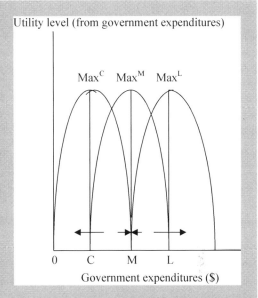

Fig. 3.2 Relationship between utility level and voter preference for government expenditure based on political ideology: (C) conservative, (M) mainstream, and (L) liberal

their true preference. In spite of this apparent weakness, the theorem provides a useful framework for empirical studies to explain how different individuals or groups would prefer government expenditure, given their social, economic, and political background. Two good examples are studies by Borcherding and Deacan (1972), and Bergstrom and Goodman (1973), which found a strong relationship between the theorem and local public expenditure. Another study by Holcombe (1989) found the theorem to be a good approximation of demand aggregation in the public sector for various issues, while others found the model to work better in a direct democracy than in a representative democracy (Pommerehne 1978). Regardless, the model serves as a valuable guide for understanding public (voters) preference for government expenditure.

3.5   Optimal Government Expenditure

This brings us to the obvious question: Is there an optimal provision of government expenditure, one that will best meet the needs of society? While the studies by Clark, Armey and others provide an interesting framework for determining the level of government expenditure that can be construed in some ways as optimal, Hugh Dalton, an early twentieth-century British economist (1922), uses a more conventional approach to determine optimal government expenditure. Known as the Principle of Maximum Social Advantage, he uses the standard microeconomic tools, such as marginal social benefit, MSB (the benefit society derives from the consumption of an additional unit of government expenditure) and marginal social sacrifice, MSS (the sacrifice society will have to make for an additional unit of tax), to determine the optimal level. According to Dalton, for government expenditure to be optimal, it must take place at the point where the marginal social benefit (from additional expenditure) equals the marginal social sacrifice (from additional taxes); that is, MSB = MSS (Fig. 3.3).

As the figure shows, each additional unit of tax contributes to additional burden (marginal sacrifice) that increases with increasing taxes, hence the upward sloping marginal social sacrifice curve. In contrast, each additional unit of government expenditure leads to decreasing social benefit that decreases with increasing expenditure, hence, the downward sloping marginal social benefit curve. At the point where the two curves intersect, which is Q^0, the gain to society will be maximum. Dalton calls it the point of maximum social advantage.

As the figure further shows, any point above Q^0, say, Q'', will result in higher marginal social sacrifice than marginal social benefit since the MSS curve lies above the MSB curve. What this means is that any further increase in tax and expenditure will diminish the maximum social advantage; as such, it will not be optimal. Similarly, any point below Q^0, say, Q', would produce a net social gain that will be below its potential in that it will leave some potential net social advantage unrealized; as such, it will not be optimal. In other words, it would make sense for government to increase the level of taxes and expenditure to realize additional net social advantage until the point when no additional net social advantage is possible. It will be the point at Q^0, where MSB = MSS.

Fig. 3.3 Point of maximum social advantage (B = Benefit; S = Sacrifice)

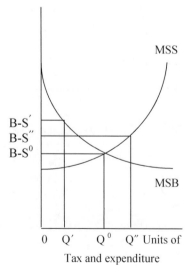

Marginal social benefit and sacrifice ($)

While the model provides an interesting framework for determining optimal government expenditure, it is also based on a number of assumptions that one may find restrictive. For instance, the model assumes that government revenue comes principally from taxes and not any other sources, which probably was close to the revenue structure at the time it was formulated. It also assumes that for the provision to be optimal the revenue (from taxes) must be equal to expenditure. In other words, it assumes a balanced budget, which does not allow much room for budget surplus or deficit. Finally, all taxes produce sacrifice and all expenditures produce benefits, which may be an overgeneralization of the reality. However, it is important to recognize that all models are based on a set of assumptions and, from that point of view, Dalton's model was no exception.

3.5.1   Theory Versus Reality

Although in theory it is possible to determine the point at which the expenditure will be efficient (optimal), in reality, it is much more complex. This is due, in part, to the fact that it is difficult to know the point at which the quantity provided via-a-vis the level of expenditure will be optimal. This is also due to the fact that expenditure decisions are often influenced by political rather than by pure economic considerations, such as the need to keep the constituents satisfied to get reelected, among others. Since neither situation provides the government with a precise knowledge of the level of expenditure that would be optimal the logical alternative for the government would be to provide less, but that would in all likelihood lead to underprovision of goods and services.

Underprovision has three important implications: First, to underprovide would mean a decrease in the overall provision that would be below what is necessary for collective consumption, which will be an inefficient allocation of resources, from society's point of view. Second, this would also lead to a possible reduction in the aggregate welfare of society because the consumption will be less than what is socially desirable. Third, from a political point of view, any decrease in collective welfare will not bode well with the public and the elected officials who want to get reelected, as well as the bureaucrats who would not like to see a reduction in the bureau budget from reduced expenditure. Consequently, this often results in overproduction vis-à-vis more expenditure than is necessary.

It is worth noting that, unlike the economic marketplace where exchanges between buyers and sellers determine the exact quantity of goods to be bought and sold, expenditure decisions take place in the political marketplace which determines the level of expenditure the government should provide, at what cost, and who will benefit from the provision. Similar to the economic marketplace, the political marketplace allows exchanges between different political interests to determine an outcome that would be acceptable to the majority under a democratic system of government.[6] However, unlike the economic marketplace where price serves as the medium of exchange, exchange in the political marketplace takes place through bargaining, negotiation, and logrolling (vote trading). The end product is a compromise—an equilibrium that results from this process (Hyman 2014), and as in any compromise, there will be gains for some and losses for others. While the process may sound simple, in reality, it is quite complex. Political interests, collusion, information asymmetry, tax share at the margin, and a variety of other factors can easily affect the equilibrium in the political marketplace, therefore, the provision of government expenditure.

A Note on Optimal Size Government

Theoretically, if it is possible to have an optimal provision of government expenditure, then, by extension, one could also argue that it is possible to have an optimal size government. In reality, it is much more complex than that. Part of the problem lies in the difficulty in determining what approach one should use because whatever approach one would use, whether it is based on population size, geographic area, spatial externality (when benefits or costs spill over adjacent geographic areas or political jurisdictions), or any other, it is likely to produce a different size government in each case.

Wallace Oates (1972) introduced an interesting approach for determining the optimal size government based on the geographic area of benefit. Although his approach was primarily used for public goods, it can be easily extended for government expenditure. Defined as the correspondence rule, it suggests that there is a hierarchy of governments, each corresponding to a given area of benefit for the goods it provides, with no externalities, similar to hierarchy of public goods, discussed earlier. A good example would be national defense, which is provided at the national level because it needs a large threshold population such as the entire nation, and also because of the high cost of defense that can take up a significant portion of GDP. Similarly, goods (expenditures, in our case) such as state-funded higher education are more appropriate at the state level because of high cost of education and the need for a threshold population large enough to support it, while goods such as police, fire, recreation, public works, elementary and secondary education make good sense at the local level since these goods can be consumed by many within the confines of a limited geographic area.

The point to keep in mind here is that different criteria will produce different size governments. For instance, if spatial externality is brought into the picture it will change the dynamics of optimal size government in that it would call for a larger government which can absorb the externality yet provide public goods (expenditures, in our case) uniformly that would benefit the public equally. In reality, it is unlikely that both can be met at the same time—a large government that would absorb the externality and a uniform provision that would benefit the public equally. The result may be a tradeoff between the two, which may not necessarily be optimal. Oates' alternative to this is to cluster the goods with similar sizes into a single government that would reduce the layers of government as well as the number within each layer, but, again, there is no guarantee that it will produce an optimal size government. Another drawback of the argument is that since the service areas will not remain constant over time, it may be necessary to adjust the clusters frequently, which would be both time consuming and costly.

3.6   Summary and Conclusion

Government expenditure deals with money a government spends each year on various public goods and services, ranging from national defense, to health care, to education, to public safety, to recreation, among others. The total spending on these goods runs from a few million dollars a year, to hundreds of millions, to billions of dollars. The expenditures are necessary to stabilize the economy, to maintain a strong national defense, to provide infrastructure, and to deal with specific needs of society that a free market system will not address on its own. Interestingly, government expenditures do not remain constant; they grow over time. The growth has been significant, especially at the federal level, where it has increased from a few hundred million dollars at the turn of the last century to over several trillion dollars today. This is a significant increase by any measure and has become a major concern because of the pace of growth. Although there have been numerous attempts to limit this growth, it is likely that the trend will continue into the future, at least, for a while. This chapter has provided a broad overview of government expenditure, in particular, its growth trend and some of the causes that may explain this growth. The chapter concluded with a brief discussion on the limits to growth in government expenditure.

Review Questions

Q1. Why is it necessary to classify government expenditures? What effect, if any, the classification has on budget allocation?

Q2. What is the difference between classification by function and classification by aggregation? How would you distinguish between (1) mandatory and nonmandatory spending, (2) expenditure for consumption and expenditure for investment, and (3) off-budget and on-budget items? Give an example of each.

Q3. There has been a significant growth in government expenditure over time at all three levels of government. What has primarily contributed to this growth, especially the growth in federal expenditure?

Q4. What is centralization ratio? How does it explain the shift in government expenditure over time, especially from local to federal government?

Q5. Why is distributional question important in government expenditure? What types of measures or programs the government, in particular the federal government, uses to deal with the distributional question? Give an example of the measures currently used by the government.

Q6. What is the difference between the theory of path dependence and the law of increasing state activity, also known as Wagner's law? How does the Peacock and Wiseman study further expand the Wagner's law when examining the effects of expenditure growth?

Q7. What can you tell from a cursory examination of the theories when applied to growth in government expenditure? Which of these theories, in your assessment, would best explain the growth in government expenditure? Why?

Q8. How does each of the following theories explain the growth in government expenditure: Interest group politics, unbalanced productivity expenditure growth theory, fiscal illusion theory, and collusive oligopoly model?

Q9. Are there limits to expenditure growth in government? Why? What is difference between the Critical Limit Theory and the Armey curve? What is the central theme of the two theories and how are the theories used to explain expenditure limits?

Q10. What is the median voter theorem? How can the theorem be used to explain the limits to expenditure growth? What are some of the constraints in using the theorem?

Q11. What is optimal government expenditure? What criteria are commonly used in measuring optimal expenditure? Explain Dalton's Principle of Maximum Social Advantage in limiting government expenditure?

Q12. Is there an optimal size government? Discuss, with reference to Wallace Oat's model of optimal size government. What are some of the limits of Oat's model?

Notes

1. Outlays are government expenditures during a fiscal year that include current expenditures plus unspent authority from previous years. For example, an outlay of $100 million in FY 2015 may include $75 million in current authority out of a total of $125 million allocated for the year, plus $25 million in unspent authority from prior years.
2. The data included in this source are mostly based on estimates and, as such, can deviate somewhat from the actual Values.
3. Social insurance programs primarily include Social Security, unemployment insurance, and Medicare. Public assistance programs, on the other hand, include both cash transfers such as Temporary Assistance to Needy Families (TANF), Supplemental Security Income (SSI) for the aged, blind, and disabled, and earned Income Credit (EIC) for the low-income working families, and in-kind benefits such as food stamps, Medicaid, low income housing assistance, national school lunch program, and work-employment program such as job training. These

programs are also called "means-tested programs" because the programs are available only to those whose incomes are sufficiently low (low income), or are considered poor.

4. The program has an interesting background that goes to the creation of Food Surplus Commodities Corporation (FSCC) in 1935 to dispense commodities by encouraging domestic consumption of surpluses. For instance, in May 1939, the Rochester County, New York, began an experimental program by providing blue stamps to the poor, free of cost, to purchase designated surplus food at retail establishments, which many consider to be the forerunner of the current Food Stamps (and of late the SNAP) program.

5. The median voter theorem states that majority voting will yield the outcome preferred by the median voter if preferences are single-peaked, where the median voter is the voter whose tastes are in the middle of the set of voters, so an equal number of other voters prefer more and prefer less of the public good (Gruber 2005). Put simply, when the voters have single-peaked preferences, under the majority rule, the outcome will be at the median.

6. In a majority rule with two choices, under a traditional democratic system, the one that receives more than 50% of the votes wins, but when multiple choices are involved, as in a pluralist system, the one that receives most votes than the rest wins. However, the majority rule in a democratic system, whether simple or pluralist, has raised serious questions about the effect it will have on the minority, which has also been a concern of the founding fathers. For instance, James Madison, concerned with the "tyranny of the majority" rule strongly advocated for the protection of minority rights. In fact, the Bill of Rights, which includes the first ten amendments of the Constitution, guarantees that. The uniqueness of the Constitution is that just as it prohibits the tyranny of the majority over the minorities it also prohibits the "tyranny of the minority" over the majority.

References

Amadeo, K. (2018, August). Current Federal Mandatory Spending. *The Balance*. https://www.thebalance.com/current-federal-mandatory-spending-3305772.

Amadeo, K. (2019, May). Interest on the National Debt and How It Affects You. *The Balance*. https://www.thebalance.com/interest-on-the-national-debt-4119024.

Army, R. (1995). *The Freedom of Revolution*. Washington, DC: Regency Publishing.

Aschauer, D. A. (1989). Is Public Expenditure Productive? *Journal of Monetary Economics, 23*, 177–200.

Barro, R. (1991). Economic Growth and a Cross-Section of Countries. *Quarterly Journal of Economics, 106*, 407–441.

Baumol, W. J. (1967, June). Macroeconomics of Unbalanced Growth: The Anatomy of the Urban Crisis. *American Economic Review, 57*, 415–426.

Bergstrom, T. C., & Goodman, R. D. (1973). Private Demand for Public Goods. *American Economic Review, 63*(3), 280–296.

Borcherding, T. E., & Deacon, R. T. (1972). The Demand for Services of Non-Federal Governments. *American Economic Review, 62*(5), 891–901.

Breton, A., & Wintrobe, R. (1975, February). The Equilibrium Size of a Budget-Maximizing Bureau: A Note on Niskanen's Theory of Bureaucracy. *Journal of Political Economy, 83*(1), 195–208.

Buchanan, J. M. (1967). *Public Finance in Democratic Processes*. Chapel-Hill: University of North Carolina Press.

Casas-Pardo, J., & Puchades-Navarro, M. (2001, April). A Critical Comment on Niskanen's Model. *Public Choice, 107*(1–2), 147–167.

Dalton, H. (1922). *Principles of Public Finance*. London, UK: George Routledge.

Elliot, J. (2010). The Future of Social Security. *Ameriprise Financial*. https://www.ameriprise-advisors.com>top-social-security-questions-answered.

Garrett, T., Kozak, A., & Rhine, R. (2010). Institutions and Government Growth: A Comparison of the 1890s and 1930s. *Federal Reserve Bank of St. Louis Review, 92*(2), 109–119.

Government Accountability Office (GAO). (1997, May 21). *Federal Investment Outlays, Fiscal Years 1981–2002*. Washington, DC: GAO/AIMD-97-88.

Gruber, J. (2005). *Public Finance and Public Policy*. New York, NY: Worth Publishers.

Holcombe, R. G. (2006). *Public Sector Economics: The Role of Government in the American Economy*. New York, NY: Pearson Prentice-Hall.

Holcombe, R. G. (1989). The Median Voter in Public Choice Theory. *Public Choice, 61*, 115–125.

Hyman, D. N. (2014). *Public Finance: A Contemporary Application of Theory to Policy*. New York, NY: Cengage Learning.

Ighodaro, C. A. U., & Oriakhi, D. E. (2010). Does the Relationship Between Government Expenditure and Economic Growth Follow Wagner's Law in Nigeria? *Annals of the University of Petroşani, Economics, 10*(2), 185–198.

Joint Economic Committee. (1995, December). *The Impact of the Welfare State on the American Economy*. Washington, DC: U.S. Congress.

Koop, G., & Poirier, D. J. (1995). An Empirical Investigation of Wagner's Hypothesis by Using a Model Occurrence Framework. *Journal of the Royal Statistical Society Series A: Statistics in Society, 158*(1), 123–141.

Landau, D. (1983). Government and Economic Growth in the Less Developed Countries: An Empirical Study for '1960–1980'. *Economic Development and Cultural Change, 35*, 35–75.

Lederle, J. W. (1949). The Hoover Commission Reports on Federal Reorganization. *Marquette Law Review, 33*(2) (Fall), 89–98.

Maxwell, W. E., Crain, E., & Santos, A. (2012). *Texas Politics Today*. New York, NY: Thomson-Wadsworth.

Mohammadi, H., Cak, M., & Cak, D. (2008). Wagner's Hypothesis: New Evidence from Turkey Using the Bounds-Testing Approach. *Journal of Economic Studies, 35*(1), 94–106.

Mueller, D. C. (2003). *Public Choice*. Cambridge: Cambridge University Press.

Musgrave, R. A. (1969). *Fiscal Systems*. New Haven, CT: Yale University Press (Chapter 3).

New, M. J. (2004, October 28). The Gann Limit Turns 25. *Cato Institute*. https://www.cato.org/publications/commentary/gann-limit-turns-25.

Niskanen, W. A., Jr. (1971). *Bureaucracy and Representative Government*. New York: Aline, Atherton.

Oates, W. (1972). *Fiscal Federalism*. New York, NY: Harcourt Brace Jovanovich.

Office of Management and Budget. (2011). *Historical Tables: Budget of the US Government*. Washington, DC.

Office of Management and Budget. (2018). *Historical Tables: Budget of the US Government*. Washington, DC.

Office of Management and Budget. (2019). *Historical Tables: Budget of the US Government*. Washington, DC.

Olson, M. (1965). *The Logic of Collective Action: Public Goods and the Theory of Groups*. Cambridge, MA: Harvard University Press.

Peacock, A. T., & Wiseman, J. (1961). *The Growth of Public Expenditure in the United Kingdom*. London: Oxford University Press.

Pechman, J. A., & Mayer, T. (1952, August). Mr. Colin Clark on the Limits of Taxation. *The Review of Economics and Statistics, 34*(3), 232–242.

Pommerehne, W. W. (1978). Institutional Approaches to Public Expenditure: Empirical Evidence from Swiss Municipalities. *Journal of Public Economics, 9*(2), 255–280.

Rueben, K. S., & Randall, M. (2017). *Tax and Expenditure Limits: How States Restrict Revenues and Spending*. Washington, DC: The Urban Institute.

U.S. Bureau of Census. (2005). *Projected Population by Single Year of Age, Sex, Race, and Hispanic Origin for the United States: July 1, 2000 to July 1, 2050*. Washington, DC.

US Government Defense Spending. (2018). https://www.usgovernmentspending.com/defense_spending.

US Government Spending. (2018, January). https://www.usgovernmentspending.com/us_spending.

An Overview of Government Revenues

4

A budget is not simply a collection of revenues and expenditures; it is much more than that. It is a reflection of the general economic condition of a political jurisdiction, its revenue base, the critical needs for public goods and services, and how the government plans to meet those needs. Therefore, to understand the budgetary activities of a government, in particular the range of goods and services it provides, it is important to have a good knowledge of the totality of the revenue base from which the government collects its revenues, including the process by which it raises those revenues and spends them on public goods and services. Having a good knowledge of the revenue base and its structure is also important to understand how much flexibility a government has in raising the needed revenue from the various sources. Accordingly, the chapter begins with a general discussion of the principal sources of government revenue, in particular, tax revenue—their underlying structure, characteristics, and some common concerns. This is followed by a discussion of alternatives to current taxes, especially income tax, which has become important in recent years. The chapter also looks at various other sources of revenue, besides taxes, that play an important role in the overall revenue structure of a government, and concludes with a brief discussion on the tradeoff between tax and non-tax revenue.

4.1 Primary Sources of Revenue

All governments collect their revenues from multiple sources, but there is one principal source that serves as the mainstay which for the federal government is income tax, for state governments it is sales tax, and for local governments it is property tax. The division of the tax base from which a government collects its revenues is not arbitrary; it is partly economic and partly political and administrative. The underlying rationale that ties the two components together is critical to understanding the tax structure that divides the responsibility between the three

© The Author(s) 2019

A. Khan, *Fundamentals of Public Budgeting and Finance*,
https://doi.org/10.1007/978-3-030-19226-6_4

levels of government—federal, state, and local; in particular, the responsibility to raise revenue for each level to carry out its assigned responsibilities. The division serves as a necessary condition for improving the performance of each level of government by ensuring a proper alignment of fiscal responsibilities, commonly known as fiscal federalism (Oates 1972). Although one may raise questions whether the alignment improves performance, most would agree that it provides considerable autonomy to individual jurisdictions as to how much revenue each level of government can raise from a given source (revenue base) and how that revenue is spent. The following sections provide a brief overview of the principal sources from which a government collects its tax revenues—income, sales, and property.

4.1.1   Income Tax

Income tax constitutes the single most important source of revenue for the federal government, as well as for a large number of states that rely on it to supplement their income from sales tax and other revenue sources. It includes both personal and business income taxes that are levied on the income of an individual or a firm based on the earnings from all sources in a given year. There is no precise definition of income, but the one that has been accepted by most economists and policy makers is the Haig-Simons definition that gives an individual the ability to convert purchasing power into consumption or savings for future use (Hyman 2014). In common parlance, it means the ability of an individual to purchase goods and services, given his or her income, and save the unused portion of income for future consumption. Two things are necessary before a tax can be imposed: One, a taxing unit, which would be an individual for personal income and a firm or business for business income; two, a time period for measuring personal or business income over a certain length of time such as a month, a quarter, and a year. Personal income by and large includes earnings from all possible sources, regardless of age or amounts earned, while business income such as corporate income includes earnings from profit, dividends received from other corporations, and profits from other investments.

4.1.1.1   Personal Income Tax

For a long time, especially during the early years of the country, the dominant source of income for the federal government was tariff on imported goods, interspersed with limited taxes such as taxes on distilled spirits, carriages, and refined sugar. Most of these taxes were withdrawn once tariff became the principal source beginning in 1817. Since the government was small, the tariff was considered sufficient for running the everyday operation of the government. As the government began to grow, the need for additional revenue increased, which eventually saw the introduction of income tax in 1913. Although it was not formally introduced until 1913, the government did introduce a rudimentary form of income tax for a brief spell in 1862, in particular to defray the costs of the Civil War. It was levied at 3% on incomes above $800 and at 5% on incomes above $10,000. The tax was repealed in 1872, but a new income tax was introduced in 1894 at a flat rate of 2% for income over $4000. It was subsequently challenged, found unconstitutional, and was repealed in 1896 (Groves 1939).

In 1913, Congress was formally given the power to levy and collect taxes on income under the 16th Amendment of the Constitution, although corporate income tax was introduced four years earlier in 1909. The tax was initially levied at 1% on net personal incomes above $3000, with a surtax (an add-on tax when income exceeds a certain level) on income over $500,000. By the end of World War I, the top marginal rate increased to 77% on personal income over $1 million to cover the war effort but eventually went down to 24% in 1929. During the depression period and all through World War II the top marginal rate continued to increase, reaching as high as 94% on incomes over $200,000 in 1945, mostly to cover the costs of the war and began to gradually decline as the war ended (Goode 1976). From 1965 through 1981, the rate remained at 70%. It was reduced to 50% in 1981, under the Economic Recovery Tax Act (ERTA), also known as Kemp-Roth Act, and further to 28% under the 1986 Tax Reform Act (TRA). The rate increased to 31% in 1991 and again to 39.6% in 1993, and remained at that level through 2000; it went down to 35% in 2003 and back up again to 39.6% in 2013. It was reduced again to 37% under the Tax Cuts and Jobs Act (TCJA) on December 22, 2017.[1] If the past is any indication of the future, the rates will change in either direction in the coming years, depending on the general condition of the economy, the political mood of the general public, and the priorities of the government.

Characteristics of the Current Structure

The current income tax structure has several basic characteristics that are unique to the system. Most of these characteristics evolved over time as the economic and political conditions changed which may partly explain why it may not be quite as simple to make any major changes in the system quickly. Regardless, the structure is well established. There are four basic characteristics that highlight the current income tax structure (Stiglitz 2000). One, it is based on adjusted rather than gross income. There are several provisions built into the system that allow individuals to adjust their income and pay taxes on net (taxable) rather than on gross income. Two, it is based on annual rather than on lifetime income. This means that individuals having the same lifetime but different current incomes may pay at different rates annually. This may also mean that individuals with variable annual incomes pay at different rates than those with stable incomes. Three, the basic unit of taxation is the family, not the individuals. When two individuals get married their tax liabilities change, even though they have identical incomes. Similarly, families with dependent children pay at different rates than families without children. Four, there is an underlying progressivity in the system that requires individuals with high incomes to pay more in taxes, at least up to a point, than individuals with low incomes.

Built-in Provisions

An important characteristic of the current tax structure which applies to all three major taxes (income, sales, and property) is that there are built-in provisions in each that provide cushions for individuals and families with varying incomes. For personal income tax, these provisions are considered necessary for job-related growth such as professional training, for encouraging certain types of activities such as purchasing homes, and for maintaining vertical equity to deal with income gaps, among others. For business tax, they are considered necessary to encourage savings, capital refurbishing, and investment. Because they are so crucial to understanding how the system works, the provisions need a little elaboration.

Three sets of provisions are built into the current personal income tax structure: exclusions, deductions, and exemptions. Exclusions usually do not appear on the tax return, but are considered income such as social security benefits (depending on income level), gifts, employer-paid health insurance, and interests earned on investments in state and local government bonds. Deductions attempt to improve both horizontal and vertical equity by allowing individuals to subtract from their adjusted gross income for uncontrollable forces such as medical expenses or casualty, for socially desirable expenses such as charitable contributions, and for special circumstances such as educational or professional expenses or interest paid on mortgage loans. Finally, exemptions are per capita subtractions from the tax base that allow taxpayers to earn a minimum amount of income before being obligated to pay income taxes. Taxpayers are allowed exemptions for themselves and each member of their family by a flat amount so that the amount of income exempted from income tax increases with family size. Therefore, the taxes individuals pay are based on their final (taxable) income after taking into consideration all the provisions in the system; that is, taxable income = gross income − adjustments (exclusions + deductions + exemptions).

To give an example, suppose that a couple, married with two dependent children, filing jointly, has a gross income of $65,000 and can use all the allowable tax provisions. Let us say that they are allowed to take $4000 in exclusions, $8500 in standard deductions such as those provided to individuals who are married, filing jointly, and no itemized deductions (additions of all expenses that are considered deductible), and $18,000 in exemptions (four in all, each at $4500). The couple's taxable income, after all the provisions, will be $34,500; that is, $65,000 − ($4000 + $8500 + $18,000) = $65,000 − $30,500 = $34,500. Assume now that the tax liability on the final income is $4900; we can use this information to calculate their average and effective tax rates, which are often used to determine the relationship between a tax rate and its tax base. An average tax rate (ATR) shows the relationship between tax liability (how much an individual or firm has to pay in taxes) and taxable income that is subject to tax. It is obtained by dividing tax liability by the amount of taxable income. The effective tax rate (ETR), which is often referred to as the actual rate because it is based on gross rather than on adjusted income, on the other hand, is obtained by dividing the tax liability by the gross income. Thus, using the procedures above, the couple's ATR will be 14.20% [$4900/$34,500 = 0.1420 × 100 = 14.20%] and ETR will be 7.54% [$4900/$65,000 = 0.0754 × 100 = 7.54%].

Built into the current system are also a number of provisions that provide special treatments to certain groups or activities such as low-income allowance and credit, tax-exempt securities, preferential tax treatment of capital gains and dividends.[2] The term often used to describe these and similar provisions, including those described earlier, is tax expenditure. For instance, the low-income allowance is a special condition attached to the standard deduction that sets a minimum standard deduction that benefits all taxpayers with adjusted gross income below a certain level, while earnings subsidies are given to low wage earners to supplement their income such as Earned Income Tax Credit (EITC). Tax-exempt securities are based on the concept of "reciprocal immunity," in which one level of government does not tax the earnings of another level of government. For instance, the state and local governments do not tax the earnings on federal securities such as treasury bills, notes, and bonds and, by the same token, the federal government does not tax the earnings on state and local bonds. Prior to 1986, tax-exemptions applied to all types of state and local securities, but the 1986 Tax Reform Act restricted it to those that can be financed using mostly general obligation (GO) bonds.

As for capital gains, which are increments in the value that results from the sale or improvement of an asset, the tax is usually much lower than the income tax to promote capital improvements. For instance, between 1986 and 2003 the capital gains rate was 28%, as opposed to ordinary tax rates that ranged between 28 and 39.6%. In general, short-term capital gains (assets held for a year or less) are taxed at the normal rate than long-term capital gains (assets held longer than a year). The rates also vary by income brackets, meaning that those in the higher-income brackets pay at a higher rate than those in the lower brackets. For instance, taxpayers in the tax brackets between 10 and 15% currently pay no taxes on long-term gains, while those in the upper-income brackets pay at a rate as high as 20% (Tax Policy Center 2017). As one would expect, this has led to considerable arguments on both sides of the tax provision. On the one hand, the provisions are necessary since the gains are taxed at a much lower marginal rate in order to provide the firms and businesses an incentive to remain productive at all times. On the other hand, one could argue that they benefit the rich and lower the tax base. Interestingly though, unlike most other tax provisions, capital gains tax lacks a clear conceptual rationale and may not easily qualify as a desirable characteristic of a tax system, discussed earlier.

Graduated Tax Structure

Another important aspect of the current tax system is that it is based on multiple tax brackets with progressively higher rates with rising incomes, known as the graduated or step-up tax (Fig. 4.1). The brackets are necessary to determine the rates at which individuals pay taxes as their incomes move from one level to the next. The difference in rates between any two adjacent brackets is called the marginal tax rate, mentioned earlier, which serves as the basis for computing the tax liability. The brackets are flexible and can change with the tax policy of an administration. Currently, there are seven such rates, with the lowest marginal

Fig. 4.1 A sample graduated
tax structure

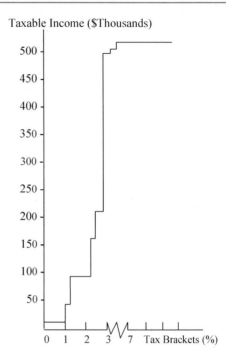

rate at 10% on income up to $9525 for single filers and $19,050 for married individuals, filing jointly, and the highest marginal rate at 37% on income over $500,000 for single filers and over $600,000 for filing jointly (Tax Foundation 2018).

The calculation of the liability is rather straightforward once the taxable income and the marginal tax rates are known. To give an example, suppose that we have two tax filers—a married couple, filing jointly, and a single individual, both with a taxable income of $85,000. Assume that there are six marginal rates: 10, 15, 25, 28, 33, and 35%. Table 4.1 shows the calculations and the liability for each filer. As the table shows, the liabilities are different for the two filers, with the single individual at $18,664 and the married couple at $14,675, indicating further that the single filer is paying $4089 more in taxes ($18,664 − $14,575). This is because the last portion of the single filer's income falls into a higher tax bracket than the married couple, filing jointly.

Let us further suppose that we have the following information on the two filers' gross annual incomes—$143,500 for the single individual and $186,750 for the married couple, filing jointly. We can use this information to calculate their average and effective tax rates. Applying the procedures discussed earlier, the ATR will be 21.96% [$18,664/$85,000=0.2196 × 100=21.96] for the single individual and 17.15% [$14,575/$85,000=0.1715 × 100] for the married couple. On the other hand, the ETR will be 13.01% [$18,664/$143,500=0.1301 × 100=13.01] for the single individual and 7.8% [$14,575/$186,750=0.78 × 100=7.8] for the married couple, filing jointly, which is much lower than the ATR, as expected.

Table 4.1 Tax rates and tax calculations

Marginal tax rate (%)	Married, filing jointly ($)	Tax liability[a] (cumulative total) ($)	Single filer ($)	Tax liability[b] (cumulative total) ($)
10	0–4500	1450	0–7250	725
15	14,501–59,500	1450+6750=8200	7251–29,750	725+3375=4100
25	59,501–119,900	8200+6375=14,575	29,751–59,950	4100+7550=11,650
28	119,901–182,800	–	59,951–91,400	11,650+7014=18,644
33	182,801–325,500	–	91,401–162,750	–
35	>325,500	–	>162,750	–

[a]$(\$14,500 \times 0.10)+(\$59,500-\$14,500) \times 0.15+(\$85,000-\$59,500) \times 0.25=\$1450+\$6750+$
$\$6375=\$14,575$ (married—filing jointly)
[b]$(\$7250 \times 0.10)+(\$29,750-\$7250) \times 0.15+(\$59,950-\$29,750) \times 0.25+(\$85,000-\$59,950) \times$
$0.28=\$725+\$3375+\$7550+\$7014=\$18,664$ (single filer)

The approach we have used thus far to calculate the tax liability is known as the "standard approach." The current system also uses a second approach which is more restrictive, called the Alternative Minimum Tax (AMT), in that, unlike the standard approach, it does not take into consideration many of the tax preferences available under the various tax provisions. AMT uses a reduced number of tax brackets than the standard approach (e.g., 26 and 28%) and the income is taxed on the higher bracket. The idea is to prevent individuals with higher incomes from taking advantage of the tax loopholes but given the fact that tax avoidance and noncompliance still remain a major problem for IRS it is difficult to say if the measure has produced the intended result.

Adjustments for Inflation

The graduated tax system often has a tendency to move individuals automatically to higher income brackets, especially during times of high inflation, known as the bracket creep. The current system has a provision called indexation that protects individuals from the effects of inflation. Indexation adjusts the rates for inflation so that the tax one pays is independent of the changes in the general price level. For instance, if during the tax year a family's real income remains the same, while inflation goes up, say, by 5%, the family will have to receive a 5% increase in nominal income to compensate for inflation. If no adjustment is made to the tax rate schedule, this nominal increase (due to inflation) could push the family to a higher tax bracket and the family may end up paying more in taxes. For instance, if an individual (or a family) has an income of $45,000 and because of inflation his income goes up by 5% (the rate of inflation) to $47,250 [$45,000+($45,000 ×0.05)=$45,000+$2250=$47,250], this will automatically put him in a higher income bracket; thereby, increasing his tax liability. Therefore, if no adjustment is made, he will end up paying at a higher rate for the entire income rather than the portion of the increase in income due to inflation. One way to avoid bracket creep is to adjust the tax brackets periodically so that the tax bracket remains the same in real terms.

4.1.1.2 Corporate Income Tax

Like personal income tax, the corporate income tax is an important source of revenue for the federal government, although its importance has declined over the years. For instance, throughout the entire 1950s and early 1960s it used to constitute over 30% of all federal receipts. Today, it is barely around 10%, while the share of personal income tax has gone up from around 14% in 1934 to an estimated 50% in 2018 (Tax Foundation 2018). Like personal income tax, the corporate income tax is also a graduated tax, with the lowest marginal rate starting at 15% and the highest at 35% on income over $18.3 million, putting it at the same level as the marginal rate for personal income through 2017; it was lowered to 21% under the current tax act (Tax Foundation 2018). The tax is primarily levied on corporate net income or profit, but a part of the profit that goes toward dividend payments produces tax liabilities for the shareholders are also taxed, even though the earnings from which the shareholders receive their dividends were already taxed at the corporate level. This is known as double taxation.

While corporate income is subject to double taxation, the interest paid on debt is deductible from taxable income. This reduces the cost of debt relative to equity, thus encouraging higher levels of leverage in the corporate capital structure. Furthermore, firms such as partnership, proprietorship, limited liability companies (firms with mixed characteristics of partnership, proprietorship, and sole ownership) and occasionally large corporations are exempted from the corporate income tax. Interestingly, the double taxation further adds to the problem in that it encourages businesses to choose these alternative organizational forms to avoid tax, which has resulted in serious erosion in the corporate tax base in recent years.

A Note on Tax Expenditures

Earlier we introduced the term tax expenditure to describe the various tax provisions in the current tax system that allow individuals, firms and businesses tax reliefs by lowering their adjusted incomes. Although the term "tax expenditures" is generally used, from a budgetary perspective, they are considered a loss of revenue for the government as a result of these provisions in the tax codes. For instance, in 2017, the government spent over a $1.5 trillion on these expenditures, which, by some estimates, is likely to increase considerably in the coming years (Center on Budget and Policy Priorities 2018). In fact, tax expenditures constitute the third largest group of government expenditure (about a fourth of total expenditures), following the discretionary and nondiscretionary expenditures of the government. While the number of these provisions runs into dozens, the areas that constitute the largest tax expenditures are exclusion for employer contribution for medical insurance and health care, net exclusion of individual and employer-provided pension contributions and earnings, and deductibility of mortgage interest on owner-occupied homes, followed by accelerated depreciation for machinery and equipment, deductibility of non-business state and local taxes, and deductibility of charitable contributions, among others.

In some ways, tax expenditures operate like direct expenditures, although they are not considered as such since they benefit thousands of business activities and individuals. As noted earlier, an interesting aspect of these expenditures is that they do not show up in the actual expenditure calculations of the government, although the Department of Treasury, along with the Joint Committee on Taxation, have been keeping tracks of these expenditures. Additionally, like most mandatory (entitlement) programs, they do not go through the normal appropriation process; as such, they tend to expand as the economy grows. This has raised some questions in recent years whether these expenditures should go through the yearly appropriation process, similar to other expenditures of the government.

4.1.1.3 Payroll Tax

In addition to personal and corporate income tax, there are also taxes on the wage and salary portion of an individual's income paid either by the employee or the employer, or both. Since they are directly withdrawn from an individual's payroll (hence, the term payroll tax), they are difficult to avoid. There are three basic components of the payroll tax, the largest of which is the Social Security tax (previously known as Federal Insurance and Contributions Act, or FICA), followed by Medicare tax, and a small fraction to support unemployment insurance. The Social Security contribution currently constitutes 12.4%, divided equally between the employee and the employer. The Medicare contribution, on the other hand, stands at 2.9%, of which 1.45% comes out of the employee's income and the other 1.45% paid by the employer. As for the component on unemployment insurance, the rate is 1.2% on earnings to $9000 (taxable wage base) currently paid by the employer. The contributions are not constant, especially for unemployment insurance; they change from time to time, depending on the condition of the economy and the costs of supporting the programs.

The tax is coordinated with the states that have unemployment insurance, so that the contributors are not double taxed. However, there is an element of regressivity in the tax structure which is directly tied to the maximum-taxable amount (cutoff level of income), currently set at $128,700 for the Social Security component, meaning that individuals above this income level do not pay tax on the portion above $128,700. Thus, an individual with an income over $350,000 pays 2.75% of his income in taxes [($128,700 × 0.0765)/$350,000 = $9730.8/$350,000 = 0.0275 × 100 = 2.75%], where 7.65% is the employee's share of the total payroll tax [12.4 + 2.9)/2 = 15.3/2 = 7.65]. On the other hand, an individual earning, say, $57,500 pays at the full 7.65% rate of his income. Therefore, anyone making less than $128,700 per year would see a higher percentage of their income taxed away than those making above that level. Although the cutoff level has increased considerably in recent years, from $90,000 in 2005 to the current level (2018), many would consider the rate of growth to be negligible considering the wide gaps in income levels.

Like the personal income tax, the reliance on payroll tax has also increased dramatically over the years with the highest in 2009 at 42.3% since the government started collecting it in 1934. It has been declining steadily in recent years, although by a small margin, as revenue from personal income tax began to increase (Tax Foundation 2018). Historically, much of this growth can be attributed to the growth in Social Security and Medicare. Most economists and policy makers believe that at their current rate of growth it will be difficult to sustain them in the long-term. Several alternatives have been suggested in recent years to deal with the problem, especially with respect to Social Security reform, ranging from increasing the retirement age to 70, to eliminating the pay-as-you-go (PAYGO) nature of the program, to financing the welfare component of the program from general revenue of the government, while supporting the benefit component from the retirement fund, to fully or partially privatizing the system, among others. Each alternative has its strengths and weaknesses, but a final solution may involve a combination of alternatives rather than any one in particular to distribute the burden equitably between different income brackets, as well as over time. Medicare is a more complex issue and may require a careful examination of all parts of the system, from hospital care, to doctor's visit and out of hospital care, to prescription drugs that make up the system, to waste and abuse, among others.

4.1.1.4 Alternatives to Income Tax

Several questions have been raised in recent years about the long-term viability of the current tax structure, the most important of which is that it is far too complex for an average taxpayer to understand. Much of this complexity comes from the intricate tax codes, regulations, and tax rulings that are not easy for an average taxpayer to understand. Not only that, it costs the taxpayers enormous amount of time and resources to prepare the tax returns and follow the guidelines. According to some calculations, there are over 65,000 pages of federal tax rules, with 580 IRS tax forms that take up over 6.0 billion hours a year on tax compliance. As noted previously, the compliance costs alone run over hundreds of millions of dollars each year in record keeping, understanding tax rules, and other related activities (Edwards 2006). The complexity also creates confusion, causes frequent errors, and exacerbates noncompliance with the tax laws, costing the government enormously each year in lost revenues.

The system understandably needs a change, but it must be done in a manner that will make it transparent so that taxes are visible to the average public and easy for the taxpayers to comply. The process will not be easy because of the years it took to build the current system. Nevertheless, if the current system has to survive as the principal instrument of revenue generation for federal government, some changes are necessary. Failure to do so will require the need to develop alternative systems of taxation. Three such systems that have received considerable attention in recent years are flat tax, national sales tax, and cash-flow tax.

Flat Tax

Known also as the flat-rate tax, flat tax was popularized by Steve Forbes, when he was running as a Presidential candidate during the 1996 Republican Presidential primary, as an alternative to the current (federal) income tax structure. In fact, in 1985, Hall and Rabuschka of Stanford University published a book on the subject which provided much of the foundation for the debate. It is based on a single marginal tax rate, rather than a progressive tax system that varies according to income ranges. Theoretically, the rate could be anywhere, but most scholars believe that it should be more toward the middle of the current stepped-up system, somewhere around 20%. The justification for a lower rate is that it will minimize the excess burden or deadweight loss which is normally associated with higher marginal tax rates. For instance, if a 40% tax rate produces four times as much deadweight loss as a 15 or 20% rate, a lower uniform rate will be economically more efficient than a combination of high and low taxes, as we have under the present system because it will produce less deadweight loss.

Another important aspect of the tax is that it will eliminate the special provisions, including double taxation on dividends which will make it easier to comply since it will not have many of the provisions of the current system. Similarly, firms and businesses will also pay at the same rate, that is, no distinction between corporations, limited partnerships, or sole proprietorships. From an administrative point of view, it will be easier to administer because everyone will be paying at the same rate. Also, like the current income tax, it will be family based in that households will receive a generous exemption based on family size, which may, in fact, lower the tax base. However, the question the flat tax faces the most is the age-old question of how to take into consideration the "fairness" issue that lies at the heart of the tax provisions under the current system. It is difficult to say to what extent it will be able to address this issue because the debate over what is fair or not fair goes back to the question of what constitutes taxable and non-taxable income, and what basis to use to tax the income one considers taxable.

There are a number of other issues that are also important to consider when it comes to flat tax: One, as with the current system, the rate may need to be adjusted frequently to accommodate the changing needs of the economy and income distribution. Two, it is not clear how different types of incomes are going to be treated under this tax. Three, and more importantly, it may reduce charitable contributions since the current system allows individuals to take tax deductions if they contribute to charitable organizations, which will not be available under a flat tax in its current form. On the other hand, it has an obvious advantage in that it will substantially lower the administrative costs from tax simplification and the loss of revenue resulting from various tax provisions under the current system.

National Sales Tax

A second alternative to the current system that has drawn considerable attention in recent years, especially among the policy makers, is the national sales tax, also called a fair tax. The argument for a national sales tax is that it is simple and easy to collect since individuals will be taxed at the same rate. Additionally, it will not be involuntary in that individuals will not have to pay a tax unless they are will-ing to consume and only in proportion to the amount they consume or at a fixed percentage of the value of the good (ad valorem); thereby, giving them greater control over their spending behavior. Let us briefly look at some of these points.

A national sales tax would be simple because, like the current sales tax, it will be collected by the businesses selling goods and services. Individuals will not have to file tax returns, so compliance will not be a problem. Collection would be easy, so tax avoidance will not be a concern but sales tax on underground economy in all likelihood will remain a problem. The general idea is that the federal gov-ernment would collect the tax and, in turn, return a portion of the revenue to the states, based on established criteria. This would, in turn, scale back the Internal Revenue Service (IRS) and the tax code, although IRS will still be required to insure that businesses paid their share of sales tax. However, in order for the fed-eral government to implement the tax, the US Congress and the states will need to repeal the 16th Amendment of the Constitution, which will not be an easy task considering that it will require two-thirds majority in Congress and three-fourths of the states to ratify it.

The idea to pay at the same rate, while sounds attractive, will be regressive, espe-cially for low-income families who spend a disproportionately higher percentage of their income on basic necessities. Consequently, it will impose a much greater bur-den on them than on high-income families. Although some goods will be tax exempt, as under the current tax structure such as food, medicine, and some professional ser-vices, it will still be disproportionate since the exemptions would apply equally to all incomes. The problem could be partially addressed by giving the low-income fami-lies a rebate on their tax, based on family size or income level to lower their tax bur-den, but it is unlikely that the measure would resolve the equity issue fully. On the other hand, it will increase savings and investments because the propensity to save is much higher for high-income families, although it is difficult to predict how much savings the tax will produce in spite of its relative stability as a revenue source.

From an economic point of view, a national sales tax would be a major depar-ture from the current tax structure, which is predominantly based on income. In other words, it will be based on consumption rather than production, which means that while under the present system the marginal tax rate will increase with income, it will be flat under a national sales tax, adding further to the equity issue. It is also not clear how the distribution issue will be addressed since the tax will eliminate the current tax provisions (Tax Policy Center 2016).

Two other issues relevant to the national sales tax alternative are the questions of what would be an appropriate tax rate and whether this rate would be sufficient to generate the needed revenue to support government expenditures. There is no clear agreement among the economists and policy makers as to what will consti-tute an "ideal" rate, but speculations range from 15 to 40%. Obviously, at a higher rate more revenue will be generated, but only up to a point, if the relationship between tax rate and tax revenue, as the Laffer curve suggests, is to hold. Also, as noted earlier, a higher rate always has the potential to work as a disincentive for individuals to be productive if additional incomes are going to be taxed away.

Cash-Flow Tax

A third alternative to the current system is the cash-flow tax that some believe would correct some of the problems, especially those related to corporate income tax. Proponents of the tax suggest several reasons why an alternative system is needed (Edwards 2003). One, although lowered considerably under the current tax act, one could argue that the current rate is still high. Two, the tax on net income or profit is inherently complex because it relies on concepts such as capital gains and capitalization of long-term assets that are difficult to calculate in a consistent manner. Three, as with personal income tax, the system is marred with complex codes that vary between different types of organizations. The proponents of cash-flow tax believe that it would eliminate some of these problems.

Procedurally, a cash-flow tax would be imposed on net cash flow rather than on net income or profit. A net cash flow is the difference between cash inflow and cash outflow, adjusted for beginning cash balance (i.e., beginning balance + cash inflows − cash outflows = net cash flow). Under the new proposal, the tax base would include receipts from the sale of goods and services (inflows) and less current and capital expenses (outflows), and would not include interests, dividends, and capital gains. In other words, it would not include the financial flows, which has been the crux of the problem. This is known as the basic cash-flow or R-based tax (R for real). According to Edwards (2003), it is possible to include the financial flows, in which case it would be called an R + F base. While the proposal has a great appeal because of its apparent simplicity, it may pose some serious implementation problems, especially with issues such as tax avoidance where multinational firms are concerned (Shome and Schutte 1993). For instance, what would happen when a firm transfers profits from high-tax countries to low-tax countries through various noneconomic means or through practices that are difficult to measure in conventional economic terms? Other problems may involve inflation adjustments, the need for special rules for various financial institutions to utilize the R-base and, more important, how to move from the old system to the new system.

4.1.2 Sales Tax

The second most important tax, next to income tax, is the sales tax. It is the primary source of revenue for most states and an important source for a large number of local governments that have come to rely on it in recent years to supplement their revenue from property tax. In the latter case, it is known as local option sales tax (LOST) since it can be withdrawn any time if it is no longer considered necessary. Sales tax was first introduced by West Virginia in 1921, followed by Georgia in 1929; by 1940, over 40 states had a sales tax of one form another, although the early history traces it back to the Pennsylvania mercantile tax introduced in 1821 (Buehler 1940). Today, almost every single state has a sales tax with the exception of Alaska, Delware, Montana, New Hampshire, and Oregon[3]; Vermont was the last state to formally adopt the tax in 1969 (ACIR 1993).

The term sales tax is often used interchangeably with "consumption tax" because the tax is levied on the actual quantity or value of goods and services individuals consume. The tax is usually collected at the point of origin at a predetermined rate. The revenue generated from sales tax has been steadily increasing over the years, for instance, from less than $40 billion in 1962 to over $165 billion in 2000. Approximately three-fourths of this revenue comes from general sales tax and one-fourth from selective tax. Combined with local sales tax, the total collection currently exceeds $500 billion a year, with the state share roughly at 80% of the total (Tax Policy Center 2017), although it has been declining somewhat in recent years to reflect the general slowdown in the national economy. For instance, between 2006 and 2008, at the height of the economic downturn, it declined by about 10%, the highest decline in many years (*Wall Street Journal* 2009), and picked up gradually as economy improved.

In general, the state governments are hit harder by any economic downturn than the local governments since it is the principal source of revenue for most state governments. Local governments generally have a tendency to react at a much slower pace to any fluctuation in the national economy than the state governments, especially in the short-term, in part because it is difficult to avoid property tax and in part because the property owners tend to hold on to their properties, even in tough economic times. Economists often use a term to define this kind of reactive behavior called "perversity hypothesis" (Gist 2008).

4.1.2.1 Forms of Sales Tax

As noted previously, based on how it is levied and the manner in which it is collected, a sales tax can be defined as general or selective. A general sales tax applies to most goods we consume except for certain basic necessities such as food and medicine, and is usually imposed at the same rate. A selective tax, also referred to as excise tax, is imposed at different rates on different goods such as tax on gasoline. A special case of excise tax is a sumptuary tax imposed on tobacco, alcohol, gambling, or illegal substance such as drugs; it is called "sin tax" because society considers the consumption of these goods as socially undesirable. The revenue generated from sin tax can be used for any activity as with any other tax but is mostly used for special programs such as alcohol or drug rehabilitation. A common concern with this tax is that it is regressive and discriminates against low-income groups who may end up spending a disproportionately higher percentage of their income on these goods.

Sales taxes usually take one of two forms: unit tax and ad valorem tax. A unit tax applies to each physical unit of a good purchased such as tax one pays on gasoline. For instance, if a gallon of gasoline costs $3.75 and the tax on each gallon is $0.20, the cost per gallon of gasoline will be $3.95 ($3.75 + $0.20). Thus, if a person buys 10 gallons of gasoline, the total cost, including the tax, will be $39.50 [$3.95 × 10 = $39.50 or ($3.75 × 10 + $0.20 × 10) = $37.50 + $2.00 = $39.50]. An ad valorem tax, on the other hand, is a tax on the value of a good calculated as a percentage of the total value of the purchase. For instance, if the price of a commodity, say, a small screen television set is $125 and there is an applicable tax rate of 8.5%, the total price of the good will be \$135.63 [\$125.00+(\$125 × 0.085)= \$125+\$10.63=\$135.63], which includes a tax of \$10.63. Another good example of ad valorem tax is property tax.

4.1.2.2 Some Common Concerns with Sales Tax

Although the sales tax is relatively easy to collect, the process of generating the tax revenue and administration can be complicated. Several factors contribute to this such as the reduction in tax base (the number of goods that are exempted from taxation), location of tax levy (the difficulty in determining where to levy the tax—at the point of origin, on the final product at the retail level), or on intermediate goods (i.e., goods used in the production of other goods), the cost of administering and collecting the tax, and the distributional effect the tax can have on the consumers.

Reduction in Tax Base

Earlier, we defined sales tax as a consumption tax on the goods and services we consume. Theoretically, if we are to pay taxes on all the goods and services we consume, then a jurisdiction's tax base will approximate the value of the total consumption but that is seldom the case. This is because certain goods are exempted from taxation, although the nature of these exemptions varies from jurisdiction to jurisdiction. In general, sales taxes typically apply to consumer goods rather than to services. Thus, housing services, whether owner-occupied or rental, are exempt from direct taxes in most states. By the same token, professional services such as medical, legal, and financial are not taxed, while personal services such as laundry, grooming are. Exemptions erode the tax base. To give an example of how exemptions lower the tax base, suppose that we have an initial tax base for personal consumption at 100%, meaning that all the goods and services we consume will be taxed. Now, if we subtract from this an exemption of 10% for food, 8% for housing, 12% for medical, and 15% for miscellaneous other services, the tax base is reduced to 55% [100 − (10+8+12+15)=55]. The net effect of these exemptions is that it will produce less revenue for the government, although they may be considered necessary from equity perspective. Interestingly, as we noted earlier, exemption is a form of tax preference and all tax preferences lower the tax base.

Location of Tax Levy

A common concern with sales tax is where to levy the tax. There are three basic options available to a government as to where the tax should be levied: at the retail level, at various stages of production with taxes paid at each stage, called multistage taxation, and at the point of origin before the final sale at the retail level. If a tax is collected at the retail level, it means that intermediate goods are not taxed; it is a single-stage tax. The multi-stage taxation applies to all sales at various stages of production. The classic example of multi-stage taxation is the value-added tax (VAT). However, multi-stage taxation does not mean that the intermediate stages are fully taxed, although in theory they are. In reality, very few states do that, especially if the items such as machines, tools, and equipment are used for production in the future or for production of other goods. The third option is to levy the tax at the initial stage of the production (i.e., at the point of origin) before the final good is produced and delivered which means that no taxes are collected from the retailer vis-a-vis the consumer. While this may avoid some of the problems of multi-stage taxation, it can create other issues such as what happens to the stages prior to the stage where the tax is levied or between the levied stage and the final sale.

Costs of Administration and Collection

The greatest advantage of sales tax is that it is relatively simple to administer and collect. However, this does not mean that the administration and collection of the tax are not without any problem. The biggest challenge for the policy makers is what specific criteria to use to determine which goods should be taxed and which should not. For instance, "food" is exempt from tax, while soft drinks are not. Similarly, clothing is exempt up to a certain amount in some states but goods such as headgear are not. This is clearly reflected in the differences that exist between states on the goods that are subject to tax liability. Part of the problem lies in the fact that there is a certain amount of arbitrariness in defining the base for a sales tax because of the myriad of goods and services we consume that vary in price and degree of usefulness.

Collection can also be a problem for certain types of goods, especially those that are sold underground such as illegal drugs, copyrighted materials, firearms, and so forth. Each year, governments lose hundreds of millions of dollars in revenue from the underground economy, which is difficult to monitor. Cross-border shopping, including Internet, telephone, and mail order purchases, where individuals can shop across borders at lower taxes has further added to the collection problem (Goolsbee 2000). A significant amount of tax dollars is lost each year as a result of cross-border shopping, even though there is a provision on individual income-tax returns to report and remit use-tax liability (self assessed and remitted by the end user). Interestingly, in spite of some of these difficulties, sales tax is still considered much easier to collect and administer than most other taxes, in particular income tax.

Distributional Effects

All taxes, including sales tax, have some elements of regressivity. What explains this regressivity is the fact that individuals with high incomes pay less of their income in sales tax than individuals with low incomes; thereby, producing a disproportionately greater burden on the latter. While the argument has some merits, it also has a weakness in that it looks at sales tax as a percentage of annual income and not lifetime income, which tends to increase over time. Some economists argue that the proportion of income individuals spend on consumption goods over their lifetime is essentially the same at all levels (Metcalf 1993). If this were to be the case, then the regressivity argument loses some of its merits. Additionally, one could argue that taxes on most goods and services are selective in that certain goods are taxed at a much higher rate while others such as basic food and medicine are completely tax exempt; therefore, making after-tax income more equitable.

This is known as the incidence of selective taxation. The point is there are arguments on both sides. On the one hand, individuals with high incomes consume the same goods as individuals with low incomes, although not necessarily at the same relative proportion to their income while, on the other, high-income individuals also pay at a higher rate for goods that cost more such as luxury cars, boats, jewelry, etc.

4.1.2.3 Value-Added Tax

In recent years, there has been a serious interest in value-added tax or VAT, in short. As noted earlier, unlike the single-stage tax, which applies to either production or distribution, VAT is a multi-stage tax that applies to all stages of production and distribution. It is basically a percentage tax on the value added to a commodity as it goes through each stage of the production process. To give an example, suppose that a farmer sells wheat to a local miller for $200, who adds $200 worth of value by making flour and sells it to a baker for $400, who, in turn, adds $100 value by making bread and sells them to a retailer for $500; the retailer adds another $75 of value by packaging and marketing, and sells the final product to the consumers for $575. Assume that there is a 10% tax on the value added (VAT), the total amount of tax collected from the process will thus be $57.50 [($200 \times 0.1) + ($200 \times 0.1) + ($100 \times 0.1) + ($75 \times 0.1) = $20.0 + $20.0 + $10.0 + $7.50 = $57.50]$, which is the same if the tax would have been collected on the total value of the product ($575 \times 0.1 = $57.50)$. Table 4.2 shows the calculation of the VAT.

As can be seen from the example above, VAT has an obvious advantage in that it is difficult to avoid since it is collected at each stage of the production process, but it would also increase the costs of administration because of the additional time and resources that would be needed to collect the tax. However, economists and policy makers are not quite certain if the gains from the increase in tax collection would outweigh the costs of added administration. This partly explains why the tax has not been implemented in the country, although it has been extensively used in a number of countries, especially Europe. There is another potential problem with VAT in that since it primarily applies to general sales it may not be quite as easy to deal with some of the distributional questions, especially those related to vertical equity. There is also a perception problem with the tax that it is regressive in that it puts an undue burden on consumers at the lower end of the income strata, which may not necessarily be true; it depends on how much value is added

Table 4.2 Computation of a value-added tax

Producer	Buys ($)	Sells ($)	Value added ($)	Tax amount[a] ($)
Farmer	–	200	200	20.00
Miller	200	400	200	20.00
Baker	400	500	100	10.00
Retailer	500	575	75	7.50
Total	$1100	$1675	$575	$57.50

[a]VAT at 10% rate

to the final stage of production process, who consume the good and how much of the good. Since many of the basic necessities such as food and medicine are tax exempt, theoretically they should not pose a heavy burden on individuals and families with low incomes.

> **A Note on Wealth Tax**
>
> Two types of variables are generally used when calculating taxes: flow variables and stock variables. Flow variables have a time dimension in that they are related to time. Income and sales taxes are based on flow variables. For instance, if someone's income is $45,000 it makes sense only if it is defined as weekly, monthly, quarterly, or annual income. Similarly, revenue from sales tax is related to weekly, monthly, quarterly, or annual sales. On the other hand, there are variables called stock variables that have no time dimension because they refer to the value of the assets one has accumulated over a period of time such as gold, stocks, bonds, property, etc. Taxes on these types of variables (assets, to be precise) are called wealth taxes. Taxes on wealth are generally higher than taxes on flow variables because of their higher accumulated value, but the problem with wealth tax is that it does not always take into consideration the liabilities of the owners. For instance, two individuals who own two properties of equal value—one owns his in that it is fully paid, while the other pays a huge mortgage on his property—cannot be treated as having the same amount of wealth because of the differences in their liabilities. Interestingly, property tax is a classic example that does not allow deductions for liabilities.

4.1.3   Property Tax

Property tax constitutes the single most important source of revenue for local governments. Although it has declined considerably in importance in recent years, it still generates a significant amount of revenue for county governments, municipalities, townships, school districts, and special districts. For instance, in the early 1960s, property tax produced almost one-half of all revenues for local governments; today, it produces on average about a third. Several factors have contributed to this declining trend: the rising costs of expenditures, increasing demand for public goods and, more importantly, the taxpayers' unwillingness to pay more for increased expenditures. The decline in reliance on property as the primary source of revenue has produced greater reliance on other sources such as user fees and charges, fines and forfeitures, and intergovernmental revenue.

Property tax has certain unique characteristics that make it considerably different from either income or sales tax. One, it produces a relatively stable source of income for local governments that is not easily affected by economic downturns, especially in the short-term. Most property owners would hold on to their property to the extent possible, even under dire economic circumstances. Two, while income and sales taxes which are determined by the level of private economic activity, the property tax is determined by the government. In other words, while the level of private economic activity determines the tax base for income or sales, for property tax it is determined largely by the government based on the value of the property. Part of the reason for this is that property is considered, as noted earlier, as wealth and, as wealth, its value can be assessed using the conventional rules of taxation on wealth. Three, unlike income or sales tax, the responsibility for property tax assessment, collection, and administration falls on multiple jurisdictions. For instance, while the tax is appraised and assessed by the county government, the state governments usually set the upper limit of the tax rate. Four, property tax is difficult to avoid because of its close proximity to the government; in fact, the collection rate for property, on average, is over 90% and can be as high as 95% or more.

4.1.3.1 Property Tax Cycle

Property taxes go through a cyclical process each year consisting of four of distinct steps or phases. The phases typically include (1) preparing the tax roll, (2) determining the assessed value of property, (3) making adjustments, (4) levy and collection. Before taxes could be levied and collected, a tax roll has to be prepared, properties have to be appraised and they have to be assessed for tax purposes. Three types of properties are generally included in this process: land (e.g., farmland, open space, and minerals), improvements on land (e.g., buildings, infrastructure, and underground improvement), and personal (tangibles such as inventory, machinery, vehicles, jewelry, artwork, and furniture, and intangibles such as stocks and bonds, insurance policies, bank deposits, patents and copyrights, trademark, and accounts receivables). As noted earlier, personal properties, which are often considered as wealth, are taxed at a higher rate than real property. However, most discussions on property tax revolve around real property, which includes land and improvements on land.

Preparing the Tax Roll

The process begins with the identification of all taxable and non-taxable properties and their legal owners, and preparing the tax roll. This is typically done using declarations by the property owners, surveyors, and collecting information on the number of building permits issued by the government. The process is time consuming, as it requires a careful recording of properties in all their details, including improvements to the structure.

Determining the Assessed Value of Property

The next phase in the process is the determination of assessed value of property. This takes place in two stages: Stage 1 determines the appraised value (of all taxable properties) and approval by the Appraisal Board, which must then be certified by the Chief Appraiser before the assessed value can be determined. Stage 2 determines the assessed value, which serves as the basis for determining the taxable value of a property based on the current market value. In an appraisal, a report is prepared by the appraiser (usually a third party) to determine the current market value of a property. In other words, the appraisal determines the current market value of property, while the assessment determines the taxable value of the property, which is usually set at full or a certain percentage of fair market value.[4]

Two approaches are commonly used to determine the appraised value vis-à-vis the current market value of a property: comparison approach and use value. The market value of a property is generally obtained from the most recent sales data, but the two are not the same. The market value can be higher or lower than the sale price, and vice versa, depending on the condition of the market, condition of the property, and so forth. The method commonly used for this purpose is the comparison approach, where an appraiser locates sales of comparable properties and adjusts the selling price to reflect the market value of the property. It is given by the expression

$$MV = P_{sale} \pm Adjustments \qquad (4.1)$$

where MV is the market value, in short for current market value, and P_{sale} is the sale price. Adjustments are quantified characteristics of properties such as time, size, acreage, amenities, and so forth that cause the prices to vary. To give an example, suppose that we are interested in the market value of a property. To find its market value, we look at the price of a comparable property that was sold recently, say, for $160,000 and add to it $15,000 for the quantifiable characteristics. The market value of the property we are interested will therefore be $175,000; that is, $160,000+$15,000=$175,000. If the property we are interested lacks some of those characteristics, say, worth $15,000, then we will subtract this amount from the sale price of the comparable property to determine its market value which, in this case, will be $145,000; that is, $160,000−$15,000= $145,000.

The use value, also called the cost approach, on the other hand, involves estimating the value of the property based on the current cost of construction, less a depreciable allowance for the age of the structure, plus the current value of land. In general, the land value is appraised separately using the current market price or the sale price of parcels under similar condition. The appraisal of the building, on the other hand, depends on several factors such as location, square footage, physical condition, age of the structure, number of bedrooms, bathrooms, fireplace, garage, and other improvements. We can use the following expression to obtain the market value of a property, using the cost approach:

$$MV = [C - ((C/L) \times A)] + V_L \qquad (4.2)$$

where MV is the appraised value of property, C is the current cost of construction, L is the useful life, A is the age of the structure, V_L is the current value of the land, and the expression $[(C/L) \times A]$ is the depreciation.

To give an example, suppose that it would cost $180,000 to construct a building today and the age of the building is 10 years. Assuming the building has a useful life of 60 years, the structure will be appraised at $150,000 using a straight-line depreciation (depreciated at a constant rate for the useful life of an asset, with adjustments for the age of the structure), plus the value of the land at $25,000, obtained in the following way:

$$
\begin{aligned}
\text{MV} &= [C-((C/L) \times A)] + V_L \\
&= [\$180,000 - \{(\$180,000/60) \times 10\}] + \$25,000 \\
&= [\$180,000 - (\$3,000 \times 10)] + \$25,000 \\
&= (\$180,000 - \$30,000) + \$25,000 \\
&= \$150,000 + \$25,000 \\
&= \$175,000
\end{aligned}
$$

Note that the depreciation is $3000 times the age of the structure, which turns out to be $30,000 [($180,000/60) \times 10 = $3000 \times 10 = $30,000]. If it were a brand new structure, the depreciation would be $3000 and no adjustments for age would be necessary, which will increase the appraised value of the property by $27,000 to $202,000; that is, ($180,000 − $3000) + $25,000 = $177,000 + $25,000 = $202,000.

In addition to the market and the use value, two other approaches are also used on occasion to determine the appraised value vis-à-vis the market value of a property: capitalized value and statistical approach. Capitalized value, also known as income approach, uses capitalization rate as the basis for obtaining the current value of a property. Capitalization rate is the ratio of net operating income from an asset (property) to its capital cost (purchase or sale price) obtained by dividing the net operating income by the purchase price; that is, net operating income/purchase or sale price = capitalization rate (CR). Used primarily for income-earning property, the method is applied in two stages: In the first stage, we calculate the capitalization rate of the property in question. In the second stage, we determine the average capitalization rate for a number of properties of comparable size, including the property in question, and use the average to estimate the value of the property.

To give an example, suppose that we have $15,000 in net operating income for a property with a sale price of $200,000; the capitalization rate for the property would be 7.5% [$15,000/$200,000 = 0.075]. Let us further suppose that we have the capitalization rates for five comparable, income-earning properties producing an average capitalization rate of 0.079 (Table 4.3).[5] We can now use this average to estimate the appraised value of the property by dividing the net operating income by the average capitalization rate, which produces a value of $189,873 [$15,000/0.079 = $189,873]. The method is frequently used to determine the value of an income-generating property.[6]

The statistical approach, on the other hand, relies on conventional statistical methods such as regression analysis to estimate the current value with the help of sales data and other available information on property characteristics such as square footage of the structure, number of bedrooms, bathrooms, stalls in the garage, and so forth. In reality, the market value is used for residential property, whereas the capitalized value is used for commercial and industrial properties.

Table 4.3 Capitalization rate calculation[a]

Property	Sale price ($)	Net operating income ($)	Capitalization rate (CR)
A	200,000	15,000	0.075
B	225,000	20,000	0.089
C	170,000	12,000	0.071
D	230,000	23,000	0.100
E	165,000	10,000	0.061

[a]Average capitalization rate, $ACR = \Sigma CR/n = 0.396/5 = 0.079$

To give an example how the market value is determined using a statistical approach, suppose that we have a regression model for single-family homes in a middle-income residential community with the following characteristics:

$$MV = \alpha + \beta_1 SF + \beta_2 BR + \beta_3 BTH + \beta_4 GAR + e \qquad (4.3)$$

where MV is market value of the property, SF is the square footage, BR is the number of bedrooms, BTH is the number of bathrooms, GAR is the garage with the number of cars that can be parked such as a two or three-car garage, α and β's are the parameters of the model (intercept and slopes, respectively), and e is the error term.

Assume now that we have collected data for a number of comparable single-family homes in the area and have estimated the model. The results of the estimated model are presented below:

$$MV = 25,000 + 45.75SF + 4,500BR + 5,750BTH + 3,500GAR$$

Therefore, to find the market value of a property, we would simply multiply the estimated coefficients (β's) by the value of the respective terms and then add the result to the intercept (α) (assuming the observed test statistics for the estimated coefficients such as t, F, and so forth are statistically significant). Thus, if a property is 2100 square feet in size, has 3 bedrooms, 2 bathrooms, and a 2 car garage, the estimated market value of the property will be $153,075 [$25,000+($45.75 × 2100)+($4500 × 3)+($5750 × 2)+($3500 × 2)=$25,000+$96,075+$13,500+$1 1,500+$7000=$153,075]. The intercept usually represents the land value, which is the value of the property without the structure. We could have also included additional variables in the model such as the number of living rooms, storage facility, office space, and so forth, but as long as there is parsimony in the variables, the model should be good enough to reflect the market price.

An important consideration in estimating the market value, regardless of the method used, is that it should produce or come as close as possible to the true market value of the property, which then must be assessed for tax purposes by the tax assessor. The convention is to multiply the estimated value by the assessment rate (e.g., by a uniform percentage) typically set at 80 or 90% of the appraised value to bring about some uniformities in assessment. Thus, if the appraised value of a property is \$175,000 and the assessment rate is 90%, the assessed value of the property will be \$157,500; that is, $\$175,000 \times 0.9 = \$157,500$.

Making Adjustments

Once a property has been appraised and its assessed value ascertained, several adjustments are made on this value to determine the tax amount or tax liability for the property owners. Like income and sales taxes, the adjustments are considered necessary to provide tax relief for property owners in order to minimize the tax burden. The simplest and most widely used among the adjustments is the homestead exemption, which is an exemption from tax of a specific amount of homestead value, similar to personal exemptions for income tax, as long as the owner of the property uses it as the primary residence. The actual amount of exemption varies from state to state. The exemption reduces the tax liability by the amount of exemption times the tax rate. For instance, if the exemption is \$15,000 and the corresponding tax rate is 3%, the amount by which tax will be lowered would be \$450 [$\$15,000 \times 0.03 = \$450$]. The important thing to keep in mind about homestead exemption is that it is not affected by changes in the assessed value of a property in that the amount of relief will remain the same, regardless of increase or decrease in assessed value.

Besides homestead exemption, governments often use a variety of other measures of adjustments to determine the final tax liability such as circuit breakers, limits on assessed value, caps on tax rates, income-tax deduction for property tax, tax freeze, veteran's exemption, and exception for old age. One of the more widely used measures, circuit breakers are designed to prevent "tax overload" (excess property tax) by limiting the amount of property taxes paid, based on the total income of the household, and are currently used by a majority of the states in the country. Two methods are generally used to determine the tax overload: threshold approach and sliding-scale approach (ACIR 1975). Under the threshold approach, an acceptable burden is defined as some percentage of household income and any tax above this level is considered "excessive" and qualifies for a tax relief. The portion of income that is considered an acceptable tax burden is the threshold level and is given by the expression

$$\text{TAX}_{\text{Relief}} = (\text{OR})[\text{PTX} - (\text{INC} \times \text{TO})] \tag{4.4}$$

where $\text{TAX}_{\text{Relief}}$ is the amount of tax relief, OR is overload relief, PTX is the property tax, INC is family or household income, and TO is the of threshold overload. Both OR and TO terms are usually expressed in percentages.

To give an example, suppose that we have a household with an annual income of \$37,500, a property tax bill of \$2275, based on an assessed value of \$130,000 and assessed at the rate of \$1.75 per \$100 of assessed value [($\$130,000/\$100) \times \$1.75 = 1300 \times \$1.75 = \$2275$]. Suppose further that we have a threshold overload of 3% (TO) and an overload relief of 40% (OR). Now, applying the expression in Eq. 4.4 will produce a tax relief of \$460, as shown below:

$$\begin{aligned}
\text{TAX}_{\text{Relief}} &= (\text{OR})[\text{PTX}-(\text{INC} \times \text{TO})]\\
&= 0.4\big[\$2275-(\$37,500 \times 0.03)\big]\\
&= 0.4(\$2275-\$1125)\\
&= 0.4(\$150)\\
&= \$460
\end{aligned}$$

Under the sliding-scale approach, on the other hand, a fixed percentage of property tax relief is provided for each eligible taxpayer within a given income class, while the amount of relief is obtained by multiplying the tax bill by this percentage; that is,

$$\text{TAX}_{\text{Relief}} = (\text{PTX})(R_C) \tag{4.5}$$

where $\text{TAX}_{\text{Relief}}$ is the amount of tax relief, R_C is the tax relief for an income class c, and PTX is the amount of property tax.

To illustrate, suppose that the government has set the threshold percentage at 20% for the income class of \$35,000–\$40,000 to which our family in the above example belongs. Therefore, the tax relief for the family under this approach will be \$455 [\$2275 × 0.2 = \$455]. In general, the percentage of relief decreases with rising income. Currently, two dozen or so states and the District of Columbia have some forms of circuit breakers with maximum allowable benefit that varies from state to state (Davis 2018). For instance, Maine currently has one of the highest benefits at around \$2000, while Oklahoma has one of the lowest at around \$200. Circuit breakers are simple, flexible, and easy to administer. Also, they do not impose any real burden on local governments since they are financed by the state.

To ensure that tax rates on property do not increase to a point where it will be financially too constraining for the property owners, some states have imposed limits on increase in assessed value to a fixed percentage such as less than 5%, although they allow the properties to be assessed at the full market value when they are sold. Another measure that has been found to be quite effective is the millage rate cap, especially for tax jurisdictions where millage rate is used. A mill is \$1 of tax for each \$1000 of assessed value of a property, or 0.001 (1/1000), called one part per thousand, or simply 0.1% [1/1000 = 0.001 × 100 = 0.1%]. Thus, a property with an assessed value of \$150,000 with a millage rate of 12.5% or 125 mills [125/1000 = 0.125 × 100 = 12.5%] will pay a tax of \$1875 [(\$150,000 × 12.5)/1000 = \$1875]. Imposing a limit on the growth in assessed value or putting a cap on the millage rate means that local governments cannot increase the rate or the assessed value of property at will without the approval of the state. Property taxes are also reduced for those who use itemize deductions on their federal income tax returns and to taxpayers who itemize on state taxes in majority of the states.

On occasion, a government may impose a tax freeze for a certain number of years to provide a temporary tax relief for property owners. Usually when that happens, there is a tradeoff with other taxes or options available to the government. For instance, a local government may decide to introduce a temporary income or sales tax in order to undertake a major capital improvement project, but in exchange it will put a freeze on property tax increase for the duration of the new tax. A government may also exempt properties from taxation or remove them from the tax-rolls, if the properties are likely to be used for economic development activities. This will lower the tax base in the short term, but once the development takes place it will generate new revenues for the government from increased economic activities which will more than compensate for the loss of revenue from the reduced tax base initially. The process is generally known as tax-increment financing and has been extensively used by local governments to promote economic growth and development.

Two other forms of exemptions that have become quite important in recent years, as the population distribution is getting more skewed toward the elderly, are veteran's exemption and exemption for old age. Veteran's exemption usually applies to disabled veterans over the age of 55 or their unmarried dependents under the age of 18. Like homestead exemption, it is a fixed amount deducted from the property value based on the percentage of disability, which can range anywhere from 10 to 100%. The higher the percentage of disability, the greater is the amount of deduction. Like the veteran's exemption, the old-age exemption is also a fixed amount deduction from the property value once the owners reach the age of 65, although the amount varies from state to state. The deduction applies primarily to school district tax, where the school districts grant a fixed amount of exemption for qualified owners over the age of 65.

To give an example, suppose that a property assessed at $100,000, subject to a tax rate of $3 per $100 of assessed value (3%), is entitled to the following exemptions: $15,000 in homestead, $7500 in veteran's exemption, $10,000 in old-age exemption (assuming the property owner will qualify for both), and a circuit breaker of $350. The tax liability for the owner will be $1675; that is, $[(\$100,000 \times 0.03) - ((\$15,000 + \$7500 + \$10,000) \times 0.03) - \$350] = [\$3000 - (\$32,500 \times 0.03) - \$350] = \$3000 - \$975 - \$350 = \$1675]$.

Levy and Collection

The last two steps of the property tax cycle are tax levy and collection. The property tax levy, also known as the tax bill, is determined by multiplying the taxable value of a property, after adjustments, by the tax rate. As noted earlier, determining this rate is an important component of the assessment process. Table 4.4 shows how the tax is calculated for a residential and a commercial property. As the table shows, for a residential property with an assessed value of $130,000, adjusted for $15,000 in homestead exemption, and a tax rate of 2.5% ($2.50 per $100 of taxable value), the tax will be $2875 $[(\$130,000 - \$15,000)(\$2.50/100) = (\$115,000 \times 0.025) = \$2875]$, while for the commercial property it will be $25,000 $[(\$1,400,000 - \$150,000)(\$2/100) = (\$1,250,000 \times 0.02) = \$25,000]$. We could have also obtained the same information by subtracting independently the amount of tax relief for homestead exemption from the assessed value; that is, $(\$130,000 \times 0.025) - (\$15,000 \times 0.025) = \$3250 - \$375 = \$2875$ and $(\$1400,000 \times 0.02) - (\$150,000 \times 0.020) = \$28,000 - \$3000 = \$25,000$.

Table 4.4 Property tax and effective rate calculation

Tax variable	Residential property ($)	Commercial property ($)
Market value (MV)	150,000	2500,000
Assessed value (AV)	130,000	1400,000
Exemptions	15,000	150,000
Taxable value (TV)	115,000	1250,000
Tax rate	2.5% ($2.50 per $100 of TV)	2% ($2 per $100 of TV)
Tax	2875	25,000
Effective tax rate	1.92% (2875/150,000)	1% (25,000/2500,000)

Applying the procedures we used for income tax, the average tax rate will be 2.5% [$2875/$115,000 = 0.025 × 100 = 2.5%] for the residential property and 2% [$25,000/$1,250,000 = 0.02 × 100% = 2%] for the commercial property. On the other hand, the effective tax rates would be much lower, as expected, at 1.92% [$2 875/$150,000 = 0.0192 × 100 = 1.92%] for the residential property and 1% [$25,0 00/$2,500,000 = 0.01 × 100 = 1%] for the commercial property. In practice, however, individual states may use their own procedures to determine the average and effective tax rates.

As with all adjustments, property tax adjustments are additive in that a property owner may be entitled to multiple adjustments or breaks which can lower his tax liability considerably, as we saw in an earlier example. Returning to the current example, suppose that our property owner is entitled to two additional tax breaks, in addition to a homestead exemption of $375—a circuit breaker in the amount of $350 and an income tax deduction of $275. His tax liability, including the homestead exemption will, therefore, be $2250 [$3250 − ($375+$350+$275) = $3250 − $1000 = $2250], which will lower the effective tax rate further to 1.5% [$2250/ $150,000 = 0.015 × 100) = 1.5%].

In the example above, we assumed a tax rate of 2.5% ($25/$1000) for the residential property. In reality, it is possible to determine the tax rate for a government if we know the projected expenditure and the amount of non-property revenue. The following expression can be used to show how this rate can be obtained:

$$PTXR = \left(EXP_{proj} - NPR_{proj}\right)/NAVP \qquad (4.6)$$

where PTXR is the property tax rate, EXP_{proj} is the projected expenditure, NPR_{proj} is the projected non-property revenue, and NAVP is the net assessed value of property (after adjustments).

To give an example, suppose that we have a government with an annual operating budget of $155 million. The government expects to collect $55 million in non-property revenue (user fees and charges, intergovernmental revenue, fines and forfeitures, etc.) and the remaining $100 million then must come from property taxes—residential, as well as commercial. Let us assume that of the $100 million, $75 million must come from residential properties and the remaining $25 million from commercial properties. Let us further assume that the net assessed

Table 4.5 Distribution of tax dollars between different jurisdictions

Jurisdiction	Mills (millage rate)	Percentage distribution (%)	Share of the tax ($)
School district	8.25 (0.00825)	0.4967 (49.67)	1291.42
County	3.57 (0.00357)	0.2149 (21.49)	558.74
City	2.41 (0.00241)	0.1451 (14.51)	377.26
Local library	1.25 (0.00125)	0.0753 (7.53)	195.78
Special district	0.75 (0.00075)	0.0451 (4.51)	117.26
Others	0.38 (0.00038)	0.0229 (2.29)	59.54
Total	16.61 (0.01661)	1.0000 (100.00)	$2600.00

value of residential property for the government has been projected to be $3750 million. Now, applying the expression in Eq. 4.6 will produce a tax rate of 0.02 or 2%; that is, [(($155 million $-$($55 million$+$$25 million))/ $3750 million$=$$75 million/$3750 million$=0.02$]. Thus, a property worth $130,000 will have a tax bill of $2600 [($130,000 $\times$ 0.02)$=$$2600].

Interestingly, the entire tax amount of $2600 will not go to the government itself; it will be distributed between different jurisdictions of the government (county, school district, city library, various special districts, and so on), based on the millage rate or any other measure used for each jurisdiction. Table 4.5 shows how the amount is distributed between different jurisdictions of the government. As the table shows, the largest share will go to the school district, followed by the county government, the city, local library, and special districts in that order, although the order may change depending on the condition of the economy or the priority of the government, but, by and large, the lion share goes to the school district.

Finally, the collection rate for property tax, as noted earlier, is quite high for most governments averaging between 90 to 95% for residential property, with some as high as 99% depending on the location of the property. For commercial property, it can vary considerably depending on the type of activity, location, general condition of the economy, and so forth. The assessment rates are also different for commercial properties, depending on the type of business activity, location, etc. Part of the reason why property tax has a much higher collection rate than most other taxes is because property is immobile and, as noted earlier, the close proximity of the taxpayers to the government makes it difficult to avoid the tax.

A Note on Rollback Rate

A term that frequently appears alongside property tax rate, especially during the budget time, is the rollback rate. A rollback rate is the rate that would produce the same amount of property tax revenue as the previous year, after adjusting for new constructions, additions, deletions, and improvements, and is usually determined by the state without voter approval. Thus, if it would require a government a 5% increase in tax rate to maintain the same level of expenditure for operation and maintenance, as last year, the rate will be 1.05. The rollback rates are typically used by a jurisdiction as a means to limiting the overall growth of a property class within the jurisdiction. Operationally, the rate divides property taxes into two categories—the portion that goes toward the operation and maintenance of the government, and the portion that goes toward debt service (principal and interest), usually on General Obligation debt since it is financed out of the credit and taxing authority of a government. It is obtained by dividing the taxes, after adjustments, for a given year by the corresponding tax base (the total value of taxable property) and is usually given by $100 of property value.

To give an example, suppose that we have the following information on property taxes for a government last year: Operating taxes of $1,250,000, with a tax base of $1,125,000,000, producing an effective tax rate of $0.001111 per $1 [$1,250,000/$1,125,000,000 = $0.001111] or $0.1111 per $100 [$0.001111 × $100 = $0.1111] of property value. From this, we can obtain the effective tax rate for this year by dividing the operating taxes for last year, adjusted (subtracted) for lost taxes by the tax base for this year as well as adjusted (subtracted) for new property values, which, let us say, are $1,200,000 (after all the adjustments) and $1,250,000,000, respectively. This will produce an effective rate of $0.00096 per $1 [1,200,000/$1,250,000,000 = $0.00096] or $0.096 per $100 [$0.00096 × $100 = $0.096] of property value. Assume now that the maximum operating rate for this year is 5% above the rate needed to maintain the same level of operating expenditure, as last year (determined by the state). The effective rollback rate for this year will, therefore, be $0.001008 per $1 [$0.00096 × 1.05 = $0.001008], or $0.1008 per $100 [$0.001008 × $100 = $0.1008] of property value.

Interestingly, for most governments, if the adopted rate is above the rollback rate, the voters can sign a petition to reduce it to the rollback rate. Conversely, if the rollback rate is below the adopted rate it can be raised to equal the adopted rate, in which case it is called the rollup rate. In general, debt service rate is not considered important for rollback rate; it is the portion that goes toward operation and maintenance that is considered more important, although both are often used to determine the overall rate.

4.1.3.2 Some Common Concerns with Property Tax

Like most taxes, property taxes have a number of concerns that are unique to the tax vis-à-vis the property owners who are affected by it. Important among these concerns are the fear of frequent appraisal, fear of rising taxes, inequality in assessment, and tax incidence (Lynch 1995). Let us briefly go over the concerns.

Fear of Frequent Appraisals
Theoretically, a property can be appraised multiple times during a year or within a span of two to three years if there are sudden changes in the market value or if it can be justified for structural improvements and other changes in the physical

characteristics of the property. Appraisals frequently lead to an increase in property tax—a prospect that most property owners do not like, although there are circumstances when it may actually lower taxes, especially during times of economic crisis or when the real estate market experiences a downward spiral. Both of these concerns are genuine and can lead to taxpayer's revolt, if not addressed properly, as it happened in California in the mid-1970s.[7] To avoid the problem, some states have introduced strict appropriation limits. A good example is California's Gann Limit, introduced by Governor Paul Gann, under Proposition 4, and adopted by the state on November 6, 1979. The act imposed broader restrictions on state and local spending by limiting the growth in spending to the rate of growth in cost of living and the rate of growth in state or local population—the latter for property tax.[8]

The following provides a simple expression for calculating the limit:

$$CYL = LYL \times (PR \times PCCLR) \tag{4.7}$$

where CYL is the current year limit, LYL is the last year's limit, PR is the population ratio, and PCCLR is the per capita cost of living ratio. The following expressions are typically used for PR and PCCLR: $PR = ((PGP + 100)/100)$ and $PCCLR = ((PGI + 100)/100)$, where PGP is the projected growth in population and PGI is the projected growth in inflation, assuming the personal income will increase by the rate of inflation. The product of PR and PCCYL produces the adjusted factor which, when multiplied by the last year's limit, will produce the current year limit, CYL.

To give an example, suppose that we have the following information for a local government in the state: LYL = $150 million, PGP = 2.5%, and PGI = 3.5%. Thus, applying the expression in Eq. 4.7 will produce the current year limit of $1,500,090,000, as shown below:

$$
\begin{aligned}
CYL &= LYL \times (PR \times PCCLR) \\
&= LYL \times [((PGP + 100)/100) \times ((PGI + 100)/100)] \\
&= \$150{,}000{,}000 \times [((0.025 + 100)/100) \times ((0.035 + 100)/100)] \\
&= \$150{,}000{,}000 \times (1.00025 \times 1.00035) \\
&= \$150{,}000{,}000 \times 1.0006 \\
&= \$150{,}090{,}000
\end{aligned}
$$

which is $90,000 ($150,090,000 − $150,000,000), or roughly 0.06% [($90,000/$150,000,000) × 100 = 0.0006 × 100 = 0.06%] above last year's limit. In other words, it is the available capacity for the government as a percentage of appropriation limit.

Inequality in Tax Assessment

The inequality in tax assessment which has a direct bearing on appraisal is often suggested as a major weakness in the current property tax structure. Although there have been significant improvements in assessment practices in recent years, the process often lacks uniformity which raises questions about the validity of the assessment process. From an empirical point of view, the real issue is how to measure this inequality. There are no cut-and-dried measures that one can use for this purpose, but simple statistical measures such as coefficient of dispersion (CD) have been found to be quite useful. The CD is based on the variation in assessment ratios (assessed value divided by the market value of property) for different properties within the same jurisdiction.

The following expression shows how to calculate the coefficient of dispersion:

$$
\begin{aligned}
\text{CD} &= \frac{|\text{MAD}|}{\text{MAR}} = \frac{\left(\sum_{i=1}^{n} |\text{AR}_i - \text{MAR}|\right)/n}{\text{MAR}} \\
&= \frac{(|\text{AR}_1 - \text{MAR}| + |\text{AR}_2 - \text{MAR}| + \cdots + |\text{AR}_n - \text{MAR}|)/n}{\text{MAR}}
\end{aligned} \tag{4.8}
$$

where AR is the assessment ratio, MAR is the mean (median) assessment ratio, MAD is the mean absolute deviation of assessment ratios, and n is the number of observations (properties).

To give an example, suppose that we have data on property values for five residential properties—A, B, C, D, and E. Table 4.6 presents the data for the five properties along with their assessed and market values. According to the table, Property C is assessed at 64% of its market value, which is the assessment ratio, obtained by dividing the assessed value of property by the market value; that is, $\$48{,}000/\$75000 = 0.64$. Properties A and B are overassessed by 6 and 3%, respectively, when compared against the mean (median) ratio of 64% for Property C, while Properties D and E are underassessed by 4 and 7%, respectively.

We can now apply the expression in Eq. 4.8 to obtain the coefficient of dispersion to determine the degree of inequality in assessment, as follows:

$$
\begin{aligned}
\text{CD} &= \frac{(|\text{AR}_1 - \text{MAR}| + |\text{AR}_2 - \text{MAR}| + \cdots + |\text{AR}_n - \text{MAR}|)/n}{\text{MAR}} \\
&= \frac{(|0.70 - 0.64| + |0.67 - 0.64| + |0.64 - 0.64| + |0.60 - 0.64| + |0.57 - 0.64|)/5}{0.64} \\
&= \frac{|0.06 + 0.03 + 0.00 + 0.04 + 0.07|/5}{0.64} \\
&= 0.04/0.64 \\
&= 0.0625
\end{aligned}
$$

or 6.25%.

The coefficient of dispersion in the above example appears to be low. Theoretically, there is no cutoff point as to where the percentage should be, but the rule of thumb is that it should be as low as possible. In general, the lower the CD, the better is the assessment. A conservative estimate would put it at about 10%; that is, as long as it is 10% or less, the quality of assessment should be considered good, indicating a reasonably uniform assessment of properties, although it is not unusual to use 15 or 20% as acceptable (depending on the location of the properties). Since inequality in assessment remains a serious concern, most states have organizations such as Tax Equalization Board that periodically assesses the level of inequality and makes the necessary adjustments by making sure that the percentage does not exceed a specified margin, as noted previously.

Table 4.6 Coefficient of dispersion for the sample properties

Assessment characteristics	Property A ($)	Property B ($)	Property C ($)	Property D ($)	Property E ($)
Market value	50,000	60,000	75,000	90,000	100,000
Assessed value	35,000	40,000	48,000	54,000	57,000
Assessment ratio[1]	0.70	0.67	0.64	0.60	0.57
Absolute deviation	0.06	0.03	0	0.04	0.07

Mean assessment ratio[2]: $\Sigma AR/n = (0.70+0.67+0.64+0.60+0.57)/5 = 3.18/5 = 0.64$

Mean absolute deviation (MAD) $= \Sigma \left| \text{absolute deviations} \right|/n$

$$= \left| 0.06+0.03+0.00+0.04+0.07 \right|/5$$

$$= 0.04$$

Coefficient of dispersion (CD) $=$ MAD/mean or median assessment ratio

$$= 0.04/0.64 = 0.0625 \ (6.25\%)$$

[1]Assessment ratio = assessed value/market value = $35,000/$50,000 − 0.70
[2]Both mean and median come out to be 0.64 in this example. While both measures could be used, median is preferred if the data are skewed or unevenly distributed

Alternatively, we could use a measure that is often used to determine the regressivity associated with assessments, known as bias in assessment (BIA) and is given by the expression

$$\text{BIA} = \frac{\sum\limits_{i-1}^{n} AR_i/n}{\left(\sum\limits_{i-1}^{n} AV_i / \sum\limits_{i-1}^{n} MV_i \right)} \tag{4.9}$$

where BIA is the bias in assessment, AR is the assessment ratio, AV is the assessed value of property, MV is the market value of property, and n is the number of observations (properties), (for $i = 1, 2,\ldots, n$). The numerator represents the mean assessment ratio and the denominator the ratio of total assessed value to total market value.

In general, BIA ranges between 0 and 1; that is, $0 \leq \text{BIA} \leq 1$. If it is equal to 1, it indicates no assessment bias and if it is equal to 0, the converse is true. Thus, applying the expression to the example in Table 4.6, we obtain a BIA coefficient of 1.0256 [0.64/($234,000/$375,000) = 0.64/0.624 = 1.0256] indicating an absence of bias. The result appears to be consistent with the coefficient of dispersion, obtained earlier.

Regressivity of Property Tax

Another frequent concern with property tax is that it is regressive. In a classic empirical study, Dick Netzer (1966) found that property tax on balance is more regressive, especially when compared against money income. For instance, if an individual pays a significantly higher percentage of his income in property tax relative to another individual, it is considered regressive. The underlying logic behind regressivity is that property tax is similar to tax one pays on consumer goods; as such, it makes a real difference as to how much one pays in taxes in relation to his income. However, the argument may not hold if property tax is treated as a tax on capital rather than on consumer goods, if we assume that it is both an investment and a consumer good. Thus, when viewed as a tax on capital, the tax burden can be treated the same way as a tax on profit, wage, or land rent, in addition to consumption, which makes the incidence argument somewhat less contentious (Aaron 1975).

Put differently, if property tax can be viewed as a national tax on capital ownership, which must be borne by the owners in proportion to their ownership of capital and the fact that capital is disproportionately owned by individuals with different incomes, the burden of tax will also be disproportionately high on individuals with higher incomes. In other words, the more expensive the property the higher is the tax. Therefore, according to Aaron, the incidence of property tax would be progressive, not regressive. Also, questions have been raised in recent years if property ownership can be treated as an investment if the market rate remains constant, or declines, especially during prolonged recessions, or when a residential community experiences gradual economic decline or blight from out-migration of business and labor, with mixed results.

A Note on Property Tax Multiplier

Another term that frequently appears alongside property tax is property tax multiplier. The term is often used to determine the rate at which the assessment rates will be uniform across a jurisdiction called equalization factor. Since different types of properties are assessed at different rates, the equalization factor brings about a sense of equity in the rate structure. The responsibility for adjusting the rate usually falls on individual state's equalization board which does so by comparing the actual selling price of individual properties for several years, usually three to five, to their assessed value, and adjusting the rate accordingly. Typically, it is obtained by dividing the statuary percentage (determined by the state) by three or five-year average (median) assessment for different classes of property (e.g., residential, commercial, industrial, vacant land, and so forth). For instance, if the statutory rate is 20% and the five-year average is 16%, the multiplier will be 1.25 [(20/16) = 1.25]. In general, a multiplier of 1 is considered neutral, meaning that it does not increase or decrease assessments; if it is greater than 1, it increases assessments and if it is less than 1, it decreases assessments.

It is worth noting that equalization serves an important purpose for a taxing district in that it ensures that the district has the sufficient capacity to raise revenues. For instance, if the average assessment for a county government is less than the statutory percent, it is likely to receive more in state aid relative to other counties to make up for less revenue; conversely, it will receive less if the average assessment is higher than the statutory percent.

4.2   Other Sources of Revenue

As noted earlier, each level of government relies heavily on a specific tax to support its activities—the federal government predominantly on income tax, the state governments on sales tax, and the local governments on property tax. Over time, the revenues generated from these sources have not kept up with the growing needs of the government. Consequently, all three levels of government have come to rely on a variety of other sources to supplement their income. The federal government relies on excise tax, estate and gift tax, borrowing (which, ideally, should not be considered a source since it has to be paid back with interest), and other sources to supplement its revenue from income tax. By the same token, state governments rely on income tax, user fees and charges, fines and forfeitures, franchise tax, intergovernmental revenues and, in some cases, lottery to raise the needed revenue. Over three-fifths of the states currently have an income tax and a large number of states have introduced lottery in recent years to fill the revenue gap. Similarly, most local governments use a variety of sources such as sales tax, user fees and charges, fines and forfeitures, franchise tax, and intergovernmental revenue to supplement their own revenue from property tax.

In general, state and local governments tend to rely more on non-tax revenue when there is a general decline in the economy or when there is a strong public resentment against raising taxes. In recent years, this reliance has increased considerably to the extent that user fees and charges, as well as intergovernmental revenue now account for a significant portion of the overall revenue of most state and local governments. According to one estimate, approximately 20% of all state and around 30% of all local revenues come from intergovernmental transfers (Holcombe 2006). The dependence is likely to be even greater during times of economic crisis, especially on intergovernmental revenue.

Let us briefly look at some of these alternative sources that have become important in the overall revenue structure of state and local governments.

4.2.1   User Fees and Charges

User fees and charges, expressed commonly as user charges, constitute a significant portion of government revenue, especially at the local level. User charges are a form of price individuals pay for the consumption of those goods and services that are provided in a business-like manner, defined earlier as proprietary goods such as water, sewer, electricity, toll roads, and so forth. There are several advantages of using user charges: One, they are directly related to the amount of goods and services individuals consume which makes it possible to exclude those who do not or are not willing to pay for their consumption. Two, since the consumption can be directly traced to individuals consuming the goods it makes it easier for a government to estimate the demand for these goods, as opposed to traditional public goods such as roads, bridges, and highways. Three, since there are no easy substitutes for many of these goods, one would expect the price to be rigid but, in reality, consumers can control the levels of their consumption and, therefore, the price they will pay. As such, the fees and charges individuals pay can be treated as a benefit tax in that it is directly related to the amount of benefit they receive from their consumption and the cost that underlies their provision. Finally, it is relatively easy to apply the marginal rule when it comes to user fees and charges because the individual decision to consume depends on the benefits they derive from each additional unit of consumption. However, applying the marginal rule can lead to underconsumption, especially for those who cannot afford the full price of the service.[9]

To give an example how user charges are calculated, let us look at the water fees charged by a government. The fees usually have three separate components priced differently: a connection charge, a capital and distribution charge, and a supply charge. The connection charge is a one-time cost, the capital and distribution charge is usually a fixed charge based on the meter size, and the supply charge is variable in that it varies in proportion to the quantity consumed. In general, the supply charge is determined to cover the marginal cost of consuming additional units of the service such as gallons of water and, as such, depends on the quantity consumed. If we assume the cost of providing an additional gallon of water to be constant, since there is no additional cost involved once the line has been connected, we can calculate this fee using a simple expression

$$UF_{water} = FC + VC(Q) \tag{4.10}$$

where UF_{water} is the user fee for water department, FC is the fixed cost, VC is the per unit variable cost, and Q is the quantity produced or consumed. To give an example, suppose that a household consumes 5000 gallons of water on average a month and the price per gallon of water is 0.045 cents a gallon (variable cost) with a fixed cost of $15. Therefore, the total cost of water for the household will be $17.25 [$15 + $0.00045(5000) = $15 + $2.25 = $17.25]. To this, we can add a one-time connection charge, say, of $150, which will be added to the initial cost but not the subsequent costs of supply.

User charges are usually set at a level where they are below the average cost of provision to make it easy for the public to consume the goods and services a government provides. The difference is frequently bridged by providing subsidies to consumers that is financed by taxes (Hyman 2014). However, the amount of subsidy individuals receive varies depending on the nature of the good and according to the income levels of the consumers. In fact, for most public goods and services for which user charges are used include subsidies of one form or another. Interestingly, subsidies are not necessarily restricted to public goods; they can also be provided to firms and businesses to offset production costs, in which case they are called production subsidy. Other examples of subsidy for non-governmental activities would be employment subsidy to encourage employment, export subsidy to promote export, environmental subsidy to deal with externality problems, and so forth.

4.2.2   Intergovernmental Revenue

Intergovernmental revenues are transfers from a higher level government to one or more lower-level governments such as from the federal government to state and local governments, and from a state government to various local governments. Most of the transfers take place in the form of grants and subsidies, commonly known as grants-in-aid. There are several reasons why these grants are necessary other than the need to supplement the revenue gaps of these governments.

First of all, intergovernmental revenues are necessary to correct for fiscal imbalances that often result from the differences in the taxing powers of the sub-national governments. For instance, state governments have greater authority, as well as flexibility to impose sales tax than do local governments. The absence of relative flexibility makes it difficult for local governments to use sales tax to the same degree the state governments do to raise the needed revenue. In the absence of intergovernmental transfers, many of these governments will simply not have the means to take new initiatives or fully meet their existing needs. Secondly, intergovernmental revenues are necessary to correct for inter-jurisdictional externalities these governments may produce in the course of providing goods and services such as constructing a sewer treatment plant close to a bordering community that may create health problems for the neighboring population. Without external financial support, the government producing externalities will not have the incentive to correct the problem, while the affected parties would bear the cost.

Thirdly, intergovernmental revenues are necessary to correct for macroeconomic problems such as recession or poor economic growth that has a direct bearing on the economic well being of the state and local governments. Although these problems are considered national in dimension, their manifestations take place at the subnational level and without external support many of these governments will not be able to address them. Fourthly, intergovernmental revenues are necessary to correct for inequities in service provision that result from qualitative differences in the goods and services the subnational governments provide for their residents such as education, health care, transportation, and so on. Without external support, the differences will not only affect the welfare of the residents of these jurisdictions, but also affect the aggregate welfare of society. Fifth, and lastly, perhaps the greatest benefit of intergovernmental revenues is that they can free-up resources of the recipient governments that they can spend on programs and activities as they see fit without any external constraints.

The grants and subsidies an upper-level government provides for lower-level governments typically fall into two major categories: general and categorical. General grants are provided for general purpose without any specific requirements or conditions which gives the recipient governments considerable latitude to use the funds as they see fit. On the other hand, categorical grants are provided for a specific purpose to achieve a specific goal or objective which takes away some of the latitudes of the general grants but, on the positive side, they minimize the chances of competition with other governments for the funds.

In both cases, the grants are often formula based which determines the amount the recipient governments can receive, depending on quantifiable factors such as population, income, housing density, and so forth, unless they are provided for a specific purpose or activity. In the latter case, they may require the recipient governments to match a certain percentage of the total cost of the activity. Grants of these kinds are commonly known as matching grants. Interestingly, contrary to conventional wisdom, the matching amount is usually higher than the matching percentage. For instance, if the matching requirement for a recipient government for a federal grant is 20% and the federal share is 80%, then for a grant of $100,000, the recipient's share will not be $20,000, as common sense would suggest, but rather it will be $25,000. This is because the grantors typically use an allocation formula based on a ratio of grant amount divided by the share of the grantor times the recipient's share; that is, $(\$100,000/0.8) \times 0.2 = \$125,000 \times 0.2 = \$25,000$. For non-matching grants, which are provided in lump-sum, no such conditions or requirements are necessary.

There has been a significant decline in general grants in recent years, as majority of the grants the federal government currently provides are categorical grants. A classic example of general grant that received considerable attention in the seventies because of its flexibility is the General Revenue Sharing grant the federal government introduced in 1972. It was phased out in the early 1980s, as the government was experiencing severe financial crisis and began to slowly shift some of the cost burden to the subnational governments under what was termed as "new federalism." However, a special case of categorical grant that enjoys considerable support among the recipient governments today is the Community Development Block Grant (CDBG). The grant is primarily used to fund a broad range of community development activities but may also be used to match the tax dollars or expenditures of the recipient government. When categorical grants are consolidated to provide assistance for a broad range activities, they are called block or broad-based grants. Since these grants come with less restrictions and government control, they are relatively easy to administer.

On average, about a fourth of state and a third of local revenue presently come from intergovernmental transfers. The percentage tends to increase during times of economic hardships. In fact, there is an inverse relationship between the general economic condition of a recipient government and the amount of intergovernmental revenue it receives. The degree to which a government relies on external support is often measured by a ratio called the dependency ratio, expressed as the amount of grants as a percentage of own revenue, as shown below:

$$DR = (IGR/GR) \tag{4.11}$$

where DR is the dependency ratio, IGR is the intergovernmental revenue, and GR is the general revenue of a government. Thus, a government receiving $3.5 million in grants-in-aid from upper-level governments out of total general revenue of $10 million will have a dependency ratio of 0.35 or 35%, meaning that only 65% of the total revenue comes from its own sources.

$$[(1 - (\$3.5\,\text{million}/\$10.0\,\text{million} \times 100)) = (1 - 0.35) \times 100 = 0.65 \times 100 = 65\%]$$

Historically, the federal contribution to local revenue has been considerably low compared to state contribution, constituting less than 10% of the total revenue for the most part but it has other ways to compensate for the difference. This may include establishing federal tax exemptions that can lower municipal borrowing costs or it may include tax exemptions the federal government can provide for local property, sales, and income taxes. The latter, in particular tends to encourage homeownership and consumption of goods and services; thereby, increasing local revenue from property, sales, and income taxes.

Although intergovernmental revenues bridge a major gap in the overall financial needs of the subnational governments, it is difficult to generalize the full effect of these grants because of the differences in the way in which the recipient governments respond to the grants. There is a general sense that unconditional grants tend to have more support among the recipient governments because of the flexibility they provide the recipient governments to use them as they see fit. On the other hand, a categorical matching grant will not produce the same amount of support, even though the funds are needed to increase local expenditures because of the conditions associated with them. The response to an external grant by a subnational government is often measured by elasticity (defined as how a recipient government responds to a grant an upper-level government provides under varying conditions). For most unconditional grants the response is generally considered elastic, while for conditional grants it is mostly inelastic.

4.2.3   Franchise Tax

Franchise taxes, also known as franchise fees, are levied against firms and partnerships that operate within a state. They are considered a privilege tax because of the rights given to them to operate in the state. The amount of levy varies from state to state, depending on the tax rules of the jurisdiction. Some states may use the capital stock of the firms, while others may use their net worth to determine the amount of tax. In general, the states with a high corporate income tax have a low franchise tax, and vice versa. For instance, Texas has one of the highest franchise taxes in the country, but no corporate income tax. As with any tax, a high franchise tax can work as a disincentive and may, in some cases, drive the businesses away to jurisdictions with low or no taxes. At the local level, these taxes constitute a small fraction of the total revenue but, nonetheless, they have become important in recent years.

4.2.4   Payment-in-Lieu-of-Taxes

Federal and state governments have a long-standing tradition of granting exemptions from taxes, in particular property taxes for organizations that provide valuable services to a community or geographic area. Tax exemptions given to hospitals, colleges, and universities, and various non-profit organizations are good examples but, unfortunately, these exemptions cost governments considerable sums in lost revenue in property taxes. For instance, the federal government owns a significant portion of land in Alaska, Utah, Wyoming, and other states, which in some cases can constitute over a third of the total land of the states. Since federal properties are tax exempt, the states have been losing a substantial income in lost revenue from property taxes yet these properties often generate revenues for the federal government. In 1976, Congress authorized the federal land management agencies to share federal income with state and local governments by providing payment-in-lieu-taxes (PIOLT) to help offset their lost revenues in taxes. Similarly, a number of states have initiated these programs where they reimburse the local governments for not taxing the land owned by public institutions. Today, over a third of the states have PILOT programs of one kind or another. Although these programs do not offer a blanket solution to their revenue problems, they can provide considerable financial relief, especially for governments that are desperately in need of new sources of revenue.

4.2.5 Interfund Transfers

In recent years, governments, in particular local governments have come to rely heavily on another source of revenue, called interfund transfer, as a means to supplement the revenue shortfall in a particular fund. Usually, the transfers take place from a fund that has been accumulating surpluses or where the funds would not be needed immediately, so that they can be used more effectively by other funds to make up for shortages without having to reduce or disrupt service provisions, or raise taxes, or service fees. Theoretically, interfund transfers should not be considered as new sources of revenue because they are essentially transfers from one fund to another and, as such, there is no change in the aggregate revenue situation of the government.

In addition to the above, governments have also been using a variety of other means to generate the needed revenue such as borrowing, reducing contribution to pension funds, and revenue from sale of government assets. Although there is a tendency to treat these sources as revenues, ideally they should not be because, as payments to governments, they are not made in exchange for goods and services.

4.3   Revenue Capacity

In spite of extensive reliance on other sources of revenue in recent years, taxes remain the mainstay of a government's revenue base, but governments do not have unlimited ability to raise revenue from taxes. They are often constrained by economic, legal, and political realities that restrict their ability to raise revenue from a given tax base. Theoretically, all tax bases have an upper limit that can produce the maximum amount of revenue for a government, which is its revenue capacity. This capacity, less the actual revenue raised, is a government's revenue reserve. In general, the larger the reserve the greater is the ability of a government to generate the needed revenue from that base. For instance, if a government collects $10.5 in property tax revenue and has a capacity of $11.7 million, then its revenue reserve is $1.2 million. While changes in income levels and other measures used by a government ultimately influence its capacity to raise revenue, it is the revenue capacity that forms the reality with which the government must deal to address its revenue needs.

There is no hard and fast rule for determining revenue capacity, but the convention is to compare the general revenue situation of a government against a comparable government or a reference group of similar governments. The rationale for using a reference group for measuring revenue capacity is that it provides a fairly reliable basis for assessing where a government stands, given its revenue potential, relative to other governments of similar size or characteristics. In this sense, the notion of "capacity" takes on an average or representative character, but, nonetheless, provides a standard for comparison with the actual data (Berne and Shramm 1986).

Consider a case where a government wants to determine its revenue capacity before making a decision on how much revenue it can raise from a particular source. Table 4.7 shows the per capita revenue for various sources of the government against the average for a reference group of comparable governments. Per capita revenue is a standard measure used for comparison purposes since it adjusts for the differences in population size. According to the table, it appears that per capita revenue for the government is considerably low for most of its revenue sources (property tax, franchise tax, charges for services, intergovernmental transfer, and miscellaneous revenues) compared to the average for the reference group. This means that there is room for additional increase in revenue from these sources, with the possible exception of intergovernmental revenue since the government does not have any control over it. In the same vein, the government does not appear to have much room for increase in revenue from sales tax, licenses and

Table 4.7 Per capita tax and non-tax revenue: reference-group comparison

Sources of revenue	Reference group ($)	Government in question ($)	Revenue reserve ($)
Property tax	211.36	165.35	+46.01
Sales tax	142.44	143.57	−1.13
Franchise tax	74.35	14.63	+59.72
Charges for services	47.84	18.24	+29.6
Fines and forfeitures	15.30	28.76	−13.46
Licenses and permits	13.21	12.42	+0.79
Intergovernmental revenue	125.34	59.80	+65.54
Miscellaneous	24.36	7.29	+17.07

permits, and fines and forfeitures since they are either close to or above the average for the reference group.

Besides using visual comparison of data, one can also use statistical measures such as multiple regression analysis to determine the revenue capacity of a government (Akin 1973). The advantage of using statistical analysis such as multiple regression analysis is that the results can be easily tested for reliability of the observed estimates. The procedure is not complicated if sufficient data are available: Simply identify the variables appropriate for analysis, develop a multiple regression model, collect data for each variable in the model for the reference group, estimate the regression coefficients (intercept and slopes), and determine the capacity.

To give an example, suppose that we want to estimate the per capita revenue capacity of a government (dependent variable). Assume that the government has collected per capita revenue data for 50 local governments of comparable size and characteristics on five (independent) variables: intergovernmental revenue (IGR), sales tax revenue (STR), real property tax revenue (PTR_R), commercial property tax revenue (PTR_C), and industrial property tax revenue (PTR_I). Assume further that the government has run a regression model using the five independent variables and obtained the following result:

$$R_{PC} = \alpha + \beta_1 PCIGR + \beta_2 PCSTR + \beta_3 PCPTR_R$$
$$+ \beta_4 PCPTR_C + \beta_5 PCPTR_I + e \tag{4.12}$$

$$\widehat{R}_{PC} = -15.25 + 0.217 PCIGR + 0.174 PCSTR + 0.325 PCPTR_R$$
$$+ 0.251 PCPTR_C + 0.225 PCPTR_I$$

where R_{PC} is the per capita revenue, PCIGR is the per capita intergovernmental revenue, PCSTR is the per capita sales tax revenue, $PCPTR_R$ is the real per capita property tax revenue, $PCPTR_C$ is the per capita commercial property tax revenue, and PC per capita industrial property tax revenue.

We can apply the estimated model to the actual values for each of the five variables to obtain the per capita revenue. Let us say that we have the following information on the five revenue variables for our government: \$725 in PCIGR, \$635 in PCSTR, \$125 in $PCPTR_R$, \$350 in $PCPTR_C$, and \$475 in $PCPTR_I$. Now, plugging these values to the estimated equation will produce the per capita revenue for our government, as shown below:

$$\widehat{R}_{PC} = - \$15.25 + 0.217(\$725) + 0.174(\$635) + 0.325(\$125)$$
$$+ 0.251(\$350) + 0.225(\$475) = -\$15.25 + \$157.325 + \$110.490$$
$$+ \$40.625 + \$87.850 + \$106.875 = \$487.915 \text{ or } \$487.92.$$

Let us assume that the estimated coefficients and the equation as a whole are statistically significant. What this means is that if our government had collected revenue at the same rate as the average of the governments in our sample, it would have a per capita revenue of $487.915 instead of its current per capita revenue. In other words, this would be the revenue capacity of the government so far as per capita revenue is concerned. Let us say that the government currently has a per capita revenue of $450. Since the per capita revenue based on the estimated model is greater than the current per capita revenue, the government has the potential to raise additional revenue from these variables, especially the ones that are below the average in our example.

In the event that it is difficult to find a comparable group, an alternative would be to take the maximum allowable tax rate for a given base at any given time and multiply it by the value of the base from which the revenue would be collected. For instance, if the sales tax of a government has an upper limit of 10% under the current law and the value of the tax base is $150 million, then its revenue capacity (the maximum amount that can be generated) from sales tax would be $15 million ($150,000,000 × 0.10). If the government currently collects $12 million in sales tax revenues, it has a reserve of $3 million, assuming everything else remaining the same. The process can be repeated for any number of sources and then added to obtain the total revenue capacity for the government.

The following shows the expression for revenue capacity:

$$RC_t = \sum_{i=1}^{n} B_i r_i^u = B_1 r_1^u + B_2 r_2^u + \cdots + B_n r_n^u \tag{4.13}$$

where RC is the revenue capacity, B_i is the tax base for the ith source, and r_i^u is the upper limit, u, of tax rate for the ith revenue source (for $i = 1, 2, \ldots, n$).

To give an example, suppose that we have the following rate information for our government on property tax, local option sales tax (LOST), and franchise tax: 4.25 mills for property ($4.25 for every $1000 of taxable value of property or $4.25/$1000), 0.01% for sales, and 0.02% for franchise tax. Assume that the corresponding tax base for each of the sources, respectively, are $8250 million for assessed value of property, $2357 million for sales tax, and $785 million for franchise tax. Therefore, the revenue capacity for the government will be

$$RC_t = \left[(\$8,250,000,000) \times (\$4.25/\$1000) \right] + (\$2,357,000,000 \times 0.01)$$
$$+ (\$785,000,000 \times 0.02) = \$35,062,500 + \$23,570,000 + \$15,700,000$$
$$= \$74,332,500$$

or $74.3325 million, which is the maximum amount of revenue it can generate from the three sources.

Suppose now that the total revenue from these sources currently stands at $55.3 million, with $24.6 million from property taxes, $18.3 million from sales tax, and $12.4 million from franchise tax. Thus, subtracting the current revenue from the revenue capacity will produce a revenue reserve of $19,032,500 ($74,332,500 − $55,300,000) for the government. However, it should be pointed out that our example includes only three revenue sources; ideally, it should include all possible sources to provide a full assessment of revenue reserve.

4.4   Summary and Conclusion

Understanding the revenue base of a government, in particular the sources from which it collects its revenues and their structure is important to understand the budget behavior of a government. This chapter has provided a general discussion of the principal sources from which a government collects its revenues such as income tax for the federal government, sales tax for state governments, and property tax for local governments, as well as the manner of collection and some common concerns with these revenues. The chapter has also provided a brief overview of various other sources, such as user fees and charges, fines and forfeitures, franchise tax, intergovernmental revenue, and payment-in-lieu-if-taxes, from which a government collects revenues to supplement its income from the principal sources. Of these, user fees and charges and intergovernmental revenue have become increasingly important in recent years as revenues from the traditional sources continue to decline as a percentage of total revenue. However, in spite of the growing importance of user fees and charges, intergovernmental revenue and other sources, taxes remain the primary sources of revenue for all three levels of government. Interestingly, governments do not collect revenues from taxes to their fullest capacity level. Political, economic, and other constrains make it difficult to raise tax revenues to their fullest capacity. As a result, most governments collect revenues that are less than their fullest capacity, producing a difference between revenue capacity and the actual revenue called revenue reserve. In general, the higher the reserve, the greater is the potential to raise revenue from a given base. The chapter concluded with a brief discussion of revenue capacity.

Review Questions

Q1.   What are the primary sources of revenue for federal, state, and local governments? Why is it necessary to supplement the tax revenues of a government? What are some of the measures commonly used to supplement the tax revenues of the governments?

Q2.   How is income defined under the current tax structure? When was the income tax, personal as well as corporate income, introduced in the country? What is the marginal tax rate? Why do the marginal rates change over time? Discuss the marginal tax rates currently used by the federal government for both personal and corporate income.

Q3.   What is built-in provision in a tax structure and why is it necessary? What are the built-in provisions in the current income-tax structure? Why do the elements of the provisions change?

Q4.   What is a graduated income tax? Why is a graduated tax system necessary? Why do the brackets in a graduated system do not remain constant?

Discuss the changes in the brackets in the two most recent income-tax structures.

Q5. Suppose that a married couple, filing jointly, with two dependent children, have a gross income of $112,000 for the year, plus $1500 in interest earnings on non-taxable government bonds. They are entitled to $3500 in exclusions, $13,500 in other itemized deductions, and $4500 in exemptions. Assume that we have the following tax rates and the corresponding income (tax) brackets: 10% ($0–$17,850), 15% ($17,851–$72,500), 25% ($72,501–$146,400), 28% ($146,401–$223,050), 33% ($223,051–$398,350), 35% ($398,351–$450,000), and 39.5% ($450,001 and above). Based on the information presented above, do the following: Calculate (a) their taxable income, (b) the tax liability (c) average tax rate, and (d) effective tax rate. [Hint: Use the most recent tax schedule from IRS, which can be easily downloaded from IRS Web site.]

Q6. Suppose that a single filer, with no dependents, has a gross income of $98,000 and can use all the allowable tax provisions. Let us say that he is allowed to take $4000 in exclusions, $8500 in standard deductions such as those provided to individuals who are married, filing jointly, and no itemized deductions (additions of all expenses that are considered deductible), and $18,000 in exemptions (four in all, each at $4500). Using the rate structure used in Q5, calculate the filer's (a) taxable income, (b) his tax liability, (c) average tax rate, and (d) effective tax rate. [Hint: Use the most recent tax schedule from IRS, which can be easily downloaded from IRS Web site.]

Q7. What are the two most frequently suggested alternatives to income tax? How feasible are the alternatives? Discuss their strengths and limitations.

Q8. What is a payroll tax? Like income tax, government's reliance on payroll tax has also increased in recent years. Why? What are the principal components of the payroll tax? What are the current rates of component contribution?

Q9. Why sales tax is often called a consumption tax? What are the two basic forms of sales tax? What are some of the common concerns with sales tax?

Q10. What is a sumptuary tax? What is another term used for sumptuary tax? Why are the rates usually high for sumptuary tax?

Q11. What is a value-added tax (VAT)? How does it differ from the conventional sales tax? What are some of the strengths and limitations of value-added tax?

Q12. Suppose that a farmer sells wheat to a local miller for $1200, who adds $400 worth of value by making flour and sells it to a baker for $1600, who, in turn, adds $150 value by making bread and sells them to a retailer for $1750; the retailer adds another $100 of value by packaging and marketing, and sells the final product to the consumers for $1850. Assume that there is a 10% tax on the value added (VAT). Calculate the total value-added tax (VAT).

Q13. What is the difference between real and personal property tax? Why is personal property taxed at a higher rate than real property?

Q14. What is a property tax cycle? Discuss the steps of the cycle with examples.

Q15. Suppose that a property is assessed at $150,000, subject to a tax rate of $2.50 per $100 of assessed value of property (2.5%). The owner is entitled to the following adjustments: $15,000 in homestead exemption, $3000 in veteran's exemption, $2000 in old-age exemption, all on the assessed value, and a circuit breaker of $500. Based on the information presented above, what would be (a) the taxable value of property, (b) the tax liability, (c) the average tax rate, and (d) the effective tax rate for the property owner.

Q16. What is a market value of a property? What approaches are commonly used to determine the market value of a property? Discuss, with an example of each.

Q17. Suppose that it would cost an individual $250,000 to construct a building today and the age of the building is 10 years. Assuming the building has a useful life of 75 years. The value of the land is $55,000. What would be the market value of the property?

Q18. What is a circuit breaker? What methods are commonly used to determine the circuit breaker? Discuss, with an example of each.

Q19. Suppose that a household with an annual income of $45,000 has a tax bill of $2500 on a property assessed at $75,000. The state determines a threshold overload of 4% and an overload relief of 50%. Assume the household income belongs to the income class of $40,000–$50,000 with a threshold percentage at 25%. What would be the tax relief for the household under (a) the threshold approach and (b) the sliding scale?

Q20. Let us say that you have information on the following properties: Parcel A ($120,000; $75,000), Parcel B ($180,000; $160,000), Parcel C ($250,000; $200,000), Parcel D ($100,000; $75,000), Parcel E ($75,000; $60,000), Parcel F ($60,000; $50,000), and Parcel G ($50,000; $45,000), where the first number within the parentheses represents recent market price and the second number the assessed value of property. Do you think there has been an inequality in assessment? Why?

Q21. Why property tax is often called a regressive tax? Some would argue that it is progressive, not regressive. Why?

Q22.   What is a property tax multiplier? How is it determined? Discuss, with a example.

Q23.   What is a user fee? How is it determined? Why is the user fee usually set below the average cost? How is the difference made up?

Q24.   Suppose that a household consumes on average 7000 gallons of water a month. The price of water is \$0.05 a gallon with a fixed cost of \$25. What would be the total cost of water for the household?

Q25.   Intergovernmental revenue has become a major source of revenue for subnational governments. Why? But it also creates dependency. How would you calculate the dependency on the revenue for a recipient government?

Q26.   What is the difference between revenue capacity and revenue reserve? How would you estimate the revenue capacity of a government? Explain how you would determine the revenue reserve of a government for prop erty tax, as an example.

Q27.   Suppose that a government wants to estimate its revenue capacity based on per capita income (dependent variable). It has collected per capita income or revenue data for 25 governments of similar size and character- istics on five independent variables: intergovernmental revenue (PCIGR), sales tax (PCSTX), real property tax ($PCPTX_R$), commercial property tax ($PCPTX_C$), and industrial property tax ($PCPTX_I$), it has run a regression model using the data for the 25 governments and estimated the following equation:

$$\widehat{R}_{PC} = -10.75 + 0.215 PCIGR + 0.125 PCSTX + 0.375 PCPTX_R \\ + 0.375 PCPTX_C + 0.325 PCPTX_I$$

The government's most recent per capita revenue are as follows: \$250 in intergovernmental revenue, \$350 in sales tax revenue, \$450 in revenue from real property tax, \$300 in revenue from commercial property tax, and \$450 in revenue from industrial property. Now using this informa- tion, calculate its (a) per capita revenue capacity and (b) revenue reserve. Interpret the result.

Notes

1. On September 27, 2017, President Trump submitted his tax plan under the title Tax Cuts and Jobs Act (TCJA) to Congress. On December 22, 2017, the bill was passed by both chambers with some changes in the original plan, including a reduction in personal income tax from the highest 39.6 to 37% and corporate income tax from the highest 35 to 21% in 2018. The plan cuts incomes tax rates, doubled the standard deductions, and eliminated personal exemptions (through 2025); it will be reverted back in 2026. While the President's initial plan called for

a substantially reduced number of tax brackets, four in all, the revised plan kept the current seven tax brackets (10, 12, 22, 24, 32, 35 and 37%) at least for now, while lowering most rates (12 from 15, 22 from 25, 24 from 28, and 37 from 39.6%).

2. There is a difference between capital gains and dividends. As noted earlier, capital gains are increases in the value of an asset from improvements or investments from the original price, whereas dividends are earnings from corporate profits paid out to stockholders. In general, short-term capital gains (if held for less than a year) are treated the same way as dividends, whereas long-term capital gains (if held for longer than a year) are treated differently, usually at a much lower rate.

3. Although Alaska does not have a sales tax, it allows its local governments to impose sales taxes that are much higher than most local option sales taxes in the country. Delaware does not have a sales tax, but it uses gross-receipts tax on firms and businesses on total receipts on goods and services.

4. What constitutes a fair market value has been a subject of academic and non-academic debate for a long time, but, by and large, it is defined as the value at which a seller is willing to sell and a buyer is willing to buy a property, once all the information is available to both the buyer and the seller. In other words, it is the value both parties agree on, with full information about the property, in an open market.

5. If the rates of the comparable properties are not close to the property in question, the capitalized rate of the property in question can be included in the sample which will bring the average closer to the property; if they are, it is not necessary to include the property in question.

6. In the example we used, we assumed that the net operating income will grow at a constant rate; if it does not, the method commonly used for calculating the value of the property is the Gordon Rule, given by the expression CF/(DR-GR), where CF is the cash flow, DR is the discount rate (usually the investor's required rate of return), and GW is the growth rate. Thus, using the NOI (net operating income) of $15,000 as the substitute for (net) cash flow, with a DR of 10% and GR of 1.5%, the approximate value of the property will be $15,000/(0.10 − 0.015) = $176,470.59 ≈ $176,471. However, the Gordon Model is not without its limitations; for instance, if DR = GR, the result will be infinity. As such, one has to be careful how the rule is used.

7. The revolt ended with the passage of Proposition 13 on June 6, 1978, that reduced the property tax rate substantially across the board. Prior to that, the property tax rate in the state averaged 3% below the market value with no restrictions on increases in tax rates, and some properties were reassessed 50–100% within the same year. The proposition limited the rate to no more than 2% as long as the property was not sold and reassessment at 1% of the sale price, if sold.

8. The act further required the state to reimburse the taxpayers any funds in excess of the amount appropriated for a given fiscal year, as well as to reimburse the local governments for the cost of complying with the requirements. Interestingly, on June 5, 1990, the state passed the Proposition 111, also known as the Traffic Congestion Relief and Spending Limitation Act, which made some changes in the Gann Limit in order to reduce its effects on state and local budgeting. For instance, the new act required the excess funds to be determined for a two-year period, rather than for a single fiscal year; thereby, making it less likely for the state to have excess revenue.

9. This is due in part to the fact that under the marginal rule the price is set equal to marginal cost, which means that if the price of a good (which reflects the marginal utility the consumers derive from the consumption of an additional unit of the good) is higher than the marginal cost (the cost of producing an additional unit of the good), the consumers are likely to consume less of the good, leading to underconsumption.

References

Aaron, H. J. (1975). *Who Pays the Property Tax?* Washington, DC: The Brookings Institution.

Advisory Commission on Intergovernmental Relations (ACIR). (1975). *Property Tax Circuit-Breakers: Current Status and Policy Issues*. Washington DC: Government Printing Office.

Advisory Commission on Intergovernmental Relations (ACIR). (1993, February). *Significant Features of Fiscal Federalism 1993, Volume 1* (Report M-185). Washington, DC: ACIR.

Akin, J. S. (1973, June). Fiscal Capacity and the Estimation Method of the Advisory Commission on Intergovernmental Relations. *National Tax Journal, 26*, 275–291.

Berne, R. M., & Shramm, R. (1986). *The Financial Analysis of Governments*. Englewood Cliffs, NJ: Prentice-Hall.

Buehler, A. G. (1940). *Public Finance*. New York, NY: McGraw-Hill Book.

Center on Budget and Policy Priorities. (2018, May 2). *Policy Basics: Federal Tax Expenditures*. https://www.cbpp.org/research/federal-tax/policy-basics-federal-tax-expenditures.

Davis, A. (2018, September 17). *Property Tax Circuit Breakers in 2018*. Institute of Taxation and Economic Policy (ITEP). https://itep.org/property-tax-circuit-breakers-in-2018/.

Edwards, C. (2003, August). *Replacing the Scandal-Plagued Corporate Income Tax with a Cash-Flow Tax* (Policy Analysis of the Cato Institute No. 484, pp. 1–43). Washington, DC.

Edwards, C. (2006, April). *Income Tax Rife with Complexity and Inefficiency* (Tax and Budget Bulletin of the Cato Institute No. 33). Washington, DC.

Gist, J. R. (2008). Economic Recession and the Fiscal Conditions of City Governments. *Journal of Urban Affairs, 10*(3), 253–272.

Goode, R. B. (1976). *The Individual Income Tax*. Washington, DC: Brookings Institution.

Goolsbee, A. (2000). In a World Without Borders: The Impact of Taxes on Internet Commerce. *Quarterly Journal of Economics, 115*(2), 561–576.

Groves, H. M. (1939). *Financing Government*. New York, NY: Holt.

Holcombe, R. G. (2006). *Public Sector Economics: The Role of Government in the American Economy*. New York, NY: Prentice-Hall.

Hyman, D. N. (2014). *Public Finance: A Contemporary Application of Theory to Policy*. New York, NY: Cengage Learning.

Lynch, T. D. (1995). *Public Budgeting in America*. New York: Prentice-Hall.

Metcalf, G. E. (1993, January). *The Life-Time Incidence of State and Local Taxes: Measuring Changes During the 1980s* (Working Paper No. 4252). Cambridge, MA: National Bureau of Economic Research.

Netzer, D. (1966). *Economics of the Property Tax*. Washington, DC: The Brookings Institution.

Oates, W. (1972). *Fiscal Federalism*. New York, NY: Harcourt Brace Jovanovich.

Shome, P., & Schutte, C. (1993). Cash-Flow Tax. *International Monetary Fund, Working Paper, 93*(2), 1–30.

Stiglitz, J. E. (2000). *Economics of the Public Sector* (pp. 456–468). New York: W. W. Norton.

Tax Foundation. (2018). *2018 Tax Brackets*. https://taxfoundation.org/2018-tax-brackets/January.

Tax Policy Center. (2016). *National Retail Sales Tax: Effects on Economic Growth*. http://www.taxpolicycenter.org/briefing-book/what-would-be-effect-national-retail-sales-tax-economic-growth.

Tax Policy Center. (2017, October 18). http://www.taxpolicycenter.org/statistics/corporate-rate-schedule.

The Wall Street Journal. (2009, April 15). Sales-Tax Revenue Falls at Fastest Pace in Years.

Part II
The Operating Budget

Understanding the Budget Process

Budgeting is an ongoing exercise, consisting of a number of distinct phases. Each phase consists of a sequence of activities and each activity, in turn, takes place in a specific time period. The phases of the process from one fiscal year often overlap phases from other fiscal years. Most fiscal years are twelve months long, which is a reasonable length of time to execute the budget. However, there are a handful of state and local governments that deviate from this practice. When a budget is prepared for execution over a two-year period, as opposed to twelve months, it is called a biennial budget.[1] Considering the budget size of some governments, state as well as local, the length of the session for a biennial budget may appear rather short to have a lengthy discussion on budgetary issues than an annual budget, but one can argue that it saves government money in additional costs of meeting every year. While both annual and biennial budgets have their strengths and limitations, governments have a choice to move from a biennial to an annual budget, and from an annual to a biennial budget, although the process is complicated.[2] Given the cyclical nature of the budgetary activities, there is a mechanical undertone to the process, but budgeting is more than a mechanical exercise; it is also political in that it takes place in a political environment. This chapter looks at the budget process both from a cyclical process and also from a political process. Interestingly, the current process evolved over a period of time; as such, the chapter begins with a brief history of budget development, especially at the federal level. Although it focuses on the federal budget, its development has a significant impact on how budgeting is done at the subnational level.

5.1 A Brief History of Budget Development

Historically, budgeting in the United States, especially at the federal level, has gone through several developmental changes. This is clearly evident from the number of budget and related acts Congress passed over the years, two of which

A. Khan, *Fundamentals of Public Budgeting and Finance*,
https://doi.org/10.1007/978-3-030-19226-6_5

are worth noting: the 1921 Budget and Accounting Act and the 1974 Budget and Impoundment Control Act. The 1921 Act provided the foundation for modern federal budgeting, allowing the President to formally submit the budget to Congress. Prior to this, there was an ongoing struggle between Congress and the President over the control of the budget process because, according to conventional wisdom, whoever controls the process controls the "power of the purse" (Fenno 1966).[3] The Act produced two other major results: One, it created the Bureau of Budget (BOB), which later on became the Office of Management and Budget (OMB), to review funding requests from various departments and agencies and to assist the President in formulating the budget. Two, it established the General Accounting Office (GAO), known today as the Government Accountability Office, with the authority to conduct independent audits of the federal agencies and departments and report directly to Congress, as an arm of the legislative branch of the government.

The 1921 Act gave the President and the executive branch considerable authority over the budget process until 1974, when Congress took away some of the authority by passing the 1974 Budget and Impoundment Control Act.[4] Like the 1921 Act, it created a budget office, similar to OMB, called the Congressional Budget Office (CBO), to allow Congress the ability to conduct independent economic analysis and to counterbalance OMB's monopoly over budgetary information. The Act also created two budget committees, one for the House of Representatives and one for the Senate, and moved the beginning of the fiscal year from July 1 to October 1. In addition, it introduced a number of procedural changes in the process, including the requirement to incorporate a multi-year revenue projection (forecast) in the President's budget, which has since become a standard practice for many state and local governments. The idea was to make some major institutional changes in the budget process that would strengthen Congressional budget authority, while reducing the President's ability to impound funds appropriated by Congress (Pfiffner 1979).

In between, Congress passed a number of acts to deal with various aspects of the budget, though not all necessarily to deal with the process. Of particular significance is the Balanced Budget and Emergency Deficit Control Act, also known as Gramm-Rudman-Hollings Act, or GRH-I, in short, passed in 1985, to deal with the growing federal budget deficit. It was ratified in 1987, under GRH-II. The act introduced, among others, budget caps on discretionary spending, set strict deficit reduction targets, and kept sequestration (involuntary reduction in government spending—domestic and defense, by GAO) as an option in the event that the government failed to meet the target reductions within a specified time. Realizing that it would be difficult to fully achieve the deficit reduction targets within the prescribed time, Congress passed in 1990 the Budget Enforcement Act (BEA) with softer reduction targets to allow for unpredictable changes in the economy, so sequestration would not be necessary. The Act also introduced PAYGO as a procedure for any new legislation that would impact direct spending, among others.

Although BEA is often credited with helping in the reduction of budget deficit in the late 1990s, which has been a major issue for a long time, there were other factors that also contributed to its success. Of particular significance is the windfall gain from the breakup of the Soviet Union that allowed the government to cut defense spending, along with some reductions in domestic spending and, more importantly, the emergence of a high-tech economy in the 1990s that saw a tremendous growth in demand for skilled labor in the new economy. Several variations of BEA have since been passed to provide additional flexibility, or add constraints, as needed, under which the government currently operates. For instance, in 2011, Congress passed the Budget Control Act raising the debt ceiling, with the option to allow the President to increase it more the following year, although by a small margin. Fortunately, the spending reduction in 2011 was less than the increase in the debt limit. In 2018, Congress further increased the spending caps under the Bipartisan Budget Act that was put in place under the 2011 Act. In all likelihood, we will see similar measures by Congress in the coming years, as the situation demands.

5.1.1   Budget Budget Acts as Reforms

An interesting aspect of the Congressional budget acts is that, for the most part, these were reforms in response to changing social, economic, and political conditions of the time. For instance, the 1921 Budget and Accounting Act, which gave the President the authority to formulate the budget, was based on the recommendations of the Taft Commission Report[5] that was given the responsibility by President Taft to look into a number of reforms the government was proposing at the time, including a presidential budget. The reforms were considered necessary as the country was growing economically and political changes were taking place in various parts of the world, including the prospects of a major war in Europe.

Several decades later, President Truman established a similar commission, under the leadership of former President Herbert Hoover, to make recommendations for reorganizing the federal government, which the President thought was long overdue. The commission report, published in 1949, made a number of recommendations (Lederle 1949), including the need to have a separate capital budget for the federal government and a performance budgeting system for government, away from the traditional line-item budget, to increase budgetary accountability (Lynch 1995). Interestingly, both Taft and Hoover Commissions were established right about the time when Europe was politically changing and, in the latter case, following the World War II, when Eastern Europe was falling into the hands of Soviet Union, eventually becoming a part of the socialist block. In fact, every single act Congress passed in between, and since then, is a reform—a response considered necessary to address the pressing problems of the time.

5.1.2   The Need for an Effective Budget Process

All budget reforms have a single goal—to have an effective budget process that will allow the government to carry out its budgetary activities in a timely manner, with maximum efficiency. The National Advisory Council on State and Local Budgeting (NACSLB)[6] defines budget process as consisting of activities that encompass the development, implementation, and evaluation of a plan for the provision of services and capital assets (GFOA 1999). According to NACSLB, a good budget process must have five essential characteristics: One, it must incorporate a long-term perspective; two, it must establish linkages to broad organizational goals; three, it must focus budget decisions on results and outcomes; four, it must involve and promote effective communication with stakeholders; and five, it must provide incentives to government management and employees. In other words, a good budget process should be more than developing a legal document that appropriates funds for a series of line items. A good budget process must go beyond the traditional concept of line items for expenditure control; it must provide incentive and flexibility to managers that can lead to improved program efficiency and effectiveness (GFOA 1999).

Based primarily on the conditions of an effective budget process, as suggested by NACSLB, Government Finance Officers Association (GFOA) has developed four principal criteria and several sub-criteria for budget development. The criteria are used to award a Certificate of Excellence each year to state and local governments, and related entities such as a school district, a water district, and a fire district, as well as community colleges that meet those criteria.[7] The four criteria are (1) budget as a policy document, (2) budget as a financial plan, (3) budget as an operations guide, and (4) budget as a communications device. Similarly, the International City Management Association (ICMA) also awards a Certificate of Performance Management to local governments for instilling a culture of performance management, pursuing comparative analysis and data-informed decision making, and promoting transparency.[8] However, the criteria used by the two organizations for their certificate programs are not permanent; they are refined from time to time, as budgetary conditions change.

5.2   A Digression on Fund Structure

Before discussing the budget process, it is important to introduce a couple of terms that are integral to budget development, especially the state and local budgets: fund structure and basis of accounting. Understanding the fund structure is important because government resources are organized by funds. A fund is an accounting entity with its own set of self-balancing accounts. Unlike a for-profit organization, which operates as a single accounting entity because its revenue comes primarily from a single source vis-a-vis the price individuals pay for the goods and services they consume, a government collects its revenues from multiple different sources, segregated into multiple funds and accounts. The segregation of accounts by funds allows the government to carry out specific functions and activities, as determined by legal and other requirements. Figure 5.1 shows the relationship between funds, functions, and line items of a government budget.

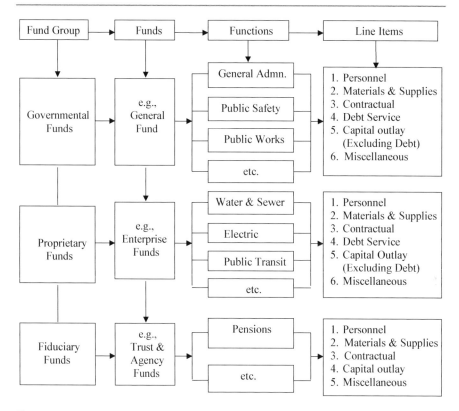

Fig. 5.1 Relationship between fund structure, funds, functions and line items

Budgeting deals with the flow of resources; that is, how revenues are collected from different sources (inflows) and how those revenues are spent on various functions and activities (outflows) through a process, known as financial transactions. From an accounting perspective, it is important to understand how these transactions are recognized, recorded, and reported, and the timing of recognition. Timing of recognition is particularly important because it determines when the transactions are recorded and how the transactions are reported in a financial statement. In most instances, it follows a set of principles, known as Generally Accepted Accounting Principles (GAAP). GAAP consists of a set of rules, procedures, and conventions that set the standards for most accounting and reporting procedures for governmental and nonprofit organizations. However, some of the procedures used in budgeting are slightly different, though not entirely, from those used for reporting under GAAP. The differences between the two are reconciled in the notes to the financial statements in the annual financial report.

5.2.1   Fund Groups

Although most organizations have the latitude to maintain as many funds as they want, the Governmental Accounting Standards Board (GASB), which sets the standards for state and local governments in the United States, recommends that the number be limited to a few, usually around a dozen or so, divided into three broad categories, called fund groups: (1) governmental, (2) proprietary, and (3) fiduciary. Each group contains a number of associated funds, each serving a specific purpose. However, each of these funds may contain additional funds (sub-funds), if necessary—thus, raising the total to a much large number. Each fund, in turn, consists of multiple accounts, such as accounts payable or taxes receivable that can run into dozens, depending on the number of transactions that take place in a government. An account is simply a record that appears on a journal (book of initial entry) or ledger (book final entry) to keep track of the transactions.

GASB modifies the fund structure from time to time using various statements, as it deems necessary. For instance, in June 1999, it introduced Statement 34 which established new financial reporting requirements for state and local governments to make the annual financial report more comprehensive and easier to understand (Patton et al. 2019). The following provides a brief description of each group and its associated funds.

5.2.2   Governmental Funds

These funds, which account for the majority of the functions and activities of a government, are supported by general revenue of the government such as taxes, intergovernmental revenue, user fees and charges, and fines and forfeitures. Governmental funds include several associated funds, namely the General Fund, Special Revenue Funds, Capital Projects Funds, Debt Service Funds, and Permanent Funds.

5.2.2.1 The General Fund

Largest of all governmental funds, the General Fund accounts for activities that are financed out of general revenue of a government such as those mentioned above. Since these revenues are used primarily for general operations of the government, they are not restricted for special purposes—hence, the term general.

5.2.2.2 Special Revenue Funds

Unlike the General Fund, these funds account for activities that are designated for a specific purpose. For instance, a local option sales tax may be legally designated to support a specific program such as a recreation facility or a public library. Another example will be street maintenance that is frequently financed out of motor vehicle tax. Community development projects that are largely supported by Community Development Block Grant (CDBG) would fall into this category.

5.2.2.3 Capital Projects Funds

These funds account for the acquisition and construction of major capital projects such as roads, bridges, and highways and are generally financed out of General Fund revenues of the government or through borrowing, or a combination of both. In general, when the projects are completed, the funds are usually discontinued and any unused portion of the fund is transferred back to the General Fund or Debt Service Fund.

5.2.2.4 Debt Service Funds

These funds account for the payment of principal and interest on general long-term debt, usually out of general revenue of the government. For the most part, these funds remain empty, except for the time when the payments become due.

5.2.2.5 Permanent Funds

The last in this category, Permanent Funds, account for activities that are legally restricted to be financed out of interest earnings, but not principal. Many state governments maintain these funds to provide support for higher education.

5.2.3   Proprietary Funds

These funds are used to account for activities of a government that are similar to those found in the private sector. In other words, proprietary funds account for goods and services that are sold to public the same way a business enterprise sells goods and services to consumers. Included in this category are Enterprise Funds and Internal Service Funds.

5.2.3.1 Enterprise Funds

Larger of the two funds, Enterprise Funds account for activities that are similar in nature to those provided by the private sector in that one must be willing to pay a price for the quantity one consumes such as water, sewer, and electricity.

5.2.3.2 Internal Service Funds

These funds account for services produced and sold by a department to other departments within the same organization. A good example of an Internal Service Fund is the data processing service provided by the IT department of a government to all other agencies and departments.

5.2.4   Fiduciary Funds

Finally, these funds are used to account for assets held by a government in a trustee capacity or as an agent for individuals, private organizations, or other governmental units. As such, they are restricted in use by individuals outside of government. Governments do not have exclusive control over these funds, but are expected to manage these funds in a trustee capacity. Included in this category are Trust Funds, Agency Funds, and Pension Funds.

5.2.4.1 Trust Funds

These funds account for assets held by a government in a trustee capacity, or as an agent for individuals, private organizations, and other entities. For instance, a donation made to a public library for the purchase of books or an endowment made to a college for scholarship purposes would be a good example of trust funds.

5.2.4.2 Agency Funds

These funds account for money collected by a government for another government or an entity of a government. A good example would be a county government that collects property taxes for a school district, which it retains in an Agency Fund until the money is disbursed to the district.

5.2.4.3 Pension Funds

These funds account for money collected for the retirement of employees. The employer has the option to retain and invest the contributions the employee and the employer make to these funds, as long as they meet the legal requirements for doing so and the money is available for employee pensions.

In addition to the above, governments also maintain two account groups—a General Fixed Asset Account Group to keep record of fixed assets such as land, buildings and facilities purchased with the general revenue of the government, and a General Long-Term Debt Account Group to keep record of long-term obligations that are financed out of general revenues of the government.

5.2.5   Basis of Accounting

As noted earlier, the timing of recognition vis-à-vis when the results of transactions should be recognized is important in governmental accounting, especially for preparing financial statements. Basis of accounting deals with the timing of recognition. Three types of accounting bases are commonly used in government: cash basis, accrual basis, and modified accrual basis. In a cash basis accounting, revenues are recorded when they are received in cash and expenditures are recorded when they are paid out in cash. Very few governments these days use cash basis accounting and most use a combination of accrual and modified accrual basis accounting. In an accrual basis of accounting, revenues are recorded when they are earned, but not received in cash, and expenditures are recorded when they are incurred, but not paid out in cash. In a modified accrual basis of accounting, on the other hand, revenues are recorded when they are received in cash and expenditures are recorded when they are incurred, but not paid out in cash. As a matter of practice, funds that focus on total economic resources, such as proprietary and trust funds mostly use accrual basis of accounting.

While GAAP serves as the basis of accounting for financial reporting, it may not be the case when preparing the budget document. As noted previously, most governments use a slightly different basis than GAAP in preparing their budgets, known as budgetary basis. The differences can be summarized in terms of four principal elements: timing of recognition, basis of accounting, reporting structure, and reporting of entities.

Timing of recognition may be different for the two bases. For instance, under GAAP basis, revenue is recognized when it is measurable and available, whereas under budgetary basis revenue is recognized when it is received in cash. Also, the fiscal year used for financial reporting may be different from the one used for budget period. The basis of accounting may also be different for the two bases. For instance, under GAAP basis, governmental funds are required to use a modified accrual basis of accounting, whereas under budgetary basis the same funds may be required to use a cash basis, or cash plus encumbrance basis (reserved for a specific activity or restricted for future use). Likewise, the reporting structure may be different for the two bases. For instance, under GAAP basis, debt service payment is reported in a debt service fund, whereas under budgetary basis it is accounted for in the General Fund. Finally, reporting of entities for which funds have been allocated may be different for the two bases. For instance, under GAAP basis, each entity is reported and recorded, whereas under budgetary basis not every entity for which funds have been appropriated will show up in the budget and general account. This is known as entity difference (Copeland 2011).

Understanding the difference between the two, GAAP basis and budgetary basis, is important so a user will know how to interpret the information in both documents. In fact, GFOA recommends that budget document should make it clear at the beginning what basis of accounting it is using (GFOA 1999). It should be worth noting that the governments are not obligated to use a budgetary basis; it is up to the individual government what basis it prefers to use. For instance, should a government prefer to use a GAAP basis for budget development, as opposed to a budgetary basis, GFOA recommends that it should be made clear at the beginning.[9]

5.3   Budget as a Cyclical Process

Returning to budget process, all budgets, whether it is prepared for federal, state, or a local government, and whether it is prepared annually or biennially, have to go through a process, called budget cycle. The cycle consists of four distinct, but interrelated phases and each phase consisting of a number of distinct activities. The phases are: preparation, appropriation, implementation, and evaluation. The process is time-consuming, detailed, and involved in that a budget has to be prepared, it has to be appropriated, it has to be implemented, and finally, it has to be evaluated. Interestingly, the process is similar for all governments, but varies in complexity depending on the size of the budget and the level of government.

5.3.1 Preparation Phase

The cycle begins when the various agencies and departments receive instructions from the chief executive and the central budget office to prepare their budget requests for the upcoming budget year. Instructions are fairly detailed and clear to avoid the potential for any ambiguity, as the agencies put together their requests. At a minimum, it is expected that the requests would include the following: mission and goals of the agency, consistent with those of the organization; budget assumptions, including any changes in service provision, explanations for change, and their effects on the budget; details of the service provision in quantitative terms; performance measures; expense calculations by line items; funding sources; and putting together the budget package, including a cash budget. In addition to asking the agencies what to include in the requests, the instructions also provide information on the economic outlook of the government, its policy changes, if any, and priorities that will serve as the background for budget preparation. Also included in the instructions are standard forms the agencies need to use to provide the information and to maintain consistency across agencies.

The time it takes to prepare the budget varies from government to government and depending on the size of the budget. Obviously, the larger the government and the bigger the budget, the more time it will take to prepare the budget. After the budget has been prepared and submitted, hearings begin with the chief executive, the budget director, the finance director, and other responsible decision makers for the agencies to justify their requests. During the hearing process, an agency may be asked to revise and resubmit the requests. The process continues until the requests are finalized, the budget is put together, called the proposed budget, and ready to be submitted to the legislature for appropriation of funds.

For the federal government, the process begins at least nine months before the budget is submitted to Congress and about 18 months before the fiscal year begins. The work begins when the agencies receive instructions from OMB to prepare their budget requests. Agencies are assigned budget examiners to guide them in preparing the budget and also to serve as go-between the agencies and the OMB. The completed requests are submitted to OMB by late summer or early fall; the requests are reviewed by OMB and its staff in consultation with the President and his aides. The 1921 Act requires the President to set forth the budget in as much details as the President considers it necessary; however, over the years the information contents, including explanatory materials, have increased considerably, as the size of the budget has increased.

The President's budget mostly includes the administration's policy proposals and priorities for individual departments, including proposals for changes in the budget process and tax laws. It also includes an estimate of country's economic outlook and a multi-year revenue projection, among others. The format of the budget is fairly standard and partly determined by law. It is important to keep in mind that the requests are estimates and often change as the budget goes through internal review and the normal appropriation process. To ensure that the activities are completed on time, it is expected that the agencies, as well as OMB, follow the

Table 5.1 Time line for the federal budget process

Time line	Specific activity
Early Fall	• Agencies submit their budget requests
November	• OMB review of the agency budget requests
December	• Incorporate revisions; agencies submit their final requests
January	• President outlines budget priorities (in his State of the Union Address)
First Monday in February	• President submits the proposed budget to Congress
February 15	• CBO submits its analysis of the President's budget to the House and Senate Budget Committees
April 1	• Senate Budget Committee submits its Concurrent Resolution on the budget
April 15	• Congress passes budget resolution
May 15	• House formally approves appropriation bills drafted by appropriation and authorizing committee
June 10	• House Appropriations Committee submits last appropriations bill to committees
June 15	• Congress adopts Reconciliation Bill
June 30	• House approves annual appropriations bill (deadline)
September	•President accepts or rejects the Congressional (proposed) budget within 10 days after receiving it
October 1	• Fiscal year begins

budget calendar. Table 5.1 presents the highlights of the federal budget calendar (Haughey 2018).

The process is very similar at the state and local level. State constitutions, for instance, allow the governors to formulate and submit the budget to the legislature. It takes somewhere between 12 and 18 months to prepare the budget depending on the size of the government. The process begins with the central budget office, often called the Governor's Budget Office or Office of Management and Planning issuing policy guidelines to various departments to prepare the budget requests. The guidelines include a range of assumptions, from revenue changes, to economic adjustments, to intergovernmental revenues. The guidelines also include instructions for the preparation of different levels of expenditures for each department. As with the federal budget, departments submit their budget proposals to the central budget office within a specified time. The state budget directors make preliminary budget recommendations to the governors based on staff evaluations and funding proposals.

During the time the budget preparation is taking place, states hold revenue estimation conference to iron out any differences so as to build a consensus on the revenue projection for the upcoming budget year, commonly known as consensus forecasting. The conference recommendations are fine-tuned during this time with additional evaluations, including internal hearings, as new information becomes available, following the revenue projection. The governors make the final budget decision before submitting the budget to the state legislature.

For local governments, the process usually starts with the setting forth of the budget calendar, at least six to eight months before the fiscal year begins. This is followed by the departments receiving instructions from the central budget office for budget preparation, while the chief administrative officer, along with the budget director, in consultation with the Mayor, makes the revenue projections for the upcoming budget year. Once the budget requests are prepared and submitted, the internal hearings with the budget director and the chief administrative officer begin. There is also a public hearing that takes place during this time to allow the public the opportunity to raise questions about the proposed budget (Table 5.2). In most instances, hearings produce budget revisions that are then compiled and put together in the form of a proposed budget, ready to be submitted to the local council or commission for budget appropriation.

Table 5.2 Time line for a local budget process[a]

Time line	Specific activity
First week in January	• CAO (Chief Administrative Officer) meets with the BD (Budget Director) and others to review current year spending
Second week in January	• CAO and BD meet with the Mayor and Council to review the current year budget and discuss policies and priorities for the upcoming budget year
Last week in January	• BD distributes worksheets for departmental budget preparation, including the budget calendar
First week in February	• Departments begin budget preparation (estimation)
Second week in February	• BD makes the initial revenue projection and discusses with CAO and the Mayor
Third week in February	• CAO, along with BD, provides additional budgetary information to the departments in light of the projections (e.g., budget cuts, salary increase, etc.)
First week in March	• Budget requests are submitted by the departments
Second week in March	• Internal hearings are held with the department heads
Third week in March	• Public hearings are held
Last week in March	• BD asks the departments to make revisions and resubmit the budget requests
Second week in April	• Departments resubmit the requests
First week in May	• CAO and the Mayor, with the assistance of BD, put together the proposed budget and send it to the Council
Second week in May	• Council holds open budget meeting, deliberates key issues, and makes final budgetary decision on the budget
First week in June	• Council adopts the budget
July 1	• Fiscal year begins

[a]Dates are approximate. Actual completion time may vary with FY beginning at a later date.

A separate capital budget calendar is also prepared during this time that goes through a similar process. The rationale for a separate capital budget calendar is that, unlike the operating budget, the capital budget deals with non-recurring expenditures on projects and programs that are costly, have a longer life span, and frequently require different methods of financing.

5.3.1.1 Developing the Budget Forecasts

Central to budget preparation are budget forecasts—forecasts of expenditures and forecasts of revenues. The responsibility for forecasting expenditures usually falls on the respective agencies and departments that are preparing the budget requests since the entities have a much better knowledge of what goods and services they are going to provide next year and the costs of their provision. The forecasts typically include costs by object classification such as personal services (salaries and wages), including benefits, materials and supplies, debt service, contract obligations, capital outlays, and miscellaneous other costs.

The simplest way to forecast the cost of these items in a budget would be to use basic arithmetic calculations. For instance, to estimate salaries for next year one would simply add the salaries of all full-time employees next year, plus the fringe benefits, plus overtime, if allowed for salaried personnel. For wages, usually for part-time employees, one would simply multiply the number of part-time employees by the number of hours each employee will work times the corresponding wage rate, plus overtime, if allowed, and add them to obtain to total wages for next year. In general, fringe benefits are not included in calculating wages for part-time employees, while full-time employees who are paid on an hourly basis are generally entitled to fringe benefits, including overtime.

To give an example, suppose that we have a service unit within a department of a government, we will call it Unit X, with five full-time and two part-time employees, and we have information on the pay scale of the employees for next year, including pay raise and fringe benefits. Assume that the fringe benefits are set at 10% of the gross pay. Let us say that the five full-time employees will have a combined gross salary, without fringe benefits, for next year of $300,000. Add to that 10% for fringe benefits, which will bring the total salary for next year to $330,000 [$300,000 + ($300,000 × 0.10) = $300,000 + $30,000 = $330,000]. Now, to calculate the wages for the two part-time employees, assume that each employee will be paid $20 an hour and will work 25 hour a week for 52 weeks a year, excluding weekends. The total wages for two employees will be $52,000 [($20 × 25 × 52) × 2 = $26,000 × 2 = $52,000]. Therefore, the combined salaries and wages for our service unit next year will be $382,000 ($330,000 + $52,000). Additionally, if overtime is allowed, especially for full-time employees, it should be included in the calculation, which will further increase the cost of personal services vis-à-vis the budget for next year.

Calculations of debt service payment and payments for contract obligations are relatively straightforward because the rate and payment structure are pretty much determined at the time of borrowing and when getting into contract obligations. Calculations of cost of materials and supplies also should be relatively simple because the costs are determined by the price and the quantity of items purchased.

However, for the most part, the calculations for the latter are done by the Central Purchasing Office since it can take advantage of volume discount and pass the savings to the respective departments.

Alternatively, when it is difficult to estimate the cost objects in a budget, one could use simple forecasting methods that require very little knowledge of mathematics or statistics such as naïve forecasting, engineering cost estimates, and the average method, among others, to estimate the expenditures. It is worth noting that when preparing the budget for next year, the agencies are often required to include, in addition to the above, detailed cost estimates of the programs the agencies will undertake next year, especially the new programs.

Unlike the expenditure forecasts, revenue forecasts are much more complicated because of the nature of the forecast variables. This is, in part, due to the fact there are considerable uncertainties as to how much revenue a government can exactly collect from variables such as income tax, sales tax, intergovernmental revenue, user fees, charges, fines, and forfeitures because so many factors influence the behavior of these variables over which the government does not have much control. On the other hand, forecasting revenues for variables such as property tax is relatively uncomplicated because it is based on assessed value of property and the rate at which the property will be assessed for the forecasting period, which is known a priori.

While the expenditure forecasts are mostly done by respective agencies, the responsibility for forecasting revenues often falls on multiple entities, depending on the government doing the forecast. For instance, for the federal government, the responsibility falls on the Department of Treasury, along with the Council of Economic Advisors on the economic outlook, and the CBO on the budget aggregates. At the state level, the responsibility typically falls on the Comptroller of Accounts, while at the local level it falls on the central budget office and the finance department. Ideally, forecasting should be done in-house, but given the demand it places on in-house expertise, especially for revenue forecasts, where such expertise is not readily available. Governments can engage outside consultants or firms.

5.3.2 Appropriation Phase

The budget of a government is essentially a proposal; it does not automatically guarantee the funding requests made in the proposed budget—appropriations must be made. Appropriation is a legislative decision on how the government spends money on various functions and activities, and it is where the greatest political battle takes place.[10] Legislative consideration of the budget begins immediately, as soon as the budget is submitted to the legislature. Like the preparation phase, the process is very similar at all three levels, except that it gets more complicated at the federal level because of the sheer size of the budget.

5.3.2.1 Federal Appropriation Process

The appropriation process for the federal government begins as soon as the President submits the budget to Congress. The budget is sent immediately to various committees for hearings and recommendations. Following the hearings, the committees put together a report and send it to the Senate and House Budget Committees outlining their spending and revenue proposals. The proposals are often at variance with the President's proposals. Next, Congress passes a resolution, adopted by both chambers with a simple majority, called concurrent resolution, setting targets for total spending, revenue and deficit for the next several years, usually for five years but can be up to ten. The responsibility for drafting the resolution falls on the budget committees, but, unfortunately, it lacks the force of the law; in other words, it lacks the legal authority to enforce because it does not require President's signature (Stone 2014). The resolution is supposed to pass by April 15, but often takes longer.

Once the budget resolution is passed, the Appropriations Committees begin their appropriation process on the various budget bills, called the appropriations bills.[11] Each Appropriations Committee has 12 subcommittees and each subcommittee is responsible for drafting a separate appropriations bill corresponding to the programs that are within its jurisdiction. The drafted bills are then ready for legislative action, which is a multi-stage process. The bills need to be voted by the respective subcommittees, the full committee, the Congressional floor, and the conference committee, if necessary, on a compromised bill[12] in the event that there is a disagreement between the two chambers before the bill is ready to go to the President for his signature (Stone 2014).

The President has the right to accept or reject the appropriation decision of the legislature in its entirety, or a specific bill. Unfortunately, unlike a governor or mayor, the President does not have the right to veto individual provisions in a bill called line-item veto; as such, the President has to accept or reject an entire bill.[13] Once the bill is rejected and sent back to Congress, it has the right to override the President's decision with two-thirds majority, which is not easy to garner and, as such, ends up making the necessary changes in the bill and resending it for approval. As soon as the President signs the bills, in other words, approves the budget, it becomes law and effective immediately.

> **A Note on Continuing Resolution, Budget Reconciliation, and Omnibus Bill**
> Three terms that frequently appear during the Congressional appropriation process are worth noting here; they are continuing resolution, budget reconciliation, and omnibus bill. In the event that Congress fails to pass legislation to fund the government, it can pass a legislation called continuing resolution to keep the government functioning at the current level of spending. Continuing resolutions are often used as a stop-gap measure to allow Congress time to complete actions on the appropriations bills. On occasion, Congress makes use of a special procedure, known as "reconciliation" to

expedite the consideration of mandatory spending and tax legislations. It was used by several administrations in the past and most recently by the Bush and Trump administrations to enact tax cuts (Center on Budget and Policy Priorities 2018). Like the concurrent resolution, the reconciliation bill needs a simple majority to pass.[14] Also, from time to time, when Congress fails to pass the twelve appropriations bills separately, it packages them into a single bill, known as omnibus bill. Interestingly, the bill often contains many unrelated pieces of legislation. Since the omnibus bill contains the twelve separate bills and some unrelated pieces of legislation, it tends to be voluminous—consequently, receiving cursory examination by the committees (Tucker 2014).

5.3.2.2 State and Local Appropriation Process

The appropriation process for states is considerably similar to that of the federal process because, like the federal government, the states have a bicameral legislature and follow some of the same procedures. For instance, in Texas, following the receipt of the governor's budget, the House Appropriations and Senate Finance Committees hold their hearings on the general appropriations bill[15] and put together their own report. The committees then send their individual report (in the form of a bill) to the full House and Senate for approval. In the event of a disagreement between the two chambers, the two bills go to a conference committee consisting of members from both chambers. As with the Congressional appropriation process, the conference committee irons out the differences between the (two) bills, puts together a compromised bill, which is then voted by both chambers. If approved, which is usually the case, the bill is ready to go to the governor for his signature. The process is pretty much the same for other states.

Some states, in particular Texas, require that the bill is certified by the Comptroller's Office to make sure that the spending amount approved in the bill is within the limits of the revenue projection (Texas Comptroller of Public Accounts 2018). This is particularly important for state and local governments because of the requirement to balance their operating budget (proposed). Interestingly, unlike the President, the governors have the right to veto individual items in the bill, called "item veto." Like Congress, the legislature has the right to override the governor's veto with two-thirds majority, but, in most instances, the governor's veto stands and the legislature makes the necessary adjustments. Once signed by the governor, the budget becomes law and effective immediately.

The process is identical at the local level, but much less complex. Once the budget is put together and approved by the chief executive (manager or mayor, depending on the form of government), the budget goes to the council or commission for appropriation. The council debates and discusses the budget, makes the necessary changes in the request, and sends the revised budget to the mayor for his approval. The mayor has the right to veto the budget and the council the right to override the veto with two-thirds majority, but, in most cases, a compromise is reached. Once the mayor signs the budget, it becomes binding and effective immediately.

A Note on Budget Ordinance

Before the fiscal year begins and the budget is formally implemented, governments, in particular local governments, are required, under the respective state charters, to pass and adopt a budget ordinance. The policy applies to all component units of a government, such as a school district or special district that operates under a separate budget. The ordinance allows the governments to levy taxes and appropriate revenues for the fiscal year. The ordinance serves as the legal basis by which the proposed expenditures are measured for accounting and reporting purposes (Millonzi 2012). Although it is a legal document, the stipulation is that the ordinance must be sufficiently intelligible and clear for an average taxpayer to understand the purpose and the basis of spending. Ordinances are not permanent; they can be amended, as necessary.

5.3.3   Implementation Phase

The passage of the bills and their signing by the chief executive set the stage for the next set of activities. The approved budget must be implemented (executed). Implementation allows the funds to be used by various agencies and departments to carry out the approved programs and policies of the government. The executive and the legislative budget offices, the Department of Treasury, as well as all affected agencies and departments get involved in this process to maintain control of the appropriated funds to ensure that expenditures do not exceed the budget authority.[16] If, under extreme circumstances, the agencies use up the funds before the fiscal year is over, or need additional funding, they have to go for supplemental appropriations. The funds available for supplemental appropriation are usually much less than the original appropriation and the appropriation process also much shorter, as such, less complicated, than the original appropriation process.

As noted earlier, appropriations are legal authorization to spend funds; they do not provide an iron-clad guarantee that the agencies will receive all the funds that have been appropriated. The chief executive has the authority (with some limits, for instance, for the federal government, under the 1974 Budget and Impoundment Control Act) to hold back, supplement, or transfer funds when faced with serious economic, financial, and other problems. Thus, there is often a difference between the budget that has been adopted (for implementation) from the one that was proposed and submitted by the chief executive, and the one approved by the legislature and signed into law by the chief executive. The final budget is usually the one at the end of the fiscal year when the implementation has been completed (actual).

5.3.3.1   Implementation Process

The actual implementation of the budget begins when the agencies and departments receive the authority or permission to incur obligations that will result in immediate or future government expenditures, called budget authority. Three types of authority are commonly used during this process: contract authority, spending authority, and borrowing authority. In a contract authority, agencies are allowed to enter into a contract agreement with a private firm (vendor) or another government to acquire goods and services within a specified time up to an established level, as determined under the appropriation guidelines. This is a standard procurement practice since, with some exceptions, governments do not produce goods; they acquire (procure) and deliver. In a spending authority, the agencies are allowed to make expenditures from a specific fund (governmental fund, enterprise fund, and so forth) for a specific purpose within a specified time up to an established level, again, as determined under the appropriation guidelines. Finally, agencies are also allowed to borrow from another fund or from the Treasury to incur obligations, called borrowing authority.

There is a relationship between budget authority and a term frequently used in budgeting called outlays. Outlays are total expenditure in a given year from current and prior years' budget authority. To give an example, suppose that new authority for spending for a government is $100 million, of which $60 million will be spent in the current year and the remaining $40 million will be spent in future years. It also has an unspent authority of $50 million, of which $30 million will be spent in the current year and the remaining $20 million will be spent in future years. The outlays for the current year, therefore, will be $90 million ($60 million + $30 million). Similarly, the outlays for future years will be $60 million ($40 million + $20 million), plus any new authority (Fig. 5.2).

It is worth noting that agencies do not receive the entire amount of appropriation in one go, or at one time; it is provided in installments over the entire length of the fiscal year, usually in quarterly installments, to ensure that the agencies do not run out of funds before the fiscal year is over or before a job is done. The process is known as allotment. The allotments are typically made for line items such as personnel services (salaries and wages), maintenance and operating expenses

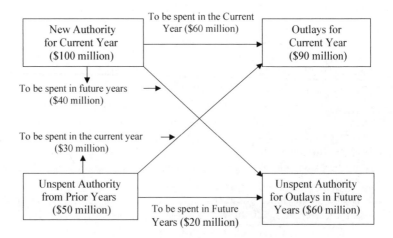

Fig. 5.2 Relationship between budget authority and outlays

(materials, supplies, and utilities), financial services (fees and interest expenses), and capital outlays.

Once the implementation process begins, it is important for a government to prepare two documents: one, a cash budget to keep track of cash flows and, the other, a cash accounting report to keep track of cash position. A cash budget is a budget of expected cash receipts (inflows) and cash disbursements (outflows). A good starting point for a cash budget is a cash-flow analysis, which is prepared using three simple pieces of information: cash inflow, cash outflow, and net flow, which is the difference between inflows (flow of funds from all revenue sources) and outflows (disbursements for all expenditure items). The analysis serves an important purpose by identifying in advance the cash position an organization will be in, and how to deal with any potential problem in the future such as cash shortage (Khan 1996).

Cash budgets can be prepared on a weekly, monthly, or quarterly basis, but usually on a weekly or monthly basis. Daily cash budgets are not uncommon, depending on the availability of information and the interest of the government. The following steps are typically used in preparing a cash budget: cash balance at the beginning of the reporting period, called the beginning balance, cash receipts (inflows), cash disbursements (outflows), and changes in cash balance at the end of the period, called the ending balance. Table 5.3 presents a simple cash budget for a local government based on monthly receipts and disbursements for a three-month period.

According to the table, the ending balance for the government at the end of the first period, which is the month of January, is −$247,000; this then becomes the beginning balance for the next period, which is February. In general, if the ending balance (the balance at the end of a period) is positive, it adds to the total revenue for the next period and the converse is true, when it is negative. The process can be repeated for as many time periods as the government wants. In reality, a cash-flow analysis for more than six months may not be useful because of the likelihood of error that increases with time in forecasting future flows, although theoretically it can be prepared for any number of months. It should be worth noting that the forecasts presented in the table were not actual forecasts, but used here for illustrative purposes, although one could use any standard forecasting methods, especially those suitable for short-term forecasts such as simple moving average.

A cash accounting report, on the other hand, is prepared to keep track of cash position at the end of a reporting period. Like a cash budget, the reports are usually prepared on a daily, weekly, monthly, and quarterly basis. Preparing the report beyond the daily report is not complicated since one only needs to add the daily balances to get the weekly balance, add the weekly balances to get the monthly balance, and so forth, but always keeping the same reporting structure. Table 5.4 presents a simple daily cash accounting report for a government; it includes a sample of two funds and five accounts, but can be easily extended to include additional funds and accounts. Ideally, two sets of cash accounting reports should be prepared—one for the government, as a whole, and one separately for each fund that produces an income or revenue for the entity. This would mostly include the

Table 5.3 A simple cash budget

Cash flows	Monthly flow ($) ($1000)		
	January	February	March
Beginning Balance (BB)	(100)	(247)	295
Cash receipts (inflows)			
Tax revenue			
Property tax	27,238	28,165	28,956
(Local) sales tax	6285	5987	5823
(Local) Franchise tax	7347	7549	7450
Non-tax revenue			
Charges and fees	2455	2138	2107
Fines and forfeitures	1570	1296	1325
Intergovernmental revenue	5216	6295	6794
Miscellaneous	1079	1512	1928
Total inflows (Excl. BB)	51,190	52,942	54,383
Cash disbursements (outflows)			
Salaries and wages	31,514	32,925	32,975
Materials and supplies	3295	2764	2516
Debt service	5760	5760	5760
Benefit payments	2127	2479	2863
Capital outlay	7295	7387	7956
Miscellaneous	1346	1085	1215
Total outflows	51,337	52,400	53,285
Changes in cash balance	–	–	–
= Net cash flow	(147)	542	1098
+ Beginning balance	(100)	(247)	295
= Ending balance (EB)	(247)	295	1393

proprietary funds such as water fund, sewer fund, electric utility fund, parking meter fund, and so forth. As the table shows, all five accounts, with the exception of parks and recreation, had a positive beginning balance. The position appears to remain the same at the end of the day.

There is a similarity between a cash accounting report and a cash budget in that both start with a beginning balance and conclude with an ending balance, with one difference: While the cash accounting reports are prepared at the end of the reporting period, the cash budgets are prepared at the beginning of the reporting period. This makes sense because a cash budget, like an operating budget, includes forecasts—forecasts of cash inflows and cash outflows.

Table 5.4 A daily cash accounting report[a]

Fund No.	Fund name	Beginning balance ($000)	Receipts ($000)	Disbursements ($)	Ending balance ($)
000–00	General Fund				
001–01	General Govt.	1150	125	250	1025
001–05	Parks & Recreation	(15)	20	10	(5)
002–00	Enterprise Funds				
002–01	Water	375	140	135	380
002–02	Electric Utility	450	175	200	425
002–03	Parking Meter	150	15	25	140
	Total	2110	475	625	1965

[a]Excluding payroll

5.3.3.2 Implementation Challenges

The budget comes full circle once it is ready for implementation by various agencies and departments (since it is the agencies and departments which initiated the process by putting together their budget requests). Unfortunately, implementation is not as simple and cut-and-dried as it may sound; the process is complete with challenges that the implementing agencies must be prepared to address. The greatest challenge is the likelihood of a revenue shortfall. If funds were available as appropriated; in other words, if there are no revenue shortfalls, or cost overruns, implementation would be straightforward, but that is seldom the case. Revenue shortfalls are difficult to avoid because of forecast errors, unforeseen increase in expenditure, poor management practice, and so forth.

Since implementation challenges are a common occurrence, several measures are available to a government that can prevent or minimize the effects of the challenges on the budget. Important among the measures are variance analysis, interfund transfer, supplemental appropriation, and cost control.

Variance Analysis

Budget variance is the difference between budgeted and actual revenue and expenditures. Before proper measures can be taken to deal with revenue shortfalls, it is important to do a variance analysis to determine the amount of variance and, more importantly, what contributed to the variance, so that proper measures can be taken to correct the problem. The goal is to keep the variance as small as possible, since zero variance is difficult to achieve. Table 5.5 presents a simple example of budget variance for the General Fund operation of a government. As the table shows, both revenues and expenditures have a negative variance for two of the four quarters—revenues in quarters 3 and 4, and expenditures in quarters 1 and 3.

Table 5.5 Budget variance: general fund operation

	Quarter 1 ($000)	Quarter 1 ($000)	Quarter 3 ($000)	Quarter 4 ($000)
Revenues				
Budgeted	175,000	225,000	150,000	125,000
Actual	180,000	240,000	125,000	115,000
Variance	5,000	15,000	(25,000)	(10,000)
% Variance[a]	2.86%	6.67%	(16.67%)	(8%)
Expenditures				
Budgeted	165,000	230,000	130,000	120,000
Actual	175,000	215,000	135,000	110,000
Variance	(10,000)	15,000	(5,000)	10,000
% Change[b]	(6.06%)	6.52%	(3.85%)	8.33%

[a][{Actual-Budgeted)/Budgeted] × 100;
[b][(Budgeted-Actual)/Budgeted] × 100

Interfund Transfer

One of the methods frequently used to deal with revenue shortfalls is interfund transfer. Interfund transfers allow the decision makers to move money from one fund or an account to another, usually from the one with a surplus to the one running a shortfall. As noted earlier, one needs to be careful when transferring money between funds, so as not to constrain the funds or accounts from which the money is transferred.

Supplemental Appropriation

As noted earlier, in the event of a budget shortfall, agencies are allowed to ask for supplemental appropriation during the fiscal year, in addition to funds already provided in the initial appropriation. The appropriations are generally provided for emergencies or unanticipated revenue shortfall over which the agency did not have much control. The actual amount of supplemental appropriation is usually much smaller than the initial appropriation; however, the agencies have to go through a formal appropriation process, although it is much less rigorous than the original process.

Cost Control

Regardless of what causes a revenue shortfall, all governments must make an effort to control their costs. Cost control deals with a set of measures that are necessary for an organization to ensure that its resources are used for the intended purposes without incurring cost overruns. The measures are essentially the same for all organizations, although their application may vary. Some of these measures are simple requiring very little efforts and resources, while others are exhaustive requiring detailed and careful analysis throughout the process. Three such measures frequently used in cost control are expenditure control, cash control, and fraud, waste and abuse control.

Expenditure Control

The first and foremost control measure an organization can use to bring its expenditures within the limits of its resource capabilities is expenditure control. Expenditure control takes place in two ways: through regulating timing of obligations and actual expenditures, and publishing a number of financial and accounting reports on a regular basis such as cash accounting report. Regulating timing ensures that funds are obligated for the intended purposes and that their misuse is kept to a minimum. Most organizations use variance analysis, similar to the ones discussed earlier, to show the amount of funds an agency has received and the actual amount it has spent on a specific activity within a given period. Also, publishing financial and accounting reports is essential to show what type of expenditures an organization has incurred and how the actual expenditures compare with those proposed and approved before implementation. These reports, which should be published on a quarterly basis, if not on a weekly or monthly basis, can also serve as principal source documents for the annual financial report that governments are required to publish at the end of each fiscal year.

Cash Control

Frequently used in government, cash control is the means by which an organization ensures control of its cash (cash receipts and cash disbursements). The simplest way to control cash is to develop a cash budget, discussed earlier. Cash control is extremely important in government, especially at the local level, where governments receive the bulk of their revenues during certain times of the year, while the expenditures take place more or less consistently throughout the year. This creates two operational problems: a cash surplus, when more revenues are received than expenditures, and a cash shortage, when expenditures exceed revenues received. Cash control helps a government maintain a balance between the two by ensuring that it has enough cash to carry out its normal, day-to-day operation, while keeping in mind that any surplus that is generated in the process does not remain idle.

When surpluses accumulate, they are usually invested in securities earning additional income for the government. Similarly, when shortages occur, money is either transferred from funds with surpluses or withdrawn from interest earnings, or both, to avoid borrowing. Additionally, to ensure safety of funds, it is important that accounts are properly segregated and are reconciled on a daily basis. Reconciliation ensures that money withdrawn from an account matches the money actually spent indicating that the account balance is correct. Also, it is important that no cash transactions are made other than petty cash and that vouchers are issued before making cash payments. The process is known as cash internal control.

Fraud and Waste Control

Every year governments lose hundreds of millions of dollars from fraud, waste and abuse at all three levels of government, but more so at the federal level. In fact, the GAO, in its annual report, provides a detailed listing of government programs and activities where waste, fraud and abuse have occurred during a fiscal year costing the government hundreds of millions of dollars. Although the government has undertaken measures to control the problem, unfortunately, it remains a serious concern. From the perspective of cost management, an organization can control fraud, waste and abuse by taking measures that would eliminate waste such as by clearly identifying where the problem has occurred, increasing the speed of response to minimize time, improving quality, and reducing costs, among others. Interestingly, these measures constitute the essence of a process called the lean operating system (LOS).

5.3.4 Evaluation Phase

The cycle ends with an audit of government finances, including the budget, and evaluation of various programs carried out during the fiscal year. The objectives of these activities are to ascertain the extent to which the government (1) has complied with the spending requirements, (2) presented the results of its financial operations and reported its financial position in accordance with the Generally Accepted Accounting Principles, or any other accepted measure, and (3) the extent to which the completed programs have achieved their stated goals and objectives. The first two together are called "financial audit" and the third "performance audit."

While financial audits are based on a set of accepted standards, such as GAAP by which one can measure and evaluate the financial position of a government, performance audits are much broader in scope. There are no set standards that can accurately guide and measure the performance of an organization. However, by focusing on goals and objectives, performance auditing can address the broader question of efficiency and effectiveness—in particular, how an organization carries out its operations and the manner in which it utilizes its resources in achieving those goals and objectives. In other words, by placing emphasis on goals and objectives, and their achievement, performance auditing can measure an organization's bottom-line performance (Aminian et al. 1912).

Auditing, in general, and financial auditing, in particular, are highly skilled activities; as such, it is expected that government uses a licensed auditor for its audit, especially the financial audit. At the federal level, it is usually done in two stages: first, internally, by the inspector general associated with a department or agency and, second, independently, by GAO. At the state level, it is usually done in-house by the state auditors,[17] while at the local level it is mostly done by external auditors, although in-house evaluations are not uncommon and frequently used for internal reporting purposes. For performance audits, these can be done internally, or a government can use outside sources, if necessary.

5.4 Budget as a Political Process

As it should become obvious, budgeting is an involved process. It involves all branches of government—in particular, the executive and the legislative branch. However, the activities that take place during the course of the cycle are not simple and smooth. The constant battle over "who should get what" and "how much" keeps the process contentious yet, in the final analysis, conflicts have to be resolved, compromises have to be made, and resources have to be allocated. Interestingly, there is a political undertone behind these activities that determines the final outcome. Aaron Wildavsky was among the first to recognize this aspect of budget behavior in his classic work the Politics of the Budgetary Process (1964), which describes in detail the role politics plays in public budgeting. A keen observer of budget process, especially the federal budget process, he did so with such thoroughness that to this day it remains the cornerstone of much of the discussion on budget politics.

5.4.1 Budget as a Political Game

Widavsky's depiction of budget politics resembles a political game. Although he does not describe it in precise game-theoretic terms, he lays out the groundwork that provides the foundation for a game-theoretic approach. All games have three essential characteristics: players, strategies, and outcome. Wildavsky begins his model of budget behavior with a group of individuals in the budget process; we will call them "players" in the typical game-theoretic sense. As in any game with established rules, the players in the budget game know the rules of the game, understand the process, have a set of "strategies" that they try to use to influence the game plan of the other players, and eventually the outcome. The success of the players is determined by their ability to fully utilize the strategies to their own advantage.

Three groups of players are critical to the game: the agencies, the chief executive and, by extension, the director of the central budget office, and the members of the Appropriations Committees. To this, we can add a fourth group—the clientele vis-à-vis the public, who do not directly participate in the budget game but whose interests all three groups claim to serve (Mikesell 2014; Lewis and Hildreth, 2011; Axelrod 1995; Gosling 1992; Lynch 1995).

Each group of players has a unique name based on the political-institutional role they play in the budget process. For instance, the agencies are called "the spenders" or "advocates" because they serve as advocates of agency interests by making the best possible case for maximum funding for agency operation. The chief executive and the director of the central budget office are called "the reviewers" because, the budget being an executive responsibility, it is the prerogative of the reviewers to ensure that the agency requests are in congruence with the goals, objectives, and priorities of the administration. Finally, the members of the Appropriations Committees are called "the cutters" because, as elected members of the legislature, they regard themselves as true representatives of public interest and, as such, the true guardians of the purse (Fenno 1966).

The roles change somewhat as the game moves through different stages of the process, although the basic expectations of the players remain the same throughout the process. Reviewers change role and become defenders as the budget enters the appropriation phase and, on unusual occasions, the cutters have been known to become advocates (Wildavsky and Caiden 2004). In reality, two sets of games take place during a budget season: the first, during the preparation stage, between the agencies and the chief executive and the central budget office. This is less difficult of the two stages: The rules are simple, strategies are less complex, and the outcomes are predictable in most cases. The second, the more important game, takes place during the appropriation phase, where all three groups of participants, in particular the agencies and the members of the Appropriations Committees, get actively involved. The battle over the purse is hard and complex during this stage, placing extraordinary demand on the skills of the players to achieve the most from the process. The tug-of-war that takes place here ultimately determines the budget outcome; in other words, who gets what, and how much.

5.4.2   Strategies and Constraints

Budgeting is a game of strategies and calculations (Wildavsky 1984). The success of the game depends on the successful use of the strategies by each player. Strategies vary in number and choices (Mikesell 2014). Some of the strategies are standard, such as padding the requests, playing the number games, demonstrating confidence during budget hearings, or simply asking for more, while others are essentially counterstrategies against the calculations of other players. The reviewers' strategies are one of cautious reminder to the spenders of the budget battle that lies ahead in the legislature or simply the need to balance the budget. On the other hand, the strategies employed by the cutters are more direct because they need only to ask questions, while the burden of proof falls on the spenders. At the same time, the cutters must exercise "judgment" in using strategies that do not adversely affect the interests of the clients they represent.

In using the strategies, as in any game, the players must take into consideration the constraints which set the parameters of the game. Each group of players is aware of these constraints. For instance, the constraints of the spenders are relatively simple in that they need the support of the public vis-à-vis the constituents they serve, the chief executive and the central budget office, and the legislature—the latter because, in all likelihood, the spenders will have to deal with the same individuals for the next budget appropriation. The constraints of the reviewers are somewhat more restrictive in that they have to take into consideration the larger picture of the government. These include, among others, budget inflexibility (difficult to cut expenditures), budget instability (unpredictable economy), balanced budget requirement (need to balance the budget) laws and mandates that impose additional restrictions, and public expectations (need to serve all constituents, regardless of their political support). The cutter's constraints are also somewhat limited in that they operate in a political environment that is fragmented, with independent committees, divided legislature, too much power with some committees, partisan pressure, and their own self-interest to get re-elected.

5.4.3   Budget Outcome

This balancing act by the players to gain as much as possible from the process forces them to bargain, negotiate, and compromise. The end product, as suggested by Wildavsky, is a budget that is "incrementally" different from last year's allocation. Interestingly, Wildavsky never makes it clear what incrementalism is, or how to measure it, other than what should be intuitively obvious when referring to budget politics. This notion of incrementalism, which lies at the heart of his budget game, has also raised serious questions about its validity as an outcome for all situations (Leloup 1978; Wanat 1978). Wildavsky believed that incremental change is both desirable and necessary to maintain the continuity of service provision, as well as to maintain the stability of the political process within which budget decisions are made. However, in a subsequent, but more conciliatory work, Wildavsky (1992, 1978) tries to relax somewhat his view of incremental outcome under certain conditions, such as major economic downturns, but, nevertheless, contends that incremental change is a much better alternative from a decision-making point of view than most.

5.5   Summary and Conclusion

Budgeting is a complex undertaking. It is probably the only function in government that involves all three branches of government, especially the executive and the legislative branch, including every single department and agency of the executive branch. Even the public at some points gets involved in the process. It is, therefore, not difficult to see why the budget process is so complex. This chapter has presented a broad overview of the budget process, highlighting the activities that are important at different stages of this process. The process is cyclical, but it is also political. Although politics may not seem obvious on the surface, it plays a major role in public budgeting, in part, because budgeting deals with public money and, in part, because the allocation decisions have to go through a political process to ensure that those responsible for spending public money can be held accountable in the event that they fail to do so. The chapter has presented the elements of both, including a brief history of budget development and how it shaped the current budget process, especially at the federal level.

Review Questions

Q1. Budget is historical. Why? How did the federal budget evolve over time? Name two Congressional Acts that changed the course of budgeting in the country, especially the federal budget?

Q2. Why are budget acts considered as reforms? Why is it important to have an effective budget process? How do budget reforms contribute to it?

Q3. What is a budget process? What role do the executive and legislative branches play in this process? Why government budgets are called "executive budgets?"

Q4. What is a fund? What is the relationship between funds, functions, and activities? Why is it important to understand the fund structure when preparing a budget?

Q5. What are the differences between the fund groups governments use for accounting and reporting purposes? Discuss the funds currently maintained under each fund group.

Q6. What is basis of accounting? What are the difference between a GAAP basis and a budgetary basis? Discuss, with examples.

Q7. What is a budget cycle? What are the phases of this cycle? Discuss the specific activities that take place during each phase of the cycle.

Q8. What are some of the similarities and dissimilarities among the federal, state, and local budget process? What makes the process complex?

Q9. What role does forecasting play in budget process? Why is it difficult to forecast government revenues than expenditures? Give an example of how you would estimate a personnel budget.

Q10. What is a budget bill? How many bills are there in the federal budget? What is a compromised bill? Why is it necessary to have a compromised bill?

Q11. What is the difference between budget appropriation, budget authority, budget outlays, and budget allotment?

Q12. What is the difference between a budget resolution, budget reconciliation, and an omnibus bill? What is an important weakness of an omnibus bill?

Q13. Who are responsible for implementing (executing) a budget? What are some of the implementation challenges? What contributes to these challenges?

Q14. What is a cash budget? How does it differ from a cash accounting report? What are the steps in preparing both? Give an example of both.

Q15. What is a variance analysis? When should a government do a variance analysis? What are the typical steps in a variance analysis?

Q16. Suppose that a government has the following quarterly revenue and expenditure data for General Fund operation of a government (Table 5.6).

Table 5.6 Review question (Q16)

	Quarter 1 ($000)	Quarter 1 ($000)	Quarter 3 ($000)	Quarter 4 ($000)
Revenues				
Budgeted	250,000	450,000	230,000	150,000
Actual	245,000	460,000	240,000	135,000
Variance	–	–	–	–
% Variance	–	–	–	–
Expenditures				
Budgeted	265,000	430,000	240,000	160,000
Actual	275,000	420,000	255,000	150,000
Variance	–	–	–	–
% Change	–	–	–	–

Given the information above, do a variance analysis. How would you interpret the results?

Q17. Why is budgeting called a political game? Who are the actors in this game? What strategies do they use? What is the outcome of the game?

Notes

1. Texas state budget is a good example which operates on a biennial cycle, divided into twelve-month period. The fiscal year begins on September 1, following a legislative session that lasts for 140 days. The state constitution permits the legislature to meet once every two years, on the second Tuesday in January of every odd-numbered year, although the governor has the authority to call special sessions as necessary, but cannot last for more than 30 days (Senate Research Center 2011).
2. Interestingly, 44 states used biennial budgeting in 1940; today, less than two dozen states do. Since 1968, some 18 states have changed their budget cycles—15 from biennial to annual, and 3 from annual to biennial (Kogan et al. 2012).
3. By all counts, it is the US House of Representatives that controls the "power of the purse" because it has the authority to raise taxes and spend money for the federal government. In fact, the power was given by the US Constitution, under Article 1, Section 7, which says that "All Bills for raising revenue must originate in the House of Representatives; but the Senate may propose or concur with amendments as on other bills."
4. The Act was inspired, in part, by President Nixon's overuse of impounding authority when, for instance, the President impounded, vis-à-vis refused to disburse Congressional appropriated fund to the tune of several billion dollars through the executive power of impoundment and, in part, for fear of running into serious budget deficit. The Act requires that the President's decision to impound funds be approved by the House of Representatives and the Senate within 45 days. Interestingly, 43 states currently give their governors the authority to impound, while the states such as Indiana, Nevada, New Hampshire, North Carolina, Rhode Island, and Vermont do not.

5. President McKinley is credited with the establishment of the first Taft Commission in 1900, headed by William Taft, to look into the US-Philippines Affairs (the country under the direct sovereign control of the United States at the time), who later became the Civil Governor of the Philippines. The commission was subsequently headed by a number of individuals. He was later appointed by President Theodore Roosevelt to be the Secretary of Wars in 1904 and became the 27th President of the United States in 1909. It is during his presidency that President Taft established the commission to look into major reforms in the federal government, including the federal budget, and the commission report published in 1912 popularly came to be known as the Taft Commission Report.

6. NACSLB was created in 1995 by eight associations of state and local government, including the Government Finance Officers Association (GFOA), to achieve three specific goals: (1) to educate public decision makers on the merits of budget systems as an effective tool for planning, analysis, and management of the financial resources of their jurisdictions; (2) to help them better understand and assess their own budget and resource-allocation systems; and (3) to provide them with a set of good budget practices that can serve as a model.

7. GFOA uses a total of 27 sub-criteria focusing on organization-wide goals, financial structure, policy and process, capital and debt, long-term financial plan, including a multi-year forecast, agency goals and performance, and quality of presentation, among others. Some of the criteria are mandatory that a document must include, as a minimum requirement, to receive the certificate.

8. ICMA's Certificates of Performance include three categories—Certificate of Excellence, Certificate of Distinction, and Certificate of Achievement, based on the level of information provided in the document and the quality of their presentation.

9. GFOA recommends that the budget document clearly define the basis of accounting used for budgetary purposes. If the budgetary basis of accounting and the GAAP basis of accounting are the same, this fact should be clearly stated. If the budgetary basis of accounting and the GAAP basis of accounting are different, major differences and similarities between the two bases of accounting should be noted. Disparities may include basic differences, timing differences, fund structure differences, and entity differences. The description of the differences between the GAAP basis of accounting and the budgetary basis of accounting should be written in a manner that is clearly understandable to those without expertise in either accounting or budgeting. The use of technical accounting terms should be avoided whenever possible. In cases where the use of technical accounting terms cannot be avoided, those terms should be clearly defined and fully explained.

10. The committees responsible for passing the appropriations bills are the House and Senate Appropriations Committees, considered to be the most powerful committees in the entire legislature. The way the process works is that when the two committees receive allocations, they divide the allocations for appropriation among the various subcommittees. The subcommittees then decide how to distribute the funds within their allocation to different components (functions) of their respective bills. Interestingly, the allocations are voted by the respective appropriate committees and are not subject to review or vote by the entire House or the Senate.

11. One can think of an appropriations bill as grouping of federal agencies, based on their specific functions for funding purposes. There are 12 bills altogether, each generated by a specific subcommittee. The 12 subcommittees and their corresponding bills are: (1) Agriculture; (2) Commerce, Justice and Science; (3) Defense; (4) Energy and Water; (5) Financial Services and General Government; (6) Homeland Security; (7) Interior and Environment; (8) Labor, Health and Human Service, and Education; (9) Legislative Branch (legislation includes only the House and Senate items); (10) Military Construction and VA; (11) State and Foreign Operations; and (12) Transportation, Housing and Urban Development. Thus, funding covering student financial aid, such as Pell grants, will fall under Labor, HHS, and Education appropriations bill.

12. A conference committee is a temporary committee composed of select members from both chambers, usually senior members, including those who have introduced the bill, to reconcile the differences in a legislation that has already been passed by the individual chamber.
13. The 1996, the 104th Congress, under Public Law 104-130, granted the President the power to line-item veto budget bills passed by Congress. It was immediately challenged in the US District Court of Columbia by several senators, found unconstitutional, and was repealed in 1998. The ruling was subsequently upheld by the Supreme Court by a vote of 6-3.
14. Under certain circumstances, such as if the bill falls under the Byrd's rule, which considers any provision in the reconciliation bill "extraneous" to the purpose of amending a mandatory spending, an entitlement, or tax laws, it will require a minimum of 60 votes.
15. Unlike the federal government, state governments deal with a single bill, commonly known as the general appropriations bill.
16. It is the authority given by Congress or a legislative body to individual agencies and departments to spend funds. In other words, it allows the agencies to borrow, to contract, to obligate, and to spend funds, as appropriated. However, the legislative body may have restrictions as to how the funds are to be spent such as within a year, over several years, and so forth.
17. Currently, in over two dozen states, the auditor is an elected official, while in others they are appointed by the governor or the state legislature. In the latter case, some states may want the governor to appoint the auditor and the legislators to confirm the appointment.

References

Aminian, H., & Samaneh, S. S. (1912). The Relationship between Performance Audit and Management Tendency to Strive towards Organizational Goals Achievement. *Australian Journal of Basic and Applied Sciences, 6*(13), 149–153.

Axelrod, D. (1995). *Budgeting for Modern Government.* New York: St. Martin's Press.

Center on Budget and Policy Priorities. (2018, May 2). *Policy Basics: Federal Tax Expenditures.* https://www.cbpp.org/research/federal-tax/policy-basics-federal-tax-expenditures.

Copeland, P. A. (2011). *Essentials of Accounting for Governmental and Not-for-Profit Organizations.* New York: McGraw-Hill/Irwin.

Fenno, R. F., Jr. (1966). *The Power of the Purse: Appropriations Politics in Congress.* Boston: Little, Brown.

Government Finance Officers Association (GFOA). (1999, June). *Basis of Accounting vs Budgetary Basis.* https://www.gfoa.org/basis-accounting-versus-budgetary-basis.

Gosling, J. J. (1992). *Budgetary Politics in American Governments.* New York: Routledge.

Haughey, J. (2018, February 27). 14 Steps to the Federal Budget Process Time-Line. *Congressional Quarterly.* https://info.cq.com/resources/14-steps-federal-budget-process-timeline/.

Khan, A. (1996). Cash Management: Basic Principles and Guidelines. In J. Rabin et al. (Eds.), *Budgeting: Formulation and Execution* (pp. 313–322). Athens, GA: Carl Vinson Institute of Government, University of Georgia.

Kogan, R., Greenstein, R., & Horney, J. R. (2012, January). *Biennial Budgeting: Do the Drawbacks Outweigh the Advantages?* Washington, DC: Center on Budget and Policy Priorities. https://www.cbpp.org.

Lederle, J. W. (1949). The Hoover Commission Reports on Federal Reorganization. *Marquette Law Review, 33*(2), 89–98.

LeLoup, L. T. (1978). The Myth of Incrementalism: Analytical Choices in Budgetary Theory. *Polity, 10*(Summer), 488–509.

Lewis, C. W., & Hildreth, W. B. (2011). *Budgeting: Politics and Power.* Oxford: Oxford University Press.

Lynch, T. D. (1995). *Public Budgeting in America.* New York: Prentice-Hall.

Mikesell, J. L. (2014). *Fiscal Administration: Analysis and Applications for the Public Sector*. New York, NY: Wadsworth.

Millonzi, K. (2012, June 14). Budgeting and Appropriations, Finance and Tax. *Coat's Cannons: NC Local Government Law*. https://canons.sog.unc.edu/faqs-on-adopting-the-budget-ordinance/.

Patton, T., Patton, S., & Ives, M. (2019). *Accounting for Governmental and Nonprofit Organizations*. Cambridge, UK: Cambridge University Press.

Pfiffner, J. P. (1979). *The President, the Budget, and Congress: Impoundment and the 1974 Budget Act*. New York: Westview Press.

Senate Research Center. (2011, January). *Budget 101: A Guide to the Budget Process in Texas*. Austin, TX: Senate Budget Center, Sam Houston Building.

Stone, C. (2014). The Federal Budget Process. In S. Payson (Ed.), *Public Economic in the United States, 2*, 679–698.

Texas Comptroller of Public Accounts. (2018). *The Texas Budget Process: A Primer*. https://comptroller.texas.gov/transparency/budget/primer.php.

Tucker, J. (2014, January 14). What Is an Omnibus? *National Priorities Project*. https://www.nationalpriorities.org/blog/2014/01/14/what-omnibus/.

Wanat, J. (1978). *Introduction to Budgeting*. Monterey, CA: Brooks/Cole Publishing.

Wildavsky, A. (1964). *The Politics of the Budgetary Process*. Boston, MA: Little, Brown. (Revised 4th edition, 1984).

Wildavsky, A. (1978, November–December). A Budget for All Seasons? Why the Traditional Budget Lasts? *Public Administration Review, 38*, 501–509.

Wildavsky, A. (1984). *The Politics of the Budgetary Process*. Boston, MA: Little, Brown. (Revised 4th edition).

Wildavsky, A. (1992, November–December). Political Implications of Budget Reform: A Retrospective. *Public Administration Review, 52*(6), 594–599.

Wildavsky, A., & Caiden, N. (2004). *The New Politics of the Budgetary Process*. New York: Pearson-Longman.

Budget Systems, Underlying Structures and Characteristics

6

Budgets are prepared using a formal structure that ties the various elements of a budget into a coherent document. The structure provides the foundation that guides the development of the budget, which, for convenience, we will call "budget systems." Although terms such as "budget formats," "budget approaches," and "budget types" are often used, "budget systems" seem more appropriate because, like any system,[1] budgets have a formal structure with interrelated components that are tied together in a coherent fashion to achieve the goals and objectives of a government. Understanding the systems and their structure is important to understand how budget decisions are made and the results those decisions have on individual agencies and departments, their functions, programs, and activities, as well as on the public vis-a-vis society at large. Budgeting is also a management function, where the responsibility for managing the systems falls on the chief administrative officer, along with the central budget office and the budget director, the agency and department heads, all the way down to the unit managers. This chapter provides a brief discussion of the role the budget systems play in the overall budget process, followed by a detailed discussion of some of the commonly used systems in government.

6.1 Budget Systems and Their Role in the Budget Process

Historically, government budgets were prepared on an ad hoc basis without any formal structure until the beginning of the twentieth century when the New York Bureau of Municipal Research, which has been at the forefront of municipal research, introduced the line-item budget (Lynch 1995). Since then, the systems have grown both in number and complexity. Today, all government budgets are prepared using one or more of these systems. Unfortunately, there are no precise guidelines as to what system or systems a government should use to develop its budget; it depends on time, available skills, and the resources of the organization.

© The Author(s) 2019
A. Khan, *Fundamentals of Public Budgeting and Finance*,
https://doi.org/10.1007/978-3-030-19226-6_6

However, once developed and formally adopted, the system usually remains in place for a long time until it is replaced by another system that can better reflect the needs and directions of the organization.

Budget systems are not abstract constructs; they are tools with direct practical applications. Although they vary in structure and complexity, the systems serve a number of useful purposes. First and foremost, they provide consistency in the way in which the various elements of a budget are presented in the document. Consistency makes it possible to create a database that can be used to compare the information contained in the document over time, as well as across organizations using similar systems. Secondly, they improve organizational efficiency. A well-designed budget system can help develop data measures that can be used for measuring efficiency in service provision. Thirdly, they improve coordination between different operating units of an organization. A well-designed budget system can improve understanding between different functional units of a government by ensuring congruence between their mission, goals, and objectives. Fourthly, and most important, they improve public's understanding of the budget. A well-designed budget system can provide greater insight into how allocation decisions are made, who are involved in the decision process, and the results of those decisions.

From a process perspective, there is a direct relationship between a budget system and the budget process. Besides helping a government develop its budget, a well-designed budget system can help improve the allocation decisions during the appropriation phase. Although to what extent the appropriation decisions rely on these systems is difficult to say, a well-designed budget system can nevertheless help the decision makers make rational choices on how best to allocate the limited resources of a government based on its mission, goals, objectives, challenges, and priorities. The systems can be equally effective during the execution phase. Ideally, one can think of a budget system as a road map that can be used as an operational guide during the execution phase by developing tasks an agency needs to undertake consistent with the mission, goals, and objectives of the organization. Finally, it can be just as effective during the evaluation phase. A well-designed budget system can improve organizational accountability by establishing a direct linkage between program goals and their accomplishments, as well as by identifying the areas where deviations have occurred in the process and the factors that have contributed to those deviations. This is particularly important from a decision-making point of view and also from the point of view of the public of knowing how best the government is utilizing their tax dollars.

6.2   Types of Budget Systems

There is a common perception about the systems that they are inflexible and mutually exclusive in that if an organization uses System A it cannot use System B or C at the same time. In reality, the systems are quite flexible and can be easily coordinated to develop an integrated system, consisting of elements of individual

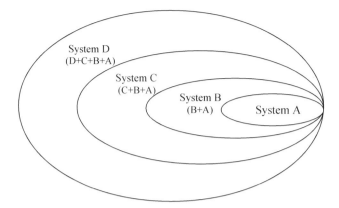

Fig. 6.1   An integrated budget system

systems. The process is not complex and can be carried out in such a way that best serves the goals and objectives of the organization. Figure 6.1 shows an integrated budget system with four sub-systems: A, B, C, and D. As the figure shows, system D contains all or some of the elements of systems C, B, and A; System C contains all or some of the elements of systems B and A; and System B contains all or some of the elements of A, while System A serves as the core system, which, in most instances, is the line-item budget.

Interestingly, when the systems are integrated into a larger system, they add something of value to the new system without fundamentally altering their own characteristics. This apparent flexibility makes it possible to constantly refine a system by incorporating the relevant elements of other systems consistent with the needs of the organization. In reality, most budget documents today contain elements of two or more systems. This section discusses five most frequently used budget systems in government: line-item, program, performance, zero-based, and strategic.

6.2.1   Line-Item Budget

Oldest among the budget systems, the line-item budget constitutes the core or skeletal budget, for lack of a better a term, that provides the foundation for all other systems. It is simple in structure, easy to understand, and less demanding on time to develop. Central to line-item budgeting is line itemization (a process that allocates funds by individual cost objects), which allows the decision makers to exercise control over budget operations by keeping track of funds allocated on individual line items. Formally, it can be defined as a system that allocates money for expenditure on specific cost objects, called line items, without any reference to goals or objectives the allocated funds will achieve, or the purpose they will serve. The items typically include personal services (salaries and wages), materials and supplies, contractual, capital outlay, debt service, and miscellaneous other items. Each of these cost items can be further divided into sub-items. For instance, personal services can be divided into full-time, part-time, over time, retirement benefits, health insurance, worker's compensations, and so forth. Similarly, materials and supplies can be divided into office supplies, general supplies, printing, and so on. Likewise, contractual can be divided into various contract obligations, and capital outlay into expenditures on land, buildings, equipment, and so forth. Finally, debt service can be broken down into payments on principal and interest for long-term debt.

To keep track of the cost items, the items are often presented using numerical or accounting codes that can vary in number from six to ten or twelve digits. For instance, a nine-digit accounting code (00-00-00-000) will account for fund type (the first two digits), specific department or function (the second two digits), specific program (the third two digits), and cost objects (the last three digits). The numbers typically vary depending on the complexity of the system, size of the government, and how detailed the government wants the information to be.

6.2.1.1 The Basic Structure

Operationally, a line-item budget is the simplest of all budget systems since it uses a minimum set of information to develop the budget—line items or costs associated with each line item. Structurally, it resembles a simple table with rows and columns, but, from an analytical point of view, one can present it as a matrix, where each element of the matrix represents the budget for a particular line item and the sum total of the rows and columns represents the total budget for the government, or any of its functional units such as a department or program (Appendix A). The advantage of using a matrix structure is that the elements of the rows and columns can be easily subjected to arithmetic operations such that they can be added, subtracted, multiplied, and transposed. Also, it gives us a bird's-eye view of the entire budget of a government, its component units and the corresponding line items.

Preparing the Budget

Preparing a line-item budget is simple and relatively uncomplicated. Basically all one needs to do is develop a list of cost or line items for individual agencies and departments based on the past history of the government, or as determined by the appropriation process, and determine the dollar amount to be spent on each item. Table 6.1 presents a simple a line-item budget, consisting of six items (personal services, materials and supplies, contractual, debt service, capital outlay, and miscellaneous) for the Water and Sewer Department of a hypothetical government. The table includes three years of budget data: last year's actual (FY_{t-1}), current year (FY_t), and the proposed budget for next year (FY_{t+1}), although we could have included additional years.

Presenting data for multiple years makes it possible to compare the changes in budget allocation over time. For instance, the current year budget in our example shows a modest increase of 2.49% over last year's budget, while the budget for next year (proposed) shows a significant increase of 10.89% over the current

Table 6.1   A simple line-item budget

Water and Sewer Fund: Expenditure Budget
Fiscal Year: 2XXX-2XXX

A/C Codes	Line Items/ Cost Objects	FY_{t-1} (Last Year/ Actual)	FY_t (Current Year)	FY_{t+1} (Next Year/ Proposed)
07-000*				
001	Personal Services	$7,860,000	$8,140,000	$8,570,000
002	Materials and Supplies	350,000	525,000	650,000
003	Contractual	710,000	750,000	780,000
008	Debt Service	1,450,000	1,450,000	1,450,000
011	Capital Outlay	1,050,000	1,275,000	1,950,000
023	Miscellaneous	530,000	620,000	750,000
	Total:	$11,950,000	$12,760,000	$14,150,000

Sources of Funding: Local (Sewer) Fund		$9,750,000
State Fund		4,250,000
Federal Fund		150,000
Total:		$14,150,000

*07 = Water and Sewer Fund, 000 = Line Items

year budget, much of which is due to increase in personal services and capital outlay. As the table shows, personal services constitute the largest segment of all line items. In most cases, it takes up somewhere between 60 and 70% of the total budget, the bulk of which goes to salaries and wages.

6.2.1.2 Strengths and Limitations of the System

As with any system, a line-item budget has its strengths and limitations. The greatest advantage of a line-item budget is its simplicity—it is simple in structure and easy to construct. Another advantage of the system is that itemizing a budget by individual line items enables a government to control its costs by keeping track of money spent on each item. Furthermore, the process allows for accumulation of expenditure data by individual agencies and departments that can be used for trend or historical analysis. However, this advantage is offset by the fact that the system does not provide any information on the purpose the allocated funds will serve. It does not tell us anything about the program or programs for which the allocated funds will be used, or the goals the funds will try to achieve for the organization, or any of its functional units (operating departments). This apparent lack of focus on specific programs, goals, and objectives makes it difficult to plan and evaluate organizational performance. Also, building a budget on pure line items has a tendency to promote incremental budgeting since no other information is available other than cost objects, which does not give much flexibility to the decision makers in making allocation decisions.

6.2.2   Program Budget

Unlike a line-item budget, in a program budget money is allocated for expenditure on specific programs rather than on specific cost objects, although line itemization remains an integral part of the budget. Programs are generally targets for action by individual functional units such as public works, public safety, education, health and human services, parks and recreation, and so forth. The difference between a line-item and a program budget is that in a program budget the focus is on specific programs and activities and not on specific line items or cost objects, which makes it possible to tie the allocation decisions to expenditure goals and objectives. In other words, in a program budget the allocation decisions are made in such a way as to ensure that there is congruity between budget allocation and program goals and objectives of the organization, although line items remain integral to the system.

6.2.2.1 The Basic Structure

A program budget has three key elements: (1) the establishment of program goals and objectives for individual departments or agencies, (2) the development of plans to achieve the goals and objectives within a specified time frame, and (3) the determination of resources that will be required to achieve the program goals and objectives. Goals summarize the general purpose the programs will serve; they are broad and generally ambitious. Objectives, on the other hand, translate the goals into measurable terms to make it possible for the organization to achieve them. They are quantitative statements of the amount of work a program will need to undertake in order to achieve the goals of the agency vis-à-vis the organization. Since the focus is on program goals and objectives, careful attention must be given to identify the program structure (elements of the program) and define the goals to justify budget allocation. In general, this information must be included in the budget request for internal review, in particular for legislative approval. The last step completes the process and is required of all systems that use a formal program structure with program goals and objectives.

   Since structurally a program budget is similar to a line-item budget, except that it focuses on programs, in particular program goals and objectives rather than on individual cost objects or line items, we can use similar algebraic expressions to describe a program budget (Appendix B). As noted earlier, presenting the budget in matrix form makes it easy to see the differences in budget allocation for different departments and their programs, as well as for different line items both within and between departments. Understanding the differences in budget allocation helps one to understand how the process works and the program needs the allocation decisions are trying to address. For instance, it can provide valuable information that can help explain why a department has been receiving consistently more funds than other departments, or what a department can do to improve the likelihood of its receiving additional funding next year, or what it can do to avoid the potential for funding reduction in the future. It should be noted, however, that since the programs are not identical or do not have the same goals and objectives, it may be difficult to compare the allocations on their face value. To a degree that may also apply to line items. Nevertheless, the structure provides a good basis for understanding the variations in budget allocation.

Preparing the Budget

Preparing a program budget, like a line-item budget, is also quite simple. Since it is structurally similar to a line-item budget, all one needs to do is describe the goals and objectives for individual programs as clearly as possible, then develop a list of cost items for the programs consistent with program goals and objectives. Given that most programs in government are repetitive, the past history of budget allocation, including current allocation, can provide the basis for determining the dollar amount to be spent on each program, with appropriate adjustments for inflation, discretionary changes, and a safety margin for uncertainties (if allowable). Table 6.2

Table 6.2   A simple program budget

Water and Sewer Fund: Expenditure Budget
Fiscal Year: 2XXX-2XXX

Program: Garbage Collection
Program Goal: To pick up garbage in a timely manner to prevent health hazard
Program Objective: To pick up garbage twice a week throughout the year, including holidays

Codes	Line Item/ Cost Object	FY$_{t-1}$ (Last Year/Actual)	FY$_t$ (Current Year)	FY$_{t+1}$(Next Year/Proposed)
07-02-01-000*				
001	Personal Services	$925,000	$980,000	$1,060,000
002	Materials and Supplies	115,000	125,000	130,000
003	Contractual	100,000	110,000	125,000
008	Debt Service	45,000	45,000	45,000
011	Capital Outlay	20,000	20,000	25,000
017	Vehicles	75,000	80,000	85,000
023	Miscellaneous**	210,000	215,000	230,000
		$1,490,000	$1,575,000	$1,700,000
	Total:	=========	=========	=========
001	Personal Services			
001-01	Salaries (Full-time)	$510,000	$ 590,000	$680,000
001-02	Wages (Part-time)	35,000	50,000	60,000
001-07	Overtime	80,000	65,000	40,000
001-10	Supervision	65,000	70,000	90,000
001-15	Supplemental Retirement	45,000	45,000	45,000
001-27	Workman's Compensation	60,000	40,000	35,000
001-63	Benefits (including paid leave)	130,000	120,000	110,000
	Sub-total:	$925,000	$980,000	$1,060,000
		========	=======	=========

Sources of Funding: Local (Sewer) Fund		$1,520,000
State Fund		150,000
Federal Fund		30,000
Total:		$1,700,000
		=========

*07= Water & Sewer Fund, 02 = Sewer Department, 01 = Garbage Collection, 000 = Line items

presents a simple program budget for the Water and Sewer Department of our hypothetical government. Let us say that the program is Garbage Collection.

As shown in the table, the program goal is to collect garbage in a timely manner to prevent health hazard. The program objective is to collect garbage, say, twice a week throughout the year, including holidays. In reality, a program can have multiple goals and objectives, but, for convenience, we are using a single goal and a single objective. Since the items in the table are exactly the same as those in the line-item budget, their interpretations will remain very much the same, but related to the program.

6.2.2.2 Strengths and Limitations of the System

There are several advantages of using a program budget. First of all, focusing on program goals and objectives provides a rational basis for budget allocation. Since the goals and objectives must reflect what a government plans to achieve, it can help the government plan its activities and set targets for goal achievement. Secondly, developing a budget with clear goals and objectives allows one to do an effective evaluation, in particular to determine the extent to which the program goals and objectives have been achieved. More importantly, it allows one to identify the areas where deviations have occurred from the goals and explain the causes of the deviations. Finally, since in a program budget the allocations are tied to program goals and objectives rather than to specific line items, it avoids the incremental approach that underlies line-item budgeting. On the other hand, it has an important weakness in that since the focus is on goals and objectives, and not on performance, it does not provide much information on the amount of job performed, or service provided, with the allocated funds. As such, it is difficult to measure efficiency of service provision.

6.2.3   Performance Budget

Performance budget represents one of the earliest budget reforms in the country, dating back to the Taft Commission Report in 1912 which called for a work-based classification of government expenditures. It was reinforced by the Hoover Commission in 1949, which recommended its adoption by the federal government (Lederle 1949), and has since become one of the most widely used budget systems for governments across the board. As the name implies, the objective of performance budgeting is to allocate money for expenditure on various programs and activities based on the levels of service these programs will perform rather than on cost objects or line items. The service levels are determined by performance measures. While the central focus in a line-item budget is how each dollar is spent on a specific cost or line item, the central focus in a performance budget is how each dollar achieves the desired level of service consistent with program goals and objectives. Put simply, it tells the public what they will be receiving for their money in measurable terms.

6.2.3.1 Importance of Performance Measures

At the heart of a performance budget are performance measures, also known as performance indicators, which are quantitative expressions for measuring capacity, process, or results of a program or activity. Quantitative expressions are descriptions that can be measured using numerical values that usually appear alongside a budget to allow the decision makers use the information for funding decisions. Conceptually, performance measures establish a cause-and-effect relationship between program goals, budget allocation, and program results. By linking resource allocation to performance, the performance budget sets forth the services to be provided by a government, the level at which the services will be provided, and the resources that will be needed to provide the services in measurable terms.

Since the performance measures are critical to the development of a performance budget, it is important that they are constructed using certain guidelines in mind. At a minimum, they must address the following: First, the measures must indicate the progress that needs to be made toward a program goal. Second, the measures must be based on a common framework for gathering data for measurement and reporting. Third, the measures must be able to describe complex concepts in simple, easy-to-understand operational terms. Fourth, they must be constructed in such a way as to enable review of goals, objectives, and policies of the government. Fifth, they must focus on key strategic areas that are vital to the success of an organization. Sixth, but not least, they must be developed in such a way as to be able to provide feedback to the organization, especially the key decision makers as well as those who are directly responsible for providing the services.

Ideally, and as noted earlier, the selection of performance measures should be based on a set of criteria that can establish a clear linkage between program goals and objectives, and its performance. This brings a certain amount of specificity to the system that will be easy to understand and measure. A recent study by Castro (2011) provides an interesting framework that can serve as a useful guide for developing performance measures, called SMART, where each letter of the term has a specific meaning. For instance, they must be **S**pecific (precise and unambiguous) **M**easurable (appropriate to the problem), **A**chievable (at a reasonable cost), **R**elevant (serve to assess performance), and **T**ractable (easy to validate and verify). Although developed primarily for developing countries, it can be easily applied to all types of governments and organizations. If the criteria suggested in SMART are not adequate, additional criteria can be used, depending on program goals and objectives of individual organizations. The rule of thumb is that whatever criteria one uses, they must be parsimonious yet produce maximum information for program existence and to justify budget allocation.

To give an example, suppose that a local Emergency Medical Service (EMS) sets, as one of its goals, improving the quality of service based on response time. The objective of the department is to reduce average response time for ambulance to produce savings in time and cost. The corresponding performance measure would be the percentage of calls with a response time, say, of 10 minutes or less. To give another example, suppose that the human resource department of a government is planning to improve its hiring practice and one of its goals is to create a paperless application process. The objective is to promote online applications to increase efficiency in processing time. The department could use, for performance measure, the number of online applications received as a percentage of total applications and the average processing time for both online and conventional applications for comparison purposes.

6.2.3.2 The Basic Structure

Structurally, a performance budget consists of five basic elements that make up the system: workload, input, process, output, and outcome, if necessary. Workload is the amount of work (job) to be done within a specified time such as the number of water meters to be read, tons of snow to be removed, the number of pot holes to be fixed, number of school lunches to be provided, and so forth, say, in a month. Workloads are essentially estimates based on past performance or most recent information and frequently serve as the benchmark for assessing how well a job can be done. Inputs are monetary and non-monetary resources necessary to produce an output quantity. These mostly include labor (e.g., man hours), capital (e.g., buildings, machines, tools, equipment, computer hardware and software), data, materials and supplies, as well as workload.

The process converts inputs into outputs; as such, it plays an important role in the entire system as it determines the efficiency with which the inputs are converted into outputs. Formally, it can be defined as a sequence of events or activities that converts the inputs into output by gathering relevant data, processing the data, and making sure that it produces the outputs or intended results. Outputs, on the other hand, are measurable results of an activity. However, to be measurable, the outputs must be consistent and homogenous, so that they can convey the same meaning in every case. Examples of outputs will be the number of children immunized, tons of garbage collected, amount of electricity produced, number of applications processed, number of students graduated, number of citations given, and so forth. In situations where it is difficult to measure outputs in discrete units, one can use surrogates or proxies, as long as they are close approximations or substitutes of actual measures.

Finally, outcomes are intended or unintended results of an activity. Since one cannot quite predict the unintended results, the process primarily focuses on outcomes that are predictable; in other words, the results an activity is likely to produce. As such, they provide a measure of effectiveness, called effectiveness measures, indicating how well the money spent on an activity has produced the intended results. Outcomes can also be related to process, in which case they are called process measures, indicating how the process has helped an organization and its component units achieve the stated goals and objectives. For instance, have the results been due to oversight activities of an organization? In general, the outcomes are broader in scope as they try to capture the underlying objectives, which may have a social or political overtone. Examples of outcomes will be reduction in crime rates, improvement in the quality of healthcare, improvement in air quality, prevention of health hazards, satisfaction with a government service, and so forth. Figure 6.2 illustrates the structure of a performance budget in terms of input, process, output, and outcome.

Budgeting does not take place in a vacuum; it takes place within the larger environment of which it is a part. As shown in Fig. 6.2, factors external to an organization play a critical role in the entire process, from input, to process, to output, and, finally to outcome. Therefore, any change in the environmental vis-à-vis external conditions, will have a direct effect on the budget. Unfortunately, organizations do not have much control over these conditions. For instance, a natural disaster like the Hurricane Katrina that devastated New Orleans in 2005 can cost a state, city, and the federal government billions of dollars. Similarly, at the global level, what happens globally, say, in the global financial market or the political turmoil in a different part of world can have a serious impact on a budget, depending on how much interaction the government has with the outside world. Put differently, is highly export-oriented, any increase or decrease in external demand for its goods will have a direct effect on the economy and, consequently, the revenue it will generate for the government. As one would expect, it is difficult to predict the cost-effect of external factors on the budget, especially if they are outside the realm of an organization.

Similarly, changes in internal factors, such as institutional or procedural changes, can also have an effect on the budget, but, unlike the external factors, the budgetary effects of these changes are usually predictable. Nevertheless, whether the effects are difficult to predict or they can be predicted with some degrees of certainty, the government should be prepared at all times to deal with the consequences of changes in external and internal events. One way to deal with the problem is to maintain contingency provisions in the budget for events such as natural disasters, economic uncertainties, structural changes, and the like.[2]

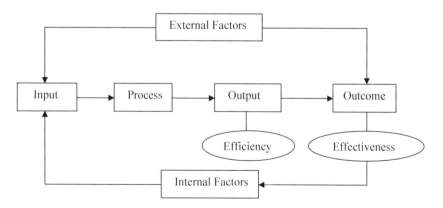

Fig. 6.2 A typical performance budgeting system with feedback loop

Preparing the Budget

Preparing a performance budget is much more involved than either a line-item or a program budget because of the need to develop meaningful performance measures that will provide the necessary data for budget development. The following steps are typically used in developing a performance budget: (1) select an agency or department for which the budget will be prepared; (2) select a program or program of activities for the agency; (3) determine the workload, as well as output units for each program; (4) determine the input units, in particular the amount of inputs (resources) to be used to produce the output quantity; (5) calculate the cost per unit of output; and (6) multiply the cost per unit of output by the total amount of output to determine the total cost of the program.

While the steps indicated above are simple and easy to follow, they can be extremely time consuming if they are to be developed for every single program or program activities. Also, agencies may spend an enormous number of hours trying to develop measures for activities that may not add much value to the decision process. To avoid the problem, one could identify the key strategic activities that are most important to the government, the community, and the larger population it serves. Table 6.3 presents a simple performance budget for the garbage collection example.

Since the development of a performance budget depends heavily on cost data, in particular input costs, it is necessary to pay careful attention how the data are collected and used to produce the output. Operationally, it is not difficult to obtain cost data for most organizations since they are available from past history, current market price, and other sources. However, frequent changes in price due to inflation, introduction of new products or substitute goods in the market, delivery delays, and other factors can affect unit costs of resources (inputs) used. Additionally, if an analysis of cost data indicates that cost of resources, such as machines, tools, equipment, and so forth varies with man-hours, then alternative measures should be used instead of unit costs.

6.2.3.3 Measuring Efficiency of a Performance Budget

An important underlying objective of all budget systems, with the exception of the line-item budget, is to provide goods and services as efficiently as possible consistent with the goals and objectives of an organization. Efficiency lies at the heart of a performance budgeting system. Since the system requires the use of performance measures, one can use these measures to evaluate performance to determine the efficiency of service provision. The simplest way to measure efficiency is to compare performance of two or more organizations of similar size and characteristics providing similar service. For instance, if it costs two governments, X and Y, providing an identical service, say, service S, $10,000 and $9500, respectively, under similar conditions, then government B is doing a better job of providing the service in cost terms than government A.

We can easily extend it to include time to have a better sense of performance over time. Let us say that it cost government A $9000 last year, $t-1$, to provide the service and government B also $9000 last year, $t-1$, assuming no changes in

Table 6.3 A simple performance budget

Water and Sewer Fund: Expenditure Budget
Fiscal Year: 2XXX-2XXX

Program: Garbage Collection
Program Goal: To pick up garbage in a timely manner to prevent health hazard
Program Objective: To pick up garbage twice a week throughout the year, including holidays

---

Performance Statistics[+]

I.   Workload

	Number of Units/Customers	25,000
	Number of Garbage Collections	2,600,000/Year
	[25,000 x (52 Weeks x 2)]	

II.   Input

	Personal Services*	52,000 Man hours (MH)/Year
	[2,600,000/(50 Units/PMH)]	
	Supervision	10.12 % of other personal services
	Materials and Supplies	$0.05/Collection/Year
	Contractual/Lease	20 Vehicles/Year
	Debt Service	---
	Vehicles	75,000 Miles/Year
	Overhead**	20% direct costs

III. Cost Per Input Unit

	Personal Services	$17.10/Man hour
	Materials and Supplies	$0.05/Collection/Year
	Contractual/Lease	$6,250/Vehicle/Year
	Debt Service	$11,250/Quarter
	Vehicle	$1.13/Mile

IV.   Cost For the Year (Estimated)

Personal Services = $17.10 x 52,000 = $889,200 ≈ $890,000**
Supervision = $890,000 x 0.1012 = $90,068 ≈ $90,000
Materials and Supplies = $0.05 x 2,600,000 = $130,000
Contractual = $6,250 x 20 = $125,000
Debt Service = $11,250 x 4 = $45,000
Vehicles = $1.13 x 75,000 = $84,700 ≈ $85,000
Overhead = $1,075,000 x 0.2 = $215,000**
Miscellaneous = $15,000 (excluding overhead)

V.   Total Cost of Operation: $1,595,000 + $45,000 (Supplemental Retirement)
+ $35,000 (Workman's Compensation) + $25,000 (Capital Outlay)
= $1,700,000

VI.   Output: Tons of garbage to be collected: 1.25 million (estimate)

VII. Cost per ton of output: $1,700,000/1,250,000 = $1.36/ton

VIII. Total cost of service provision 1,250,000 x $1.36 = $1,700,000

Sources of Funding:	Local (Sewer) Fund	$1,520,000
	State Fund	150,000
	Federal Fund	30,000
	Total:	$1,700,000

---

*Personal Services = Salaries + wages + ov ertime + benefit = $680,000 + $60,000 + $40,000
+ $110,000 = $890,000 (excludes supplemental retirement and workman's compensation;
Supervision, which is part of direct personal services, is calculated separately)
**Overhead = Direct costs x Percent age of Direct Costs = (Salaries + Wages + Overtime
+ Supervision + Materials and Supplies + Vehicles) x 0.2 = $680,000 + $60,000 + $ 40,000
+ $80,000 + 130,000 + $85,000) x 0.2 = $1,075,000 x 0.2 = $215,000. Note that we included
overtime as part of overhead calculation because we assumed it was not planned and as such,
was not absorbed under salaries and wages, or expended on materials or vehicle use.

service provision. We can now convert the cost changes in percentage terms to see if there has been any change in efficiency for the two governments. Interestingly, government B still appears to be doing a better job than A since it has a lower cost increase: 5.56%, as opposed to 11.11%; that is $[((\$9500 - \$9000)/\$9000) \times 100 = 5.56\%]_B < [((\$10,000 - \$9000)/\$9000) \times 100 = 11.11\%]_A$. We can further extend the example to include multiple years and look at the trend to see how efficiently each government has been providing the service over time, taking any two time periods at a time.

There is a major weakness of the measure suggested above in that it takes into consideration only output, and not input, but, in reality, one needs both to measure efficiency. In other words, it does not tell us anything about the productivity of the input used in producing an output quantity. Therefore, a better measure of efficiency would be to include both input and output into the calculation.

Productivity Index

The measure commonly used that takes both input and output into consideration is productivity index. In common sense terms, productivity index simply measures the relationship between input and output. There are different ways to measure productivity that takes both into consideration, but the simplest way to develop the index is to express it as a ratio, as shown below:

$$PI = O/I \tag{6.1}$$

where PI is the productivity index, O is the output, I is the input, and O/I is the ratio of output to input.

We can use the garbage collection problem, as an example, to measure the productivity, say, of labor, while keeping the effects of all other input factors constant. Thus, using the number of man-hours for garbage collection next year (the proposed budget) as input and the amount of garbage to be collected as output, the productivity index (PI) for our problem would be 24.04, or simply 24.04 tons per man hour; that is, $1,250,000/52,000 = 24.04$.

The productivity index we thus obtained is a measure of labor productivity since we used labor as the input. If, instead of labor, we had used capital vis-à-vis the amount of capital used (usually expressed in dollar terms) in collecting 1.25 million tons of garbage, the result would have been tons per unit of capital (tons per dollar of capital), indicating the productivity of capital used. Similarly, if we had used materials vis-à-vis the amount of materials used in collecting 1.25 million tons of garbage, the result would have been tons per unit of material, indicating the productivity of materials used, and so forth.

While the expression used in Eq. 6.1 is simple, it is static in that it does not show the changes in productivity resulting from changes in input and output. Therefore, to reflect the measure of change in productivity we can expand the expression in Eq. 6.1 by incorporating time periods. The following provides a productivity index based on two time periods:

$$PI = \left[(O_t/I_t)/(O_{t-1}/I_{t-1})\right] \times 100 \tag{6.2}$$

where PI is the productivity index, O_t is the output at time t (which is the current year), I_t is the input at time t (the current year), O_{t-1} is the output at time $t-1$ (which is last year), and I_{t-1} is the input at time $t-1$ (last year).

The expression in Eq. 6.2 is really a ratio of two productivities—the current year productivity, which is the numerator, and the base year productivity, which is the denominator. Note that the current year (t) is the reference year or the reference point, and last year ($t-1$) is the base year against which the performance of past and future years is measured. In general, the most recent year usually serves as the base year, although any year in a time series can serve as the base year.

We will use the garbage collection example again to measure the change in productivity. Let us say that we have the following information for our problem: $O_{t-1} = 1000,000$ tons; $O_t = 1,100,000$ tons; $I_{t-1} = 50,000$ man-hours, and $I_t = 50,000$ man-hours—the same amount of man-hours used in both years. Thus, applying the expression in Eq. 6.2, we can obtain the productivity index for our garbage collection problem, as given below:

$$PI = \left[(O_t/I_t)/(O_{t-1}/I_{t-1})\right] \times 100$$
$$= \left[(1,100,000/50,000)/(1,000,000/50,000)\right] \times 100$$
$$= [22/20] \times 100$$
$$= (1.1) \times 100$$
$$= 110(\%)$$

The result produces a 10% $[(1.1 - 1.0) \times 100 = 10\%]$ increase in labor productivity from the previous year. Looking at the productivity ratio for individual years, we can see that it was 22 tons per man hour in the current year (t), as opposed to 20 tons last year ($t-1$)—an improvement of 2 tons over last year. We can easily extend the process to include any number of years.

Interestingly, we could have obtained the same result by calculating the productivity index separately for each year and then taking the difference between the two indices, and expressing the difference in percentage change terms, as shown below:

$$PI = \left[(PI_t - PI_{t-1})/(PI_{t-1})\right] \times 100$$
$$= \left[((O/I)_t - (O/I)_{t-1})/(O/I)_{t-1}\right] \times 100$$
$$= [(1,100,000/50,000) - (1,000,000/50,000)/(1,000,000/50,000)] \times 100$$
$$= [(22 - 20)/(20)] \times 100 \qquad\qquad (6.3)$$
$$= (2/20) \times 100$$
$$= 10(\%)$$

As before, the result shows a 10% increase in productivity from last year. An advantage of using the expression above is that it gives us a direct measure of productivity change; there is no need to subtract the result from 100 to obtain the change. Had there been a loss of productivity, the result would have a negative value.

It should be worth noting that the measure suggested above uses a single input—labor. When a single input is used to measure productivity, it is called partial productivity. Likewise, when a combination of inputs is used to measure productivity, it is called multifactor productivity. For instance, in addition to labor, if we had also used materials and capital (a total of three input variables), and aggregated the variables in some fashion (add, divide, multiply, etc.) to measure productivity, the result would be a multifactor productivity. However, if we had measured the productivity separately for each input factor, it would be a partial productivity, not a multifactor productivity since the input factors were not considered together. On the other hand, if we had used an aggregate output, such as the output of all the activities for the department taken together, and an aggregate of inputs, such as a weighted average of the input factors, it would not be a multifactor productivity, but it would be total factor productivity because aggregates were used for both input and output, in particular for output.

Interestingly, the method frequently used to measure productivity with multiple inputs is production function (PF). A production function measures the relationship between an output and two or more inputs. There is a family of production functions from which one can choose to measure productivity, depending on the interest of the researcher. Besides production functions, there are other methods, such as those based on mathematical programming or stochastic frontiers that one can use for measuring productivity (Khan and Murova 2015; Murova and Khan 2017), and the methodology is expanding.

On occasion, it may be necessary to compare the productivity of a government against a standard for a specific service that can be used as benchmark. In the event that a standard is not available, one can take an average of productivity measures for a number of governments with similar size and characteristics providing similar service, and use it as benchmark for comparison.

6.2.3.4 Strengths and Limitations of the System

While a performance budget has obvious advantages over a line-item or program budget, some of which were discussed earlier, the greatest advantage of performance budgeting is that it creates a performance culture in an organization by promoting accountability of employees and agencies in utilizing the resources to ensure that its goals and objectives are met. If observed carefully, the process can guide capacity building for better governance by linking program goals and resource use, thereby, contributing to overall goal achievement of the organization. As a system, it brings together policy making, planning, and budgeting to program implementation, followed by assessment and feedback, and then cycling back to policy making.

In spite of its strengths, performance budgeting has its weaknesses. The greatest weakness of the system is that it focuses on volume and not on the quality of job performed. Although outcome measures try to address the quality issue somewhat, it is often not clear how these measures are used to determine the effectiveness of a program. Unfortunately, measuring effectiveness is far more difficult than measuring efficiency, especially if the outcomes are difficult to express in measurable terms and also because of social, political, and other considerations that often underlie the outcome measures. Harry Hatry and Donald Fisk (1971) suggested a simple yet interesting approach for quality assessment by incorporating the percentage of population satisfied with a service based on citizen survey. In fact, citizen surveys have been extensively used in government for measuring public satisfaction with government services for a long time.

Although somewhat dated, their approach has an interesting appeal in that it uses survey methodology that allows one to include any type of quality measure, besides citizen satisfaction (Hatry 1997, 2006; Simonsen and Robbins 2000). Another approach that does not rely on survey methodology would be to develop a mechanism for monitoring performance, similar to a tracking device, as the system goes through the various stages of the process, from setting goals and objectives, to the production of final goods and services (output), to achieving desired results (outcomes). The process can be time consuming, but useful in tracking where the deviations have occurred in the system and finding means to correct them.

A Note on GPRA

In 1993, Congress passed an act called the Government Performance and Results Act (GPRA) to address a range of issues, dealing with government accountability and performance. The primary objective of the act was to build confidence in government by focusing on results of government activities, improve the managerial and internal workings of agencies within the government, and extend support to Congressional oversight and decision making. Although the federal government has a long history of budget management systems, GPRA adds a new dimension that requires the results of agency performance to be integrated in the decision-making process. One other feature that separates GPRA from the preceding practices is that, while many of the earlier reforms were initiated by the executive branch without any legal requirements, GPRA is statutory meaning that the inclusion of performance measures are required by law (GAO 1996).

The GPRA is founded on three basic elements: (1) the development of a strategic plan, (2) the development of a performance plan, and (3) the preparation and submission of a performance report. At the core of GPRA is the development of a strategic plan. A strategic plan provides a framework for achieving the missions, goals, and objectives of an organization through a set of well-defined strategies within a defined time frame. The plan is required to cover at least five years from the fiscal year in which it is submitted and be updated every three years. The development of a performance plan requires the agencies to follow a set of steps consistent with a performance budget. The steps typically include the development of quantifiable performance measures, identifying resources required to achieve performance goals, establishing performance indicators for measuring relevant outputs, service levels, and outcomes of a program activity, and evaluating the observed performance results against target performance goals. Finally, the Act requires the agencies to prepare and submit an annual performance report detailing the success and failure in meeting the program goals.

In 2002, the Office of Management and Budget (OMB) developed a system for formally evaluating the effectiveness of the federal programs called Program Assessment Rating Tool (PART). What distinguishes it from GPRA is that it focuses entirely on program effectiveness. Based, in part, on survey design, PART uses four broad criteria to evaluate a program: program design, strategic planning, program management, and program results. Using a series of questions based on the four criteria, the instrument rates the programs on a scale of 0 to 100 and ranks them as effective (85–100), moderately effective (70–84), adequate (50–69), and ineffective (0–49). A fifth category has been added recently, called results not demonstrated yet, indicating the programs that have not been able to develop acceptable performance goals. Additional changes are likely, as the programs and the criteria go through further evaluation by OMB and others.

6.2.3.5 Alternative Formulation: Cost-Based Budget

The cost data used in performance budgeting serve an important purpose; in addition to providing information on unit costs, they can be variously analyzed to develop a budget in pure cost terms depending on how the costs are classified called cost-based budget or cost budget, in short. A cost budget is based on traditional cost structure that divides costs into two basic categories: fixed costs and variable costs. Fixed costs are costs that do not change, regardless of the quantity produced, whereas variable costs change with changes in the quantity produced. Thus, in the current example, the total cost (TC) of the program for next year will be the sum of the fixed and the variable costs of garbage collection. The fixed costs (FCs) would include the costs of leasing, debt service, the portion of personal service that is salaried, supplemental retirement benefits, including paid leave, since these costs will remain unchanged during the budget period. The variable costs (VCs), on the other hand, would include materials and supplies, capital outlay, the portion of personal service that is based on hourly wages, overtime, since these costs would vary depending on the amount of labor and materials used. Table 6.4 gives the cost breakdown of the budget for next year.

Costs can also be classified as direct and indirect. Direct costs are costs that can be directly attributed to an activity, whereas the indirect costs cannot; as such, the term used to define these costs is overhead. Overhead costs for individual activities are often difficult to determine. As a result, most organizations use overhead cost as a fixed percentage of the total cost of operation for the entire organization and use it as the overhead for the respective activity. Let us suppose that the overhead cost of operation for the entire government in our example currently is 20%; thus, applying it to the garbage collection problem will produce an overhead of $340,000 ($1,700,000 x 0.2). The remaining $1,360,000 will then go toward direct

Table 6.4 A simple cost structure

Water and Sewer Fund: Expenditure Budget
Fiscal Year: 2XXX-2XXX

Program: Garbage Collection
Program Goal: To pick up garbage in a timely manner to prevent health hazard
Program Objective: To pick up garbage twice a week throughout the year, including holidays

Cost Categories	Cost ($)
07-02-01-000*	
I. Fixed Costs	
Personal Services	
Salaries (Full-time)	$680,000
Supplemental Retirement	45,000
Workman's Compensation	35,000
Supervision (Fixed)	90,000
Benefit (including Leave)	110,000
Total Personal (Fixed)	$960,000
Contractual/Lease	125,000
Debt Service	45,000
Overhead	215,000
Total Fixed Cost	$1,345,000
II. Variable Costs	
Personal Services	
Wages (Part-time)	$60,000
Overtime (Salaried)	40,000
Total Personal (Variable)	$100,000
Materials and Supplies	130,000
Capital Outlay	25,000
Vehicles	85,000
Miscellaneous (Excluding overhead)	15,000
Total Variable Cost	$355,000
III. Total Cost of Operation	$1,700,000
($1,345,000 + $355,000)	

*Fund and account information

labor and direct materials. The process can be further extended by breaking down direct labor and materials into different types of direct labor and direct materials, etc. Overhead, on the other hand, is usually treated as an all-inclusive category or item.

Activity-Based Costing

The difficulty in dealing with overhead has produced several alternatives over the years, but the one that has drawn the most attention in recent years, especially in the 1970s through the 1990s, is activity-based costing (ABC). ABC assigns costs to cost objects through a set of activities rather than assigning them directly from a cost pool (defined as a group of accounts from which costs are allocated to a cost object). The purpose of activity-based costing is to determine what is driving the costs, called cost driver, and charge a cost object for only the overhead it actually consumes (Burch 1994). There are five major building blocks that make up ABC: resources (inputs), resource drivers (measures the amount of resources used up or consumed), activities (unit of work that converts inputs to outputs), activity cost drivers (activities consumed), and cost objects (outputs, e.g., products, services, jobs, etc.). Although every element of the process is important, the cost drivers play a pivotal role in the entire process, as it provides the justification for the activities and also for costs. As such, it is used as the cost-allocation base (allocates costs to cost objects). Figure 6.3 illustrates the structure of an ABC process.

When a budget is prepared using activity-based costing, it is called an activity-based budget (ABB). Conceptually, one can treat ABB as a variation of performance budget. From that perspective, ABB is not a new concept in government, although it has received more attention in recent years. For instance, the federal government has been using it for a long time, going back to 1951 when it moved from the traditional line-item to performance budgeting based on the recommendations of the Hoover Commission. It is not clear, however, how expenditure estimates by activities were made or to what extent they were based on input–output analysis of a performance budgeting system.

6.2.4   Zero-Based Budget

Zero-based budget (ZBB) was first introduced by the US Department of Agriculture in the early 1960s, though without much success, as a means to justify program needs, expenditure requests, and cost structure. Several years later, Peter Pyhrr (1973) revitalized interests in ZBB by successfully implementing it in Texas Instruments as a method of controlling the overhead costs. Impressed with its success, Governor Carter of Georgia invited Pyhrr to help him implement the system in the state and, in 1976 when he became the President, decided to adopt it in the

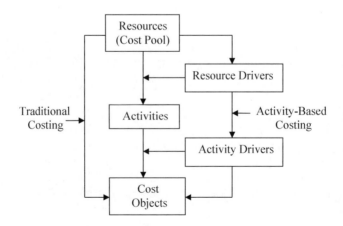

Fig. 6.3 A typical ABC process

federal government. Today, a large number of state and local governments, along with numerous private and nonprofit organizations, use ZBB or some variations of it.

ZBB has been variously defined. In its bare essence, it means constructing a budget with zero base, from scratch, that is, without any reference to what has gone before based on a fundamental reappraisal of organizational goals, methods, and resources (Taylor 1977). It makes no assumption about the past and every operation is questioned, scrutinized, and justified on the basis of its own merits (costs and benefits). In some ways, the process can be construed as a departure from traditional incremental budgeting associated with line-item budget, although line-item budget remains as the core system. Conceptually, it involves a bottom-up approach where managers at all levels of decision-making participate in the process by systematically evaluating how activities and resources of a government should be allocated to accomplish its goals, objectives, and priorities.

6.2.4.1 The Basic Structure

An important characteristic of ZBB, which distinguishes it from all other budget ing systems, is its flexibility. It does not require a rigid structure, or procedure, and can be easily tailored to meet the specific needs of a government. Although the specifics may differ, the steps involving a ZBB process are essentially the same; it uses a three-step process: (1) selection of decision units, (2) development of a set of packages, called decision packages, and (3) ranking of the packages in some priority order. Together, the steps serve as the building blocks of ZBB.

Decision Units

The decision units are the basic building blocks of ZBB. They are the focal points in the organization where the decision makers at the operating level (the operating managers) make decisions as to how much they will need to spend, the scope, and the quality of work that will need to be performed. Theoretically, a decision unit can be anything; it can be a functional unit, a program, or an activity, depending on the level of detail the organization wants for budget decision making. Although ZBB can be designed within the traditional object-classification system, it is more adaptable to a program budgeting structure. This is due to the fact that the decision packages are by their very nature oriented toward governmental functions, programs, and activities than specific line items. Besides, the program structure is important in all agencies because the requests for budget appropriations are usually justified at the program and activity levels.

Decision Packages

The decision packages provide the rationale for various programs and activities of a program structure. They are an important building block of a ZBB process since they are prepared for individual programs and related activities. Formulating a decision package requires that each agency determines appropriate objectives for individual programs, as well as for associated activities. Once a choice regarding the objectives of a program or activity has been made, several different levels of effort, called funding levels, can be made. In general, the funding levels generally express an incremental cost and benefit, built upon a base that provides support for other levels. By using different levels of funding, the decision makers can avoid elimination of a program or activity by choosing, for instance, a lower level of funding.

To give an example, suppose that a government using a ZBB system decides to use four levels of funding. Level 1, defined as "the minimum-level effort," specifies a level below which a program or activity will not be considered viable. It can be set at any level below the current level, or set at, say, 90% of the last year's budget.[3] What constitutes this minimum can vary from year to year, and from government to government, depending on program needs. Level 2, defined as "the current services level," represents funding at the 100% of the current year budget. Funding is not expected to exceed this level unless major changes take place in the program or its activities. Level 3, defined as "the intermediate level," represents funding at a slightly higher level than the current services level, but below the full amount requested. Level 4, defined as "the most desired level," represents an agency's full request. It is used only in those circumstances where the total request for a program exceeds those prescribed at Level 3. Together, the sum total of the budget requests for the decision packages constitutes the total budget request for an agency.

Ranking the Decision Packages
The final element in the ZBB process is the ranking of the decision packages in order of priority. Usually, the high priority packages rank at the top and the low priority packages at the bottom. Prioritization gives the decision makers the flexibility to consider the packages that are at the top when faced with budget constraints. The way the process works is that the manager at the lowest level evaluates and ranks the packages of his unit, sends them to the next higher level; the manager at the next level then re-evaluates the packages, re-ranks them, and sends them to the next higher level. The process continues until the decision is made at the highest level of decision making. Figure 6.4 shows how the process works.

The ranking of the decision packages during the entire process requires a careful analysis. It can become complex if the list of packages and the number of decision units become far too large for the decision makers to be able to do a thorough analysis of the requests. At the agency level, where the manager has the added responsibility of consolidating the packages, the complexity can increase multiple-fold. Nevertheless, the process gives the decision makers at various levels some control over the substantive mix of programs and activities, which is crucial to a ZBB system.

Preparing the Budget
Preparing a budget using ZBB follows the stages mentioned above in proper sequence: selection of decision units, followed by decision packages, and ranking of the packages. Table 6.5 shows the ZBB formulation of the garbage collection example we used earlier. According to the table, garbage collection is one of five decision packages for the department, although, ideally, we could have many more

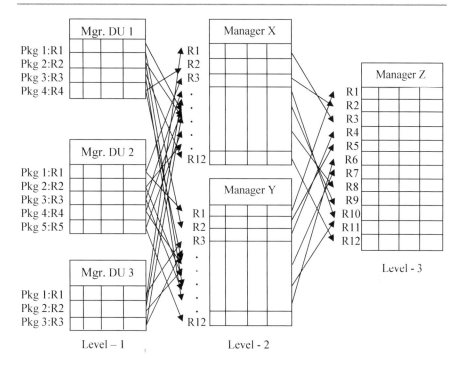

Fig. 6.4 Ranking of decision packages and the consolidation process. First column—last year's budget, second column—current year budget, third column—next year's (proposed) budget, fourth column—cumulative total (proposed)

such packages. The rule of thumb is to have between two to seven packages, ideally five, so that one is able to compare them without being inconsistent. Having more than seven packages can make the comparison difficult. The packages are rank-ordered, from highest to lowest, with a cumulative cost, in this case, of $6.185 million, which is the proposed budget for the department for next year, FY_{t+1}.

The advantage of presenting budget allocations in cumulative terms is that it establishes a cut-off line to indicate the maximum number of packages an agency can undertake, given the amount of resources available. For instance, if the maximum amount available to the department next year is $4.3 million, then the most it can undertake are the first three packages, and so forth.

Table 6.5 also shows the funding levels for the package. As noted earlier, at Level 1, the funding is below the current year budget, assuming it will not reduce the overall service quality. This may, however, mean that the agency will have to make some cuts elsewhere such as in benefits, overtime, or salaries. The Level 2 funding will keep the budget at the same level, as it is for the current year, while the last two levels show increased funding from the current year. The table also shows the workload measures to indicate how the performance statistics can be easily integrated into a ZBB process.

Table 6.5 A simple Zero-based budget

Water and Sewer Fund: Expenditure Budget
Fiscal Year: 2XXX-2XXX

Decision Unit: Sewer Department
Decision Package (1 of 5): Garbage Collection
Program Goal: To pick up garbage in a timely manner to prevent health hazard
Program Objective: To pick up garbage twice a week throughout the year, including holidays

Ranking of Packages	Cost ($000)	Cumulative Cost ($)			
Package 1 of 5: Rank 1	1,700,000	1,700,000			
Package 2 of 5: Rank 2	1,250,000	2,950,000			
Package 3 of 5: Rank 3	1,325,000	4,275,000			
Package 4 of 5: Rank 4	1,195,000	5,470,000			
Package 5 of 5: Rank 5	715,000	6,185,000			
Line Item/Cost Object	FY_t ($)	FY_{t+1} Level 1($)	FY_{t+1} Level 2($)	FY_{t+1} Level 3($)	FY_{t+1} Level 4($)
07-02-01-000					
001 Personal Services	980,000	882,000	980,000	1,025,000	1,060,000
002 Materials & Supplies	125,000	113,000	125,000	127,000	130,000
003 Contractual	110,000	110,000	110,000	110,000	125,000
008 Debt Service	45,000	45,000	45,000	45,000	45,000
011 Capital Outlay	20,000	18,000	20,000	23,000	25,000
017 Vehicles	80,000	80,000	80,000	80,000	85,000
023 Miscellaneous	215,000	194,000	215,000	225,000	230,000
Total:	1,575,000	1,442,000	1,575,000	1,635,000	1,700,000
Workload Measures					
N of Units to Serve/Month	25,000	25,000	25,000	25,000	25,000
N of Collections to be Made/Year	2,600,000	2,600,000	2,600,000	2,600,000	2,600,000
Sources of Funding	FY_t ($)	FY_{t+1} Level 1($)	FY_{t+1} Level 2($)	FY_{t+1} Level 3($)	FY_{t+1} Level 4($)
Local (Sewer) Fund	---	1,322,000	1,430,000	1,480,000	1,520,000
State Fund	---	100,000	120,000	130,000	150,000
Federal Fund	---	20,000	25,000	25,000	30,000
		1,442,000	1,575,000	1,635,000	1,700,000

6.2.4.2 Strengths and Limitations of the System

In spite of its popularity as a budget system, ZBB has several important limitations. First of all, while the use of decision units gives the decision makers considerable flexibility in deciding on the level of details, having too many decision units
and packages can increase the volumes of paper works, which can limit the coordination between different agencies. Secondly, the ranking of decision packages
in priority order can be a frustrating experience for most agencies. Although each
agency is expected to prioritize its program and activity packages on the basis of
a set of criteria that are consistent and methodologically sound, political and other
considerations can make it difficult to do so. The presence of other factors, such as
legal constraints, earmarked, or court-mandated programs, can make it even more
difficult for the upper-level management to consolidate the decision packages. The
problem can be minimized by isolating programs that are mandated from those

that are not mandated and leaving prioritization only for non-mandated programs. Thirdly, and most important, a common concern that seems typical of the ZBB process is the incremental level of funding. There is no clear evidence that justifies the cut-off points generally established for these levels. This is in direct contrast to the notion that ZBB begins by looking at the budget afresh, each year, especially if the allocations are to be made not based on last year's budget.

6.2.5   Strategic Budget

As the name implies, strategic budget (SB) is a forward-looking system built on the position, strengths, and weaknesses of an organization. While the traditional budget systems take an inward view of an organization by focusing on the internal factors (activities), strategic budgeting takes a broad, open approach directed toward both internal and external factors (activities). This adds a new dimension to the traditional budget process by enlarging an organization's view of management and making it more useful as an approach to deal with the changing forces that influence its management functions. However, like any other budget system, its objective is to provide a structure that would allow an organization to better allocate its resource to meet the competing needs of society. Although not entirely a new concept, strategic budgeting is considered an important development in the long history of budget reforms, going back to line-item budget.

Strategic budget has its roots in strategic planning. Strategic planning is a process that deals with the future based on current decisions. It starts by defining an organization's philosophy, along with its mission (focus) and vision (direction), identifying its goals and objectives, defining strategies, outlining policies and, finally, mapping out concrete actions to achieve the stated mission, goals, and objectives. As a process, strategic planning is continuous because the formulation of strategies takes place in an environment that is constantly changing. It is also feedback-oriented because the changing environment requires constant updating of information generated at each stage of the process. Most important of all, it is an action-oriented system that tries to bridge the gap between what is designed as a process and what is achieved in reality; in other words, it tries to bridge the gap between theory and practice. In conventional terminology, this is known as operationalization—a process that ties strategic planning to tactical or operational planning.

6.2.5.1 The Basic Structure

As a budgeting system, strategic budgeting is not complicated and can be easily tailored to suit an organization's structure, needs, and circumstances. This apparent flexibility also makes it suitable for adapting it to a program budgeting structure, similar to ZBB, by explicitly orienting it toward an organization's philosophy, mission, vision, values, goals, objectives, strategies, and actions. Organizational philosophy is the global view of an organization, its purpose toward which it must strive. It consists of statements concerning a set of beliefs and preferences that serve as the guiding principles of the organization. Mission is the focus that establishes a link between the philosophy of an organization and its vision and core values. Vision provides the direction the organization must use to achieve its mission, while values explain the behavior that safeguards those values. Together, they represent the core values and principles that provide the rationale for the existence of an agency. Goals, as noted previously, are general ends to which an agency must direct all its effort. Objectives, on the other hand, are quantitative statements of what an agency plans to achieve within a given time frame. Strategies, the core elements of the structure, are methods or approaches employed by an agency to achieve its goals, objectives, and the results of its actions. Finally, actions transform strategies into a series of tasks.

Understanding the relationship between different components of the system is crucial, especially in government where requests for appropriation are justified at the program and activity level based on a sound understanding of the goals, objectives, and strategies. Although the details may differ, the objectives of a strategic budgeting system are essentially the same as in any other budgeting system in that they must be clear (to indicate the direction of change), flexible (to accommodate the changing needs of an organization), and rational (to ensure that the elements of the structure are logically connected). Figure 6.5 illustrates the relationship between the different components of a strategic budget.

Structurally, a strategic budget has four basic elements that constitute the essence of the system: strategic planning, budgeting, reporting, and evaluating. The process begins with the development of a strategic plan, which encourages agencies to budget for needed resources, implement sound management strategies, document and report the results of their programs, and evaluate the results. During this phase, individual agencies are asked to develop programs of activities, along with performance plans that identify the agency mission, goals, objectives, strategies, and actions based on a set of agreed upon performance measures for the upcoming budget year. Budgeting allocates the resources of an organization in a balanced and systematic manner between different departments, while maintaining

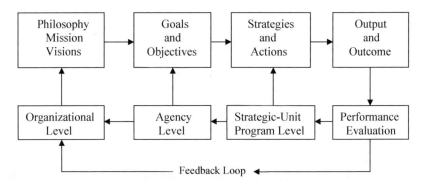

Fig. 6.5 A typical strategic budgeting system with feedback loop

its financial stability. Finally, reporting requires the agencies to use the program and performance plans to measure their performance on an ongoing basis, and make strategic adjustments, as needed, to achieve the overall goals, objectives, and performance targets.

Operationally, a strategic budget is close to a zero-based budget in that the strategies and actions are often decided at the strategic-unit level, similar to the decision units in ZBB. The strategies are similar to the decision packages of ZBB, but with a long-term focus. As in ZBB, developing the strategy set (similar to decision packages) is crucial to the entire process since much of the decision on budget allocation depends on these strategies and how well they have been put together to achieve the goals and objectives of the agency vis-à-vis the organization. In general, before selecting the strategies, each (strategic) unit must do a careful analysis of relevant data to justify their selection. In particular, the units must ask how feasible and attainable the strategies are in light of the available resources, time, and other constraints.

Since structurally a strategic budget is similar to a zero-based budget, to construct the budget one could follow essentially the same steps: identify the strategic units, define the strategies, and decide on the appropriate actions. Theoretically, each unit can have a strategy set consisting of multiple strategies and each strategy, in turn, can have multiple actions. While they must be clear and unambiguous, the strategies must have some flexibility to accommodate any possible changes in the budget. There is a parallel here with ZBB where flexibility is often incorporated through a rolling budget (i.e., continually updated), so that new fiscal years can be added as the old ones are deleted. Additionally, strategies should have some options for contingency plans providing information on contingencies, possible counter-measures, establishment of trigger points (measurements specifically designed to signal important changes at critical performance levels), and any other consideration necessary to deal with the likely problems. The contingencies do not have to be exhaustive, as long as they cover the plan period.

Table 6.6 shows the strategic formulation for the garbage collection example, discussed earlier. The table also shows the strategy for the example and a corresponding action. As noted previously, we could have used multiple strategies and actions but, for the sake of simplicity, we have used one of each. In reality, the actual number should be determined by the size of the strategic unit, the number of programs it plans to undertake, the history of its budget and, like ZBB, it is possible to rank the strategies and actions.

The example presented above is simple, but the steps suggested here can be applied to any unit of the organization. As the scale of the budget gets larger, it becomes critically important that the agency mission, goals, objectives, and strategies are synchronized to minimize any potential conflict between agency mission and the mission of the organization. In the same vein, careful attention must be given to develop the strategic units to minimize duplication of programs and activities, among others.

Table 6.6   A simple strategic budget

Water and Sewer Fund: Expenditure Budget
Fiscal Year: 2XXX-2XXX

Strategic Unit: Sewer Department
Mission: To maintain community health and prevent disease
Goal: To pick up garbage in a timely manner to prevent health hazard
Objective: To pick up garbage twice a week throughout the year, including holidays

Strategy: Use the agency guidelines for weekly collection
Action: 100 percent of collections to be made/Week

Line Item/Cost Object	FY_t ($)	FY_{t+1} Level 1($)	FY_{t+1} Level 2($)	FY_{t+1} Level 3($)	FY_{t+1} Level 4($)
07-02-01-000					
001 Personal Services	980,000	882,000	980,000	1,025,000	1,060,000
002 Materials & Supplies	125,000	113,000	125,000	127,000	130,000
003 Contractual	110,000	110,000	110,000	110,000	125,000
008 Debt Service	45,000	45,000	45,000	45,000	45,000
011 Capital Outlay	20,000	18,000	20,000	23,000	85,000
017 Vehicles	80,000	80,000	80,000	80,000	85,000
023 Miscellaneous	215,000	194,000	215,000	225,000	230,000
Total:	1,575,000	1,442,000	1,575,000	1,635,000	1,700,000
	=======	=======	=======	=======	=======
Workload Measures					
N of Units to Serve/Month	25,000	25,000	25,000	25,000	25,000
N of Collections to be Made/Year	2,600,000	2,600,000	2,600,000	2,600,000	2,600,000

Sources of Funding	FY_t ($)	FY_{t+1} Level 1($)	FY_{t+1} Level 1($)	FY_{t+1} Level 1($)	FY_{t+1} Level 1($)
Local (Sewer) Fund	---	1,322,000	1,430,000	1,480,000	1,520,000
State Fund	---	100,000	120,000	130,000	150,000
Federal Fund	---	20,000	25,000	25,000	30,000
		1,442,000	1,575,000	1,635,000	1,700,000
		=======	=======	=======	=======

6.2.6   Other Budget Systems

In addition to the above, there are a number of budget systems that have been in use at different levels for sometimes. Most of these systems are variations or extensions of the major budget systems. For convenience, we will call these systems—sub-systems. Four budget systems would fall into this category, Planning, Programming, and Budgeting System, outcome-based budget, target-based budget, and priority-based budget. This section also highlights three other budget systems that have been receiving considerable attention in recent years, including one that has a long history going back to 1954; they are management by objectives, sustainability budget, and participatory budget.

6.2.6.1 Planning, Programming, and Budgeting System

In the early 1960s, the Department of Defense introduced a variation of program budget, called Planning, Programming, and Budgeting System (PPBS), that marked a significant departure from the traditional budgeting practice. While the

objective of PPBS remains essentially the same as a program budget in that it allocates the resources of a government to various programs and activities based on
a set of goals and objectives, there is a major difference that sets it apart. PPBS
relies on a systematic analysis of program goals and objectives and their alternatives to justify budget allocation. It does so by integrating various methods of
planning and evaluation into the budget process, such as cost-benefit analysis and
systems approach, to establish priorities and strategies for goal achievement.

PPBS is based on three basic elements that make up the system: Planning,
Programming, and Budgeting System. Planning allows a government to establish
goals and objectives, and determine the criteria by which to achieve those goals
and objectives. It is essentially an output-oriented function that ties the goals
and objectives to goal achievement in such a way as to prevent possible conflicts
between programs (Solem and Werner 1968). In general, the responsibility for
developing the goals and objectives rests with the upper-level management of an
organization.

Programming allows a government to develop a formal structure by which to
analyze the programs. The structure divides the programs into a series of output-
oriented activities that tie the various inputs such as personnel, materials and supplies, and capital outlay to a specific output (Fig. 6.6). Budgeting involves the
development of a crosswalk showing the linkage between a program, its goals,
objectives, and budget allocation. The last element, the system, indicates the use
of a systematic approach that coherently ties the goals and objectives of individuals programs to the larger goals of the organization to minimize overlap and inefficiency in resource use. Completing the tasks for each element is an involved and
time-consuming process that needs to take into consideration a variety of factors,
including some that are noneconomic in character.

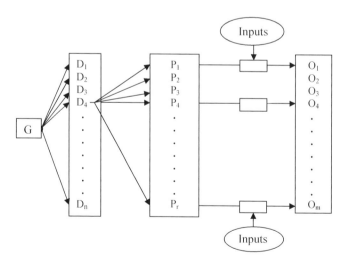

Fig. 6.6 A simple program structure: Government (G), Departments (D), Programs (P), and
Program Outputs (O)

In spite of its thoroughness and early success, PPBS (which subsequently was changed by the Department of Defense to PPBE—Planning, Programming, Budgeting, and Execution—to include a wide range of programs) has not been as well received as some of the other systems. The effort by the Johnson administration to use it across the board for all federal agencies did not quite materialize, although it remains the dominant system in use for the Defense Department, today.

There are several explanations as to why the system did not do well outside of the Defense Department: First of all, it was too analytical for traditional bureaucracy at the time when it was introduced, especially its over-reliance on methods such as cost-benefit analysis and systems approach, although that has changed considerably in recent years as governments have become much more analytically sophisticated. Secondly, it uses a top-down approach that does not have much room for feedback from lower-level management that is directly responsible for providing goods and services. This may partly explain why it is much more suitable for agencies with a top-down structure such as the Defense Department. Thirdly, it relies too much on a rigid structure that discourages coordination between different agencies and departments, while the general structure of bureaucracy does not allow such rigidity.

On the positive side, the system focuses on efficiency and goal achievement through programming and resource allocation, which lie at the heart of all budget decisions in government.

6.2.6.2 Outcome-Based Budget

Outcome-based budget (OBB) is an extension of performance budgeting system and focuses primarily on the outcomes budgetary decisions have on the public vis-à-vis society at large. As mentioned earlier, outcomes are intended and unintended consequences of a budget decision. Since it is difficult to predict the unintended consequences of a budget decision, the focus of an outcome-based budget is mostly on the intended consequences. For instance, if the goal of a public safety department is to reduce traffic infractions by a certain percentage by next year, the output will be the number of citations given and outcome will be the actual reduction in infractions within the target date. The question that is appropriate in outcome-based budgeting is to what extent the program performance produces the intended results (outcomes).

Different approaches have been suggested over the years for developing outcome-based budgets. A good example is an approach suggested by Osborne and Gaebler (1992) which uses a two-pronged approach: linking approach and purchase approach. In a linking approach, the outcomes are linked to the budget process, from input, to process, to output, to outcome (as shown in Fig. 6.2), so that there is a cause-and-effect relationship between the goals and objectives of an organization and the outcomes to help achieve those goals. In a purchase approach, on the other hand, the emphasis is on how the specific resources of an organization are allocated to accomplish specific outcomes, so that there is a one-to-one correspondence between budget allocation and the planned outcomes. This enables the stakeholders (whose interests the system vis-à-vis the government serves) to see what specific resources are allocated to accomplish what specific outcomes. However, the process may be somewhat more difficult than the linking approach because of multiple stakeholders and their interests in budget decisions that are not always in congruence. Regardless, according to the authors, the first approach should serve as a necessary first step to develop the budget (Martin 2002).

Similarly, GFOA (2007) recommends an eight-step process to develop an outcome-based budget that is simple, practical, and easy to follow. The following provides a summary of the steps: One, determine how much revenue is available to carry out the budgetary activities based on revenue forecasts. This is where good and accurate forecasts become useful. Two, develop outcomes and prioritize them. The number of outcomes should not be to be too many or too few, so that the outcomes will be consistent and easy to prioritize. The rule of thumb is that the number should be ten or less. Three, allocate resources to the desired outcomes. Since resources are often limited, the allocation should be on the basis of those with higher priorities first. Four, determine what strategies, programs, and activities will achieve the desired outcomes. Five, select the proposals that best meet the program priorities to be included in the budget. Six, set measures to monitor progress on achievement; this will close the feedback loop. Seven, analyze the results to compare the actual and budgeted outcomes. In other words, determine the achievement of outcomes. Eight, and finally, communicate the performance results to the public.

Interestingly, like any budget system with the exception of line-item, an outcome-based budget can be built on an existing process. In fact, it should be relatively easy to build since it is an extension of a performance budgeting system. Operationally, it can use the same input measures as in performance budgeting to determine the relationship between input and outcomes, as opposed to input and output, such as outcome per unit of labor, outcome per unit of material, and so forth, assuming one is able to define the outcomes in quantitative terms. Where it is difficult to express the outcomes in quantitative terms, efforts should be made to use proxies or surrogates, as long as they are close substitutes of the intended outcomes. Also, since outcomes are direct measures of effectiveness, defining outcomes in clear and precise terms, consistent with the goals and objectives of individual agencies and departments vis-à-vis the organization as a whole, is critical to the development of the budget.

Ultimately, the success of a government policy depends on how effectively it has been able to provide goods and services to meet the needs of the public. There is a caveat here that one has to be careful when developing an outcome-based budget. There may be a tendency to deliberately set the intended outcomes (target results) at a lower level to demonstrate success at the end of the fiscal year or the completion of the programs. This is an important weakness of the system unless proper attention is given to avoid the trap.

6.2.6.3 Target-Based Budget

Target-based budget (TBB), as a system, was developed out of necessity to deal with the financial hardships many state and local governments, in particular the latter, were experiencing in the 1970s. As a result, the system takes a pragmatic approach to budget development that tries to find the most effective way to meet the spending needs of an organization. The process begins when the chief executive, with the help of the budget director and others responsible, sets the expenditure targets (hence, the name target-based budgeting) for individual agencies and departments. Targets are based on past history of expenditure, or strategic priorities, or any other criteria that reflect the critical needs of the organization. Once set, the targets are pretty much locked in that the operating agencies do not have any flexibility to deviate from the targets, except under extreme circumstances such as unforeseen disasters or events over which they do not have any control. Most governments have contingency provisions to deal with these types of situations to ensure that normal operations of the government are not disrupted.

There is a similarity between expenditure targets and nondiscretionary spending. A nondiscretionary spending, as noted earlier, is a spending over which the operating agencies do not have any control, as opposed to discretionary spending over which the agencies have some control. When the expenditure targets are set for an agency that portion of the budget automatically becomes nondiscretionary spending. In reality, the discretionary spending under target-based budgeting is allowed only after the requirements for nondiscretionary spending targets have been met. To give an example, suppose that a government expects to collect $350 million in revenue next year which are to be allocated among different agencies and departments. Let us say that Department X will receive $35 million for next year's budget, the bulk of which will go toward specific expenditure targets, say, $20 million, as set by the upper-level management. The balance of the amount after the targets has been met, which is $15 million, the department will have the discretion to spend, as it deems necessary (Fig. 6.7).

Procedurally, target-based budgeting requires each agency to submit two sets of spending requests: One that is based on spending targets and the other that is discretionary. For the discretionary portion of the spending, the agencies are often required to prioritize their requests since the requests often exceed the available amount, so that the funds can be allocated on the basis of the priorities. This is where the knowledge of ZBB becomes useful since prioritization plays an important role in the ZBB process. As such, target-based budgets are often regarded as a variant of ZBB. However, for the system to work effectively, the government must have good and reliable revenue estimates since the spending targets are based on these estimates. In general, the better the estimates, the more effective is the target-based budget. Unfortunately, revenue estimates are seldom perfect, which makes it necessary to have some flexibility in the system to allow for deviations from the targets.

6.2.6.4 Priority-Driven Budget
The budget systems we have discussed, with the exception of the line-item budget, are non-incremental in nature. Incremental budgeting works well in situations where the general condition of the economy is good, revenue growth is predictable, and budget shortfall is unlikely. On the other hand, when the economy is performing at less than its full potential, revenue growth is below the expected level, and the government is faced with the prospect of a budget shortfall, incremental budgeting does not provide a realistic solution. One way to deal with the problem is to reduce the budget by a fixed percentage across the board for all programs.

Fig. 6.7 A simple target-
based budgeting structure

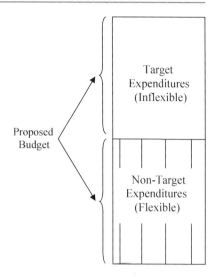

While the decision may appear reasonable for maintaining uniformity, it does not offer a rational alternative since programs do not have the same size, scope, or objectives. Priority-driven budget (PDB), which combines elements of both ZBB and a strategic budget, is considered an effective alternative to incremental budgeting in that it can help a government avoid decisions such as arbitrary cuts which can lead to inefficient service provision. The use of a priority-driven budget system allows a government to identify important strategic priorities, rank various programs, and activities according to how well they align with the priorities and allocate resources consistent with the ranking (Kavanagh et al. 2010).

The development of a priority-driven budget is relatively straightforward. It involves a sequence of steps built on the framework of the earlier systems, but without some of their inherent weaknesses. Steven Chapman (2007) suggests a multi-step process for developing a priority-driven budget: One, identify the available resources, similar to the step GFOA recommended for an outcome-based budget. Most organizations begin the budget process by identifying the needs for next year's budget, but priority-driven budget begins by identifying what will be available from all possible sources. This allows it the opportunity to deal with budgetary problems more effectively since it is not based primarily on needs, but on what is available. Two, identify organizational priorities. The priorities are similar to mission statements in a strategic budget, but they differ in one important respect in that they are based on the outcomes that are of value to the public.

Three, define priority results clearly. This emphasizes the need for developing organizational or agency goals more precisely. For instance, if one of the goals of a government is to have a safe community, then it must clearly define what "safe" means, so that it is possible to develop a set of measures that are operational. Four, identify decision units. These are very similar to the decision units of ZBB or strategic units of a strategic budget. Five, score decision units vis-à-vis programs against results. This involves developing a process to objectively evaluate how the programs achieve the priority results. Six, compare scores between programs.

The objective here is to be able to come up with the final ranking of the programs to ensure that it is clear, precise, and consistent. Seven, allocate resources consistent with the final ranking. Eight, and finally, evaluate the results to see the extent to which the programs have produced the intended results.

While it has its advantages, priority-driven budgets also have some weaknesses that are inherent in any budget system that deals with priorities in a social setting such as how are they identified, who identifies them, what measures are used to evaluate them, and so forth. Nevertheless, it offers an alternative that attempts to correct some of the problems of ZBB and strategic budgeting system, first, by starting with a realistic assumption of a revenue base and, second, by suggesting steps for objectively evaluating priorities until a final ranking of programs and activities is obtained.

6.2.6.5 Management by Objectives

A somewhat different in approach, the management by objectives (MBO) gained limited popularity as a budget system under the Nixon Administration. Developed originally by Peter Drucker (1954), it is more of a planning and performance monitoring system than an actual tool for developing a formal budget. Since the focus of the system is on management of an organization by objectives, to be effective the objectives of an MBO process have to meet at least three criteria: One, they must be specific providing a clear statement of activities; two, they must be measurable permitting formal evaluation and analysis of the objectives; and, three, they must be attainable allowing a realization of success (Lynch 1995).

The guiding principle that underlies MBO is that once the objectives have been defined, it would help the employees better understand their role and the expectations the management has of their responsibilities. More importantly, it would allow them to see how their activities relate to the larger goals and objectives of the organization. This would then serve as an important motivating force for employees to be productive members of the organization, knowing the impact their activities will have on the success of the organization. To ensure that the objectives can be realized within a specified time frame, the process requires periodic review of results and making revisions of the objectives to allow for contingencies. The review is critical to the entire process because it promotes interaction between the management and the employees to help maintain a good working relationship within the organization. It also allows the participants an opportunity for solving problems, as they emerge. However, a major weakness of the system is that since so much emphasis is placed on the objectives and their achievement, the organization may have a tendency to select only those objectives that are relatively easy to achieve and ignore the ones that are challenging.

6.2.6.6 Sustainability Budget

Although not a budget management system per se in the conventional sense of the term, a sustainability budget combines elements of different systems to provide a pragmatic approach to budget development in the same tradition of a target-based or priority-driven budget. However, unlike the traditional budgeting systems, which focus on specific elements of budgeting such as control of money (line-item budgeting), goal achievement (program budgeting), efficiency in resource use (performance budgeting), budget allocation under constraints (zero-based budgeting), and so forth, sustainable budgeting takes a comprehensive approach to achieve planned change that can be sustained over a long period of time, usually over 30 years or more. Developed initially for developing and emerging market economies with fragile capital structure, rising debt, an expanding public sector that is vulnerable to cyclical disturbances, the concern for sustainability has expanded to advanced economies in light of the financial problems many of these economies have been facing in recent years.

Regardless of the circumstances under which it was developed and the initial objectives, the goals of a sustainability budget are essentially the same as any other budget systems. Allen Schick (2005) suggests four principal criteria that should be central to sustainability budgeting, although they may overlap: (1) solvency—the ability of a government to pay its financial obligations, (2) growth—the capacity of a government to meet the growing needs of its population, (3) stability—the capacity of government to meet future obligations without increasing the tax burdens, and (4) fairness—the capacity of government to pay current obligations without shifting the cost to future generations. There are no specific methods for analyzing sustainability, but conventional approaches such as baseline projections (projections based on the condition that current trend will continue in the future), balance-sheet analysis (analysis of assets, liabilities, and fund balance, or equity), fiscal-gap analysis (analysis of a government's combined expenditure and indebtedness exceeding its available resources), generational accounting (how current policies of a government affect future generations), and other similar measures can be used to assess the long-term economic and financial viability of a government. The real issue, however, is how to integrate sustainability into the budget process.

Different governments have developed different measures for dealing with the sustainability problem based on their unique financial conditions, needs, and challenges. For instance, the State of Washington (2010) developed a 9-step process for budget sustainability. They are (1) managing the size of compensation to improve efficiency, (2) improving budget transparency, (3) reinstating a firm expenditure limit, (4) implementing sound pension reforms, (5) expanding the use of state efficiency and restructuring account, (6) examining inventory of real property assets for possible sale, (7) leveraging the rainy-day fund to protect against future downturns, (8) better managing debt service, and (9) integrating priority-based budgeting with performance reviews. Interestingly, the steps adopted by the state are unique to the state and, by no means, conclusive in that the steps must be continually updated to ensure the success of the program. Other state and local governments have also developed measures that best fit their immediate financial needs, while ensuring long-term economic viability.

6.2.6.7 Participatory Budget

One of the more recent budget systems, participatory budget has its roots in direct democracy that encourages citizen participation in almost every stage of the budget process, from budget development, to budget execution, to budget evaluation, to ensure greater accountability in governance. The system was formally introduced by the Workers Party in 1989 in Porto Alegre (the capital of the southernmost state of Brazil) which won the mayoral election in 1988 with a mandate to reverse the budgetary politics that historically favored spending public money in affluent neighborhoods, eventually bankrupting the government. Termed as the "inversion of spending priorities," the new administration reversed the spending trend focusing more on poorer citizens and neighborhoods (Wampler 2007). By 1990, 12 cities in Brazil adopted the system and, by 2004, it spread to more than 300 municipalities worldwide (Wampler and Avritzer 2004). Several Western democracies, including the United States (the City of New York, Chicago, Cambridge, Long Beach, and Greensboro), Canada (Toronto), Central and Eastern Europe countries, as well as several Asian, Middle-Eastern, and African countries have experimented with the system since then, mostly at the local level (Folsher 2007; Shall 2007).

Operationally, there are no hard and fast procedures for developing a participatory budget system; individual communities can develop their own format, but keeping in mind the importance of citizen participation in the overall budget process. Julie Garrigues (2016) has recently suggested an eight-step process for developing the budget: (1) citizen engagement meeting, (2) proposition (developing ideas and setting priorities), (3) selection, (4) voting, (5) consensus (on final budget recommendations), (6) approval, (7) implementation (including technical plan and contracts), and (8) monitoring. However, for the budget to be effective, it must meet, at a minimum, three conditions: One, decision-making power (the government must have the power to administer and resources to implement the budget); two, citizen engagement (the public must be a part of the process); and, three, accountability and repetition (the public must be apprised of the specific projects and programs the budget would implement).

While, in principle, participatory budgeting is useful as an instrument of direct democracy and has merits in societies with widespread income gap between communities, the idea of citizen participation in the budget process is nothing new. For instance, although somewhat different in style, it has been part of the US budget process for a long time. As noted earlier, the current budget process at the local level allows citizen feedback on the budget during public hearing before the budget is finalized and prepared for submission to the legislature for appropriation. In addition, public referendums, required by law, and frequently used by both state and local governments for major legislations on matters related to taxes, expenditure, and various social and economic issues are consistent with citizen participation in decision making in government.

6.3   Some Common Misconceptions

In spite of their long history and usefulness as management tools, there are several misconceptions about the budget systems: (1) the systems are a panacea for government; (2) allocation decisions are frequently based on these systems; and (3) they are instruments of efficiency and effectiveness. The foremost misconception about the systems is that the systems are answers to all budgetary problems and challenges facing a government; they are not. While a budget system can improve budget management practices by providing a formal structure, it cannot correct budgetary problems resulting from economic, social, and political realities. For instance, ZBB was hailed for a long time as a cure for all budgetary challenges, but it failed to cut nondiscretionary spending when President Carter tried to apply it to the federal budget. Unfortunately, it was not the fault or inability of the system, but the way Congress preset the spending levels which could not be changed without new legislations.

Regarding allocation decisions, as noted earlier, although the decision makers often look at the information produced by the systems, there is no conclusive evidence that they rely entirely on the systems for allocation decisions. Party politics, budget constraints, and self-maximizing interest such as interest to get reelected, among others, often shape how allocation decisions are made. Finally, the systems, by themselves, are not instruments of efficiency and effectiveness, but, if properly designed, they can produce information that can be used for measuring efficiency and effectiveness.

6.4 Summary and Conclusion

This chapter has presented an overview of budget systems used in government, from line-item, to program, to performance, to ZBB, among others. Several things become apparent from our discussion of the budget systems. First and foremost, the systems have a unique feature in that they are flexible and can be modified to fit the needs of a government. In reality, there is no canned system that can fit all governments. No model can be applied directly from theory to practice without adjustments and budget systems are no exception. Secondly, old systems do not quite disappear; they are incrementally adapted to new systems. Thirdly, no system is capable of meeting all the budgetary needs of every government. There is no "all-encompassing" system that can deal with every situation. Fourthly, to select a system because it is "new and exciting" will not guarantee a successful budget; only a careful and thorough assessment of the circumstances to which it is applied will increase the likelihood of its success. Along these lines, certain future trends seem likely: One, there will be continuous expansion of these systems and their adaptations. Two, the focus on efficiency and effectiveness will remain integral to the budgetary practices of a government. A system that allows both measures to be addressed will have a greater empirical appeal, which may partly explain why performance budgeting has received so much attention over the years. Three, proper implementation will be needed for a system to work. Even the best systems cannot produce the "best results" if they are not implemented properly. This means that the systems must be modified and continuously updated to fit the circumstances to which they are applied and not the other way round.

Review Questions

Q1. What is a budget system? What role does a budget system play in the budget process?

Q2. What is a line-item budget? Why is it called a core budget? What are the strengths and limitations of a line-item budget? Give an example of a line-item budget.

Q3. What is a program budget? What are strengths and limitations a program budget? Give an example of a program budget.

Q4. What is a performance budget? What role do performance measures play in a performance budget? Why is it important to select appropriate criteria for measuring performance? Give an example.

Q5. Suppose that you have just been appointed the Budget Director of ABC city. One of your new responsibilities includes the development a performance budgeting system for the government, but before you could develop the new system you have decided to develop a miniature budget for the Customer Accounting Department to see how it works. The primary service of the department is Meter Reading.

Below are the statistics for the department:

1. Outputs (i.e., number of meters to be read per month): 21,000

2. Number of customers billed per month: 18,000 (some customers have two separate meters)
3. Inputs (i.e., resources to be used):
   A. Direct: a. personal services (non-salaried), b. personal services (salaried), c. materials and Supplies, c. fringe benefits, d. vehicles and equipment (capital outlay), and e. debt
   B. Indirect (Overhead): a. personnel (administration), b. materials and supplies
4. Cost per unit of input:
   A. Direct Costs:
      a. Personal Services (non-salaried) = $10.50 per hour
      b. Personal Services (salaried) = 15% of non-salaried personal services
      c. Fringe Benefits (Personnel):
         1. Leave (salaried: 14 days vacation + 7 days of sick leave) = $12,125 (annual)
         2. Insurance (salaried: health and dental) = 5% of direct personal cost (annual)
      d. Materials and Supplies= $8,750 (annual)
      e. Vehicles and Equipment (Capital Outlay):
         1. Contractual (lease rental) = $6,250 (annual, including insurance)
         2. Equipment (one time) = $7,500 (annual)
         3. Mileage Cost = $0.25/per vehicle mile
      f. Debt Service = $15,750 (annual)
   B. Indirect Costs:
      a. Personnel: 20% of direct personnel
      b. Materials and Supplies: 10% of direct material
   C. Miscellaneous: 5% of direct and indirect cost (annual)
5. Number of work units (WU) per input unit (IU):
   a. Personnel services = 24 meters per man -hour,
   b. Total vehicle miles = 36,000 a year (i.e., 1.7143 vehicle miles per meter)

Given the information above, develop a performance budget for the depart-ment, with a program structure—the agency name, program description, program goal, and program objectives make sure to include the following line items: [1] personnel services, including fringe benefits, [2] materials and supplies, [3] capital outlay, [4] debt service, and [5] miscellaneous.

Q6. Define efficiency. How can one use performance measures to measure the efficiency of service provision?

Q7. What is a productivity index? What is the difference between a single and a multi-factor productivity? Under what circumstances would one use a single factor, as opposed to a multifactor productivity?

Q8. Suppose that a local school district is trying to measure student perfor-mance based on recent test scores for several schools in the district against the amount of money the district spends on each student a year, on average. Assume that the maximum score a student can receive is 1600, divided equally between writing and math skills. The following table shows the student test scores (output) and per capita expenditure (input) for two recent years (Table 6.7).

Given the information above, do the following: [a] construct an output index for each school, [b] construct an input index for each school, [c] construct a productivity index for each school, and [d] interpret the results.

Table 6.7   Review Question (Q8)

Schools	Test scores last year ($t-1$)	Test scores current year (t)	Expenditure ($) last year ($t-1$)	Expenditure ($) current year ($t$)
S1	1000	1100	12,000	14,000
S2	1100	1150	13,000	14,000
S3	1300	1350	16,000	15,000
S4	1100	1000	15,000	14,000
S5	1200	1250	14,000	15,000
S6	1300	1250	15,000	16,000
S7	1200	1300	17,000	16,000

Q9. What is a cost-based budget? How does it differ from a performance budget?

Q10. What is a zero-based budget? What are the building blocks of a zero-based budget? What are the strengths and limitations of a zero-based budgeting system?

Q11. What role do funding levels play in a zero-based budget? Give an exam-ple of a zero-based budget with different funding levels.

Q12. What is a target-based budget? Why is it called a variation of zero-based budget? Why is good forecasting important in a target-based budget?

Q13. What is a strategic budget? How does it differ from a zero-based budget? What are the strengths and limitations of a strategic budgeting system? Give an example of a strategic budget.

Q14. What is the difference between a priority-driven, sustainability, and participatory budget? What are some of the misconceptions about the budget systems?

Notes

1. A system is a collection of elements, connected together in an organized way. The elements of a system can be concepts (language), objects (a machine consisting of component parts), and subjects (a man-machine system consisting of concepts, objects, and subjects). A system may exist in nature as a natural aggregation of component elements found in nature, called natural system, or it may be contrived by man as an aggregation of elements that are related and constituted as a system, called man-made system (Checkland 1976).
2. A good example is reserve funds most governments maintain. Two types of funds are commonly associated with reserve funds are rainy-day funds and contingency funds. Known often as budget stabilization funds, "rainy-day funds" allow governments to set aside excess revenue for use in times of unexpected revenue shortfall or budget deficit. Some governments may require a small fraction of their surpluses to be set aside for a rainy-day fund. A contingency fund, on the other hand, is a reserve fund set aside to deal with unexpected circumstances or emergencies outside of the operating budget. Another term for contingency fund is disaster-relief or disaster-recovery fund. Interestingly, the two terms are often used synonymously, although they are not exactly the same.
3. Setting the levels against the current year budget makes most sense, although the convention has been to use the last year's budget because it represents the actual budget. On the other hand, the current year budget reflects the most recent allocation and, therefore, the levels will provide a more accurate picture of choices the decision makers can make in light of next year's budget scenario.

References

Burch, J. (1994). *Cost and Management Accounting, Modern Approach*. St. Paul, MN: West Publishing.

Castro, M. F. (2011, July). *Defining and Using Performance Indicators in Government M&E Systems* (Special Series in the Nuts and Bolts of M&E Systems No. 12). Washington, DC: The World Bank.

Chapman II, S. G. (2007). *Priority-Driven Budgeting: An Alternative to Incremental Budgeting*. Washington, DC: Government Finance Officers Association (GFOA) (Module 15).

Checkland, P. B. (1976). Toward a System-Based Methodology for Real-World Problem Solving. In J. Beishon & G. Peters (Eds.), *Systems Behavior* (pp. 51–77). New York, NY: Harper & Row (for Open University Press).

Drucker, P. F. (1954). *The Practice of Management*. New York: Harper Business.

Folsher, A. (2007). Participatory Budgeting in Central and Eastern European Countries. In A. Shah (Ed.), *Participatory Budgeting* (pp. 127–156). Washington, DC: The International Bank for Reconstruction and Development (IBRD), The World Bank.

Garrigues, J. (2016, December 27). Eight Steps to Effective Participatory Budgeting. *CitizenLab*. https://www.citizenlab.co/blog/civic-engagement/steps-to-effective-participatory-budgeting/.

General Accountability Office (GAO). (1996). *Executive Guide: Effectively Implementing the Government Performance and Results Act*. Washington, DC: Office of the Comptroller General of the United States.

Government Finance Officers Association (GFOA). (2007). *Recommended Budget Practice—Budgeting for Results and Outcome*. http://www.gfoa.org/downloads/budgetingforresults.pdf.

Hatry, H. P., et al. (1997). *Customer Survey for Agency Managers: What Managers Need to Know?* Washington, DC: The Urban Institute.

Hatry, H. P., et al. (2006). *How Effective Are Your Community Services? Procedures for Performance Measurement*. Washington, DC: The Urban Institute.

Hatry, H. P., & Fisk, D. M. (1971). *Improving Productivity and Productivity Measurement in Local Governments*. Washington, DC: The National Commission on Productivity.

Kavanagh, S. C., Johnson, J., & Fabian, C. (2010, April). Anatomy of Priority-Based Budget Process. *Government Finance Review, 26*(2), 9–16.

Khan, A., & Murova, O. (2015). Productive Efficiency of Public Expenditures: A Cross-State Study. *State and Local Government Review, 47*(3), 170–180.

Lederle, J. W. (1949). The Hoover Commission Reports on Federal Reorganization. *Marquette Law Review, 33*(2), 89–98.

Lynch, T. D. (1995). *Public Budgeting in America*. New York: Prentice-Hall.

Martin, L. L. (2002). Budgeting for Outcomes. In A. Khan and W. B. Hildreth (Eds.), *Budget Theory in the Public Sector* (pp. 246–260). Westport, CT: Quorum Books.

Murova, O., & Khan, A. (2017). Public Investments, Productivity, and Economic Growth: A Cross-State Study of Selected Public Expenditures in the US. *International Journal of Productivity and Performance Management, 66*(2), 251–265.

Osborne, D., & Gaebler, T. (1992). *Reinventing Government: How the Entrepreneurial Spirit is Transforming the Public Sector*. Reading, MA: Addison-Wesley.

Pyhrr, P. A. (1973). *Zero-Base Budgeting: A Practical Tool for Evaluating Expenses*. New York, NY: Wiley.

Schick, A. (2005). Sustainable Budget Policy: Concepts and Approaches. *OECD Journal on Budgeting, 5*(1), 107–126.

Shall, A. (2007). Sub-Saharian Experience with Participatory Budgeting. In A. Shah (Ed.), *Participatory Budgeting* (pp. 191–224). Washington, DC: The International Bank for Reconstruction and Development (IBRD), The World Bank.

Simonsen, W., & Robbins, M. D. (2000). *Citizen Participation in Revenue Allocation*. New York, NY: Westview Press.

Solem, J., & Werner, H. D. (1968). PPBS: A Management Innovation. *Journal of Cooperative Extension, 6* (Winter), 221–228.

State of Washington. (2010). *Thrive Washington: Nine Steps to Budget Sustainability in Washington State*. Olympia, WA: A Joint Research Series of the Washington Roundtable and Washington Research Council.

Taylor, G. M. (1977). Introduction to Zero-Base Budgeting. *The Bureaucrat, 6*(Spring), 33–55.

Wampler, B. (2007). A Guide to Participatory Budgeting. In A. Shah (Ed.), *Participatory Budgeting* (pp. 21–54). Washington, DC: The International Bank for Reconstruction and Development (IBRD), The World Bank.

Wampler, B., & Avritzer, L. (2004). Participatory Publics: Civil Societies and New Institutions in Democratic Brazil. *Comparative Politics, 36*(3), 291–312.

Elements of Budget Forecasting

7

Budgeting is about future—future revenues and future expenditures. For a government to be able to function effectively, in particular to be able to carry out its activities in a planned and organized manner, it has to have a sound knowledge of future revenues and expenditures. Forecasting provides that knowledge by producing a set of estimates of revenues and expenditures based on past and current information to indicate whether the government will have sufficient resources to effectively carry out these activities. Without good and accurate forecasts, a government will not only find it difficult to plan its activities, but will also find it difficult to cope with the increasingly complex environment in which it has to operate. This notion of forecasting is more appropriate at the subnational level where the state and local governments are required by law to balance their budget, especially the operating budget, which means that the projected revenues of a government must balance the projected expenditures for it to be able to run its everyday operations without incurring a deficit. This does not mean that the governments will not have a budget deficit; in all likelihood, they will, but without good and reliable forecasts it will be difficult to determine the measures that will be necessary to balance the budget. This chapter provides a broad overview of budget forecasting; in particular, some of the methods commonly used in forecasting government revenues and expenditures.

7.1   Background and Purpose

Forecasting government budget is not a recent development, although it has received more attention in recent years. Early history of forecasting indicates that an act of Congress in the 1800s required the Secretary of Treasury to submit revenue estimates to Congress along with plans and analyses of specific levels of expenditure. There is no concrete evidence as to how seriously and the extent to

© The Author(s) 2019
A. Khan, *Fundamentals of Public Budgeting and Finance*,
https://doi.org/10.1007/978-3-030-19226-6_7

which the department followed this requirement (Buck 1929). As noted earlier, the 1974 Budget and Impoundment Control Act requires that the federal budget include a multiyear revenue forecast as part of the regular budget submission process to Congress. Today, all fifty states and a large number of local governments prepare multiyear revenue and expenditure forecasts as part of their ongoing budgetary activities. Two other factors have also contributed to this trend: the development of a wide range of forecasting methods over the years and the easy availability of microcomputers with enormous computational and data storage capacity that were not available a few years ago. The latter, in particular, has made it possible to take advantage of many of these methods that were previously difficult to use without high speed mainframe computers.

While forecasting is critical as an effective tool for budget development, it is important to keep in mind that a forecast is not an end rather it is an input into the decision process. It is a prediction of what will happen or likely to happen in the future based on an analysis of the past and current activities of an organization. Put simply, forecast values are not the actual values one would observe at some future points in time, but rather they are estimates of the actual values that will occur in the future. The probability that the prediction will be successful depends, to a large measure, on the process that can identify the forecasting activities and their sequence, so that important elements (of the process) are not left out. Although one will seldom find forecasts that are perfect, decisions will have to be made with the best possible information available. The real challenge in forecasting is not whether forecasts are good and reliable, although that is the ultimate objective, rather how to continue to develop and use the existing methodologies to produce better forecasts.

7.2   Forecasting Process

The process begins with a number distinct, but interrelated steps that must take place in a structured and systematic fashion called the forecasting process. These steps and the manner in which they are carried out are vital to the successful completion of a forecast. Budget practitioners who are actively engaged in this process need to understand this; in particular, the purpose these steps serve within the larger forecasting environment. Although the underlying circumstances may vary the steps remain essentially the same, whether the forecasts are made to guide the budget development by an administrative agency or help improve the legislative understanding of the budget situation, or simply to identify the need for a new revenue source.

Six steps are commonly used in a forecasting process: They are (1) define the forecasting objective, (2) select a time horizon, (3) determine the forecasting method or methods to be used, (4) gather relevant data, (5) do the forecast, and (6) evaluate the forecasting results.

7.2.1 Define the Forecasting Objective

Defining the forecasting objective is probably the most critical phase in the entire process as it sets the tone and direction of the forecast. It is necessary at the very outset of the process to define the problem, specify the purpose for which the forecasts will be used, and establish the criteria for successful completion of the forecast. Such criteria must include a clear knowledge of the type as well as the number of activities the government will undertake, the current costs of these activities and the resource base from which the revenues will be generated to provide them. This will give the forecaster a clear sense of the time and the effort he will have to put into the process.

7.2.2 Select a Time Horizon

Once the forecasting objective has been defined, the forecaster must determine the time length of the forecast. Three sets of time frames are generally used in a forecast: short-term, intermediate-term, and long-term. Short-term forecasts have a time length of less than a year, intermediate-term a length of one to two years, and long-term a length of three to five or six years. Budget practitioners use a somewhat different terminology for forecasts that range from two to six or seven years, called "multiyear forecasting," which is essentially a combination of intermediate- and long-term forecasts. Forecasts beyond six or seven years are not uncommon in government but are primarily used for assessing the impact of a policy change on the budget, rather than on short-range effects of changes in economic conditions. Examples of these types of forecasts are land use development, population growth, changes in economic base, employment, and income.

7.2.3 Determine the Forecasting Method

The next step in the process is to specify the method or methods the forecaster will use to do the forecast. During this stage, the forecaster must identify and list all possible methods suitable for forecasting along with their strengths and weaknesses. This is frequently referred to in the forecasting literature as "green lighting." The number of methods available to a forecaster has increased significantly over the years, giving the forecaster considerable flexibility in selecting the method that will be most appropriate for a forecasting problem. Since the data collected on revenues, expenditures, and other variables have different characteristics, it may not be appropriate to use the same method across the board for all variables. Similarly, methods have their own distinctive characteristics that may not make them suitable for all forecasting problems, in which case the forecaster may find it necessary to use multiple methods to avoid the problems inherent in a particular method.

A key element in selecting a forecasting method is the data consideration. Generally speaking, forecasting methods should be selected on the basis of how well they fit the data, not the other way round. Two types of data are of general interest to a forecaster: cross-sectional, where data are collected on a single point in time for multiple jurisdictions and, time series, where data are collected over successive periods of time usually for a single jurisdiction. In determining a forecasting method, especially where time-series data are concerned, it is important to look at the pattern that underlies the series first. The simplest way to identify patterns in a series is to plot the data on a two-dimensional plane, make a visual examination, look for turning points (when the series takes a sudden turn), count the number of turning points, determine the nature of the curve, select the appropriate method, and obtain the estimated value.

In general, the pattern in a series falls into four distinct categories: trend, seasonal, cyclical, and irregular (Fig. 7.1). The trend pattern reflects the growth or decline in the data over a long time period. The cyclical pattern reflects the fluctuations around the trend. The seasonal pattern reflects changes in the data that repeat themselves over time, while the irregular pattern is more difficult to predict.

While the underlying pattern or length of a series is crucial in determining the appropriate forecasting method, other factors such as the time available to complete a forecast, the degree of accuracy expected in the forecast, and the length of the forecast period also play an important role in the process. Additionally, the knowledge of the forecaster and his ability to define the forecasting problem as well as his understanding of the environment in which forecasting will take place are equally important in selecting a forecasting method.

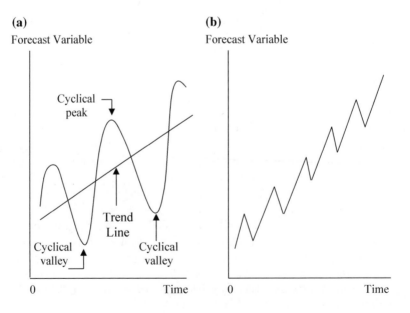

Fig. 7.1 (a) Trend and cyclical series. (b) Seasonal series

7.2.4 Gather Relevant Data

Gathering appropriate data to produce reliable forecasts is extremely important in forecasting, especially in government where data are not always maintained in a consistent fashion. There are several reasons for that: First of all, governments frequently change programs, undertake new measures, and add new sources of revenue—all of which can create a major data gap. Secondly, the process of a sudden change in a policy can drastically affect the variables that are impacted by the decision, creating extreme values called "outliers" in the data with the likelihood for producing misleading forecasts. Thirdly, problems can further occur if the data do not conform or if there is a mismatch in the data. For instance, revenue and expenditure data for most governments are collected on a fiscal year basis, while economic and demographic data are collected on a calendar year basis; thereby, creating a mismatch of data.

All three problems—data gap, the presence of outliers, and data mismatch, while common in forecasting, are not difficult to overcome. For instance, the problem with missing data can be easily corrected with interpolations, as long as there are not too many missing observations in the same series. Similarly, the problem with outliers can be corrected by throwing them out from the data set or treating them separately, if there are too many outliers, or using a dummy variable if the problem is the result of a policy change. Finally, the problem of non-conformity or data mismatch can be corrected by lagging the calendar year sequences to correspond with the fiscal year, among others.

There are at least four other situations where data problems can seriously impair the forecasting results if they are not properly addressed. One, the data collection process can consume too much time if the method requires a large data series, as is frequently the case with methods such as Box-Jenkins and transfer function models. Two, there may be a tendency in government to overly aggregate the data when reporting them in the budget, creating an "aggregation bias" that may over-generalize the results. To correct the problem, one can use numbers that are not rounded to their nearest values (since rounding off numbers may mean a discrepancy of thousands or even millions of dollars in budgetary terms) or use data that will not require too many adjustments such as those available from federal government publications. Three, time-series data may sometimes contain discretionary changes in rates or base components, as in sales, income, or property taxes. If that is the case, the data need to be cleaned by factoring out the effects of discretionary changes in tax rate or base definition, which may be a lengthy exercise. Finally, data may not always be available in time or they may be available in purely descriptive terms, in which case dummy or proxy variables such as national income or demographic data can be used as substitutes for local or state data. However, caution should be exercised when using proxy variables for they can lead to measurement problems from oversimplification of data use.

The point to recognize here is that the quality of data a forecaster uses has a significant bearing on the forecast. What primarily restricts a forecaster from producing reliable forecasts is not so much the quantity as much as the quality of data with which the forecaster has to work. If a forecaster has to work with data that are of poor quality, it will inevitably produce results that will be suspect even though the method used is the most appropriate for the forecasting problem.

7.2.5   Do the Forecast

Once the data have been collected, cleaned, and prepared, the forecaster can proceed to do the forecast. It is a straightforward process but can be time consuming depending on the forecasting method used. Obviously, the more complex the method, the more time and resources it will take to do the forecast, and vice versa.

7.2.6   Evaluate the Forecast

The process concludes with an evaluation of forecasting results where the forecaster must verify the forecast values against those available to check for their accuracy. Accuracy determines the quality of a forecast by indicating how far the forecast values are from the observed values. The closer the forecast values are to the observed values, the better the forecasts. The conventional wisdom that a forecast should be considered "good" if it is within a 5% margin of error does not always work. For instance, a 5% error on a trillion dollar budget is not quite the same as a 5% error on a million dollar budget, although the impact of the error on the budget could be just as severe for both. The idea of a good forecast is to keep the errors as low as possible, but that may not always be possible, even for an experienced forecaster. Since it is difficult to say in advance how accurate the forecasts will be until the values are actually observed, forecasters often look at the forecasts on past observations called "backcasts" to see how accurate the past predictions have been. If the results (backcasts) turn out to be good, it is safe to assume that the forecasts will also be good, everything else remaining the same.

7.3   Forecasting Methods

There has been a significant increase in the number of forecasting methods available to a forecaster over the years that vary in complexity and data requirements. Regardless, all forecasting methods fall into four basic categories: qualitative, deterministic, time series, and causal. Qualitative forecasts are mostly used when historical data are not available or when one needs an impromptu forecast. They rely on the effective use of judgmental process and management experience of the experts, rather than on exclusive historical data. Typical examples of qualitative methods are panel consensus, Delphi, visionary forecast, and historical analogy. Deterministic forecasts are often based on simple arithmetic calculations that do not require any formal statistical analysis. As such, these methods have limited data requirements and are generally based on the knowledge of projected changes in the variables that directly affect the forecast values. Two good examples of deterministic forecasts are naïve forecasts and engineering cost estimates (for lack of a better term).

Time-series methods use past or historical observations to predict the future values of a forecast variable. The primary purpose of these methods is to discover the pattern that underlies these observations and to extrapolate them into the future to produce the desired forecasts. While there is a wide range of time-series methods that one can use, two methods frequently used are the average method and trend line. Finally, the causal methods are based on a cause-and-effect relationship between a dependent and one or more independent (explanatory) variables. When the variables in a causal method are mostly economic, or when the underlying relationship is based predominantly on economic theory, they are commonly known as econometric methods.

Local governments, in general, use a combination of deterministic and time-series methods that are simple, have low data requirements, and are easy to use. In contrast, the federal government as well as most state governments use both time-series and econometric methods, especially the latter. Econometric methods are relatively complex to design, have considerable data requirements, and cost more in time and resources, which may explain why these methods are used more at the federal and state level than at the local level. On occasion, especially when there are disagreements on forecasts or when expert opinions are needed, qualitative methods such as panel consensus or Delphi are frequently used to supplement the forecasts (Klay 1983).

This section discusses some of the most commonly used methods in budget forecasting, in particular those mentioned above. They are naïve forecasts, engineering cost estimates, the average method, trend line, and causal forecasts.

7.3.1 Naïve Forecasts

The simplest way to forecast a government budget (revenue as well as expenditure) is to assume that next year's budget will be exactly the same as the current year, which means that there will be no change in demand or the cost of providing government services and, consequently, no change in the level of revenue that will be needed to provide them. This is known as the naïve forecast. Since a naïve forecast assumes the current conditions to be the same as last year, it can serve as an initial decision tool from which to make the appropriate changes in a budget.

We can use a simple expression to describe it, as shown below:

$$\widehat{Y}_{t+1} = Y_t \qquad (7.1)$$

where $\widehat{Y}_{t+1}$ is the value of Y at time $t+1$, and Y_t is the current value of Y.

To give an example, suppose that a government wants to forecast its General Fund expenditure for various line items for next year. The government starts with

Table 7.1 General fund budget: expenditure forecasts by line items

Expenditure by object classification	FY_t ($000)	FY_{t+1} Unadjusted ($000)	FY_{t+1} Adjusted* ($000)	FY_{t+1} Partially adjusted ($000)
Personnel services	1,010,000	1,010,000	1,040,300	1,040,300
Materials and supplies	115,000	115,000	118,450	118,000
Contractual	110,000	110,000	113,300	110,000
Insurance	45,000	45,000	46,350	46,350
Capital outlay	75,000	75,000	77,250	75,000
Miscellaneous	12,000	12,000	12,360	12,000
Total	$1,367,000	$1,367,000	$1,408,010	$1,401,650

*Assuming a 3% increase due to inflation

an initial assumption that next year's expenditure will be exactly the same as the current year, t, which will serve as its base. Table 7.1 shows the naïve forecasts for the General Fund (GF) operation for next year, $t+1$.

Assume, for the sake of argument that the expenditure for our government will change, say, increase by a constant amount across the board next year. The constant could be inflation rate or any other measure the forecaster may find useful to define the change. We can then plug the constant term into the expression in Eq. 7.1 to show the change in next year's expenditure, so that the new expression will be

$$\hat{Y}_{t+1} = cY_t + Y_t \tag{7.2}$$

where c is the constant and the rest of terms are the same as before.

We can easily expand the expression in Eq. 7.2 to develop a line-item budget for the General Fund, consisting of n line items, for next year, $t+1$, so that

$$\hat{Y}_{t+1,1} = cY_{t1} + Y_{t1} \tag{7.3}$$

$$\hat{Y}_{t+1,2} = cY_{t2} + Y_{t2}$$
$$\begin{matrix} . & . & . \\ . & . & . \\ . & . & . \end{matrix} \tag{7.4}$$

$$\hat{Y}_{t+1,m} = cY_{tn} + Y_{tn} \tag{7.5}$$

where the second subscript represents line items.

Assume further that c is the inflation rate, which, let us say, will increase by 3% next year and the government has decided to adjust the expenditures across the board for all the line items in the fund to reflect the increase. Table 7.1 also shows the adjusted expenditure for the government. Theoretically, the constant term can take on any value specified by the forecaster, or as seems appropriate. Going back to the example, suppose now that instead of increasing expenditure across the board the government decides to increase it for three items (personal services, materials and supplies, and insurance), while keeping the rest constant (Table 7.1). The process can be used for any number of cost items in the table to produce the desired changes in the forecast. The end product will no longer be a naïve forecast because once a change has been made in the original forecast the results will no longer be the same as the current year; that is, $\hat{Y}_{t+1} \neq \hat{Y}_t$. However, when it is assigned a value of 1; in other words, when $c = 1$, the equation converts to $\hat{Y}_{t+1} = Y_t$ and becomes the same as the naïve forecast.

It should be pointed out that the basic assumption underlying a naïve forecast is that past relationship will continue into the future unchanged, but in reality that is seldom the case. Even if it were to remain the same, it is unlikely that the factors that affect a government budget such as the price of labor, materials, and supplies will remain constant over time. On the other hand, if a forecaster has past information on the changes in any of these factors, the information can be used to develop simple expressions to produce suitable forecasts. Engineering cost estimates would fall into this category.

7.3.2 Engineering Cost Estimates

These methods are primarily used to estimate the future costs of a specific service or program based on a set of predetermined values. Once the relevant information or data have been gathered on all the activities related to a good or service, it is a simple process of constructing suitable expressions to do the forecast. However, there are no set procedures for constructing these expressions; they vary depending on the nature of the problem. As with naïve forecasts, the forecasts based on engineering cost estimates do not involve any complex statistical analysis or assumptions and, consequently, one cannot readily apply conventional tests for statistical reliability of the forecasts. Nevertheless, they are known to produce reasonably good forecasts in the short term, especially where costs or expenditures are concerned.

The simplest way to construct these estimates is to assume that the forecaster has information on the base of an activity, as well as on the costs associated with the activity (Hirsch 1970). As long as one has that information, the total cost or expenditure can be easily obtained by multiplying the base by the cost per unit of base. That is,

$$E_t^i = N_t(c_t^i) \tag{7.6}$$

where E^i is the expenditure on ith activity, N is the number of base units (b), and C^i is the cost per unit base for the ith activity (for $i = 1, 2, ..., n$).

Although simple in structure, the expression in Eq. 7.6 has a weakness in that it does not show the likely changes in the base. This may give the appearance of the forecast being static, or the same as a naïve forecast. Therefore, to reflect the likely changes, Eq. 7.6 can be rewritten as

$$\hat{E}_{t+1}^i = (b_t)(c_t)[(1 + \Delta b)(1 + \Delta c)]^t \tag{7.7}$$

where Δb and Δc represent the changes in the base and the cost per unit base, respectively, and the rest of the terms are the same as before.

To give an example, suppose that a government wants to know what will be the cost of running its police department (PD) next year, $t+1$. The department serves a modest-size community with a population of 120,000, which, let us say, will grow to 121,500, next year—a 1.25% increase over the current year. The current cost of running the department is $18 million a year with an average cost of $150 per person [$18,000,000/120,000 = $150], which is projected to increase by 3.1% next year to keep up with the cost of inflation. Suppose that the department presently employs 2.5 police officers for every 1000 people with an average annual operating cost of $45,000 per officer. Assume that there are no other costs involved and that the same service ratio will be maintained next year. Therefore, the cost of running the department next year, $t+1$, will be

$$
\begin{aligned}
\hat{E}_{t+1}^{PD} &= (b_t)(c_t)[(1 + \Delta b)(1 + \Delta c)]^{t=1} \\
&= (120,000)(\$150)[(1 + 0.0125)(1 + 0.031)]^{1} \\
&= (\$18,000,000)[1.0438875] \\
&= \$18,789,975
\end{aligned}
$$

or approximately $18.79 million.

Interestingly, since we know the projected population for next year, $t+1$, we can use this information to determine the number of additional police officers the department will need next year at the current ratio of officers to population, which will be 4 [(((121,500 − 120,000)/1000) × 2.5 = 3.75 ≈ 4 (after rounding off)]. We can do the same for $t+2$, or any number of years in the future, as long as we have the relevant information.

Assume now that the population of the community will grow by 0.75% the following year, $t+2$, and there will be no changes in any of the other factors. The operating cost of running the department at $t+2$ will thus be

$$
\begin{aligned}
\hat{E}_{t+2}^{PD} &= (b_t)(c_t)[(1 + \Delta b)(1 + \Delta c)]^{t=2} \\
&= (120,000)(\$150)[(1 + 0.0075)(1 + 0.031)]^{2} \\
&= (\$18,000,000)[1.0789652] \\
&= \$19,421,374
\end{aligned} \tag{7.8}
$$

or $19.421 million, and the process can be continued for any number of years.

Similar computations can be made to determine any future expenses for other services, assuming the same level of growth in population, but, as always, caution should be exercised when using these results because they may not be consistent for all governments or their services. For instance, measures such as manpower-to-service ratio, residential-to-nonresidential development ratio, the average cost of services, tax rate for real estates, and sales tax or taxes on income are likely to be different for different communities. Therefore, to use these methods uniformly across the board for all governments without making proper adjustments in the methods can produce grossly inaccurate results.

7.3.3 The Average Method

The simplest among the time-series methods is the average method. Its simplicity lies in the fact that it uses measures such as simple arithmetic average to do the forecast. The method is based on the assumption that the future values of a forecast variable tend toward the average of its past occurrences. In other words, the average of the past values of a variable can provide a good basis for its future values. The procedure for using the method is quite simple: Simply take the percentage differences between any two adjacent observations in a series, calculate their average, and use that as a basis for forecasting the future values, say, for next year, $t+1$, as shown below:

$$\hat{Y}_{t+1} = Y_t + (Y_t)(\text{Average Change}) \tag{7.9}$$

where Y is the forecast variable.

Now, expanding the expression for change in Eq. 7.9, we can write it as

$$\hat{Y}_{t+1} = Y_t + (Y_t)\left[\left\{\left(\frac{(Y_t - Y_{t-1})}{Y_{t-1}}\right) + \left(\frac{(Y_{t-1} - Y_{t-2})}{Y_{t-2}}\right) + \cdots \right.\right.$$
$$\left.\left. + \left(\frac{(Y_{t-n} - Y_{t-n-1})}{Y_{t-n-1}}\right)\right\}/(n-1)\right] \tag{7.10}$$

where $\hat{Y}_{t+1}$ is the predicted value of the forecast variable Y at time $t+1$, Y_t is the current value of the forecast variable Y, Y_{t-i} is the past value of the forecast variable Y (for $i = 1, 2, \ldots, n$), and n is the number of observations.

To give an example, suppose that a local government wants to forecast the parking meter revenue (PMR) for next year, $t+1$. Let us say that we have the data on parking meter revenue for the government for the last 15 years (Table 7.2). Now, to forecast the revenue for next year we simply apply the expression in Eq. 7.10 to the data, as shown below:

$$\hat{PMR}_{t+1} = PMR_t + (PMR_t)\left[\left\{\left(\frac{(PMR_t - PMR_{t-1})}{PMR_{t-1}}\right) + \left(\frac{(PMR_{t-1} - PMR_{t-2})}{PMR_{t-2}}\right) + \cdots \right.\right.$$
$$\left.\left. + \left(\frac{(PMR_{t-n} - PMR_{t-n-1})}{PMR_{t-n-1}}\right)\right\}/(n-1)\right]$$
$$= (\$7650) + (\$7650)\left[\left\{\left(\frac{(\$7650 - \$7490)}{\$7490}\right) + \left(\frac{(\$7490 - \$7190)}{\$7190}\right) + \cdots \right.\right.$$
$$\left.\left. + \left(\frac{(\$4690 - \$4370)}{\$4370}\right)\right\}/(15-1)\right]$$
$$= (\$7650) + (\$7650)[(0.0214 + 0.0417 + \cdots + 0.0732)/14]$$
$$= (\$7650) + [(\$7650)(0.0409)]$$
$$= \$7962.885$$

or $7.963 million, which is the amount of revenue the government will collect from parking meters for next year, $t+1$.

Table 7.2 Revenue from parking meters (RPM) and other statistics

Time (*T*)		Revenue, *Y* ($000)	Percentage change (%Δ)	Rank order by time	Rank order by revenue	*d*	*d²*
t − 14	1	4370.00	–	1	1	0	0
t − 13	2	4690.00	7.32	2	2	0	0
t − 12	3	4780.00	1.92	3	3	0	0
t − 11	4	5040.00	5.44	4	4	0	0
t − 10	5	5280.00	4.76	5	5	0	0
t − 9	6	5520.00	4.55	6	6	0	0
t − 8	7	5750.00	4.17	7	7	0	0
t − 7	8	5980.00	4.00	8	8	0	0
t − 6	9	6230.00	4.18	9	9	0	0
t − 5	10	6460.00	3.69	10	10	0	0
t − 4	11	6740.00	4.33	11	11	0	0
t − 3	12	6950.00	3.12	12	12	0	0
t − 2	13	7190.00	3.45	13	13	0	0
t − 1	14	7490.00	4.17	14	14	0	0
t	15	7650.00	2.14	15	15	0	0
t + 1	16	–	–	–	–	–	–
			$\bar{Y} = 0.0409$			$\Sigma d = 0$	$\Sigma d^2 = 0$

We can repeat the process to produce forecasts for any number of years. For instance, for year 2, $t+2$, the forecast value for $t+1$ will serve as the constant, instead of Y_t, so that $PMR_{t+2} = PMR_{t+1} + (PMR_{t+1})[(\ldots)/(n-1)]$, and so forth. However, it is worth pointing out that when past forecasts are used to forecast future values of a variable, the errors contained in the past forecasts are added to the series that will become part of the error in any future forecasts. A second problem with the method which is common to arithmetic averages in that if a series contains extreme values (outliers) it will skew the average, which, in turn, will distort the forecasts. The problem can be easily corrected by discarding the outliers and replacing them with interpolated values, or increasing the length of the series which will even out some of the skewness in the data.

7.3.4 Trend Line

One of the most popular time-series methods among the budget practitioners is the trend line, partly because of its analytical simplicity and partly because of its statistical appeal. A trend is a continuous movement in a time series. For certain types of revenue, as well as expenditure, it is possible to obtain a fairly accurate forecast with a simple trend line than with advanced or sophisticated methods, especially if the forecast variables are affected by long-term trends due to economic or demographic factors. For instance, cities and states with growing population and economic activities will have an upward trend in their property tax base and sales tax collections. In contrast, if the same cities and states have consistently declining economic activities it will show a downward trend in their tax base and revenue collections. Trend-line projections are quite useful in both of these cases.

7.3.4.1 The Basic Model

Trend lines are generally expressed in terms of degrees. A first-degree trend is a straight line, the second degree is a curve that increases or decreases at an increasing or decreasing rate, called quadratic form, the third degree is a curved line that depicts a wave-like pattern, known as cubic form, and higher degree polynomials show more complex patterns. The number of degrees indicates the number of times the curve shifts directions. The first degree does not change direction, the second degrees changes once, the third degree twice, and so forth. Although higher degree polynomials can be used in forecasting, in most instances the first, second, and third degrees are what one would need.

The following presents a simple expression for a first-degree trend line:

$$Y_t = \alpha + \beta T \tag{7.11}$$

where Y is the dependent (explained) variable representing the variable whose values are being forecast, T is the independent (explanatory) variable representing time, and α and β are the intercept and slope coefficients, respectively.

The expression in Eq. 7.11 assumes a linear or straight-line relationship (degree one) between the dependent variable, Y, and time meaning that for any value of T, Y will change by a constant amount equal to the value of the slope, β. The slope indicates the amount by which the forecast variable Y will change for one unit change in the independent variable T, and can be obtained by the expression

$$\hat{\beta} = \frac{\sum (Y - \bar{Y})(T - \bar{T})}{\sum (T - \bar{T})^2} \tag{7.12}$$

where $\bar{Y}$ and $\bar{T}$, respectively, are the arithmetic means of Y and T, and $\hat{\beta}$ is the estimated value of β. The intercept, α, on the other hand, measures the value Y will assume in the absence of the independent variable T, and is obtained by the expression

$$\hat{\alpha} = \bar{Y} - \hat{\beta}\bar{T} \tag{7.13}$$

where $\hat{\alpha}$ is the estimated value of α and the rest of the terms are the same as before.

7.3.4.2 The Model Parameters

In general, the slope of the method in Eq. 7.11 can be positive or negative, although the convention is to express the relationship in positive term, $Y = \alpha + \beta T$. A positive slope indicates a positive relationship between the dependent variable Y

and the independent variable T, meaning that Y will change in the same direction as the direction of change in T; that is, if T goes up, so will Y, and vice versa. A negative slope, on the other hand, indicates an inverse relationship between Y and T, meaning that as T goes up, Y will go down, and vice versa. The slope, however, cannot be 0, because if it is zero it will mean a total redundancy of the explanatory variable.

On the other hand, the intercept term can be positive, negative, or 0. When it is 0, it means that Y will have a value 0 when $T=0$. In other words, there is no intercept. When the intercept is negative, it means that Y has a negative value when $T=0$, in which case the forecaster has to decide if it is the right model to use. On the other hand, when it is positive, which is usually the case in most studies, it means that Y will have a positive value when $T=0$. The equation is solved by the ordinary least squares method (OLS), which allows for a unique solution of the method. (For a detailed discussion of OLS, see any standard econometrics textbook).

7.3.4.3 Significance of the Estimated Parameters and the Model

Once the model has been estimated, in particular the model parameters, it is important to determine the significance of the estimated model and the parameters. Five sets of statistics are typically used for this purpose: t-values, F ratio, R-square (coefficient determination), DW statistic (Durbin-Watson) when using time-series data, and MAPE (mean absolute percentage error) for measuring accuracy of the forecasts, among others.

The following provides a brief description of t-values, R^2 and F ratio, while DW static is discussed later under second-order tests and MAPE under measuring forecasting errors.

t-Values

These values are primarily used to determine the significance of the estimated coefficients in a causal model. The values are obtained by dividing the estimated coefficients by their corresponding standard errors, called the standard error of the estimate, and are given by the expression: $t_{\hat{\alpha}} = \hat{\alpha}/SE_{\hat{\alpha}}$ (for intercept) and $t_{\hat{\beta}} = \hat{\beta}/SE_{\hat{\beta}}$ (for slope), where SE is the standard error. Standard errors measure the accuracy of predictions, which is the difference between the observed and estimated values of the observations, $Y_i - \hat{Y}_i$ (where Y is the forecast variable). In general, if the standard errors are small, the t-values will be large indicating the significance of the estimated coefficients. The converse will be true when the standard errors are large.

R^2

The Coefficient of Determination, or R^2, which is the square of correlation coefficient R, measures the amount of variation in the dependent variable Y that is explained by the amount of variation in the independent variable, usually expressed as a percentage. It ranges between 0 and 1. For instance, a R^2 of 0.96

means that 96% of the variation in Y is explained by the variation in the independent (explanatory) variables (assuming there is more than one independent variable). In general, the R^2 tells us how well the estimated equation fits the sample observations. In other words, the close the estimated equation to the observations, the better is the fit. It is given by the expression

$$R^2 = \sum_{i=1}^{n} (\hat{Y}_i - \bar{Y})^2 / \sum_{i-1}^{n} (Y_i - \bar{Y})^2 \tag{7.14}$$

where Y_i represents the ith value of the dependent variable Y (for $i = 1, 2, 3, \ldots, n$), $\bar{Y}$ is the mean of the dependent variable, and $\hat{Y}$ is the estimated value of the dependent variable. The numerator represents the explained variance (variation due to the independent, explanatory variables) and the denominator represents the total variance (variation due to the explanatory variables, as well as the error term), and the equation becomes the ratio of explained to total variance.

F Ratio
Finally, the F ratio is used to see if the model as a whole is significant; in other words, if the model as a whole is a good fit of the data. As such, it is often called the goodness of fit test, or simply the F-test. It is given by the expression

$$F = \left[\sum_{i=1}^{n} (\hat{Y}_i - \bar{Y})^2 / (k - 1) \right] / \left[\sum_{i=1}^{n} (Y_i - \hat{Y})^2 / (n - k) \right] \tag{7.15}$$

where $\bar{Y}$ is the mean of the dependent variable, $\hat{Y}$ is the estimated value of the dependent variable Y, k is the number of parameters in the model, including the intercept term, n is the number of observations. The numerator of the expression is the explained variance due to the presence of the independent variables (adjusted for the degrees of freedom) and the denominator is the error variance due to the presence of the error term (adjusted for the degrees of freedom).

It should be worth noting that F-tests are not necessary for models with a single independent variable; they are more appropriate for models with multiple independent variables. For a model with one independent variable, the estimated slope coefficient and the observed t-value should be sufficient in most instances to assess the overall quality of the model. In general, t, R^2, and F ratios are good when they are high and the standard error is good when it is low. Put simply, the higher the t-value, R^2, and the F ratio, the better is the estimated model.

7.3.4.4 Model Illustration
To illustrate the method, let us use the data on parking meter revenue we used for the average method. As before, our objective is to forecast the parking meter revenue (PMR) for next year, $t + 1$. Table 7.3 shows the data, as well as some of the steps involved in estimating the model parameters.

The results of the estimated model are presented below:

Table 7.3 Estimation of trend line for parking meter revenue

Revenue, Y ($000)	Time (T)		$(Y - \bar{Y})$	$(T - \bar{T})$	$(T - \bar{T})^2$	$(Y - \bar{Y})(T - \bar{T})$	$\hat{Y}$ ($000)
4370.00	$t - 14$	(1)	−1638.00	−7.0	49.0	11,466.00	4353.25
4690.00	$t - 13$	(2)	−1318.00	−6.0	36.0	7908.00	4589.64
4780.00	$t - 12$	(3)	−1228.00	−5.0	25.0	6140.00	4826.04
5040.00	$t - 11$	(4)	−968.00	−4.0	16.0	3872.00	5062.43
5280.00	$t - 10$	(5)	−728.00	−3.0	9.0	2184.00	5298.82
5520.00	$t - 9$	(6)	−488.00	−2.0	4.0	1952.00	5535.21
5750.00	$t - 8$	(7)	−258.00	−1.0	1.0	258.00	5771.61
5980.00	$t - 7$	(8)	−28.00	0.0	0.0	0.00	6008.00
6230.00	$t - 6$	(9)	222.00	1.0	1.0	222.00	6244.39
6460.00	$t - 5$	(10)	452.00	2.0	4.0	904.00	6480.79
6740.00	$t - 4$	(11)	732.00	3.0	9.0	2196.00	6717.17
6950.00	$t - 3$	(12)	942.00	4.0	16.0	3768.00	6953.57
7190.00	$t - 2$	(13)	1182.00	5.0	25.0	5910.00	7189.96
7490.00	$t - 1$	(14)	1482.00	6.0	36.0	8892.00	7426.36
7650.00	t	(15)	1642.00	7.0	49.0	11,494.00	7662.75
$\bar{Y} = 6008$	$\bar{T} = 8.0$		0.00	0.0	280.0	66,190.00	$\hat{\bar{Y}} = 6008$

$$\hat{\beta} = \frac{\sum (Y - \bar{Y})(T - \bar{T})}{\sum (T - \bar{T})^2} = \frac{66,190.00}{280.00} = 236.3929$$

$$\hat{a} = \bar{Y} - \hat{b}\bar{T} = 6008.00 - (236.3929)(8.0) = 4116.8568$$
$$\hat{Y}_t = \hat{\alpha} + \hat{\beta}T$$

$$\hat{Y}_{1,t-14} = \hat{\alpha} + \hat{\beta}T = 4116.8568 + 236.3929(1) = 4116.8568 + 236.3929 = 4353.2497$$

$$\hat{Y}_{2,t-13} = \hat{\alpha} + \hat{\beta}T = 4116.8568 + 236.3929(2) = 4116.8568 + 472.7858 = 4589.6426$$

(and so on)

$SER = \sqrt{\frac{\sum (Y_i - \hat{Y}_i)^2}{n-k}} = 39.4157$ (where SER is the standard error of regression, i.e., standard error of the estimate, n = Number of observations; k = Number of parameters in the model)

$t_{\hat{\alpha}} = \hat{\alpha}/S_{\hat{\alpha}} = 4116.857/21.41685 = 192.2251 (p < 0.01)$

$t_{\hat{\beta}} = \hat{\beta}/S_{\hat{\beta}} = 236.3929/2.35554 = 100.3561 (p < 0.01)$

$r = \frac{\sum_{i=1}^{n} (Y_i - \bar{Y})(T_i - \bar{T})}{\sqrt{(Y_i - \bar{Y})^2}\sqrt{(T_i - \bar{T})^2}} = \frac{66,190}{66,236} = 0.9993; R^2 = 0.9986$

$R^2 = (r)^2 = (0.9993)^2 = 0.9986; r = \sqrt{R^2} = \sqrt{0.9987} = 0.9993$

$F = \frac{\hat{\beta}^2 \sum_{i=1}^{n} (T - \bar{T})^2}{\sum_{i=1}^{n} e^2/(n-k)} = \frac{(236.3929)^2(280)}{(20,196.8)/(15-2)} = \frac{15,646,848.89}{1553.60} = 10,071.35 (p < 0.0001)$

(where $e^2 = (Y - \hat{Y})^2$, n = Number of observations; k = Number of parameters in the model; $(n - k) = 15 - 2 = 13$)

$$\text{MAPE} = \frac{\sum |\text{PE}|}{n} \times 100$$

$$= \left[\sum (|\text{Observed} - \text{Estimated}|/\text{Observed})/n \right] \times 100$$

$$= [(|4370.00 - 4353.25|/4370.00) + \cdots + (|7650.00 - 7662.75|/7650.00)/15]$$
$$\times 100$$

$$= 0.4911(\%)$$

$$\hat{PMR}_t = 4116.857 + 236.3629T$$

$$(192.2251)(100.3561)$$

$$R^2 = 0.9987 \ F = 10071.35 \ DW = 2.06989 \ MAPE = 0.4911$$

where $\hat{PMR}$ is the estimated parking meter revenue, \$4116.857 is the estimated intercept indicating the revenue the government would earn, if $T=0$; that is, if time was not a factor, \$236.3629 is the estimated slope indicating the revenue the government would earn for each additional period, and R^2 appears to be quite high explaining 99.87% of the variation in PMR (forecast variable) explained by the explanatory variable, T (Time).

Overall, the model appears to be reasonably good, as evidenced by the t-values (within parentheses), R^2, and F ratio. Both t-values turned out to be quite high and statistically significant at less than 1% level ($p<0.001$) which can be easily checked against the critical t-value found in any standard statistical textbook. The R^2 also came out to be high. The model as a whole appears to be quite good, as given by the high F value, and significant at less than 1% level ($p<0.01$) which can be easily checked against the critical value of F found in any standard statistics textbook.[1] The soundness of the estimated model is also supported by DW statistic and low MAPE, discussed later. In general, if the estimated coefficients are significant, the chances are high the model will be significant, and vice versa. Figure 7.2 shows the estimated trend line.

We can now use the above statistics to forecast the revenue for next year, $t+1$. To do so, all we need to do is plug in the value of T for next year, which is 16 $(15+1)$, where 15 is the current year, t, multiply it by the estimated slope coefficient, and add the result to the intercept, so that

$$\begin{aligned}\hat{PMR}_{t+1} &= \$4116.857 + \$236.3629(16) \\ &= \$4116.857 + \$3781.806 \\ &= \$7898.663\end{aligned}$$

the revenue for parking meter next year will be approximately \$7.899 million. The result appears to be close to the amount we obtained earlier from the average method.

To forecast the revenue for $t+2$, we do the same; that is, plug in the new value of T for year after next, which will be 17 $(15+2)$, multiply it by the slope coefficient, and add the result to the intercept, so that the revenue for $t+2$ will be

$$\begin{aligned}\hat{PMR}_{t+2} &= \$4116.857 + \$236.3629(17) \\ &= \$4116.857 + \$4018.169 \\ &= \$8135.026\end{aligned}$$

which is a little over \$8.135 million, and repeat the process to produce forecasts for any number of years into the future.

It should be pointed out that since the model uses a linear trend, the revenue will increase by a constant amount, but it is unrealistic to assume that growth will

Fig. 7.2 Estimated trend line

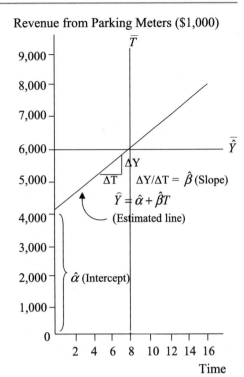

take place at the same rate for all future years. This may explain why this type of model is useful for short and intermediate-term rather than long-term forecasts. To avoid the problem, the data must be updated continuously as new information becomes available and repeat the forecast. Ideally, all forecasts should be updated on a regular basis, regardless of the method or methods used.

Diagnostic Checks

In general, time series with trends are more common for economic than for non-economic data because economic data tend to reflect underlying patterns much better than noneconomic data. Consequently, forecasters often find it useful to fit a trend model when they are dealing with revenue or expenditure forecasts. In most instances, the trend is obvious and detailed testing is not necessary, but in the event that one has some doubts it is important to use applicable measures to see if there is a trend in the data before running the model.

The simplest way to detect a trend in a series is to plot the data on a two-dimensional plane (with forecast variable on the vertical axis and time on the horizontal axis) to see if there is a discernible trend. As long as the data do not take a turn upward or downward, or move in a wave-like fashion, it is an indication that there is a trend in the data. Alternatively, we can use formal statistical tests that can tell us if there is a trend in the series, in particular the direction of the trend—if it is positive or negative. Two types of tests are generally used for this purpose:

parametric and non-parametric. Parametric tests, such as t and F, are based on a set of assumptions about the distribution of the population from which a sample (data) has been drawn such as normal, approximately normal, binomial, rectangular, and so forth, while non-parametric tests do not make such assumptions; as such, they are often called distribution-free methods.

A good example of a non-parametric test applied to trend line is the Spearman's rank correlation coefficient, ρ (rho).[2] It is given by the expression

$$\rho = 1 - \left[6 \left(\sum_{i=1}^{n} d_i^2 \right) / n(n^2 - 1) \right] \tag{7.16}$$

where ρ is the Spearman's rank correlation coefficient, which ranges between ± 1 ($-1 \le \rho \le +1$), d_i is the ith rank deviation, and n is the number of observations in a data series (for $i = 1, 2,\ldots, n$).

The deviation, d, in Eq. 7.16 is obtained by taking the difference between the rank orders for time and the values of the forecast variable. In general, if ρ is positive the trend is upward, and if it is negative the trend is downward. Thus, applying the equation to the data in our parking meter revenue example would produce a positive coefficient of 1, as shown below:

$$\rho = 1 - \left[6\Sigma d^2 / n(n^2 - 1) \right]$$
$$= 1 - \left[(6)(0)/(15)(15^2 - 1) \right]$$
$$= 1 - 0$$
$$= 1$$

The result indicates a strong upward trend in the series. Interestingly, the reason we have a perfect relationship is because there were no differences between the two rank orders, which is not always the case (Table 7.2).

In spite of its apparent simplicity and the ease of use as a forecasting method, there are circumstances where it may be difficult to fit a trend line to a series such as when a major turning point occurs that can bring about a permanent change in the series. This is usually the case when there is a major change in a government policy that substantially shifts the direction of movement in the data. The trend line may also be difficult to fit to a series if there are random changes that cannot be easily explained. For instance, a sudden increase in government expenditure for a single period or two because of an unforeseen event that could not have been predicted would be a good example, assuming that the event is unlikely to recur in the near future or during the forecast period.

7.3.4.5 Causal Forecasts

Unlike time-series forecasts, causal forecasts are based on a cause-and-effect relationship between a dependent and one or more independent (explanatory) variables. An important aspect of forecasting with causal models is that these models not only take into consideration one way (individual) effect, but also multi-way (simultaneous) effects among the variables in a system; as such, they provide a much greater insight into the workings of the system than most conventional time-series models. In general, when we are dealing with individual effects in a causal relationship we use a single-equation causal model, as opposed to when we are dealing with simultaneous effects among the variables, both dependent and independent, we use a multi-equation model. However, there is a commonality between time-series and causal models in that both rely on time-series data to do the forecast.

In general, single-equation models are more frequently used in budget forecasting than multi-equation models because they are conceptually simple, have low data requirements, and are relatively easy to construct. On the other hand, multi-equation models are more complex yet versatile than single-equation models since they take into consideration all possible interactions among the variables in a model. In reality, what specific model a forecaster will use depends on a variety of factors such as the nature of the relationship between the variables, the properties of the coefficients to be estimated, the skill level of the forecaster, the availability of data, and time and cost associated with each model, among others. The simplest form of causal relationship between a dependent and a set of explanatory, independent variables is a linear one, although non-linear models are not uncommon. In sum, the advantage of using a linear model is that it is simple, easy to understand, and apply.

The first step in building a causal model is to specify the model. This requires a forecaster to correctly identify the variables to be included in the model, specify the relationship between the dependent and the independent variables, such as linear or non-linear, present the relationship in a mathematical form, and determine a priori the signs and magnitude of the model parameters. These a priori definitions eventually become the theoretical criteria on the basis of which the results of the estimated model are evaluated. Thus, the specification of the model presupposes knowledge of theory, as well as familiarity with the problem. Previous works, empirical evidence, and a familiarity with the problem, including the environment in which forecasting will take place are necessary for effective causal modeling.

The following presents a simple linear causal (regression) model with one independent variable:

$$Y_t = \alpha + \beta X_t + e_t \qquad (7.17)$$

where Y is the dependent variable, X is the independent variable, α and β are the intercept and slope coefficients, respectively, and e is the error term, representing the variables not included in the model.[3]

Once the model has been specified, the next step is to collect the relevant data and estimate the model using conventional statistical procedures. The method commonly used for this purpose is the ordinary least squares (OLS) method, as noted earlier.[4] However, before the results of the estimated model could be used for forecasting purposes it is important that the results are tested for statistical significance, called the first-order tests, as well as to ensure that the conditions (assumptions) under which the model was built are satisfied, called the second-order tests.

Tests of Model Assumptions

The tests we conducted for the significance of estimated model (trend line), t and F, are called the first-order tests. The evaluation of the estimated model also requires a series of tests to assess the robustness of the model, called the second-order or econometric tests, since the econometricians have popularized the use of these tests. These tests are geared more toward model assumptions. While the first-order tests, such as z-test, t-test, and F-test, are used to test the significance of the estimated coefficients or the model, the second-order tests are generally used to see if the estimated model has violated the assumptions on which it was built. Important among these assumptions are zero mean, normality, homoskedasticity, independence, and no multicollinearity. All of these assumptions with the exception of multicollinearity are based on the distribution of the error term, e. The following provides a brief description of each:

Zero mean indicates that the error term, e, has a zero mean; that is, for any combination of the levels of explanatory variables, X's (X_1, X_2, ..., X_n), the error term e has an expected value of zero, $E(e_i) = 0$ (for $i = 1, 2,..., n$). The violation of zero mean indicates that we may have a biased estimate of the intercept. However, this may not have much empirical significance because in many practical situations the intercept term is of little importance to the researcher. Interestingly, the regression coefficient (slope), which is of much greater importance, remains unaffected by the violation of this condition.

Normality means that the error terms, e's, corresponding to the Xs, are normally distributed. Symbolically, the term can be written as $e \sim N(0, \sigma_e^2)$, which means that it is normally distributed with a zero mean and constant variance; that is, for any combination of levels of the explanatory variables, X_1, X_2,..., X_n, the random term follows a bell-shaped distribution which is usually assured with large samples. The violation of normality condition means that it will not be possible to conduct various tests of significance of the estimated parameters such as t, z, and other tests and construct confidence intervals. Interestingly, even if the normality assumption is violated we can still proceed as if it were true, as long as we have a large enough sample of data.

Homoskedasticity means that the error term e_i has a constant variance, $\text{var}(e) = \sigma_e^2$, regardless of the level of explanatory variables, X_1, X_2,..., X_n. In other words, its values do not depend on the values of the X's. When this condition is violated, we have a heteroskedasticity problem. Heteroskedasticity is a condition that is often associated with cross-sectional data that may include observations that vary in size for the same study producing what is known as "scale-effect," but can also apply to time-series data. The presence of heteroskedasticity means that the estimated coefficients will not be efficient in that they will not have minimum variance, although they will still be unbiased. This also means that the forecasts based on the estimated coefficients will be inefficient and, as such, may not be reliable.

Independence means that the successive values of the error term e, both temporally (over time) and across space (for different cross-sectional units), are independent meaning that they are not related to each other. In other words, there is no serial or autocorrelation. Autocorrelation generally occurs when the mathematical form of the model is misspecified, or when it includes omitted explanatory variables, or when there are too many interpolated data in a series. The presence of autocorrelation means that the forecasts based on OLS estimates will be inefficient, although the estimated coefficients may be unbiased.

Finally, no multicollinearity means that the explanatory variables are not highly related; in other words, the Xs are not highly correlated with each other to make their contribution to the dependent variable redundant. Multicollinearity can occur for a variety of reasons such as when there are too many lagged values for the same variable in a model, or when the model contains too many powers (X^2, X^3, X^4,..., etc.) of the same variable, or when the variables have a strong trend in common. Multicollinearity can also occur when the data collected over too small a range (small data set), or when the explanatory variables are linearly related with each other, as noted above. The presence of multicollinearity means that the standard errors of the estimates will be large making the t-values small and the coefficients indeterminate. In other words, they will be statistically insignificant.

Detecting the Problem

In each of the above situations, there are specific tests that can be conducted to see if any of the conditions have been violated and take specific measures to correct the problem. For instance, the assumption of normality can always be taken as satisfied if the sample size is large. The rule of thumb is that if the sample size $n \geq 30$, we can safely assume the distribution to be approximately normal. Alternatively, we can use formal tests, such as chi-square test, Jarque-Bera[5] test, and so forth to determine the presence of normality. Interestingly, there is no specific test for the verification of the zero mean for the error term since we set $E(e)$ at the beginning of our estimation procedures, which means that its plausibility should be examined in each case on a priori grounds (Pindyck and Rubinfeld 1988).

To see if there is a multicollinearity problem in the model, the convention is to look at the signs of the estimated model or the size of standard errors. If the signs are reversed, or the standard errors are high which will produce low t-values (since $t_{\hat{b}} = \hat{b}/\text{SE}_{\hat{b}}$) making the estimated coefficients insignificant. Alternatively, we can conduct formal tests, such as Farrar-Glauber test, Frisch's confluence analysis, and a host of other tests found in any standard econometrics textbook, to see if there is a multicollinearity problem.

Similarly, to see if there is a heteroskedasticity problem in the model the simplest way to find it would be to plot a graph on a two-dimensional plane with the squared residuals ($\hat{e}^2$'s) on the vertical axis and the dependent variable (X) on the horizontal axis. If the coordinates cluster more or less uniformly around the estimated (regression) line, it is an indication that there is no heteroskedasticity in the model; if they do not, it would indicate otherwise (Fig. 7.3). Alternatively, we can use formal tests to evaluate the presence of the problem. This would involve conducting tests such as Spearman's rank correlation test, Park test, Goldfeld-Quandt test, Glejser test, Breusch-Pagan-Godfrey test, White test, and so forth, which, again, can be found in any standard econometric textbook.

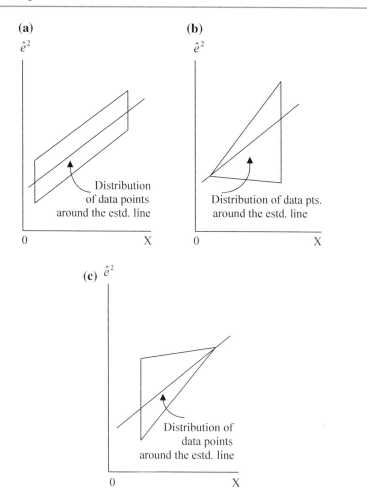

Fig. 7.3 (**a**) Homoskedasticity (constant variance). (**b**) Heteroskedasticity (increasing variance). (**c**) Heteroskedasticity (decreasing variance)

Finally, to see if there is an autocorrelation problem in the model, the rule of thumb is to plot the error terms against time on a two-dimensional plane with time (t) on the horizontal axis and the error term (e_t) on the vertical axis. Alternatively, we can use a lagged scatterplot, where the lagged-error term (e_{t-1}) appears on the horizontal axis and the error term (e_t) on the vertical axis (Fig. 7.4). Another alternative would be to use a correlogram, which is a plot of autocorrelation coefficients against lagged time. Autocorrelation coefficients are essentially the Pearson's product-moment correlation coefficients (r), where the correlations are computed between one time series against the same series lagged by one or more time unit.

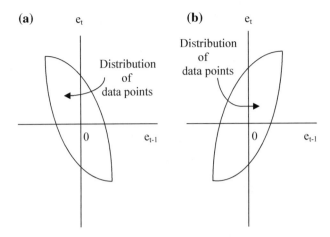

Fig. 7.4 (a) Negative autocorrelation. (b) Positive autocorrelation

While the visual plots are useful as a first step to detect the problem, they do not provide a precise measure of the extent of the problem in a model. The alternative is to use formal tests such as the Durbin-Watson (DW) test,[6] although there are other measures that can also be used such as Von Neumann ratio (ratio of the variance of the first difference of an independent variable with any other independent variable), Breusch-Godfrey test (for higher-order autocorrelation), Durbin's h test (for large samples), and so forth. Incidentally, Durbin's h can also be used in causal analysis with lags of the dependent variables, in which case DW test would be biased toward 2. (Details of these and other measures can be found in any standard econometrics textbook).

Measures to Correct the Problem
In each of the cases mentioned above where a problem occurs, there are specific measures one can take to correct the problem once it has been properly identified. Starting with multicollinearity, there are different ways in which to address the problem depending on how severe it is. The simplest way to correct the problem is to increase the sample size, which tends to lower the standard error of the estimated coefficients. Alternatively, one could use formal procedures, such as stepwise regression (both forward and backward), principal components analysis (for data reduction), introduce additional equations in the model (as long as they do not increase standard errors), or use methods such as two- or three-stage least squares.

As for dealing with the autocorrelation problem, one needs first to identify the sources that cause the problem. If the problem is due to omitted variables in the model, then the alternative will be to include the variables. If the problem is due to misspecification of the mathematical form of the model, then the remedy would be to use the correct form. By the same token, if the problem is due to the presence of too many interpolated data in a series, the alternative will be to reduce the number of interpolations. One could also use formal procedures such as first differencing, generalized difference equations, Cochrane-Orcutt two-step procedure, Durbin's two-step procedure, and so forth.

Finally, with regard to heteroskedasticity there are different ways one can address the problem. The simplest would be to transform the original model in such a way as to obtain a form in which the transformed disturbance term will have a constant variance. Alternatively, one could use formal measures such as weighted least squares, Generalized Least Squares,[7] White's heteroskedasticity correction procedure, and so forth. (A detailed discussion of these and others procedures as well as those suggested for multicollinearity and autocorrelation problems can be found in any standard econometrics textbook.)

7.3.4.6 A Single-Equation Model with One Independent Variable

Let us now look at a simple linear model with one independent (explanatory) variable. Suppose that a government wants to forecast the revenue from user fees and charges for next year, $t+1$. Table 7.4 shows the data on the variable over a ten-year period.[8] We will make a simple assumption in order to estimate the model that the revenues from user fees and charges depend on their most recent values, so that

$$\text{UFC}_t = \alpha + \beta \text{UFC}_{t-1} \tag{7.18}$$

where UFC is the revenue from user fees and charges, UFC_{t-1} is the lagged value of UFC, and α and β are the parameters of the model

The model presented above is generally known as the lagged model, where the value of a dependent variable depends on the past values of one or more independent variables. The lagged models are based on the assumption that there is often a substantial time lapse between the time when a decision is made and the time when

Table 7.4 Revenue from user fees and charges (UFC)

Time (T)		Y UFC ($000)	X UFC($t-1$) ($000)
$t-10$	(1)	707.000	–
$t-9$	(2)	800.210	707.000
$t-8$	(3)	968.320	800.210
$t-7$	(4)	1013.380	968.320
$t-6$	(5)	1171.820	1013.380
$t-5$	(6)	1254.020	1171.820
$t-4$	(7)	1317.270	1254.020
$t-3$	(8)	1465.530	1317.270
$t-2$	(9)	1584.400	1465.530
$t-1$	(10)	1557.790	1584.400
t	(11)	1610.370	1557.790
$t+1$	(12)	1660.671	–

the decision begins to produce a measurable effect, but people hardly change their behavior patterns overnight meaning that most recent data will have a far greater impact on the behavior of a dependent variable than the data further into time.

The results of the estimated model (which can be obtained using any standard statistical software) are presented below:

$$\hat{\text{UFC}}_t = 201.5144 + 0.9061 \text{UFC}_{t-1}$$

$$(2.7133) \quad (14.8777)$$

$$N = 11 \quad R^2 = 0.9651 \quad F = 221.3445 \quad \text{SER} = 56.2347$$

$$\text{DW} = 2.7140 \quad \text{MAPE} = 29.6171$$

The results seem to indicate that the model is a reasonably good fit of the data, as given by the high R^2. Both t and F values came out to be significant at $p < 0.05$ (which can be easily checked against the critical values of t and F found in any standard statistics textbook). Interestingly, the standard error of regression (SER), which tells us how well the equation fitted the data, and MAPE came out to be a little higher than expected. Similarly, the DW statistic also showed a slight tendency toward negative autocorrelation. The problem can be attributed in part to the small sample used in the current example (which is likely in this case), although we could have used measures such as first-order autoregressive scheme to correct the problem, discussed later.[9]

Since the results of the estimated model came out to be reasonably good and statistically significant for the most part, we can use this information to forecast the revenue for next year, $t + 1$, by plugging in the value of UFC at time t, as shown below:

$$\hat{\text{UFC}}_{t+1} = \$201.5144 + 0.9061 \text{UFC}_t$$

$$= \$201.5144 + 0.9061 (\$1610.370)$$

$$= \$1660.6707$$

which turns out to be approximately \$1.661 million. What the result tells us is that it is the amount of revenue the government will collect from user fees and charges next year, $t + 1$.

To see how good the forecast is we can forecast the value UFC at time t (current period) by plugging in the value of UFC at time $t - 1$ (backcasting). The result of the backcast produces a value of \$1613.028; that is, $\hat{\text{UFC}}_t = \$201.5144 + 0.9061 \text{UFC}_{t-1} = \$201.5144 + (0.9061)(\$1557.79) = \$1613.028$, which is close to the observed value of \$1610.370 at time t. We can now repeat the process to forecast the value of UFC at time $t + 2$ as $\hat{\text{UFC}}_{t+2} = \$201.5144 + 0.9061 \text{UFC}_{t+1}$, at time $t + 3$ as $\hat{\text{UFC}}_{t+3} = \$201.5144 + 0.9061 \text{UFC}_{t+2}$, and so forth.

7.3.4.7 A Single-Equation Model with Two Independent Variables

Let us look at another example; this time, a single-equation model with two independent (explanatory) variables without any lag. Our objective is to forecast the revenue from local option sales tax (LOST) for a government for next year, $t + 1$.

LOST constitutes an important source of revenue for local governments, in particular those that find it difficult to raise property taxes. Let us assume that LOST depends on two things: the median family income and the percentage of single-parent homes (Table 7.5). We make an additional assumption to set up the model that LOST is positively related to median family income (MFI) and inversely related to percentage of single-parent homes (PSPH). The assumption makes good sense, since the higher median family income the more likely it is that a family will have more disposable income to spend, which, in turn, will produce more sales tax revenue for the government. The converse will be true if there is a large pool of single-parent homes with limited income and spending ability.

The relationship between the three variables can be expressed in the following way:

$$\text{LOST}_t = \alpha + \beta_1 \text{MFI}_t - \beta_2 \text{PSPH}_t + e_t \tag{7.19}$$

where LOST is the revenue from local option sales tax, MFI is the median family income, PSPH is the percentage of single-parent homes, α and β are the parameters of the model, intercept and slopes, respectively, and e is the error term.

As before, we estimate the model using the OLS method. The results of the estimated model are presented below:

Table 7.5 LOST revenue and related data for the two-variable causal model

Time (T)		LOST Y ($million)	MFI X_1 ($million)	PSPH X_2 (%)	LOST (Estimated) ($million)	$\hat{e}$	$\hat{e}_{t-1}$
$t-14$	(1)	7.127	49.110	8.6	7.223	−0.096	–
$t-13$	(2)	8.135	51.870	8.6	8.763	−0.628	−0.532
$t-12$	(3)	9.867	52.113	8.5	9.494	0.373	1.001
$t-11$	(4)	10.671	53.832	8.4	11.048	−0.377	−0.750
$t-10$	(5)	11.416	54.134	8.4	11.217	0.299	0.676
$t-9$	(6)	12.481	54.586	8.4	11.469	1.012	0.713
$t-8$	(7)	14.142	55.125	7.8	15.342	−1.200	−2.212
$t-7$	(8)	15.715	55.760	7.8	15.696	0.019	1.219
$t-6$	(9)	16.819	55.937	7.8	15.795	1.024	1.005
$t-5$	(10)	17.983	61.219	7.8	18.742	−0.759	−1.783
$t-4$	(11)	19.125	61.784	7.8	19.058	0.067	0.826
$t-3$	(12)	20.431	61.875	7.5	20.894	−0.463	−0.530
$t-2$	(13)	21.272	62.024	7.5	20.978	0.294	0.757
$t-1$	(14)	22.031	62.327	7.3	22.337	−0.306	−0.600
t	(15)	23.784	62.521	7.2	23.041	0.743	1.049
$t+1$	(16)	24.428	–	–	–	–	–

$$\hat{\text{LOST}}_t = 31.33524 + 0.55627\text{MFI}_t - 5.9816\text{PSPH}_t$$
$$\quad\quad\quad (2.6026)\quad\ (5.9587)\quad\quad (-6.7751)$$

$$N = 15 \quad R^2 = 0.9855 \quad F = 4027.0957 \quad \text{SER} = 0.6931$$
$$\text{DW} = 2.8548 \quad \text{MAPE} = 3.5715$$

where the values in parentheses are the t-values, all of which came out to be significant at less than 5% level of significance ($p < 0.05$).

Diagnostic Checks and Corrections

The results of the estimated model appear to be reasonably good, as given by high R^2, t-values, F ratio, low SER and MAPE; thereby, indicating that it has satisfied the basic model conditions, described earlier. For instance, it does not seem to have a multicollinearity problem since the signs of the parameters did not change and all three t-values came out to be significant at $p < 0.05$ (which can be checked against the critical values of t and F found in any standard statistical tables). However, on close examination, the model appears to have a slight negative auto-correlation problem since the DW statistic is close to 3, which is higher than the standard acceptable level of 2.0 for no autocorrelation, similar to the previous example. To correct the problem, we use the first-order autoregressive scheme, or AR(1), in short (a standard practice for autocorrelation problems). The use of the first-order autoregressive schemes assumes that the problem is not due to omitted variable or misspecification of the mathematical form of the model. It also rules out that there are not too many interpolated data in the series.

In general, if the autocorrelation is of the first-order scheme it means that the error term at time t is directly related to the error term of the previous period, $t - 1$, plus a random variable, as can be seen below:

$$e_t = p e_{t-1} + v_t \tag{7.20}$$

where p is the corresponding slope, and v is the new random variable. The procedure requires that we transform the original data in such a way as to produce a model that will not have or substantially reduce the autocorrelation problem.

To apply the method, we proceed in three steps: First, we estimate the residual term, $\hat{e}$, then regress the estimated residual term, $\hat{e}$, on $\hat{e}_{t-1}$. Next, we use the estimated coefficient to obtain a new set of values for the explanatory variables and, finally, apply the OLS method to the transformed variables to re-estimate the model. The result of the first step appears to be significant, as shown below, by the t-value (in parentheses) at $p < 0.05$:

$$\hat{e}_t = 0.516442 \hat{e}_{t-1}$$
$$(6.2893)$$

We can now use the estimated coefficient to obtain a new set of values for our revenue variable, as well as for the median family income and the percentage of single-parent homes, as shown below:

$$LOST_t^* = LOST_t - 0.516442LOST_{t-1}$$
$$MFI_t^* = MFI_t - 0.516442MFI_{t-1}$$
$$PSPH_t^* = PSPH_t - 0.516442PSPH_{t-1}$$

where LOST*, MFI*, and PSPH* are the new (transformed) variables.

Next, we re-estimate the model with the transformed variables using the OLS method. The results of the re-estimated model are presented below:

$$\hat{LOST}_t^* = 31.5231 + 0.00056MFI_t^* - 5.99761PSPH_t^*$$
$$(3.9826) \quad (9.1051) \quad \quad (-10.4001)$$

$$N = 14 \quad R^2 = 0.9956 \quad F = 1234.337 \quad SER = 0.3600$$
$$DW = 2.1636 \quad MAPE = 1.7269$$

The results appear to be reasonably good as all the relevant coefficients came out to be significant at $p<0.05$. There also does not appear to be any autocorrelation problem since the Durbin-Watson (DW) statistic came down to a little over 2.0. We could have conducted a second-order autoregressive scheme on the re-estimated model but, in all likelihood, it would not have made any significant difference since the DW was already close to the acceptable level for no autocorrelation.

Although heteroskedasticity is a common problem for cross-sectional data, it is not unusual to find the problem in time-series data. As noted earlier, there are ways to detect the presence of a heteroskedasticity problem in a model, which ranges from a simple graphical method to conventional second-order tests. To see if there is a heteroskedasticity problem in our model as well as for the purpose of illustration, we use the White test, considered to be the simplest among all the tests of heteroskedasticity. It is basically a chi-square (χ^2) test that relies on the R^2 obtained from a regression of the squared residuals of the original model, $\hat{e}^2$, called auxiliary regression. The test is done in two steps: In the first step, we estimate the model and obtain the residuals, $\hat{e}_t$. In the second step, we take the squared values of the residuals and regress them on each of the explanatory variables, their squared values, and squared products. Higher powers of the regressors can also be used, if necessary, but in most instances, squared values usually produce the desired results.

The chi-square is computed in the following way: $nR^2 \approx \chi^2_{df}$, where n is the number of observations, and df represents the degrees of freedom (number of parameters in the model, excluding the intercept term). A low χ^2 would indicate the presence of heteroskedasticity and a high χ^2 would indicate the opposite.

The results of the initial test are provided below:

$$e_t^2 = \alpha + \beta_1 MFI_t - \beta_2 PSPH_t + \beta_3 MFI_t^2 + \beta_4 PSPH_t^2 + \beta_5(MFI_t)(PSPH_t) + v_t$$
$$\hat{e}_t^2 = 1133.046 - 0.01481MFI_t - 178.0986PSPH_t + 4.59e^{-08}MFI_t^2 + 6.8817PSPH_t^2$$
$$(1.3646) \quad (-1.2765) \quad \quad (-1.4027) \quad \quad (1.0641) \quad \quad (1.3839)$$
$$+ 0.0012(MFI)(PSPH)$$
$$(0.0009)$$

$$R^2 = 0.4369 \quad 15(0.4369) \approx \chi^2 = 6.5535$$

where 15 represent the number of observations (n) in the data series.

As can be seen from the above results, both R^2 and χ^2 came out to be rather low. The low χ^2 suggests the presence of a minor heteroskedasticity problem. To correct the problem, we run a second regression with the transformed variables to see if there were any significant improvements in the results. The results appear to have improved the heteroskedasticity problem considerably, as shown below:

$$\hat{\text{LOST}}_t^* = 31.52314 + 0.00056\text{MFI}_t^* - 5.99761\text{PSPH}_t^* + 1.33e^{-17}\text{MFI}_{t*}^2 + 1.71e^{-09}\text{PSPH}_{t*}^2$$

$$\quad\quad (4.12e^{08}) \quad (5.19e^{08}) \quad\quad (-5.05e^{08}) \quad\quad\quad (3.3524) \quad\quad\quad (3.6548)$$

$$+ 3.00e^{-13}(\text{MFI}^*)(\text{PSPH}^*)$$

$$\quad (3.7332)$$

$$R^2 = 0.9998 \quad 14(0.9998) \approx \chi^2 = 13.9972$$

As the results indicate, the chi-square coefficient more than doubled the previous value and came out to be significant at $p<0.05$ (with 5 degrees of freedom for the five explanatory variables, which can be easily checked against the critical χ^2 value found in any standard statistics textbook). Likewise, the R^2 also more than doubled to 0.9998, indicating a strong explanatory power of the model.

Doing the Forecast

With the correction of the autocorrelation and heteroskedasticy problems in our model, we can now use the estimated coefficients of the transformed model to forecast the LOST revenue for next year, $t+1$. Let us assume that we know the next year's values of MFI and PSPH, or that they are given to us. In the event that we do not know these values a priori, we can estimate the values using any of the time-series models, discussed earlier.

The estimation of the forecast for next year's LOST revenue based on the information we have for MFI and PDPH produces the following results:

$$\hat{\text{LOST}}_{t+1} = 31.5231 + 0.00056\hat{\text{MFI}}_{t+1} - 5.99761\hat{\text{PSPH}}_{t+1}$$

$$= 31.5231 + 0.00056(64,442) - 5.99761(7.2)$$

$$= 24.4278(\$24,427,800)$$

We can repeat the process for any number of years into the future, provided that we have the corresponding forecast values for MFI and PSPH. The process would be the same if we had additional explanatory variables.

It is important to recognize, however, that each time we do a forecast using the forecast values of the explanatory variables we are including errors that are contained in the previous forecasts. This also means that the further we forecast into the future the greater is the likelihood that it would contain more errors from the previous forecasts. This may partly explain why it is necessary to periodically update the forecasts, as new data become available.

Setting up Confidence Intervals

The forecasts produced so far are what one would call "point forecasts." They are expected values, not actual values, but they allow us to set up intervals about them called "interval forecasts" to indicate with a certain degree of confidence where the actual values are expected to lie. This is important, especially from a decision-making point of view since it gives the decision makers a range of options when making policy decisions, rather than restricting themselves to a single value. The confidence intervals for LOST revenue for next year are calculated in the following way:

$$C[\hat{Y} - (t_{\alpha/2})(\mathrm{SE}_{\hat{y}}) < Y < \hat{Y} + (t_{\alpha/2})(\mathrm{SE}_{\hat{y}})] = (1 - \alpha)$$
$$C[24.4278 - (2.145)(0.3600) < Y < 24.4278 + (2.145)(0.3600)] = 0.95$$
$$C[23.6556 < Y < 25.2000] = 0.95$$

where C is the notation for confidence intervals, $\hat{Y}$ is the estimated value of Y, $t_{\alpha/2}$ is the t-value for a two-tailed distribution corresponding to $(1 - \alpha)$, $SE_{\hat{Y}}$ is the standard error of estimate, and $(1 - \alpha)$ is the confidence level.

According to the interval estimates, there is a 95% chance that the actual revenue the government will collect from LOST next year will be between $23,655,600 and $25,200,000. It is important to note that the selection of the confidence level is the discretion of the forecaster. For instance, we could have used a different confidence level such as 90 or 99%, but 95% is considered fairly standard. In general, the higher the confidence level the greater is the reliability of the estimated coefficients. Note that we used a t-value instead of a z value (for large samples) because we are dealing with a small sample. However, for large samples it makes no difference since at a higher level, that is, as the sample size (number data points in a series) increases, the t distribution approximates a standard normal distribution (z). In other words, they become one and the same.

There is a much simpler way to construct these intervals that does not require the same confidence level to be used for different forecast values. It is a rule of thumb approach that relies on less restrictive assumptions than the conventional intervals, although it takes into consideration high and low estimates based on the expected value and the notion of confidence limits. It is less demanding on time and can be used as ballpark approximation for actual intervals. The following provides the expression, showing how to set up the intervals for sales tax revenue using this approach:

$$\left[\left\{\hat{Y}_{t+i} \times (1 - \alpha)\right\} < Y_{t+1} < \left\{\hat{Y}_{t+i} \times (1 + \alpha)\right\}\right] \tag{7.21}$$

where Y is the sales tax revenue and $(1 - \alpha)$ is the confidence coefficient.

Now, applying the expression in Eq. 7.21 to the observed estimates we can easily obtain the approximations for the actual intervals, as shown below:

$$(24.4278 \times 0.95) < Y < (24.4278 \times 1.05) = (23.2064 < Y < 25.6492)$$
$$(25.8943 \times 0.95) < Y < (25.8943 \times 1.05) = (24.5996 < Y < 27.1890)$$
$$(26.7373 \times 0.95) < Y < (26.7373 \times 1.05) = (25.4004 < Y < 28.0742)$$
$$(27.5990 \times 0.95) < Y < (27.5990 \times 1.05) = (26.2191 < Y < 28.9790)$$
$$(27.8466 \times 0.95) < Y < (27.8466 \times 1.05) = (26.4543 < Y < 29.2389)$$
$$(28.4016 \times 0.95) < Y < (28.4016 \times 1.05) = (26.9815 < Y < 29.8217)$$

where the first terms of the expression are the forecast values. The intervals appear quite reasonable, but caution should be exercised when using these intervals since the procedures suggested here do not follow the conventional rules of interval estimation based on inferential statistics. Also, most statistical software these days produce these intervals; as such, interval estimations by hand are somewhat redundant. Nevertheless, they could provide useful ballpark approximations for the actual intervals.

7.3.4.8 Single-Equation Models with Multiple Independent Variables

The single-equation models described above dealt, first, with one, and then with two independent variables but, in reality, we often have to deal with not one or two, but several independent variables, in which case we need to expand the basic linear model to include multiple independent variables. The general form of a single-equation model with multiple independent variables in linear form can be expressed in the following way:

$$Y_t = \alpha + \sum_{i=1}^{m} \beta_i X_{it} + e_t$$

$$= \alpha + \beta_1 X_{1t} + \beta_2 X_{2t} + \cdots + \beta_m X_{mt} + e_t$$

(7.22)

where the terms in the expression are the same as before, except that it includes multiple independent variables, m.

Although it may appear simple, operationally when one is dealing with multiple independent variables in a single equation it is difficult to use the same computational procedures, as opposed to when dealing with multiple independent variables. It will involve far too many computations that will require the knowledge of matrix algebra to solve the problem. In reality, that is seldom necessary since any standard statistical software should be able to deal with multiple regression problems with a large number of independent variables and observations.

7.3.5 Cash-Flow Forecasts

Besides estimating revenues and expenditures for multiple years, governments also estimate the future cash flows, called cash-flow forecasts, especially in the short term. Cash-flow forecasts are frequently used in government to determine if the government will have enough cash to meet its obligations in the short term, usually less than year—a week, a month, a quarter, or six months. Although annual cash-flow forecasts are not uncommon, the forecasts are mostly based on weekly, monthly, and quarterly data.

Since cash-flow forecasting deals with short-term periods, it is useful to use methods that are particularly suitable for short-term forecasts such as the average method, discussed earlier. Another method that is frequently used for short-term forecasting is simple moving average (SMA), discussed next.

7.3.5.1 Simple Moving Average

SMA is one of the simplest and most widely used methods among the family of time-series methods, especially where short-term forecasts are concerned. Like the average method, it relies on arithmetic average, but instead of using a single average it uses a series of averages called moving averages (MAs), which are obtained by taking the average of the most recent observations in a series. The procedure is quite simple: As new observations become available, a new average is calculated by dropping the oldest observation from the average and including the newest one. The newest average is then used to forecast the value for the next time period. Thus, the number of observations used in the average always remains constant and includes the most recent observations.

However, the method requires that the number of observations included in the average is specified in advance such as three months, six months, or nine months. The number of months included in a series defines the type of moving average method being used for forecasting. Thus, a series containing three months of data is called a three-month moving average, six months of data is called a six-month moving average, and so on.

The following presents the mathematical expression for the method:

$$\hat{Y}_{t+1} = \frac{Y_t + Y_{t-1} + \cdots + Y_{t-n+1}}{n} \tag{7.23}$$

where $\hat{Y}_{t+1}$ is the forecast value of Y at time $t+1$, Y is the actual observation, Y_{t-i} is the past observations (for $i = 1, 2,..., n$), and n is the number of observations in the moving average

To give an example, suppose that a government wants to forecast its cash flows (inflows and outflows) for the Water Department. Inflows in this case will be cash receipts from the sale of water and outflows will be cash disbursements. Let us say that the government has the cash receipt and disbursement data for the last 12 months, from January through December. The objective of the government is to forecast the cash receipt (inflow) and cash disbursement (outflow) for the month of January, next year, using a three-month moving average. Table 7.6 shows the monthly receipt and disbursement data for the government, except for the forecast month of January ($t+1$).

To obtain the receipt for January ($t+1$), we simply plug in the data for the three most recent months in the expression in Eq. 7.23 and calculate the average, as shown below.

$$\hat{Y}_{t+1(\text{January})} = \frac{Y_{\text{Dec}} + Y_{\text{Nov}} + Y_{\text{Oct}}}{3}$$

$$= \frac{\$220,000 + \$235,000 + \$255,000}{3}$$

$$= \$236,667$$

The result produces a value of \$236,667, which is the projected cash receipt for the month of January.

We can repeat the process to forecast the cash receipt for the month of February, $t+2$, in the similar fashion, so that

$$\hat{Y}_{t+2(\text{February})} = \frac{Y_{\text{Jan}^*} + Y_{\text{Dec}} + Y_{\text{Nov}}}{3}$$

$$= \frac{\$236,667^* + \$220,000 + \$235,000}{3}$$

$$= \$230,556$$

and so on.

Now, to forecast the cash disbursements for the months of January and February, we do the same, as shown in Table 7.6. A quick glance at the results, especially the revenue forecasts, would indicate that the projected cash receipts for January are lower than the receipts for December, which is the most recent month, indicating a decrease of \$18,330 over December, but much higher than the receipts for the previous January. The fluctuations in receipts are usually explained by the underlying fluctuations in the data, which is not uncommon in government. This is evident in the higher receipts for the summer months when water consumption is usually high, as shown in Fig. 7.5. It could also be due to the fact that the data used in the example are not actual data, but randomly generated for illustrative purposes. While fluctuations are inherent in seasonal data, they can make it difficult to see the underlying changes in a series because of seasonal influence; as such, it may be necessary to adjust the data to measure the real changes in the series such as increase or decrease in growth, turning points, and so forth. A wide range of methods are available that can be used for this purpose such as Winter's seasonal exponential smoothing, among others.

In general, governments tend to collect more revenue during certain times of the year, such as sales tax during holiday season and property taxes when they become due, producing surpluses (revenues not immediately needed for expenditures). Some of these surpluses are invested in different instruments to produce non-tax revenue or can be used to make up for revenue shortfall in other areas. Overall, the forecasts appear to be consistent with this underlying pattern. The disbursements (outflows) tend to depict less fluctuation because, unlike receipts (inflows), they tend to remain more or less consistent throughout the year.

Besides the influence of seasonal variation in the data, there are other concerns with moving averages such as how to find the initial value when no previous forecasts are available. The rule of thumb is to substitute the first observation of the

Table 7.6 Three-month moving average for the Water Department

Month	Time	(Inflow) Cash receipts ($000)	(Outflow) Cash disbursements ($000)	Net flow ($000)	3-month MA receipts ($000)	3-month MA disbursements ($000)	Net flow ($000)
January	$t-10$	215.00	225.00	−10.00	–	–	–
February	$t-9$	225.00	220.00	5.00	–	–	–
March	$t-8$	230.00	225.00	5.00	–	–	–
April	$t-7$	240.00	230.00	10.00	223.33	228.33	–
May	$t-6$	255.00	240.00	15.00	231.67	225.00	–
June	$t-5$	270.00	245.00	25.00	241.67	231.67	–
July	$t-4$	290.00	250.00	40.00	255.00	238.33	–
August	$t-3$	285.00	245.00	40.00	271.67	245.00	–
September	$t-2$	275.00	240.00	35.00	281.67	246.67	–
October	$t-1$	255.00	240.00	15.00	283.33	245.00	–
November	$t-1$	235.00	240.00	−5.00	271.33	241.67	–
December	t	220.00	230.00	−10.00	255.00	240.00	–
January[a]	$t+1$	–	–	–	236.67[a]	236.67[a]	0.00[a]
February[a]	$t+2$	–	–	–	230.56[a]	235.56[a]	−5.00[a]

[a]Forecast month

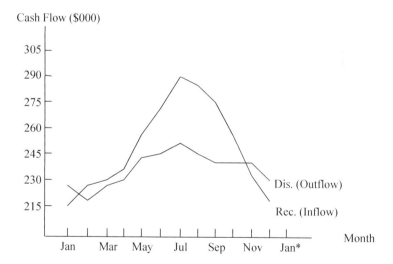

Fig. 7.5 Monthly cash flow for the Water Department

series (October, in the current example) for the first forecast. Another alternative would be to take the average of three or four most recent observations and use that average as the forecast for the initial value. Although these are considered ad hoc measures, their use tends to be quite effective when no information is available on previous forecasts. Another important concern with simple moving average is that it assigns equal weight to all the observations used in a forecast, which can easily produce a different result than one would normally expect for a given distribution (data set). This was clearly evident in the higher value for the month of January, next year, since we expect it to be lower than the value for the month of December. The problem can be easily corrected by assigning differential weights to different observations, usually the highest for the most recent observation since it tends to contain the most information in the series. The method commonly used for this purpose is the weighted moving average. Alternatively, one could use methods such as exponential smoothing to correct the problem.

In the example presented above, we considered a single revenue variable, sale of water, but, in reality, the method can be applied to any number of revenue variables, as long as we are interested in short-term forecasts. We could do the same for the expenditure side for outflows since we need both inflows and outflows to forecast the cash flows. Table 5.5, presented earlier under cash budgeting, is a good example of cash-flow forecast for a local government based on monthly receipts and disbursements over a three-month period. Although the forecasts presented in the table were not based on actual forecasts, any of the time-series methods suggested here can be used to do the forecast.

7.4   Measuring Forecast Errors

The decision to use a particular forecasting method is based on the assumption that, when completed, it will produce reliable and accurate forecasts. In reality, it is unrealistic to expect a model to produce perfect forecasts, but it is not unrealistic to expect a model that produces relatively accurate forecasts with small errors. Therefore, knowing the accuracy of a forecast is important to have any meaningful application of the results. The simplest way to measure the accuracy of a forecast is to plot the actual values against the predicted values to see the level of error in a forecast, but, unfortunately, the plots do not give a precise measure of accuracy other than providing an optical impression of performance. A more effective way to deal with the problem is to use measures that would provide a better picture of accuracy that are simple and also easy to interpret.

There is a wide range of such measures that can be used for this purpose such as mean squared error (MSE), mean absolute deviation (MAD), and mean absolute percentage error (MAPE). Most of these measures are based on simple statistical concepts such as mean, variance, standard deviation, and covariance. Of the three, MAPE is considered a better measure because it contains elements of both MSE and MAD. Although MAPE is widely used, ideally, one should use more than one measure to ensure greater accuracy of the forecasts.

In general, MAPE provides an indication of how large the forecast errors are in comparison with the actual values of the series. It is obtained by averaging the magnitude of absolute percentage errors and is given by the expression

$$\text{MAPE} = \frac{\sum_{i=1}^{n} |\text{PE}_i|}{n} = \frac{\sum_{i-1}^{n} \left| \frac{(O_i - E_i)}{O_i} \right|}{n} \times 100 \qquad (7.24)$$

where $\text{PE}_i = i$th percentage error (for $i = 1, 2, \ldots, n$) and $n =$ Number of observations.

7.5   Forecast Evaluation

While the use of conventional approaches to measure forecast errors such as MAD, MSE, MAPE, and so forth is a good way to determine the accuracy of a forecast, it may be useful to use other measures, such as comparing the forecasts obtained with a particular model with those obtained by other models, to see how well they compare. This is a common practice at the national level, where various research organizations (e.g., Data Resources Incorporated, Chase Econometrics, Wharton Econometric Associates, and others) develop forecasts on the same set of variables. Most of these variables are macroeconomic variables such as unemployment, inflation, gross domestic product, budget deficit, and so forth. The forecasts can easily serve as benchmark against which individual forecasts can be compared to measure their accuracy.

Another, perhaps, more effective way to produce reliable forecasts is to take an average of the forecasts produced by different methods into a single forecast. This is known as composite forecasts. Composite forecasts are useful in situations where the forecaster is not sure of the forecasting results. By taking an average of the forecasts, the forecaster can avoid large errors. The rule of thumb is to use at least five different forecasts on the same set of variables. A common assumption in selecting multiple methods is that they should belong to the same family of methods. However, if the methods selected are substantially different in nature; in other words, if there are qualitative differences among the methods, the forecaster should assign weights to the forecasts produced by each method and take a weighted average.

The following provides a simple expression for a composite forecast for a forecast variable for next year, $t + 1$:

$$\hat{Y}_{t+1} = \left(\sum_{j=1}^{m} \hat{F}_j \right) / m \qquad (7.25)$$

where $\hat{F}$ is the forecast for the variable Y at time $t + 1$, with jth forecasting method (for $j = 1, 2, \ldots, m$), and m is the total number of forecasting methods.

To give an example, suppose that a government wants to forecast revenue from excise tax for next year, ETX_{t+1}, where ETX stands for excise tax. The government uses five different forecasting methods which produce the following forecasts: $ET\hat{X}_1 = \$25.7$ million, $ET\hat{X}_2 = \$23.5$ million, $ET\hat{X}_3 = \$26.3$ million, $ET\hat{X}_4 = \$24.6$ million, and $ET\hat{X}_5 = \$22.8$ million, where the subscript indicates the method used. If there are no major qualitative differences in the methods, we can simply take an average of the five forecasts, which will be $24.58 million [($2 5.7m + \$23.5m + \$26.3m + \$24.6m + \$22.8m)/5 = \$24.58m$]. However, if there are qualitative differences in the methods, then it may be necessary to use a weighted average method but one has to be careful how the weights are assigned.

7.5.1 Interim Review

As noted earlier, it is important that once a forecast has been made for any number of years into the future it is periodically updated, as new data become available. This is known as interim review. Interim review is fairly common in government for both short-tern and long-term forecasts. The idea is not necessarily to determine how good the forecasts are, although that is important, but to see if substantial deviations have occurred; if so, how significant are the deviations and, more importantly, what contributed to the deviations. Also, it is natural to expect that forecasts would be good and reliable; however, it is not uncommon for a forecast user to expect accuracy level that may not be realistically achieved. It is then up to the forecaster and others involved in the process to explain what can or cannot be achieved, given the results, in which case the user may very well need to establish a contingency plan to deal with potential errors in the forecast.

7.6   Summary and Conclusion

Forecasting lies at the heart of a budget. Without good and reliable forecasts, it would be difficult for any government to plan and effectively carry out its operations. This chapter has introduced some of the basic forecasting methods used in budget forecasting. Most of these methods are conceptually simple, have low data requirements, and also easy to use. As noted earlier, the number of methods available to a forecaster has increased considerably over the years yet there is no one particular method that can be considered superior—much depends on the quality of data, the knowledge and skills of the forecaster, and his ability to effectively utilize the available information to do the forecast. Given the range of options available to a forecaster, it is natural to expect that forecasts would be good and reliable, but that is not always the case. Consequently, it is not uncommon for a forecast user to expect an accuracy level that may not be realistically achieved; the user must be aware of that. The responsibility usually falls on the forecaster and others involved in the process to explain what can or cannot be achieved, and why, in the likely case of negative forecasts, the administrator may very well need to establish a contingency plan to deal with future budget deficits.

Review Questions

Q1. Why is forecasting important in public budgeting? How should the decision makers use budget forecasts?

Q2. What is a forecasting process? Discuss the steps of the process.

Q3. What are the different types of methods commonly used in budget forecasting? What are the strengths and weaknesses of the methods? How would you select a forecasting method?

Q4. What is a naïve forecast? Write the equation for naïve forecast. Look at the example on naïve forecasts in the chapter. Redo the forecast for next year using 2.5% inflation rate (1) for some of the items, and (2) all the items.

Q5. What is an engineering cost estimate? Why is it considered a better method than naïve forecasting? For the problem discussed in the chapter, assume that the community will experience a 2.5% growth population next year What will be the cost of running the department next year, assuming everything will remain the same? How many police officers will be needed to meet the growing needs of the community? What would be the cost of running the department if the population actually declines by 1.5% next year?

Q6. What is a constant average method? Suppose that we have the following revenue data for the Water Department of a local government (Table 7.7):

Using the information above, do a revenue forecast for the department for next year $(t+1)$.

Table 7.7 Review Question (Q6)

Year (T)	Revenue, Y ($000)	Percentage change ($\%\Delta$)
$t-9$	6180.00	–
$t-8$	6230.00	–
$t-7$	6370.00	–
$t-6$	6410.00	–
$t-5$	6490.00	–
$t-4$	6540.00	–
$t-3$	6610.00	–
$t-2$	6720.00	–
$t-1$	6890.00	–
t	7140.00	–
$t+1$	–	–

Q7. Let us say that you want to use the same data for a trend-line forecast? What would be the revenue for the department for next year, $(t+1)$? And year after next, $(t+2)$?

Q8. What is a non-parametric test? Give an example of a non-parametric test to measure trend in a series. Use now the test to determine the trend for the data in Q6.

Q9. What is a parametric test? Give an example of a parametric test to measure trend in a series and calculate the test statistics for the data in Q6. Now, based on the test statistics, make an appropriate inference about the parameters.

Q10. Explain the square of correlation coefficient R^2, Interpret the value of $R^2 = 0.98$. Give the expression to calculate R^2.

Q11. Discuss the following terms: F ratio, t-values, normality assumption, assumption of independence, homoscedasticity, and no multicollinearity in a linear regression.

Q12. Suppose that a government wants to forecast the revenue from user fees and charges (UFC) for next year. It has the following data for the forecast variable (Table 7.8):

Table 7.8 Review Question (Q12)

Year (T)	UFC (t) Y ($000)	UFC ($t-1$) X ($000)
$t-7$	917.19	784.32
$t-6$	1013.21	917.19
$t-5$	1152.94	1013.21
$t-4$	1289.16	1152.94
$t-3$	1351.89	1289.16
$t-2$	1471.23	1351.89
$t-1$	1543.73	1471.23
t	1619.20	1543.73
$t+1$	–	–

Given the data above, do the following: (1) fit the model $UFC_t = \alpha + \beta UFC(t-1)$, (2) forecast the value of UFC at time $t+1$, $t+2$, and $t+3$, (3) determine the value of R^2 and χ^2, and (4) interpret the results. Also, Find the confidence intervals for $UFC_{(t+1)}$ and interpret the results.

Q13. What is a cash-flow forecast? Write the mathematical expression for a simple moving average method. Let us say that we have the following revenue data from sale of electricity for a local government (Table 7.9):

Now, using the data above, forecast the revenue for the government for the months of February, March, and April.

Table 7.9 Review Question (Q13)

Month	Time (T)	Actual revenue ($000)	Projected revenue ($000)
July	$t-5$	40,773	–
August	$t-4$	41,631	–
September	$t-3$	35,519	–
October	$t-2$	31,830	–
November	$t-1$	29,789	–
December	t	51,538	–
January	$t+1$	33,266	–
February	$t+2$	–	–
March	$t+3$	–	–
April	$t+4$	–	–

Q14. Why is it necessary to measure forecasting errors? What methods are commonly used to measure forecasting errors? Why and when should a forecaster use averages to measure the accuracy of a forecast?

Q15. Define MAPE and write the expression for calculating MAPE. What are the advantages and disadvantages of using MAPE?

Q16. Why is the choice of methods important in forecasting? Do advanced and sophisticated methods always produce the best forecast? Why is it relatively easy to do an expenditure forecast than revenue forecast?

Notes

1. The following expression for the F value is generally used for the trend line: $F = \left[\hat{\beta}^2 \sum_{i=1}^{n} (T - \bar{T})^2 \right] / \left[\left(\sum_{i=1}^{n} e^2 \right) / (n - k) \right]$, where $e^2 = (Y - \hat{Y})^2$, n is the number of observations in a series, and k is the number of parameters in the model, which will be 2 in the current example.

2. There are other non-parametric tests that one can also use such as runs test, turning points test, sign test, Kendall's tau, Fischer-Yates coefficient, and Daniels' test, among others. Of these, Daniel's test, which is similar to Spearman's rank correlation, is considered the simplest yet useful.

3. The error term has a special meaning in regression analysis. For instance, when a linear equation is expressed, say, as $Y = a + \beta X$, it implies that the relationship is exact in that all the variations in Y is due entirely to the variation in X. If this were true, then all the data points on a two-dimensional plane would fall on a straight line. However, when the observations come from the real world and are plotted on a graph, one will most certainly observe that they will not fall on a straight line. In other words, there will be some deviations of the observations from the line, however small they may be. There are several explanations as to why the deviations occur such as omission of variables, random or

unpredictable behavior of human beings, imperfect specification of the mathematical form of the model, errors in aggregation, and errors in measurement. Of these, the first four are called the errors of omission, and the fifth the error of measurement. In order to correct for these errors, the convention is to introduce an error term into the equation, so that it will now appear as $Y = a + \beta X + e$. Therefore, the true relationship that connects the variables in the equation (model) consists of two components—one represented by the line, $a + bX$, and the other by the error term, e.

4. The attractiveness of OLS method is that it has a number of properties that are considered desirable characteristics of least squares estimators. They include, among others, (1) *unbiasedness*, where the difference between the expected value and the true parameter is assumed to be 0, (2) *minimum variance*, where an estimate has the lowest variance compared to any other estimates in the model, (3) *efficiency*, where it is both unbiased and has minimum variance, and (4) BLUE, called the Best Linear Unbiased Estimator, where the estimator is linear, unbiased, and has the least variance. Another notable property of the estimators is *sufficiency*, where the estimator utilizes all the available information in a sample about the parameter.

5. The Jarque-Bera test, also known as JB test, is based on the skewness and kurtosis of the distribution of data. It is given by the expression $\left[\left(\frac{n}{6} \right) \left(s^2 + \frac{1}{4} k^2 \right) \right]$, where n is the sample size (or degrees of freedom), s is the skewness, given by $(\bar{X}_3 / S^3)$, and k is the kurtosis, given by $[(\bar{X}/s^4) - 3]$.

6. This statistic is primarily used in situations where one is dealing with time-series data to see if the successive error terms, e's, are correlated with each other called autocorrelation. Considered a part of the second-order tests, its objective is to test the null hypothesis that there is no autocorrelation problem in a model; if there is, it violates one of the conditions of causal modeling, described in the next section. The DW statistic extends between 0 and 4 ($0 < d < 4$), where d stands for DW statistic. The rule of thumb for interpretation is that there is no autocorrelation if DW statistic is around 2, usually between 1.5 and 2; it is positive if it is between 0 and 2, and it is negative if it is between 2 and 4.

7. When the OLS estimator is no longer BLUE, the Generalized Least Squares (GLS) estimator can solve the problem by transforming the model into one with homoskedastic errors leaving the structure of the model intact; in other words, by turning the heteroskedastic model into an homoskedastic one.

8. As a rule of thumb, one must have at least 15 data points when dealing with a time-series model and 10 data points when dealing with a cross-sectional model, although the actual requirement will vary depending on the method used. For cross-sectional models, in particular, the common-sense rule is that the number of observations must be higher than the number of parameters in a model to have any meaningful result. For models such as Box-Jenkins (discussed in the next chapter), the requirements are much higher. Box-Jenkins themselves preferred over 50 observations, while some practitioners use even more. There are two simple explanations for large sample (data) requirements: (1) when one is dealing with a small data set, it is harder to see statistically which autocorrelation or partial autocorrelation coefficients are significant, making it difficult to identify the correct model, and (2) larger series produce more accurate parameter estimates; therefore, more accurate forecasts. Interestingly, some recent studies suggest that a large data set may not be necessary for Box-Jenkins.

9. The model suggested here is based on an actual study conducted by the author; the name is withheld for maintaining anonymity of the city.

References

Buck, A. E. (1929). *Public Budgeting*. New York, NY: Harper & Row.

Hirsch, W. Z. (1970). *The Economics of State and Local Government* (pp. 280–290). New York, NY: McGraw-Hill.

Klay, W. E. (1983). Revenue Forecasting: An Administrative Perspective. In J. Rabin & T. D. Lynch (Eds.), *Handbook of Public Budgeting and Financial Management* (pp. 287–316). New York, NY: Marcel Dekker.

Pindyck, R. S. & Rubinfeld, D. L. (1988). *Econometric Models and Economic Forecasts*. New York, NY: Irwin-McGraw-Hill.

Capital Budgeting and Improvement Process

8

Capital budgeting plays a vitally important role in the overall budgetary activities of a government. In some ways, it can be considered much more important than the routine operations of a government because of the impact these activities have on long-term economic growth and development of a jurisdiction. The activities, commonly referred to as capital improvement activities, involve investments in capital assets such as roads, bridges, highways, land, buildings, vehicles, equipment, physical plants, and so forth. The level as well as the quality of capital assets in a government and how well they are maintained indicate how well an economy is performing. In general, the better the condition of capital assets the stronger is the economy. Understanding the characteristics of a capital budget and, more importantly, the process that underlies these activities is important to understand what makes capital budgeting so unique and different from the operating budget and why it is necessary to have a separate capital budget, as most state and local governments do. The chapter has twofold objectives: One, it provides a brief discussion of the characteristics of a capital budget, types of capital assets a government maintains, and the relationship between a capital budget and long-term planning. Two, it provides an at length discussion of the capital budget process which, like an operating budget, is complex, detailed, and often time consuming. The chapter concludes with a brief discussion of the impact a capital budget has on the operating budget.

8.1   Characteristics of a Capital Budget

A capital budget has several distinguishing characteristics that separate it from an operating budget. First and foremost, it deals with expenditures that involve investments in capital assets that are non-recurring and have a life span of several years.[1] As such, a capital budget is prepared for multiple years, usually for five or six years. The idea behind a five- or six-year capital budget is that it matches the

© The Author(s) 2019
A. Khan, *Fundamentals of Public Budgeting and Finance*,
https://doi.org/10.1007/978-3-030-19226-6_8

Capital Budgeting and Improvement Process

long-term development needs of a jurisdiction consistent with the funding sources. Second, although the expenditures are non-recurring in that the construction or acquisition of an asset involves one-time expenditure, the operation and maintenance of the assets require recurring operating expenditures. What this means that even though the budget is prepared for five or six years, it is adopted and updated annually which establishes a direct linkage with the operating budget where they appear as annual capital outlays. Third, expenditures on capital assets involve large commitments of resources, which, depending on the assets, can run into hundreds of millions of dollars. Fourth, and as noted earlier, investments in capital assets are vitally important for long-term economic growth and development of an economy. A strong and vibrant economy needs well-developed and maintained capital assets to sustain its pace of economic growth and development. Fifth, last but not least, once constructed or acquired, the assets remain in place for a long time, which makes it difficult to reverse or change the decision once they have been put in place.

The long-term aspect of capital budgeting also means that expenditures on capital assets can produce income that can substantially add to the revenue stream of a government. For instance, the construction of a capital project, say, a sports arena can create direct employment for the community in which it is located from construction and maintenance of the facility, which, in turn, can generate new revenues for the government from income, sales, and property taxes. Not only that, the multiplier effect of the facility from support industries and service activities can further add to the growth and expansion of the economy, producing additional revenues for the government. On the other hand, not all capital assets are non-recurrent or one-time. For instance, the construction of a large-scale project such as a bridge or highway will be non-recurring but items such as replacing a piece of machinery or equipment for sewer or electric utility will be recurring, although they may not recur annually.

8.2 Types of Capital Assets

Capital assets are not uniform. They vary in size, characteristics, resource requirements, and complexity. As such, it is important that a clear distinction is made between different types of capital assets before undertaking the improvement activities. Unfortunately, there are no precise guidelines for classifying capital assets that can serve as benchmark for all governments. Individual governments can develop their own classification systems, based on the needs for capital improvement and the strength of their resource base, or they can use established criteria such as those suggested by GFOA. GFOA, for instance, classifies capital assets into a number of distinct categories such as land, buildings and improvements (other than buildings), furnishings and equipment, infrastructure, construction/development in progress, and other capital assets (GAAFR 2012). The last category includes those assets that do not fit into any of the other categories. This would include vehicles, capital leases, and assets such as computer software, easements, and land use rights, among others. The list is not all-inclusive and can be expanded further to include variations within each category. For instance, a local public school system may report library holdings or museum collections as assets, in addition to the buildings that house them, as long as they meet Government Accounting Standard Board's (GASB's) codification (Freeman et al. 2006).[2] Similar procedures can be used to classify other activities, as well.

While the classification systems suggested by GFOA and others rely on basic physical characteristics, capital assets can also be classified based on their size, physical condition, as well as on their relationship with other assets.

8.2.1   Classification According to Size

Since capital assets vary in size, cost, complexity and life span, another way to classify capital assets would be according to the nature of the assets, the length of time it takes to construct or acquire an asset and their relative costs (size). Based on this, three types of capital assets are generally recognized when developing a capital budget: capital projects, capital items, and inventory items. A capital project is a non-recurring expenditure, involving a large commitment of resources on infrastructure (such as roads, bridges, and highways), facilities (such as public buildings and physical plants) acquisition of real property (such as land), and major additions that are not consumed within a year, but have a life span of several years. A capital item, on the other hand, costs less, requires less time to complete or acquire, and can be both recurring and non-recurring such as a vehicle, a machinery, or a piece of equipment. If it is non-recurring and costs above a specified level, but below the costs of a capital project, it is a capital item. If it is recurring but does not recur annually and costs below a specified level, it is considered operating rather than a capital item. Finally, an inventory item is relatively inexpensive and does not meet the threshold of a capital item but may still require regular accountability. As such, these items are considered part of routine operating budget requests. Examples of inventory items will be desktop computers, printers, copiers, scanners, and other similar and relatively inexpensive items.

Unfortunately, there is no uniform cutoff line that separates a capital project from a capital item, or a capital item from an inventory item. However, a government can set an upper and lower limit of expenditure to determine an approximate boundary for each category, based on the size of the government, its asset characteristics, and their estimated costs. For instance, a large government with a fairly large budget a capital project could include any asset that costs at least $100,000, a capital item that would cost, say, between $25,000 and $100,000, and an inventory item that would cost less than $25,000. Similarly, for a small government, a capital project may include assets that would cost over $25,000, a capital item anything between $5000 and $25,000, and an inventory item anything below $5000. Ideally, it should be up to the individual government to decide what it would consider an appropriate cutoff line.

8.2.2   Classification According to Physical Condition

At its core, the decision to construct or acquire capital assets depends on their physical condition. Obviously, an asset that is in good working condition, there is no need to replace it or acquire a new one, as long as it is producing the desired result. However, based on the physical condition of an asset, it can be classified as a replacement asset, an expansion asset, and a new asset. A replacement asset replaces an existing asset that is no longer operating at its fullest capacity or has served its useful purpose, while an expansion asset adds to an existing asset because of changes in need or demand such as expanding a highway, a building, or a physical plant. A new asset, on the other hand, is an asset that was not part of the current inventory; it may be a replacement asset or acquired for the first time.

Additionally, a government may be required by law to improve its capital facilities in order to meet the operating standards. Mandated assets have higher priorities over non-mandated assets. A county-operated prison facility or healthcare center that relies on state funding would be good examples of mandated assets.

8.2.3   Classification According to Level of Dependency

Capital assets can be self-standing or dependent, based on the degree of their relationship with other assets. Four types of capital assets are generally recognized when considering relationships with other assets: independent, mutually exclusive, not mutually exclusive, and dependent. An asset is considered independent if its acquisition or construction does not depend on any other asset. In other words, it can be evaluated based entirely on how it will contribute to the function for which it was acquired without having to evaluate the effect it will have on other assets. A good example of an independent asset will be the acquisition of a patrol vehicle or fire truck that may not have any direct effect on the valuation of other assets.

Similarly, an asset is considered mutually exclusive if its acquisition or construction automatically precludes the construction or acquisition of any other asset. However, there are circumstances when it is technically or financially impossible to consider more than one asset. For instance, if a government is faced with two alternatives—repair and retain or replace, both are not feasible since one cannot retain and replace at the same time. Mutually exclusive assets also apply to situations where a government can consider one or a limited number of assets, given its budget and other constraints. Thus, if a government can undertake, say, one out of three, or three out of a maximum of seven capital projects, given the availability of funds, this will automatically preclude the rest of the projects from being considered. It will not be mutually exclusive, if all three or seven can be undertaken.

Finally, an asset is considered dependent if its acquisition or construction depends on the construction or acquisition of other assets. A good example of a dependent asset will be a government-owned garage for repair and maintenance, only if it has a large number of vehicles to have its own facility that will be economically viable. Assets of this type are also called contingent assets. A special case of dependent assets is a complementary asset, where investment in an asset complements the functioning of one or more assets. For instance, if a government acquires a software package for a specific function that will not only improve its performance but will also improve the performance of other functions of the government will be a good example. Assets can also be mixed in that they can belong to more than one category. For instance, an asset can be both independent and mutually exclusive or independent and not mutually exclusive.

In sum, having a clearly defined classification system is important, especially from an operational point of view, as this would allow a government to recognize the inherent differences that exist among different capital assets. This would also allow the government to pay proper attention to their acquisition, construction, and maintenance.

8.3 Capital Budgeting and Long-Term Planning

Capital budgeting generally functions within the larger plan of a government such as a comprehensive or a master plan. The long-term nature of the capital budget, which is prepared for several years into the future, makes it possible to identify capital needs, establish capital asset standards, and select appropriate capital improvement projects. While both comprehensive and master plans are long-term in nature, covering a wide range of developmental activities that extend over multiple years, usually ten, fifteen, or more, a master plan is more specific in nature, providing a vision for an organization that reflects its mission, goals, objectives, and priorities.[3] As such, it provides a foundation for the best way to achieve them.

Frequently, the term capital improvement plan (CIP) is used to identify and select capital assets, their projected costs, sources of funding, and the time when they will be acquired. In this sense, it provides a structure for undertaking capital improvement activities. Although integral to capital budgeting, the CIP is often used interchangeably with a capital budget, but the two are not necessarily the same. A capital budget, like an operating budget, is a formal budget with clearly defined goals and objectives, except that it deals with actual physical assets, and funds are appropriated for these assets consistent with those goals and objectives. Since the assets have a life span of several years, the budget is prepared and implemented for multiple years without the requirements of annual appropriation, unless there is a major departure from the stated goals or expenditure targets. A capital improvement plan, on the other hand, is not a budget but rather an intermediate-range plan, usually five to seven years, or longer, designed to help a government with its capital budget by recommending what assets to consider, when to consider, and how to implement them consistent with its goals, objectives, priorities, and available resources.

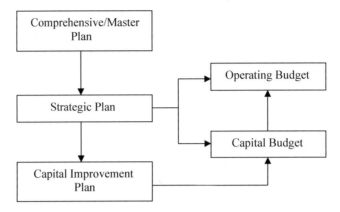

Fig. 8.1 Relationship between comprehensive, strategic and capital improvement plan and the capital budget

From a practical point of view, the operationalization of a capital improvement plan generally takes place through a process known as strategic planning. As noted earlier, strategic planning allows the decision makers to search for the best way (strategies and actions) to undertake budgetary activities, in particular, capital improvement activities, consistent with the mission, goals, objectives, and internal financial resources of an organization. As such, it serves as the direct link between a master plan and a capital improvement plan. However, the actual task of implementing a capital improvement plan, in particular its full-fledged operation, often falls under what is commonly known as tactical planning. Tactical planning deals with the development of plans for operation and maintenance of capital improvement programs. The difference between a strategic plan and a tactical plan is that the former sets the stage vis-a-vis develops the strategies, while the latter takes specific steps (tasks) to achieve them. Figure 8.1 shows the relationship between a comprehensive/master plan, strategic plan, and a capital improvement plan/program.

Finally, a capital improvement plan brings a structure into the decision process by coordinating the various components of a capital budget, thereby providing a rationale for allocating resources. The process increases transparency when the activities are well-coordinated and helps with the implementation of the capital budget. At the same time, the decision makers, as well as those involved in the execution of the budget, need to ensure that the process is precise and clear so that it does not take up unnecessary time and resources that can jeopardize successful implementation of the plan.

8.4 Capital Budget Process

As with an operating budget, capital budgeting involves a sequence of activities that parallels the operating budget process called the CIP process. Like the operating budget, the activities of the process typically include preparation and executive review, public hearings, especially at the local level, legislative review, approval, amendment, and supplemental appropriation. All these activities take place within a defined time frame, similar to an operating budget calendar, called the capital budget calendar.[4] However, unlike the operating budget, preparing the capital budget is the single most important activity in the entire process that is largely determined by the condition of the infrastructure, commitments of resources which are considerably large, irreversibility of decisions once the projects are put in place, and the potential for risk and uncertainty. Nevertheless, the essential structure remains the same in that the budget has to be prepared, funds have to be appropriated, projects have to be implemented and, finally, evaluated.

Operationally, the activities of a CIP process can be summarized in terms of eight basic steps or phases: (1) organize the CIP process, (2) conduct a needs assessment analysis, (3) set priorities, (4) do a cash flow analysis, (5) determine the financing options, (6) appropriate funds, (7) execute the budget, and (8) evaluate the budget.

8.4.1 Organize the CIP Process

The process begins once a decision has been made to develop a capital budget and the designation of the lead department that will be responsible for coordinating the activities. In most instances, the budget or the finance department takes the initiative with the assistance of the planning department by setting up a CIP committee, consisting of senior members from various departments, in particular those with recognized capital needs such as public works, transportation, water, sewer, electricity, police, and fire. The committee is generally headed by the chief administrative officer. Additionally, and where appropriate, a second group of individuals may be involved, working closely with the principal committee, which would carry out the actual tasks. This would include staff personnel, in particular, the physical planner, project engineer, construction engineer, purchasing manager, and project accountant, among others.

The responsibility for carrying out the activities of the process is divided among different members of the committee, based on their knowledge of the field such as overall design to planners, physical design to planning engineers, purchasing to acquisition or purchasing managers, construction to construction engineers, budget allocation to budget managers, cost reporting to cost accountants or cost engineers, and overall responsibility to the project manager. To assign the responsibilities, it may be necessary to construct a responsibility-assignment matrix, indicating the individuals who will be responsible for each component of the project. Table 8.1 presents a simple responsibility-assignment matrix. During this stage, it is important for the responsible managers to determine if the project calls for any special design standards, safety requirements, and compliance with government regulations. These tasks, although appear simple compared to other activities of the process such as the actual construction or acquisition of assets, can cause unnecessary delay and add to the total cost of project implementation. As such, they must be completed before beginning the actual work on the projects.

Table 8.1 A simple responsibility-assignment matrix

	Manager						
Responsibility	X_1	X_2	X_3	X_4	X_5	X_6	X_7
Planning	Δ	•		•			
Physical design		Δ		•			
Purchasing/acquisition			Δ				
Construction		•		Δ			
Budget allocation					Δ		
Cost reporting	•	•	•	•	•	Δ	•
Time management	Δ	Δ	Δ	Δ	Δ	Δ	Δ
Funds management	Δ	Δ	Δ	Δ	Δ	Δ	Δ
Overall management	•	•	•	•	•	•	Δ

X_1 = Planner; X_2 = Planning Engineer/Architect; X_3 = Purchasing/Acquisition Manager; X_4 = Construction Engineer; X_5 = Budget Manager; X_6 = Cost Accountant/Cost Engineer; X_7 = Project Manager; Legend: Δ = Primary Responsibility; • = Secondary Responsibility

Three things must take place during this stage, especially once the team has been put together: (1) forms must be prepared to solicit proposals for capital projects from individual departments, (2) criteria must be developed for evaluating and selecting projects, and (3) initial projections must be made for non-earmarked revenues to serve as the basis for financing the selected projects. Forms can vary in length and content, depending on how detailed the decision makers want them to be. Appendix C presents a simple example of a form for soliciting proposals. Developing criteria for project selection can be complex and time-consuming, but the end product must be consistent with goals, objectives, and the critical needs of the government. For instance, for an established community with well-developed infrastructure, the goal will be maintaining the existing assets in excellent working condition. On the other hand, for a community that is experiencing a slow growth or decline, the goal will be revitalizing the infrastructure. Similarly, the goals will be different for a community that is experiencing rapid growth. The point is the criteria developed must reflect the goals of an organization based on the existing condition of its capital assets and the critical needs for capital improvement.

8.4.2 Conduct a Needs Assessment Analysis

Needs assessment analysis begins with an analysis of the existing stock or inventory of capital assets to determine the needs for capital improvement. Inventory analysis is more of a management than a budgeting function since all organizations need to maintain an up-to-date inventory of their capital assets, in addition to maintaining an inventory of materials and supplies. The analysis is generally done at the end of each fiscal year by providing an up-to-date account of existing stock of capital assets, their current condition, and developing an estimate of costs of maintaining inventory, known as inventory analysis, followed by an analysis of needs assessment.

8.4.2.1 Needs Assessment Matrix

Once the assets have been classified and an inventory has been taken, the next step in the process is to do a needs assessment analysis. Needs assessment analysis is a systematic process of determining the needs for capital improvement, given the existing condition of the capital assets of a jurisdiction. The assessment provides the decision makers the needed information as to which assets to abandon, which ones to retain, and which ones to replace or acquire. The simplest way to do a needs assessment analysis is to construct a needs assessment matrix, showing the types of capital assets, the dates when constructed or acquired, the extent of use, current condition, and suggestions for improvement. Table 8.2 illustrates a sample needs assessment matrix. Ideally, the analysis should be done by individuals who are well-qualified or licensed to provide an objective assessment of the condition of the assets.

Four things typically result from a needs assessment analysis: (1) retain an asset in its current condition, (2) repair the asset, (3) replace the asset, and

Table 8.2 A simple needs assessment matrix

| Type of capital asset | Physical condition | | | |
	Year acquired/ constructed	Extent of use	Current condition	Comments
Land				
Parcel A	1923	Hardly	Good	None
Parcel B	1948	Occasionally	Very good	None
etc.	–	–	–	–
Buildings		–		
City hall	1975	Heavy	Good	Needs major plumbing
Public library	1987	Heavy	Very good	Needs extension
Police building	2015	Heavy	Excellent	None
etc.	–	–	–	–
Infrastructure				
4th street bridge	1976	Heavy	Poor	Needs major repair
35th street tunnel	2013	Moderate	Excellent	None
Main street	1958	Heavy	Good	Restrict traffic flow
etc.	–	–	–	–
Equipment				
Fire truck (1)	2018	Moderate	Excellent	None
Garbage truck (2)	2007	Heavy	Poor	Needs replacement
Patrol vehicles (3)	2012	Heavy	Poor	Need replacement
etc.	–	–	–	–

(4) acquire a new asset. Retaining an asset in its current condition means that no improvement is necessary at least in the short-term, although all physical assets must be evaluated on a regular basis to ensure that they are in good working condition. Maintaining assets in good working condition improves performance and adds to their longevity. With time and frequent use, assets deteriorate and may require additional repair beyond their normal maintenance. Repairing an asset can be costly over time if it continues to deteriorate, in which case it may be cost-effective to replace the asset. However, before an asset can be replaced, it is necessary to do a thorough analysis of the existing condition of the asset to justify its replacement. The term commonly used for this purpose is called replacement analysis.

8.4.2.2 Decision to Retain or Replace an Asset

Capital assets are dynamic in that they do not have a fixed life—they vary over time, depending on the nature and frequency of use. As such, a capital investment cannot be considered a commitment until the end of the asset's useful life. Once the assets have been put in place, it is necessary to evaluate their physical condition on a regular basis to assess their performance. As time goes by and the conditions begin to deteriorate, they may need more frequent evaluations to determine whether they should be retained, abandoned, or replaced. The decision is frequently guided by four major considerations: physical deterioration, changes in demand, technological change, and financial factors.

Physical deteriorations are changes that occur in the physical condition of an asset from continuous use, resulting in less than efficient performance. Once the conditions deteriorate, routine maintenance and repair costs tend to increase, adding to energy costs, operating time, unexpected incidents, and so forth. Changes in demand for goods and services are a common occurrence in both public and private organizations. Governments frequently encounter demand changes either due to changes in population, changes in economic condition, or due to changes in the design of a good or service it provides vis-a-vis the technological change.

In any event, when a change occurs it becomes necessary to abandon, replace, or upgrade the existing assets to meet the changing needs of the jurisdiction. In the case of technological change, it has a direct effect on the efficiency of capital assets. In general, technological changes affect the efficiency of manufacturing equipments more rapidly than they affect, say, the road or highway construction equipments. Nevertheless, the changes have a direct bearing on the cost of production or delivery of a good or service.[5] Furthermore, the financial conditions can determine whether or not and how often a government should replace its existing assets. A government that is financially sound will have the needed resources to replace their assets more frequently than a government that is financially strapped. Although the presence of any of these considerations can justify the need for replacement, ideally all four should be taken into consideration before making a decision to replace.

Decision Criteria

There are different ways in which one can determine whether to retain or abandon a capital asset, but the approach most frequently used is the present value of cash flows. A present value of cash flow (PVCF) is the difference between the discounted stream of cash flows (inflows and outflows) from an investment. In general, if the present value of cash flow of an asset is greater than its abandonment value (AV) the asset should be retained, assuming it is in good working condition. In other words, if PVCF>AV, retain the asset; if not, abandon the asset. Conversely, if PVCF<AV, abandon the asset. To give an example, suppose that the present value of cash flow of a patrol vehicle at the end of the sixth year of seven years of its useful life is $7500, which includes the normal cost of repair and maintenance. It has an abandonment value of $8500. Since the abandonment value is higher than the present value of cash flows of the vehicle, it should be abandoned or replaced. Interestingly, there is no clear definition of what constitutes an abandonment value, although it is often treated the same way as the salvage value but the two are not necessarily the same. The salvage value, by definition, has a value at the end of the useful life of an asset, whereas the abandonment value may be zero or even negative if there is a cost associated with abandonment such as disposing a used car at owner's expense.

If an asset has costs (outflows) but no direct returns (inflows), the replacement decision could be based on the present value of costs of the asset. Since the costs of operation and maintenance of an asset tend to increase over time, one can look at the point of inflexion when the cost will begin to increase and use it as a basis for replacement. Assuming the cost increases monotonically (increases without changing signs; that is, positive monotone for increases and negative monotone for decreases) after a certain period, the following rules would generally apply: Replace the asset if the present value of cost in the next period is higher than the weighted average of previous costs; do not replace, if it is less. Formally, we can present the criteria as follows:

$$\text{Replace, if } C_t < \left[\frac{I + \sum_{t=1}^{T} C_i \text{DF}^{t-1}}{\sum_{t=1}^{T} \text{DF}^{t-1}} \right] \tag{8.1}$$

$$\text{Do not replace, if } C_t > \left[\frac{I + \sum_{i=1}^{T} C_i \text{DF}^{t-1}}{\sum_{t=1}^{T} \text{DF}^{t-1}} \right] \tag{8.2}$$

where C_t is the cost at time t, I is the initial cost of an asset, and DF is the discount factor (the factor by which a stream of cash flows are multiplied to obtain their present values—present value of inflows and outflows). The expression on the right-hand side of inequality is the weighted average of all costs up to and including period $t - 1$ (for $t = 1, 2, \ldots, T$).

To give an example, suppose that a government has recently purchased a heavy-duty equipment for the Water Department at a cost of $20,000. It has a maintenance cost that increases every year. The government wants to know at what point it will need to replace the equipment. Table 8.3 shows the costs and related data for the equipment. The first column is obvious. The second column in the table represents the costs of maintenance, the third column is the discount factor (DF),

Table 8.3 Replacement cost data and results

Year (i)	Cost ($)	DF[a] $[1/(1+r)^i]$	PV of cost ($)	Cumulative PV of costs ($)[b]	Cumulative DF	Weighted average ($)[c]
1	000	1.0000	0.0000	20,000.00	1.0000	20,000.00
2	450	0.9524	428.58	20,428.58	1.9524	10,463.32
3	1000	0.9070	907.00	21,335.58	2.8594	7461.56
4	1500	0.8638	1295.70	22,631.28	3.7232	6078.45
5	2800	0.8227	2306.56	24,825.08	4.5459	5460.98
6	4200	0.7835	3290.70	28,115.78	5.3294	5275.60
7	5700	0.7462	4253.34	32,369.12	6.0756	5327.72
8	7500	0.7107	5330.25	37,699.37	6.7863	5555.22
9	9800	0.6768	6632.64	44,332.01	7.4631	5940.16
10	11,300	0.6446	7283.98	51,615.96	8.1077	6366.29

[a]Discount Factor, where r is the Discount Rate, $r = 0.05$
[b]Includes the cost of purchase
[c]Weighted Average Cost (Year 2) = $20,428.58/1.9524 = $10,463.32

the fourth column represents the present value of costs, the fifth column is the cumulative costs that include the purchase price, the sixth column is the cumulative discount factors, and the last column is the weighted average cost of the vehicle, obtained by dividing Column 5 (cumulative PV of costs) by Column 6 (cumulative discount factors).

As shown in the table, the minimum weighted average cost occurs at the end of the sixth year, meaning that the equipment will need to be replaced at that time. It should be noted that our discussion does not include what if the equipment fails completely before the sixth year, in which case the government may not have any choice but to replace it. It also does not take into consideration any salvage or abandonment value, although it can be easily incorporated into the formulation. If cost increase is not monotonic, the formulations will need to be changed to adjust for the deviations. Other constraints may need to be built into the formulation, depending on the type of asset being considered.

In addition to providing information on the need to retain or replace an existing capital asset, needs assessment analysis is also useful to determine if a government needs to invest in new capital assets. There is a broad consensus among economists, physical planners, and policy makers that scaling-up capital investments in government that is experiencing slow or no growth, particularly in infrastructure (roads, bridges, highways, physical plants, and so forth), is critical to achieving economic growth. Improvements in infrastructure or adding to existing infrastructure can improve productivity through economies of scale and also raise the quality of human and physical capital (Straub 2008). In sum, a thorough needs assessment analysis can determine the gap that currently exists in the capital stocks of a government, including infrastructure, and identify where the investments should take place and how much. However, the decision to invest in new capital infrastructure must be based on a sound economic plan that takes into consideration the revenue base of the jurisdiction, its tax structure, current debt levels, the quality of its labor force, and the condition of existing infrastructure, among others.

A Note on Sunk-Cost Trap

Managers often have a tendency to hold on to losing assets rather than abandoning them, even if they have served their intended purpose. This may be due to the psychological difficulty a manager may have in ignoring the sunk costs that have already been incurred but are irrelevant from an economic point of view. This is known as sunk cost trap and is generally recognized as a behavioral accounting problem. To give an example, suppose that a government is faced with two options from the use of an existing asset that has already cost the government $50,000 from repair and maintenance and is likely to cost more in the coming years: Option 1 will produce a fixed return of $75,000 if abandoned, assuming it is the same as the salvage value. Option 2 has two equiprobable outcomes: (1) it will produce a zero cash flow, if retained; and (2) it will produce a positive cash flow of $150,000 at the end of the accounting cycle. A risk-avoiding manager will obviously go with the first option because it assures a guaranteed return of $75,000, although there is a sunk cost of $50,000 that has already been incurred which the manager must ignore. A risk-taking manager, on the other hand, will go with the second option since it has the likelihood of a much larger return, although there is a risk associated with it.

8.4.3   Set Priorities

Each year, governments receive far more requests for capital projects than their available resources can permit, which makes it necessary to prioritize them to ensure that they are selected in an orderly fashion. Prioritization helps a government determine the assets that are more important to the government, gives it the lead time for effective decision making and, more importantly, brings objectivity into the decision process. Unfortunately, there are no precise measures for developing criteria by which to prioritize, but most would agree that the criteria must be consistent with the goals and objectives of an organization (Hatry 1988). Oftentimes, experience is substituted for prudence and objectivity. While experience is useful, it may not always reflect the dynamic nature of capital improvement needs that change with budget constraints, technological changes, and the wide differences that exist among the decision makers on their preferences for capital improvement activities.

Since projects vary in size and scope, a simple approach would be to select criteria that make good, common sense and also have an appeal to the general public such as essential to community health and safety, maintaining the existing levels of service, meeting emergency needs, and so forth. If a community has a strong political orientation, one could also add political consideration such as strengthening public support or community interest. Alan Walter Steiss (1975) recommended six basic criteria that can cover the breadth of needs most governments have for capital improvement: urgent, essential, necessary, desirable, acceptable, and deferrable. Others have developed similar criteria to fit the needs of their budget development. Although most of these criteria are broad and cover a diverse range of attributes, they do not fully explain why the decision makers make the choices they do. Nevertheless, they provide an ordering mechanism for setting priorities. Lawrence and Vogt (2007) make an interesting observation that whatever criteria one uses, as long as they are used consistently, the priorities derived from the use of the criteria must drive both the capital and the annual operating budgets.

8.4.3.1   Methods of Priority Setting

Once the criteria have been developed, the next step is to decide what method to use to determine the priorities for the projects. There is a wide range of methods that can be used for this purpose, ranging from simple rule of thumb approach which relies on subjective judgment, to the use of point systems (assignment of points or numbers to objects, categories, or events in a systematic fashion, similar to an interval or ratio scale), to net present value that relies on time value of money, and so forth. This section focuses on measurement scales based on point systems, used frequently for prioritizing capital projects, especially where multiple projects are involved with different goals and objectives.

Use of Point Systems

Point systems are primarily used for intangible factors and can vary anywhere from 1 to 5, to 50, and even to 100 points, depending on how fine the shades of preferences the decision makers want to use. The advantage of using a point system is that, besides ranking the projects, it is possible to identify a cutoff line (point) that would correspond to the budget available for funding capital improvement activities. Jon Vogt (1995) suggests a simple point system based on a two-dimensional matrix, where the first dimension represents the degree of urgency and the second dimension the priority of functions. Several categories are considered under each dimension that range from high to low on a seven-point scale for degree of urgency (1 for highest and 7 for lowest) and an eight-point scale for priority of functions (1 for highest and 8 for lowest). Table 8.4 presents a simple example of how the matrix is used.

As shown in the table, to rank a capital request, all one needs to do is assign a rating from the matrix. In general, a low score indicates high priority and a high score indicates the opposite. While the structure of the matrix appears simple and easy to follow, the point system it uses relies typically on an interval scale. The problem with conventional point systems, in particular the use of interval scales is that while they generate scores that can be easily aggregated to produce the overall ranking of a project, they do not readily allow for comparison of alternatives. Comparison allows the decision makers to determine the relative importance of a project to the overall goal of an organization. Put simply, a project that ranks high

Table 8.4   A two-dimensional rating matrix for capital projects

Degree of urgency		Priority of functions		
Categories	Public safety (1)	Health and human services (2)	Public works and transportation (3)	Recreation (4)
Legislation (1)	1	2	3	4
Safety/hazard (2)	2	4	6	8
Efficiency (3)	3	6	9	12
Maintenance (4)	4	8	12	16
Renovation (5)	5	10	15	20
Replacement (6)	6	12	18	24
Acquisition (7)	7	14	21	28

must be superior to all other projects in comparison, given the goals and objectives of an organization and the criteria used.

One way to correct the problem is to use a ratio scale, which allows for easy comparison of attributes, characteristics, activities, etc. The following section discusses a method that uses a ratio scale and has been extensively used for setting priorities for a wide variety of problems and situations called the Analytic Hierarchy Process, or the AHP, in short.

Use of a Ratio Scale

Developed by Thomas Saaty (1980), the AHP has been extensively used over the years in a variety of situations, involving all kinds of social, economic, and behavioral problems. The attractiveness of AHP as a decision tool lies in its ability to compare both discrete alternatives and their attributes. The method requires the decision makers to provide fundamental comparison between elements taken pairwise in all possible combinations and construct a tabular matrix containing those comparisons expressed as numerical ratios. The final product is a vector of normalized weights which summarize the judgments of the decision makers who assigned the weights.

The AHP begins by breaking down a complex problem into a hierarchy consisting of a number of levels. Each level consists of a number of elements and each element, in turn, consists of some other elements and the process of decomposition continues until the most specific elements of the problem have been identified. The elements are chosen in such a way as to ensure that they are important in some ways with regard to the problem, although their importance may not be equal. The underlying notion behind structuring a problem into a hierarchy is to seek understanding at the highest level from the interactions of the various levels of the hierarchy rather than the elements of the levels (Manheim 1966).

Choice of a Scale

An important characteristic of the AHP is that, unlike most ranking methods, it uses a ratio scale to assign weights (priorities) to the elements in each level of the hierarchy. The way it works is that each participant in the decision process is asked how he or she would evaluate or compare the elements of a given level in a pairwise fashion with respect to each element in the immediate preceding (higher) level. The intensity of preference is expressed as a rank on a 9-point scale. The distribution of points on this scale is as follows: 1 = equal importance, 3 = weak importance, 5 = essential or strong importance, 7 = demonstrated importance, 9 = absolute importance. The even number, 2, 4, 6, and 8 are considered intermediate values between two adjacent judgments. The 9-point scale, according to Saaty, represents a sufficient enough range within which respondents can offer their preference.

Quantifying the relative importance of the elements on this scale is the essence of the method since it provides us with the necessary data by producing a matrix of pairwise comparisons. Mathematically, solving this matrix of pairwise comparisons to extract suitable priorities boils down to solving an eigenvalue problem.[6]

Formulation of the Problem

To illustrate how the method works, let us look at the capital budgeting problem for a government with seven capital projects: X_1, X_2, X_3, X_4, X_5, X_6, and X_7 with three levels. We start with a global goal (G) at Level 1, three criteria at Level 2 (C_1, C_2, and C_3), and seven capital projects at Level 3. Theoretically, one can have as many levels as possible depending on the problem but three levels are usually adequate for most problems. The global goal, which sets the overall purpose for the decision exercise, say, is to improve the overall community welfare by undertaking the projects in light of the three criteria or sub-goals: C_1—ensure public safety, C_2—create a better living environment, and C_3—foster economic growth. The seven projects are: X_1—construct a technology center, X_2—upgrade the water treatment plant, X_3—construct a new community health center, X_4—renovate the civic center, X_5—repair the old pedestrian bridge, X_6—undertake downtown redevelopment, and X_7—expand the Southside commercial strip.

The primary task of AHP is to find the relative weights of various projects according to their overall contributions to the global goal, subject to a set of criteria, which will be the sub-goals in our case. The relative weights are then compiled using a pairwise comparison matrix to produce the necessary priorities. Figure 8.2 shows the hierarchical structure for the problem with the global goal, the sub-goals or criteria, and the projects under consideration.

To apply the method, one needs to proceed in two stages. In the first stage, the elements of Level 2 are compared with each other against the element at Level 1, which is the global goal. In the second stage, the elements of Level 3 are compared with each other against each element of Level 2, and the process continues until the elements of every level are compared with each other against each and every single element of the preceding levels. The rationale for this is quite simple: While the elements of a level may be important collectively to the elements at the next higher level, they may not be of equal importance to the decision makers responsible for assigning weights. Therefore, one needs to know which of these elements at a given level are more important with respect to the elements of preceding level, so that one has a clear sense of the elements that are at the top of the priority ranking.

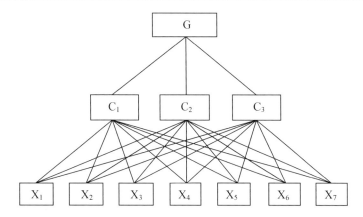

Fig. 8.2 The CIP hierarchy

Analysis of Choices Among Criteria

The process begins by asking a decision maker or the individual assigning weights how he or she will compare the elements of a level with each other against the elements of the preceding level. The result would produce a series of matrices for each level, except for the global goal at Level 1 since it is the reference element. For the current problem, we will have a 3×3 matrix for Level 2 where the three criteria or sub-goals will be compared in a pairwise fashion with each other against the global goal, and three initial matrices for Level 3 where the seven projects will be compared in a similar fashion with each other against each sub-goal. The matrices will then be synthesized to produce the final vector of priorities. We will start with a single decision maker.

Table 8.5 presents the matrix of pairwise comparisons of the three criteria with respect to the global goal. As the table shows, each cell value of the matrix represents the weight the decision maker assigns to a criterion 1 (C_1) in comparison with another criterion with respect to the global goal. Thus, a value of 3 corresponding to C_1 and C_3 indicates the relative importance of criterion 1 (C_1) when compared with criterion 3 (C_3), meaning that C_1 is 3 times as important as C_3. Conversely, C_3 is 1/3rd as important as C_1 with respect to the global goal, and so forth. The diagonal elements, on the other hand, always have a value of 1 since an element compared with itself is always equally important.

Table 8.5 Level 1: Pairwise comparison matrix of criteria

G	Criteria		
	C_1	C2	C3
C_1	1	3	1
C_2		1	1/5
C_3			1

Once the initial matrix of pairwise comparison has been developed, we can calculate the priority for each criterion by synthesizing the judgments or weights assigned to them. The purpose of synthesizing judgments is to obtain an overall estimate of the relative importance of the elements of a given level of the pair-wise comparison matrix. To achieve this synthesis, we do the following: One, add the values in each column of the matrix (e.g., $1+(1/3)+1=2.33$ and repeat the process). Two, divide each element in a column by the total of that column to obtain a normalized matrix to permit meaningful comparison among elements (e.g., $1/2.33=0.43$ and repeat the process), Three, calculate the average for each row by adding the values in each row of the normalized matrix and dividing the row total by the number of elements in that row (e.g., $1.21/3=0.403$ and repeat the process). The synthesis yields the relative importance or priorities for elements of the matrix. The results of this synthesis are presented in the priority vector in Table 8.6.

According to the table, economic growth (C_3) came on top with a priority weight of 0.480, followed by public safety (C_1) with a priority weight of 0.403, and better living environment (C_2) with a priority weight of 0.117.

Consistency of Weights

A key consideration in AHP is the calculation of consistency of weights assigned by the decision makers on a hierarchy. For instance, if A is preferred to B, and B is preferred to C, then in a perfectly consistent relationship A must be preferred to C. Unfortunately, as hard as we may try, our feelings and preferences are seldom consistent. Therefore, a realistic assessment of the situation in preference comparison is to account for inconsistency in judgments. Interestingly, the AHP uses a measure, called consistency ratio (CR), to determine the overall level of consistency in judgments, according to which the judgments are considered consistent if the ratio is less than or equal to 10%.[7] The calculation of this ratio is simple and can be achieved in five easy steps.

Table 8.6 Level 2: Synthesis of judgments for criteria

G	Criteria				
	C_1	C_2	C_3		
C_1	1	3	1		
C_2	1/3	1	1/5		
C_3	1	5	1		
Total	2.33	9.00	2.2		
	Normalized weights			Total	Priority vector
C_1	0.43	0.33	0.45	1.21	0.403
C_2	0.14	0.11	0.10	0.35	0.117
C_3	0.43	0.56	0.45	1.44	0.480
Total	1.00	1.00	1.00	3.00	1.000

First, multiply the matrix of comparison by the priority weights to obtain a new vector:

$$\begin{bmatrix} 1 & 3 & 1 \\ 1/3 & 1 & 1/5 \\ 1 & 5 & 1 \end{bmatrix} \begin{bmatrix} 0.403 \\ 0.117 \\ 0.480 \end{bmatrix} = \begin{bmatrix} 1.234 \\ 0.346 \\ 1.468 \end{bmatrix}$$

Second, divide each element in the new column vector by its corresponding element in the priority vector to get vector:

$$1.234/0.403 = 3.062$$
$$0.346/0.117 = 2.957$$
$$1.468/0.480 = 3.058$$

Third, calculate the average of these values to obtain a number, called λ_{max} (maximum eigenvalue), which turns out to be

$$(3.062 + 2.957 + 3.058)/3 = 3.026 = \lambda_{max}$$

Fourth, determine the consistency index (CI), which is given by the expression $(\lambda_{max} - n)/(n - 1)$, where n is the size of the matrix. Applying the relevant values to the expression, we obtain the following consistency index:

$$CI = (\lambda_{max} - n)/(n - 1) = (3.026 - 3)/(3 - 1) = 0.026/2 = 0.013$$

Fifth, and finally, divide the consistency index by the random value of this for $n = 3$, which is 0.58, to obtain the consistency ration (CR). That is,

$$CR = CI/\text{Random Consistency} = 0.013/0.58 = 0.0224$$

The consistency ratio thus obtained is 0.0216 or 0.022, which indicates a good consistency for the three criteria in our problem. Since it is much less than the cutoff point of 10%, we can consider it an acceptable level of consistency.

Analysis of Choices Among Projects

With the rankings of the criteria thus obtained, we can now continue with our analysis. The next step in the process is to rank the projects against each of the criteria. We do so by taking a pair of projects at a time and asking the decision maker which of the two projects would he would consider more important with respect a given criterion and continue the process until the comparisons for all pairs of projects are exhausted. Table 8.7 shows the pairwise comparison matrices for the seven projects with respect to each of the three criteria. The table also includes the normalized weights and their corresponding priority vectors. (Incidentally, the table shows the calculations only for the first normalized matrix and the corresponding priority vector; the remaining normalized matrices and their corresponding priority vectors are obtained the same way. Appendix D provides the detailed calculation of the comparison matrices of the projects.)

A consistency analysis run on each of the three pairwise comparison matrices of projects, obtained the same way as Level 2 indicates that they are all consistent, as shown below[8]

$$CI_1 = (\lambda_{max} - n)/(n - 1) = (7.41 - 7)/(7 - 1) = 0.0683; \; CR = 0.0518$$
$$CI_2 = (\lambda_{max} - n)/(n - 1) = (7.33 - 7)/(7 - 1) = 0.0550; \; CR = 0.0417$$
$$CI_3 = (\lambda_{max} - n)/(n - 1) = (7.76 - 7)/(7 - 1) = 0.1267; \; CR = 0.0959$$

Looking at the values in Table 8.7, it becomes apparent that the priorities obtained for the seven projects do not have exactly the same order of preference for each criterion, as one would expect, yet, from a decision-making point of view, it is important that these differences are somehow aggregated into a single, coherent set. In other words, we need to synthesize these differences in such a way as to be able to derive a final ranking of the projects. To achieve this, the AHP requires that we construct a matrix where each column of this matrix represents the corresponding priority vector from Table 8.7, and then multiply the matrix by the priority vector obtained for the criteria set in the preceding level of the hierarchy.

The result will produce a composite vector for the hierarchy, as shown below:

$$
\begin{bmatrix}
0.091 & 0.381 & 0.186 \\
0.250 & 0.155 & 0.041 \\
0.063 & 0.129 & 0.057 \\
0.036 & 0.061 & 0.094 \\
0.037 & 0.032 & 0.162 \\
0.366 & 0.032 & 0.243 \\
0.157 & 0.134 & 0.217
\end{bmatrix}
\begin{bmatrix}
0.403 \\
0.117 \\
0.480
\end{bmatrix}
=
\begin{bmatrix}
0.170 \\
0.138 \\
0.067 \\
0.131 \\
0.105 \\
0.267 \\
0.183
\end{bmatrix}
=
\begin{bmatrix}
X_1(R3) \\
X_2(R4) \\
X_3(R7) \\
X_4(R5) \\
X_5(R6) \\
X_6(R1) \\
X_7(R2)
\end{bmatrix}
$$

As can be seen from the composite vector above, X_6—undertake downtown redevelopment came on top with a priority weight of 0.267 (R1), followed by X_7—expand the Southside Commercial Strip with 0.183 (R2), X_1—construct a technology center with 0.170 (R3), X_2—upgrade the water treatment plan with 0.138 (R4), X_4—renovate the civic center (R5) with 0.131, and X_5—repair the old pedestrian bridge with 0.105 (R6), and X_3—construct a new community health center with 0.067 (R7).

Multiple Decision Makers

Up to this point, we have considered a single decision maker. Let us assume that there is more than one decision maker whose judgments are as important and who may not quite agree with the judgments of the first decision maker. Thus, we need to find out the level of disagreement or inconsistency the two decision makers have on their choices of the project rankings. We can use the standard Root Mean Square (RMS) for this purpose:

$$d(D_1, D_2) = \sqrt{\frac{1}{n}\left[\sum_{i=1}^{n}(w_{i1} - w_{i2})^2\right]} \qquad (8.3)$$

Table 8.7 Level 3: Pairwise comparison matrices of projects

	Projects								
C_1	X_1	X_2	X_3	X_4	X_5	X_6	X_7		
X_1	1	1/5	2	3	3	1/3	1/4		
X_2	5	1	7	6	5	1/3	2		
X_3	1/2	1/7	1	2	3	1/5	1/4		
X_4	1/3	1/6	1/2	1	1	1/7	1/4		
X_5	1/3	1/5	1/3	1	1	1/8	1/3		
X_6	3	3	5	7	8	1	4		
X_7	4	1/2	4	4	3	1/4	1		
Total	14.16	5.21	19.83	24.00	24.00	2.38	8.08		
	Normalized weights							*Total*	*Priority vector*
X_1	0.07	0.04	0.10	0.13	0.13	0.14	0.03	0.64	0.091
X_2	0.35	0.20	0.35	0.25	0.21	0.14	0.25	1.75	0.250
X_3	0.04	0.03	0.05	0.08	0.13	0.08	0.03	0.44	0.063
X_4	0.02	0.03	0.03	0.04	0.04	0.06	0.03	0.25	0.036
X_5	0.02	0.04	0.02	0.04	0.04	0.06	0.04	0.26	0.037
X_6	0.21	0.57	0.25	0.29	0.33	0.42	0.49	2.56	0.366
X_7	0.28	0.09	0.20	0.17	0.13	0.10	0.13	1.10	0.157
Total	1	1	1	1	1	1	1	7.00	
C_2	X_1	X_2	X_3	X_4	X_5	X_6	X_7	NWs[a]	*Priority vector*
X_1	1	5	4	5	6	7	2	2.68	0.381
X_2		1	3	2	1/2	5	2	1.09	0.152
X_3			1	3	1	4	2	0.91	0.129
X_4				1	1/2	3	1/3	0.35	0.061
X_5					1	3	1/2	0.76	0.109
X_6						1	1/4	0.26	0.032
X_7							1	0.94	0.134
C_3	X_1	X_2	X_3	X_4	X_5	X_6	X_7	NWs	*Priority vector*
X_1	1	5	3	2	3	1/2	1/2	1.30	0.186
X_2		1	1/2	1/3	1/2	1/5	1/4	0.29	0.041
X_3			1	1/2	1/2	1/5	1/4	0.40	0.057
X_4				1	1/2	1/2	1/3	0.66	0.094
X_5					1	1	1/2	1.13	0.162
X_6						1	2	1.70	0.243
X_7							1	1.52	0.217

[a]Normalized Weights (All the numbers have been rounded off to the nearest integers)

where d is the level of disagreement between two decision makers, D_1 and D_2, and w is the weight assigned to the ith project (for $i = 1, 2, ..., n$).

Suppose the weights assigned by the second decision maker are as follows: X_1 (0.275), X_2 (0.160), X_3 (0.115), X_4 (0.030), X_5 (0.065), X_6 (0.125), and X_7 (0.150). To calculate the disagreement between the two decision makers, we take the square root of the difference (variance) of their weights, which produces the following result:

$$
\begin{aligned}
d &= \sqrt{\begin{array}{l}[(0.170 - 0.275)^2 + (0.138 - 0.160)^2 + (0.068 - 0.115)^2 + (0.131 - 0.030)^2 \\ +(0.105 - 0.065)^2 + (0.267 - 0.125)^2 + (0.193 - 0.150)^2]/7]\end{array}} \\
&= \sqrt{\begin{array}{l}[0.010936 + 0.000463 + 0.002242 + 0.010244 + 0.001623 \\ +0.020425 + 0.001113]/7\end{array}} \\
&= \sqrt{0.0470475/7} \\
&= 0.0819(8.19\%)
\end{aligned}
$$

which is quite low, suggesting that the decision makers in general do not disagree much in their judgments of the projects. In general, the lower the value of d, the higher is the agreement, and vice versa. We can repeat the process for any number of decision makers. In the event there is a significant disagreement among the decision makers, it may be necessary to reevaluate the criteria as well as the projects.

The Final Ranking

Although the two decision makers do not disagree much in their judgments, there was no one-to-correspondence in the weights they assigned which means that we need to synthesize the differences to produce the final ranking. We can do this by taking the average of the two rankings. The AHP recommends the use of geometric mean since it uses a ratio scale. The geometric mean of the two sets of rankings is presented below:

$$
\left(\prod_{i=1}^{n} w_i\right)^{1/n} = \sqrt[n]{w_1 w_2 w_3 \ldots w_n} \tag{8.4}
$$

$$
\begin{aligned}
X_1 &= \sqrt[2]{(0.1704)(0.275)} = 0.2164 \text{ (R1)} \\
X_2 &= \sqrt[2]{(0.1384)(0.160)} = 0.1488 \text{ (R4)} \\
X_3 &= \sqrt[2]{(0.0676)(0.115)} = 0.0882 \text{ (R5)} \\
X_4 &= \sqrt[2]{(0.1312)(0.030)} = 0.0627 \text{ (R7)} \\
X_5 &= \sqrt[2]{(0.1053)(0.065)} = 0.0827 \text{ (R6)} \\
X_6 &= \sqrt[2]{(0.2679)(0.125)} = 0.1830 \text{ (R2)} \\
X_7 &= \sqrt[2]{(0.1834)(0.150)} = 0.1658 \text{ (R3)}
\end{aligned}
$$

With the exception of two projects, X_2 and X_5, the results do not appear to correspond to the initial ranking, indicating the wide differences in the weights they assigned. (However, we need to keep in mind that the ranking by the second decision maker was arbitrarily assigned and not based on actual comparison, as in the case of the first decision maker.)

Limitations of the Method
Like most analytical methods, the AHP has its strengths and limitations. As noted earlier, as a method, it offers a useful aggregation procedure for multicriteria problems by breaking them down into their constituent components (hierarchy). It is relatively easy to use in spite of the fact that it involves some technical computations. At the operational level, its greatest contribution is the use of a ratio scale that makes comparison between criteria relatively easy. On the other hand, the decision makers can spend an enormous amount of time shifting between criteria and assigning weights, especially if they are not familiar with the problem or if there are too many levels in a hierarchy. Also, there is no guarantee that a single answer will emerge; ties are not unlikely in rank ordering but too many ties can lead to an imprecise decision. Nevertheless, methods such as the AHP can be tremendously useful in providing a rational approach for making choices when confronted with multiple alternatives that are imprecise, competing, and conflicting.

8.4.4   Do a Cash Flow Analysis

Once the projects have been prioritized and a decision has been made as to which projects to undertake, it is necessary to do a financial analysis to see if enough resources would be available to fund the accepted projects. The convention is to do a cash flow analysis to look at the changes in the cash flow situation of a government that is likely to result from the current and future capital improvement activities. As noted earlier, a typical cash flow statement has four components: a beginning balance, cash flow from operation (inflows and outflows), net flow (difference between inflows and outflows), and an ending balance. The information produced by a cash flow statement can serve as a useful guide to determine the current and future financial condition of an organization and, more importantly, to determine the amount that needs to be financed.

Two types of cash flow statements are generally used for financial analysis: A historical statement to facilitate the systematic evaluation of past cash flows and projected or pro-forma statement to provide insights into future cash flows but the two statements are not mutually exclusive. The historical statement, with appropriate adjustments for change in price, volume, inflation, and so forth, provides the necessary data to develop the projected cash flow statements. Table 8.8 presents a sample cash flow statement for the CIP problem we discussed under project prioritization.

As shown in Table 8.8, it will cost the government approximately $65 million to finance the seven capital projects. The statement includes the projected costs of the

Table 8.8 Cash flow statement for capital improvements based on existing and new projects ($million)

Activities/categories (Funding projection)	FY_t	FY_{t+1}	FY_{t+2}	FY_{t+3}	FY_{t+4}
Beginning balance	15.00	(45.00)	(10.00)	5.00	10.00
(+) Projected operating revenue	245.00	275.00	270.00	275.00	–
Total operating revenue	260.00	230.00	260.00	280.00	–
(−) Projected operating expenditure[a]	225.00	210.00	220.00	230.00	–
Gross cash flow from operation	35.00	20.00	40.00	50.00	–
(−) Debt service on existing debt	5.00	10.00	10.00	10.00	–
Net flow of funds (after debt service)	30.00	10.00	30.00	40.00	–
(−) Current (capital) expenditure	10.00	10.00	15.00	15.00	–
Net flow of funds (adjusted for current)	20.00	0.00	15.00	25.00	–
(−) Proposed (new) capital expenditure[b]	65.00	10.00	10.00	15.00	–
New funds required	(45.00)	(10.00)	5.00	10.00	–

[a]Excludes both current and (previously) approved capital expenditures, but includes normal repair and maintenance
[b]Approximate cost of seven capital projects

projects. It also shows that the government will need at least $45 million to fund the projects at the end of the current period, assuming they will be funded from current operations. If the projects are to be funded through borrowing, which is a common practice for all three levels of government, there will be no need to include the amount of debt in the statement, except for the payments on debt service.

8.4.5   Determine the Financing Options

Financing choices are critical to determining whether or not a government should be able to successfully carry out its capital budgeting activities. In fact, the term "capital" has come to imply resources used by an organization to finance its capital assets. How these resources are used together to finance capital assets is generally known as capital structure. There is a whole body of literature that has grown over the years that deals with capital structure, in particular, to determine an optimal mix of resources that can be used to finance these assets without putting heavy cost burden on an organization. This section looks at resources that are commonly used by a government to finance its capital assets.

Governments fund their capital assets from internal as well as external sources but the decision to use one or the other, or both, depends on a variety of factors such as the size of the government, its economic and revenue base, credit history, ability to meet expenditure needs from current and future revenues, among others. Ideally, given a choice, most governments would prefer to finance their capital assets from current operations but that is seldom the case. Unless a government is in a strong financial situation, financing assets from current operations will tie up resources that can be used to fund other activities of government or to balance the operating budget. Consequently, most governments rely on external sources to meet their capital improvement needs.

While the upper-level governments have more latitude in using both internal and external sources to finance their capital assets, local governments have certain restrictions when using external funding. The restrictions come from the fact that local governments are the products of their states which often set limits as to how much money they can borrow, how often they can borrow, and what kinds of instruments they can use to borrow. One can construe this relationship between the state and local governments as one of principal-agent, where the local governments (agents) must provide goods and services that benefit their constituents vis-à-vis the public, consistent with the larger goals of the state governments (principals). The benefit principle lies at the heart of most economic decisions a government makes which also applies to capital financing in that those who benefit from the assets must pay for their costs, at least, in principle.

8.4.5.1 Internal Sources of Financing

There is a wide variety of sources a government can use to finance its capital assets internally without having to rely on external sources. This section looks at six of the most commonly used sources: (1) current operating revenues, (2) earmarked revenues, (3) fund reserves, (4) special assessment, (5) development fees, and (6) leasing.

Current Operating Revenues

These are revenues from taxes, fees, charges, and other conventional sources raised principally to fund current operations of government that are also used to finance capital assets, usually with shorter life span such as patrol vehicles, fire trucks, or heavy equipment. They can also be used to fund recurring expenditures such as sidewalks, ramps, and street lights. The principle underlying the use of current operating revenues is that they should be used to finance assets that produce benefits in the present, not necessarily in the future. Consequently, they are not generally used to finance assets with longer life spans, partly because they are too costly to support them out of current revenues and partly because they can violate intergenerational equity (current generation funding assets that benefit future generations).

Earmarked Revenues

These are revenues from taxes, fees, and charges that are set aside or earmarked for specific capital improvement projects. A good example is the revenue from motor fuel tax that is earmarked for public transportation or highway construction. There is an advantage of using earmarked revenues in that one can see the direct relationship between the projects where the money will be spent and the benefits they will produce for the community which increases transparency and accountability.

Fund Reserves

Governments often maintain reserves for dealing with budget shortfalls or contingencies but they can also use reserves for funding capital projects. If the reserves are created with the sole objective of funding specific projects, they in essence become earmarked revenues but, in most instances, they are open, as long as they are used for capital improvements. In the latter case, they can be used for recurring as well as non-recurring expenditures such as acquisition of land, buildings, vehicles, and equipment, depending on the size of the reserve.

Special Assessments

These are levies on real property used primarily to pay for capital improvements that benefit the property (owners). They can be used for a variety of improvement projects, from replacing water main, to constructing fire stations, to upgrading storm and sewer systems, to building pedestrian skyways, among others. Special assessments are not property taxes in conventional sense of the term since they must be used for special purposes; as such, they require legal authority to specially assess the property to raise the needed revenue. There are two general rules most governments use for special assessments: One, the value of the assessment should not be higher than the benefit it produces for the property, based on the market value. Two, the assessment must uniformly apply to all properties of the same class. Although as an approach the assessments do not generate much revenue for a government, they can still produce the needed revenue to finance specific capital projects.

Development Fees

Used interchangeably with impact fees, these are mostly charges applied to offset the costs of new development—residential as well as commercial; they can also be applied to redevelopment activities. Development fees are different from the permit fees most governments use to cover the cost of processing application permits and development plans. The charges are generally fixed at a specific dollar value per lot, say, per acre that a developer must pay for the privilege of development. They have traditionally been used to finance water systems, sewer treatment plants, and local roads. The primary objective of these fees is to cover the increased costs for providing existing and improved infrastructure. Many consider the development fees to be fair since it is easy to see the direct benefit the assets produce for the public, although it is not unlikely for a developer to pass on the burden to the consumers.

Special Purpose Local Option Sales Tax

Most local governments use local option sales tax (LOST) to supplement their revenue from property tax and other revenue sources. As noted earlier, LOST constitutes a small fraction of the overall sales tax, ranging usually between 0.5 and 1.5%. Governments also have the option to use a variation of LOST, called special purpose local option sales tax (SPLOST) for construction, alteration, relocation, and improvement of roads, bridges, and means of public transportation, and the purchase of facilities or equipment necessary for the operation of the government, as needed.

Leasing

It is a process by which an organization acquires a capital asset, based on contractual agreement between a lessor (the owner of the asset) and a lessee (the user), for a series of payments at periodic intervals. Leasing is a common practice for most governments for financing their capital assets, in particular, capital or inventory items and is often considered a better option than outright purchasing. There are several reasons why it is so: (1) it provides a viable alternative for acquiring assets, especially for governments that are financially hard-pressed, (2) it can free-up existing resources that can be used to meet other financial needs, (3) it provides a flexible alternative to raising taxes or borrowing funds to pay for a capital asset, (4) it avoids the risk of technological obsolescence and, more importantly, (5) it does not affect a government's ability to borrow and does not lower its credit rating.

Although the advantages are obvious, a government considering leasing must do a thorough analysis to ensure that the benefits outweigh the costs of purchase. In reality, the actual analysis does not have to be all that complicated and can be accomplished in three easy steps: (1) determine the costs of buying, as well as leasing, (2) calculate the difference between the two options, and (3) select the one that produces a lower cost to the government. We can formally express this relationship between buying and leasing in terms of a simple algebraic expression, as shown below:

$$W_C = \left[\left(P_0 + \sum_{t=0}^{T} OC_t \right) - SV_T \right] - \sum_{t=0}^{T} (LC_t + OC_t) \tag{8.5}$$

where W_C is the cost of ownership, P_0 is purchase price at time 0, OC_t is the operating cost, including maintenance at time t, LC_t is lease cost at time t, and SV_T is the salvage value at time T (for $t = 1,..., T$). The first part of the equation represents the cost of ownership and the second part the cost of leasing, assuming the operating and maintenance costs rest with the government, if purchased.

While the expression in Eq. (8.5) seems simple enough to be useful for everyday purpose, it has a major weakness in that it does not take into consideration the time value of money, which is important, especially for capital assets that have a life span of several years. Interestingly, when the time value of money is incorporated into the expression, Eq. (8.5) becomes

$$NPV_W = \left[\left(P_0 + \sum_{t=0}^{T} \frac{OC_t}{(1+r)^t} \right) - \frac{SV_T}{(1+r)^T} \right] - \sum_{t=0}^{T} \left(\frac{LC_t + OC_t}{(1+r)t} \right) \tag{8.6}$$

where NPV_W is the net present value of ownership (difference between the present value of ownership or purchase and the present value of lease), r is the discount rate, and the rest of the terms are the same as before. It should be noted that the expression $OC_t/(1+r)^t$ can also be written as $OC_t[1/(1+r)^t]$, where $1/(1+r)^t$ is the discount factor (DF).

To give an example, suppose that the public works department of a government needs a heavy-duty truck for running its normal departmental activities. The department has two choices: buy the truck or lease it. If the department has to buy the truck, it will cost it $65,000. If it has to lease, it will cost the department $18,000 in rent, payable at the end of each period for three years (assuming it will be leased for three years). If purchased, there is a salvage value of $23,000 at the end of the asset's useful life. There is also an operating cost of $5000, which includes repair and maintenance, if the vehicle is purchased; if leased, it will be included in the lease price. Assume a discount rate of 9%. Table 8.9 shows the present value (PV) of ownership of the vehicle for the department.

As shown in Table 8.9, the net present value of ownership is $2788.97, which is obtained by taking the difference between the sum of the present value of purchase and the present value of lease. That is,

$$NPV_W = \sum (PV \text{ of Purchase}) - \sum (PV \text{ of Lease})$$
$$= [(\$65,000.00 + \$4587.40 + \$4208.40 + \$3860.92) - \$16,647.99]$$
$$- [\$21,100.91 + \$19,358.64 + \$17,760.21]$$
$$= \$61,008.73 - \$58,219.76$$
$$= \$2788.97$$

Next, to determine whether the department should purchase or lease the vehicle, we apply a simple decision rule: if $NPV_W > 0$, lease; if $NPV_W < 0$, purchase. Since the net present value of ownership is positive, the department should go with

Table 8.9 Present value of ownership vs present value of lease

Year	P ($)	O ($)	SV ($)	DF	PV of purchase ($)
0	65,000	–	–	–	65,000.00
1	–	5000	–	0.917431	4587.16
2	–	5000	–	0.841680	4208.40
3	–	5000	–	0.771830	3859.15
4	–	–	23,500	0.708425	16,647.99
Year	L ($)	O ($)	Total cost ($)	DF	PV of purchase ($)
0	–	–	–	–	–
1	18,000	5000	23,000	0.917431	21,100.91
2	18,000	5000	23,000	0.841680	19,358.64
3	18,000	5000	23,000	0.771830	17,752.09
4	–	–	–	0.708425	–

the option to lease. Alternatively, if the sum of the PV of purchase > the sum of the PV of lease, lease; if not, purchase. Since the ΣPV of purchase is greater than the ΣPV of lease, the government should lease the vehicle.

A couple of points are worth noting here: One, although it takes into consideration the time value of money, the model suggested here has a weakness in that it ignores intangible factors such as convenience, location, and personal relationship between a lessor and lessee which can affect the final cost of the asset. Two, it does not take into consideration the factors that may affect the final cost such as restrictions on the use of the asset once acquired or a special clause requiring the government to buy a safety insurance for the protection of the asset against potential loss, theft, or damage. In each of these instances, there is a monetary implication that must be incorporated in the final calculation before making a decision to buy or lease.

8.4.5.2   External Sources of Financing
External sources of financing capital assets can be an attractive alternative if they do not impose any serious cost burden or take away resources from current operations of a government. A prudent manager should explore all possible sources of external financing before turning his attention to internal sources. Four sources of external financing are commonly used for this purpose: grants-in-aid, public trust funds, public–private partnership, and borrowing.

Grants-in-Aid
Intergovernmental transfers provide a sound alternative for governments that lack resources to finance their capital improvement activities. Most of these transfers take place in the form of grants-in-aid, which are usually provided for activities that generate spillovers. As noted previously, grants-in-aid often come with conditions and, in some cases, with matching requirements that may limit a recipient government's flexibility in deciding where they can invest the funds, which projects they can undertake, and what pricing policy they can use to earn a return. In extreme cases, they can increase dependency on upper-level governments but without which they would find it difficult to support many of the improvement activities on their own. On the positive side, intergovernmental transfers can free-up resources of the recipient governments that can be used for funding projects that otherwise would not be possible; as such, they provide a viable alternative.

Public Trust Funds
Although not as common as some of the other measures suggested here, public trust funds (where a government serves in a trustee capacity) are occasionally used to finance capital assets such as parks and recreation facilities, museums, sports arenas, and college buildings. In most instances, the funds are designated for a specific development project that cannot be used for any other purpose yet they provide a stable source for funding capital assets. Depending on the size of the trust funds and the conditions under which they are provided, governments can invest all or a fraction of these funds to generate interest earnings which can be used for funding capital assets.

Public–Private Partnership

As noted previously, public–private partnership has become an attractive alternative in recent years as an instrument of financing capital projects, in particular physical infrastructure. The partnership can help a government that is financially struggling by freeing up resources for other activities and reducing its debt burden. It can also draw on the private sector expertise to minimize cost of development and increase efficiency of operation. However, like most options, it has some disadvantages in that there is no certainty that the commitments will be there for the long-term and that costs will be low. There is also the possibility that the government may eventually lose control of the facility to the private sector. Some of these problems can be avoided by having a clear and binding contract agreement between the parties but that may discourage some firms to participate.

Borrowing

Borrowing, also known as pay-as-you-use, is one of the principal sources of financing capital projects, used mostly when current revenues are not sufficient to provide for their expenditures on a pay-as-you-go (PAYGO) basis. There is also a simple explanation why borrowing is sometimes preferred to PAYGO: Since capital projects have a long life that can serve current as well future users, it makes good sense to use borrowing so the burden can be distributed between the current and future generation of taxpayers. In general, capital projects that are eligible for debt financing must satisfy two basic conditions: One, the average life of the asset must be as long as the life of the debt to ensure that the government does not have to pay for the debt when the asset is no longer in use. Two, the full cost of the asset must not be borne by other potential revenue sources such as user fees and charges, grants-in-aid, and private contributions, exception being revenue debt which is mostly financed out of revenue generated from the sale of service such as water, sewer, and electric utility.

Decision Criteria

Borrowing is an exhaustive process, from the time a decision is made to borrow, to the time when the debt is issued and sold to an investor. Several factors must be taken into consideration before making a decision to borrow: One, the government has the right or statutory authority to issue a debt and the maximum amount it can borrow. This is particularly true for local governments which are required by law to hold a public referendum before issuing certain types of debts such as general obligation (GO) bonds. Two, the government must able to afford the debt. In other words, if resources are to be used, say, from the operating budget to finance the debt service (principal and interest) it should not impair the government's ability to finance its current operations. Three, the government must carefully evaluate all available financing options that will maximize its ability to finance the capital asset at the lowest cost, while maintaining flexibility to address future financial needs. Put simply, the debt should produce the least financial burden on the taxpayers and must not affect the ability of the government to borrow in the future. Four, the government must ensure that the issuance of debt will not affect its credit rating for future debt.

Types of Debt

There is a wide range of debt instruments currently used by all three levels of government to finance their capital improvement activities. They fall into two broad categories: short-term and long-term. Short-term debt typically includes notes issued by a government in anticipation of revenue it will earn (1) from various revenue sources other than taxes, called revenue anticipation note (RAN), (2) from various taxes, called tax anticipation note (TAN), and (3) from sale of bonds or bond proceeds, called bond anticipation note (BAN). As the term implies, notes are of short-term duration, usually a year or less. In addition, governments can also use their line of credit, if needed, for acquisition of small capital items. However, most debt instruments governments use for capital budgeting are long-term and these include mostly bonds. Two types of bonds are typically used—those that are backed by full faith and the credit of a government to allow it to use its taxing authority to issue the debt and those that do not have any such requirements. The former primarily includes general obligation (GO) bonds, certificates of obligation, limited tax notes, bond banks, while the latter includes mostly revenue bonds. The following provides a brief discussion of each:

General Obligation Bonds These instruments are primarily issued for the construction of major capital assets that require significant outlay. They are backed by full faith and the credit of the government. They require voter approval and are issued with a promise to levy ad valorem (property) taxes in an unlimited amount as necessary to pay for debt service.

Certificates of Obligation Similar to GO bonds in that they are backed by full faith and the credit of the government, these instruments do not require voter approval. However, the voters can force an election for the issuance of the debt by presenting a petition with a certain percentage of registered voters, usually less than 10%. Interestingly, unlike the GO bonds, they are payable from ad valorem taxes, revenues, or a combination of both.

Limited Tax Notes Issued for a limited time period such as five or seven years, these types of debts are backed by full faith and the credit of the government. Although they do not require voter approval, they frequently require the action of the council or commission to approve the debt issue. The proceeds from the issues are used to finance the construction of a major facility or an expensive piece of equipment.

Revenue Bonds These bonds are typically issued to finance the construction, improvement, and repair of capital assets, operated mostly by enterprise operations of a government such as water, sewer, and electric utility, and repaid through the sale of goods or services. They do not require voter approval and are not backed by full faith and the credit of the government but may need indirect support similar to certificates of obligation. There is a wide range of revenue bonds, besides those issued by enterprise operations such as industrial revenue bonds, lease revenue bonds, certificates of participation, and tax increment bonds, among others.

Industrial Revenue Bonds. These bonds are issued by a government to encourage relocation and expansion of industries to promote economic growth. The government is not generally responsible for debt payment and often serves as a conduit to provide a lower interest rate for the borrower responsible for industrial development. However, the firm may receive a break in property taxes for land and equipment.

Lease Revenue Bonds. Unlike the industrial revenue bonds, these bonds are used to construct a facility such as a toll bridge or an office building for lease purposes, which will be paid off from the lease revenue the establishment will earn from leasing the facility.

Certificates of Participation. These are a variation of lease revenue bonds, usually arranged through public sale of certificates, where the holder of the certificate owns a beneficial interest in the lease. If issued by an enterprise operation, it in essence becomes a revenue bond.

Tax Increment Bonds. Also known as tax allocation bonds, these bonds are issued to pay upfront for the purchase and reclamation of land and installation of infrastructure such as streets, landscaping, curves, gutters, and water and sewer line. Once the property is prepared, it is sold to a private developer at a price that is usually below the cost of preparing the land called cost write-down. Write-down costs are generally funded by the bonds that are repaid through a special increment fund (created to accumulate tax increments from the increase in value of the property above the base from redevelopment).

Bond Banks Bond banks are an arrangement among a large number of governments, especially smaller municipalities and special districts within a state to pool their general obligations to create a bond bank. Creating a bond bank makes it possible to offer larger issues that can attract more investors and lower interest costs. It can also lower the risk that is frequently associated with small, unrated issuers. Bond banks are generally created by the state legislatures, often as an independent agency, and administered by a board of commissioners appointed by the governor. The bank works closely with the local governments to provide cost-effective and competitive financing programs.

While borrowing remains the principal instrument of debt financing, it has several weaknesses. One, it can easily add to the existing debt burden of a government, even though there are legal debt limits as to how much some governments can borrow, especially local governments. Two, as noted previously, borrowing can easily crowd out the capital market; in particular, if capital is in short supply, which can easily raise the interest cost to the government that has to compete with the private sector for capital. Three, the interest cost can be prohibitive for a government that is experiencing financial troubles and slow its economic growth. There are ways, however, by which a government can lower the borrowing costs such as by having a good credit rating, having an upper-level government guarantee the debt, shifting the administrative costs to an upper-level government, maintaining a consistent income from reserve funds that can offset some of the costs of debt financing, and purchasing debt (bond) insurance, among others.

As critical borrowing is to finance capital improvement activities, a government cannot borrow ad infinitum to support its capital improvement activities; there is often a legal (statutory) debt limit as to how much a government can borrow, usually set as a percentage of a government's tax base. Bond issues covered by this limit are those that are financed by property taxes, including special assessments and tax increments. The difference between legal debt limit and the bonds outstanding that are covered by the legal debt limit is frequently referred to as the legal debt margin. To give an example, suppose that the market value of real property of a government is \$500 million, with a statutory limit of 5% and an existing debt applicable to the debt limit of \$5 million, the legal debt margin for the government will be \$20 million, that is, $[(\$500,000,000 \times 0.05) - \$5,000,000 = \$25,000,000 - \$5,000,000 = \$20,000,000]$. In other words, that is, how much the government should be able to borrow, given the market value of its real property and the existing debt.

A Note on Build America Bonds

In 2009, the federal government introduced the American Recovery and Reinvestment Act (ARRA) which contained a provision for a new type of municipal security, designed to assist localities to raise funds for local infrastructure projects. The program, called Build America Bonds (BABs), was established as part of President Obama's stimulus legislation to lower the borrowing costs for state and local bond issuers. The goal was to direct more funds toward construction projects that would, in turn, generate jobs. An important characteristic of these bonds was that they provided a federal subsidy of 35% of interest directly to investors through tax credits, thereby lowering their tax liability. Unfortunately, the program died in 2010 when Congress failed to extend it. Part of the problem with the program was that it was not entirely tax-free in spite of the tax credit. While many municipal bonds generate income that is free of federal, state and local income tax, the Build American Bonds were taxed at the federal level which worked as disincentive for most investors.

8.4.5.3 Cost of Capital

An important consideration in capital financing is the cost a government incurs when borrowing is used as a means to finance capital projects, known as cost of capital.[9] Although various other means are used to finance capital projects, as we have seen in the preceding discussion, the fact that debt constitutes the primary source of financing these activities, the cost of debt essentially becomes the cost of capital. Thus, if a government has to pay 4.5% in interest rate on a debt, assuming no other financing options are involved, it will be the cost of capital for the government. In general, for a government to be able to use debt as a means to finance capital projects it must have a sound revenue base from which the debt can be financed. This is important because when a government borrows, it gets into a legal obligation to make periodic payments on debt until it is fully paid off. Having a sound revenue base helps a government get a better bond rating (an important consideration for marketing bond), lower its interest cost, and provide a safety cushion for the investors.

Since governments use multiple means to finance their capital improvement activities, the question is how to calculate the cost of capital. Ideally, the calculation should be based on weighted average of all forms of financing the government uses, including debt. The calculation should also be based on current market costs of debt rather than on historical costs since decisions for investments are made in the present, based primarily on current rather than on past information. The following provides a simple expression for weighted average cost of capital:

$$\text{WACC} = \left[\sum_{i=1}^{n} (w_i C_i) / \sum_{i=1}^{n} w_i\right] \times 100 \tag{8.7}$$

where WACC is the weighted average cost of capital, w_i is the weight assigned to ith debt (for $i = 1, 2, \ldots, n$), and C_i is the interest cost associated with ith debt

Assume, for convenience, that the sum of the weights is equal to 1, the expression would then become

$$\text{WACC} = \sum_{i=1}^{n} (w_i C_i) \times 100$$
$$= (w_1 C_1 + w_2 C_2 + \cdots + w_n C_n) \times 100 \tag{8.8}$$

To give an example, suppose that a government uses five different debt instruments to finance its capital investment needs—GO bonds, certificates of obligation (CO), and three revenue bonds (RB_1, RB_2, and RB_3). Let us say that the total amount of debt for the government for all five instruments together is \$50 million, used in varying proportion for each instrument: $GO = 30\%$, $CO = 10\%$, $RB_1 = 20\%$, $RB_2 = 15\%$, and $RB_3 = 25\%$. Assume further that the corresponding interest cost to the government for individual instruments are as follows: $GO = 0.03$, $CO = 0.04$, $RB_1 = 0.06$, $RB_2 = 0.07$, $RB_3 = 0.05$.

The weighted average cost of capital for the government, therefore, would be

$$\begin{aligned}
\text{WACC} &= (w_1)(C_1) + (w_1)(C_1) + (w_1)(C_1) + (w_1)(C_1) + (w_1)(C_1) \\
&= [\{(0.3)(0.03)\} + \{(0.10)(0.04)\} + \{(0.20)(0.06)\} + \{(0.15)(0.07)\} \\
&\quad + \{(0.25)(0.05)\}] \times 100 \\
&= (0.0090 + 0.0040 + 0.0012 + 0.0105 + 0.0125) \times 100 \\
&= 0.0372 \times 100 \\
&= 3.72\%
\end{aligned}$$

which is the (weighted) average cost of debt to the government. From the point of view of the investors, that is, those who will invest in these instruments, it is the minimum they must earn on their investments. Some investors may prefer to add a safety margin to the estimates to protect against potential loss, which will raise the cost somewhat.

Interestingly, each method of debt financing also requires an estimate of cash outflows, in particular, the amount of money the government will need to pay in interest and principal. Since the payments are going to be made over the life span of the debt, it is necessary to estimate the present value of these payments (cash outflows) to determine the explicit cost of debt in real terms.

8.4.6   Appropriate Funds

Once the capital budget is prepared and reviewed internally, it has to go through an appropriation process, similar to the operating budget process. The process consists of the same basic steps, discussed earlier: executive review, public hearings, especially for local governments, and legislative review. The executive review culminates in final decisions and executive recommendations to the legislature for appropriation. Public hearings give the citizens an opportunity to ensure that their concerns about the use of tax revenues as well as future growth and development of the community are reflected in the budget. Legislative review begins by delegating responsibility to specific committees to look into different components of the budget. The committees can call for hearings with respective agency representatives, if necessary, to provide additional information or clarification on the recommended budget before making their own recommendations. This is followed by legislative decisions on committee recommendations and final action on individual projects.

Budget decisions are not cast in stones; they can be amended. As with the operating budget, the capital budget can also be amended, as need be, with the approval of the legislature and preferably before the assets are put in place. Additionally, agencies responsible for executing the budget can request for supplemental appropriation, special appropriation (for unforeseen circumstances), and transfer of appropriation between funds, departments, or between different divisions within the same department.

8.4.7   Execute the Budget

Implementing a capital budget requires careful planning and organization until they are fully operational. The process can take anywhere from a few weeks to a few years, depending on the nature of the projects. For instance, installing a network system for data management and intra-organizational communication may take a few weeks, as opposed to constructing a road or highway that may take several years. Nevertheless, all capital improvement activities need to go through a series of steps to ensure that the projects are completed on time and cost, as scheduled and within the approved budget, and can deal with change, as well as risk and uncertainty. This involves careful review and control of projects being implemented called in-progress functions. The functions typically include managing costs, managing time, managing change, and managing risks, and are part of what is commonly known as project management functions and should be integral to capital budgeting process. The following sections provide a brief overview of the functions.

8.4.7.1 Managing Costs

Cost management is an essential function of project implementation. While there are individuals who specialize in cost management, managing costs is the collective responsibility of the entire management responsible for the implementation of a project. The primary objective of cost management is cost control to ensure that there are no cost overruns, in particular, that no preventable wastes of money can take place or any unauthorized increase in costs can occur during the implementation process. Accurate and timely cost control measures are critical to avoid the cost problems that can slow down the implementation of a project.

An important aspect of this process is that there must be an auditing of cash outflows related to the acquisition of the assets to avoid any cost overruns. Two things are necessary to ensure this: One, the establishment of internal accounting control procedures to accumulate all relevant project-related costs and, two, the use of periodic progress reports. These reports should be prepared on a timely basis, especially during the construction or acquisition phase to allow for easy comparison of actual expenditures against initial estimates of project costs and to provide explanations of significant variations that may occur, similar to variance analysis during the execution of an operating budget, discussed earlier.

Additionally, governments should constantly search for innovative approaches to improve their cost management practices. A good example would be total cost management (TCM), an approach that has a long history of effective cost control. Unlike conventional cost control measures that look at individuals components of a project, TCM takes a holistic approach to cost management, where the managers responsible for different segments of a project come together to decide on the best way to deal with the implementation difficulties so as to keep the cost to a minimum. The approach is particularly suitable for large projects, with multiple phases, requiring extended completion time where potentials exist for cost overruns.

8.4.7.2 Managing Time

Time management is vitally important for successful implementation of a project. Failure to complete a project on time can not only cost a government delays, but also add substantial cost overruns. While individual managers are responsible for making sure that their activities are completed within the specified time and cost, the overall responsibility of seeing a project through falls on the project manager. Many things can happen during the implementation phase that can cause project delays, including some over which the management may not have any control, but all can add to the total cost of the project. The goal of the project manager, as well as individual managers, is to ensure that the cost overruns from delays are kept to a minimum. Projects managers who are successful in meeting their project schedules have a good chance of staying within their budget.

To ensure that delays do not occur, or kept to a minimum, the project manager must break down the project into a number of distinct tasks that need to be performed in a structured and systematic manner. The manager must decide the order in which the tasks will be performed, what resources they will require, and how much time they will need. Each of these tasks has a direct bearing on the project and could lead to project delays or result in a faulty project. One way to keep track of the activities is to construct a time chart such as a Gantt chart, named after the gentleman who developed it over a hundred years ago (Gantt 1910). Used widely in project management, it is essentially a line graph, showing all the activities, from the beginning to the end. The chart highlights the activities by identifying major milestones when a major task is completed to indicate significant progress made toward completing the project. This is often followed by a brief account of the amount of work completed or remains to be done. It can also be used to indicate the percentage of allocated funds used up for the completed work, similar to the variance analysis discussed in a previous chapter.

Although a Gantt chart provides a visually attractive means for illustrating the status of a project at various phases of development, it has several weaknesses: One, it does not tell us if there is an optimal completion time; two, it does not provide much information on the savings a project will generate if completed ahead of time, called crashing; three, and most important, it does not tell us much about the cost of delay. These are important considerations that must go into the decision process before undertaking a project. Two methods that are ideally suited when faced with these types of questions are the critical path method (CPM) and program evaluation and review technique (PERT).

8.4.7.3 Managing Change

It is not unusual for a project to go through changes during the implementation phase, although ideally it should not. Changes may be necessary because of faulty designs, specification errors, material defects, and so forth. Most project managers are aware that these changes can occur any time during the implementation process, but, as long as it is not due to the change in scope (change in focus or dimension of the project), it should not be difficult to address the problem. A realistic approach would be to take a flexible view that allows the management team to accommodate some changes as they emerge. This is part of what one would call change management that project managers often use to recognize potentials for change. Once a change is recognized as necessary, the manager should document the change, review it with the management, submit the proposed change to the responsible authority, and make appropriate accommodations for change.

On the other hand, scope management is much more complex and should be thoroughly addressed before beginning work on the project. To avoid the problem later in the process, the scope should be clearly defined at the beginning as part of the project definition. Much of the work during this time should be directed at developing an acceptable definition of the project in terms of its mission, goals, objectives, deliverables, and how it will operate. Once the scope has been defined, it serves as the basis against which potential changes are assessed and performance measured. However, regardless of the nature of change, all participants in a project must understand that changes cost time and resources; therefore, they must surface as early as possible.

8.4.7.4 Managing Risks

Risks and uncertainties are inevitable in everything we do. Although the two terms are used interchangeably, there is a difference between what the terms actually mean. Uncertainty is a situation where the outcomes of a decision are difficult to predict with any degree of certainty and, consequently, difficult to assign a priori probabilities to their occurrence. In the case of risk, on the other hand, it is possible to predict the outcomes and, as such, assign a priori probabilities, which makes it easier to use than uncertainty. For instance, it is possible to predict the likelihood of a project member getting sick, or finding a defective item, or a project producing less than optimum result under certain conditions.

Since risks are unavoidable, a prudent manager must make every effort to recognize the likelihood of risks and prepare a range of possible courses of action as part of project management. Among the things the manager can do are (1) take actions now to avoid the risk, reduce its likelihood, or its likely impact, (2) make contingency plans for dealing with any potential outcome of a risk, (3) take no action, if it is recognized as an acceptable risk, (4) share the risk with others, if possible, such as with other agencies or governments, and (5) where possible, transfer the risks to a third party for a fee or premium such as buying insurance. The last option, in particular, buying insurance against any liability that may occur in the course of implementing a project can significantly offset the costs of risks. Also, legal requirements may obligate a government to obtain adequate insurance to cover against some risks.

The point is it is difficult to implement a project, especially large-scale projects, without the likelihood of any serious problems occurring along the way, including occasional risks and uncertainties; even the most experienced team is not immune from their occurrences. A successful project manager, therefore, must recognize the possibility of their occurrences early on and take all possible preventive measures to minimize project delays and the costs they may produce for the organization.

Two important considerations in controlling in-progress capital projects are worth noting here: One, the establishment of internal accounting control procedures to accumulate all relevant project-related costs; two, the use of periodic progress reports, especially during the construction or acquisition phase that compare actual expenditures against initial estimates of project costs and provide explanations of significant variations that may occur, similar to variance analysis during the execution of an operating budget, discussed earlier. Furthermore, it is important to key the reports to critical events in the construction or acquisition of an asset.

8.4.8 Evaluate the Budget

Finally, once implemented, the capital budget should be evaluated on a regular basis to ensure that the acquired items or installed projects are operating to their fullest capacity and producing the desired results and, most important, are within the specified limits or targets. This includes activities both during and after the capital budget has been implemented. Evaluation can be informal, conducted internally, or they can be formal, requiring formal analysis such as those suggested for the operating budget.

8.5   Impact on the Operating Budget

No discussion of a CIP process is complete without some discussions of the impact the capital expenditures will have on the operating budget. This stems from the fact that since a government has a finite amount of resources to spend between the operating and the capital expenditures, it needs to make a trade-off between the two.[10] In other words, any decision to spend money on capital expenditures will have a direct impact on the operating budget and vice versa, although the degree of impact will be different for different governments depending on the size of their capital assets, how the funds are generated to finance the assets, and the manner in which the costs are distributed over time. For instance, if the assets are financed using debt, then the amount of debt that can be optimally as well as legally supported by the government through debt service payments, given the level of existing debt, will determine the amount of debt the government can issue. Conversely, the size of the operating budget can also determine the level and composition of the capital budget.

Another impact the capital budget has on the operating budget is the cost of operation and maintenance. Capital expenditures involving construction and acquisition of assets will result in new costs in operation and maintenance, as well as in additional staffing required for management of capital assets. Most governments are concerned that the costs do not exceed the ability of the operating budget to support the normal operations of the government. In some cases, a government may decide to restrict the debt service to a fixed percentage of the operating budget to ensure that the debt service payments do not overburden the operating revenues of the government. However, the impact of capital expenditures on the operating budget can also be positive in that, if executed properly, it can lead to substantial cost savings for the government. For instance, if infrastructure maintenance such as road resurfacing can be funded through the capital budget, it can produce considerable cost savings for the operating budget by eliminating an important cost commitment from the operating budget. Also, maintaining capital assets in good working condition can prevent frequent breakdowns and potential loss of service, thereby saving government considerable sums of money over time.

From a practical point of view, understanding the impact of the capital budget on the operating budget is important to have a sense of the effect the capital expenditures will have on specific operating expenditures and the time it will take for the operating budget to make the necessary adjustments. In general, the greatest impact occurs with new projects, as opposed to existing projects requiring normal operation and maintenance. For instance, in a study of forty-eight largest US cities, Bland and Nunn (1992) found that labor-intensive services such as police and fire protection are more sensitive to capital expenditures than most other services. Their findings further noted that since the operating and the capital budgets are often prepared independently, there is a need for close coordination between the two budget cycles, especially in those cases where the impact on the operating budget is clear and positive.

Interestingly, the Chief Executive's recommendations generally incorporate these impacts in the budget request and the costs the capital budget will produce in terms of additional operating expenditures, including the timing of expenditures. The information is useful in aiding the review process.

8.6   Summary and Conclusion

The budgetary activities of a government fall into two distinct groups—activities that deal with routine (recurring) operations, called the operating budget activities, and those that deal with non-routine (non-recurring) operations, called the capital budgeting activities. While both sets of activities are necessary in a government, capital budgeting plays a major role in the overall budgetary activities because of the long-term impact a capital budget has on the growth and development of an economy. This chapter has provided a fairly detailed overview of capital budgeting activities in government; in particular, the distinction between different types of capital assets and the relationship between capital budgeting and long-term planning. The chapter has also provided a detailed discussion of the capital budget process. Like an operating budget, the capital budget process is detailed, time-consuming, and complex, in part, because of large commitments of resources and, in part, because of irreversibility of decisions once the assets have been put in place, as well as the potential for risk and uncertainty. The chapter concluded with a brief discussion of the impact a capital budget will have on the operating budget.

Review Questions

Q1. What is a capital budget? How does it differ from an operating budget? What is the relationship between capital budgeting and long-term planning?

Q2. What is a capital asset? How would one classify a capital asset? Discuss the various methods of classification, with an example of each.

Q3. What is a capital budget process? What are the steps of this process and why the process is considered analytically more detailed and time-consuming than an operating budget process?

Q4. What is a needs assessment matrix? Why is necessary to carefully evaluate a capital asset before deciding whether to retain or replace? What decision criteria one would use to retain or replace an asset? What is a sunk cost trap?

Q5. Suppose that a government has recently purchased a utility vehicle at a cost of $25,000, with maintenance costs that will increase over time, as shown in Table 8.10.

Table 8.10 Review Question (Q5)

Year	Maintenance cost ($)	DF*1/(1+r)^i	PV of cost ($)	Cumulative PV of cost ($)	Cumulative DF	Weighted average ($)
1	700	—	—	—	—	—
2	1500	—	—	—	—	—
3	2700	—	—	—	—	—
4	3500	—	—	—	—	—
5	5800	—	—	—	—	—
6	7300	—	—	—	—	—
7	9400	—	—	—	—	—
8	11,500	—	—	—	—	—

Using the information presented in the table, complete the table and determine at what point the government will need to replace the vehicle. [Hint: Use a discount rate of 5 percent (5%)].

Q6. Why is it necessary to prioritize capital projects? What are the advantages of using a ratio scale as opposed to an interval scale, when prioritizing? Discuss, with reference to the methods suggested in the chapter.

Q7. A local community hospital needs a state-of-the-art X-Ray machine to replace the one it has been using for several years. The hospital has the option to buy or lease the equipment. If the hospital decides to buy the equipment, it will cost $125,000; if it decides to lease, the rental cost will be $15,000 per year. If purchased, there is a salvage value of $25,000 at the end of the asset's productive life. There is also a maintenance cost of $3000 if the equipment is purchased. The equipment has a useful life of seven years. Calculate the PV of ownership and indicate if the hospital should buy or lease. [Hint: Use a discount rate of 5 percent]

Q8. How do we calculate normalized weights? What is a priority vector? Complete the following in Table 8.11.

Table 8.11   Review Question (Q8): Synthesis of judgments for criteria

G	Criteria				
	C_1	C_2	C_3		
C_1	1	4	1/3		
C_2	1/4	1	1/7		
C_3	3	7	1		
Total	4.25	–	–		
	Normalized weights			*Total*	*Priority vector*
C_1					–
C_2					
C_3					
Total	1.00	1.00	1.00		1.000

Note For example normalized weight for $(C_1 = 1) = 1/4.25$

Q9. Define Consistency Index (CI) and Consistency Ratio CR). Use the table from Q8 to find CI and CR. What do the results tell us?

Q10. Why is important to rank capital projects in government? Discuss two different methods of project ranking.

Q11. What is WACC and how is it calculated? Suppose that a government uses seven different debt instruments to finance its capital investment needs—GO bonds, certificate of obligation (CO), certificate of participation (CP), and four revenue bonds (RB_1, RB_2, RB_3, and RB_4). Let us say that the total amount of debt for the government for all seven instruments together is $100 million, used in varying proportion for each instrument: $GO = 20\%$, $CO = 15\%$, $CP = 10\%$, $RB_1 = 20\%$, $RB_2 = 15\%$, $RB_3 = 5\%$ and $RB_4 = 15\%$. Assume further that the corresponding interest cost to the government for individual instruments are as follows: $GO = 0.05$, $CO = 0.03$, $CP = 0.02$, $RB_1 = 0.08$, $RB_2 = 0.06$, $RB_3 = 0.09$, $RB_3 = 0.05$. Find the value of WACC.

Q12. How are capital projects financed? What are some of the internal sources of financing capital projects?

Q13. Why and under what circumstances should a government use external financing, i.e., borrowing to finance its capital improvement activities? Discuss some of the commonly used sources of external finance used by government?

Q14. What is a weighted average cost of capital? What are the advantages of using a weighted average cost of capital?

Q15. Suppose that a government uses three different debt instruments to finance its capital investment needs – GO bond, certificate of obligation (CO), and a revenue bond (RB). Let us say that the total amount of debt for the government for all three instruments together is $100 million, used in varying proportion for each instrument: $GO = 50\%$, $CO = 10\%$, $RB_1 = 40\%$. Assume further that the corresponding interest costs to the government for individual instruments are as follows: GO=0.03, CO=0.04, and RB=0.05. What will be the weighted average cost of capital?

Q16. What is in-progress function? What role do these functions play in capital budgeting? Discuss some of these functions with examples.

Q17. Capital budgeting has an impact on the operating budget that varies in size and scope. Discuss some of the impacts a capital budget has on the operating budget.

Notes

1. When discussing the life span of an asset, it may be necessary to make a distinction between types of lives such as economic life, ownership life, physical life, and useful life. Economic life is the time (usually expressed in years) over which an asset is expected to operate with minimum cost to its owner. In other words, the net return from the use of the asset will be the maximum. The ownership life is the time when an asset is acquired to the time it is disposed. The ownership life will vary depending on how long an asset is held by an owner. If the ownership changes hands three times, then the time the asset is held by an owner will be the ownership life of the asset for the owner. Physical life is the time when an asset is acquired to the time when it is no longer able to produce goods and services. If an asset is managed properly with due care, the chances are that physical life of an asset will coincide with the time of its acquisition to the time it is abandoned or replaced. Finally, useful life is the time when an asset is kept in productive use with normal repair and maintenance.

   Most discussions on capital assets revolve around useful life. In general, vehicles and computers hardware have a life span of five years, software about three years, non-residential buildings about 20 years, and roads, bridges and highways are much longer. Land does not have a life span in conventional sense of the term since it does not go through normal wear and tear.

2. GASB's Codification Section 1400—Reporting Capital Assets, under Statement 34, recommends the following classification systems for capital assets: land, land improvements, land preparation-roads, land easements-intangible, buildings, machinery and equipment, library books, computer software-intangible, construction in progress, and infrastructure such as roads, bridges, streets, curbs and gutters, sidewalks, drainage systems, lighting systems, historic monuments, and smaller assets that are immovable.

3. The term comprehensive plan is often used interchangeably with a master plan, although the two are not necessarily the same. A comprehensive plan usually has a minimum set of requirements that need to be met and has laws that guide those requirements (such as land use, noise level reduction, and so forth). A master plan is not necessarily restricted by such requirements, although it can be more narrowly focused than a comprehensive plan; however, both have a long-term focus, which may explain why capital facilities constitute a part of both.

4. A capital budget calendar typically follows the same structure as the operating budget: It starts with the development of budget goals (CIP goals, in this case) and strategies, say, in the spring, followed by budget development in the summer, followed by review of requests by the chief administrative officer (City or County Manager, for a local government) and recommendations for change in the early fall. This is followed by submission of the budget for legislative review in the spring and recommendations, followed by formal adoption in the summer before the fiscal year begins on the first of September or October. If it is a local budget, there is a public hearing that usually takes place in the spring simultaneously with the legislative review.

5. Technological changes, together with demand change, are often called obsolescence. Even financial changes can be considered a form of obsolescence.

6. The principle underlying eigenvalues can be described as follows: Given a square matrix A, if it is possible to find a vector $V \neq 0$ and a scalar λ such as $AV = \lambda V$, where the scalar is called the eigenvalue and the vector eigenvector, then the expression $AV = \lambda V$ can be written as $AV = \lambda IV$, where I is the identity matrix. One can also write it as $AV - \lambda IV = 0$, or $(A - \lambda I)V = 0$, where $(A - \lambda I)$ is the characteristics matrix of A. By cause by assumption $V \neq 0$, the characteristic matrix must be singular and, therefore, its determinant must disappear. This determinant, on expansion, yields a polynomial in λ, and the various roots become the eigenvalues.

7. The following argument is given by Saaty for the calculation of this ratio. If numerical judgments were taken from the scale 1/9, 1/8, 1/7,…, 1/2, 1, 2, 3,…, 9, then using a reciprocal matrix would have the following average consistencies for different order matrices:

Size of matrix	1	2	3	4	5	6	7	8	9	10
Random consistency	0.00	0.00	0.58	0.90	1.12	1.24	1.32	1.41	1.45	1.49

8. A computer program run to obtain the λ_{max} for the three matrices produced slightly different results: 7.50425, 7.72805, and 7.70716, respectively. The difference, which is marginal, can be attributed to the number of digits used after the decimal points to calculate the λ_{max} in each case.

9. Cost of capital also includes the cost of equity, in addition to the cost of debt. The cost of equity is the return investors require on an investment, which is usually much higher than investment in government bonds and notes such as investments in high yielding securities. As such, the cost of capital for government does not include the cost of equity.

10. For a long period of time, especially between the 1950s and 1960s, the capital budget used to constitute about 30% of the total budget; today, it is barely around 10% across the board, which partly explains the current condition of the physical infrastructure in the country.

References

Bland, R. L., & Numm, S. (1992, June). The Impact of Capital Spending on Municipal Operating Budgets. *Public Budgeting & Finance, 12*(2), 32–47.

Freeman, R. J., Shoulders, C. D., & Allison, G. S. (2006). *Governmental and Nonprofit Accounting: Theory and Practice*. New York, NY: Prentice-Hall.

Gantt, H. L. (1974). *Work, Wages, and Profit*. Easton, PA: Hive Publishing (Originally published in *The Engineering Magazine* in 1910).

Gauthier, S. J. (2012). *GAAFR: Governmental Accounting, Auditing, and Financial Reporting*. Chicago, IL: Government Finance Officers Association (GFOA).

Hatry, H. P. (1988). *Guide to Setting Priorities for Capital Investment*. Washington, DC: Urban Institute Press.

Lawrence, D. M., & Vogt, A. J. (2007). *Capital Planning, Budgeting, and Debt Financing*. Chapel Hill: School of Government, University of North Carolina.

Manheim, M. L. (1966). *Hierarchical Structure: A Model for Planning and Design Processes*. Cambridge: MIT Press.

Saaty, T. L. (1980). *Analytic Hierarchy Process: Planning, Priority setting, Resource Allocation*. New York, NY: McGraw Hill.

Steiss, A. W. (1975). *Local Government Finance: Capital Facilities Planning and Debt Administration*. Lexington, KY: Lexington Press.

Straub, S. (2008). *Infrastructure and Growth in Developing Countries: Recent Advanced and Research Challenges* (World Bank Policy Research Working Paper No. 4460). Washington, DC: World Bank.

Vogt, J. A. (1995). Budgeting Capital Outlays and Improvements. *Budget Development*. Athens, GA: Carl Vinson Institute of Government.

Evaluating Capital Projects and Budget Decisions

9

Each year governments receive more funding requests for capital projects from various agencies and departments than the governments can realistically undertake. This makes it necessary for the decision makers to carefully evaluate each project before deciding which ones to accept and which ones to reject. Whether the projects are selected independently or in conjunction with other projects, each must be justified, first and foremost, on the basis of the critical needs of the government. Additionally, the decision must take into consideration the resource base of the government and, more importantly, the costs and benefits the projects will produce for the government and the political jurisdiction it serves. This chapter discusses some of the commonly used methods for evaluating capital projects. Of the methods discussed here, cost-benefit analysis has been extensively used in government than any other method because of its versatility and established history. Although not as common in government as they are in the private sector, the chapter also looks at risk and uncertainty associated with capital projects, as well as measures to deal with the problems. Finally, the chapter concludes with a brief discussion on the need to use depreciation for capital assets.

9.1 Project Evaluation in Capital Budgeting

Considering the resource constraints within which budget decisions have to be made, in particular the capital budget decisions, it is not difficult to understand why the capital budget process requires a careful evaluation of the projects. The process of evaluating capital projects is important to ensure that the selected projects meet the needs of the government. Project evaluation is a systematic process for analyzing the merits of a project. The process can be complex and time consuming depending on the need, the nature and size of the projects, as well as the number of projects being considered for evaluation.

© The Author(s) 2019
A. Khan, *Fundamentals of Public Budgeting and Finance*,
https://doi.org/10.1007/978-3-030-19226-6_9

However, notwithstanding the complexity of the process, a successful evaluation must follow several basic steps; in particular, the following: (1) define the goals and objectives of the project or projects being considered for evaluation, (2) determine the specific method or approach to be used for evaluation, (3) develop a set of criteria by which to evaluate the projects, (4) analyze and compare the results, and (5) select the appropriate project(s).

In general, goals summarize the general purpose the projects will serve for an organization; they are broad and generally ambitious. Objectives translate the goals in measurable terms that would make it possible for the organization to achieve the goals within a defined time frame. Methods are specific tools used to produce information necessary to determine the acceptability of a project. Criteria, on the other hand, set the parameters for evaluation, defined by the specific methods used, but are often within the discretion of the decision makers. Finally, once the first three steps of the process have been successfully completing, the last two steps—comparing and selecting projects—becomes relatively simple.

9.2   Methods of Project Evaluation

Since capital budgeting decisions have a direct impact on long-term economic growth and development of a government, how the projects are selected and the methods used in selecting the projects play a critical role in the overall evaluation process. Just as there are different types and variations of capital projects, so are there different types of methods that one can use for project evaluation. Interestingly, many of these methods have evolved over time in response to the changing needs of an organization. The methods vary in scope and complexity, including some that have been in existence for a long time. For the most part, the methods are based on financial assessment of the organization and continue to serve as the essential tools in capital budgeting decisions.

The following sections discuss four such methods that have been widely used in project evaluation: payback period, cost-benefit analysis, cost-effectiveness analysis, and equivalent annual cost. Of these, cost-benefit analysis has a long history of use in government for a wide range of projects and improvement activities, and, to this day, it remains the single most important decision tool in project evaluation.

9.2.1   Payback Period

An important consideration in capital budgeting decision is how much time it will take to pay off the resources (money) spent in acquiring a project. In project evaluation, this is typically known as the payback period. Payback period simply means the time during which cash inflows from an operation will equal its cash outflows. In other words, it is the amount of time a government will need for the earnings (cash inflows) to equal the cost of undertaking a project (cash outflows).

Put differently, it is the time when the cash flow (the difference between cash inflows and outflows) from a project operation will be zero.

The definition above has an interesting implication for project evaluation in that it focuses primarily on recovery time, but not on what happens after the costs have been recovered. Since payback is mostly concerned with recovery time, it is often used as the benchmark for project acceptance. The "benchmark" in this case means the maximum number of time periods it will take to recover the full cost of a project. Thus, if it takes seven years to recover the cost of a project, it is the time that should be used as benchmark for the project. However, the time to recover the cost would vary from project to project, depending on the project size and the flow of funds. For instance, a small project with low positive net flow can take a much longer time to realize the full cost of investment than a large project with high positive net flow.

There are several advantages of using payback. First, it can help a government determine how fast it can recover the cost to avoid the problem of holding up cash for a long period of time. This is particularly important for governments that are strapped for cash. Second, it is flexible in that it can be used as a supplementary tool or in combination with other decision tools such as discounted cash flows. Third, and most important, it is simple to use since it requires only three sets of information: inflows, outflows, and the initial cost of investment.

To give an example, suppose that a county-run hospital wants to replace one of its old MRI machines with a new, state-of-the-art, equipment. The machine will be primarily used for outpatient services. Assume that the new machine will cost the government $1.35 million, including installation, which is a one-time cost. Let us further assume that it will produce a cash flow (inflow minus outflow) from operation of $450,000 year for the duration of the life of the machine. To find the payback period, we simply divide the cost of the machine by the annual cash flow, which will be 3 years, that is, $1,350,000/$450,000 = 3 years. In reality, cash flows are seldom constant; they vary over time. Let us now suppose that the hospital expects to recover the cost from the operation of the machine at different amounts. Table 9.1 shows the expected cash flows from the machine operation.

As shown in the table above, it will take the government a little over 3 years to recover the cost of the project, which is the payback period. However, looking at the cash flows, it appears that the project will continue to produce positive return

Table 9.1 Expected outflow, inflow, net flow, and cumulative net flow

Year	Outflow ($)	Cash flow ($)	Cumulative net flow ($)	Cumulative net flow (with cost of funds) ($)
0	(1,350,000)	–	(1,350,000)	(1,350,000)
1	–	310,000	(1,040,000)	(1,175,000)
2	–	425,000	(615,000)	(867,500)
3	–	545,000	(70,000)	(409,250)
4	–	550,000	480,000	99,825
5	–	495,000	975,000	–

beyond the payback period. As noted earlier, payback period is not concerned about what happens once the cost has been recovered. This is a major weakness of the method since it fails to take into account the returns that most projects continue to generate beyond the period of cost recovery.

Cost of Funds in Payback Calculation

Payback has a couple of other weaknesses, in addition to the one mentioned above. One, it takes a fragmented approach to project investment. What this means is that it does not consider the overall liquidity of cash-flow position (the ease with which an asset can be converted to cash) of a government; rather, it focuses on the cash flow resulting from a single project. Two, it frequently fails to consider the cost of funds necessary to support an investment, even during the payback period. Cost of fund is the return on an investment after all the adjustments have been made for costs. This is an important factor that should not be ignored in payback calculation because it could result in underestimating the payback.

To illustrate how one would incorporate the cost of funds into payback calculation, let us look at the cumulative net flow column in Table 9.1. According to the table, the net flow for the current year (t_0) is negative $1.35 million since there is no cash inflow during this period. Let us assume that the hospital would like to have a return of 10% on this investment. Therefore, at a return rate of 10% on $1.35 million, the cost of funds corresponding to the net flow in the first year would be $135,000, obtained by multiplying the net flow by the rate of return ($1,350,000 \times 0.10$). Now, to obtain the cumulative net flow for the first year, we simply add this cost of fund to the net flow of $1,350,000 and then subtract the total from the cash flow for the first year, which will produce a cumulative net flow of $1,175,000, as shown below:

$$
\begin{aligned}
CNF_{t+1} &= [CNF_0 + (CNF_0 \times RR)] - INF_{t+1} \\
&= \left[\$1,350,000 + (\$1,350,000 \times 0.10)\right] - \$310,000 \\
&= \$1,485,000 - \$310,000 \\
&= \$1,175,000
\end{aligned}
\tag{9.1}
$$

where CNF is cumulative net flow in the first year $(t+1)$, RR is the return rate, and INF is the inflow in the first year $(t+1)$.

It is worth noting that taking the cost of funds into consideration will increase the cumulative net flow by $135,000 in the first year, from $1,040,000 to $1,175,000, which means that it will increase the payback period. In other words, it will take a little longer to recover the cost of the machine. We can repeat the computation for the second year, which will produce a cumulative net flow of $867,500; that is,

$$
\begin{aligned}
CNF_{t+2} &= [CNF_1 + (CNF_1 \times RR)] - INF_{t+2} \\
&= \left[\$1,175,000 + (\$1,175,000 \times 0.10)\right] - \$425,000 \\
&= \$1,295,500 - \$425,000 \\
&= \$867,500
\end{aligned}
$$

and continue to repeat the process until the costs are fully recovered.

As shown in Table 9.1, the recovery period, when the cost of funds is included, will be approximately the fourth year, not the third year. In other words, if we did not consider the cost of funds we would have underestimated the payback period by close to a year. It is important to note that since the cash flows take place over a period of time into the future, it would be useful to adjust (discount) the flows for the time value of money, which may change the recovery period further.

9.2.2   Cost-Benefit Analysis

One of the oldest and most widely used methods for evaluating public projects is cost-benefit analysis (CBA) dating back to at least the seventeenth century when Sir William Petty introduced it as an operational tool, while studying the public health cost of combating the plague in London, England in 1667 (Thompson 1982). It was popularized by Jules Dupit, a nineteenth-century French economist, and subsequently by other European economists, such as Pareto, Kaldor, Hicks, and others. In the United States, it achieved statutory authority with the passage of two pieces of legislation early in the nineteenth century, the River and Harbor Act of 1902 and the Flood Control of 1936. In the 1950s, the Interagency Committee on Water Resources tried to use it to evaluate economic decisions. In 1952, the Bureau of Budget (BOB) adopted its own set of criteria for appraising public projects. With the advent of President Lyndon Johnson's Great Society Program in the mid-1960s, CBA formally entered the public decision-making arena. In 1965, when PPBS was officially introduced, CBA became an integral part of it and twelve years later when ZBB was introduced by the Office of Management and Budget (OMB), it retained some of the elements of cost-benefit analysis. Although PPBS did not have a good record of success, it did lay out the foundations for spreading the benefits of CBA at all levels of government.

Considering its long history, cost-benefit analysis still remains the single most important method for evaluating public projects. When resources are scarce and the demand for public projects exceeds the available resources, the rational choice for a decision maker is to undertake those projects that will produce the greatest amount of return (benefits) for the resources utilized (costs). This fundamental rule of efficiency that guides the allocation decision of a household or firm also guides the allocation decision of a government when considering competing needs of its jurisdiction.

9.2.2.1 Steps in Cost-Benefit Analysis
Like most decision tools, cost-benefit analysis follows a structured process involving a number of distinct steps. These steps typically include (1) define the goals and objectives an organization is trying to achieve, (2) select one or more projects for evaluation, (3) determine the costs and benefits associated with each project, (4) evaluate the projects, and (5) select the project or projects.

Define Goals and Objectives

All cost-benefit analysis begins with a clear statement of goals and objectives. Unlike the private sector, where the goals are generally stated in terms of maximizing profit for a firm or business, defining goals and objectives for government is much more complex. The complexity arises from the imprecise and often conflicting nature of the goals a government tries to achieve as well as the projects whose costs and benefits are not always easy to measure. However, in situations where a government functions like a business organization such as providing a good or service for a price, it is possible to apply some of the same behavioral rules of market operations to define the goals and objectives. On the other hand, in situations where a government cannot function like a business organization, that is, sell goods and services for a price such as national security or local public safety, it must base its decisions on the objectives that underlie the service provision rather than on the financial criteria. In other words, it is not the financial, but the social or collective goal that a government tries to achieve must serve as the principle determining factor in making public decisions. Thus, social goal or objective which serves as the basis for most public decisions must also provide the foundation for cost-benefit analysis.

Given that collective or social objectives must provide the basis for most public decisions, the question then is how does one define and measure these objectives. Unfortunately, there is no cut-and-dried answer to the question; nevertheless, the discussion on the subject has led to two strands of arguments over time (Mishan 1981). The first strand, which is deeply rooted in mainstream welfare economics, states that cost-benefit analysis must be based on a set of normative considerations as to what social objectives ought to be. The underlying notion here is that these objectives can be obtained from a consensus on value judgments of the individuals who make up the society. However, generating consensus on value judgments is extremely difficult, if not impossible, in that one cannot simply add, say, individual welfare to produce the aggregate welfare of society (Arrow 1959). According to the second strand, social objectives can be defined as those pursued by someone who is responsible for making decisions that affect society at large and who is also accountable to the public for those decisions. From this point of view, cost-benefit analysis is a process of appraising decision problems, as viewed by a decision maker or a group of decision makers who hold the same view of society and how its welfare is measured. This is more consistent with the logic used in financial decision making in the private sector and is the one used in the current discussion.

Select a Project or Projects for Evaluation

Once the goals and objectives have been defined, the next step in the process is to identify and select the project or projects for evaluation. Theoretically, there is no limit as to the number of projects a government can consider at any given time, but, in practice, it depends on the goals and objectives of the government, as well as the resources the projects will consume and the benefits the projects will produce. Two things are necessary during this stage: first, a clear distinction between the types of projects that are being considered for evaluation (mutually exclusive, not mutually exclusive, independent, dependent, and so forth) because the decision rules for project acceptance are not necessarily the same for different types of projects, and second, projects should not be lumped together unless there are no restrictions on project selection other than cost. For instance, purchasing a patrol vehicle is not the same as constructing a bridge or highway, although both are defined as capital projects.

Determine the Costs and Benefits Associated with Each Project

The central problem in any cost-benefit analysis is not how many projects are selected for consideration, but rather how one values the costs and benefits associated with each project. In government, where one has difficulty in measuring social objectives, the tasks of valuing costs and benefits of a public project can be a real challenge for the decision makers. From a practical point of view, however, one can always use the private sector experience as a starting point, where dollar values are commonly used for measuring costs and benefits. In situations where it is difficult to readily use dollar terms, especially for projects with intangible costs and benefits, it may be necessary to use proxy variables such as the amount of property damage prevented by local fire service or the amount of money saved in hospital care from the early vaccination of children, and so forth, so that one is able to use dollar values. However, care should be exercised when using proxy or surrogate variables, as they may not reflect the true measures of costs and benefits associated with the problem under consideration.

Evaluate the Project(s)

Once the goals and objectives have been defined, projects have been identified for evaluation, and some determinations have been made as to their costs and benefits, the next step in the process is to evaluate the projects. The convention is to use one or more criteria by which to analyze and compare the projects. Comparison makes it possible for the decision makers to assess the merit of each project individually or against each other before selecting the one that will meet the goals and objectives of the organization.

Select the Project(s)

The process completes with the selection of the project or projects.

9.2.2.2 Measures for Evaluating Costs and Benefits

The primary concern in cost-benefit analysis is deciding what measures to use when evaluating a project. The decision is particularly important in government where projects vary sharply in characteristics, as well as in size and the effect a particular measure can have on project evaluation. Four sets of measures are generally used in cost-benefit analysis: net benefit (NB), benefit-cost ratio (B:C), net present value (NPV), and internal rate of return (IRR). In each case, the decision is generally based on the rule that for a project to be considered for acceptance its benefits must outweigh its costs, although in theory a government can accept projects as long as their benefits equal their costs (since governments are not in the business of making profit). From a practical point of view, however, it does not make much sense if the investment in a project does not produce any net gain to society.

Let us briefly look at these measures in some details.

Net Benefit

Net benefit (NB) is the difference between benefits a project will produce (total benefits) and the costs it will incur (total costs) over its life span. According to this, a project is considered acceptable if its net benefit is positive; that is, the sum of its benefits exceeds the sum of its costs. If more than one project is involved, the decision rule is to select the one that produces the highest net benefit, assuming the projects are mutually exclusive. If they are not mutually exclusive, then select the projects as long as their net benefits are positive; in other words, the sum of their benefits exceeds the sum of their costs.

We can formally express net benefit as

$$\text{NB}_i^j = \sum_{i=1}^{n} B_i^j - \sum_{i=1}^{n} C_i^j \tag{9.2}$$

where NB is the net benefit for project j, B and C are benefit and cost, respectively, for the ith benefit and cost (for $i = 1, 2, \ldots\ldots, n$), corresponding to project j.

To give an example, suppose that a government wants to renovate its civic arena which is used for hosting various public events. Let us say that the renovation will include the following: (1) replace the existing heating system, (2) increase the seating capacity by 10%, and (3) complete a number of other repairs to upgrade the facility. The government believes that the improvement will significantly increase its revenue, reduce maintenance costs, and will be cost-effective in the long run than constructing an entirely new facility. The decision facing the government is to determine if the economic benefits from the project will be worth the outlay. Since the problem deals with a single project, the only requirement is to determine whether to accept or reject the project Table 9.2 shows the benefits and costs associated with the project.

As shown in the table, it will cost the government approximately $3.55 million to renovate the facility. The total yearly benefit from the renovation will be $1.39 million (assuming the project will have a useful life of several years), thus producing a net negative benefit of $2.16 million in the first year ($1,390,000 − $3,550,000). The negative benefit will decline to $0.77 million in the second year [($1,390,000 × 2) − $3,550,000), but in the third year, it will produce a net positive benefit of $0.62 million [($1,390,000 × 3) − $3,550,000 = $4,170,000 − $3,550,000 = $620,000] and, in all likelihood, will continue to produce positive benefits for most of the remaining years of its useful life.

Benefit-Cost Ratio

Benefit-cost ratio (B:C)[1] measures the return one will earn for each dollar worth of investment. According to this, a project is considered acceptable if it produces

Table 9.2 Net-benefit calculation for project renovation

Description of costs and benefits	Costs and benefits ($)
Direct costs	
Replacing the heating system	650,000 (One-time)
Increasing the seating capacity	2,750,000 (One-time)
Indirect costs	
Other repairs for upgrading	150,000 (One-time)
Total Cost	3,550,000 (One time)
Direct benefits	
Increase in revenue	1,250,000 (Annual)
Indirect benefits	
Savings on energy cost	125,000 (Annual)
Savings on maintenance costs	15,000 (Annual)
Total Benefits	1,390,000 (Annual)
Net benefit	
First-year differential	−2,160,000[1]
Second-year differential	−770,000[2]
Third-year differential	+$620,000[3]

[1]$1,390,000 − $3,550,000 = −2,160,000
[2]($1,390,000 × 2) − $3,550,000 = $2,780,000 − $3,550,000 = −$770,000
[3]($1,390,000 × 3) − $3,550,000 = $4,170,000 − $3,550,000 = +$620,000

a B:C of greater than 1; that is, B:C > 1. For instance, a benefit-cost ratio of 1.65 ($1.65/$1.00) means a return of $1.65 for each dollar invested, with a net gain of 65 cents ($1.65 − $1.00), while a ratio of 0.65 ($0.65/$1.00) would indicate a net loss of 35 cents ($0.65 − $1.00). When more than one project is involved, the decision rule is to accept the one with the highest positive ratio, assuming the projects are mutually exclusive. If they are not mutually exclusive, then select the projects with positive benefit-cost ratios.

Formally, it can be expressed as

$$\text{B:C}_j = \sum_{i=1}^{n} B_i^j \Big/ \sum_{i=1}^{n} C_i^j \qquad (9.3)$$

where B:C_j is the benefit-cost ratio for project j, and the rest of terms are the same as before.

Consider a case where a government is looking into six relatively small, but mutually exclusive projects for downtown redevelopment. Since the projects are mutually exclusive, only one of the six projects can be accepted but we do not know which one. Suppose that the government is indifferent between the projects, as long as the selected project produces the highest positive return. Since the focus is on the highest positive return for the capital invested, we will use benefit-cost ratio as a measure for acceptability. Table 9.3 shows the relevant data on benefit-cost ratio for each project.

A quick glance at the table would indicate that all six projects except one, Project D, meet the minimum requirement for acceptance since they all have a B:C of at least 1. However, when the projects are ranked according to their B:C the order changes: Project B comes up on top with a ratio of 2.57, followed by Project E with a ratio of 2.01, Project F with a ratio of 1.65, and so forth. Given that the projects are mutually exclusive, that is, only one of the five projects which meets the minimum requirement for acceptance, which is Project B since it has the highest B:C. In other words, the government should select Project B for redevelopment.

Let us relax the assumption that the projects are mutually exclusive; instead, assume that they are not mutually exclusive in that the selection of one will not preclude the selection of any other. With the assumption relaxed, it appears that all five projects would qualify for acceptance since they all meet the minimum acceptance requirement of B:C>1 and it will cost the government $12.025 million to undertake all five projects. Consider now for a moment that our government has a budget constraint that restricts the maximum allowable expenditure on downtown redevelopment to $11 million. Therefore, given the amount of resources available, it can undertake only four of the five projects: B, E, F, and C, in that order, at a cost of $10.675 million without exceeding the budget. However, if we lower the constraint, say, to $6 million, only three of the projects—B, E, and F—can be considered without exceeding the budget, and so forth. It should be worth noting that the order of projects is important in cost-benefit analysis in that where a project stands in a rank order determines whether or not it will be accepted.

While B:C produces a relatively accurate measure for acceptability, it may not always be useful for comparing acceptable projects. Consider a government that is looking into two alternatives for disposing toxic wastes. Alternative 1 is a toxic waste dump that produces a benefit worth $200 million and costs the government $100 million, thereby producing a B:C of 2.0. Alternative 2 involves sending the wastes to a distant location outside the jurisdiction of the government. It produces

Table 9.3 Benefit-cost ratio for downtown redevelopment projects

Project	Cost ($)	Benefit ($)	B:C	Project rankings	Cost ($)	Cumulative cost ($)
A	1,350,000	1,450,000	1.07	B (R1)	1,460,000	1,460,000
B	1,460,000	3,750,000	2.57	E (R2)	2,350,000	3,810,000
C	5,325,000	6,825,000	1.28	F (R3)	1,540,000	5,350,000
D	2,175,000	1,650,000	0.76	C (R4)	5,325,000	10,675,000
E	2,350,000	4,740,000	2.01	A (R5)	1,350,000	12,025,000
F	1,540,000	2,540,000	1.65	D (R6)	2,175,000	14,200,000

a benefit of $150 million and costs the government $100 million with a B:C ratio of 1.5.

Obviously, Alternative 1 is preferable because it has the higher benefit-cost ratio of the two. However, we could add a constraint to the scenario for Alternative 1 by suggesting that it would produce a seepage-induced crop damage of $25 million, which will bring the benefit-cost ratio down to 1.75 [($200m − $25m)/$100 m = $175m/$100m = 1.75], but will still be higher than the benefit-cost ratio for Alternative 2 and the toxic dump should be preferred. Interestingly, twenty-five million dollars can also be considered as an increase in cost, in which case the B:C would be 1.6 [$200m/($100m + $25m) = $200m/$125m = 1.6]. If we further assume that the seepage-induced crop damage would be higher than $25 million then, in all likelihood, Alternative 2 will be the preferred choice. In sum, B:C can lead to incorrect decisions, depending on how one calculates costs and benefits and what is included in those calculations.

Net Present Value

Most public projects, including the ones discussed above, have useful lives that extend over several years. This means that one cannot simply compare the dollar amounts from different periods because the value of money, called the time value of money, does not remain constant over time. It decreases with increasing time. Inflation, if nothing else, contributes to this general decline in the value of money. However, the problem can be easily resolved by using a simple concept called present value (PV). Present value is the current value of a future stream of money (costs and benefits). Since money generally loses its value over time, the present value is usually less than or equal to the future value.

To give an example, suppose that a government wants to invest an amount, X, today, $t = 0$, at an interest rate of 5% that will produce exactly $100 next year, $t + 1$, what would be the present value of $100? It will be $95.24. That is,

$$
\begin{aligned}
X(1 + r)^{t+1} &= \$100 \\
X(1 + 0.05)^1 &= \$100 \\
X &= \$100/(1 + 0.05)^1 \\
&= \$100/1.05 \\
&= \$95.24
\end{aligned}
\tag{9.4}
$$

In other words, $100 next year will be worth $95.24 today, which is the same as saying that if the government had invested $95.24 today at an interest rate of 5%, it would be worth $100 next year. Put differently, the $100 next year would be the future value (FV) of $95.24, a year from now. That is,

$$
\begin{aligned}
FV_{t+1} &= PV_t(1 + r)^{t+1} \\
&= \$95.24(1 + 0.05)^1 \\
&= \$95.24/(1.05) \\
&= \$100.00
\end{aligned}
\tag{9.5}
$$

Interestingly, we could have also expressed PV in terms of FV, so that

$$
\begin{aligned}
PV_t &= FV_{t+1}/(1+r)^{t+1} \\
&= \$100/(1+0.05)^1 \\
&= \$100/(1.05) \\
&= \$95.24
\end{aligned}
\tag{9.6}
$$

Going back to the example, the present value of $100 two years from now, $t+2$, in terms of FV, will be

$$
\begin{aligned}
PV_t &= FV_{t+2}/(1+r)^{t+2} \\
&= \$100/(1+0.05)^2 \\
&= \$100/(1.05)^2 \\
&= \$100/(1.1025) \\
&= \$90.70
\end{aligned}
$$

and, as before, the FV of $90.70, two years from now, $t+2$, will be

$$
\begin{aligned}
FV_{t+2} &= PV_t(1+r)^{t+2} \\
&= \$90.70(1+0.05)^2 \\
&= \$90.70(1.1025) \\
&= \$99.997
\end{aligned}
$$

or $\approx\$100.00$. Similarly, the PV of $100 three years from now, $t+3$, will be $86.38; that is, $PV_t = FV_{t+3}/(1+r)^{t+3} = \$100/(1+0.05)^3 = \$100/(1.1576) = \$86.38$, and so forth.

In general, when the interest rate is given by r, the present value of a future stream of money in t years is $\$V(1+r)^t$, where $\$V$ is the value of money at any future point in time, and t is the tth time period (for $t=1, 2,\ldots\ldots, T$). Thus, even without inflation, a dollar in the future is worth less than a dollar today and, as such, must be discounted by an amount equal to the return (interest) rate. The rate at which future returns are discounted to their present value is called the discount rate (DR). We can now extend this notion to calculate the present value of a future stream of costs and benefits, and if we take their differences, the result will be net present value (NPV).

Net present value, therefore, is the discounted net benefit, adjusted for time value of money, and is expressed as

$$
NPV_j = \sum_{t=0}^{T} \frac{B_t^j}{(1+r)^t} - \sum_{t=0}^{T} \frac{C_t^j}{(1+r)^t}
\tag{9.7}
$$

Expanded, we can write Eq. 9.7 as

$$NPV_j = \left[\frac{B_0^j}{(1+r)^0} + \frac{B_1^j}{(1+r)^1} + \frac{B_2^j}{(1+r)^2} + \cdots + \frac{B_T^j}{(1+r)^T} \right]$$
$$- \left[\frac{C_0^j}{(1+r)^0} + \frac{C_1^j}{(1+r)^1} + \frac{C_2^j}{(1+r)^2} + \cdots + \frac{C_T^j}{(1+r)^T} \right] \quad (9.8)$$

where NPV_j is the net present value of project j, r is the discount rate, t is the time stream (for $t=0, 1, 2,\ldots\ldots, T$), and B_t and C_t are the benefit and cost stream at time t, respectively.

For computational purposes, we can further write the expression in Eq. 9.8 as

$$NPV_j = \left[B_0^j \frac{1}{(1+r)^0} + B_1^j \frac{1}{(1+r)^1} + B_2^j \frac{1}{(1+r)^2} + \cdots + B_T^j \frac{1}{(1+r)^T} \right]$$
$$- \left[C_0^j \frac{1}{(1+r)^0} + C_1^j \frac{1}{(1+r)^1} + C_2^j \frac{1}{(1+r)^2} + \cdots + C_T^j \frac{1}{(1+r)^T} \right] \quad (9.9)$$

where $1/(1+r)^t$ is the discount factor (DF), which, when multiplied by the corresponding benefits and costs, will produce the discounted streams of benefits and costs, in other words, the present value of benefits and costs.

The decision rule for a project to be considered acceptable when using NPV is that it must be positive. For more than one project and assuming the projects are mutually exclusive, the rule is to select the project with the highest NPV; if they are not mutually exclusive, then select the projects with positive NPVs.

If there is a salvage value at the end of the useful life of a project, Eq. 9.7 can be written as

$$NPV_j = \left[\sum_{t=0}^{T} \frac{B_t^j}{(1+r)^t} + \frac{SV_T^j}{(1+r)^T} \right] - \sum_{t=0}^{T} \frac{C_t^j}{(1+r)^t} \quad (9.10)$$

where SV is the salvage value at time T, and the rest of the terms are the same as before.

If, instead of having a stream of costs, we have one-time cost with no salvage value, Eq. 9.10 will become

$$NPV_j = \sum_{t=0}^{T} \frac{B_t^j}{(1+r)^T} - C_0^j \quad (9.11)$$

where C_0 is one-time cost, and the rest of the terms are the same as before.

It should be pointed out that one-time cost means that there are no subsequent costs a project would incur other than the costs of normal repair and maintenance. Ideally, these costs should be treated as part of the operating cost for a government. However, if costs occur over the entire length of a project's useful life and

Table 9.4 Net present value calculation for the two construction projects

Project A

Year	Outlay ($)	Benefits ($)	DF[a]	PV of benefits ($)
0	10,000,000	–	1.0000	–
1	–	1,750,000	0.9434	1,650,950
2	–	3,850,000	0.8900	3,426,500
3	–	4,625,000	0.8396	3,883,150
4	–	2,575,000	0.7921	2,039,658
5	–	1,950,000	0.7473	1,457,235
6	–	1,435,000	0.7050	1,011,675
Total	$10,000,000	$16,185,000	–	$13,469,168

Project B

Year	Outlay ($)	Benefit (S)	DF	PV of benefits (S)
0	10,000,000	–	1.0000	–
1	–	1,900,000	0.9434	1,792,460
2	–	2,650,000	0.8900	2,358,500
3	–	3,750,000	0.8396	3,148,500
4	–	4,525,000	0.7921	3,584,253
5	–	3,850,000	0.7473	2,877,105
6	–	2,695,000	0.7050	1,899,975
Total	$10,000,000	$19,370,000	–	$15,660,793
$NPV_A =$	$3,469,168			$B{:}C_A = 1.3469$
$NPV_B =$	$5,660,793			$B{:}C_B = 1.4237$

[a]Based on 6% rate of discount

can be treated as outflows, they can be discounted the same way as one would discount a stream of benefits.

Consider a case where a government is looking into two mutually exclusive construction projects, A and B, each with a life span of 6 years. Let us say that the initial cost of construction for both projects is the same at $10 million (although we could have assumed a different initial cost for each), but they produce different amounts of benefits over their life spans. Assume a discount rate of 6%. The decision problem facing the government is to select the project that would produce the higher positive NPV of the two. Table 9.4 shows the streams of discounted benefits for both projects, along with their corresponding NPV and B:C. Since the projects have one-time cost only, there was no need to discount it.

According to the table, Project B has a higher NPV, as well as a higher discounted B:C ratio than Project A, which means that it is the one the government should select. In the example presented above, Project A was high on both NPV and B:C, which makes it relatively simple to decide which one to accept, but that may not always be the case. Assume for a moment that one project has a higher

NPV and a lower B:C such that there is no clear choice, in which case it will be up to the decision makers to make a value judgment whether the return on a dollar worth of investment is more important than a positive net present value, and vice versa.

Internal Rate of Return

Finally, the internal rate of return is the rate at which the sum of a discounted stream of benefits equals the sum of a discounted stream of costs such that the two sides will break even. In other words, it is the rate that equates the net present value to zero and is given by the expression

$$
\text{NPV}_j: \sum_{t=0}^{T} \frac{B_t^j}{(1+i)^t} = \sum_{t=0}^{T} \frac{C_t^j}{(1+i)^t}
$$

$$
\text{or} \sum_{t=0}^{T} \frac{B_t^j}{(1+i)^t} - \sum_{t=0}^{T} \frac{C_t^j}{(1+i)^t} = 0
\tag{9.12}
$$

where NPV_j is the net present value for the jth project, i is the internal rate that equates the NPV to 0, and the rest of the terms are the same as before.

It should be worth noting that the notation i is deliberately used in Eq. 9.12 to distinguish it from r because when i is used one can compare it to r to see whether a project will produce a positive or negative NPV. In general, when $i>r$, the NPV is positive and when it is less r, $i<r$, the NPV is negative. Operationally, IRR can be defined as the rate that sets the present value of a stream of cash flows for a project equal to the initial investment outlay. For most projects, it is expected that the net cash flows from operation over time will be higher than the initial investment to justify the project selection. In general, the higher the cash flows relative to the initial investment, the greater will be the IRR and the project will be worth undertaking.

Formally, we can write it as

$$
\sum_{t=1}^{T} \frac{CF_t^j}{(1+i)^t} = I_0
$$

$$
-I_0 + \sum_{t=1}^{T} \frac{CF_t^j}{(1+i)^t} = 0
\tag{9.13}
$$

Expanded, we can further write Eq. 9.13 as

$$
-I_0 + \frac{CF_1^j}{(1+i)^1} + \frac{CF_2^j}{(1+i)^2} + \frac{CF_3^j}{(1+i)^3} + \cdots + \frac{CF_T^j}{(1+i)^T} = 0
\tag{9.14}
$$

where I_0 is the initial investment or outlay at time $t=0$, CF is the cash flow at time t, and the rest of the terms are the same, as before.

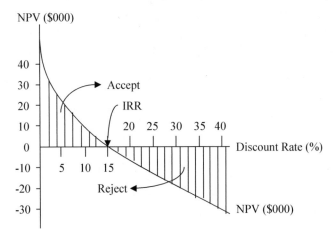

Fig. 9.1 A diagrammatic representation of IRR

There is an advantage of using IRR, as opposed to NPV, although the latter is most frequently used in cost-benefit analysis in that IRR can be quite effective if the decision makers do not have a priori knowledge of the discount rate since it can be empirically determined through a process of trial and error, as can be seen in Fig. 9.1. As shown in the figure, the internal rate of return at which the NPV becomes 0 is 15.0%. The figure also shows that there is an inverse relationship between NPV and the discount rate in that the higher the discount rate the lower the net present value, and vice versa.

However, for smaller problems involving two or three time periods it is possible to determine this rate algebraically using the expression in Eq. 9.13; as such, one does not have to use trial and error, which can be exhausting. To give an example, suppose that we have a project with a life span of two years, 0 and 1, where 0 represents current year (the year the project is undertaken) and 1 the next year, with corresponding cash flows of $-\$100$ and $\$110$. Since the NPV is 0 for IRR, we can present the discounted cash flows for the project as

$$-\$100 + \frac{\$110}{(1+i)} = 0$$

With slight algebraic manipulations, such as multiplying both sides of the above expression by $(1+i)$ and rearranging the results, we can easily obtain the value of i as

$$-\$100(1+i) + \$110 = 0$$
$$-\$100 - \$100i + \$110 = 0$$
$$\$10 - \$100i = 0$$
$$\$10 = \$100i$$
$$0.1 = i$$

or $i = 0.1$, which is 10%. To see if the rate produces a net present value of 0, we can plug in the value of i and calculate the NPV for the project; that is, $-\$100(1+i)^0 + \$110(1+i)^{-1} = -\$100(1+0.10)^0 + \$110(1+0.10)^{-1} = -\$100(1) + \$110(0.909) = -\$100 + \$100 = 0$, which it does, as the case should be.

Assume now that the project has a life span of three years, including the current year (0, 1, 2), and we have the following cash flows corresponding to 0, 1, and 2: $-\$100, \$60$, and $\$75$. As before, we set it first as a discounted cash-flow problem

$$-\$100 + \frac{\$60}{(1+i)^1} + \frac{\$75}{(1+i)^2} = 0$$

and then multiply both sides by $(1+i)^2$, so that

$$-\$100(1+i)^2 + \frac{\$60}{(1+i)^1}(1+i)^2 + \frac{\$75}{(1+i)^2}(1+i)^2 = 0(1+i)^2$$

$$-\$100(1+i)^2 + \$60(1+i) + \$75 = 0$$

which produces a quadratic equation. Now, solving it using the standard procedure for a quadratic equation, we get

$$
\begin{aligned}
(1+i) &= \frac{-b \pm \sqrt{b^2 - 4ac}}{2a} \\
&= \frac{-60 \pm \sqrt{(60)^2 - 4(-100)(75)}}{2(-100)} \\
&= \frac{-60 \pm 183.3}{-200}
\end{aligned}
\tag{9.15}
$$

$$(1+i) = -243.3/-200 = 1.2165, \text{ and}$$
$$(1+i) = 123.2/-200 = -0.6165$$

The second value can be easily ignored since a negative discount rate makes no sense.[2] Therefore, the correct rate will be $(1+i) = 1.2165$, that is, $i = 1.2165 - 1 = 0.2165$ (21.65%). Although it may appear quite simple, finding the rate beyond two or three-year period can be problematic because it will require the use of higher-order polynomials, which will not be easy to solve by hand. The alternative is to use a trial-and-error procedure or use any standard spreadsheet such as Excel.

In general, a high IRR is associated with high early returns, indicating that benefits will occur at a faster rate during the early years of a project's useful life and then decline as time progresses. By the same token, a low IRR would indicate a gradual increase in benefits with higher returns taking place toward the later years and declining as time progresses. Thus, if the objective is to realize as much return as possible in the early years of a project's useful life, then a project with high IRR should be selected. This may partly explain why firms and businesses have traditionally preferred IRR over NPV for a long time since it is to the advantage of the owners or stockholders to know when the returns will be highest for their investments and when they will begin to decline, although the trend has changed considerably in recent years in favor of NPV.

However, project selection based on internal rate of return can be misleading, especially when projects vary in size. Consider a government looking into two projects, A and B, where Project A requires an initial expenditure of $100 and yields a return of $108 a year from now, so that its IRR is 8%.[3] Project B, on the other hand, requires an initial expenditure of $1000 and produces a return of $1070 a year from now, generating an IRR of 7%.[4] Assume that neither project can be duplicated and that the government has the option to borrow at 6% rate of interest. Thus, if the government were to use IRR, Project A should be preferred to Project B since it produces a net positive return of $2 ($8−$6 in interest cost on an initial expenditure of $100), which is closer to 0 than Project B's net return of $10 ($70−$60 in interest cost on the initial expenditure of $1000). Although, theoretically, Project A should be selected if one has to go by IRR; in reality, Project B should be preferred because it has a much higher (absolute) return for the same period. Therefore, when projects are of different sizes, the IRR does not always serve as an ideal guide. On the other hand, the NPV provides a more realistic scenario in terms of the actual situation.

Overall, IRR works better when projects share the same discount rate, have predictable cash flows, and have a shorter life span. However, when the discount rate changes, which is a common occurrence for longer-life projects or when there are multiple positive and negative cash flows, it is not an effective measure since it cannot account for changes in the rates without modifications.

A Note on Modified Internal Rate of Return

As noted earlier, IRR does not work well if there are multiple positive and negative cash flows, especially where borrowing rate may differ from investment rate, in which case the alternative is to use a modified IRR, called MIRR, in short. It is given by the expression

$$MIRR = \left[\left(\sum_{t=1}^{T-1} FV_{\text{Inflows}} + \text{Inflow}_T \right) \Big/ (-) \left(\sum_{t=0}^{T} PV_{\text{Outflows}} \right) \right]^{1/T} - 1 \quad (9.16)$$

$$= \left[\left(\sum_{t=1}^{T-1} (\text{Inflows})(1+r)^t + \text{Inflow}_T \right) \Big/ (-) \left(\sum_{t=0}^{T} \frac{\text{Outflows}}{(1+r)^t} \right) \right]^{1/T} - 1$$

where FV is the future value, given by $(\text{inflows})(1+r)^t$, PV is the present value, given by $(\text{outflows})/(i+r)^t$, and t is the time period that ranges from 0 to T.

To give an example, let us look at the project we discussed earlier under IRR with a life span of three years (0, 1, 2) and the following cash flows: −$100, $60, $75, where the first value represents the cash outflow at time 0 (current period) and the last two values represent the cash inflows at times 1 and 2 (remaining periods), with an IRR of 21.65%. Suppose that the government borrowed the funds to finance the project at 8% (borrowing rate), which will produce a present value of cash outflow of $-\$100$; that is, $PV_{Outflow} = -\$100/(1+0.08)^0 = -\$100$. Suppose further that the rate on the cash inflows is 10%, which is the investment rate (assuming the funds can be invested or reinvested). This will produce a future value of positive cash flow (through the end of the last period) of \$141; that is, $FV_{Inflows} = (\$60)(1+0.1)^1 + \$75 = \$66 + \$75 = \$141$. The resultant MIRR will be $[\$141/(-)(-\$100)]^{1/3} - 1 = (\$141/\$100)^{1/3} - 1 = 1.1213 - 1 = 0.1213$ or 12.13%. As expected, the MIRR < IRR (12.13% < 21.65%).

9.2.2.3   Comparisons of B:C, NPV, and IRR

Although all four measures (NB, B:C, NPV, and IRR) discussed above are useful, there are some fundamental differences among them that are worth noting here, especially those related to B:C, NPV, and IRR. Net present value generally provides an absolute measure of a project's worth, whereas both B:C and IRR provide a relative measure of the viability of a project. In particular, NPV shows the dollar amount by which a project's discounted benefits exceed its discounted costs. On the other hand, B:C shows the ratio of (discounted) benefits to (discounted) costs, and IRR shows a return percentage. Therefore, decision makers looking to rank projects must have a clear notion as to what they are looking for in a project since the conclusions will likely be different if they are using absolute measures, as opposed to relative measures.

9.2.3   Cost-Effectiveness Analysis

An important requirement of cost-benefit analysis is that one must be able to express the benefits and costs in monetary terms. However, expressing costs and benefits, in particular, the latter in dollar terms is not always possible, especially where the benefits are intangible in nature. The difficulty lies in determining how to assign dollar values that will reflect the true measures of these benefits. For instance, how would one assign dollar values to the benefits a public safety program produces for children or to the improvement in public welfare a particular social policy generates for certain income groups? When benefits are difficult to measure in monetary terms the alternative is to use cost-effectiveness analysis that does not require one to convert benefits in dollar terms. In cost-effectiveness analysis, as in cost-benefit analysis, costs are presented in monetary terms, while the benefits are presented by the amount of non-monetary effects a project produces for a given cost, rather than by its dollar value. The objective, however, is the same in that it purports to select the best alternative from several possible choices. The only difference is that in cost-effectiveness analysis the comparison is made in terms of costs and their effectiveness without the requirement of expressing the latter in dollar terms (Quade 1982).

9.2.3.1 Cost-Effectiveness Ratio

Like the benefit-cost ratio (B:C), in cost-benefit analysis the cost-effectiveness of a project is measured by a ratio called cost-effectiveness ratio (C:E). It is determined by comparing the monetary effects of a project or program with its non-monetary effects and can be expressed as

$$C:E = \frac{C}{NME} \tag{9.17}$$

where C:E is the cost-effectiveness ratio, C is the cost or monetary effects, and NME is the non-monetary effect.

Looking at the expression in Eq. 9.17, one could see that there are some similarities between cost-effectiveness ratio and benefit-cost ratio in that both measure the effectiveness (benefits) of resources used in one or more projects in relation to the results they produce. However, unlike CBA, the decision rule for cost-effectiveness analysis does not revolve around a single measure, but rather, it depends explicitly on the goals and objectives a decision maker hopes to achieve from a given investment. To give an example, suppose that a government wants to build a neighborhood recreation center to reduce juvenile crimes. It will cost the government approximately \$250,000 to build the facility, but will reduce crime by 65% in the next five years. The cost-effectiveness ratio for the project will be \$250,000/65.0 = \$3,846.15. What this means is that it will cost the government on average \$3,846.15 to reduce the crime rate by 1%. Put simply, it is the cost per percentage reduction in crime for the neighborhood recreation center.

The method can be easily extended to compare multiple projects. When multiple projects are involved, the decision rule is similar to B:C in that select the project that produces the highest cost-effectiveness ratio (assuming the projects are comparable). If they are not comparable, they can be grouped into distinct categories based either on project characteristics or their aggregate costs.

Consider a case where a local school district is considering constructing a computer laboratory for one of its premier schools. Similar facilities have been built in a select number of school districts around the country, and student performance on math and science was tested on 1000 high school students with the newly introduced facility that produced varying results. Table 9.5 shows a three-year test result (average), including the most recent year, on a scale of 0 to 100 for five

Table 9.5 Cost-effectiveness analysis for computer learning facilities

School districts	Cost of the facility per 1000 students (\$)	Effectiveness measure (average performance score on a scale of 0 to 100)	C:E (\$/Score)
A	1,160,000	75	15,466.67
B	2,875,000	90	31,944.44
C	1,720,000	80	21,500.00
D	4,395,000	95	46,263.16
E	1,380,000	85	16,235.29

school districts, randomly selected, that have similar facilities (A, B, C, D, and E), along with their costs which include, among others, costs of equipment, instruction, operation and maintenance. According to the table, District A has the lowest cost-effectiveness ratio with a value of $15,466.67, which means that it will cost the district on average $15,466.67 for each successful score on a scale of 1 to 100. In other words, it is the cost per achievement score for District A. Similarly, it is $31,944.44 for District B, $21,500.00 for District C, and so forth.

The result produces an interesting dilemma for the decision makers in that the district that produces the best result, which is D, is also the most costly district. It costs almost $15,000 more for each additional score than District B, which has the second best performance. On the other hand, District E produces a reasonably good result (3rd highest) at a cost that is about one-third of the cost of District D. From a decision-making point of view, if cost is not a factor, the choice for the decision makers is obvious: Select District D, which costs more but produces the best performance, but if cost is an important consideration, which it is in most cost-benefit or cost-effectiveness analysis, then an acceptable alternative would be District E, which costs less but produces a reasonably good result.

Interestingly, the critical issue in cost-effectiveness analysis, as in cost-benefit analysis, is how to calculate the present value of cost-effectiveness, especially where the benefits or returns are intangible. This was not a problem in the current example because the results (performance scores) are measurable in terms that do not have a time dimension in the sense that the value of a test score does not increase or decrease relative to time, as monetary benefits or returns do. If the returns were expressed in terms that change in value over time, it would pose a real challenge for the decision makers. The alternative would be to discount them the same way one would discount a stream of costs and benefits. However, discounting a stream of intangible returns could pose an additional problem because of the difficulty in selecting a discount rate that would be appropriate.

9.2.4 Equivalent Annual Cost

There are situations in project evaluation where cost, more than benefit, is the primary consideration, in which case the method commonly used is the equivalent annual cost (EAC). EAC is the annual cost of acquiring, operating, and maintaining a physical asset over its useful life. The method is particularly suitable for comparing multiple projects with unequal lives, but with equal risks. The objective is to select one or more projects from a number of alternatives that would produce the greatest cost savings for an organization. This is where EAC has an advantage over cost-benefit analysis in that where in cost-benefit analysis the goal is to find the relative merits of a set of alternatives, in EAC the goal to find the alternative or mix of alternatives that would achieve the goal at the lowest cost.

The following presents an expression typically used in calculating EAC:

$$\text{EAC} = (\text{PC})[\frac{r}{1 - (1 + r)^{-t}}] + \text{MC} \tag{9.18}$$

where EAC is the equivalent annual cost, PC is project cost or the cost of an asset, r is the discount rate, and MC is the annual maintenance cost.

To give an example, consider a case where the federal Environmental Protection Agency (EPA) wants to purchase an analyzer for chemical analysis. It receives bids from two vendors, A and B. The bid cost for the analyzer by vendor A is \$150,000 with an annual maintenance cost of \$5000, while the bid cost for the analyzer by vendor B is \$175,000 with an annual maintenance cost of \$3000. The analyzer A has a useful life of 4 years and B a useful life of 5 years. Assume a discount rate of 8%. Now, applying the expression in Eq. 9.18, we obtain the following equivalent annual costs for the two analyzers:

$$EAC_A = (PC)\left[\frac{r}{1-(1+r)^{-t}}\right] + MC$$

$$= (\$150,000)\left[\frac{0.08}{1-(1+0.08)^{-4}}\right] + \$5000$$

$$= (\$150,000)\left[\frac{0.08}{1-0.7350}\right] + \$5000$$

$$= \left[(\$150,000)(0.3019)\right] + \$5000$$

$$= \$45,288 + \$5000$$

$$= \$50,288$$

for analyzer A, and

$$EAC_B = (PC)\left[\frac{r}{1-(1+r)^{-t}}\right] + MC$$

$$= (\$175,000)\left[\frac{0.08}{1-(1+0.08)^{-5}}\right] + \$3000$$

$$= (\$175,000)\left[\frac{0.08}{1-0.6806}\right] + \$3000$$

$$= \left[(\$175,000)(0.2505)\right] + \$3000$$

$$= \$43,838 + \$3000$$

$$= \$46,838$$

for analyzer B.

As the results would indicate, analyzer B is the more cost-effective option for the agency, with an annual cost savings of \$3450 [\$50,288 − \$46,838]. The example can be easily extended to include multiple assets. It is worth noting that the scenario may change if we include the salvage value for each asset. There are other advantages of using the method, besides cost savings. For instance, it takes into consideration the time value of money and flows over the entire life span of a project. Another advantage of the method is that it can provide a baseline for rate structure for a public project, if we know a priori the return rate for the project to remain operationally viable, which is often a problematic issue. Finally, as noted earlier, it is extremely useful for projects with unequal lives, a frequent concern the decision makers have with conventional cost-benefit or cost-effectiveness analysis.

9.2.5   Some Common Concerns

Up to this point, our discussion of cost-benefit and cost-effectiveness analysis was relatively straight forward. As long as we have the relevant information, selecting one or more projects for capital investments should not pose any problem for decision makers. In reality, the process is complex, as there are issues that need to be addressed before undertaking a full-fledged analysis. This section discusses some of these issues, in particular selecting a discount rate, projects with different life spans, projects with different sizes, and projects with risks and uncertainty.

9.2.5.1 Selecting a Discount Rate

As noted earlier, time plays an important role in all cost-benefit analysis. When time is brought explicitly into cost-benefit calculation, it changes the valuation of a project because of the need to discount it for costs and benefits that would occur over its entire life span. The critical element in this calculation is the rate one must use to discount these benefits and costs since setting this rate high or low will have a direct impact on the decision whether to accept or reject a project. For instance, a high discount rate will make a project less attractive to future consumption because, from the point of the consumer, they will be better off (derive more satisfaction) by consuming the resources now than postponing the consumption at some future points in time.

This leads one to the difficult choice of selecting a discount rate that will better reflect an individual's ability or willingness to sacrifice current consumption in favor of consumptions in the future. The conventional wisdom is to use the inflation rate as a proxy for the discount rate. Unfortunately, the use of inflation rate as a proxy provides a less than adequate measure because it fails to take into account the real earning capacity of funds invested in public projects. However, nobody quite knows what the real earning capacities of these funds are and how to utilize that information to determine a rate that could be effectively used to discount a stream of benefits and costs. Several methods have been suggested over the years to deal with this problem. Important among them are (1) opportunity cost of capital, (2) marginal rate of time preference, (3) weighted average cost of capital, (4) social rate of time preference, and (5) borrowing rate of capital.

Opportunity Cost of Capital

Opportunity cost simply means the cost of opportunity forgone. When the concept is applied to capital investments, it means the return a given capital could have earned from an alternative investment, as opposed to the current investment. Suppose that a government decides to undertake a project at a substantial cost of money that would benefit a particular community within the jurisdiction.

To finance the project, the government must impose a new tax which the community will have to bear but will be eventually repealed once the project takes off. Assume for a moment that if instead of paying tax to support the project, the taxpayers could have invested the money in high-yielding securities that would have earned them a return of, say, 10.5% a year on their investments. It is the opportunity the taxpayers will have to forgo should the government decide to undertake the project. From a decision-making point of view, it is the rate the government should use to discount the streams of costs and benefits for the project.

The opportunity cost of capital is based on a simple assumption that money, in particular savings, if not withdrawn through taxes, would have gone into private investment; that is, it will not remain idle but that is hardly the case. Individuals do not spend all their savings on investments; some of them are held as cash or placed in demand deposits to meet short-term needs. Alternatively, they may decide to spend all of it on additional consumptions such as going on a vacation or buying luxury goods. This trade-off between investment and consumption makes it further difficult to determine the rate that will reflect the true opportunity cost of capital.

Marginal Rate of Time Preference
Assume now that money comes not from private investment, but from private consumption. The appropriate discount rate will then be the rate at which the gain one realizes from the consumption of a dollar at the margin today is equal to the gain one will realize from a marginal dollar next year. In common-sense terms, this means that the value of, say, $1 consumed today is equal to $(\$1)(1+0.03)^1=\$1.03$ next year, or $(\$1)(1+0.03)^2=\$1.0609\approx\$1.06$ the year after, and so forth, assuming a discount rate of 3% and that this relationship will hold for all consecutive years. As long as this relationship holds and the rate remains relatively low, people will be indifferent between current and future consumption. This is known as the marginal rate of time preference. Thus, when funding for a project comes from private consumption, the appropriate discount rate is the marginal rate of time preference. This will be 3% in the current example.

Weighted Average Cost of Capital
In reality, public investments include funds that come from both private investment and consumption. Since funds come from private investment as well as from private consumption, a better alternative will be to take an average of the both, known as the weighted average cost of capital (Gramlich 1981). We can formally write this as

$$C_w = Sr_0 + \hat{S}r_m \tag{9.19}$$

where C_w is the weighted average cost of capital, with w as the weight, S is the proportion of resources that comes from private investment, r_0 is the opportunity cost of capital, $\hat{S}$ is the proportion of resources that comes from private consumption (which is really $1-S$), and r_m is the marginal rate of time preference. The S and $\hat{S}$, respectively, are the weights corresponding to r_0 and r_m.

Since the total amount of resources available to a government can come from either private investment or private consumption, or both, $S + \hat{S}$ must be equal to 1. For instance, assume that we have information on each of the terms in Eq. 9.19, where $S = 0.75$, $r_0 = 0.08$, $\hat{S} = 0.25$, and $r_m = 0.06$, the weighted average cost of capital will be

$$
\begin{aligned}
C_w &= Sr_0 + \hat{S}r_m \\
&= Sr_0 + (1 - S)r_m \\
&= (0.75)(0.08) + (0.25)(0.06) \\
&= 0.060 + 0.015 \\
&= 0.075
\end{aligned}
$$

or 7.5%.

Although useful as a concept, the weighted average cost of capital is not without its weaknesses. The existence of market imperfections such as financial regulations and taxes can greatly diminish the attractiveness of both the opportunity cost of capital and the marginal rate of time preference. This is because most taxpayers do not find financial regulations or taxes attractive, especially if they were to come at the expense of their investment or consumption decisions. Therefore, by simply taking the average of the two alternatives as a means for discounting costs and benefits will not necessarily be accurate. A better alternative would be to use the social rate of time preference since the projects a government deals with are public projects that affect society in part or as a whole.

Social Rate of Time Preference

Social rate of time preference measures the valuation a society places on its current consumption, as opposed to consumption in the future. The assumption here is that there exists for society a collective rate that relates the value of net benefit received at some future points in time to the value of an equivalent net benefit available today. This collective rate is generally regarded as the market rate of interest represented by government securities such as Treasury bills (T-bills). The rationale for using government securities as a case in point is that they are riskless since they have guaranteed returns and principal repayment at maturity and, as such, are safe to invest. Economists argue that the social rate of time preference as measured by the market rate of interest on riskless securities is equal to the marginal rate of return on private capital, which represents the opportunity cost of capital (Mikesell 1977). If this equality does not hold, society will increase or decrease its savings until the social rate of time preference equals the marginal rate of return on invested capital (after allowing for risks).

Borrowing Rate of Capital

While the approaches discussed above appear attractive from a conceptual point of view, they are not always easy to operationalize. As a result, most governments prefer to use what is commonly known as the borrowing rate of capital.

Governments, like individual consumers, firms, and businesses, frequently borrow money to finance their capital projects and other development activities but to be able to borrow they must compete with the private sector for capital in the capital market. This increases the aggregate demand for capital and, consequently, the rate of interest at which they can borrow. However, the amount of capital that is available in the market at a given point in time and the extent to which the market is able to meet the demand depends on the credit rating of the borrowers (including government) and the rate at which they can borrow, among others.

As noted previously, the competition for capital between government and the private sector has a tendency to crowd out the capital market, leaving less capital for private borrowing and investment. While there is an appeal to the controversy, one could also argue that this would be true only if the returns from private investments are much higher than the returns from public investments. Assuming that is the case, the comparison may not be easy to make because of the inherent differences between private and public investments and the intergenerational effects the public investments produce for society at large. Furthermore, public borrowing is necessary to provide for economic and social infrastructure such as roads bridges, highways, public utilities, education, public safety, and the like that are vital for creating conditions for private investment. If the private sector has to pay for these and other public investments, it is likely that many of these goods and services will not be provided or the return on private investments will have to be substantially higher to recover the costs of these expenditures. Therefore, the argument that public borrowing comes at the expense of private investments does not entirely bear out, especially in the long run.

9.2.5.2 Projects with Unequal Life Span

In our earlier example of two projects with time value of money, A and B, both had exactly the same life span of six years. In reality, projects seldom have identical life span, meaning that their costs and benefits cannot be readily compared without making some adjustments for the differences in their useful lives. Without this adjustment, one may end up with projects that are less desirable, even though they may have higher B:C or NPV. This can create a real problem for the decision makers if they have to go by the outcomes of these decisions. Since time difference in projects plays a critical role in cost-benefit analysis, one way to resolve the problem is to take a number of short-lived projects and compare them with several larger ones in such a way that they end up with a common termination time.

Consider a case where we have two mutually exclusive projects, X and Y, where X has a life of 4 years and Y has a life of 6 years, including the year in which they are acquired or constructed. To find a common denominator, we take three-type X projects and two-type Y projects so that the sum total of their useful lives will be exactly the same—twelve years each. Assume that both projects have one-time costs, but their benefits vary over their life spans. We can then express the NPV for the two sets of projects as

$$NPV_X = \left[\sum_{t=1}^{4} \frac{B_t^X}{(1+r)^t} - \frac{C_1}{(1+r)^1}\right] + \left[\sum_{t=5}^{8} \frac{B_t^X}{(1+r)^t} - \frac{C_5}{(1+r)^5}\right]$$
$$+ \left[\sum_{t=9}^{12} \frac{B_t^X}{(1+r)^t} - \frac{C_9}{(1+r)^9}\right] \tag{9.20}$$

$$NPV_Y = \left[\sum_{t=1}^{6} \frac{B_t^Y}{(1+r)^t} - \frac{C_1}{(1+r)^1}\right] + \left[\sum_{t=7}^{12} \frac{B_t^Y}{(1+r)^t} - \frac{C_7}{(1+r)^7}\right] \tag{9.21}$$

where NPV_X and NPV_Y are the net present values of X and Y, and the rest of the terms are the same as before.

If we ignore the assumption of one-time cost and assume instead that the projects have costs that are spread over their entire useful lives, Eqs. 9.20 and 9.21 will, respectively, become

$$NPV_X = \left[\sum_{t=1}^{4} \frac{B_t^X}{(1+r)^t} - \sum_{t=1}^{4} \frac{C_t^X}{(1+r)^t}\right] + \left[\sum_{t=5}^{8} \frac{B_t^X}{(1+r)^t} - \sum_{t=5}^{8} \frac{C_t^X}{(1+r)^t}\right]$$
$$+ \left[\sum_{t=9}^{12} \frac{B_t^X}{(1+r)^t} - \sum_{t=9}^{12} \frac{C_t^X}{(1+r)^t}\right] \tag{9.22}$$

$$NPV_Y = \left[\sum_{t=1}^{6} \frac{B_t^Y}{(1+r)^t} - \sum_{t=1}^{6} \frac{C_t^Y}{(1+r)^t}\right] + \left[\sum_{t=7}^{12} \frac{B_t^Y}{(1+r)^t} - \sum_{t=7}^{12} \frac{C_t^Y}{(1+r)^t}\right] \tag{9.23}$$

where the terms of the equations are the same as before.

Although the expressions appear simple and relatively straightforward, the actual process of selecting appropriate projects for comparison can be quite difficult. Part of the problem is in finding projects that will be similar in characteristics, so that they can be combined in some meaningful ways to find a common time denominator. In other words, projects should not be arbitrarily lumped together simply because their combined life spans will come out to be the same. Doing so may not produce any better solution than when they are treated as individual projects. Ideally, when one is dealing with projects with different life spans and cost is the primary consideration, a better alternative would be to use a method called equivalent annual cost (EAC), discussed earlier.

9.2.5.3 Projects with Unequal Size

A frequent problem facing the decision makers in government is how to deal with projects that have different sizes. Ideally, it should not pose a problem if one is dealing with mutually exclusive projects with no capital rationing, that is, no restriction on resource availability, in which case all that decision makers have to do is select the project that produces the highest net present value or return on a given investment. On the other hand, if they are not mutually exclusive and there are constraints on resource availability, then a common-sense approach would be to divide the projects into distinct groups or categories by their functional characteristics such as transportation projects into one category, recreation projects into another category, public safety projects into another category, and so forth and then select a subset from each category based on their rankings as the available resources would permit.

Another alternative would be to group the projects by their cost size such as between $100,000 and $250,000, $250,000 and $1 million, $1 million and $10 million, and so forth and then select a subset from each group as the available resources would allow. A third alternative would be rank all the projects according to some established criteria and select as many as the available sources would permit, similar to the example discussed previously. The assumption here is that, once the projects go through a careful evaluation process, the decision makers are indifferent as to which projects get selected as long as they are high on the priority ranking and their benefits exceed the costs.

9.2.5.4 The Problem of Uncertainty

Up to this point, we assumed that the decision makers know for sure the costs and benefits associated with a project, but it is quite likely that it may not always be the case. The costs and benefits we use in calculating B:C or NPV are not actual costs and benefits, but rather, they are estimates of costs and benefits that will occur at some future points in time. For instance, a project that will cost $18 million to complete and will produce $35 million in benefits over its life span is expected, but not actual costs and benefits. Although in theory one expects the difference between the estimated costs and benefits to be negligible, in reality, it is unavoidable and, therefore, must be recognized in cost-benefit calculations. The point here is that without some knowledge or acceptance of uncertainty, decision makers may find themselves faced with situations that they did not anticipate such as project delays, unexpected cost overruns, and reduction in benefits.

As noted previously, the term "uncertainty" is often used in cost-benefit analysis to reflect a degree of "risk" associated with an investment decision, but the two are not exactly the same. Uncertainty is generally regarded as a situation in which it is difficult to know or assign a priori probabilities to the outcomes of a decision, whereas in the case of risks they are known and it is possible to assign probabilities without much difficulty. As such, the convention is to focus more on risk than on uncertainty, although the generic term used for both is uncertainty. There are several ways in which the problem of uncertainty can be addressed in public projects. We discuss here two such methods that have received considerable attention in recent years with potential for use in government: certainty-equivalent method and risk-adjusted discount rate.

Certainty-Equivalent Method

The certainty-equivalent method allows adjustments for risks by converting uncertain future costs and benefits to certainty equivalents. The method is particularly useful when decision makers perceive different levels of risks associated with the streams of estimated costs and benefits. In other words, it reflects the decision makers' perception of the degree of risk associated with the estimated costs and benefits. Since it is difficult to forecast with accuracy the future values of costs and benefits, it is frequently represented by the expected value of probability distribution[5] associated with costs and benefits and is given by the expression

$$\text{NPV}_j = \sum_{t=0}^{T} \frac{\alpha_t \hat{B}_t^j}{(1+R)^t} - C_0^j \qquad (9.24)$$

where NPV_j is the net present value for project j, $\hat{B}$ is the expected benefit at time t (for $t = 0, 1, 2, \ldots, T$), α_t is the risk coefficient that converts expected benefits and costs into certainty-equivalent value at time t, R is the risk-free rate (usually given by the rate for T-bills), and C_0 is the one-time cost for project j at time 0. The first part of the expression represents expected certainty-equivalent value over the life span of a project, while the second part represents the typical one-time cost.

If costs extend over the entire life span of a project, they should be discounted the same way as the stream of benefits. In general, certainty equivalent ranges between 0 and 1. The higher the value, the lower the penalty the decisions makers assign to the distribution of net benefits. For instance, a value of 1 indicates that the decision makers do not associate any risk with the future streams of benefits and costs and, therefore, are willing to accept the expected value of the streams as certain. The risk-free rate of a return is the return rate normally associated with the Treasury bills because, as noted earlier, they are safe to invest.

To give an example, suppose that a government wants to construct a children's amusement park at a cost of $1 million that will produce a return of $275,000 in the first year, $300,000 in the second year, $320,000 in the third year, $315,000 in the fourth year, and $310,000 in the fifth year. The risk coefficients assigned by the administration, respectively, are 0.95 for year 1, 0.90 for year 2, 0.87 for year 3, 0.82 for year 4, and 0.75 for year 5. Assume a risk-free discount rate of 5%. The corresponding net present value of the project will be $128,854, as given by

Table 9.6 Net present value calculation for certainty-equivalent method

Year	Benefit ($)	Risk coefficient, α	Certainty-equivalent value ($\alpha \times$ $benefit)	DF at the risk-free rate of 5%	Present value ($)
1	275,000	0.95	261,250	0.9524	248,815
2	300,000	0.90	270,000	0.9070	244,890
3	320,000	0.87	278,400	0.8638	240,482
4	315,000	0.82	258,300	0.8227	212,503
5	310,000	0.75	232,500	0.7835	182,164
				ΣPV = $1,128,854 Initial cost = $1,000,000 NPV = $128,854	

the computations in Table 9.6. Since the net present value is positive, the investment should be worth undertaking.

It should be worth noting that the risk coefficients, as assigned by the decision makers, decrease in value with time. This is because it is easier to predict with a greater certainty (higher probability) the estimates of costs and benefits of a project's useful life during its early years than those corresponding to the later years.

Risk-Adjusted Discount Rate

The risk-adjusted discount rate, on the other hand, is used to reflect the amount of risk inherent in a project. The rationale behind using this rate is that projects that have higher variability in the probability distribution of their returns should be discounted at a higher rate than projects with lower variability. Thus, a project with no variability or risk should be discounted at the risk-free rate, while a project with any risk should be discounted at a rate in excess of the risk-free rate. It is given by the expression

$$NPV_j = \sum_{t=0}^{T} \frac{\hat{B}_t^j}{(1+R')^t} - C_0^j \tag{9.25}$$

where NPV is the net present value for the jth project, $\hat{B}_t$ is the expected value of the distribution of benefits of project j at time t (for $t = 1, 2,\ldots\ldots, T$), R' is the risk-adjusted discount rate, and C_0^j is the one-time cost for project j at time 0.

The first part of the expression in Eq. 9.25 represents the expected value of the distribution of discounted benefits over the life span of the project, and the second part represents one-time cost. As before, if the costs of a project extend over its entire life span, they should be discounted the same way as the stream of benefits. Like the certainty-equivalent method, the amount of risk adjustment is also based on how the decision makers perceive the risks associated with the project. Let us go back to the amusement park example again. Assume now that we have the following probability distribution for the benefit stream: 0.1 for year 1, 0.2 for year 2, 0.3 for year 3, 0.3 for year 4, and 0.1 for year 5. Table 9.7 shows the probability distribution and the expected value for the project.

Table 9.7 Net present value calculation for risk-adjusted discount rate

Year	Benefit stream		Expected value of benefit ($)
	Probability (P)	Benefit ($)	
1	0.1	275,000	27,500
2	0.2	300,000	60,000
3	0.3	320,000	96,000
4	0.3	315,000	94,500
5	0.1	310,000	31,000
	Expected value $= \Sigma P_i B_i / \Sigma P_i$		$= \$309,000$

Assume a risk-adjusted discount rate of 6%, although in practice it could be much higher. The risk-adjusted net present value for the project can then be calculated in the following way:

$$
\begin{aligned}
NPV_j &= \sum_{t=0}^{T} \frac{\hat{B}_t^j}{(1+R')^t} - C_0^j \\
&= \left(\frac{\hat{B}_1^j}{(1+R')^1} + \frac{\hat{B}_2^j}{(1+R')^2} + \cdots + \frac{\hat{B}_5^j}{(1+R')^5} \right) - C_0^j \\
&= \left(\frac{\$309{,}000}{(1+0.06)^1} + \frac{\$309{,}000}{(1+0.06)^2} + \cdots + \frac{\$309{,}000}{(1+0.06)^5} \right) - \$1{,}000{,}000 \\
&= (\$291{,}509.434 + \$275{,}008.900 + \$259{,}442.359 \\
&\quad + \$244{,}756.942 + \$230{,}902.775) - \$1{,}000{,}000 \\
&= \$1{,}301{,}620.410 - \$1{,}000{,}000 \\
&= \$301{,}620.410
\end{aligned}
$$

This is the NPV of the project after adjusting for risk. Since the value is positive, the project should be worth considering. If there are multiple projects involved, the same procedure can be applied and the projects can be ranked on the basis of their risk-adjusted NPVs.

Despite its apparent simplicity in calculation, there are several inherent weaknesses of the method. One, it assumes the same riskiness for each project when multiple projects are involved and, consequently, the same risk-adjusted rate over the entire life of the project. Certainty-equivalent method, on the other hand, requires individual examination of projects in each time period, since riskiness associated with a project can change over its useful life. Two, the risk-adjusted discount rate, as opposed to the risk-free rate used in certainty-equivalent method, is subjective and, therefore, subject to error.

9.2.5.5 Need for Sensitivity Analysis

When dealing with decision tools, it is important to sensitize the data to see what kind of changes will take place in the result if the value of any of the key terms included in the analysis will change. The certainty-equivalent method and the risk-adjusted rate discussed above are two cases in point where one could see how to incorporate the condition of uncertainty when evaluating a project. However, a variety of other situations may emerge once a project gets under way that may significantly affect the initial estimates of a project. One way to deal with the problem is to do a sensitivity analysis. Sensitivity analysis provides a systematic procedure for analyzing the effects of a change in the values of the key variables in a project such as changes in the discount rate, benefit level, construction schedule, production cost, and price of labor and materials. It is really the "what if" question in project evaluation.

There are different ways to do a sensitivity analysis. The simplest is to develop a set of scenarios such as likely, most likely, least likely, and so forth for the variables in question in terms of a range of values for the key parameters. Once the values have been determined, the next step would be to calculate a series of NPVs or B:Cs or IRRs for each scenario, depending on which one is preferred in the study. The idea is to have a sense of the likely effect a change in the values of the key parameters can produce for a project and develop a contingency plan to deal with the problem, as the situation arises.

9.2.5.6 Other Related Issues

Generally speaking, the computation of costs and benefits is rather simple if one is dealing with private sector projects. The costs are simply the payments a firm makes for inputs, and the benefits are the revenues it receives, and both are measured by the market prices. The process is more complicated for government because the costs and benefits governments deal with are typically social costs and social benefits which may not be reflected in the market prices. Also, the analysis may vary depending on whether the local, state, or federal government is the decision maker. Even within a government, the values assigned to different levels of benefits and costs will vary depending on their composition and how individuals view them. Nevertheless, for cost-benefit analysis to be useful to decision makers, the process should accurately reflect their values. There are several ways in which this could be achieved.

Use of Market Prices

The price one pays for a commodity in the market reflects the marginal cost of its production and the marginal benefit it produces for the consumer. If the government uses inputs or produces goods that are traded in the private market, then market prices should be used for valuation. A good example will be electric utility. Let us say that a community has the option to buy electricity from its own government or from a private provider. Since the government has to compete with the private provider, ideally, it should use the market price but where the government is the sole provider it becomes difficult to use the market price because it will not reflect the competitive price. There are also other imperfections in the market such as externalities and uncertainties that often make it difficult for the market price to reflect the true social costs and benefits of publicly produced goods and services. Therefore, market prices may not always accurately reflect the true costs and benefits of a public project.

Use of Shadow Prices

Since the price of a good or service in imperfect markets generally does not reflect its true marginal social cost, one can use the shadow price to replace the market price. A shadow price assigns value to a good or service not traded in the market place (Abt 1977). In some sense, it is the true value the consumers are willing to pay for a good or service. To give an example, suppose that a government stops providing public safety, say, police protection for its residents. In the absence of the service, it will invariably increase crimes of all sorts, which will make life unbearable for the residents and will induce them to ask the government for the service. Therefore, the price society is willing to pay for a service in the absence of it is the shadow price. (More on shadow price in the next chapter.)

Monopoly

Suppose that a government uses monopolistically produced inputs for one of its projects such that the price is above marginal cost. The question then is: Should the government value the input at its market price (monopoly price, in this case) or at its marginal production cost (under competitive conditions)? The answer would depend on the impact of the government purchase on the market. If the use of the inputs by the government would lead to an increase in the production of inputs by an exact amount, the social cost would be the value of the additional production. On the other hand, if there is no additional production of inputs, the use of the inputs by the government would come at the expense of private use of the inputs. Assuming the consumers are willing to pay the market price for the inputs, an appropriate measure would be to use a combination of the two responses—a weighted average of price and marginal cost.

Unemployment

Cost-benefit analysis assumes that all resources are fully employed but a public project may involve hiring workers who are currently involuntarily unemployed. Because hiring an unemployed worker does not affect output elsewhere in the economy, the wage the worker is paid does not represent an opportunity cost. The worker only forgoes leisure when hired, the value of which is low if unemployment is involuntary. If the government is running an effective stabilization policy to maintain a constant rate of unemployment, hiring an unemployed worker may mean reducing employment and output elsewhere in the economy and the social cost of the worker will be his or her wage. Even if the worker is involuntarily unemployed, it is difficult to predict at what point he or she will no longer be unemployed, which makes pricing of unemployed resources such as labor a serious problem. Therefore, in the absence of a serious recession or depression, valuation of unemployed labor at the going wage rate would be a good approximation for practical purposes.

Taxes

Government taxes on inputs can also have an effect on cost-benefit analysis. For instance, if an input that goes into the production of a commodity that is used in cost-benefit analysis is taxed, the price received by the producer of the input is less than the price paid by the purchaser since a portion of the purchase price will go to the tax collector. If that is the case, the question is which price should be used to value the input: producer's price or the purchaser's price? The rule of thumb is if the production is likely to increase, then the producer's supply price should be used. If the production is likely to remain constant, the purchaser's price should be used. For a combination of both, a weighted average should be used.

Indirect Effects

When private firms change their outputs, it does not affect the market prices for their products because they are small relative to the economy, but public projects can be so large that they can induce changes in market price. For instance, if a mass transit that operates through a major city is closed, it will change the demand for other services. The demand for automobiles will increase, and the demand for housing by the transit route may decrease, which, in turn, will lead to changes in other services that are directly tied to housing and automobiles. Any of these changes will have an effect on the market price for these and related services. These indirect effects cause great problems in cost-benefit analysis. It is often difficult to predict the indirect effects that are caused by a public project or even to identify them when the projects have been undertaken. Also, when dealing with indirect effects, there is a danger of double counting (counting a single element more than once) or not knowing if the indirect effect is a benefit or cost that is independent of the direct effects of the project, which can complicate the analysis. The point is in applying cost-benefit analysis, one must be aware of the existence of these and other problems and the alternatives that could be realistically pursued.

9.3   Capital Assets and Depreciation

Earlier in the chapter, we briefly introduced the notion of salvage value (SV), which is the value of an asset at the end of its useful life. Most capital assets have a useful life of several years, but with wear and tear the value depreciates over time. When assets depreciate, they lose some or all of their use values because they are wearing out and, as such, fail to perform to their fullest capacity. This is particularly important in capital budgeting since the rate and level of depreciation determine when and how fast an asset needs to be replaced. Fire trucks and patrol vehicles are classic examples of capital assets that easily depreciate from wear and tear. Assets may also lose their value because of technological change. As technology improves, the current assets tend to become obsolete, that is, less efficient, although they may continue to function. Computers, medical equipment, and other high tech gadgets that we use on a regular basis are good examples where technology tends to change at a much faster rate than the pace at which the assets can be replaced. Thus, both wear and tear and technological obsolescence can depreciate the value of an asset.

Although depreciation is a common occurrence and can be easily recognized, the determination of its magnitude in advance is a difficult task. In most instances, the actual amount of depreciation can seldom be established until the assets have been retired from service. Nevertheless, there is a wide range of methods that can be used for this purpose. This section discusses one of the most frequently used methods used in depreciation calculation, especially in government called straight-line depreciation. It is called straight line because it depreciates the value of an asset by a constant amount, meaning that depreciation will be the same for each year of the useful life of the asset.

The following expression shows how to determine the depreciable value of an asset using the straight-line method:

$$d_t = V_0/T \tag{9.26}$$

where d_t is the amount of depreciation at time t, V_0 is the initial value or cost of the asset, and T is the depreciable life (for $t=0, 1, 2,\ldots\ldots, T$).

To give an example, suppose that a government has recently purchased a patrol vehicle for its police department at a cost of $60,000. Let us say that the average life span of a patrol vehicle in a mid-size urban area is 5 years, with no salvage value (the residual value at the end of the useful life after taking into consideration all the depreciations). Therefore, dividing the purchase price by the life span of the vehicle will produce an annual depreciation of $12,000 [$60,000/5]. At this rate, the vehicle will be fully depreciated by the end of the fifth year in that there will be no salvage or residual value at the end of the fifth year. That is,

$$V_0 - \sum_{t=1}^{5} d_t = 0$$

$$= V_0 - (d_1 + d_2 + d_3 + d_4 + d_5)$$
$$= \$60,000 - (\$12,000 + \$12,000 + \$12,000 + \$12,000 + \$12,000)$$
$$= 0$$

Table 9.8a shows the straight-line depreciation without the salvage value. As the table shows, the book value at the beginning of the first year is the original cost of the vehicle, while the book value at the end of the year, called the ending or net book value, is the beginning book value minus the accumulated depreciation.[6] Depreciations are generally calculated by multiplying the initial book value at the beginning of the year by the depreciation rate, where the depreciation rate is obtained by taking the reciprocal of the life span of an asset. Thus, the depreciation rate for a vehicle with a life span of 5 years will be $1/5 = 0.2$ or 20%. Returning now to the example, let us say that we want to find the book value of the vehicle at the end of the first year (net book value). Therefore, subtracting the accumulated depreciation from the initial book value for year 1 will produce the ending or net book value at the end of the year 1, which is $48,000; that is,

Table 9.8a Straight-line depreciation (without the salvage value)[a]

Year	Annual depreciation ($)	Accumulated depreciation ($)	Net book value[a] ($)
0	–	–	60,000
1	$60,000 \times 0.2 = 12,000$	12,000	48,000
2	$60,000 \times 0.2 = 12,000$	24,000	36,000
3	$60,000 \times 0.2 = 12,000$	36,000	24,000
4	$60,000 \times 0.2 = 12,000$	48,000	12,000
5	$60,000 \times 0.2 = 12,000$	60,000	0

[a]Net Book Value = (Initial Cost − Salvage Value) − Accumulated Depreciation

Table 9.8b Straight-line depreciation (with the salvage value)[a]

Year	Annual depreciation ($)	Accumulated depreciation ($)	Net book value[a] ($)
0	–	–	40,000
1	$40,000 \times 0.2 = 8000$	8000	32,000
2	$40,000 \times 0.2 = 8000$	16,000	24,000
3	$40,000 \times 0.2 = 8000$	24,000	16,000
4	$40,000 \times 0.2 = 8000$	32,000	8000
5	$40,000 \times 0.2 = 8000$	40,000	0

[a]Net Book Value = (Initial Cost − Salvage Value) − Accumulated Depreciation

$60,000 − $12,000 = $48,000. For year 2, it will be $60,000 − $24,000 = $36,000. We can repeat the process to obtain the net book value for the remaining years of the useful life of the vehicle.

Assume now that there is a salvage value of $20,000 at the end of fifth year of the vehicle, which will require us to modify the expression in Eq. 9.26. To do so, we simply need to subtract the salvage value from the initial value of the vehicle and divide the difference by the depreciable life, T, to obtain the annual depreciation.

The following expression shows the salvage value in depreciation calculation:

$$
\begin{aligned}
d_t &= \frac{V_0 - SV_T}{T} \\
&= (\$60,000 - \$20,000)/5 \\
&= \$8000
\end{aligned}
\tag{9.27}
$$

Interestingly, if the government were to sell the vehicle at a price above the salvage value, it would be considered a gain, and, by the same token, if it were to sell the vehicle below the salvage value, it would be a loss. Table 9.8b shows the straight-line depreciation for the vehicle with the salvage value. The calculation of the ending or net book value at the end of a given period is the same as that used without the salvage value.

Besides straight line, there are other methods that one can also use depending on the purpose of depreciation such as declining balance, sum-of-the-years' digits, and units-of-production. Of the three, the first two belong to a category known as accelerated depreciation. In an accelerated depreciation, depreciations are usually high in the early years of an asset's life and decline gradually with time. For instance, in a declining balance, the depreciation is high in the first year and declines gradually in subsequent years, hence the term declining balance. In sum-of-the-years' digits, depreciation is higher than the straight line, but less than declining balance. Accelerated depreciations are common in the private sector because of the tax benefits they can produce for a firm for high early depreciations.

However, unlike the declining balance or the sum-of-the-years' digits, the units-of-production method is based on the output of an asset rather than on its useful life.

To determine the depreciation, the rule of thumb is to calculate first the total output of an asset and then take the depreciation for each year based on the fraction of the total output in that year. If estimated correctly, the method can produce fairly accurate depreciation than most other methods, especially for capital assets such as public utilities.

9.4   Summary and Conclusion

Each year governments receive more requests for capital improvement projects from various departments and agencies than the available resources would allow them to undertake. This makes it necessary for the decision makers to carefully evaluate the projects before making decisions to appropriate funds. This chapter has briefly presented some of the commonly used methods for evaluating capital projects, in particular payback period, cost-benefit analysis, equivalent annual cost, and cost-effectiveness analysis. Although all four methods are useful, cost-benefit analysis has been used more frequently in government than any of the other methods because of its versatility and established history. In spite of its widespread application, one has to be careful when using cost-benefit analysis, especially when selecting a discount rate, dealing with projects with different size and life span, uncertainties, intangibles, and so forth. These are challenging problems, but not difficult to address if one is careful about the rules that are needed to deal with the problems. Although not as common in government as they are in the private sector, the chapter also looked at risk and uncertainty, as well as the measures to deal with the problems. The chapter concluded with a brief discussion on depreciation of capital assets.

Review Questions

Q1. What is payback period? Why is it important for a government to do a payback period calculation before purchasing a major capital item? Should the item be discounted in calculating the payback period? Why?

Q2. What is a discount rate? Why is it difficult to select a discount rate? What method is commonly used in government to select the rate? Why?

Q3. Suppose that the Central Printing Office of a small local government wants to buy a multi-purpose high speed copying machine at a cost of $5,000. It hopes to recover the cost of the machine from the copying service it will provide to various departments of the college. The following presents the cash inflows for the office over a six-year period: Year 1—$1000, Year 2—$1500, Year 3—$2000, Year 4—$1700, Year 5—$1, 200, Year 6—$1000, Year 7—$800, and Year 8–$500. What would be payback period for the investment? [Hint: Use a discount rate of 5%]

Q4. What is the difference between a present value and a future value? Suppose that a government wants to invest $1.2 million in a project with a return rate of 10%, what would be the future value after the 3 years of the initial investment?

Q5. Suppose that a county-run hospital wants to buy two state-of-the-art MRI machines, one for the hospital and one for the outpatient clinic, at a one-time cost $2.5 million. The hospital expects a 10% return on its investment. The following provides the cash flow data for the equipments (Table 9.9).

Table 9.9 Review Question (Q5)

Year	Outflow ($)	Cash inflow ($)	Cumulative net flow ($)	Cumulative net flow (with cost of funds) ($)
0	2,500,000	—	—	—
1	—	525,000	—	—
2	—	675,000	—	—
3	—	755,000	—	—
4	—	650,000	—	—
5	—	595,000	—	—

Given the information above, calculate the payback period with and without discounting.

Q6. What is cost-benefit analysis? Why is it important for a government to do a cost-benefit analysis before undertaking a project? What are the steps in a cost-benefit analysis?

Q7. What are the differences between benefit-cost ratio, net present value, and internal rate of return? Given a choice, which one would you use? Why? What are some of the limitations of benefit-cost analysis?

Q8. A government is evaluating two investment projects, each with a one-time cost of $1 million and a life span of six years. The estimated benefits for the projects are as follows (Table 9.10).

Table 9.10 Review Question (Q8)

Project A	Project B
Cost: $1,000,000 (one time)	Cost: $1,000,000 (one time)
Benefit stream	Benefit stream
Year 1: $350,000	Year 1: $375,000
Year 2: $425,000	Year 2: $425,000
Year 3: $575,000	Year 3: $530,000
Year 4: $925,000	Year 4: $750,000
Year 5: $850,000	Year 5: $825,000
Year 6: $750,000	Year 6: $950,000

Assume that the government will use net present value (NPV), which project should the government select? Why? Would the decision be different if it were using a discounted benefit-cost ratio instead of NPV? Why? [Hint: Use a discount rate of 6.0%]

Q9. Suppose that you have been asked by the City of Misfits to evaluate three public projects each with a one-time cost and a life span of six years. The estimated costs and benefits associated with the projects are as follows:

Project A: Initial (One-time) Cost: Yr0—$1,250,000; Benefit Stream: Yr1—$450,000, Yr2—$625,000, Yr3—$850,000, Yr4—$1,125,000, Yr—$950,000, and Yr6—$775,000;

Project B: Initial (One-time) Cost: Yr0—$1,250,000; Benefit Stream: Yr1—$350,000; Yr2—$775,000; Yr3—$925,000; Yr4—$1,350,000; Yr5—$1,450,000; and Yr6—$1,125,000;

Project C: Initial (One-time) Cost: Yr0—$1,250,000; Benefit Stream: Yr1 $870,000; Yr2—$950,000; Yr3—$775,000; Yr4—$650,000, Yr5—$500,000, and Yr6—$425,000.

A. Assuming you will use a discount rate of 7.5%, which is the borrowing rate for the government, which project would you select? Why?

B. Would the decision be the same if the discount rate was higher than 7.5%? Lower than 7.5%? Why?

Q10. What is cost-effectiveness analysis? What are the advantages and disadvantages of using cost-effectiveness analysis?

Q11. What is cost-effectiveness ratio? Suppose that a government wants to build a neighborhood recreation center to reduce juvenile crimes. It will cost the government approximately $250,000 to build the facility, but will reduce crime by 65% next year. Calculate the cost-effectiveness ratio for the project and interpret the result.

Q12. Consider a case where a local school district is planning on setting up a computer laboratory for one of its premier schools. Similar facilities have been built in a select number of school districts around the country and student performance on math and science was tested on 1000 high school students with the newly-constructed facility that produced varying results. The table below shows a three-year test result (average) for the most recent year on a scale of 0 to 100 for five school districts, randomly selected, that have similar facilities (A, B, C, D, and E), along with their costs which include, among others, costs of equipment, instruction, operation and maintenance (Table 9.11).

Table 9.11   Review Question (Q12)

School districts	Cost of the facility per 1000 students ($)	Effectiveness measure (Average performance score on a scale of 0 to 100)	C:E ($/Score)
A	1,160,000	75	—
B	2,875,000	90	—
C	1,720,000	80	—
D	4,395,000	95	—
E	1,380,000	85	—

Given the information in the table above, calculate the cost-effectiveness ratio for the school districts. What do the results tell us about cost-effectiveness of the facilities?

Q13. What is a modified internal rate of return? Under what conditions one would use a modified internal rate of return? Explain, with an example.

Q14. A state highway patrol department last year purchased a new vehicle in the amount $50,000 with a salvage value of $10,000. The vehicle has a life span of 5 years. What would be the actual cost of the vehicle, assuming a straight-line depreciation, with and without the salvage value?

Notes

1. A comparable term, especially for discounted B:C ratio used in the private sector is the profitability index (PI), defined as the ratio of the present value of cash inflows to the outflows. As a general rule, a ratio of 1 or greater indicates that the project under consideration has an expected value equal to or greater than the discount rate. Like B:C, the PI is a measure of a project's profitability (net return) per dollar of investment.
2. Although in theory a discount rate can be negative, it has no empirical meaning. A negative discount rate means that the cash flow has a negative risk, but since, by definition, the risk cannot be negative, it makes no economic sense.
3. Using the expression suggested earlier, the IRR for Project A was obtained in the following way: $-\$100+[\$108)/(1+i)^1]=0$, or $-\$100(1+i)+\$108=0$, or $-\$100-\$100i+\$108=0$, or $\$8-\$100i=0$, or $\$8=\$100i$, or $i=\$8/\$100=0.08$.
4. Similarly, for Project B, it was obtained, as follows: $-\$1000+[\$1070)/(1+i)^1]=0$, or $-\$1000(1+i)+\$108=0$, or $-\$1000-\$1000i+\$1070=0$, or $\$70 - \$1000i=0$, or $\$70=\$1000i$, or $i=\$70/\$1000=0.07$.
5. An expected value is the average or mean of a random variable. A random variable is defined as a variable that has its own probability distribution. There are two types of distribution one deals with in statistics: discrete and continuous. The expected value of a discrete probability distribution is given by the expression $E(X)=\Sigma Xf(X)$, where X is the random variable. To give an example, let us say that X has the following values: -3, 0, 2, and 4, and that $Pr(X=-3)=0.2$, $Pr(X=0)=0.1$, $Pr(X=2)=0.4$, and $Pr(X=4)=0.3$, The expected value of X will then be, $E(X)=-3(0.2)+0(0.1)+2(0.4)+4(0.3)=1.4$. The expected value of a continuous distribution is given by the expression $E(X) = \int_{-\infty}^{\infty} xf(x)dx$, where X is a bounded random variable. To give

an example, let us say that we have a continuous distribution of the form $f(x) = \{{2x \atop 0}$ for $0 < x < 1$ for the upper bound and otherwise for the lower bound. Then

$$E(X) = \int_0^1 x(2x)dx = \int_0^1 2x^2 dx = 2\int_0^1 x^2 dx = 2\left[\frac{x^3}{3}\right]_0^1 = 2\left[(\tfrac{1}{3}) - 0\right] = 2(\tfrac{1}{3}) = 2/3.$$

The expected value used in the current example is for a discrete distribution.

6. A term that frequently appears with salvage or residual value is book value. Book value is the initial cost minus the accumulated depreciation of an asset. Book value can be beginning book value (at the beginning of the year) and ending or net book value (at the end of the year). In general, the ending book value of previous period becomes beginning value of the next period. Salvage or residual value, on the other hand, is the value after all the depreciations have been taken into consideration, which is usually what an asset is worth at the end of its useful life.
Another term for salvage value is scrap value.

References

Abt, C. C. (1977). The Issue of Social Costs in Cost-Benefit Analysis of Surgery. In J. B. Bunker, B. A. Barnes, & F. Mosteller (Eds.), *Costs, Risks and Benefits of Surgery* (pp. 40–55). New York, NY: Oxford University Press.

Arrow, K. (1959). *Social Choice and Individual Values*. New Haven, CT: Yale University Press.

Gramlich, E. M. (1981). *Benefit-Cost Analysis of Government Programs* (pp. 98–100). Englewood Cliffs, NJ: Prentice-Hall.

Mikesell, R. F. (1977). *The Rate of Discount for Evaluating Public Projects*. Washington, DC: American Enterprise Institute for Studies in Economic Policy.

Mishan, E. J. (1981). *Introduction to Normative Economics*. New York, NY: Oxford University Press.

Quade, E. S. (1982). *Analysis for Public Decisions*. New York, NY: North Holland.

Thompson, M. S. (1982). *Benefit-Cost Analysis for Program Evaluation* (pp. 1–2). Beverly Hills, CA: Sage.

Capital Rationing and Budget Allocation

10

As it should become obvious by now, capital budgeting, like an operating budget, is a long, complex, and arduous process. Much of this complexity arises from the fact that there are more demands for projects, programs, and improvement activities than the available resources can permit. This is particularly true for government where agencies have to compete with each other for limited resources. This discrepancy between demand for capital expenditure on one hand and the availability of resources, on the other, makes budget allocation a complex undertaking. The process of allocating resources when faced with budget constraints is generally known as capital rationing. Capital rationing is not a problem for projects that are mutually exclusive or when one is restricted to selecting a few from multiple competing projects; there are usually physical reasons for that. Capital rationing is a problem when multiple projects have to compete for a limited amount of resources. Theoretically, if there are no resource limitations, there would not be any need for capital rationing but the fact that resources are limited, while the demand for projects, programs, and improvement activities is unlimited, it increases the need for capital rationing. This chapter provides a brief discussion of why and under what conditions capital rationing is necessary, followed by a general discussion of some of the commonly used methods in capital rationing.

10.1   The Need for Capital Rationing in Government

When faced with budget constraints, governments have basically four choices: One, do not undertake the desired projects, which is not a realistic option for most governments; two, use internal sources (including intergovernmental revenue), assuming the resources are sufficient enough to undertake the projects; three, use external financing (borrowing) if internal sources are not available; and four, but not least, use a combination of borrowing and internal sources, if internal resources are not sufficient enough to generate the necessary funds. The primary

© The Author(s) 2019   361
A. Khan, *Fundamentals of Public Budgeting and Finance*,
https://doi.org/10.1007/978-3-030-19226-6_10

reason capital rationing occurs in government is that most governments, given a choice, would prefer not to use external financing for their improvement projects because of the long-term debt burden it will produce for the taxpayers. This is particularly true for governments with substantial debt obligations that can easily add to their debt burden, in particular, long-term interest costs. Capital rationing may be used if there is a good likelihood that there may not be enough public support for a project or projects that need to be financed through new or additional taxes. Decision makers may also use capital rationing as a way to separate less desirable projects for improvement from those that are more desirable, such as a public library, a fire station, a healthcare facility, or a public safety project, that may have an immediate need for local citizens than a community swimming pool.

Unfortunately, most governments do not have the means to generate sufficient funds internally for their capital improvement activities. Consequently, they have to rely substantially on external financing, which means that governments have to compete with other governments as well as with the private sector to borrow the necessary capital. However, the extent to which a government is able to borrow and the rate at which it can borrow depend on the conditions of the capital market, as well as its own overall financial condition. In a theoretically perfect capital market, capital rationing should not be a problem because most governments, as well as firms and businesses, can always raise capital if the investments are attractive. In reality, transaction costs, information asymmetry, and other factors such as competition for available capital often create conditions that require capital rationing. In addition to that, if the capital market imposes restrictions such as limiting the supply beyond a certain amount which is possible if the market suspects an uncertain economy, capital rationing can become a real and serious problem. This is known as hard capital rationing.

Both situations—market-imposed capital rationing and rationing resulting from transaction and other costs—have an immediate effect on the market in that it raises the marginal cost of capital (the cost of borrowing an additional dollar from a competitive capital market). If organizations are able to generate the needed capital internally, it will lower the aggregate demand, which, in turn, will keep the cost of capital down, but in an expanding economy, the demand will always exceed the available supply, thereby increasing the cost. In general, the lower the supply of capital, the higher is the marginal cost of capital. The converse is true if the supply is higher. Figure 10.1 shows how the supply affects the marginal cost of capital, when the government and the private sector have to compete with each other for the available capital.

On occasion, policy makers may decide on a policy that may require a government to establish an upper limit on the total amount it can spend on capital improvement projects, even if the supply of capital is not a factor and the projects have positive net present values. A plausible scenario for this will be when a government wants to achieve certain goals and uses capital improvement activities as an instrument to achieve those goals. Capital rationing then serves as the means for implementing strategies and for avoiding projects that may not serve the goals of the government. The management can set a target budget for capital improvement and then distribute the funds to respective agencies and departments consistent with the goals and priorities.

Fig. 10.1 Demand, supply, and interest cost of capital

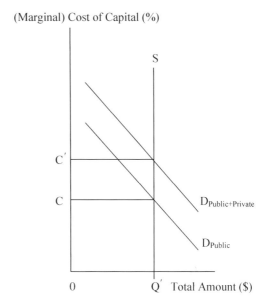

10.2 Conventional Approaches to Capital Rationing

Regardless, whether capital projects are financed internally or externally, the fact remains that most governments have a fixed amount of capital available for a given period, known as capital rationing period. Therefore, the objective of a government with finite capital should be to undertake those projects that will produce the greatest amount of return for the invested funds over their life spans. Two methods that are generally used in this context are net present value (NPV) and internal rate of return (IRR), discussed earlier. Net present value is the difference between the sum of discounted stream of benefits and costs. As long as NPV is positive, it is an indication that the project is worth undertaking. Internal rate of return, on the other hand, sets the present value of the stream of cash flows for a project to the initial investment outlay. Although both methods have their strengths and weaknesses, NPV has received considerably more attention in government than IRR. Part of the reason for this, as noted previously, is that project selection based on internal rate of return can be misleading, especially when projects vary in size, while the NPV provides a more realistic scenario in terms of the actual situation.

To give an example, consider a government that is looking into a set of nine different projects of varying sizes for capital improvement. These are essentially the same projects we considered in an earlier chapter, plus two additional projects. Table 10.1 presents the projects with their outlays and the corresponding NPV. The estimated cost of undertaking the projects is $69.03 million. Looking at the table, it appears that all nine projects are worth undertaking since all of them have

Table 10.1 Capital improvement projects, priorities, projected costs, and NPV

Project-ranking	Project description	Cost ($M)	Cumulative cost ($M)	NPV ($M)
X_1-R2	Construct a technology center	9.26	9.26	5.27
X_2-R4	Upgrade the water treatment plant	6.30	9.26+6.30=15.56	4.88
X_3-R5	Construct a new community health center	9.00	15.56+9.00=24.56	2.56
X_4-R6	Renovate the civic center	5.11	24.56+5.11=29.67	4.42
X_5-R3	Repair the old pedestrian bridge	6.16	29.67+6.16=35.83	2.35
X_6-R1	Undertake downtown redevelopment	21.15	35.83+21.15=56.98	14.27
X_7-R7	Expand the Southside commercial strip	4.69	56.98+4.69=61.67	2.31
X_8-R8	Renovate the administrative building	3.39	61.67+3.39=65.06	1.25
X_9-R9	Construct a new youth activity center	3.97	65.06+3.97=69.03	1.06

positive NPVs. If the government had unlimited funds, there will be no need for capital rationing and all nine projects will be considered for adoption but, in reality, that is hardly the case. In most instances, the funds available fall far short of the actual needs. Suppose that the maximum amount the government can spend on the projects is $32.85 million, which means that some of the projects will have to be ignored or, at least, postponed for now, given the budget constraint. The question is: which ones?

The simplest way to address the question of budget allocation is to rank the projects according to their NPVs and allocate the available funds on the basis of their rank order. This approach makes most sense if the objective is to invest in those projects and improvement activities where the PV of benefits would far outweigh the PV of costs. Therefore, according to this criterion, the government should be able to undertake a maximum of two projects, X_6 and X_3, at a cost of $30.15 million ($21.15m + $9m). On the other hand, this may not be consistent with the goal if the government wants to undertake as many projects as possible, as long as they produce positives NPVs. In other words, if the order is not important, the government should be able to undertake six out of nine projects—X_2, X_4, X_5, X_7, X_8, and X_9—at a cost of $28.48 million [$X_2 + X_4 + X_5 + X_7 + X_8 + X_9 = $6.30m + $5.11m + $6.16m + $4.69m + $3.39m + $2.83m = $28.48m), leaving a balance of $4.37 million ($32.85 million − $28.48 million), or any combination, as long as the total cost of the projects does not exceed the budget constraint. Since there were no specific restrictions for project selection other than that they must have a positive NPV, this alternative allows the government to undertake the maximum number of projects for the available capital.

The greatest advantage of conventional approaches to capital rationing such as NPV is that they are simple and easy to grasp, but they have a major weakness in that they do not readily suggest how to maximize the value of the invested capital subject to such constraints as not to exceed the capital ceiling or budget constraint. This is particularly important for a government where it is difficult to move funds around or exceed the approved funding level without further legislative approval. Although constrained maximization may produce a lower value than unconstrained maximization, it can still produce reasonably satisfactory results.[1] For instance, if a government is faced with a true capital rationing problem where the constraints cannot be lifted, the objective should be to select the projects, subject to the capital rationing constraints such that the sum of the projects' NPV is maximized (optimized). This is where alternative approaches that are better equipped to deal with constrained optimization such as those used in mathematical programming become useful.[2] The following sections provide several examples of mathematical programming applications in capital rationing.

10.3   Alternative Approaches to Capital Rationing

Among the alternative approaches to dealing with capital rationing problems, mathematical programming has a long history. In its bare essence, mathematical programming is the use of quantitative models, in particular optimization models to help the decision makers make best possible decisions. As is common with quantitative models, mathematical programming provides an abstract representation of a real-world problem with resource and other constraints, usually with the help of mathematical equations. Two types of equations are generally used in mathematical programming: objective function equation which describes the goals and objectives a decision maker hopes to achieve and constraint equations which describe the limitations on resources or restrictions imposed by the environment. This is where mathematical programming becomes useful because of its ability to deal with constraint optimization. The basic approach is to optimize the objective function, subject to these and other constraints that restrict the activities of the decision maker. As abstractions of the real world, the models try to capture the most essential elements and relationships that exist in the real system. Since most quantitative models are quite involved, mathematical programming models use solution algorithms that follow a step-by-step process to guarantee the best solution to the model formulation.

Within the broader class of mathematical programming, there are several specific models that can be used to solve a decision problem. Each one of them can be used to deal with a capital rationing problem, depending on the model assumptions and the interrelationships among the problem components. Each uses a different set of equations in the objective function or constraint equations, and each allows different assumptions about the input parameters. Some of the terms of the equations may be known with certainty, or they may be assumed to be known given by a probability distribution. This is where mathematical programming models have an advantage over conventional quantitative models in that they can precisely describe most real-world systems under conditions of both certainty and uncertainty. Operationally, the certainty models are less complex and much easier to solve than the uncertainty models since all the model conditions are known with certainty. This section discusses one of the most frequently used programming models in capital rationing, especially under conditions of certainty, namely linear programming. It also briefly touches base on two other programming methods, integer and goal programming, that are also frequently used in capital rationing.

10.3.1 Linear Programming

Developed in the 1940s as a means to deal with complex planning problems during World War II and post-war industrial operations, linear programming is the most well known among all the mathematical programming models. It has since been applied to a wide variety of problems and disciplines, from industrial technology, to medicine, to economics, to business, among others. Although it can be applied to any situation, linear programming is suitable for problems involving resource allocation, especially where resources such as labor, materials, and capital are in short supply. The primary objective of linear programming is to find an optimum solution (maximum or minimum) for a function called the objective function, subject to resource and other constraints. The objective function describes the goal or objective a decision maker hopes to achieve, while the constraints describe the resource limitations and other restrictions imposed by the environment within which the system operates.[3]

Operationally, both the objective function and the constraint equations must be expressed in linear form such that each term in these equations can be expressed with variables raised to the power 1, hence the term linear. However, solving a linear programming problem is not as complex as it may seem at a first glance, provided that one follows some basic steps. These steps typically are (1) formulate the problem by specifying the input parameters of the decision variables, the objective function, and all the relevant constraints, (2) solve the problem, using any of the following methods: a graphical method, the conventional simplex method, or a computer-based solution algorithm, (3) interpret the results, and (4) perform a sensitivity analysis on the solution, known as post-optimality analysis.

10.3.1.1 Graphical Solution
The simplest way to solve a linear programming problem is to use a graphical approach since it makes it relatively easy to visualize the problem, especially when one is dealing with two decision variables and a limited number of constraints, and follow the solution process. To give an example, consider a case where a government must allocate its capital between two projects—Project 1 and Project 2. Assume that Project 1 will produce an NPV of $1.5 million and Project 2 will produce an NPV of $1.25 million. Assume further that we have two variables, X_1 and X_2, representing the resources to be allocated to the two projects to realize the problem objective, called the decision variables.

We can formally write the above relationship, as

$$Z = \$1.5X_1 + 1.25X_2 \tag{10.1}$$

Equation 10.1 is our objective function and, by definition, it must be linear for a linear programming problem. Figure 10.2 shows the objective function and, as shown in the figure, the amount allocated on Project 1 is measured on the horizontal axis, while the amount allocated on Project 2 is measured on the vertical axis. Each of the downward-sloping lines represents the combination of X_1 and X_2 that will result in a particular value of Z, which is NPV in our case. Since there are no constraints, we can draw infinite number of such lines. Thus, an NPV of \$1.5 million can be obtained by the following combination:

$$Z\,(\text{NPV}) = 1.5\big(\$1,000,000\big) + 1.25\big(\$0\big) = \$1,500,000$$

Alternatively,

$$Z(\text{NPV}) = 1.50\big(\$0\big) + 1.25\big(\$1,200,000\big) = \$1,500,000$$

We can repeat the process for the remaining lines. The goal of the government obviously is to achieve as much NPV as possible, so that it can be on the highest possible line which means moving farthest toward the northeast in Fig. 10.2. However, once the constraints are brought into the picture, the goal of the

Fig. 10.2 Graphical solution of the LP problem

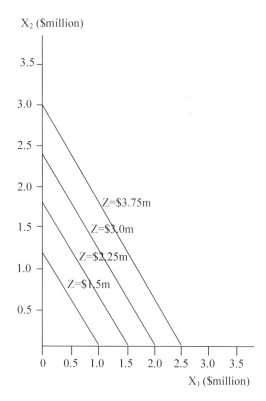

government changes in that it is no longer possible to be on the highest possible line. Instead, the goal becomes one of achieving the highest attainable line, that is, the highest attainable NPV, in our case. Note that the objective function coefficients are all in millions.

To illustrate the point, let us introduce some constraints to our capital rationing problem. Suppose that the government estimates that it will cost no more than $1.5 million for Project 1 and $2 million for Project 2. Let us further suppose that the maximum the government can spend on the two projects is $3 million. For convenience, we will call the first two constraints cost constraints and the third constraint the budget constraint. We can add to this two implied constraints, which is typical of mathematical programming in that the allocations cannot be negative; that is, they must be greater than or equal to 0 (≥ 0), called non-negativity constraints. The non-negativity constraints indicate that fractional solution (partial attainment) is possible. If a fractional solution is not preferable, there are alternative approaches such as integer programming (discussed briefly in the next section) that can be used to deal with the problem.

The complete model with the objective function and the constraint equations, including the non-negativity constraint, can now be presented, as follows[4]:

$$\text{Maximize NPV} = \$1.5X_1 + \$1.25X_2 \tag{10.2}$$

Subject to

$$X_1 \leq \$1,500,000 \tag{10.3}$$

$$X_2 \leq \$2,000,000 \tag{10.4}$$

$$X_1 + X_2 \leq \$3,000,000 \tag{10.5}$$

$$X_1, X_2 \geq 0 \tag{10.6}$$

Figure 10.3 shows the three constraints graphically. The lines in the figure are drawn by converting each of the inequality constraints to equality. The shades on one side of the lines indicate the side of the line that is allowed by the inequality constraint. The vertical line shows the upper limit of the constraint for X_1, set at $1.5 million, while the horizontal line shows the upper limit of the constraint for X_2, set at $2 million. Thus, any point to the left of the vertical line will produce a solution for X_1, called the feasible (attainable) solution, since it will not exceed the upper limit of the constraint, and any point to the right will exceed the upper limit. Similarly, any point below the horizontal line will produce a feasible (attainable) solution for X_2 since it will not exceed the upper limit of the constraint, and any point above the line will exceed the upper limit. The third constraint, which is the budget constraint, indicates the total amount the government can spend on the two services must not exceed $3 million and can be drawn by setting $X_1 = X_2 = 0$, so that when $X_1 = 0$, $X_2 = \$2$ million, or when $X_2 = 0$, $X_1 = \$1.5$ million.

The intersection of the three lines produces a region, called the feasible region, which contains the solution that will be optimal. Therefore, any point inside the

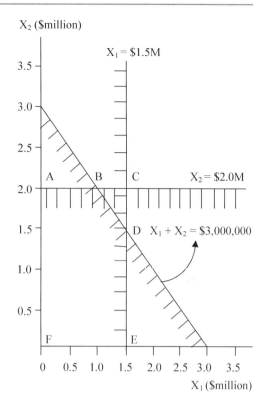

Fig. 10.3 Constraints for the LP problem

area ABCDEF will produce a feasible solution for the first two constraints, while any point inside the area ABDEF will produce a feasible solution for all three constraints. In other words, the optimal solution must lie within this region because in order to have an optimal solution it must be able to satisfy all the constraints in the problem.

In linear programming, the optimal solution always lies at the corner point called the corner point solution. This is because the highest attainable line will always touch the feasible region at one of the corners of the region,[5] but the question is which corner? As noted earlier, our goal is to select the point that is farthest as we move outward to the top right-hand corner of the feasible region, which will be point D at the intersection of the lines for the first and third constraints (Fig. 10.4). In other words, the highest attainable line is reached by allocating $1.5 million in Project 1 and, likewise, by allocating $1.5 million for Project 2. We can now plug in these values for X_1 and X_2 in the objective function to determine the optimal value of NPV. The result will produce a value of $4.125 million, that is, $1.5X_1 + 1.25X_2 = (1.5)(\$1.5 \text{ million}) + (1.25)(\$1.5 \text{ million}) = \$2.25 \text{ million} + \$1.875 \text{ million} = \$4.125 \text{ million}$, which is the maximum NPV the two projects will produce for the government, given the cost and budget constraints.

Fig. 10.4 Feasible region
for the LP problem

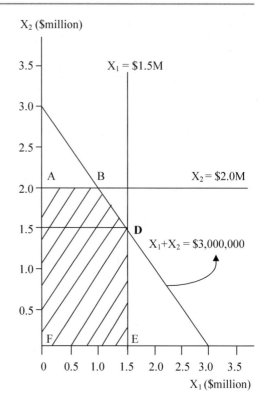

Let us try to interpret the results some more. Looking at the figure again, it appears that the government will be able to undertake Project 1 fully, set at the maximum cost of $1.5 million, but not Project 2. Since the maximum the government can spend on the two projects is $3 million and Project 2 costs $2 million, the maximum it can spend on Project 2 is $1.5 million, thereby producing a shortfall of $500,000. In other words, the $3 million budget constraint will allow the government to undertake Project 1 fully and Project 2 partially, assuming partial solution (completion) is acceptable. If partial solution is not acceptable and Project 1 has a higher priority of the two, the government obviously should be able undertake the project fully and there is no need for capital rationing. Conversely, if Project 2 has a higher priority than Project 1, it should be able to undertake it fully and leaving $1 million for Project 1, thereby producing a shortfall of $500,000 for the project and, again, there is no need for capital rationing. The underlying assumption here was that the government did not have a preference as to which one should get selected first, as long as the available resources get optimally allocated between the two projects and the result produces maximum NPV, hence the need for capital rationing.

It was considerably easy to find the optimal solution for our capital rationing problem since we had only two decision variables and three constraints to deal with, but if one has to deal with a large number decision variables and constraints, it will not be possible to show the optimal solution on a two-dimensional graph. It will be too cumbersome, if not impossible. The alternative is to use a solution method that is capable of dealing with multiple decision variables, as well as constraints, and has been a standard for solving linear programming problems for a long time called the simplex method.[6]

10.3.1.2 Simplex Solution

The simplex method provides an iterative (step-by-step) solution for the linear programming problem. It does so, first, by converting the constraints to equations; second, by defining a set of new variables called the basic variables (which can take any values other than zero, as opposed to non-basic variables which are set to be zero); third, by finding an initial feasible solution for the problem; and, finally, by continuing the search for an improved solution (by presenting the results in each of the solution in a table called tableau) until an optimal solution has been found. In common sense terms, it means that each time the method produces a solution for the objective function as large or larger (for a maximization problem) and as small or smaller (for a minimization problem) than the previous solution, it is reaching closer and closer to the optimal solution. The process continues until the optimal solution has been reached.

The method begins by requiring that all inequality constraints (constraints with less than or equal to, or greater than or equal to) are converted to strict equalities. To do so, the method introduces two new variables into the system of equations— one slack (for less than or equal to, $\leq$) and one surplus (for greater than or equal to, $\geq$). The slack variables represent an underutilization of resources (below the upper limit of capacity), while the surplus variables represent an overutilization of resources (above the upper limit of capacity) within each constraint. By adding a slack variable to a less than or equal to constraint and subtracting surplus variables from a greater than or equal to constraint, the inequalities are converted to strict equalities. This process of adding a slack or subtracting a surplus is known as augmentation.

Going back to our problem, since all three constraint equations contain less than or equal to terms, we can add a slack variable to each of the three equations. The augmented model with the slack variables added is shown below:

$$X_1 + S_1 = \$1,500,000 \tag{10.7}$$

$$X_2 + S_2 = \$2,000,000 \tag{10.8}$$

$$X_1 + X_2 + S_3 = \$3,000,000 \tag{10.9}$$

where X_1 and X_2 are the decision variables, and S_1, S_2, and S_3 are the slack variables corresponding to the three constraint equations. The interpretation of the slack variables is quite simple. For instance, if we obtain a slack of $0 for X_1 ($S_1 = \$0$) and $500,000 for X_2 ($S_2 = \$500,000$), it means that the government will be able to undertake Project 1 fully and Project 2 partially, given the budget constraint.

The following provides the complete simplex formulation of our two-project capital rationing problem:

$$\text{Maximize NPV} = 1.5X_1 + 1.25X_2 \tag{10.10}$$

Subject to

$$X_1 + S_1 = \$1,500,000 \tag{10.11}$$

$$X_2 + S_2 = \$2,000,000 \tag{10.12}$$

$$X_1 + X_2 + S_3 = \$3,000,000 \tag{10.13}$$

$$X_1, X_2, S_1, S_2, S_3 \geq 0 \tag{10.14}$$

A computer solution to the simplex problem would produce the following results:

$$X_1 = \$1.5 \text{ million}; X_2 = \$1.5 \text{ million}$$
$$S_1 = \$0; \ S_2 = \$500,000; \ S_3 = \$0$$
$$\text{Maximum (Optimal) NPV} = \$4,125,000$$

which is exactly what we obtained using the graphical method.[7]

10.3.1.3 The Dual
Every maximization (minimization) problem in linear programming has a corresponding minimization (maximization) problem. The original problem is called the primal and the corresponding problem is called the dual.[8] The primary purpose of using a dual is to determine the accuracy of the primal. Another reason why the dual is used is that it is sometimes easier to solve a linear programming problem first by solving its associated dual than solving the primal problem directly, especially when the primal has a large number of variables but few constraints. For instance, a primal problem with n decision variables and two constraints can be easily transformed into a two-variable problem that can be solved graphically or using the traditional simplex method.[9] Finally, the duality in linear programming provides useful information that can lead to a better understanding of the problem solution.

An important contribution of the simplex method other than finding the optimal solution in a more efficient manner is that it produces a variety of information that policy makers will find useful for making allocation and other decisions. Of particular significance is the shadow price. Shadow prices show the amount of latitude the decision makers have in utilizing the available resources. More specifically, they reflect the changes in the objective function as a result of marginal (one unit) changes in the right-hand side (RHS) coefficients of the constraint equations. Since the constraints are generally expressed in terms of equalities ($=$), less than or equal to ($\leq$) for slack variables, and greater than or equal to ($\geq$) for surplus variables, the changes are directly related to the nature of these constraints. For a less than or equal to constraint, the shadow prices represent the amount by

Table 10.2 Dual solution of the primal problem

	X_1	X_2	RHS	Dual value (shadow price)
Maximize	$1.5m	$1.25m		
Constraint 1	1	0	≤$1,500,000	0.25
Constraint 2	0	1	≤$2,000,000	0
Constraint 3	1	1	≤$3,000,000	1.25
Solution	$1,500,000	$1,500,000	$4,125,000	

which the value of the objective function will increase (for a maximization problem) or decrease (for a minimization problem) as a result of one unit increase (or decrease) in the input. For a greater than or equal to constraint, they indicate the amount by which the objective function will increase for one unit decrease in the input. In other words, the shadow price represents the maximum amount a decision maker will be willing to pay to acquire one additional unit of resource for a slack variable or to have a requirement relaxed by one unit for a surplus variable.

Interestingly, the information on shadow prices can be easily obtained from the final tableau of the simplex solution or directly from the dual of a primal problem. Table 10.2 provides the dual values (shadow prices) for our two-project primal capital rationing problem. According to the table, the dual value for constraint 1 is 0.25, for 2 it is 0, and for 3 is it is 1.25. What this means is that optimal solution (NPV) will increase by $0.25 for one dollar increase in the RHS coefficient of constraint 1, from $1,500,000 to $1,500,001, by $0 for one dollar increase in the RHS coefficient of constraint 2, from $2,000,000 to $2,000,001, and by $1.25 for one dollar increase in the RHS coefficient of constraint 3, from $3,000,000 to $3,000,001. Since the constraint 2 has a value of 0, it means that its marginal contribution is 0. In other words, increasing the allocation for Project 2 by an additional dollar, from $2,000,000 to $2,000,001, will not change the optimal solution in the objective function.

It is important to note, however, that shadow prices are valid within the specific range of additional units one can acquire. What this means is that one must be able to determine the amount of additional resources the government will need in order to realize the potential increases, as given by the shadow prices.

10.3.1.4 Sensitivity Analysis

Prudent decision making requires that we make an effort to determine how sensitive an optimal solution is to discrete changes in the input parameters of a linear programming problem. For instance, what would happen if the objective function coefficients were different for any of the decision variables or what would happen if there was a change in the technical coefficients of the constraint equations? Similarly, what would be the nature of the optimal solution if some of the input resources (right-hand side coefficients) were different from those included in the model? Post-optimality or sensitivity analysis provides answers to these questions by offering the flexibility a model needs to determine the optimal solution under changed conditions. We can use the current example to examine how the questions raised above affect the optimal solution. We can consider them simultaneously or one at a time.

Let us say that we change the objective function coefficients from 1.5 to 1.4 for Project 1 and from 1.25 to 1.3 for Project 2. To keep the problem simple, let us keep the same technological coefficients, as before, but increase the RHS coefficient for Project 1 to $1.6 million, lower it for Project 2 to $1.8 million, and increase the budget availability to $3.2 million. Please note that changes in technological coefficients do not occur usually during the course of an operation unless there has been a measurement error or a technological improvement, or some other factors that may actually reduce the requirement of a particular resource.

The simplex solution of the revised problem would produce the following results:

$$X_1 = \$1.6 \text{ million}; X_2 = \$1.6 \text{ million}$$
$$S_1 = \$0; \quad S_2 = \$200,000; \quad S_3 = \$0$$
$$\text{Maximum (Optimal) NPV} = \$4,320,000$$

The results of the simplex solution of the revised problem turned out to be quite similar to those obtained for the original problem in that the government should be able to undertake Project 1 fully and Project 2 partially, as it falls short by $200,000, given the budget constraint. If, on the other hand, we could increase the budget constraint by another $0.2 million to $3.4 million ($3.2 million + $0.2 million) to cover the full costs of the projects, the government should be able to undertake both projects and there will be no need for capital rationing or the use of methods such as linear programming. The dual values for the revised problem would also produce marginally different results from the earlier solution. Table 10.3 provides the dual values (shadow prices) for our revised primal capital rationing problem. The dual value for constraint 1 is 0.1, 0 for constraint 2, and 1.3 for constraint 3. Looking at the optimal solution, it appears that there will be an increase in the NPV by $195,000 [$4,320,000 − $4,125,000 = $195,000]. As before, the marginal changes in constraint 2 will not make any contribution to the optimal solution.

It should be worth noting that sensitivity analysis is useful in situations where there are some uncertainties as to the estimates used in developing the problem (model). In particular, it allows identification of the factors to which the solution is most sensitive, so the decision makers can pay additional attention to those factors.

Table 10.3 Dual solution of the revised primal problem

	X_1	X_2	RHS	Dual value (shadow price)
Maximize	$1.4m	$1.3m		
Constraint 1	1	0	≤$1,600,000	0.1
Constraint 2	0	1	≤$1.800,000	0
Constraint 3	1	1	≤$3,200,000	1.3
Solution	$1,600,000	$1,600,000	$4,320,000	

10.3.1.5 Multi-year Capital Rationing Problem

Since the capital budgets extend over multiple years, let us look at another capital rationing problem for a government involving two capital projects (X_1 and X_2), their costs, net present values, and a two-year budget allocation. Although in reality these budgets are prepared for five or six years, to keep the problem simple we will use two years of data only. Computationally, it should not make any difference how many years are included in a problem; the process will be the same, as long as one has the requisite data. Let us say that it will cost the government $5.4 million for Project 1 in year 1 and $3.7 million in year 2, and $4.2 million for Project 2 in year 1 and $2.1 million for Project 2 in year 2. The corresponding NPV for the two projects are $8.5 million and $7.1 million, respectively. The total amount of budget available for the two years is $6 million, divided into $4 million for year 1 and $2 million for year 2. Our objective is to find the value of the projects that will maximize the objective function (NPV) subject to the budget constraints. We assume that the projects are independent, but not mutually exclusive.

Following the structure used in Eqs. 10.10–10.14, we can formally present the general structure of the capital rationing problem for the government as

$$\text{Maximize NPV} = 8.5X_1 + 7.1X_2 \tag{10.15}$$

Subject to

$$5.4X_1 + 4.2X_2 + S_1 = 4.0 \quad \text{Year 1} \tag{10.16}$$

$$3.7X_1 + 2.1X_2 + S_2 = 2.0 \quad \text{Year 2} \tag{10.17}$$

$$\left. \begin{array}{l} X_1 + S_3 = 1 \\ X_2 + S_4 = 1 \end{array} \right\} \begin{array}{l} \text{Upper limits on} \\ \text{project acceptance} \end{array} \tag{10.18}$$

$$X_j, S_i \geq 0 \quad (\text{for } j = 1, 2; \quad i = 1, 2, 3, 4) \text{ Non - negativity constraints} \tag{10.19}$$

It is necessary to point out a few things about the model formulation: The general structure of the model is similar to that shown in Eqs. 10.7–10.9 in that a couple of slack variables have been added to each less than or equal to constraints to provide a more complete interpretation of the results. For instance, the slack variables S_1 and S_2 indicate the amount of budget that will remain unallocated to the two projects, while the variables S_3 and S_4 represent the percent of projects 1 and 2 that are not feasible or acceptable to the government. Furthermore, the sum of the X's and its corresponding slack variables must equal to 1.00 or 100%, meaning that the entire project must be either accepted or not accepted. A summary of the simplex solution is presented below:

$$X_1 = 0; \ X_2 = 0.9524$$
$$S_1 = \$0; \ S_2 = \$0; \ S_3 = 0; \ S_4 = 0.0476$$
$$\text{Optimal Solution: } \$6762.040$$

The results of the optimal solution are interpreted in the following way: Projects with a solution value equal to 1.0 indicate that they are perfectly feasible and should be accepted, while projects with a value less than 1.0 are partially feasible, indicating that their acceptance should be at the discretion of the decision makers. On the other hand, projects that have a value of 0 indicate that they are non-feasible and, as such, should be rejected in favor of the one attainable. Looking at the results, it appears that project 1 is not feasible since it has a value of 0, while project 2 is 95.24% feasible. In addition, S_1 and S_2 came out to be 0, indicating that the entire budget allocation of $6 million ($4 million in year 1 and $2 million in year 2) has been spent on the project that has been designated for acceptance. Furthermore, S_3 and S_4 were 0 and 0.0476, respectively, indicating that the project corresponding to the slack variable S_3 (Project 1) was not acceptable, while the project corresponding to the slack variable S_4 (Project 2) was only 4.76% not feasible ($0.9524 + 0.0476 = 1$). The result produces a maximum NPV of $6.7619 million for the accepted project.

The Extended Problem

Let us now look at the larger problem involving the nine projects, discussed earlier. As shown in Table 10.1, the nine projects together will cost the government a total of $69.03 million over a three-year period, of which $33.62 million will be in year 1, $23.07 in year 2, and $12.34 million in year 3. Let us suppose that the government has a limited budget that will allow it to spend a maximum of $21.75 million ($11.15 + $7.15 + $3.45). The objective of the government is to maximize the net present value (NPV) of the projects, subject to the budget constraints. As before, we assume the projects to be independent but not mutually exclusive. Table 10.4 shows the breakdown of the information for the problem.

Using the information in Table 10.4, we can now formulate the LP model for the extended problem as

$$\text{Maximize NPV} = 5.27X_1 + 4.88X_2 + 2.56X_3 + 4.42X_4 + 2.35X_5 + 14.27X_6$$
$$+ 2.31X_7 + 1.25X_8 + 1.06X_9 \qquad (10.20)$$

Subject to

$$5.91X_1 + 2.83X_2 + 3.46X_3 + 2.37X_4 + 2.38X_5 + 9.42X_6 + 2.74X_7 + 2.28X_8$$
$$+ 2.23X_9 \leq 11.15 \qquad \text{Year 1} \qquad (10.21)$$

$$3.35X_1 + 2.12X_2 + 3.13X_3 + 1.73X_4 + 2.14X_5 + 7.25X_6 + 1.12X_7 + 1.11X_8$$
$$+ 1.12X_9 \leq 7.15 \qquad \text{Year 2} \qquad (10.22)$$

$$1.35X_2 + 2.41X_3 + 1.01X_4 + 1.64X_5 + 4.48X_6 + 0.83X_7$$
$$+ 0.62X_9 \leq 3.45 \qquad \text{Year 3} \qquad (10.23)$$

$$X_j \geq 0 \quad (\text{for } j = 1, 2, 3, \ldots\ldots, 9) \quad \text{Non - negativity constraints} \qquad (10.24)$$

Table 10.4 Capital improvement projects, projected costs, and NPV

Projects	Project description	Cost-year1 ($M)	Cost-year2 ($M)	Cost-year3 ($M)	NPV ($M)
X_1	Construct a technology center	5.91	3.35	–	5.27
X_2	Upgrade the water treatment plant	2.83	2.12	1.35	4.88
X_3	Construct a new community health center	3.46	3.13	2.41	2.56
X_4	Renovate the civic center	2.37	1.73	1.01	4.42
X_5	Repair the old pedestrian bridge	2.38	2.14	1.64	2.35
X_6	Undertake downtown redevelopment	9.42	7.25	4.48	14.27
X_7	Expand the Southside commercial strip	2.74	1.12	0.83	2.31
X_8	Renovate the administrative building	2.28	1.11	–	1.25
X_9	Construct a new youth activity center	2.23	1.12	0.62	1.06
Projected costs: $69.03		33.62	23.07	12.34	
Budget constraint: $21.75		11.15	7.15	3.45	

As with the two-variable case, the decision variables are continuous in that partial projects are allowed and all the input parameters are known with certainty. With the slack variables added, the complete model will look like, as follows:

$$\text{Maximize NPV} = 5.27X_1 + 4.88X_2 + 2.56X_3 + 4.42X_4 + 2.35X_5 + 14.27X_6$$
$$+ 2.31X_7 + 1.25X_8 + 1.06X_9 \tag{10.25}$$

Subject to

$$5.91X_1 + 2.83X_2 + 3.46X_3 + 2.37X_4 + 2.38X_5 + 9.42X_6 + 2.74X_7 + 2.28X_8$$
$$+ 2.23X_9 + S_1 = 11.15 \qquad \text{Year 1} \tag{10.26}$$

$$3.35X_1 + 2.12X_2 + 3.13X_3 + 1.73X_4 + 2.14X_5 + 7.25X_6 + 1.12X_7 + 1.11X_8$$
$$+ 1.12X_9 + S_2 = 7.15 \qquad \text{Year 2} \tag{10.27}$$

$$1.35X_2 + 2.41X_3 + 1.01X_4 + 1.64X_5 + 4.48X_6 + 0.83X_7$$
$$+ 0.62X_9 + S_3 = 3.45 \qquad \text{Year 3} \tag{10.28}$$

$$\left.\begin{array}{lll} X_1 + S_4 = 1 & X_2 + S_5 = 1 & X_3 + S_6 = 1 \\ X_4 + S_7 = 1 & X_5 + S_8 = 1 & X_6 + S_9 = 1 \\ X_7 + S_{10} = 1 & X_9 + S_{11} = 1 & X_8 + S_{12} = 1 \end{array}\right\} \begin{array}{l} \text{Upper limits} \\ \text{on project} \\ \text{acceptance} \end{array} \tag{10.29}$$

X_j, $S_i \geq 0$ (for $j = 1, 2, 3, \ldots, 9$; $i = 1, 2, 3, \ldots, 12$) Non-negativity constraints   (10.30)

As before, several slack variables were added to each less than or equal to constraints to provide a more complete interpretation of the results. For instance, the slack variables S_1, S_2, and S_3 represent the amount of budget dollars that will remain unallocated to any of the nine projects for years 1, 2, and 3. On the other hand, the slack variables, from S_4 through S_{12}, represent the percentage of the projects that will not be acceptable to the government. In general, the sum of X_j and its corresponding slack must add up to 1.0 or 100%. This is shown in the non-negativity constraint, which has been modified to show the upper limit for each project. Table 10.5 provides a brief summary of the optimal solution of the complete model.

Looking at Table 10.5, it appears that only two of the nine projects are completely feasible (2 and 4, that is, $X_2 = 1.0$, $X_4 = 1.0$), three are partially feasible (1, 6, and 7, that is, $X_1 = 0.5040$, $X_6 = 0.1168$, and $X_7 = 0.6829$), and the rest are non-feasible, as shown under the solution value. The values corresponding to the slack variables S_1, S_2, and S_3 indicate the budgeted amount that remains unallocated for all three years. The table also introduces two new terms—basic and non-basic variables. A basic variable typically has a non-zero solution and a non-basic variable has a zero solution. Put simply, projects 2 and 4 are completely feasible, while 50.40% of project 1, 11.68% of project 6, and 68.29% of project 7 are partially feasible and the remaining four projects are not feasible at all; as such, they should be rejected. Together, the projects used up 100% of the budget for all years 1, 2, and 3 ($S_1 = 0$, $S_2 = 0$, and $S_3 = 0$) in that nothing remains unallocated and generate a maximum objective function value of $15.2 million, which is the maximum NPV for the completely and partially feasible projects.

Table 10.5 The LP solution summary: extended problem[a]

Basic variable (primal)	Solution value (primal)	Non-basic variable (primal)	Solution value (primal)	Variable (slack/ surplus)	Dual value (shadow price)
X_1	0.5040	X_3	0.0000	S_1	0.0125
X_2	1.0000	X_5	0.0000	S_2	1.5511
X_4	1.0000	X_8	0.0000	S_3	0.6489
X_6	0.1168	X_9	0.0000	S_4	0.0000
X_7	0.6829	S_1	0.0000	S_5	0.6804
S_4	0.4960	S_2	0.0000	S_6	0.0000
S_6	1.0000	S_3	0.0000	S_7	1.0517
S_8	1.0000	S_5	0.0000	S_8	0.0000
S_9	0.8832	S_7	0.0000	S_9	0.0000
S_{10}	0.3171			S_{10}	0.0000
S_{11}	1.0000			S_{11}	0.0000
S_{12}	1.0000			S_{12}	0.0000

[a]Optimal solution: $Z = \$15.2002$ million

Shadow Prices

As noted previously, shadow prices play an important role in linear programming. They tell us what kind of changes will result in the objective function for an additional unit of change in the resource constraints (RHS coefficients), which in this case will be budget constraint for each of the three years. They are associated with both slack and surplus variables and can be obtained from the objective function (Z_j) row of the final tableau of the simplex solution, as well as directly from the dual of a primal problem. The rule of thumb is that for resource constraints, the slack or surplus variables that are basic in the optimal solution their shadow prices will be zero and those that are non-basic in the optimal solution their shadow prices will be positive. For instance, the presence of variables S_1, S_2 and S_3 as non-basic variables in the optimal solution means that the budgets allocated for the three years have been completely exhausted (Table 10.5). The corresponding shadow prices for the three variables are 0.0125, 1.5511, and 0.6489, respectively (shown under the dual value column). The values indicate the amount by which the objective function (NPV) would increase for each dollar of additional budget the government could obtain. Since the values are expressed in millions of dollars, it means that for each additional million dollar of allocation the objective function would increase by $0.0125 million in NPV for S_1, $1.5511 million for S_2 and $0.6489 million for S_3.

On the other hand, if the slack variables for any of the budget constraints in the primal solution had a positive value for a given year, say, 0.4567 for year 2, it would indicate the amount ($0.4567 million) by which the budget would remain unallocated for that year. As such, its shadow price would be zero under the dual value column meaning that the government would be unwilling to spend any additional resources on it since it has some unspent resources. Operationally, it means that if we were to change the right-hand side value for the constraint (say, increase), it will not have much effect on the objective function.

In addition to indicating how the objective function will change as a result of a marginal change in the constraints, the shadow prices serve another important purpose: They allow the decision makers to rank the projects according to their relative importance, which may be different from those obtained under NPV or IRR. Part of the reason for this is that under NPV and IRR, projects are treated independently and, more importantly, without any resource limitations which is not the case with shadow prices. Therefore, based on the shadow prices, the rank order (R) of the two completely accepted projects will be X_2 (R1) and X_4 (R2).

In general, shadow prices apply to both accepted and rejected projects and, as noted above, can be obtained directly from the dual of a primal problem. Although projects that are not feasible should be rejected, there are circumstances when one may be forced to accept a rejected project, especially if their shadow prices are low. The shadow prices for rejected projects indicate the amount by which the objective function would decrease if we are to accept the rejected (non-feasible) projects. What this means is that if one is forced to accept a project that is not feasible, it is quite likely that the result will produce a less than optimal utilization of the allocated funds, but for projects with low shadow prices, the effect on the

Table 10.6 The LP solution summary: revised problem[a]

Basic variable (primal)	Solution value (primal)	Non-basic variable (primal)	Solution value (primal)	Variable (slack/ surplus)	Dual value (shadow price)
X_1	1.0000	X_3	0.0000	S_1	0.5482
X_2	1.0000	X_9	0.0000	S_2	0.0000
X_4	1.0000	S_1	0.0000	S_3	0.6373
X_5	0.4756	S_3	0.0000	S_4	2.0299
X_6	1.0000	S_4	0.0000	S_5	2.4681
X_7	1.0000	S_5	0.0000	S_6	0.0000
X_8	0.7667	S_7	0.0000	S_7	2.4770
S_2	0.0612	S_9	0.0000	S_8	0.0000
S_6	1.0000	S_{10}	0.0000	S_9	6.2504
S_8	0.5244			S_{10}	0.2788
S_{11}	0.2333			S_{11}	0.0000
S_{12}	1.0000			S_{12}	0.0000

[a]Optimal solution: $Z = \$33.226$ million

objective function would also be low. In general, the smaller the shadow prices for rejected projects, the more amenable they would be to acceptance. Project 8 would fall into that category.

As before, we can rank the rejected projects in terms of their shadow prices but, in this case, it was not possible because their shadow prices came out to be zero. Interestingly, partially accepted projects are not ranked because their shadow prices are also zero, which would be projects 1 and 6 in our example.

Sensitivity Analysis

As noted earlier, once the initial solution has been obtained for an optimization problem, it is important to do a sensitivity analysis on the solution to see what kinds of results the model formulation would produce for any changes in the problem. For example, we can change the budget allocation (RHS of the constraints) for each of the three years, assuming that the decision makers are able to find some additional resources to support as many projects as they can. (We could also assume that budget may actually decline.) Let us say that the revised allocations are now $26.15 million for year 1, $17.50 million for year 2, and $8.45 million for year 3. This would improve the solution considerably, as shown in Table 10.6. The number of projects completely feasible increased from two to five (1, 2, 4, 6, and 7), while the number of partially feasible projects remained at two (5 and 8), with two projects (3 and 9) completely unfeasible. The optimal solution for the objective function also increased from $15.2002 million to $33.226 million for the completely feasible and partially feasible projects, which is to be expected because of increased allocation.

Furthermore, the values corresponding to the slack variables S_1, S_2, and S_3 indicate that the budgeted amount for years 1 and 3 has been completely used up ($S_1=0$ and $S_3=0$), while $0.0612 million remains unallocated for year 2 ($S_2=0.0612$). In other words, projects 1, 2, 4, 6, and 7 are completely acceptable, while 47.56% of project 5 and 76.67% of project 8 are partially feasible, and the remaining two projects (3 and 9) are not feasible at all. Together, the completely feasible and partially feasible projects used up almost the entire budget for all three years.

Additional changes in the right-hand side constraints, as well as the objective function coefficients for individual projects, would have improved the solution some more. The analysis did not make any attempt to change the technological coefficients (costs associated with individual projects) because they are generally assumed to be fixed since they are often based on engineering (pre-determined) cost estimates. However, if we were to make some changes in the coefficients, the results would be reflected in the optimal solution.

10.3.2 Integer Programming

An interesting question that emerges from the fractional solution of the LP problem is whether partial projects make enough sense. There is no definitive answer to this other than the type of projects being evaluated and what is important to the decision makers in light of a given problem. Obviously, the completely feasible projects would be more attractive to a decision maker than partial projects, but the latter would give the decision makers an opportunity to reevaluate their importance in light of the given objective. However, if fractional solution is not acceptable, the alternative would be to use integer programming (IP). Integer programming is really an extension of linear programming with an added constraint that the decision variables must be integers, although there are cases where it is possible to have a combination of both. When the decision variables are all integers, it is called a pure integer programming problem, and when they are a mixture of both (fractional and integer-valued), it is called a mixed integer programming problem. Pure integer programming means that projects are either accepted or rejected which is consistent with the non-divisibility characteristics of most public projects.[10]

Structurally, integer programming is quite similar to linear programming; as such, it is often treated as an extension of linear programming and, therefore, we can use the same solution procedures for both. In other words, we can treat it as an LP problem by ignoring the integer requirement, then solving it using the standard simplex method, as in linear programming. If the solution produces all integer values, then one has an optimal solution for the problem; if not, there are other methods one can use such as Gomory's cutting-plane and the branch-and-bound method.[11]

10.3.2.1 Capital Budgeting Application

To give an example, let us go back to the problem we used for the two-year linear programming problem with two independent capital improvement projects, X_1 and X_2, with a corresponding NPV of $8.5 million for X_1 and $7.1 million for X_2. The costs of the two projects, respectively, are $5.4 million for X_1 and $4.2 million for X_2 for year 1, and $3.7 million for X_1 and $2.1 million for X_2 for year 2. The budget constraints for the two projects, respectively, were $4 million for year 1 and $2 million for year 2. As before, we assume the projects to be independent. Since the original problem had fractional values for the two projects, including their corresponding NPVs, we decided to round them off to their nearest integers (e.g., $8.5 million $\approx$ $9 million).

We can now formally write the problem as

$$\text{Maximize NPV} = 9X_1 + 7X_2 \tag{10.31}$$

Subject to

$$5X_1 + 4X_2 \leq 4 \quad \text{Year 1} \tag{10.32}$$

$$4X_1 + 2X_2 \leq 2 \quad \text{Year 2} \tag{10.33}$$

$$X_j = (0, 1) \quad (\text{for } j = 1, 2) \tag{10.34}$$

It should be worth noting that formulation of the problem compared with the (primal) linear programming formulation is that Eq. 10.34 has a 0–1 condition, which guarantees that each project is completely accepted ($X_j = 1$) or that it is rejected ($X_j = 0$). The solution of the problem using the simplex method, as before, produces the following results: $X_1 = 0$, $X_2 = 1$, and an optimal NPV of $7 million. The results indicate that project 1 is not acceptable since $X_1 = 0$, while project 2 is acceptable since $X_2 = 1$.

We can easily extend the application to our extended budget problem involving the nine projects, and present it formally as

$$\text{Maximize NPV} = 5X_1 + 5X_2 + 3X_3 + 4X_4 + 2X_5 + 14X_6 + 2X_7 + X_8 + X_9 \tag{10.35}$$

Subject to

$$6X_1 + 3X_2 + 3X_3 + 2X_4 + 2X_5 + 9X_6 + 3X_7 + 2X_8 + 2X_9 \leq 11 \quad \text{Year 1} \tag{10.36}$$

$$3X_1 + 2X_2 + 3X_3 + 2X_4 + 2X_5 + 7X_6 + X_7 + X_8 + X_9 \leq 7 \quad \text{Year 2} \tag{10.37}$$

$$X_2 + 2X_3 + X_4 + 2X_5 + 4X_6 + X_7 \quad + X_9 \leq 3 \quad \text{Year 3} \tag{10.38}$$

$$X_j = \{0, 1\} \quad (\text{for } j = 1, 2, 3, \ldots\ldots, 9) \tag{10.39}$$

As before, since the original problem had fractional values for all nine projects, including their corresponding NPVs, we round them off to their nearest integers (e.g., $5.91 million $\approx$ $6 million). Table 10.7 shows the results of the extended problem. As the table shows, only 3 of the 9 projects (X_1, X_2, and X_5) were found

Table 10.7 The IP solution summary

Projects	Project description	Solution value[a] (acceptable projects)
X_1	Expand the civic center complex	1
X_2	Renovate the police building	1
X_3	Replace the water treatment facility	0
X_4	Construct a new recreation center	0
X_5	Complete street resurfacing	1
X_6	Construct a new prison facility	0
X_7	Expand the district-5 health center	0
X_8	Renovate the administrative building	0
X_9	Expand the central library	0

[a]Optimal solution: $Z = \$12$ million

to be acceptable with a maximum NPV of $12 million. Although no attempt was made here, we could have done some sensitivity analysis, similar to the linear programming problem to see additional changes in project acceptance and optimal NPV.

10.3.3 Dealing with Multiple Goals

Up to this point, our discussion of capital rationing and budget allocation focused on a single goal or objective but, in reality, one frequently encounters not one but multiple goals of varying nature, which makes it difficult to apply the conventional linear or integer programming models to these types of problems. The model that has been frequently used for multiple goals is a variation of linear programming called goal programming (GP). It was originally developed by Charnes and Cooper (1961) and subsequently refined by Lee (1972), Ignizio (1976), Steuer (1986), and others. The way it works is that instead of maximizing or minimizing an objective function directly, as in conventional linear programming, it attempts to minimize the deviations from goals sequentially. The deviations, represented by a set of deviational variables, ds, take a special meaning in goal programming in that the objective function becomes the minimization of these variables.[12]

The procedure for goal programming is not as complicated as it may seem at a first glance. Each goal is set at a level which may not necessarily be the most attainable, but one that decision makers would be satisfied to achieve. From an operational point of view, the objective then becomes one of finding a set of solutions for these goals in light of some stated targets, along with their associated constraints. As a general rule, goal achievement starts with the most important goal, one that has the highest priority, and continues until the achievement of the least important goal with lowest priority. This is known as sequential solution. The process allows the decision makers to see the extent to which the priorities have been achieved or whether they need to make additional changes in the model.

To give an example, let us go back to the linear programming problem with two capital improvement projects, X_1 and X_2, each with a life span of two years along with their corresponding costs, and set it up as a goal programming problem. We make a minor change in the problem by setting an arbitrary NPV goal value of $10 million for the objective function. We will call the budget constraints the environmental constraints and the objective function as the goal constraint. We assume the projects are of equal importance and have the same priority.

We can now formulate the goal programming problem as

$$\text{Minimize} \quad P_1 d_1^+ + P_2 d_2^+ + P_3 d_3^- \tag{10.40}$$

Subject to
Environmental Constraints:

$$\text{Year 1:} \quad 5.4X_1 + 4.2X_2 \quad \leq 4 \tag{10.41}$$

$$\text{Year 2:} \quad 3.7X_1 + 2.1X_2 \quad \leq 2 \tag{10.42}$$

Goal Constraint:

$$\text{NPV:} \quad 8.5X_1 + 7.1X_2 + d_3^- - d_3^+ = 10 \tag{10.43}$$

$$X_1, X_2, d_3^-, d_3^+ \geq 0 \tag{10.44}$$

where Ps are the (preemptive) priority weights and ds are the deviational variables (Note 12). The weights are typically assigned by the decision makers. They could also be used from the priority weights produced by the Analytic Hierarchy Process and other similar methods, discussed earlier.

As before, we apply the simplex method to solve the problem. Table 10.8 shows the computer solution for the problem. As can be seen from the table, the project 1 came out to be not feasible ($X_1=0$), while project 2 came out to be 95.24% feasible ($X_2=0.9524$). Similarly, the goal constraint has been underachieved by $3.2381 million, meaning that NPV goal will be achieved by $6.6719 million ($10 million−$3.3281). Likewise, the results of the environmental constraints indicate that the budget allocation of $6 million for year 1 and year 2 has been fully spent on the accepted project, as given by 0 deviation values.

Table 10.8 The GP solution summary: basic problem

Project acceptance	Constraint analysis	Goal	Goal achievement	Over- or underachievement
$X_1=0.0000$	$d_1^+ = 0.0000$	NPV Goal	6.7619	3.2381 (under)
$X_2=0.9524$	$d_1^- = 0.0000$			
	$d_2^+ = 0.0000$			
	$d_2^- = 0.0000$			
	$d_3^+ = 0.0000$			
	$d_3^- = 3.2381$			

The problems such as underachievement are quite common in goal programming and can be easily fixed with some changes in the goal or environmental constraints. For instance, we could have reformulated the problem by reducing the goal value for NPVs, say, to $7 million, which would have realized the goal by $6.7619 million with an underachievement of $0.2381 million ($7 million−$0.2381 million). A further reduction of the NPV goal to $6 million would fully realize the goal value. We could have also changed the budget constraint, say, to $7 million for year 1 and $4 million for year 2. The result would be 87.89% acceptance for project 1 and 35.63% for project 2, and so forth.

The problem can be easily extended to include all nine projects, but is not considered here because of the involved process, and the problem will require to set up the model with all the attended constraints and is beyond the scope of the chapter. However, there is a wide body of literature on goal programming dealing directly with capital rationing that has grown considerably over the years that interested readers may find useful.

10.3.4 Other Programming Methods

The programming models described above are structurally simple and easy to formulate as long as the model conditions are known with certainty, but they can pose serious challenges when the conditions become uncertain. There is a whole range of models that have been developed over the years that can effectively deal with these problems. This section briefly highlights some of these models, in particular Monte Carlo simulation, stochastic linear programming, and quadratic programming.

10.3.4.1 Monte Carlo Simulation

Monte Carlo simulations are abstract representation of a real-world system that captures, with the help of mathematical models, the principal operating characteristics of the system as it moves through time-variant random variables (random variables whose values change with time). These simulations are primarily based on a systems approach consisting of three basic elements: input, process, and output. The inputs are mostly parameters (values specified by the decision makers) and exogenous variables (factors over which the decision makers do not have any control). The process includes identities and operating equations that describe the functioning of the system using parameters and exogenous variables, while the outputs include endogenous variables that show how efficiently the system is operating or is likely to operate.

Monte Carlo simulations have an advantage over the conventional methods in that they can more effectively deal with the exogenous variables, because they are mostly defined by specific probability distributions. They are also effective in dealing with interrelationships between different variables, as well as identities and operating equations that are non-linear in nature. However, one should be careful about using simulation as the input requirements for these models can put great demand on the decision makers. In the same vein, the researcher has to have a sound understanding of the mathematical properties of the real system under consideration which may not be obvious to a lay person.

10.3.4.2 Stochastic Programming

Like Monte Carlo simulation, stochastic linear programming (SLP) is quite useful in dealing with capital rationing problems with uncertainty. In stochastic linear programming, the LP components of the method usually replace the identities and operating equations of the simulation models. One of the earliest and well-known applications of stochastic programming to capital rationing was by Salazar and Sen (1968), where the authors introduced several uncertainty conditions related to economic variables that were likely to affect a capital project, in particular its cash flows. Over time, SLP models have become more complex, as efforts were made to capture the intricacies associated with various uncertainty conditions.

A special case of stochastic linear programming that has received some attention in the literature on capital rationing is chance-constrained programming (CCP). The basic idea behind CCP is to maximize an expected objective function subject to economic and other constraints that can be relaxed to accommodate for random variations in the system. In other words, unlike the LP model where the optimal solution will not violate any constraints, in chance-constraint programming there is at least one constraint for which some probability of violation is acceptable. Although both SLP and CCP deal with uncertainty conditions, the solution methodology for CCP is more complex than the standard stochastic methodologies. In general, CCP requires the derivation of deterministic equivalents for all chance constraints by taking into consideration the shape and parameters of the probability distributions of all random variables. The derivation often produces non-linear equations, which can greatly complicate the feasibility of the solution.

10.3.4.3 Quadratic Programming

Quadratic programming (QP) is another special case of mathematical programming that can be applied to capital rationing problems under conditions of both certainty and uncertainty (quadratic stochastic programming). In a typical quadratic programming, the objective is to maximize a quadratic objective function subject to a set of linear constraints. The QP models are much easier to solve than non-linear programming models, because the feasible region is convex (curved outward on a two-dimensional plane). Convexity ensures that any feasible solution is also a global optimal solution, meaning that a feasible solution that maximizes the objective function also maximizes it over the entire set of feasible solutions. Put simply, one only needs to find a local optimum, instead of an infinite number of local optima to reach the global optimum.

10.4   Application Dilemma

A question that frequently comes up in any discussion on the use of tools such as mathematical programming and similar analytical methods is how often are these methods used to solve actual problems? While there has been a growing interest in these tools, empirical evidence suggests that most organizations do not use these methods as frequently as one would like, other than problems that require their use, although the trend has been changing in recent years (Gitman and Forrester 1977; Ryan and Ryan 2002). Two things often work against their widespread use: the complexity of the methods that is not always easy to understand and, more importantly, the computational difficulties that take an enormous amount of time to obtain the optimal solution. However, with the availability of various spreadsheets and menu-driven software, it is becoming relatively easy to use these methods far more effectively than it has been in the past. A good example is a study by Jackson and Staunton (1999) which uses the MS Excel Solver for a quadratic programming problem. The study has opened up new opportunities for solving complex optimization problems with spreadsheets, although Excel software has been extensively used for small-scale problems (Emmons et al. 1992). There are plenty of other examples where Excel Solver has been used to solve conventional mathematical programming problems.

10.5 Summary and Conclusion

Capital rationing is a common occurrence in government because of the need to deal with more demands for capital projects and improvement activities than the available resources can permit. There are two basic conditions under which capital rationing occurs: internal and external. Internal capital rationing occurs when management imposes restrictions on capital expenditures either because the projects are not worth undertaking, or the resources designated for capital expenditures have to be transferred to meet the operating needs of the government. External capital rationing occurs, on the other hand, when a government is unable to raise the necessary funds through borrowing either because the government is under severe financial distress, or it has a low bond rating, or it does not have the public support to raise the necessary capital. Regardless, whether funds are internally generated or market induced, capital rationing remains a serious decision problem for a government. Traditionally, the capital rationing problem has been addressed through IRR or NPV, but the problem with these methods is that they do not provide much information on how to maximize the value of the invested capital subject to budget and other constraints that may contribute to the problem. This is where optimization methods such as those used in mathematical programming become useful. Interestingly, the number of these methods and the conditions under which the methods can be applied have increased over the years—each capable of dealing with a complex range of capital rationing problems. This chapter has provided a broad overview of two such methods, namely linear and integer programming, that have been extensively used in capital rationing problems and are also relatively easy to use.

Q1. What is capital rationing? Why is capital rationing important in government? How can cost-benefit analysis be used for capital rationing?

Q2. Suppose that a government is planning on undertaking several investment projects starting next year. It has done a preliminary analysis of the projects and obtained NPV for each. The government has $100 million to invest. The following provides the costs of the projects and their corresponding NPV: Project A: Cost $25 million, NPV $15 million; Project B: Cost $15 million, NPV $10 million; Project C: Cost $30 million, NPV $10 million; Project D: Cost $10 million, NPV $5 million; Project E: Cost $20 million, NPV $10 million; Project F: Cost $40 million, NPV $25 million; Project G: Cost $30 million, NPV $15 million. Since all the projects produce a positive NPV, indicating that they are worthwhile, the government is in a dilemma: How many of the projects can the government undertake without exceeding the budget limit? Which ones? Why?

Q3. What are the advantages of using alternative approaches to capital rationing, such as mathematical programming, to traditional cost-benefit analysis, especially net present value method?

Q4. One of the most widely used mathematical programming models in capital rationing is linear programming. Why is it called linear? What is the basic structure of a typical linear programming model? Explain the terms.

Q5. Consider that a government must allocate its available capital between two projects—Project 1 and Project 2. Assume that Project 1 will produce an NPV of $2 million and Project 2 will produce an NPV of $ 1.75 million. Assume further that we have two decision variables, X_1 and X_2, representing the resources to be allocated between the two projects. The maximum amount that could be allocated to project 1 is $3,000,000 and project 2 is $2,500,000. Total resources that could be allocated should be no more than $4,300,000. Construct a linear programming model for the problem.

Q6. Suppose that we have the following linear programming for a budget allocation problem:

$$\text{Maximize NPV} = \$3.5X_1 + \$2.75X_2$$
$$\text{Subject to } X_1 \leq \$2{,}700{,}000$$
$$X_2 \leq \$3{,}000{,}000$$
$$X_1 + X_2 \leq \$4{,}000{,}000$$
$$X_1, X_2 \geq 0$$

Find a graphical solution of the above linear programming problem and interpret the results.

Q7. What are the advantages of using the simplex method for solving a linear programming problem, as opposed to the graphical method? For the problem in Q5, use the simplex method to solve the problem and interpret the results.

Q8. Suppose that we have new information on the nine capital improvement projects, discussed earlier in the chapter, their projected costs, and NPV: Table 10.9

Given the information in the table, (1) construct a linear programming

Table 10.9 Review question (Q8)

Project	Project description	Cost-year1 ($M)	Cost-year2 ($M)	Cost-year3 ($M)	NPV ($M)
X_1	Construct a technology center	3.25	3.41	0.85	4.85
X_2	Upgrade the water treatment plant	2.52	2.32	1.65	5.28
X_3	Construct a new community health center	3.19	3.72	2.19	2.79
X_4	Renovate the civic center	2.32	2.13	1.25	4.18
X_5	Repair the old pedestrian bridge	2.27	2.42	1.83	2.65
X_6	Undertake downtown redevelopment	8.45	6.90	5.12	12.15
X_7	Expand the Southside commercial strip	3.15	1.46	0.91	2.13
X_8	Renovate the administrative building	2.20	1.27	0.57	1.40
X_9	Construct a new youth activity center	3.15	1.75	0.78	1.13
	Budget constraint: $21.75	$11.15m	$7.15m	$3.45m	

problem and solve it and (2) determine which projects are completely feasible, partially feasible, and not feasible at all.

Q9. What is the difference between a primal and its dual in linear programming? What are the advantages of using dual? Set up the dual for the problem in Q6.

Q10. What is a shadow price? What role does a shadow price play in linear programming? How can the shadow price be obtained from dual?

Q11. What is integer programming? Why should one use integer programming for capital rationing? Can the same solution procedure be used for integer programming? How?

Q12. Suppose that we have a government that is looking into three independent capital improvement projects, X_1, X_2, and X_3 with a corresponding NPV of $5 million for X_1, $8 million for X_2, and $4 million for X_3. The budget is for three years. The costs of the three projects, respectively, are $6 million, $4 million, and $3 million for year 1, and $5 million, $3 million, and $6 million for year 2. The initial budget allocation for the two projects, respectively, is $8 million for year 1, $6 million for year 2, and $4 million for year 3. Construct an integer programming problem and solve it. Also interpret the results you have.

Q13. Let us say that we have the following integer programming problem:

$$\text{Maximize NPV} = 4X_1 + 3X_2 + 5X_3 + 2X_4 + 7X_5 + 9X_6$$

Subject to

$$12X_1 + 5X_2 + 4X_3 + 8X_4 + 3X_5 + 5X_6 \leq 19 \qquad \text{Year 1}$$
$$2X_1 + X_2 + 2X_3 + 5X_4 + 3X_5 + 4X_6 \leq 12 \qquad \text{Year 2}$$
$$5X_1 + 2X_2 + X_3 + 2X_4 + X_5 + 7X_6 \leq 8 \qquad \text{Year 3}$$
$$X_j = \{0, 1\} \quad (\text{for } j = 1, 2, 3, \ldots\ldots, 6)$$

Solve the above integer programming problem, and interpret the results.

Q14. What is goal programming? What are the advantages of using goal programming, as opposed to simple linear or integer programming?

Q15. Suppose that we have the following goal programming problem:

$$\text{Minimize} \quad P_1 d_1^+ + P_2 d_2^+ + P_3 d_3^-$$

Subject to
Environmental Constraints:

	Year 1 :	$3.8X_1 + 6.3X_2$	≤ 5
	Year 2 :	$8.2X_1 + 7.3X_2$	≤ 8

Goal Constraint:
NPV:

$$8.2X_1 + 5.4X_2 + d_1^- - d_1^+ = 11$$
$$11.3X_1 + 9.8X_2 + d_3^- - d_3^+ = 15$$
$$X_1, X_2, d_3^-, d_3^+ \geq 0$$

Given the problem above, (1) define priority weight, (2) consider equal priority weight, then solve the problem and interpret the results.

Notes

1. In general, if an organization truly rations its capital, its value may not be maximized. This is because under the conventional "efficient capital market theory," an organization needs to undertake all the projects to maximize its value (such as stockholders wealth). Since rationing does not allow an organization to undertake all the projects, it obviously will not maximize the value. At the same time, no organization has unlimited resource for it to be able to undertake every single project, which makes capital rationing absolutely necessary. Interestingly, although it does not produce a perfect solution, the use of constraint optimization as an alternative produces a reasonably satisfactory solution to the problem.
2. Much of the credit for this goes to Lorie and Savage (1955) who first discovered the problem with the conventional IRR approach when applied to capital rationing problems, especially with multi-period, interdependent projects. Later on, Charnes et al. (1959) and Weingartner (1966) refined the Lori-Savage model by suggesting a linear programming alternative to the problem.

3. Structurally, all linear programming models must contain three basic components: an objective function component consisting of a set of decision variables (variables whose values are determined as part of achieving the optimal solution) and associated coefficients called the objective function coefficients; a component containing resource and other constraints, given by the capacity for each decision variable called technical coefficients, and an upper or lower limit of resource availability for each constraint equation; and a third component containing a set of non-negativity constraints, specifying the range of values the decision variables must not exceed.

The following presents a typical linear programming model with m decision variables:

$$\text{Maximize } Z = \sum_{j=1}^{m} a_j X_j \tag{10.45}$$

Subject to

$$\sum_{i=1}^{n} c_{it} X_j \leq B_t \tag{10.46}$$

$$0 \leq X_j \leq 1 \tag{10.47}$$

where Z is the objective function to be optimized (maximized or minimized, maximized in this case), X_j is the jth decision variable (for $j = 1, 2, \ldots\ldots, m$), a_j is jth objective function coefficient, c_{it} is the ith technological coefficient associated with jth decision variable at time t (for $i = 1, 2, \ldots\ldots, n$ and $t = 1, 2, \ldots\ldots, T$), and B_t is the resource constraint or resource availability at time t. The terms a, c, and B are known as input parameters of the model (the constants whose values are specified by the decision makers).

4. Extended, the general linear programming problem (maximization or minimization, maximization in this case) with m decision variables and n constraints can be written as follows:

$$\text{Maximize } Z = a_1 X_1 + a_2 X_2 + \ldots + a_m X_m \tag{10.48}$$

Subject to

$$c_{11} X_1 + c_{12} X_2 + \ldots + c_{1m} X_m \leq B_1 \tag{10.49}$$

$$c_{21} X_1 + c_{22} X_2 + \ldots + c_{2m} X_m \leq B_2$$

$$\begin{matrix} \cdot & \cdot & & \cdot & \cdot \\ & & & & \tag{10.50} \\ \cdot & \cdot & & \cdot & \cdot \\ \cdot & \cdot & & \cdot & \cdot \end{matrix}$$

$$c_{n1} X_1 + c_{n2} X_2 + \ldots + c_{nm} X_m \leq B_n \tag{10.51}$$

$$0 \leq X_j \leq 1 \tag{10.52}$$

As before, a, c, and Bs are the constants (input parameters) provided by the decision makers and Xs are the decision variables.

5. There is a simple explanation why the solution would lie at a corner point: Suppose that we are searching for an extreme function (maximum or minimum) such as maximize $z = ax + by$, as in our linear programming problem. We would typically take the first partial derivatives of z with respect to x and y, which would equal a and b. Unfortunately, since we are considering

a linear function in polygon, the system $\frac{\partial z}{\partial x} = 0$; $\frac{\partial z}{\partial y} = 0$ would not produce a solution, if a and b are not equal to 0 in any regular point (e.g., interior point in the polygon). The extremums (extreme points) do not have such problem; as such, we should be searching for extremums (corner points) on the boundary.

6. Developed by Dantzig in 1947, the simplex method remains the primary method of solution to this day, although several other methods have been suggested in recent years. Two good examples are the ellipsoid method, developed by Leonid Khaciyan in 1979 to solve any linear programming problems in a number of steps that are polynomial function of the amount of data defining a linear program. In 1984, Narendra Karmarkar introduced a method called the interior-point method that combines elements of both ellipsoid and the simplex methods. However, the popularity of the simplex method lies in the fact that it is simple yet highly efficient, requiring a few steps that are small multiple of the number of variables in a problem.

7. There is a wide variety of software programs available for solving mathematical programming problems such as Excel Solver (a product of Microsoft), LiPS (Linear Programming Solver), ASO (Analytic Solver Optimization) for larger problems, LINDO (Linear, Interactive, and Discrete Optimizer), and so forth. In addition, there is standard statistical software such as SAS that can solve basic mathematical programming problems. Most of these programs are interactive and user friendly, requiring very little knowledge of computer, as long as one is familiar with the basic methods.

8. All dual problems have three important properties. First, the optimal value of the primal objective function is always equal to the value of the dual objective function, provided that an optimal feasible solution exists. Second, if a decision variable in the objective function has a value that is non-zero, the corresponding slack (or surplus) variable in the dual problem must have an optimal value of zero. Finally, if a slack (or surplus) variable in the primal has a value that is non-zero, the corresponding decision variable in the dual must have an optimal value of zero. Although all linear programming problems have their duals, interpreting the dual solution can be complicated unless the problem is properly converted into its dual first. The rules for converting a standard linear programming problem into its corresponding dual are fairly straightforward: (1) The direction of optimization is reversed in that maximization in the primal becomes the minimization in the dual, and vice versa, (2) the inequalities of the constraint equations are reversed in that the less than or equal to becomes greater than or equal, and vice versa, while non-negativity constraints remain unchanged, (3) the constraints rows in the primal become the columns in the dual, (4) the right-hand side (RHS) constraints in the primal become the objective function coefficients in the dual, while the objective function coefficients become the right-hand side constraints (RHS) in the dual, and (5) the decision variables in the primal, X_js, become the decision variables in the dual, Y_js

9. The following provides a dual formulation of the primal problem for our two-project capital rationing problem:

$$\text{Primal:} \quad \text{Maximize NPV} = 1.5X_1 + 1.25X_2 \tag{10.53}$$

Subject to

$$X_1 \leq \$1,500,000 \tag{10.54}$$

$$X_2 \leq \$2,000,000 \tag{10.55}$$

$$X_1 + X_2 \leq \$3,000,000 \tag{10.56}$$

$$X_1, X_2 \geq 0 \tag{10.57}$$

$$\text{Dual:} \quad \text{Minimize } C = \$\,1,500,000Y_1 + \$2,000,000Y_2 + \$3,000,000Y_3 \tag{10.58}$$

Subject to

$$Y_1 + Y_3 \geq 1.50 \tag{10.59}$$

$$Y_2 + Y_3 \geq 1.25 \tag{10.60}$$

$$Y_1, Y_2, Y_3 \geq 0 \tag{10.61}$$

where Y_js are the new decision variables and C is the objective function, representing cost and other constraints to be minimized. Interestingly, the simplex solution of the dual (minimization) problem is very similar to the primal (maximization) problem. The steps are pretty much the same, except how the variables are entered in the simplex tableau, since the problem is revered; however, the optimal solution remains the same under both.

10. The following provides a typical IP formulation for a maximization problem with m decision variables and n constraints:

$$\text{Maximize } Z = \sum_{j=1}^{m} c_j X_j \tag{10.62}$$

Subject to

$$\sum_{i=1}^{n} a_{ij} X_j \leq B_j \tag{10.63}$$

$$X_j = \{0, 1\} \quad (\text{for } j = 1, 2, 3, \ldots, m) \tag{10.64}$$

where X_j is an integer. The above formulation is very similar to the original LP formulation (Eqs. 14.1–14.3) with one minor difference—the non-negativity constraint can be expressed in terms of 0 and 1, indicating that when $X_j = 1$ the project should be accepted, and when $X_j = 0$ it should be rejected.

11. One of the earlier methods, Gomory (also called the cutting-plane method) uses the standard simplex procedure by adding a constraint to the problem that transforms it to an IP problem. But the method that has received the most attention in recent years is the branch-and-bound because it is more flexible and can be easily applied to a variety of situations, including both integer and mixed-integer problems. the method is based on a two-step solution process, where the problem is first solved the standard simplex method. If the solution produces all integer values, we have an optimal solution. If not, the method proceeds by branching off a feasible non-integer solution into a subset of problems in such a way that continuous solutions that do not satisfy the integer requirement can be eliminated in favor of discrete solutions. The branching process is accomplished by introducing mutually exclusive constraints in order to satisfy the integer requirements of the problem. Since the problems we are discussing here are fairly straightforward, it is possible to deal with them directly as an LP problem with various IP constraints to achieve the same objective.

12. Structurally, goal programming uses the simplex algorithm to find the optimum solution, which makes it easy to understand as well as interpret the results. However, the objective is always to minimize the deviations from goals subject to a set of constraints, where both the objective function and the constraint equations are expressed in linear terms, although non-linear goal programming is not uncommon.
The following presents a typical GP model:

$$\text{Minimize: } \sum_{k=1}^{K} \sum_{i=1}^{n} P_k \left(w_{ik}^- d_i^- + w_{ik}^+ d_i^+ \right) \tag{10.65}$$

Subject to

$$\sum_{j=1}^{m} a_{ij} X_j + d_i^- - d_i^+ = B_j \tag{10.66}$$

$$X_j, d_i^-, d_i^+ \geq 0 \qquad\qquad (10.67)$$

where P_k is the preemptive priority weight ($P_k >> P_{k+1}$), w_{ik} is the weight assigned to ith goal on priority k, a_{ij} is the ith technical coefficients associated with jth project, $B_j =$ is the jth target level, and d_i^-, d_i^+ are deviational variables (for $i = 1, 2, \ldots\ldots, n; j = 1, 2, \ldots\ldots, m;$ and $k = 1, 2, \ldots\ldots, K$).

As can be seen from the above formulation, the deviational variables play an important role in goal programming. The specification of these variables in the objective function determines whether a particular goal is to be reached as exactly as possible, or whether either under- or over-achievement is to be avoided, or whether it is desirable to move as far from some target levels as possible.

The following provides some basic rules for using the deviational variables in the objective function: (1) if the objective is to achieve a minimum level of a goal, use negative deviations (d^-s); (2) if the objective is to not to exceed a specified level of a goal, use positive deviations (d^+s); (3) if the objective is to come as close as possible to a specified goal value, use both positive and negative deviations ($d^+ + d^-$); (4) if the objective is to achieve the maximum attainable value for a given goal, use both negative and positive deviations ($d^- - d^+$); and (5) if the objective is to achieve the minimum attainable value for a given goal level, use both positive and negative deviations ($d^+ - d^-$).

The constraints of the model also deserve some elaboration. Two types of constraints are generally used in goal programming: environmental constraints and goal constraints. Environmental constraints represent restrictions imposed by the decision environment, whereas the goal constraints represent policies imposed by the decision makers. The environmental constraints are similar to the resource constraints in linear programming, and, as such, they require the usual slack or surplus variables. On the other hand, goal constraints are specified as strict equalities that contain both positive and negative deviational variables to indicate over- or underachievement of a goal.

References

Charnes, A., & Cooper, W. W. (1961). *Management Models for and Industrial Applications of Linear Programming*. Englewood Cliffs, NJ: Wiley.

Charnes, A., Cooper, W. W., & Miller, M. H. (1959, January). Application of Linear Programming to Financial Budgeting and the Costing of Funds. *Journal of Business, 32*, 20–46.

Emmons, H., Flowers, A. D., Khot, C. M., & Mathur, K. (1992). *Storm: Quantitative Modeling for Decision Support*. Englewood Cliffs, NJ: Prentice-Hall.

Gitman, L. J., & Forrester, J. R. (1977). A Survey of Capital Budgeting Techniques Used by Major US Firms. *Financial Management, 6*(3), 66–71.

Ignizio, J. P. (1976). *Goal Programming and Extension*. Lexington, MA: Lexington Books.

Jackson, M., & Staunton, M. D. (1999). Quadratic Programming Applications in Finance using Excel. *Journal of the Operations Research Society, 50*(2), 1256–1266.

Lee, S. M. (1972). *Goal Programming for Decision Analysis*. Philadelphia, PA: Auerbach Publishing.

Lorie, J. H., & Savage, L. J. (1955, October). Three Problems of Rationing Capital. *Journal of Business, 28*(4), 229–239.

Ryan, P. A., & Ryan, G. P. (2002). Capital Budgeting Practices of the Fortune 1000: How Have Things Changed? *Journal of Business and Management, 8*(4) (Winter), 355–364.

Salazar, R. C., & Sen, S. K. (1968, December). A Simulation Model of Capital Budgeting Under Uncertainty. *Management Science, 15*, 161–179.

Steuer, R. E. (1986). *Multiple Criteria Optimization: Theory, Computation, and Application*. New York: Wiley.

Weingartner, H. M. (1963). *Mathematical Programming and the Analysis of Capital Budgeting*. Englewood Cliffs, NJ: Prentice-Hall, Inc.

Concluding Observations: Some Critical Issues

11

While budgeting remains a vitally important function of government, there are ongoing issues and challenges that policy makers, budget scholars, and practitioners need to continue to pay attention. Some of these issues are conceptual, such as the need for a budget theory, while others are of much more practical significance. We can define these issues as macro- and micro-budgeting issues, using the term LeLoup (1978) used some years ago. We can also define them as critical, needing immediate and serious attention, and ongoing, not so critical, but requiring attention, nonetheless. Of particular importance are three issues, two of which have received wide attention over the years: the federal budget deficit and debt problem that has been growing unabated for a long time and could reach a crisis proportion and the expenditure growth controversy that has been a contentious issue for a long time. The third, and not so conspicuous, is the need to have a separate capital budget for the federal government, in part, to deal with the deficit and debt problem and, in part, to simplify the budget process. At the subnational level, there are serious challenges that state and local governments need to address such as the looming pension crisis that can financially cripple many of these governments, if not addressed properly. In addition, there are issues that may appear mundane on the surface, but have practical implications for the government and the public, that will need serious attention—sooner or later. This concluding chapter briefly highlights some of these issues.

11.1 The Deficit and Debt Problem

Budget deficit is the difference between a government's revenue and expenditure, and debt is the accumulated deficits over time, both of which have been a concern for the government for a long time. There are two components of the current debt—one, held by the public, called public debt, which includes investors outside of the government such as individuals, corporations, Federal Reserve System, and

© The Author(s) 2019
A. Khan, *Fundamentals of Public Budgeting and Finance*,
https://doi.org/10.1007/978-3-030-19226-6_11

foreign investors, and the other, held by various departments or accounts within the government, called intragovernmental debt, such as Social Security Trust Fund which, for example, is allowed to invest its surpluses only in US Treasury securities. The bulk of the debt is held internally by investors and a small fraction by intragovernmental accounts totaling over 90%, while the rest are held by foreign investors, largely by China and Japan.

The US debt has a long history that dates back to the revolutionary period, although formal recording of the debt did not start until much later. Interestingly, the United States is not the only country with a long history of debt; almost every country in the world, industrialized and non-industrialized, has a debt history, but it is the size of the debt that has increasingly become a concern. For instance, in 1790, when the Department of Treasury first started recording the nation's debt, it was barely over a $71 million. By 1929, right before the country was entering the Great Depression, it rose to $17 billion, increasing rapidly to $260 billion within a span of 16 years by the time World War II ended, which is understandable, given a depression economy and a major war (US Department of the Treasury 2018). Unfortunately, the debt never came down to the pre-war level and continued to grow at an alarming rate crossing one trillion dollars in 1982 (US Department of the Treasury 2018). However, much of this growth took place in recent years, from less than a trillion dollars in 1981, to over $5 trillion in 1999, to over $22 trillion in 2019—all within a span of forty years reflecting an exponential growth (Applebaum 2019).

Like the national debt, the deficit has also been increasing over the years but often interspersed with surpluses, some as late as in the late 1990s, under the Clinton Administration. However, unlike debt, the deficit has been increasing at a slower pace for the greater part of the last century, from less than $5 billion during the depression period, to $45 billion when World War II ended, to $79 billion in 1981, to $318 billion in 2003, and then accelerating to one trillion dollars in 2019 (OMB 2019). Again, much of this growth took place within a span of forty years and, like debt, reflecting an exponential growth. While both deficit and debt have been growing at an exponential rate, it is the debt that has become a serious concern because of the long-term impact it has on the economy. However, to get a sense of the magnitude of the debt problem, one needs to measure it against a benchmark. Two measures are commonly used for this purpose: per capita debt and debt as a percentage of GDP.

Interestingly, per capita debt does not show a major shift in the growth pattern, increasing by less than $20,000 in the last one hundred years, from $46,000 in 1918 to over $61,000 in 2018. This is due in part to the fact that while the overall debt has been increasing over time, the US population was also growing during the same period. As such, debt as a percentage of GDP is considered a better measure since it is directly tied to the growth of the national economy. For instance, in 1929, the federal debt as a percentage of GDP was barely 16%, which increased to 114% by the end of World War II, largely due to the war economy, and then sliding down to 31% in 1974, the lowest it has been since the depression period. By 2000, it gradually increased to 55%, rising to 108% by 2018—an astonishing growth by any measure (US Department of the Treasury 2018). According to a recent CBO estimate, at this rate, the federal debt as a percentage of GDP will increase to 148% by 2038 (CBO 2018). Translated in purely economic terms, it will take an entire year's GDP, plus 48% more to repay the debt at that level.

For a lay person, what is important to understand about the current debt problem is not the size of the debt, but what contributed to the current situation, the impact it has on the economy, in particular the taxpayers because ultimately it is the taxpayers vis-à-vis the public who will have to bear the burden of repayment and how best to address the problem. Several factors have contributed to the current debt situation such as war, the expansionary policy to deal with the problems of unemployment and recession, and the growth in entitlement programs, among others. The United States has a long history of debt related to war, going back to the revolutionary war of 1812 which tripled the debt, war with Mexico in the late 1840s that added more than $2 billion in debt in 2019 dollars, and the Civil War which raised the debt from $64.6 million to $2 billion, which in 2019 terms will be $42 billion. Subsequent wars, in particular World War I raised the debt by $5.5 billion, which in 2019 terms would be $112 billion, and World War II cost the country approximately $323 billion, which in 2019 terms would be $5.8 trillion— an astronomical sum by any measure (Reed 2019). This does not include the cost of other wars such as Korean, Vietnam, Afganistan, and the Gulf wars, following the 9/11 terrorist attacks on US soil.

The growth in entitlement programs, from Social Security, to Medicare, to Medicaid, which have been growing consistently over the years, in all likelihood, will continue to grow, as more baby boomers reach the retirement age, adding to the aggregate debt problem. Besides the entitlement programs, government expansionary policies over the years to deal with the macroeconomic issues, known as deficit financing, also contributed to the problem. Although in theory deficit financing can more than offset the deficits when the economy bounces back, unfortunately, it has not been quite as effective in dealing with the problem largely because of slow growth in GDP. In fact, the US GDP growth has been consistently low, below 5%, for the greater part of the second half of the last century and through the early 2000s, raising serious questions about the country's ability to fully address the debt problem.

However, the real problem with debt is that it will eventually have be to paid off, but, in the interim, it adds to interest costs—money that could be spent on productive activities such as education, transportation, technology, and research and development. According to Congressional Budget Office, at the current rate of deficit and debt the interest cost will continue to grow from close to $400 billion a year in 2019 to over $900 a year in 2028. Overall, the interest cost will be close to $7 trillion during this period (CBO 2018). Unfortunately, there are no easy solutions to the debt problem other than raising taxes or cutting down expenditures, or both. Both measures will require a major sacrifice on the part of the public, and a determined political will on the part of the government, neither of which appears reasonable at this time, given the current political climate of the country.

11.2   Expenditure Growth Controversy

It is difficult to discuss public budgeting without discussing the growth in government expenditures. We briefly looked at the growth trend in an earlier chapter, including some of the causes underlying this growth. The rapid growth in government expenditures, especially at the federal level, remains and will continue to remain a contentious issue among the academics and policy makers because of the differences in opinion as to how large the expenditures should be and what kind of impact these expenditures produce for the economy. Two strands of arguments generally revolve around this issue: those who believe in the expanded role of government and those who believe in a smaller government.

Those who believe in the expanded role of government argue that government expenditures, especially social and economic expenditures, are necessary to stimulate the economy during periods of high unemployment and recession. As noted previously, higher spending during economic downturns can spur economic growth by increasing the purchasing power of the public, which is the essence of government fiscal policy. Higher spending is also necessary to minimize the distributional consequences of income gap and to ensure a minimum level of spending necessary for maintaining economic stability. In other words, government spending has a positive effect on the economy.

On the other hand, there are those who believe in a smaller government argue that higher spending can retard economic growth when resources are transferred from the productive sector to government, which is traditionally considered as less efficient in resources use. More specifically, they argue that government expenditure creates an "economic rent" over and above what is necessary for a productive economy (Krueger 1974). The rent favors special interests who use various means, including lobbying, to extract maximum benefit from government such as cash grants, subsidies, tax credits, loan guarantees, in-kind payments, and so forth. Interestingly, as the argument goes, rent-seeking is common at every level of government that includes both special interests and public employees. For instance, in a fifty-state study, Richard Vedder (1993) shows how excess payments to public employees cost the average taxpayer money that is not always reflected in higher productivity. The gist of the argument is that increased expenditures can create barriers to policies that favor tax reform, reduced spending on government redistribution programs, and a balanced budget, among others. In other words, overspending by government produces a negative effect on the economy.

While it is not difficult to find strong arguments on both sides of the expenditure growth issue, in reality, most academics and policy makers are neither for an expanded or a smaller government, but for a government that can meet the economic challenges without creating a heavy financial burden on the public vis-à-vis the taxpayers.

11.3   A Capital Budget for the Federal Government

As noted earlier, unlike most state and local governments, the federal government does not have a separate capital budget, although the subject comes up every now and then, especially during the budget season and, more importantly, when discussing the deficit and debt issue. As such, it is difficult to conclude the discussion on public budgeting without throwing some light on the state of capital budgeting in the federal government.

There is a common perception among the budget practitioners and some policy makers that the federal government will not have a deficit or debt problem to the same degree it does, if it had a separate capital budget, in particular if the government is required to balance the budget, similar to most state and local governments, which is not necessarily true. As noted earlier, state and local governments are not required to balance the entire budget—only the (proposed) operating budget. For the most part, these governments support their capital improvement activities through pay-as-you-use basis, in other words, through debt financing. According to one estimate, as of 2018, the combined state and local debt stood at approximately $3 trillion, with local share at $1.84 trillion and state debt at $1.16 trillion (US Government Spending 2019). By all counts, it will continue to increase in the coming years, as these governments try to deal with their crumbling infrastructure and other pressing issues. Therefore, having a separate capital budget will not necessarily address the deficit and debt issue, except that it will be accounted differently.

Regardless, the need for a separate capital budget has been a long-standing concern for the federal government since it was first suggested by the Hoover Commission Report in 1949 (Lederle 1949). Numerous studies have been conducted on the subject since then, both in favor and against a formal capital budget. Those who support the capital budget, for instance, offer three arguments: One, the present budget process favors current consumption, as opposed to future consumption; two, the fragmentary nature of the budget process, especially during the appropriation phase, makes it difficult for Congress to have a clear assessment of federal investments; and three, separating the capital budget from the operating budget would make it possible for the government to balance the budget (Gershberg and Benning 1997). Furthermore, the federal government can institute a constitutional amendment requiring the government to balance the budget, the same way the state and local governments balance their budgets. Unfortunately, amending the federal constitution is not quite as simple as it may sound[1], which explains why, it has been amended only 27 times, as opposed to dozens and even hundreds of times for some state governments such as Texas.

On the other hand, those who oppose the budget argue that forcing a constitutional requirement to balance the budget would encourage undesirable investments, compounded by undesirable borrowing and, in the long run, may not achieve the objectives a separate capital budget is expected to produce for the government (Gershberg and Benning, 1997). In addition, it may make it difficult for the federal government to deal with pressing, at times, unforeseen, macroeconomic issues that state and local governments do not have to deal with.

Interestingly, several models currently exist for a separate capital budget for the federal government—the most notable among these is the one suggested by Robert Eisner (1998). An ardent scholar in the Keynesian tradition, Eisner, provides an interesting framework for developing a capital budget. According to Eisner, the federal capital budget will have, at a minimum, three accounts: a capital budget account that would include all investment outlays, the operating budget account that would include depreciation for capital assets as a cost, and a consolidated account that would combine the operating and capital accounts into a unified budget. The consolidated account would show the budget deficit or surplus, as it is under the current unified budget. The model is similar to the financial accounting model used by firms and businesses, where capital investments are not treated as expenditures on the operating budget, rather they are treated as annual depreciation costs, spread over the life span of the assets.

To give an example of how the model tries to address the problem, suppose that the government decides to invest in a capital asset that costs $150 million and has a useful life of five years. Using a straight-line depreciation, say, of 20%, the operating budget will show an outlay of $30 million for depreciation ($150 million × 0.20) in the first year. At the end of the year, when the financial statements are usually prepared, it will show $120 million ($150 million − $30 million) in assets in the capital account. The process will be repeated in the second year, with $30 million in outlays in the operating budget for depreciation, and the remaining $90 million ($120 million − $30 million) assets in the capital account at the end of the year, and so forth, until all the expenses have been reported as budget outlays in the operating budget and the capital account is exhausted for the year-end reporting.

However, not having a separate capital budget does not mean that the government does not deal with the capital expenditures in the federal budget—it does. The capital expenditures in the federal budget are controlled by annual appropriations and, according to some estimates, as much as a third or more of the discretionary spending goes toward capital investments (CBO 2008), primarily for infrastructure, military hardware, and research and development. The actual investments can vary though, from year to year, depending on the general condition of the economy and the priorities of the government.

Assuming, for the sake of argument, that the government will eventually have a separate capital budget, three sets of issues will need to be addressed to develop the budget: implementation, measurement, and control. Implementation will require a clear definition of capital, in particular the depreciation rate that will be used in accounting for capital spending. Measurement problem will need to address how to mix the cash and accrual basis accounting, so it will not create measurement problems for the government. Finally, new challenges may emerge for a separate capital budget, especially for discretionary programs where the control over spending largely focuses on the year in which the funds are appropriated.

In other words, new mechanisms will have to be developed for ensuring account-ability for capital spending (CBO 2008).

11.4   The Looming State and Local Pension Crisis

The budgetary issues discussed above are what one would call macro-budgeting issues affecting the entire nation and the economy, but there are equally challeng-ing issues at the subnational level that need serious and immediate attention. The most notable among the issues is the looming pension problem facing many state and local governments that could become a major financial crisis affecting their long-term budget prospects, if not addressed properly. Unfortunately, this is a sub-ject that has hardly been addressed at the broader level, unlike some of the other issues, discussed here. According to the American Legislative Exchange Council (ALEC), as of 2019, the state and local governments are about $5.6 trillion dol-lars short when it comes to financing their pension obligations. Translated in dol-lar burden terms, it comes out to be around $17,000 per person or about $70,000 per family. However, the burden is not evenly distributed among the states, for instance, with Alaska having the highest per capita debt at about $43,000 and Indiana the lowest at around $8500 (Investor's Business Daily 2019).

A recent study by the Volker's Alliance Group, which grades the states on their ability to deal with budgetary challenges, under "Truth and Integrity in State Budgeting: Preventing the Next Fiscal Crisis," presented a cautionary note for the majority of the states in the country. The study is based on five categories: budget forecasting, budget maneuvers, legacy costs, reserve funds, and transparency. Of these, the legacy costs, which deal with pension funding, raised some serious questions about the states' ability to deal with the problem in the short run (The Volker Alliance Report 2018). Unfortunately, like the deficit and debt problem, there are no easy solutions to the potential pension crisis, other than raising taxes, which will not be an easy task, especially for local governments since the bulk of their revenue comes from property taxes and most voters are reluctant to see their property taxes go up. The alternative is to use local option sales tax (LOST), along with user fees and charges or a combination of both, since voters are less reluctant to oppose when it comes to sales tax or user fees than property or income tax.

11.5   Other Related Issues

In addition to those highlighted above, there are other serious, ongoing issues and challenges that these governments (subnational) also need to pay attention. Important among these are how to deal with budgetary demands, given the real-ities of declining revenues, demand for more and better services by the taxpay-ers, while not necessarily willing to bear the additional tax burden, infrastructure challenges and their impact on state and local budgets, and balancing economic opportunities with environmental risks (Schlachter 2012). Additionally, there are issues that are not budgetary in nature, but have serious budgetary implications, especially at the state level such as federal deregulation, cybersecurity, adjusting to federal tax reforms, improving infrastructure technology, online sales tax collection, and redistricting, among others.

At a conceptual level, issues, such as not having a formal budget theory that can fully explain the budget behavior of government, will continue to remain a challenging task for budget scholars for a long time. V. O. Key raised this issue as far back in 1940 in his classic work The Lack of a Budget Theory, followed by Lewis (1952), Mosher (1954), Smithies (1955), Wildavsky (1961, 1978), Schick (1988), LeLoup (2002), and others. Interestingly, both Key (1940) and Lewis (1952) offer a microeconomic solution to the problem using resource constraints to increase allocative efficiency (Key) and utility maximization for public goods provision (Lewis) as the framework for a budget theory. But as Wildavsky points out: Budgeting is more than allocating the scarce resources between X and Y activities; it is about meeting the conflicting needs of society by bringing about compromises in the political marketplace through incremental adjustments in budget allocation (Wildavsky 1961). Unfortunately, in a pluralist democracy with multiple conflicting interests, it is not an easy task, as the long history of budget acts in Congress, state chambers, and city halls would tell us.

However, at a more immediate and practical level, the issues facing the government are the need to simplify the current federal tax system, develop an effective budget process that will minimize conflict between competing interests, continuously update the budget systems that will meet the changing needs of the government, and determine a critical set of knowledge and skills that will enhance budget practice, among others. While it is difficult, if not impossible, to fully address each and every single issue with budgetary implications since no government has unlimited resources or know-how to address them all, it is just as important to recognize the gravity of the issues and the fact that they need serious attention.

11.6   Summary and Conclusion

Budgeting is a dynamic field; it is involved and expanding, with interests that overlap multiple disciplines—economics, politics, finance, accounting, and administration. It is also practical in that the knowledge and tools acquired have direct implications for those who carry out the budgetary activities of a government on a daily basis. On the other hand, there are issues and challenges, existing as well as new, that are constantly shaping the dynamics of the field. This chapter has provided an overview of some of those challenges. Of particular significance is the deficit and debt problem with a history that goes back to the revolutionary period, battles between those who favor an expanded government and those who do not, and balancing the federal budget constitutionally and, in the process, separating the operating budget from the capital budget.

At the subnational level, there are serious challenges that the state and local governments need to address such as the looming pension crisis that can financially cripple many of these governments, if not addressed properly. In addition, there are issues that may appear mundane on the surface, but have practical implications for the government and the public that will need serious attention—sooner or later.

Review Questions

Q1. How serious is the government deficit and debt problem? What measures can a government take to address the problem?

Q2. What is the basis of expenditure growth controversy? What explanations are provided by those who favor a larger government and those who favor a smaller government?

Q3. Why is it necessary to have a separate capital budget for the federal government? Will having a separate capital budget address the problem of budget deficit and debt? How does Robert Eisner address the issue of a separate capital budget for the federal government? What are the principal elements of his model for implementing the budget?

Q4. Why is pension funding a serious budgetary challenge for many state and local governments in the country? What can the governments do to address the problem?

Note

1. There are four ways to amend the federal constitution, contrary to conventional wisdom: (1) Both houses propose an amendment with a two-thirds vote, and three-fourths of the state legislatures approve. Twenty-six of the 27 amendments were approved in this manner; (2) both houses propose an amendment with a two-thirds vote, and three-fourths of the states approve the amendment via ratifying conventions. Only the 21st Amendment, which repealed Prohibition, was passed in this manner; (3) two-thirds of the state legislatures call on Congress to hold a constitutional convention, and three-fourths of the state legislatures approve the amendment; (4) two-thirds of the state legislatures call on Congress to hold a constitutional convention, and three-fourths of the states approve the amendment via ratifying conventions (Block 2016).

References

Applebaum, B. (2019, February 15). The Federal Debt Is Rising; Concern Is Not. The *New York Times*. https://www.thestreet.com/politics/national-debt-year-by-year-14876008.

Block, L. E. (2016, August 18). There Are Four, Not Two Ways to Amend the Constitution. *Washington Post*. https://www.washingtonpost.com/opinions/there-are-four-not-two-ways-to-amend-the-constitution/2016/08/18/058afcf2-6420-11e6-b4d8-33e931b5a26d_story.html?utm_term=.29c26dd6ffce.

Congressional Budget Office (CBO). (2008, May). *CBO Paper on "Capital Budgeting."* Washington; DC: Congressional Budget Office.

Congressional Budget Office (CBO). (2018, June 26). *The 2018 Long-Term Budget Outlook*. Washington, DC: Congressional Budget Office. https://www.cbo.gov/publication/53919.

Eisner, R. (1998, April 24). *A Capital Budget for Truth in Packaging*. Prepared for Presentation at the President's Commission to Study Capital Budgeting, Public Hearing, Washington, DC.

Gershberg, A. I., & Benning, J. F. (1997, December). *Federal Capital Investment and the Balanced Budget Amendment: The Pros and Cons of a Federal Capital Budget*. New York: The Nelson A. Rockefeller Institute of Government, New York University.

Investor's Business Daily. (2019, May 10). Will Looming State and Local Pension Crisis Bankrupt the US? *Investor's Business Daily*. https://www.investors.com/politics/editorials/the-looming-pension-crisis-of-state-and-local-governments/.

Key, V. O., Jr. (1940, December). The Lack of a Budget Theory. *American Political Science Review, 34*, 1137–1140.

Krueger, A. O. (1974, June). The Political Economy of the Rent-Seeking Society. *American Economic Review, 64*(3), 291–303.

Lederle, J. W. (1949). The Hoover Commission Reports on Federal Reorganization. *Marquette Law Review, 33*(2), 89–98.

LeLoup, L. T. (1978). The Myth of Incrementalism: Analytical Choices in Budgetary Theory. *Polity, 10*(Summer), 488–509.

LeLoup, L. T. (2002). Budget Theory for New Century. In A. Khan & W. B. Hildreth (Eds.), *Budget Theory in the Public Sector* (pp. 1–21). Westport, CT: Quorum Books.

Lewis, V. B. (1952). Toward a Theory of Budgeting. *Public Administration Review, 12*(Winter), 43–54.

Mosher, F. C. (1954). *Program Budgeting: Theory and Practice*. Chicago, IL: Public Administration Service.

Office of Management and Budget. (2006). *Historical Tables: Budget of the US Government*. Washington, DC.

Reed, E. (2019, May). What Is the National Debt Year by Year from 1790 to 2019. *The Street*. https://www.thestreet.com/politics/national-debt-year-by-year-14876008.

Schick, A. (1988). An Inquiry into the Possibility of Budget Theory. In I. S. Rubin (Ed.), *New Directions in Budget Theory* (pp. 59–69). Albany, NY: State University of New York Press.

Schlachter, B. (2012). Key *Strategies and Challenges for Local Governments* (Fiscal Policy and Governance Committee Report). Pittsburgh, PA: Institute of Politics, University of Pittsburgh.

Smithies, A. (1955). *Budgetary Process in the United States*. New York: McGraw-Hill.

The Volker Alliance. (2018, December 12). *The Volker Alliance Releases the Second Annual Study: "Truth and Integrity in State Budgeting: Preventing the Next Fiscal Crisis."* https://www.volckeralliance.org/news/volcker-alliance-releases-second-annual-study-truth-and-integrity-state-budgeting-preventing.

US Department of the Treasury. (2018). *Debt to the Penny*. Washington, DC.

US Government Spending. (2019, March). https://www.usgovernmentdebt.us/local_debt_chart; https://www.usgovernmentdebt.us/state_debt_chart.

Vedder, R. (1993, April). *Economic Impact of Government Spending: A 50-State Analysis* (NCPA Policy Report No. 178). Dallas, TX: National Center for Policy Analysis.

Wildavsky, A. (1961). Political Implications of Budgetary Reform. *Public Administration Review, 21*(Autumn), 183–190.

Wildavsky, A. (1978, November–December). A Budget for All Seasons? Why the Traditional Budget Lasts? *Public Administration Review, 38*, 501–509.

Appendix A

Algebraic Formulation of a Line-Item Budget

Algebraically, we can present the line-item budget of a government or any of its agencies as a column vector, **v**, consisting of a single column with a finite number of elements. To present the budget vector, we start with a single department of a government, say, the jth department, with n cost or line items, so that

$$B^j = \begin{pmatrix} B^j_1 \\ B^j_2 \\ B^j_3 \\ \cdot \\ \cdot \\ \cdot \\ \cdot \\ B^j_n \end{pmatrix} = \mathbf{v} \qquad (A.1)$$

where B^j stands for budget of the jth department on ith line item (for $j = 1, 2,\ldots\ldots, m;\ i = 1, 2,\ldots\ldots, n$), and **v** is a vector of line items. The first line item usually represents personal services (subscript 1), the second line item represents materials and supplies (subscript 2), the third represents contractual agreements (subscript 3), the fourth represents capital outlay (subscript 4), and so on. Thus, the term B^j_1 represents the jth department's budget on line item 1, B^j_2 represents the jth department's budget on line item 2, and so forth.

Since the money allocated on each item is additive, we can express the total budget for the jth department with i line items as

$$B^j_1 + B^j_2 + B^j_3 + \ldots\ldots\ldots\ldots + B^j_n = \sum_{i=1}^{n} B^j_i = B^j \qquad (A.2)$$

© The Editor(s) (if applicable) and The Author(s), under exclusive license to Springer Nature Switzerland AG, part of Springer Nature 2019
A. Khan, *Fundamentals of Public Budgeting and Finance,*
https://doi.org/10.1007/978-3-030-19226-6

where B_i^j is the budget for the jth department on ith line item, and the rest of the terms are the same as before. Thus, if a department has a budget, say, of \$25 million, of which it allocates \$15 million on line item 1 (salaries and wages), \$2 million on line item 2 (materials and supplies), \$4 million on line item 3 (contractual agreements), and \$3 million on capital outlay, and \$1 million on miscellaneous items, the sum total of the allocations must equal \$25 million; that is, \$15m (salaries & wages) + \$2m (materials & supplies) + \$4m (contractual) + \$3m (capital outlay) + \$1m (miscellaneous) = \$25 million.

Now, consider a government with m departments, each with n line items. Therefore, to obtain the total budget of the government we will simply add the column vectors $v_1 + v_2 + \ldots\ldots + v_n$, so that

$$B^G = v_1 + v_2 + \ldots\ldots\ldots\ldots\ldots\ldots + v_n$$

$$= \begin{pmatrix} B_1^1 \\ B_2^1 \\ B_3^1 \\ \cdot \\ \cdot \\ \cdot \\ \cdot \\ B_n^1 \end{pmatrix} + \begin{pmatrix} B_1^2 \\ B_2^2 \\ B_3^2 \\ \cdot \\ \cdot \\ \cdot \\ \cdot \\ B_n^2 \end{pmatrix} + \ldots\ldots\ldots\ldots + \begin{pmatrix} B_1^m \\ B_2^m \\ B_3^m \\ \cdot \\ \cdot \\ \cdot \\ \cdot \\ B_n^m \end{pmatrix} \qquad (A.3)$$

$$= v$$

where B^G is the budget of the government, G.

Since there are m departments in a government, each with multiple line items, n, we can show the budget of the entire government using a $(m \times n)$ matrix, with m rows and n columns, where the first term of each cell represents a department and the second term a line item (Table A.1). Thus, the term B_{11} represents the budget allocated for department 1 on line item 1, B_{12} the budget allocated for department 1 on line item 2, and so forth.

The row and column totals in Table A.1 need a little explanation. While each row total represents the budget allocated to an individual department on all line items, from 1 to n, and each column total represents the budget allocated on an

Table A.1 The structure of a line-item budget in matrix form

Departments	Line items			Total
	L_1	L_2	L_3 . . . . . . L_n	
D_1	B_{11}	B_{12}	B_{13} . . . . . . B_{1n}	$\sum_{i=1}^{n} B_{1i}$
D_2	B_{21}	B_{22}	B_{23} . . . . . . B_{2n}	$\sum_{i=1}^{n} B_{2i}$
D_3	B_{31}	B_{32}	B_{33} . . . . . . B_{3n}	$\sum_{i=1}^{n} B_{3i}$
$\cdot$	$\cdot$	$\cdot$	$\cdot$	$\cdot$
D_m	B_{m1}	B_{m2}	B_{m3} . . . . . . B_{mn}	$\sum_{i=1}^{n} B_{mi}$
Total	$\sum_{j=1}^{m} B_{j1}$	$\sum_{j=1}^{m} B_{j2}$	$\sum_{j=1}^{m} B_{j3}$ . . . . . $\sum_{j=1}^{m} B_{jn}$	$\sum_{j=1}^{m} \sum_{i=1}^{n} B_{ji}$

Table A.2 A Line-item budget in dollar terms ($million)

Department	L_1	L_2	L_3 · · · · · · · · L_n	Total ($)
			Line items	
D_1	6.5	0.5	0.3 · · · · · · · · 0.4	10.0 $\sum_{i=1}^{n} B_{1i}$
D_2	6.3	0.7	0.5 · · · · · · · · 0.7	12.5 $\sum_{i=1}^{n} B_{2i}$
D_3	9.2	0.8	0.9 · · · · · · · · 0.8	13.6 $\sum_{i=1}^{n} B_{3i}$
·	·	·	· ·	·
·	·	·	· ·	·
·	·	·	· ·	·
D_m	4.8	0.2	0.3 · · · · · · · · 0.2	7.5 $\sum_{i=1}^{n} B_{mi}$
Total ($)	62.0	7.4	6.3 · · · · · · · · 5.3	100.0
	$\sum_{j=1}^{m} B_{j1}$ $\sum_{j=1}^{m} B_{j2}$ $\sum_{j=1}^{m} B_{j3}$		· · · · · · $\sum_{j=1}^{m} B_{jn}$	$\sum_{j=1}^{m}\sum_{i=1}^{n} B_{ji}$

individual line item for all departments, from 1 to m. Thus, the row total $\sum_{i=1}^{n} B_{1i}$ represents the line-item budget for department 1, $\sum_{i=1}^{n} B_{2i}$ for department 2, and so on. Similarly, the column total $\sum_{j=1}^{m} B_{j1}$ represents the budget the entire government, taken all the departments together, on line item 1, $\sum_{j=1}^{m} B_{j2}$, on line item 2, and so forth. The last term, $\sum_{j=1}^{m}\sum_{i=1}^{n} B_{ji}$, represents the line-item budget for the entire government, B^G, where G stands for government. Table A.2 provides an example of a line-tem budget for the entire government in dollar terms.

An advantage of presenting the budget in matrix form is that we can make the necessary adjustments in the budget by adding, subtracting, multiplying, or transposing the cell values. For instance, if the budget is to increase for a department on a line item by a constant rate (fraction), k, next year, $t + 1$, then we can simply multiply the budget allocated for the line item by the constant term and add it to the original allocation to obtain the budget for next year, for a given line item, so that

$$
\mathbf{v} = (k)
\begin{pmatrix}
B_1^1 \\
B_2^1 \\
B_3^1 \\
\cdot \\
\cdot \\
\cdot \\
B_m^1
\end{pmatrix}
+
\begin{pmatrix}
B_1^1 \\
B_2^1 \\
B_3^1 \\
\cdot \\
\cdot \\
\cdot \\
B_m^1
\end{pmatrix}
=
\begin{pmatrix}
kB_1^1 + B_1^1 \\
kB_2^1 + B_2^1 \\
kB_3^1 + B_3^1 \\
\cdot \\
\cdot \\
\cdot \\
kB_m^1 + B_m^1
\end{pmatrix}
\tag{A.4}
$$

for line item 1, and $\mathbf{v}$ is the budget for m departments on line item 1, for next year. For n line items, it will be

$$
\mathbf{v}' = \begin{pmatrix} kB_1^1 + B_1^1 \\ kB_2^1 + B_2^1 \\ kB_3^1 + B_3^1 \\ \cdot \\ \cdot \\ \cdot \\ kB_m^1 + B_m^1 \end{pmatrix} + \begin{pmatrix} kB_1^2 + B_1^2 \\ kB_2^2 + B_2^2 \\ kB_3^2 + B_3^2 \\ \cdot \\ \cdot \\ \cdot \\ kB_m^2 + B_m^2 \end{pmatrix} + \cdots \cdots + \begin{pmatrix} kB_1^n + B_1^n \\ kB_2^n + B_2^n \\ kB_3^n + B_3^n \\ \cdot \\ \cdot \\ \cdot \\ kB_m^n + B_m^n \end{pmatrix} \quad (A.5)
$$

where the subscript represents the department, the superscript the line item, and k is the constant by which the budget will increase. For decrease, we will simply do the opposite.

Thus, the budget for the entire government next year, $t + 1$, after the adjustments by the constant rate, k, will be

$$
B_{t+1}^G = \begin{pmatrix} kB_1^1 + B_{1,t+1}^1 \\ kB_2^1 + B_{2,t+1}^1 \\ kB_3^1 + B_{3,t+1}^1 \\ \cdot \\ \cdot \\ \cdot \\ kB_m^1 + B_{m,t+1}^1 \end{pmatrix} + \begin{pmatrix} kB_1^2 + B_{1,t+1}^2 \\ kB_2^2 + B_{2,t+1}^2 \\ kB_3^2 + B_{3,t+1}^2 \\ \cdot \\ \cdot \\ \cdot \\ kB_m^2 + B_{m,t+1}^2 \end{pmatrix} + \cdots \cdots + \begin{pmatrix} kB_1^n + B_{1,t+1}^n \\ kB_2^n + B_{2,t+1}^n \\ kB_3^n + B_{3,t+1}^n \\ \cdot \\ \cdot \\ \cdot \\ kB_m^m + B_{m,t+1}^m \end{pmatrix}
$$

$$
\mathbf{v}' = \begin{pmatrix} \sum_{i=1}^n B_{1,t+1}^i \\ \sum_{i=1}^n B_{2,t+1}^i \\ \sum_{i=1}^n B_{3,t+1}^i \\ \cdot \\ \cdot \\ \cdot \\ \sum_{i=1}^n B_{m,t+1}^i \end{pmatrix} \quad (A.6)
$$

We can continue the process for any number of years into the future (assuming the items will increase by a constant rate each time). If the constant terms are different for different line items the process will still be the same, except that the k's will be different for each line item; that is, $k_1 \neq k_2 \neq k_3 \neq \ldots \ldots \neq k_n$.

Appendix B

Algebraic Formulation of a Program Budget

Since structurally a program budget is similar to a line-item budget, except that it focuses on programs, program goals and objectives rather than on individual cost or line items, we can use the same algebraic expressions to describe the program budget. As before, we start with a single department of a government, say, the jth department with p programs, and present the budget for individual programs as elements of a column vector, $\mathbf{v}$, as shown below:

$$B^j = \begin{pmatrix} B^j_1 \\ B^j_2 \\ B^j_3 \\ \cdot \\ \cdot \\ \cdot \\ \cdot \\ B^j_p \end{pmatrix} = \mathbf{v} \tag{B.1}$$

where B^j_k represents the budget for the jth department on kth program (for $k = 1$, $2,\ldots\ldots, p$).

As before, since the money allocated for each program is additive, we can express the total budget for the jth department with p programs as

$$B^j_1 + B^j_2 + B^j_3 + \ldots\ldots\ldots\ldots\ldots + B^j_p = \sum\nolimits_{k=1}^{p} B^j_k \tag{B.2}$$

where B^j_k is the budget of the jth department on kth program, and the rest of terms are the same as before. Thus, if a department has a budget, say, of

© The Editor(s) (if applicable) and The Author(s), under exclusive license
to Springer Nature Switzerland AG, part of Springer Nature 2019
A. Khan, *Fundamentals of Public Budgeting and Finance*,
https://doi.org/10.1007/978-3-030-19226-6

$10 million, and it spends $3 million on program 1, $2 million on program 2, $3 million on program 3, and the rest on other items, the sum total of the budget for all the programs must equal $10 million; that is, $3 million + $2 million + $3 million + $2 million (other program) = $10 million.

Since all budget allocations eventually boil down to allocations for individual line items, we can express the budget for an individual program as the sum of the budget allocated on all the line items for the program, so that

$$B_1^k + B_2^k + B_3^k + \ldots\ldots\ldots + B_n^k = \sum_{i=1}^{n} B_i^k \qquad (B.3)$$

where B_i^k stands for budget allocated for the kth program on ith line item (for $i = 1, 2,\ldots\ldots, n$). Thus, if a program has a budget, say, of $5 million, of which $2 million goes to personnel, $0.5 million to materials and supplies, $1.5 million to contractual agreements, and the rest on miscellaneous other items, the sum of the budget for the line items must equal $5; that is, $2 million + $0.5 million + $1.5 million + $1 million (miscellaneous) = $5 million.

We can easily extend the expression in Eq. B.3 to include p programs, as shown below:

$$B_{11}^i + B_{12}^i + B_{13}^i + \ldots\ldots\ldots + B_{1p}^i = \sum_{k=1}^{p} B_{1k}^i \qquad (B.4)$$

$$B_{21}^i + B_{22}^i + B_{13}^i + \ldots\ldots\ldots + B_{2p}^i = \sum_{k=1}^{p} B_{2k}^i \qquad (B.5)$$

$$B_{31}^i + B_{32}^i + B_{13}^i + \ldots\ldots\ldots + B_{3p}^i = \sum_{k=1}^{p} B_{3k}^i$$

$$
\begin{array}{ccccc}
\cdot & \cdot & \cdot & \cdot & \cdot \\
\cdot & \cdot & \cdot & \cdot & \cdot \\
\cdot & \cdot & \cdot & \cdot & \cdot
\end{array}
\qquad (B.6)
$$

$$B_{m1}^i + B_{m2}^i + B_{m3}^i + \ldots\ldots\ldots + B_{mp}^i = \sum_{k=1}^{p} B_{mk}^i \qquad (B.7)$$

where B_{jk}^i represents the budget of the jth department for the kth program on ith line item and the rest of the terms are the same as before.

Table B.1 presents the structure of a program budget in matrix form. As can be seen from the table, there is a similarity between a line item and a program budget, except that in the case of a program budget the elements (cells) of the matrix represent the budget of the individual programs by department. Thus, the element B_{11} means the budget for program 1 for department 1, B_{21} for program 2 for department 1, and so on.

The row and column sums can also be interpreted the same way, as before. For instance, the row total $\sum_{k=1}^{p} B_{1k}$ represents the budget of department 1 for all its programs, taken together, from 1 to p, $\sum_{k=1}^{p} B_{2k}$ the budget for department 2 for all its programs, taken together, from 1 to p, and so forth. Similarly, the column total $\sum_{j=1}^{m} B_{j1}$ represents the budget of the entire government for all

Table B.1 The structure of a program budget in matrix form

Department	Program				Total
	P_1	P_2	$P_3 \ldots \ldots P_p$		
D_1	B_{11}	B_{12}	$B_{13} \ldots \ldots B_{1p}$		$\sum_{k=1}^{p} B_{1k}$
D_2	B_{21}	B_{22}	$B_{23} \ldots \ldots B_{2p}$		$\sum_{k=1}^{p} B_{2k}$
D_3	B_{31}	B_{32}	$B_{33} \ldots \ldots \ldots B_{3p}$		$\sum_{k=1}^{p} B_{3k}$
.	.	.	.	.	.
.	.	.	.	.	.
.	.	.	.	.	.
D_m	B_{m1}	B_{m2}	$B_{m3} \ldots \ldots B_{mp}$		$\sum_{k=1}^{p} B_{mk}$
Total	$\sum_{j=1}^{m} B_{j1}$	$\sum_{j=1}^{m} B_{j2}$	$\sum_{j=1}^{m} B_{j3} \ldots \sum_{j=1}^{m} B_{jp}$		$\sum_{j=1}^{m} \sum_{k=1}^{p} B_{jk}$

the departments, taken together, on program 1, $\sum_{j=1}^{m} B_{j2}$ the budget for the entire government for all the departments, taken together, on program 2, and so forth. However, it is important to note that the programs would be different for different departments, although their position in the matrix would remain the same. The last term, $\sum_{j=1}^{m} \sum_{k=1}^{p} B_{jk}$, represents the total budget for the entire government, B^G. Table B.2 provides a simple example of a program budget in dollar terms.

As with the line-item budget, if the allocation for individual programs and departments increases by a constant rate, k' (fraction), we can use the same procedure to adjust the budget for next year, $t + 1$, or the year after, $t + 2$, and so forth.

Table B.2 A program budget in dollar terms (in $million)

Department	Program				Total ($)
	P_1	P_2	$P_3 \cdot \cdot \cdot \cdot \cdot \cdot \cdot P_p$		
D_1	2.5	1.2	$1.3 \cdot \cdot \cdot \cdot \cdot \cdot \cdot 2.4$		10.0 $\sum_{k=1}^{p} B_{1k}$
D_2	1.3	2.5	$4.1 \cdot \cdot \cdot \cdot \cdot \cdot \cdot 1.7$		2.5 $\sum_{k=1}^{p} B_{2k}$
D_3	3.2	1.8	$2.0 \cdot \cdot \cdot \cdot \cdot \cdot 3.1$		13.6 $\sum_{k=1}^{p} B_{3k}$
.	.	.	.	.	.
.	.	.	.	.	.
.	.	.	.	.	.
D_m	4.8	0.2	$0.3 \cdot \cdot \cdot \cdot \cdot \cdot 0.2$		7.5 $\sum_{k=1}^{p} B_{mk}$
Total ($)	35.0	15.0	$20.3 \cdot \cdot \cdot \cdot \cdot \cdot 5.7$		100.0
	$\sum_{j=1}^{m} B_{j1}$	$\sum_{j=1}^{m} B_{j2}$	$\sum_{j=1}^{m} B_{j3} \cdot \cdot \cdot \cdot \cdot \sum_{j=1}^{m} B_{jp}$		$\sum_{j=1}^{m} \sum_{k=1}^{p} B_{jk}$

Appendix C

A Sample Form for Soliciting CIP Proposals

I. Background Information

Name of the Government: _____

Department: _____ Division: _____

Project Type (construction, acquisition, etc.): _____

Project Manager: _____ Title/Position: _____

Date Submitted: _____

II. Project Detail

A. Project Description

    1. Project Title   _____

    2. Location   _____

    3. Project description   _____

                               _____

                               _____

    4. Attach a map, if necessary

B. Needs Assessment

    1. Justification for request _____

                               _____

                               _____

    2. Current condition   Excellent_____; Very Good_____; Good_____;

                               Poor_____; Very Poor_____

    3. Nature of request: Repair _____; Replace _____; Renovate _____;

                               Acquire (New) _____

    4. Part of the Master Plan? _____; Comprehensive Plan? _____

    5. Relationship to other projects _____

C. Project Benefits: Monetary (Estimated)

Direct Benefits: $ _____

Explanation: _____

_____

_____

Indirect Benefits: $ _____ (if available)

Explanation: _____

_____

_____

Project Benefits: Non-Monetary (Describe)

_____

_____

_____

D. Project Costs: Monetary (Five-Year Estimates)

1. Planning (e.g., architectural service, engineering service, inspection fees, etc.)

Cost (By Type): $ _____

Explanation: _____

_____

2. Acquisition (e.g., land, building, equipment, etc.)

Cost (By Type): $ _____

Explanation: _____

_____

3. Construction (e.g., labor, materials, equipment, furniture, etc.)

Cost (By Type): $_____

Explanation: _____

_____

4. Repair and maintenance (e.g., monthly, quarterly, annual, etc.)

Cost (By Type): $ _____

Explanation: _____

_____

5. Any other costs, specify

_____

_____

Project Costs: Non-Monetary (Describe)

_____

_____

_____

E. Estimated Time of Completion (By Months and Years)
   1. Estimated total time _____
   2. Breakdown by phase: (Include a Brief Narrative)
      Phase 1: _____ Phase 2: _____ ; Phase 3: _____
      Phase 3: _____ Phase 4: _____; Etc. _____

F. Financing Sources
   1. Internal sources, specify (Include percentage breakdown)

   _____

   _____

   2. External sources, specify (Include percentage breakdown)

   _____

   _____

G. Impact on the Operating Budget: Monetary (Estimates)
   Short-term: $ _____
   Explanation: _____

   _____

   Long-term: $ _____
   Explanation: _____

   _____

   Impact on the Operating Budget: Non-Monetary (Describe)

   _____

   _____

_____

_____

III. Any other information relevant to the proposal

_____

_____

_____

_____

Appendix D

Pairwise Comparison Matrices of Projects

See Table D.1.

Table D.1 AHP level 3: pairwise comparison matrices of projects

C_1	Projects								
	X_1	X_2	X_3	X_4	X_5	X_6	X_7	Total	
X_1	1	1/5	2	3	3	1/3	1/4	9.78	
X_2	5	1	7	6	5	1/3	2	21.53	
X_3	1/2	1/7	1	2	3	1/5	1/4	7.09	
X_4	1/3	1/6	1/2	1	1	1/7	1/4	3.39	
X_5	1/3	1/5	1/3	1	1	1/8	1/3	3.32	
X_6	3	3	5	7	8	1	4	31.00	
X_7	4	1/2	4	4	3	1/4	1	16.75	
Total	14.16	5.21	19.83	24.00	24.00	2.38	8.08	92.86	
	Normalized weights							Total	Priority vector
X_1	0.07	0.04	0.10	0.13	0.13	0.14	0.03	0.64	0.091
X_2	0.35	0.20	0.35	0.25	0.21	0.14	0.25	1.75	0.250
X_3	0.04	0.03	0.05	0.08	0.13	0.08	0.03	0.44	0.063
X_4	0.02	0.03	0.03	0.04	0.04	0.06	0.03	0.25	0.036
X_5	0.02	0.04	0.02	0.04	0.04	0.06	0.04	0.26	0.037
X_6	0.21	0.57	0.25	0.29	0.33	0.42	0.49	2.56	0.366
X_7	0.28	0.09	0.20	0.17	0.13	0.10	0.13	1.10	0.157
Total	1	1	1	1	1	1	1	7.00	

(continued)

© The Editor(s) (if applicable) and The Author(s), under exclusive license
to Springer Nature Switzerland AG, part of Springer Nature 2019
A. Khan, *Fundamentals of Public Budgeting and Finance*,
https://doi.org/10.1007/978-3-030-19226-6

Table D.1 (continued)

C_1	Projects								
	X_1	X_2	X_3	X_4	X_5	X_6	X_7	Total	
C_2	X_1	X_2	X_3	X_4	X_5	X_6	X_7	Total	
X_1	1	5	4	5	6	7	2	30.00	
X_2	1/5	1	3	2	1/2	5	2	13.70	
X_3	1/4	1/3	1	3	1	4	2	11.58	
X_4	1/5	1/2	1/3	1	1/2	1	1/3	3.87	
X_5	1/6	2	1	2	1	3	1/2	9.67	
X_6	1/7	1/5	1/4	1	1/3	1	1/4	3.18	
X_7	1/2	1/2	1/2	3	2	4	1	11.50	
Total	2.46	9.53	10.08	17	11.33	14.33	8.08	83.50	
	Normalized weights							*Total*	*Priority vector*
X_1	0.41	0.52	0.40	0.29	0.53	0.28	0.25	2.68	0.381
X_2	0.08	0.10	0.30	0.12	0.04	0.20	0.25	1.09	0.155
X_3	0.10	0.03	0.10	0.18	0.09	0.16	0.25	0.91	0.129
X_4	0.08	0.05	0.03	0.06	0.04	0.04	0.04	0.35	0.061
X_5	0.07	0.21	0.10	0.12	0.09	0.12	0.06	0.76	0.109
X_6	0.06	0.02	0.02	0.06	0.03	0.04	0.03	0.26	0.032
X_7	0.20	0.05	0.05	0.18	0.18	0.16	0.12	0.94	0.134
Total	1	1	1	1	1	1	1	≈ 7.00	
C_3	X_1	X_2	X_3	X_4	X_5	X_6	X_7	Total	
X_1	1	5	3	2	3	1/2	1/2	15.00	
X_2	1/5	1	1/2	1/3	1/2	1/5	1/4	2.98	
X_3	1/3	2	1	1/2	1/2	1/5	1/4	4.78	
X_4	1/2	3	2	1	1/2	1/2	1/3	7.83	
X_5	1/3	2	2	2	1	1	1/2	10.33	
X_6	2	5	5	2	1	1	2	18.00	
X_7	2	4	4	3	2	1/2	1	16.50	
Total	6.37	22	17.5	10.83	8.5	3.9	6.33	75.42	
	Normalized weights							*Total*	*Priority vector*
X_1	0.16	0.23	0.17	0.18	0.35	0.13	0.08	1.30	0.186
X_2	0.03	0.05	0.03	0.03	0.06	0.05	0.04	0.29	0.041
X_3	0.05	0.09	0.06	0.05	0.06	0.05	0.04	0.40	0.057
X_4	0.08	0.14	0.11	0.09	0.06	0.13	0.05	0.66	0.094
X_5	0.05	0.09	0.11	0.18	0.12	0.26	0.32	1.13	0.162
X_6	0.31	0.23	0.29	0.18	0.12	0.26	0.32	1.70	0.243
X_7	0.31	0.18	0.23	0.28	0.24	0.13	0.16	1.52	0.217
Total	1	1	1	1	1	1	1	7.00	

Bibliography

Aaron, H. J. (1975). *Who Pays the Property Tax?* Washington, DC: The Brookings Institution.

Abt, C. C. (1977). The Issue of Social Costs in Cost-Benefit Analysis of Surgery. In J. B. Bunker, B. A. Barnes, & F. Mosteller (Eds.), *Costs, Risks and Benefits of Surgery* (pp. 40–55). New York, NY: Oxford University Press.

Advisory Commission on Intergovernmental Relations (ACIR). (1993, February). *Significant Features of Fiscal Federalism 1993, Volume 1* (Report M-185). Washington, DC: ACIR.

Akin, J. S. (1973, June). Fiscal Capacity and the Estimation Method of the Advisory Commission on Intergovernmental Relations. *National Tax Journal, 26*, 275–291.

Amadeo, K. (2019, May). Interest on the National Debt and How It Affects You. *The Balance.* https://www.thebalance.com/interest-on-the-national-debt-4119024.

Amadeo, K. (2018, August). Current Federal Mandatory Spending. *The Balance.* https://www.thebalance.com/current-federal-mandatory-spending-3305772.

Aminian, H., & Samaneh, S. S. (1912). The Relationship between Performance Audit and Management Tendency to Strive towards Organizational Goals Achievement. *Australian Journal of Basic and Applied Sciences, 6*(13), 149–153.

Applebaum, B. (2019, February 15). The Federal Debt Is Rising; Concern Is Not. The *New York Times.* https://www.thestreet.com/politics/national-debt-year-by-year-14876008.

Army, R. (1995). *The Freedom of Revolution.* Washington, DC: Regency Publishing.

Arrow, K. (1959). *Social Choice and Individual Values.* New Haven, CT: Yale University Press.

Arrow, K. J., Cheney, H. B., Minhas, B. S., & Solow, R. M. (1961, August). Capital Labor Substitution and Economic Efficiency. *Review of Economics and Statistics, 43*(3), 225–250.

Aschauer, D. A. (1989). Is Public Expenditure Productive? *Journal of Monetary Economics, 23*, 177–200.

Axelrod, D. (1995). *Budgeting for Modern Government.* New York: St. Martin's Press.

Baghestani, H., & McNown, R. (1992). Forecasting the Federal Budget with Time-Series Models. *Journal of Forecasting, 11*(2), 127–139.

Barro, R. (1974, November–December). Are Government Bonds Net Wealth? *Journal of Political Economy, 82*(6), 1095–1117.

Barro, R. (1991). Economic Growth and a Cross-Section of Countries. *Quarterly Journal of Economics, 106,* 407–441.

Bator, F. M. (1958, August). The Anatomy of Market Failure. *Quarterly Journal of Economics, 72*(3), 351–379.

Baumol, W. J. (1952, November). The Transaction Demand for Cash: An Inventory Theoretic Approach. *Quarterly Journal of Economics, 66*(4), 545–556.

Baumol, W. J. (1967, June). Macroeconomics of Unbalanced Growth: The Anatomy of the Urban Crisis. *American Economic Review, 57,* 415–426.

Baumol, W. J. (1970). *Economic Dynamics: An Introduction* (3rd ed.). New York, NY: Macmillan.

Berne, R. M., & Shramm, R. (1986). *The Financial Analysis of Governments*. Englewood Cliffs, NJ: Prentice-Hall.

Bland, R. L., & Numm, S. (1992, June). The Impact of Capital Spending on Municipal Operating Budgets. *Public Budgeting & Finance, 12*(2), 32–47.

Block, L. E. (2016, August 18). There Are Four, Not Two Ways to Amend the Constitution. *Washington Post*. https://www.washingtonpost.com/opinions/there-are-four-not-two-ways-to-amend-the-constitution/2016/08/18/058afcf2-6420-11e6-b4d8-33e931b5a26d_story.html?utm_term=.29c26dd6ffce.

Bohm, P. (1972). Estimating Demand for Public Goods: An Experiment. *European Economic Review, 3,* 111–130.

Borcherding, T. E., & Deacon, R. T. (1972). The Demand for Services of Non-Federal Governments. *American Economic Review, 62*(5), 891–901.

Box, G. E. P., & Jenkins, G. M. (1976). *Time-Series Analysis: Forecasting and Control*. San Francisco, CA: Holden-Day.

Break, G. F. (1980). *Financing Government Expenditures in a Federal System*. Washington, DC: The Brookings Institution.

Breton, A., & Wintrobe, R. (1975, February). The Equilibrium Size of a Budget-Maximizing Bureau: A Note on Niskanen's Theory of Bureaucracy. *Journal of Political Economy, 83*(1), 195–208.

Brookings Institution. (2010, February). *The Tax Policy Briefing Book*. Washington, DC: Tax Policy Center, The Brookings Institution.

Bruce, N. (2001). *Public Finance and the American Economy*. New York, NY: Addison-Wesley.

Buchanan, J. M. (1962, November). Externality. *Economica*. Reprinted in W. Briet & H. M. Hochman (Eds.), *Readings in Microeconomics* (pp. 477–488). New York, NY: Holt, Rinehart, and Winston (1968).

Buchanan, J. M. (1965). An Economic Theory of Clubs. *Economica, 32*(125), 1–14.

Buchanan, J. M. (1967). *Public Finance in Democratic Processes*. Chapel-Hill: University of North Carolina Press.

Buchanan, J. M., & Tullock, G. (1962). *The Calculus of Consent*. Ann Arbor: University of Michigan Press.

Buck, A. E. (1929). *Public Budgeting*. New York, NY: Harper & Row.

Buehler, A. G. (1940). *Public Finance*. New York, NY: McGraw-Hill Book.

Burch, J. (1994). *Cost and Management Accounting, Modern Approach*. St. Paul, MN: West Publishing.

Canto, V. A., Joines, D. H., & Laffer, A. B. (1983). *Foundations of Supply-Side Economics: Theory and Evidence*. New York, NY: Academic Press.

Casas-Pardo, J., & Puchades-Navarro, M. (2001, April). A Critical Comment on Niskanen's Model. *Public Choice, 107*(1–2), 147–167.

Castro, M. F. (2011, July). *Defining and Using Performance Indicators in Government M&E Systems* (Special Series in the Nuts and Bolts of M&E Systems No. 12). Washington, DC: The World Bank.

Center on Budget and Policy Priorities. (2018, May 2). *Policy Basics: Federal Tax Expenditures*. https://www.cbpp.org/research/federal-tax/policy-basics-federal-tax-expenditures.

Center on Budget and Policy Priorities. (2019, January 31). *Policy Basics: Introduction to the Federal Budget Process*. https://www.cbpp.org/research/policy-basics-introduction-to-the-federal-budget-process.

Chantrill, C. (2010, November). *US Government Spending by Functions* (Compiled from Multiple Government Publications). https://www.USgovernmentspending.com.

Chapman II, S. G. (2007). *Priority-Driven Budgeting: An Alternative to Incremental Budgeting*. Washington, DC: Government Finance Officers Association (GFOA) (Module 15).

Charnes, A., & Cooper, W. W. (1961). *Management Models for and Industrial Applications of Linear Programming*. Englewood Cliffs, NJ: Wiley.

Charnes, A., Cooper, W. W., & Miller, M. H. (1959, January). Application of Linear Programming to Financial Budgeting and the Costing of Funds. *Journal of Business, 32*, 20–46.

Checkland, P. B. (1976). Toward a System-Based Methodology for Real-World Problem Solving. In J. Beishon & G. Peters (Eds.), *Systems Behavior* (pp. 51–77). New York, NY: Harper & Row (for Open University Press).

Choudhury, N. N. (1976, July). Integration of Fiscal and Monetary Sectors in Econometric Models: A Survey of Theoretical Issues and Empirical Findings. *International Monetary Fund, Staff Papers, 23*, 395–440.

Christensen, T., & Laegreid, P. (2003, March 15–18). *Trust in Government—The Significance of Attitudes Towards Democracy, the Public Sector and Public Sector Reforms*. Paper Presented at the 64th National Conference of the American Society for Public Administration (ASPA) on "The Power of Public Service," Washington, DC.

Clayton, E. R., & Moor, L. J. (1972, February). PERT Versus GERT. *Journal of Management Science, 23*(2), 11–19.

Cobb, C. W., & Douglas, P. H. (1928, March). A Theory of Production. *American Economic Review, 18*(1), 139–165.

Collins, B. K., & Khan, A. (2004). Information Asymmetry in Public Investment Management. In A. Khan & W. B. Hildreth (Eds.), *Financial Management Theory in the Public Sector* (pp. 25–54). Westport, CT: Praeger Publishers.

Commission on the Bicentennial of the United Stated States Constitution. (1976). *The Constitution of the United States*. Washington, DC.

Congressional Budget Office (CBO). (2008, May). *CBO Paper on "Capital Budgeting."* Washington, DC: Congressional Budget Office.

Congressional Budget Office (CBO). (2018, June 26). *The 2018 Long-Term Budget Outlook*. Washington, DC: Congressional Budget Office. https://www.cbo.gov/publication/53919.

Copeland, P. A. (2011). *Essentials of Accounting for Governmental and Not-for-Profit Organizations*. New York: McGraw-Hill/Irwin.

Curley, M., & Formica, P. (2008, December). Laboratory Experiments in the Empirical Economic Analysis of Higher-Expectation Entrepreneurship. *Industry and Education, 22*(6), 355–363.

Dalton, H. (1922). *Principles of Public Finance*. London, UK: Routledge.

Dantzig, G. B. (1963). *Linear Programming and Extensions*. Princeton, NJ: Princeton University Press.

Daunton, M. (2001). *Trusting Leviathan: The Politics of Taxation in Britain, 1799–1914*. Cambridge, UK: Cambridge University Press.

Dauten, C. A., & Valentine, L. M. (1974). *Business Cycles and Forecasting*. Cincinnati, OH: South-Western Publishing.

Davis, A. (2019, March 26). *Property Tax Circuit Breakers in 2018*. Institute on Taxation and Economic Policy. https://itep.org/property-tax-circuit-breakers-in-2018.

Davis, D. W., & Christensen, L. R. (1980). The Relative Efficiency of Public and Private Firms in a Competitive Environment: The Case of Canadian Railroads. *Journal of Political Economy, 88*, 958–976.

Deaton, A. (1997). *Analysis of Household Surveys: A Microeconomic Approach to Development Policy*. Baltimore, MD: Johns Hopkins University Press.

Deb, K., & Gupta, H. (2005). Searching for Robust Pareto-Optimal Solutions in Multi-objective Optimization. *Proceedings of the Third Evolutionary Multi-criteria Optimization (EMO-05) Conference (Lecture Notes on Computer Science), 3410*, 150–164.

Dickey, D. A., & Fuller, W. A. (1979). Distribution of the Estimators for Autoregressive Time Series with a Unit Root. *Journal of American Statistical Association, 74*, 427–431.

Domar, E. (1957). *Essays in the Theories of Economic Growth*. New York, NY: Oxford University Press.

Dornbusch, R., & Fisher, S. (1990). *Macroeconomics* (pp. 18–20, 149–157). New York, NY: McGraw-Hill.

Downs, A. (1967). *Inside Bureaucracy*. Boston, MA: Little, Brown.

Drucker, P. F. (1954). *The Practice of Management*. New York: Harper Business.

Edwards, C. (2003, August). *Replacing the Scandal-Plagued Corporate Income Tax with a Cash-Flow Tax* (Policy Analysis of the Cato Institute No. 484, pp. 1–43). Washington, DC.

Edwards, C. (2006, April). *Income Tax Rife with Complexity and Inefficiency* (Tax and Budget Bulletin of the Cato Institute No. 33). Washington, DC.

Eisner, R. (1998, April 24). *A Capital Budget for Truth in Packaging*. Prepared for Presentation at the President's Commission to Study Capital Budgeting, Public Hearing, Washington, DC.

Emmons, H., Flowers, A. D., Khot, C. M., & Mathur, K. (1992). *Storm: Quantitative Modeling for Decision Support*. Englewood Cliffs, NJ: Prentice-Hall.

Feldstein. M. S. (1976, July–August). On the Theory of Tax Reform. *Journal of Public Economics, 6*, 77–104.

Fenno, R. F., Jr. (1966). *The Power of the Purse: Appropriations Politics in Congress*. Boston: Little, Brown.

Folsher, A. (2007a). Participatory Budgeting in Central and Eastern European Countries. In A. Shah (Ed.), *Participatory Budgeting* (pp. 127–156). Washington, DC: The International Bank for Reconstruction and Development (IBRD), The World Bank.

Folsher, A. (2007b). Participatory Budgeting in Asia. In A. Shah (Ed.), *Participatory Budgeting* (pp. 157–190). Washington, DC: The International Bank for Reconstruction and Development (IBRD), The World Bank.

Folsher, A. (2007c). Participatory Budgeting in the Middle East and North Africa. In A. Shah (Ed.), *Participatory Budgeting* (pp. 225–242). Washington, DC: The International Bank for Reconstruction and Development (IBRD), The World Bank.

Forrester, J. (2002). The Principal-Agent Model and Budget Theory. In A. Khan & W. B. Hildreth (Eds.), *Budget Theory in the Public Sector* (pp. 123–138). Westport, CT: Quorum Books.

Freeman, R. J., Shoulders, C. D., & Allison, G. S. (2006). *Governmental and Nonprofit Accounting: Theory and Practice*. New York, NY: Prentice-Hall.

Friedman, M. (1962). *Capitalism and Freedom*. Chicago, IL: The University of Chicago Press.

Galbraith, J. K. (1967). *The New Industrial State*. Boston, MA: Houghton-Mifflin.

Gantt, H. L. (1974). *Work, Wages, and Profit*. Easton, PA: Hive Publishing (Originally published in *The Engineering Magazine* in 1910).

Garrett, T., Kozak, A., & Rhine, R. (2010). Institutions and Government Growth: A Comparison of the 1890s and 1930s. *Federal Reserve Bank of St. Louis Review, 92*(2), 109–119.

Garrigues, J. (2016, December 27). Eight Steps to Effective Participatory Budgeting. *CitizenLab*. https://www.citizenlab.co/blog/civic-engagement/steps-to-effective-participatory-budgeting/.

Gauthier, S. J. (2012). *GAAFR: Governmental Accounting, Auditing, and Financial Reporting*. Chicago, IL: Government Finance Officers Association (GFOA).

General Accountability Office (GAO). (1996). *Executive Guide: Effectively Implementing the Government Performance and Results Act*. Washington, DC: Office of the Comptroller General of the United States.

Gershberg, A. I., & Benning, J. F. (1997, December). *Federal Capital Investment and the Balanced Budget Amendment: The Pros and Cons of a Federal Capital Budget*. New York: The Nelson A. Rockefeller Institute of Government, New York University.

Gilchrist, W. G. (1976). *Statistical Forecasting*. New York, NY: Wiley.

Giles, D. (2004). Calculating a Standard Error for the Gini Coefficient: Some Further Results. *Oxford Bulleting and Economics and Statistics, 66*(3), 425–433.

Gist, J. R. (2008). Economic Recession and the Fiscal Conditions of City Governments. *Journal of Urban Affairs, 10*(3), 253–272.

Gitman, J. G., & Forrester, J. R. (1977). A Survey of Capital Budgeting Techniques Used by Major US Firms. *Financial Management, 6*(3), 66–71.

Goldstein, G. S., & Pauly, M. V. (1981). Tibout Bias on the Demand for Local Public Goods. *Journal of Public Economics, 16*, 131–144.

Goolsbee, A. (2000). In a World Without Borders: The Impact of Taxes on Internet Commerce. *Quarterly Journal of Economics, 115*(2), 561–576.

Gosling, J. J. (1992). *Budgetary Politics in American Governments*. New York: Routledge.

Government Accountability Office (GAO). (1997, May 21). *Federal Investment Outlays, Fiscal Years 1981–2002*. Washington, DC: GAO/AIMD-97-88.

Government Accountability Office (GAO). (1999, February 3). *Public-Private Partnerships: Key Elements of Federal Buildings and Facility Partnerships*. Washington, DC: GAO B-27865.

Government Accountability Office (GAO). (2008, March 13). *Internal Revenue Service: Fiscal Year 2009 Budget Request and Interim Performance Results of IRS's 2008 Tax Filing Season*. Washington, DC: GAO-08-567.

Government Finance Officers Association (GFOA). (1999, June). *Basis of Accounting vs Budgetary Basis*. https://www.gfoa.org/basis-accounting-versus-budgetary-basis.

Government Finance Officers Association (GFOA). (2007). *Recommended Budget Practice— Budgeting for Results and Outcome*. http://www.gfoa.org/downloads/budgetingforresults.pdf.

Gramlich, E. M. (1981). *Benefit-Cost Analysis of Government Programs* (pp. 98–100). Englewood Cliffs, NJ: Prentice-Hall.

Granger, C. W. J. (1969, July). Investigating Causal Relations by Econometric Models and Cross-Spectral Methods. *Econometrica, 37*, 424–438.

Greene, W. H. (2003). *Econometric Analysis*. New York, NY: Prentice-Hall.

Groves, H. M. (1939). *Financing Government*. New York, NY: Holt.

Gruber, J. (2005). *Public Finance and Public Policy*. New York, NY: Worth Publishers.

Guillermina, J. (1979). On Gini's Mean Difference and Gini's Index of Concentration. *American Sociological Review, 44*(5), 867–870.

Halachmi, A., & Boydston, R. (2003). The Political Economy of Outsourcing. In A. Khan & W. B. Hildreth (Eds.), *Case Studies in Public Budgeting and Financial Management* (2nd ed., pp. 65–76). New York, NY: Marcel Dekker.

Hall, R. E., & Rabuschka, A. (1985). *The Flat Tax*. Stanford, CA: Hoover Press.

Hand, L. (1947, December). Thomas Walter Swan. *Yale Law Journal, 57*(2), 167–169.

Harberger, A. C. (1974). The Incidence of the Corporate Income Tax. In A. C. Harberger (Ed.), *Taxation and Welfare* (pp. 132–162). Boston, MA: Little, Brown.

Hardin, G. (1968, December 13). The Tragedy of the Commons. *Science, 162*, 1243–1248.

Harris, S. (2004, July 8). "Promoting Public-Private Partnerships" in the Section on Business Supplement. *The Times*, p. 3. Allied Newspaper Limited, Valletta.

Harrod, R. F. (1948). *Toward a Dynamic Economics*. London: Macmillan.

Hatry, H. P. (1988). *Guide to Setting Priorities for Capital Investment*. Washington, DC: Urban Institute Press.

Hatry, H. P., et al. (1997). *Customer Survey for Agency Managers: What Managers Need to Know?* Washington, DC: The Urban Institute.

Hatry, H. P., et al. (2006). *How Effective Are Your Community Services? Procedures for Performance Measurement*. Washington, DC: The Urban Institute.

Hatry, H. P., & Fisk, D. M. (1971). *Improving Productivity and Productivity Measurement in Local Governments*. Washington, DC: The National Commission on Productivity.

Haughey, J. (2018, February 27). 14 Steps to the Federal Budget Process Time-Line. *Congressional Quarterly*. https://info.cq.com/resources/14-steps-federal-budget-process-timeline/.

Haveman, R. H. (1976). *The Economics of the Public Sector*. New York, NY: Wiley.

Heilbroner, R. L., & Thurow, L. C. (1984). *Understanding Macroeconomics*. Englewood Cliffs, NJ: Prentice-Hall.

Higgins, M. (2007). *Concepts in Federal Taxation*. Jersey City, NJ: Thomson-Southwestern.

Hirsch, W. Z. (1970). *The Economics of State and Local Government* (pp. 280–290). New York, NY: McGraw-Hill.

Hirshleifer, J. (1980). *Price Theory and Applications* (2nd ed.). Englewood Cliffs, NJ: Prentice-Hall.

Holcombe, R. G. (1989). The Median Voter in Public Choice Theory. *Public Choice, 61*, 115–125.

Holcombe, R. G. (1997). A Theory of Public Goods. *Review of Austrian Economics, 10*(1), 1–22.

Holcombe, R. G. (2001, July). Public Policy Toward Pecuniary Externalities. *Public Finance Review, 29*(4), 304–325.

Holcombe, R. G. (2002). The Ramsey Rule Reconsidered. *Public Finance Review, 30*(6), 562–578.

Holcombe, R. G. (2006). *Public Sector Economics: The Role of Government in the American Economy*. New York, NY: Prentice-Hall.

Holden, K. (1995). Vector Autoregression Modelling and Forecasting. *Journal of Forecasting, 14*(3), 159–166.

Hungerford, T. L. (2011, June 1). *Tax Expenditures and the Federal Budget*. Washington, DC: Congressional Research Service.

Hyde, A. C. (1991). The Development of Budgeting and Budget Theory: The Threads of Budget Reform. In A. C. Hyde (Ed.), *Government Budgeting: Theory, Process, and Politics* (pp. 1–6). Pacific Grove, CA: Brooks/Cole Publishing.

Hyman, D. N. (2014). *Public Finance: A Contemporary Application of Theory to Policy*. New York, NY: Cengage Learning.

Ighodaro, C. A. U., & Oriakhi, D. E. (2010). Does the Relationship Between Government Expenditure and Economic Growth Follow Wagner's Law in Nigeria? *Annals of the University of Petroşani, Economics, 10*(2), 185–198.

Ignizio, J. P. (1976). *Goal Programming and Extension*. Lexington, MA: Lexington Books.

Investor's Business Daily. (2019, May 10). Will Looming State and Local Pension Crisis Bankrupt the US? *Investor's Business Daily*. https://www.investors.com/politics/editorials/the-looming-pension-crisis-of-state-and-local-governments/.

Jackson, M., & Staunton, M. D. (1999). Quadratic Programming Applications in Finance using Excel. *Journal of the Operations Research Society, 50*(2), 1256–1266.

Joint Economic Committee. (1995, December). *The Impact of the Welfare State on the American Economy*. Washington, DC: U.S. Congress.

Kaldor, N. (1939, September). Welfare Propositions of Economics and Interpersonal Comparisons of Utility. *Economic Journal, 49*, 549–552.

Kavanagh, S. C., Johnson, J., & Fabian, C. (2011). *Anatomy of Priority-Based Budget Process*. Chicago, IL: Government Finance Officers Association.

Kenyon, D. A., & Benker, K. M. (1984, September). Fiscal Discipline: Lessons from the State Experience. *National Tax Journal, 37*, 433–446.

Key, V. O., Jr. (1940, December). The Lack of a Budget Theory. *American Political Science Review, 34*, 1137–1140.

Keynes, J. M. (1936). *The General Theory of Employment, Interest and Money*. Cambridge, UK: Cambridge University Press.

Khan, A. (1996). Cash Management: Basic Principles and Guidelines. In J. Rabin et al. (Eds.), *Budgeting: Formulation and Execution* (pp. 313–322). Athens, GA: Carl Vinson Institute of Government. The University of Georgia.

Khan, A. (1997a). Capital Rationing, Priority Setting, and Budget Allocation: An Analytical Guide for Public Managers. In R. T. Golembiewski & J. Rabin (Eds.), *Public Budgeting and Finance* (pp. 963–974). New York: Marcel Dekker.

Khan, A. (1997b). Cash Management: Basic Principles and Guidelines. In J. Rabin, et al. (Eds.), *Budgeting: Formulation and Execution* (pp. 313–322). Athens, GA: Carl Vinson Institute of Government, University of Georgia.

Khan, A. (2003). Forecasting the General Fund Budget of Local Government: The City of Pleasantville. In A. Khan & W. B. Hildreth (Eds.), *Case Studies in Public Budgeting and Financial Management* (pp. 195–2008). New York, NY: Marcel Dekker.

Khan, A., & Murova, O. (2015). Productive Efficiency of Public Expenditures: A Cross-State Study. *State and Local Government Review, 47*(3), 170–180.

Klay, W. E. (1983). Revenue Forecasting: An Administrative Perspective. In J. Rabin & T. D. Lynch (Eds.), *Handbook of Public Budgeting and Financial Management* (pp. 287–316). New York, NY: Marcel Dekker.

Kogan, R., Greenstein, R., & Horney, J. R. (2012, January). *Biennial Budgeting: Do the Drawbacks Outweigh the Advantages?* Washington, DC: Center on Budget and Policy Priorities. https://www.cbpp.org.

Koitz, D., Bobb, M. D., & Page, B. (2002, July 14). *125-Year Picture of the Federal Government Share of the Economy: 1950–2075* (A Series of Issue Summaries from the Congressional Budget Office No. 1). (Revised July 3, 2002).

Koop, G., & Poirier, D. J. (1995). An Empirical Investigation of Wagner's Hypothesis by Using a Model Occurrence Framework. *Journal of the Royal Statistical Society, Series A: Statistics in Society, 158*(1), 123–141.

Krueger, A. O. (1974, June). The Political Economy of the Rent-Seeking Society. *American Economic Review, 64*(3), 291–303.

Krugman, P. (2019, January 17). Learn About Supply-Side Economics: History, Policy, Effects. *Politics and Society.* https://www.masterclass.com/articles/learn-about-supply-side-economics-history-policy-effects#what-is-supplyside-economics.

Kumbhakar, S. C. (2011, April). *Estimation of Multiple Output Production Functions* (Working Paper). Binghamton, NY: Department of Economics, State University of New York.

Laffer, A. (2004, June 1). The Laffer Curve: Past, Present, and Future. *The Heritage Foundation.* https://www.heritage.org/taxes/report/the-laffer-curve-past-present-and-future.

Landau, D. (1983). Government and Economic Growth in the Less Developed Countries: An Empirical Study for '1960–1980'. *Economic Development and Cultural Change, 35,* 35–75.

Lanzillotti, R. V. (1958, December). Pricing Objectives in Large Companies. *American Economic Review, 48*(6), 921–940.

Lawrence, D. M., & Vogt, A. J. (2007). *Capital Planning, Budgeting, and Debt Financing.* Chapel Hill: School of Government, University of North Carolina.

Lawrence, L. L. (2002). Budgeting for Outcomes. In A. Khan & W. B. Hildreth (Eds.), *Budget Theory in the Public Sector* (pp. 246–260). Westport, CT: Quorum Books.

Lederle, J. W. (1949). The Hoover Commission Reports on Federal Reorganization. *Marquette Law Review, 33*(2), 89–98.

Ledyard, J. O. (1994). *Public Goods: A Survey of Experimental Research* (Social Science Working Paper 861). Pasadena: Division of the Humanities and Social Sciences, California Institute of Technology.

Lee, S. M. (1972). *Goal Programming for Decision Analysis.* Philadelphia, PA: Auerbach Publishing.

LeLoup, L. T. (1978). The Myth of Incrementalism: Analytical Choices in Budgetary Theory. *Polity, 10*(Summer), 488–509.

LeLoup, L. T. (2002). Budget Theory for New Century. In A. Khan & W. B. Hildreth (Eds.), *Budget Theory in the Public Sector* (pp. 1–21). Westport, CT: Quorum Books.

Lewis, C. W., & Hildreth, W. B. (2011). *Budgeting: Politics and Power.* Oxford: Oxford University Press.

Lewis, V. B. (1952). Toward a Theory of Budgeting. *Public Administration Review, 12*(Winter), 43–54.

Lipsey, R. G., & Lancaster, K. (1956–1957). The General Theory of the Second Best. *Review of Economic Studies, 24,* 11–32.

Locke, J. (1970).*Two Treatises of Government* (p. 380). Cambridge, UK: Cambridge University Press.

Lorie, J. H., & Savage, L. J. (1955, October). Three Problems of Rationing Capital. *Journal of Business, 28*(4), 229–239.

Lynch, T. D. (1995). *Public Budgeting in America.* New York: Prentice-Hall.

Makridakis, S., & Wheelwright, S. C. (1978). *Forecasting: Methods and Applications.* New York, NY: Wiley.

Makridakis, S., & Weeelwright, S. C. (1978). *Interactive Forecasting* (pp. 387–388). San Francisco, CA: Holden Day.

Manheim, M. L. (1966). *Hierarchical Structure: A Model for Planning and Design Processes.* Cambridge: MIT Press.

Manion, P. (2003). Financial a Recycling Facility Through a Public-Private Partnership. In A. Khan & W. B. Hildreth (Eds.), *Case Studies in Public Budgeting and Financial Management* (2nd ed., pp. 763–772). New York, NY: Marcel Dekker.

Maxwell, A. E., & Crain, E. (2008). *Texas Politics Today*. New York, NY: Thomson-Wadsworth.

McCarthy, M. D. (1972). *The Wharton Quarterly Econometric Forecasting Model*. Philadelphia: University of Pennsylvania.

McCreadie, K. (2009). *Adam Smith's the Wealth of Nations: A Modern-Day Interpretation of an Economic Classic*. Oxford, UK: Infinite Ideas.

McNees, S. (1988, July–August). "How Accurate Are Macroeconomic Forecasts?" Federal Reserve Bank of Boston. *New England Economic Review*, 15–36.

Meadows, D. H., Meadows, D. L., Randers, J., & Behrens III, W. W. (1972). *The Limits to Growth*. New York, NY: Universe Books.

Metcalf, G. E. (1993, January). *The Life-Time Incidence of State and Local Taxes: Measuring Changes During the 1980s* (Working Paper No. 4252). Cambridge, MA: National Bureau of Economic Research.

Mikesell, J. L. (2014). *Fiscal Administration: Analysis and Applications for the Public Sector*. New York, NY: Wadsworth.

Mikesell, R. F. (1977). *The Rate of Discount for Evaluating Public Projects*. Washington, DC: American Enterprise Institute for Studies in Economic Policy.

Miller, M. H., & Orr, D. (1966, August). A Model of the Demand for Money. *Quarterly Journal of Economics, 80*, 413–435.

Millonzi, K. (2012, June 14). Budgeting and Appropriations, Finance and Tax. *Coat's Cannons: NC Local Government Law*. https://canons.sog.unc.edu/faqs-on-adopting-the-budget-ordinance/.

Mishan, E. J. (1981). *Introduction to Normative Economics*. New York, NY: Oxford University Press.

Moder, J., Phillips, C. R., & Davis, E. W. (1983). *Project Management with CPM and PERT*. New York, NY: Van Nostrand-Reinhold.

Mohammadi, H., Cak, M., & Cak, D. (2008). Wagner's Hypothesis: New Evidence from Turkey Using the Bounds-Testing Approach. *Journal of Economic Studies, 35*(1), 94–106.

Moody's Investors Service. (2016, March 10). *US Public-Private Partnership Market Steadily Growing*.

Mosher, F. C. (1954). *Program Budgeting: Theory and Practice*. Chicago, IL: Public Administration Service.

Mueller, D. C. (2003). *Public Choice*. Cambridge: Cambridge University Press.

Murova, O., & Khan, A. (2017). Public Investments, Productivity, and Economic Growth: A Cross-State Study of Selected Public Expenditures in the US. *International Journal of Productivity and Performance Management, 66*(2), 251–265.

Musgrave, R. A. (1959). *The Theory of Public Finance*. New York, NY: McGraw-Hill (Chapters 1–2).

Musgrave, R. A. (1969). *Fiscal Systems*. New Haven, CT: Yale University Press (Chapter 3).

Mushkin, S. (1972). *Public Prices for Public Products*. Washington, DC: The Urban Institute.

National Advisory Council on State and Local Budget (NACSLB). (1999). *Recommended Budget Practices: A Framework for Improved State and Local Government Budgeting*. Chicago, IL: Government Finance Officers Association (GFOA) (Second Printing).

Netzer, D. (1966). *Economics of the Property Tax*. Washington, DC: The Brookings Institution.

New, M. J. (2004, October 28). *The Gann Limit Turns 25*. Cato Institute. https://www.cato.org/publications/commentary/gann-limit-turns-25.

Niskanen, W. A., Jr. (1971). *Bureaucracy and Representative Government*. NY: Aldine-Atherton.

Oates, W. (1972). *Fiscal Federalism*. New York, NY: Harcourt Brace Jovanovich.

Office of Management and Budget. (2006). *Historical Tables: Budget of the US Government*. Washington, DC.

Office of Management and Budget. (2011). *Historical Tables: Budget of the US Government*. Washington, DC.

Office of Management and Budget. (2018). *Historical Tables: Budget of the US Government*. Washington, DC.

Office of Management and Budget. (2019). *Historical Tables: Budget of the US Government*. Washington, DC.

Ogwang, T. (2000). A Convenient Method of Computing the Gini Index and Its Standard Error. *Oxford Bulletin of Economics and Statistics, 62,* 123–129.

Olson, M. (1965). *The Logic of Collective Action: Public Goods and the Theory of Groups.* Cambridge, MA: Harvard University Press.

Osborne, D., & Gabler, T. (1992). *Reinventing Government.* Reading, MA: Addison-Wisely.

Patton, T., Patton, S., & Ives, M. (2019). *Accounting for Governmental and Nonprofit Organizations.* Cambridge, UK: Cambridge University Press.

Peacock, A. T., & Wiseman, J. (1961). *The Growth of Public Expenditure in the United Kingdom.* London: Oxford University Press.

Pechman, J. A. (1985). *Who Paid the Taxes: 1966–1985?* Washington, DC: The Brookings Institution.

Pechman, J. A., & Mayer, T. (1952, August). Mr. Colin Clark on the Limits of Taxation. *The Review of Economics and Statistics, 34*(3), 232–242.

Perkins, H. (2017, September 12). *State Budget Process: A Comparative Analysis.* Washington, DC: The Council of State Governments. http://knowledgecenter.csg.org/kc/content/state-budget-processes-comparative-analysis.

Pfiffner, J. P. (1979). *The President, the Budget, and Congress: Impoundment and the 1974 Budget Act.* New York: Westview Press.

Pindyck, R. S., & Rubinfeld, D. L. (1998). *Econometric Models and Economic Forecasts.* New York, NY: Irwin-McGraw-Hill.

Preston, A. E., & Ichniowski, C. (1991, June). A National Perspective on the Nature and Effects of the Local Property Tax Revolt, 1976–1986. *National Tax Journal, 44,* 123–146.

Putnam, R. D. (1995, January). Bowling Alone: America's Declining Social Capital. *Journal of Democracy, 6*(1), 65–78.

Pyhrr, P. A. (1973). *Zero-Base Budgeting: A Practical Tool for Evaluating Expenses.* New York, NY: Wiley.

Quade, E. S. (1982). *Analysis for Public Decisions.* New York, NY: North Holland.

Ramanthan, R. (1998). *Introductory Econometrics with Applications* (pp. 523–527). New York, NY: The Dryden Press.

Ratti, R. A. (1985). A Descriptive Analysis of Economic Indicators. *Federal Reserve Board of St. Louis, 67*(1), 14–24.

Reed, E. (2019, May). What Is the National Debt Year by Year from 1790 to 2019. *The Street.* https://www.thestreet.com/politics/national-debt-year-by-year-14876008.

Richardson, H. W. (1972). *Input-Output and Regional Economics.* London, UK: Weidenfeld & Nicolson.

Robichek, A. A., & Van Horne, J. C. (1967, December). Abandonment Value and Capital Budgeting. *The Journal of Finance, 22,* 577–589.

Romer, C., & Bernstein, J. (2008/2009, January 13). *The Job Impact of the American Recovery and Reinvestment Plan* (p. 4). Office of the President-elect. http://otrans.3cdn.net/45593e8ecbd07413m6bt1te.pdf.

Rosell, E. (2003). The Chickens Come Home to Roost: The Publicization of Private Infrastructure. In A. Khan & W. B. Hildreth (Eds.), *Case Studies in Public Budgeting and Financial Management* (2nd ed., pp. 773–784). Yew York, NY: Marcel Dekker.

Rueben, K. S., & Randall, M. (2017). *Tax and Expenditure Limits: How States Restrict Revenues and Spending.* Washington, DC: The Urban Institute.

Ryan, P. A., & Ryan, G. P. (2002). Capital Budgeting Practices of the Fortune 1000: How Have Things Changed? *Journal of Business and Management, 8*(4) (Winter), 355–364.

Saaty, T. L. (1980). *Analytic Hierarchy Process: Planning, Priority Setting, Resource Allocation.* New York, NY: McGraw-Hill.

Salazar, R. C., & Sen, S. K. (1968, December). A Simulation Model of Capital Budgeting Under Uncertainty. *Management Science, 15,* 161–179.

Samuelson, P. A. (1938). A Note on the Pure Theory of Consumer's Behavior. *Economica, 5*(17), 61–71.

Samuelson, P. A. (1954, November). The Pure Theory of Public Expenditure. *The Review of Economics and Statistics, 36*(4), 387–389.

Schick, A. (1988). An Inquiry into the Possibility of Budget Theory. In I. S. Rubin (Ed.), *New Directions in Budget Theory* (pp. 59–69). Albany, NY: State University of New York Press.

Schick, A. (2005). Sustainable Budget Policy: Concepts and Approaches. *OECD Journal on Budgeting, 5*(1), 107–126.

Schlachter, B. (2012). Key *Strategies and Challenges for Local Governments* (Fiscal Policy and Governance Committee Report). Pittsburgh, PA: Institute of Politics, University of Pittsburgh.

Schniederjans, M. J. (1995). *Goal Programming: Methodology and Applications.* Norwell, MA: Kluwer Academic.

Scott, D. C. (1972). *Forecasting Local Government Expenditure.* Washington, DC: The Urban Institute.

Senate Research Center. (2011, January). *Budget 101: A Guide to the Budget Process in Texas.* Austin, TX: Senate Budget Center, Sam Houston Building.

Shafriritz, J. M., Russell, E. W., & Borick, C. P. (2009). *Introducing Public Administration.* New York, NY: Pearson Education.

Shall, A. (2007). Sub-Saharian Experience with Participatory Budgeting. In A. Shah (Ed.), *Participatory Budgeting* (pp. 191–224). Washington, DC: The International Bank for Reconstruction and Development (IBRD), The World Bank.

Shelley II, M. C. (1978, October). *Forecasting the National Budget with the Technique of Time-Series Analysis.* Paper Presented at the Southwest Regional Conference of the American Society for Public Administration, Charleston, SC, 17–20.

Simonsen, W., & Robbins, M. D. (2000). *Citizen Participation in Revenue Allocation.* New York, NY: Westview Press.

Smith, R. T. (2008). Forecasting Revenues and Expenditures in the Public Sector: Guidance from a Code of Ethics. In J. Sun & T. D. Lynch (Eds.), *Government Budget Forecasting* (pp. 527–550). Washington, DC: CRC Press.

Smith, V. L. (1980). Relevance of Laboratory Experiments to Testing Resource Allocation Theory. In J. Kmenta & J. Ramsey (Eds.), *Evaluation of Econometric Models* (pp. 345–377). New York: New York University Press.

Smithies, A. (1955). *Budgetary Process in the United States.* New York: McGraw-Hill.

Solem, J., & Werner, H. D. (1968). PPBS: A Management Innovation. *Journal of Cooperative Extension* (Winter), 221–228.

Solow, R. (1956, February). A Contribution to the Theory of Economic Growth. *Quarterly Journal of Economics, 70,* 65–94.

State of Washington. (2010). *Thrive Washington: Nine Steps to Budget Sustainability in Washington State.* Olympia, WA: A Joint Research Series of the Washington Roundtable and Washington Research Council.

Steiss, A. W. (1975). *Local Government Finance: Capital Facilities Planning and Debt Administration.* Lexington, KY: Lexington Press.

Steuer, R. E. (1986). *Multiple Criteria Optimization: Theory, Computation, and Application.* New York: Wiley.

Stigler, G. I. (1971). The Theory of Economic Regulation. *Bell Journal of economics and Management Science, 2*(Spring), 3–21.

Stiglitz, J. E. (2000). *Economics of the Public Sector* (pp. 456–468). New York: W. W. Norton.

Stiglitz, J. E., & Rosengard, J. K. (2015). *Economics of the Public Sector* (pp. 606–635). New York: W. W. Norton.

Stone, C. (2014). The Federal Budget Process. In S. Payson (Ed.), *Public Economic in the United States, 2,* 679–698.

Straub, S. (2008). *Infrastructure and Growth in Developing Countries: Recent Advanced and Research Challenges* (World Bank Policy Research Working Paper No. 4460). Washington, DC: World Bank.

Strauss, R. P., & Hughes, G. D. (1976). A New Approach to the Demand for Public Goods. *Journal of Public Economics, 6,* 191–204.

Suits, D. B. (1962). Forecasting and Analysis with an Econometric Model. *American Economic Review, 52*(1), 104–132.

Tax Foundation. (2018). *2018 Tax Brackets*. https://taxfoundation.org/2018-tax-brackets/January.

Tax Policy Center. (2016). *National Retail Sales Tax: Effects on Economic Growth*. http://www.taxpolicycenter.org/briefing-book/what-would-be-effect-national-retail-sales-tax-economic-growth.

Tax Policy Center. (2017, October 18). http://www.taxpolicycenter.org/statistics/corporate-rate-schedule.

Taylor, G. M. (1977). Introduction to Zero-Base Budgeting. *The Bureaucrat, 6*(Spring), 33–55.

Texas Comptroller of Public Accounts. (2018). *The Texas Budget Process: A Primer*. https://comptroller.texas.gov/transparency/budget/primer.php.

The Volker Alliance. (2018, December 12). *The Volker Alliance Releases the Second Annual Study: "Truth and Integrity in State Budgeting: Preventing the Next Fiscal Crisis."* https://www.volckeralliance.org/news/volcker-alliance-releases-second-annual-study-truth-and-integrity-state-budgeting-preventing.

The Wall Street Journal. (2009, April 15). Sales-Tax Revenue Falls at Fastest Pace in Years.

Theil, H. (1967). *Economics and Information Theory*. Amsterdam: North Holland.

Thompson, M. S. (1982). *Benefit-Cost Analysis for Program Evaluation* (pp. 1–2). Beverly Hills, CA: Sage.

Tiebout, C. (1956). A Pure Theory of Local Public Expenditure. *Journal of Political Economy, 64*, 416–424.

Tucker, J. (2014, January 14). What Is an Omnibus? *National Priorities Project*. https://www.nationalpriorities.org/blog/2014/01/14/what-omnibus/.

U.S. Bureau of Census. (Multiple Years). *Statistical Abstracts of the United States*. Washington, DC: Department of Commerce.

U.S. Bureau of Census. (Multiple Years). *Government Finances*. Washington, DC: Department of Commerce.

U.S. Bureau of Census. (2005). *Projected Population by Single Year of Age, Sex, Race, and Hispanic Origin for the United States: July 1, 2000 to July 1, 2050*. Washington, DC.

US Department of the Treasury. (2015). *The Budget in Brief: Internal Revenue Service*, FY2015. US Washington DC. FY2015. https://www.irs.gov/pub/irs-news/IRS%20FY%202015%20Budget%20in%20Brief.pdf.

US Department of the Treasury. (2018). *Debt to the Penny*. Washington, DC.

US Government Defense Spending. (2018). https://www.usgovernmentspending.com/defense_spending.

US Government Spending. (2012, June). https://www.USGovernmentSpending.com.

US Government Spending. (2018, January). https://www.usgovernmentspending.com/us_spending.

US Government Spending. (2019, March). https://www.usgovernmentdebt.us/local_debt_chart; https://www.usgovernmentdebt.us/state_debt_chart.

Van Slyke, D. M. (2013, March 9). *Building Public-Private Partnerships*. Presented to National League of Cities' Conference. https://www.nlc.org/sites/default/files/2017-06/Building%20Public-Private%20Partnerships.pdf.

Vedder, R. (1993, April). *Economic Impact of Government Spending: A 50-State Analysis* (NCPA Policy Report No. 178). Dallas, TX: National Center for Policy Analysis.

Vogt, J. A. (1995). Budgeting Capital Outlays and Improvements. *Budget Development*. Athens, GA: Carl Vinson Institute of Government.

Wampler, B. (2007). A Guide to Participatory Budgeting. In A. Shah (Ed.), *Participatory Budgeting* (pp. 21–54). Washington, DC: The International Bank for Reconstruction and Development (IBRD), The World Bank.

Wampler, B., & Avritzer, L. (2004). Participatory Publics: Civil Societies and New Institutions in Democratic Brazil. *Comparative Politics, 36*(3), 291–312.

Wanat, J. (1978). *Introduction to Budgeting*. Monterey, CA: Brooks/Cole Publishing.

Wanniski, J. (1978). *The Way the World Works: How Economies Fail and Succeed*. New York, NY: Basic Books.

Webster, T. J. (2003). *Managerial Economics*. New York, NY: Academic Press.

Weingartner, H. M. (1963). *Mathematical Programming and the Analysis of Capital Budgeting*. Englewood Cliffs, NJ: Prentice-Hall, Inc.

Widasin, D. E. (1989). Demand Estimation for Public Goods. *Regional Science and Urban Economics, 19*, 353–379.

Wildavsky, A. (1961). Political Implications of Budgetary Reform. *Public Administration Review, 21*(Autumn), 183–190.

Wildavsky, A. (1964). *The Politics of the Budgetary Process*. Boston, MA: Little, Brown. (Rev. 4th ed., 1984).

Wildavsky, A. (1984). *The Politics of the Budgetary Process*. Boston, MA: Little, Brown. (Revised 4th edition).

Wildavsky, A. (1978, November–December). A Budget for All Seasons? Why the Traditional Budget Lasts? *Public Administration Review, 38*, 501–509.

Wildavsky, A. (1992, November–December). Political Implications of Budget Reform: A Retrospective. *Public Administration Review, 52*(6), 594–599.

Wildavsky, A., & Caiden, N. (2004). *The New Politics of the Budgetary Process*. New York: Pearson-Longman.

Wilde, L. (1980). On the Use of Laboratory Experiments in Economics. In J. Pitt (Ed.), *The Philosophy of Economics* (pp. 137–143). Dordrecht: Reidel.

Williamson, O. E. (2000, September). The New Institutional Economics: Taking Stock, Looking Ahead. *Journal of Economic Literature, 38*, 595–613.

Wolf, C., Jr. (1988). *Markets or Governments: Choosing Between Imperfect Alternatives*. Boston: MIT Press.

Yang, C. W., & Stitt, K. R. (1995, January). The Ramsey Rule Revisited. *Southern Economic Journal, 61*(3), 767–774.

Yitzhaki, S. (1991). Calculating Jackknife Variance Estimation for Parameters of the Gini Method. *Journal of Business and Economic Statistics, American Statistical Association, 9*(2), 235–239.

Index

A

Aaron, H., 136, 179
Ability to pay, 33, 56, 58, 59, 95
Account group, 162
Activity-based budget (ABB), 206
Activity-based costing (ABC), 205, 206
Ad Valorem tax, 118, 119
Allocation function, 4, 42
Alternative minimum tax (AMT), 111
Analytic Hierarchy Process (AHP), 289, 290,
    292, 294, 296, 297, 384, 419
Appraised value, 62, 123–126
Appropriation bills, 165, 169, 184
Appropriations committee, 82, 165, 169, 179,
    180, 184
Armey curve, 95, 96
Assessed value (AV), 123, 127–130, 134–136,
    145, 168
Assessment ratio (AR), 134, 135
Audits, 156, 178
    financial audit, 178
    performance audit, 178
Autocorrelation, 249–254, 256–258, 270
Automatic stabilizers, 87
Average tax rate (ATR), 69–71, 108, 110, 130

B

Backcasting, 254
Balanced budget, 21, 22, 99, 156, 398
    neutral effect, 21
Balanced budget requirement, 94, 180
Balance of payment disequilibrium, 12, 26–28
Basic *vs* non-basic activities, 371, 378
Basis of accounting, 158, 162, 163, 184
    budgetary basis, 163, 184
    GAAP basis, 163
Bator, F.M., 4, 8

Baumol, W.J., 27, 91, 92
Benefit-cost ratio, 325–329, 338
Benefit principle, 56, 59, 60, 299
Bias in assessment (BIA), 135
Block grant
    Community Development Block Grant
        (CDBG), 140, 160
Borrowing
    bond banks, 306
    certificates of obligation (CO), 305, 308
    GO bonds, 305, 308
    revenue bonds, 305, 306, 308
Bracket creep, 111
Buchanan, J.M., 32, 92
Budget and Accounting Act, 156, 157
Budget and Impoundment Control Act, 156, 171
Budget authority
    borrowing authority, 172
    contract authority, 171
    spending authority, 171, 172
Budget committee, 156, 165, 169
Budget Control Act, 157
Budget cycle, 163, 183, 314
Budget Enforcement Act (BEA), 156, 157
Budget game, 179, 181
    appropriation game, 180
    preparation game, 180
Budget ordinance, 171
Budget reconciliation, 169, 170
Budget resolution, 165, 169
Budget system, 184, 187–191, 194, 198, 210,
    211, 214, 217–223, 402
Build-America bonds (BABs), 307
Built-in provisions
    deduction, 108
    exclusions, 108
    exemptions, 108

Made in the USA
Coppell, TX
11 January 2023

10914574R00256